Springer Proceedings in Business and Economics

Springer Proceedings in Business and Economics brings the most current research presented at conferences and workshops to a global readership. The series features volumes (in electronic and print formats) of selected contributions from conferences in all areas of economics, business, management, and finance. In addition to an overall evaluation by the publisher of the topical interest, scientific quality, and timeliness of each volume, each contribution is refereed to standards comparable to those of leading journals, resulting in authoritative contributions to the respective fields. Springer's production and distribution infrastructure ensures rapid publication and wide circulation of the latest developments in the most compelling and promising areas of research today.

The editorial development of volumes may be managed using Springer's innovative Online Conference Service (OCS), a proven online manuscript management and review system. This system is designed to ensure an efficient timeline for your publication, making Springer Proceedings in Business and Economics the premier series to publish your workshop or conference volume.

More information about this series at http://www.springer.com/series/11960

Nicholas Tsounis · Aspasia Vlachvei
Editors

Advances in Cross-Section Data Methods in Applied Economic Research

2019 International Conference on Applied Economics (ICOAE 2019)

Springer

Editors
Nicholas Tsounis
Department of Economics
University of Western Macedonia
Kastoria, Greece

Aspasia Vlachvei
Department of Economics
University of Western Macedonia
Kastoria, Greece

ISSN 2198-7246 ISSN 2198-7254 (electronic)
Springer Proceedings in Business and Economics
ISBN 978-3-030-38252-0 ISBN 978-3-030-38253-7 (eBook)
https://doi.org/10.1007/978-3-030-38253-7

This Springer imprint is published by the registered company Springer Nature Switzerland AG
The registered company address is: Gewerbestrasse 11, 6330 Cham, Switzerland

Organization

Program Chairs

Aspasia Vlachvei, University of Western Macedonia
Angela Besana, IULM
Nicholas Tsounis, University of Western Macedonia

Program Committee

Dimitris Serenis, Coventry University, UK
Aspasia Vlachvei, University of Western Macedonia
Ourania Notta, Alexander Technological Institute of Thessaloniki, Greece
George Polychronopoulos, University of West Attica, Greece
Ricardo Ramalhete Moreira, UFES, Brazil
Chukiat Chaiboonsri, Chiang Mai University, Thailand
Angela Besana, IULM
Nicholas Tsounis, University of Western Macedonia

Preface

This year's conference is co-organised by the International University of Languages and Media and the Department of Economics of the University of Western Macedonia, Greece, after the kind invitation by Dr. Angela Besana who is also co-chair of the conference.

The aim of the conference is to bring together economists from different fields of Applied Economic Research in order to share methods and ideas.

The topics covered include:

- Applied Macroeconomics
- Applied International Economics
- Applied Microeconomics including Industrial Organisations
- Applied Work on International Trade Theory including European Integration
- Applied Financial Economics
- Applied Agricultural Economics
- Applied Labour and Demographic Economics
- Applied Health Economics
- Applied Education Economic

All papers presented in ICOAE 2019 and published in the conference proceedings were peer-reviewed by anonymous referees. In total, 84 works were submitted from 24 countries while 56 papers were accepted for presentation and publication in the conference proceedings.

The acceptance rate for ICOAE 2019 was 67%.
The full-text articles will be published online by Springer in the series "Springer Proceedings in Business and Economics".

The organisers of ICOAE 2019 would like to thank:

- The Scientific Committee of the conference for their help and their important support for carrying out the tremendous workload in organising and synchronising the peer-reviewing process of the submitted papers in a very specific short period of time.

- The anonymous reviewers for accepting to referee the submitted to the conference papers and submit their reviews on time for the finalisation of the conference programme.
- Dr. Angela Besana for accepting to host the conference at IULM and providing the required resources.
- The local organising committee and the volunteering students for their help and the success of the conference.
- Mr. Gerassimos Bertsatos for running the reception desk on the conference and Mr. Lazaros Markopoulos and Mr. Stelios Angelis from the Department of Economics and Informatics, of the University of Western Macedonia, respectively, for their technical support.

Kastoria, Greece

Nicholas Tsounis
Aspasia Vlachvei

Contents

Chapter 1
Impact of the Corporate Governance on the Financial Performance of Insurance Companies in the Slovak and Czech Republics

Janka Grofčíková and Katarína Izáková

Abstract Numerous expert studies have been conducted looking into the factors affecting the financial performance of businesses. Similarly, the issues of corporate governance and its individual determinants have been addressed in detail. The contribution of our paper is to link the aforementioned issues and their application specifically to companies providing insurance services whose products have a trust-based characteristic. Therefore, the control and management of insurance companies and their administration of entrusted resources are under strict control and are regulated by the Solvency II Directive in European Union law. The Czech and Slovak insurance markets have a common history. Currently, both markets are part of the European Union's single insurance market. This research compares these two markets in terms of this sector development, financial performance and selected determinants of corporate governance in insurance companies. The aim of this paper is to examine the impact of corporate governance on the financial performance of insurance companies. Using correlation and multiple regression analysis, we modelled the impact of selected financial and non-financial determinants of corporate governance on the aggregate performance indicator ROA.

Keywords Corporate governance · Firm performance · Insurance companies

JEL Codes M14 · G22

J. Grofčíková (✉) · K. Izáková
Department of Finance and Accounting, Faculty of Ecomonics Matej Bel University in Banská Bystrica, Tajovského 10, Banská Bystrica, Slovakia
e-mail: janka.grofcikova@umb.sk

K. Izáková
e-mail: katarina.izakova@umb.sk

N. Tsounis and A. Vlachvei (eds.), *Advances in Cross-Section Data Methods in Applied Economic Research*, Springer Proceedings in Business and Economics,
https://doi.org/10.1007/978-3-030-38253-7_1

1.1 Introduction

Insurance is a product that is in the professional literature perceived as a "trust-based product" (Credence good), since its consumers might not ex post realize the usefulness of the product which has been provided to them. In other words, they are often not able to recognize whether the product has been of the type and quality that have been ex ante requested. A trust-based product market requires a more sensitive approach in order not to undermine the built trust. Hence, regulation of the financial market is done through the means of regulations and directives, e.g. Solvency II Directive, which relates to the insurance market. We will focus specifically on the corporate governance system (CG), which is part of the second pillar of Solvency II, in the context of its impact on the performance of insurance markets in the Czech Republic and Slovakia (Izáková and Přečková 2014).

The interdependence of the history of the Slovak and Czech nations has had a significant influence on the development of the insurance market in these countries. Slovakia, as part of the multinational Austro-Hungarian Empire, was the area where mainly Hungarian, Austrian, Czech, Italian as well as English, French and Dutch insurance companies were involved in this business until the end of the First World War. In 1919, the first national insurance company was founded. It operated under the name Prvá slovenská poisťovňa (First Slovak Insurance Company), a cooperative in Žilina, which later changed to Slovakia, a general insurance company whose main business activities focused on life and fire insurance. Subsequently, Slovenská poisťovňa (Slovak Insurance Company) was established. After nationalization in 1945, it became a part of the Czechoslovak State Insurance Company, which operated as a monopoly insurance company in the territory of Czechoslovakia. As a result of the political changes after the year 1939, the number of insurance companies in the Slovak insurance market was reduced to 19, including five domestic, five protectorate, six German and three Italian insurance companies. The domestic Tatra insurance company (later Poštová poisťovňa—Post Insurance Company) took over the insurance portfolio of the Czech insurance companies that operated in Slovakia until then. The history of Česká pojišťovna (the Czech Insurance Company) dates back to 1827, when it opened its first Česká vzájemná pojišťovna (the Czech joint insurance company) branch in Prague. In the 1950s, the insurance sector was influenced by the conditions of a centrally managed economy. After the federal arrangement of the state in the year 1969, they operated as an independent Slovak State Insurance Company and Czech State Insurance Company. After 1989, when the political regime changed, the insurance market started to loosen up and allowed other domestic and foreign companies to enter the market. These changes resulted in the gradual transformation of the Slovak Insurance Company and Czech Insurance Company, which were owned by a state, into commercial institutions. In 2001, the majority of the state share in the Slovak Insurance Company was taken by Allianz AG, which, at that time, also operated in the Slovak insurance market. 1 January 2003 is officially registered as a day when Allianz—Slovenská poisťovňa (Allianz—Slovak Insurance Company) was established. In 2008, Česká pojišťovna (Czech Insurance

Company) became a member of the Generali and PPF group. Obviously, changes of ownership relations in insurance companies and subsequent mergers require new regulatory measures and stringent conditions related to insurance business activities.

Since 1 May 2004, the Slovak and Czech insurance markets have been part of the European Union's single insurance market, but they are of a relatively lower level compared to the EU insurance markets. Apparently, this is the consequence of the aforementioned historical development. Taking the qualitative point of view into consideration (since it might be applicable to mutual comparison), we assume that despite the 25-year existence of a competitive environment in the insurance market, Slovak and Czech insurance sector still do not reach the level of the highly developed European countries.

While comparing the insurance sector in Slovakia and the Czech Republic, several factors have to be taken into consideration. Firstly, the amount of inhabitants in Slovakia (from 2009 to 2017) was around 5.424 million on average, and the Czech Republic reached almost twice the average (from 2009 to 2017), which was about 10.528 million. This was also reflected in the number of insurance companies in both compared countries. At the end of 2017, there were a total of 16 insurance companies in Slovakia (24 companies were in existence in 2007) and 26 insurance companies in the Czech Republic at the end of 2017 (33 companies in 2012). It is interesting to note that in the monitored period of 2007, 2012 and 2017, the group of best insurance companies was always represented by the same five largest insurance companies in the Czech Republic, according to the premium written. In 2007, the largest insurance company in the Czech Republic, Česká pojišťovna (the Czech Insurance Company) declined its market share from 30.56 to 21.90%. Allianz—Slovenská poisťovňa (Allianz—Slovak Insurance Company), which is the largest insurance company in the Slovak Republic and is a company with the similar development. Kooperativa poisťovňa, a.s. (Kooperativa Insurance Company) and VIG, which are the second largest insurance companies in both countries, had a similar share (in 2007, it was 22% in both the Slovak and Czech Republic, and in 2017, their share was 20% in the Czech Republic and 19.15% in Slovakia). The third largest insurance company in the Czech Republic is Allianz pojišťovna, a.s., and in Slovakia it is Generali Slovakia. These two companies had a very similar share; in 2017, in the Czech Republic it was 10% (in the Slovak Republic 9.15%), and in 2012 it was 8.03% in the Czech Republic (in Slovakia 8.57%). In 2007, Česká pojišťovna Slovensko, a.s. with its share of 6.56% was ranked as the third largest insurance company in Slovakia, and in the Czech Republic it was Allianz pojišťovna, a.s. with its share of 7.37%. Within the monitored period, Generali pojišťovna, a.s. maintained the position of the fifth largest insurance company in the Czech Republic; whereas, in Slovakia the insurance companies in the fourth and fifth positions changed. Besides these, there are other insurance companies operating on the Czech and Slovak markets, such as the insurance company Aegon, ČSOB Insurance Company, Ergo, NN, Uniqa, Insurance Company SLSP and Cardif. In total, there are 11 insurance companies with their registered offices in the Slovak and Czech Republic, but apart from these more insurers might be found on the market, e.g. AXA pojišťovna and AXA životná pojišťovna operating in the Czech Republic (in Slovakia both of them operate only as a branch of a foreign insurance company), or Credendo—Short-Term EU Risks, which is a credit insurance company in the Czech Republic (in Slovakia this company operates also as a branch of a foreign insurance company).

1.2 Comparison of Indicators of Insurance Market Development in Slovak and Czech Republic

The current state and development of insurance markets in the monitored countries are determined mainly by the indicator of premium written, which is the amount of money that insurance companies operating in the insurance market of an individual country acquire from both new and existing clients during the year. Furthermore, the share of life and non-life insurance, as well as the degree of concentration of the insurance market, and the share of foreign companies in the insurance market are taken into account to analyse insurance markets.

In the Czech Republic, the share of life insurance in total premium written corresponds to a long-term ratio of 40:60 in favour of non-life insurance, while in the developed countries of Western Europe this ratio is usually the opposite (e.g. in UK, France or Italy). However, in western countries, this significantly advanced market related to life insurance results from the fact that commercial insurance companies are involved in social and pension systems in different ways, which yet does not work in the countries that are monitored in our research. In Slovakia, since 2008, the volume of premium written in life insurance exceeded over non-life insurance for the first time in 2013, as in this year the highest share of 56.79% was recorded, but then it was gradually decreasing, and in the year 2017 the share of 52.28% was recorded.

While considering the percentage of the premium written for life and non-life insurance in the monitored countries (Fig. 1.1), we can see that it does not develop in the same way. We assume that it results from an impact of different legislative directives. In Slovakia, for example, the year 2010 was the last tax year when a deduction of the premium from the tax base could be applied. From the beginning of

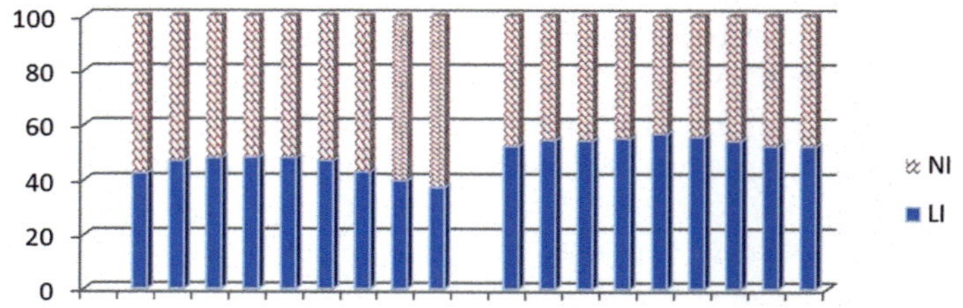

Fig. 1.1 Development of the percentage ratio of premium written in life (LI) and non-life insurance (NI) in Slovak and Czech Republic

2005, there was the law in force according to which a tax base might be lowered by the premium for life insurance (on average 12 thousand Slovak crowns). The conditions of this law were set in a way that the insurance payment period was ten years at least, and the insurance might end only when the age of 55 was reached. The tax base could be reduced by the whole life insurance premium paid in a given year, including also some extra insurance premium. In the Czech Republic, i.e. the state government still provides the subsidy (which is also in the amount of 12 thousand CZK). However, this is not fully used by citizens, and non-life insurance still prevails in the Czech Republic. Obviously, in both the Slovak and Czech Republic, the non-life insurance sector is mostly composed of three products, including a compulsory car insurance (24%), property insurance (23.6%) and motor third-party liability insurance (20%), further followed by a third-party liability insurance (16.4%) and other insurance (15.8%).

In the Czech Republic, loss ratio (as a share of insurance claims paid to the premium received) in non-life insurance was affected by the floods and heavy storms in 2010–2013. Also in the following years, an increase in loss ratio was influenced by the overall increase in non-life insurance, predominantly in the motor insurance segment (both liability and accident insurance). As seen, this is also prevalent in the Slovak Republic and presents the most significant element in non-life insurance (Fig. 1.2).

When comparing the insurance markets of different countries, it is reasonable to use ratio indicators that reflect the size of the country and its economic level. These ratios are related to insurance penetration rate (Fig. 1.3) and insurance density (Fig. 1.4). Insurance penetration reflects the percentage of total premium to GDP, and it also reflects the development of the country's insurance market in the context of the country's economic development. This is considered to be the most important indicator of the insurance market development at a national and world level.

When examining the link between GDP value and insurance penetration indicator, the direct effect of this factor is determined. The graph illustrates a decline in life insurance in 2014 in the Czech Republic. This decline resulted in the equal insurance penetration rate of 2.89% in the monitored countries in 2017. However, in comparison with other European countries where the insurance penetration rate

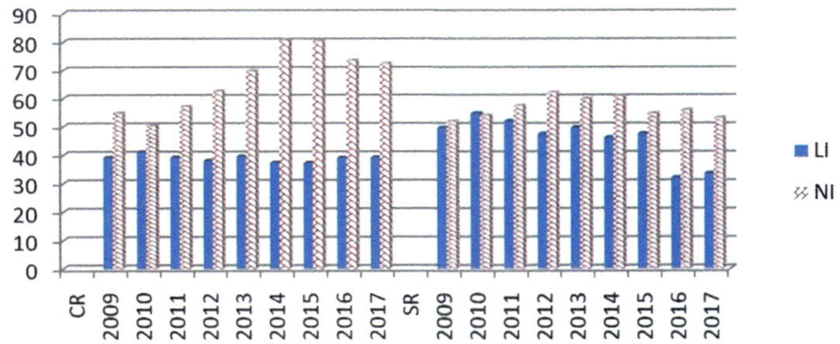

Fig. 1.2 Loss ratio life insurance (LI) and non-life insurance (NI) in Slovak and Czech Republic in %

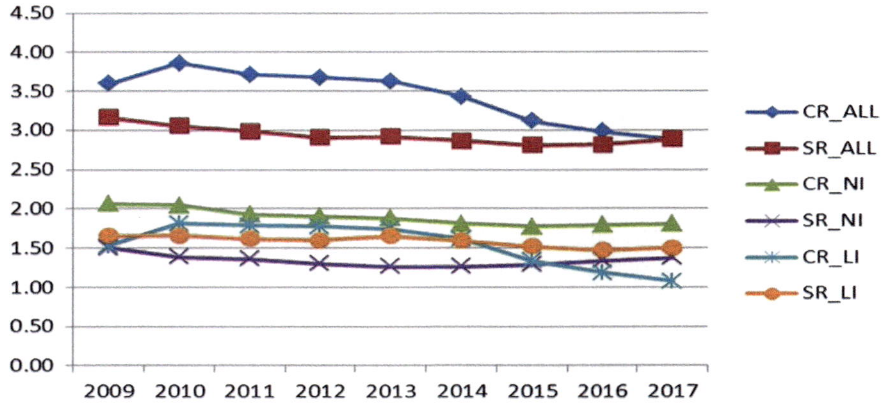

Fig. 1.3 Development of insurance to GDP (for life and non-life insurance in total) in SR and CR in %

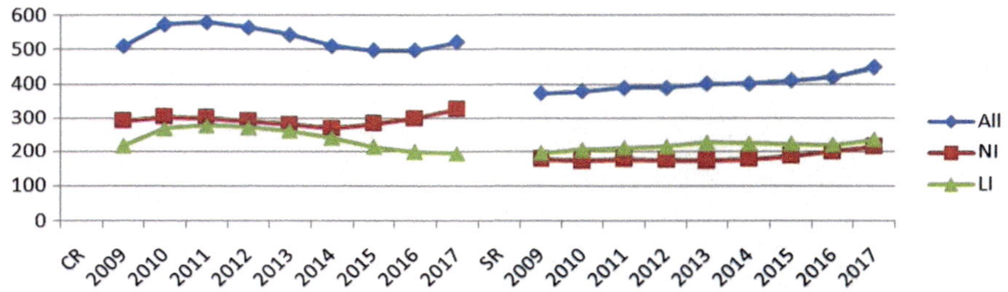

Fig. 1.4 Development of premium written (for life and non-life insurance in total) per person in CR and SR in EUR

reached 6.7% on average, the Slovak Republic and Czech Republic reached the level that is almost twice lower. With regard to the rate of the insurance penetration related to life insurance in 2017, EU countries reached 4.4%; CR reached 1.08%; SR 1.51%. On the other hand, considering the rate of non-life insurance penetration in 2017, EU countries reached 2.3%; CR 1.80% and SR reached 1.38%.

Insurance density is the average amount of money that an individual person spends on a commercial insurance in a particular country. This indicator measures the insurance market in proportion to the size of the country surveyed (premium written/country population).

In 2009, the annual per capita premium for non-life insurance in the Czech Republic was 293 EUR, and it increased to 327 EUR by 2017. In comparison with Slovakia, this is 112 EUR higher, since in the Slovak Republic the annual per capita premium for non-life insurance was 2015 EUR in 2017. In 2017, the annual per capita premium for life insurance was 235 EUR in Slovakia, which is slightly higher compared to the premium in the Czech Republic between 2010 and 2014. However, within the last three years, we can see a divergent decline to 195 EUR in 2017.

1.3 Literature Review

The results of corporate governance including financial management of companies can be measured by various financial–economic analyses indicators. According to the contribution of Afza and Nazir (2014), corporate governance models are based on the fundamental theories including agency theory, stewardship theory, stakeholder theory, resource dependence theory, transaction cost theory and political theory. The administration and management of companies and its significance have been the focus of many authors for a long time, e.g. Cadbury (1992), Shleifer and Vishny (1986), Millstein (1998) and others. Khanchel (2007) examines the issues of corporate governance from the perspective of its measurement and formulates the determinants of strong corporate governance.

Relationships between corporate performance and corporate governance are discussed in detail by the professional community, and many contributions have been published on this topic. Zahroh and Hamidah (2016) explore the relationship between corporate financial performance and corporate governance in terms of board size and independence, the independence of the audit committee, audit quality and the degree of implementation of corporate governance principles. Musa and Debnárová (2014) explore the relationship between corporate governance and selected areas of finance decision making. Other contributions examine the impact of selected determinants of corporate governance on business performance, measured most often by return on assets (ROA) and return on equity (ROE) on a sample of businesses, e.g. from Vietnam (Vo and Phan 2013), Malaysia (Fooladi et al. 2014), Singapore (Vu and Nguyen 2017), Japan (Mizuno 2010), Turkey (Ararat et al. 2017), Slovakia (Grofčíková and Izáková 2018), the United Kingdom (Akbar et al. 2016) and Poland (Bartkowiak and Borkowski 2014).

However, similar surveys in the insurance sector are rare. Bakeš and Valášková (2018) are examining the processes and methods of management with an emphasis on managing unpredictable risks arising in financial markets, with the aim of minimizing their negative impacts on the insurance companies' results. Stroe (2014) examines the management of insurance companies with an emphasis on the difference in insurance products, whose success in the market is conditioned by the perception of risk on the part of the client and the trust towards the insurance company. Research on the performance of insurance companies has been conducted by others, e.g. Uddin (2018) and Abdelkader and Lamia (2014). Selected relationships of corporate governance and performance of insurance companies are reviewed in their contributions by Saeed and Khurram (2015), Markonah et al. (2017), and Wang et al. (2007).

1.4 Methodology

The main goal of our paper is to review and compare the impact of corporate governance on the financial performance of the insurance companies based in the Czech and Slovak Republics. It had been stated in the theoretical part of the paper that research into the financial performance of enterprises has been published in many professional and scientific studies. A lot of attention has also been paid to corporate governance and its selected determinants. The major contribution of our paper is in interconnection of these two research areas and their application in the specific environment of the insurance companies.

Our sample consists of the insurance companies with the legal form of a joint-stock company, acting in the relevant markets before 31 Dec 2017. We got all necessary information from the annual reports on 2017. These are mainly the data reflecting the situation on both insurance markets. Regarding our effort to review the impact of governance on performance of the selected insurance companies, in our focus there were the subjects which create their managing authorities in compliance with the legislation in force. According to the Czech legislation, the inner structure system of the joint-stock companies can be either dualistic (managing authorities are a board of directors and a board of supervisors), or monistic (companies establish a board of directors and a statutory director). Should there be any doubt, a dualistic system is selected (§ 396 of Act No. 90/2012). As of 31.12.2017, there were 27 insurance companies based in the Czech Republic. In Slovakia, there were 16 insurance companies based on the same date. According to the Slovak legislation, joint-stock companies use dualistic inner structure system. Therefore, all the insurance companies included in the research had established a dualistic inner structure system. Two insurance companies were excluded from the original set; a Czech one because in their annual report 2017 they only reported consolidated economic results, and a Slovak one because it was declared bankrupt in January 2018. Thus, we have ensured comparability of the insurance companies both from the aspect of the data reported in their annual reports and from the moral aspect of the insurance companies' governance. Taking a statistical point of view into consideration, these entities form a basic set. Data from the annual reports of the Czech insurance companies were transformed by calculating the average annual exchange rate of the euro in a given year.

Insurance markets in the Czech and Slovak Republics are compared by these 33 indicators:

1. total assets
2. equity
3. gross premium written for life
4. and non-life insurance
5. gross claim settlement costs for life
6. and non-life insurance
7. total personnel costs
8. indebtedness
9. loss ratio
10. liquidity
11. ROA
12. ROE
13. ROS
14. asset turnover

15. gross wage profitability
16. gross profitability of directors' remuneration
17. gross profit
18. the amount of dividends paid
19. dividend ratio
20. the majority shareholder's share in equity
21. number of shareholders with qualified participation

22–29. size and structure of the board of directors and the board of supervisors
   i.(number of members
   ii.women ratio
   iii.ratio of members with university degree
   iv.and ratio of members based in a foreign country), ... there are 8 indicators

30. average amount of remuneration of a member of governing bodies
31. number of days of activity of the insurance company (before 31.12.2017)
32. number of employees
33. the proportion of managers in the total number of employees

We have processed the data in the SPSS programme with an independent sample T-test (H_0: $\mu_0 = \mu_1$; H_1: $\mu_0 \neq \mu_1$).

We intend to study corporate governance through selected financial and non-financial determinants listed in Table 1.1. Our choice of determinants was based on the stakeholders' corporate governance model according to which the interests of all the groups involved should be taken into consideration for the reason the shareholders are not the only risk bearers in the company (Škare and Hasić 2015). Our research is focused on these interested parties: shareholders, employees (executive staff and other employees), management (members of boards) and creditors. An interesting financial determinant is also the ratio of the executive staff personnel costs in total personnel costs. However, this information is only published by the Czech insurance companies, so we did not include it in the set of examined determinants.

The selected aggregated indicator of the insurance companies' financial performance is the return on assets (ROA) calculated as a ratio of gross profit and total assets of the insurance company in 2017.

The relation of the non-financial determinants to ROA, as a dependent variable, is established for each market individually by means of the correlation analysis. We shall use zero-order and partial Pearson's R, and Somers' d (H_0: $\rho = 0$; H_1: $\rho \neq 0$).

The impact of the selected corporate governance determinants on ROA is identified with multiple linear regression analysis and through assembling the following linear regression model:

$$y = \beta_0 + \beta_1 x_1 + \beta_2 x_2 + \cdots + \beta_n x_n + \varepsilon, \tag{1.1}$$

where y = an explained, dependent variable, b = a regression coefficient, x = a selected independent, explanatory variable, e = a random error and n = a number of explanatory variables.

Table 1.1 Financial and non-financial corporate governance determinants

	Symbol	Description and measurement (stakeholders identifier)
Non-financial CG determinants	SHL	Percentage of the first largest shareholder (a)
	SHQ	Number of shareholders with qualified participation (a)
	BDM	Total number of Board of Directors members (with chairman) (b)
	BDW	Ratio of women in the Board of Directors (b)
	BDUD	Ratio of the Board of Directors members with university degree (b)
	BDF	Ratio of members in the Board of Directors with residence outsite the Slovakia resp. Czech Republic (b)
	BSM	Total number of Board of Supervisors members (b)
	BSW	Ratio of women in the Board of Supervisors (b)
	BSUD	Ratio of the Board of Supervisors members with university degree (b)
	BSF	Ratio of members in the Board of Supervisors with residence outsite the Slovakia resp. Czech Republic (b)
	EMP	Total number of employees (c)
	MAN	Ratio of middle managers on total number of employees (c)
Financial CG determinants	GPWL	Gross premium written (life insurance, in EUR) (b, c)
	GPWN	Gross premium written (non-life insurance, in EUR) (b, c)
	GCPL	Claims paid (gross amount, life insurance, in EUR) (b, c)
	GCPN	Claims paid (gross amount, non-life insurance, in EUR) (b, c)
	TI	Total indebtedness ((Assets-Equity)/Assets) (d)
	LR	Loss ratio (Total gross claims paid/ Total gross premium written) (b, c)
	LIQ	Liquidity (Debitors + Cash)/Creditors) (d)
	PC	Total personnel costs in EUR (c)
	BMRA	Statutory, Executive and Supervisory Board members' remuneration (BMR) (average per person, in EUR) (b)
	DR	Dividend ratio (dividend paid in 2017/net profit for year 2016) (a)

Stakeholder identifier (a) shareholders, (b) management, (c) employees and (d) creditors

The explaining ability of the regression model is verified by F-test ANOVA (H_0: $\mu_0 = \mu_1 = \cdots = \mu_n$; H_1: $\mu_0 \neq \mu_1 \neq \cdots \neq \mu_n$). Adequacy of the respective explanatory variables included in the model is evaluated with T-test (H_0: $\mu_0 = \mu_1$; H_1: $\mu_0 \neq \mu_1$). To assess multicollinearity of the explanatory variables entering the regression model, we use the variance inflation factor (VIF) indicator with the maximum reference value of 10. Variables with VIF < 10 can be assessed as weakly, insignificantly linearly interdependent. By means of Durbin–Watson test, we assess residues ε_i independence (H_0: residues ε_i are independent; H_1: residues ε_i are interdependent). If required, this might by complement with a test of statistical relevance of the autocorrelation coefficient of the first degree.

For the purpose of assessment of the used statistical methods, we use significance level $\alpha = 0.1$.

1.5 Empirical Results and Discussion

1.5.1 Independent Samples Test

Common history and similarities in development of the Czech and Slovak insurance markets have influenced their current situation. In this chapter, we present the results of research aimed at comparison of these markets. The results are summarized in Table 1.2.

The results of the analysis have shown that the Czech and Slovak markets are the same with regard to 24 observed indicators. Despite the differences in average measures of the individual indicators, based on the test result, the zero hypotheses of variance and mean equality cannot be rejected. Therefore, we can conclude that the Slovak and Czech insurance markets have the same indicators, in Table 1.2 to be found under the entry "Equal variances assumed". An average number of the insurance companies' activity days in the Czech Republic are 7823, in Slovakia 7573 days. In favour of the Czech insurance companies, we have found differences in equity, GCPL, PC, BMRA, BDM, EMP and BSUD. As for the other indicators—GCPN, LR, LIQ, DR, gross profit, BDW, SHQ, MAN, BSM, BSW, profitability of BMR (gross profit/total BMR), profitability of PC (gross profit/PC), ROA, ROE, ROS and asset turnover, we have found variances in favour of the Slovak insurance companies.

We have identified the differences in variances in 9 out of total 33 indicators. For these indicators, in Table 1.2 to be found as "Equal variances not assumed", we accept an alternative hypothesis at the selected significance level and conclude that the Slovak and Czech insurance companies differ in these indicators. The greatest difference in favour of the Czech insurance companies has been found in total assets, and the difference of means is here up to EUR 229,565,071. The Czech insurance companies also report a greater amount of gross premium written in both life and non-life insurance, and in 2017 they paid on average EUR 7,584,440 more on dividends.

Table 1.2 Independent samples test for equality of variances and of means

	Indicator	Equality of variance		*t*-test for equality of means			
		F	Sig.	*t*	Sig.	Mean difference	SE difference
Equal variances not assumed	Assets	3.220	0.080*	−0.882	0.383	−229,565,071	260,221,666
	GPWN	3.211	0.081*	−1.049	0.301	−56,307,490	53656729,31
	GPWL	3.694	0.062*	−0.171	0.865	−4,629,227	27,075,140
	TI	15.395	0.000***	2.507	0.017**	0.150	0.060
	Dividend paid	3.489	0.069*	−1.234	0.227	−7,584,440	6,143,771
	BDUD	2.913	0.096*	1.146	0.259	0.097	0.085
	BDF	5.022	0.031**	1.188	0.074*	0.168	0.089
	SHL	8.298	0.006***	0.980	0.334	0.042	0.043
	BSF	11.185	0.002***	2.319	0.026**	0.251	0.108
Equal variances assumed	Number days of activity	0.644	0.427	−0.354	0.725	−249.233	703.278
	Equity	1.122	0.296	−0.610	0.545	−33,495,248	54,870,792
	GCPN	1.702	0.200	0.497	0.622	39,190,627	78,901,759
	GCPL	1.346	0.253	−0.061	0.952	−1,383,241	22,625,943
	LR	1.374	0.248	0.904	0.372	0.271	0.304
	LIQ	2.623	0.113	0.711	0.481	3.810	5.355
	PC	1.354	0.252	−0.415	0.681	−2,978,706	7,178,446
	BMRA	1.458	0.235	−0.231	0.819	−9284	40,260
	DR	0.033	0.856	0.985	0.331	0.159	0.161
	Gross profit	1.107	0.299	0.033	0.974	419,104	12,742,481
	BDM	0.261	0.612	−0.276	0.784	−0.097	0.353
	BDW	0.049	0.826	1.197	0.238	0.075	0.063

(continued)

Table 1.2 (continued)

	Indicator	Equality of variance		*t*-test for equality of means			
		F	Sig.	*t*	Sig.	Mean difference	SE difference
	SHQ	0.733	0.397	0.272	0.787	0.071	0.263
	EMP	1.412	0.242	−0.231	0.818	−57.884	250.517
	MAN	0.123	0.728	0.936	0.355	0.022	0.024
	BSM	1.629	0.209	1.045	0.303	0.910	0.871
	BSW	0.169	0.683	1.221	0.229	0.084	0.069
	BSUD	2.419	0.128	−0.762	0.451	−12.890	16.919
	Profitability of BMR	2.741	0.106	0.310	0.759	3.441	11.112
	Profitability of PC	1.705	0.199	0.598	0.553	0.663	1.109
	ROA	2.175	0.148	1.368	0.179	0.022	0.016
	ROE	2.516	0.121	1.489	0.145	0.109	0.073
	ROS	2.332	0.135	1.489	0.145	0.316	0.212
	Asset turnover	0.056	0.814	0.344	0.733	0.044	0.128

Mean Difference (+) Mean in Slovakia > Mean in CR; (−) Mean in Slovakia < Mean in CR
*Correlation is significant at the 0.1 level (2-tailed). **Correlation is significant at the 0.05 level (2-tailed). ***Correlation is significant at the 0.01 level (2-tailed)

Contrarily, the Slovak insurance companies report 15 percentage points (p.p.) higher total indebtedness, 9.7 p.p. higher ratio of the Board of Directors members with University Degree (BDUD), 16.8 p.p. higher BDF, 4.2 p.p. higher SHL and 2.51 p.p. higher BSF.

Significant differences in means have only been found in total indebtedness (TI, $Mean_{SR} = 27.24\%$, $Mean_{CR} = 10.45\%$, Sig. = 0.017), in the ratio of the Board of Directors members with foreign residence to the total number of members (BDF, $Mean_{SR} = 80.62\%$, $Mean_{CR} = 65.60\%$, Sig. = 0.074) and in the ratio of the Board of Supervisors members with foreign residence to the total number of members (BSF, $Mean_{SR} = 63.54\%$, $Mean_{CR} = 38.46\%$, Sig. = 0.026).

1.5.2 Correlation Analysis

By means of correlation analysis, we have identified the relation of the non-financial corporate governance determinants (see Table 1.1) to ROA, ROE, ROS and asset turnover. In the following text, we only present statistically significant outputs, calculated in SPSS.

The results of the Pearsons' R correlation coefficient for the Czech insurance companies are as follows: MAN with ROS ($r = -0.591$, Sig. = 0.001), BSW with ROA ($r = -0.346$, Sig. = 0.083), BSW with asset turnover (r = 0.436, Sig. = 0 .026), BSF with ROE ($r = 0.423$, Sig. = 0.031) and BSF with ROA ($r = 0.350$, Sig. = 0.080).

In the Slovak insurance market, we have identified these relations of non-financial corporate governance determinants with ROA, ROE, ROS and asset turnover: BDF with ROS ($r = 0.627$, Sig. = 0.012), BDF with asset turnover ($r = 0.528$, Sig. = 0.043), MAN with ROE ($r = -0.623$, Sig. = 0.013) and BSW with ROE ($r = 0.459$, Sig. = 0.086).

Strong similarities between the Czech and Slovak insurance markets allow us to evaluate them together and make just one Slovak and Czech common insurance market with a total number of 41 insurance companies. In the common market, we have identified these statistically significant relations: BDW with asset turnover ($r = -0.298$, Sig. = 0.059), BDF with ROS ($r = 0.284$, Sig. = 0 .072), SHL with asset turnover ($r = 0.283$, Sig. = 0 .077), MAN with ROE ($r = -0.334$, Sig. = 0.033), MAN with ROS ($r = -0.477$, Sig. = 0.002), BSM with ROE ($r = 0.281$, Sig. = 0.075), BSF with ROS ($r = 0.322$, Sig. = 0.040) and BSF with ROA ($r = 0.280$, Sig. = 0.077).

The above-mentioned results can be summarized as follows:

- between the selected non-financial corporate governance determinants and aggregated performance indicators (ROA, ROE, ROS and asset turnover) medium up to strong statistically significant dependence has been identified,
- positive correlation with the performance indicators has been identified for BDF, BSF, BSM and a SHL,

- ratio of women in a boards has a considerable impact in 3 out of the 4 observed performance indicators. BSW has a positive influence on ROE and asset turnover and a negative one on ROA. BDW has a negative influence on ROA,
- ratio of middle managers to total number of employees (MAN) has a negative influence on ROS in the Czech market and on ROE in the Slovak market. We have also recorded a negative correlation MAN on ROE and on ROS in the common market.

From another point of view, we can determine the impact of the Supervisory Board members on ROA. There is a positive influence of the Supervisory Board foreign members' ratio (BSF) on ROA, but a negative one of the women ratio (BSW). Supervisory Board structure also has a significant impact on ROE. We have found a medium dependence on BSW, BSF and BSM. BSF has a positive influence on ROS as well. ROS is positively influenced also by the ratio of the Board of Directors members with foreign residence (BDF). BDF has a strong impact on asset turnover, which is also positively influenced by BSW and SHL, and BDW has a negative influence.

The goal of our paper shall be met by building a linear regression model. ROA is the explained, dependent variable in the regression model. Financial and non-financial corporate governance determinants listed in Table 1.1 are the explanatory, independent variables. The regression model will be used to illustrate the impact of corporate governance on the financial performance of the insurance companies.

The results of the correlation analysis of the indicators included in the model are summarized in Table 1.3. Zero-order correlation will be supplemented with Somers' *d* indicator which measures unilateral dependence. The data set entering the regression analysis influences the results of the individual correlation coefficients. Therefore, by calculation of partial correlation between a dependent and a selected independent variable, we can control the impact of the other variables included in the model.

Zero-order correlation coefficient detects bilateral dependence of variables, the value of which can even be influenced by the existence of unquantified values. Partial correlation is used to measure the direction and intensity of the relation between the independent and dependent variables, cleaned from the impact of the other variables. Somers' *d* allows detecting one-way dependence between the selected independent and dependent variables, which can bring more accurate results. In all cases, we observe a shift in the coefficient value.

1.5.3 Regression Analysis

We use the regression analysis to shape the relation between the input independent variables listed in Tables 1.1 and 1.3 and ROA. With regard to the findings about similarities of the Czech and Slovak market, we have built one model for the common Czech and Slovak market. We have used the backward method. SPSS has built 11 models. In the process of a suitable model selection, we considered *R* value, *R* square,

Table 1.3 Zero-order, partial correlation and Somers' d for explanatory variables in regression model

Variable	Correlation coefficient (Sig.)			Variable	Correlation coefficient (Sig.)		
	Zero-order	Somers' d	Partial		Zero-order	Somers' d	Partial
GPWN	0.088 (0.583)	0.017 (0.871)	0.011 (0.966)	BDW	−0.173 (0.280)	−0.184 (0.177)	−0.265 (0.304)
GPWL	0.141 (0.378)	0.114 (0.387)	−0.147 (0.574)	BDUD	−0.031 (0.849)	0.144 (0.379)	0.178 (0.494)
GCPN	0.059 (0.715)	−0.033 (0.775)	0.511 (0.036**)	BDF	0.128 (0.423)	0.023 (0.879)	0.344 (0.176)
GCPL	0.122 (0.448)	0.077 (0.548)	0.331 (0.195)	SHL	0.104 (0.522)	0.133 (0.336)	0.310 (0.226)
TI	0.050 (0.755)	−0.168 (0.180)	−0.456 (0.066*)	SHQ	−0.011 (0.944)	−0.068 (0.715)	0.654 (0.004***)
LIQ	−0.167 (0.296)	0.005 (0.986)	0.070 (0.789)	EMP	0.094 (0.557)	0.061 (0.618)	0.103 (0.695)
LR	−0.294 (0.062*)	−0.212 (0.050**)	−0.405 (0.107)	MAN	−557 (0.119)	−0.090 (0.493)	0.069 (0.792)
BMRA	0.105 (0.521)	0.165 (0.085*)	−0.021 (0.936)	BSM	−0.006 (0.970)	−0.030 (0.827)	−0.252 (0.329)
DR	0.277 (0.080*)	0.246 (0.048**)	0.527 (0.030**)	BSW	−0.259 (0.103)	−0.209 (0.134)	−0.621 (0.008***)
PC	0.085 (0.602)	0.046 (0.691)	−0.150 (0.567)	BSUD	0.032 (0.843)	−0.050 (0.730)	0.178 (0.495)
BDM	−0.181 (0.258)	−0.158 (0.217)	0.508 (0.037**)	BSF	0.280 (0.077*)	0.142 (0.333)	0.235 (0.363)

*Correlation is significant at the 0.1 level (2-tailed). **Correlation is significant at the 0.05 level (2-tailed). ***Correlation is significant at the 0.01 level (2-tailed)

adjusted R square, standard error of the estimate and Durbin–Watson test. Informative value of the models was assessed by ANOVA analysis. Relevance of variables included in the model was assessed by the T-test; multicollinearity of the variables was assessed by VIF. The results of the regression analysis are listed in Table 1.4.

We can see that in all proposed models, there exists very strong correlation between ROA and the explanatory variables. This information comes from the multiple correlation coefficient R which is minimum 86.2%. R square presents the ROA variability ratio that can be explained by the given model. Adjusted R square revises the estimate of ROA variability ratio that can be explained by the included number of the explanatory variables in the model. The highest adjusted R square was measured in models 6 and 7. The lowest standard error of the estimation is in model 7. In this model, however, two variables with VIF higher than the reference value were included. That is why we choose model 8 as the most suitable one: it still has a reasonable informative value, and none of the variables exceeds the VIF reference value. The highest VIF was found with GCPL at 4.983.

Table 1.4 Regression analysis (backward method)

Variables	Model no	1	2	3	4	5	6	7	8	9	10	11
	Entered	all (see Tab. 3)										
	Removed		GPWN	BMRA	MAN	LIQ	GPWL	BDUD	EMP	BSF	BDW	LR
Model summary	*R*	0.904	0.904	0.904	0.904	0.903	0.901	0.896	0.889	0.885	0.875	0.862
	R square	0.818	0.818	0.818	0.817	0.816	0.812	0.802	0.791	0.782	0.766	0.743
	Adj. *R* square	0.551	0.579	0.603	0.623	00.641	0.652	0.652	0.648	0.650	0.639	0.620
	SE of the Est.	0.0308	0.0298	0.0289	0.0282	0.0275	0.0271	0.0271	0.0273	0.0272	0.0276	0.0283
ANOVA	*F* value	3.061	3.420	3.813	4.233	4.674	5.072	5.332	5.540	5.910	6.041	6.030
	Sig.	0.015**	0.008***	0.004***	0.002***	0.001***	0.000***	0.000***	0.000***	0.000***	0.000***	0.000***

*Correlation is significant at the 0.1 level (2-tailed). **Correlation is significant at the 0.05 level (2-tailed). ***Correlation is significant at the 0.01 level (2-tailed)

The value of Durbin–Watson test of residuals independence in model 8 is 2.219. This value is situated within the interval in which we cannot decide on residuals independence. Therefore, we have decided, based on the results of the test of statistical significance of the first degree autocorrelation coefficient, for unstandardized and studentized residuals. On the grounds of comparison of autocorrelation coefficients with critical value of cyclical autocorrelation coefficient for $\alpha = 0.05$ and $n = 39$, we can accept null hypothesis of residuals independence. In Table 1.5, we present regression statistics for model 8.

We formulate the following regression model for explanation of the impact of selected variables on the aggregated performance indicator ROA:

$$\begin{aligned} \text{ROA} = & -0.018 - 0.015\ \text{BDM} - 0.040\ \text{BDW} + 0.037\ \text{BDF} + 0.096\ \text{SHL} \\ & + 0.042\ \text{SHQ} - 0.003\ \text{BSM} - 0.079\ \text{BSW} + 1.650\text{E}{-}04\ \text{BSUD} \\ & + 0.015\ \text{BSF} + 6.798\text{E}{-}11\ \text{GCPN} + 3.642E{-}10\ \text{GCPL} - 0.091\ \text{TI} \\ & - 0.012\ \text{LR} - 7.789\text{E} - 10\,\text{PC} + 0.053\ \text{DR} + \varepsilon. \end{aligned} \tag{1.2}$$

The model contains total of 15 explanatory variables. Nine variables have a character of non-financial corporate governance determinants, and six variables are of a financial character. We regard the variables BDM, SHL, SHQ, BSW, GCPN, GCPL, TI, LR, PC and DR as significant on the selected significance level $a = 0.1$. By means of this model, we can explain 79.1% (R square), or 64.8% (Adj. R square) of variability of the dependent variable ROA, which can be considered as a very good result.

Regression coefficients for BDM, BDW, BSM, BSW, PC, TI and LR are negative. PC presents an interest group of employees attempting to negotiate favourable payroll and social benefits for themselves and thus being a cost item for the insurance company. Another cost is remuneration paid to the managing authority members. The higher the number of the managing authority members, the higher the total amount of paid remuneration is, and the lower the profitability is. Regression coefficients for BDM, BDW, BSM and BSW also have a higher absolute value when compared to the PC coefficient. The reason is a 2.94 times bigger average amount of remuneration to one managing authority member (Mean = EUR 83,803) when compared to an average amount of remuneration to one employee (EUR 28,548). TI and LR are financial corporate governance determinants presenting the interests of creditors and company clients. Their interests are of a cost to insurance companies.

Regression coefficients for shareholders (SHL, SHQ, DR) have positive values. Their interest is the growth of the company's assets value. We also have measured positive coefficients for the ratio of foreign management members (BDF, BSF) who most frequently represent the interest of a foreign parent company and the ratio of managers with a university degree. We have also measured a very low positive coefficient for gross claims payments. The ratio of female managers has a negative regression coefficient. This finding may be related to a more sensitive social responsiveness of women, which is consequently reflected in the company costs.

Table 1.5 Multiple regression for model 8

Var.	Unstd. Coeff. B	Std. Error	*t*-value	Sig.	VIF	Var.	Unstd. Coeff.	Std. Error	*t*-value	Sig.	VIF
Constant	−0.018	0.058	−0.318	0.753		BSUD	1.650E–04	9.703E–05	1.699	0.103	1.362
BDM	−0.015	0.005	−2.872	0.009***	1.618	BSF	0.015	0.016	0.928	0.364	1.954
BDW	−0.040	0.030	−1.338	0.194	1.684	GCPN	6.798E–11	2.702E–11	2.516	0.020**	2.258
BDF	0.037	0.023	1.620	0.119	1.650	GCPL	3.642E–10	1.422E–10	2.562	0.018**	4.983
SHL	0.096	0.051	1.873	0.074*	2.855	TI	−0.091	0.030	−2.985	0.007***	2.162
SHQ	0.042	0.010	4.297	0.000***	2.710	LR	−0.012	0.006	−1.890	0.072*	1.820
BSM	−0.003	0.003	−1.140	0.267	2.329	PC	−7.789E–10	4.207E–10	−1.851	0.078*	4.202
BSW	−0.079	0.023	−3.476	0.002***	1.222	DR	0.053	0.013	4.208	0.000***	1.954

*Correlation is significant at the 0.1 level (2-tailed). **Correlation is significant at the 0.05 level (2-tailed). *** Correlation is significant at the 0.01 level (2-tailed)

1.6 Conclusion

The insurance market of the Slovak and Czech Republics was similar not only due to their common history, but we also find similarity from the data presented in the 2017 annual reports. We compared a total of 33 financial and non-financial indicators. Based on the independent samples T-test, we found a statistically significant difference in mean and variance in only three indicators (TI, BSF, BDF). All three showed higher values for the Slovak insurance market.

By correlation analysis, we examined the direction and tightness of the dependence of non-financial determinants of corporate governance listed in Table 1.1 on selected aggregated indicators of financial performance. In the test of the impact of MAN on the financial performance of insurance companies measured by ROA, ROE, ROS and asset turnover, we identify in all cases a strong indirect correlation. Thus, the growth in the number of executives to the number of employees strongly reduces the financial performance of insurance companies.

The results of the multiple regression analysis are presented in the conclusion of this paper. They were used to quantify the impact of selected financial and non-financial determinants of corporate governance on the aggregate indicator of the financial performance of ROA and compile a regression model. We consider our research to be beneficial, as we have not found similar research on this issue in the insurance sector.

Acknowledgements This paper has been supported by the Scientific Grant Agency of Slovak Republic under project VEGA No. 1/0749/18 "Research on the application of corporate governance principles in companies in Slovakia". The authors would like to express their gratitude to the Scientific Grant Agency of The Ministry of Education, Science, Research and Sport of the Slovak Republic for financial support of this research and publication.

References

Abdelkader, D., & Lamia, J. (2014). Determinants of performance of Tunisian insurance companies: Case of life insurance. *International Journal of Innovation and Applied Studies, 6*(1), 90–96. https://doi.org/10.1016/j.ribaf.2015.10.013.

Act No 90/2012 on commercial companies and cooperatives.

Afza, T., & Nazir, M. S. (2014). Theoretical perspective of corporate governance: A review. *European Journal of Scientific Research, 119*(2), 255–264.

Akbar, S., Poletti-Hughes, J., El-Faitouri, R., Zulfiqar, S., & Shah, A. (2016). More on the relationship between corporate governance and firm performance in the UK: Evidence from the application of generalized method of moments estimation. *Research in International Business and Finance, 38,* 417–429.

Ararat, M., Black, B. S., & Yurtoglu, B. B. (2017). The effect of corporate governance on firm value and profitability: Time-series evidence from Turkey. *Emerging Markets Review, 30,* 113–132.

Bakeš, V., & Valášková, K. (2018). Assessment of financial risks in the insurance sector using the sensitivity analysis. In N. Tsounis, & A. Vlachvei (Eds.), *Advances in panel data analysis in applied economic research. ICOAE 2017. Springer proceedings in business and economics*. Cham: Springer. https://doi.org/10.1007/978-3-319-70055-7_39.

Bartkowiak, P., & Borkowski, M. (2014). Financial review as an element of corporate governance in the Polish legal regulations. *Journal of International Studies, 7*(2), 70–82. https://doi.org/10.14254/2071-8330.2014/7-2/6.

Cadbury, A. (1992). *Report of the committee on the financial aspects of corporate governance*. London: Gee & Co., Ltd.

Fooladi, M., Zaleha, A. S., Norman, M. S., & Romlah, J. (2014). The effect of corporate governance and divergence between cash flow and control rights on firm performance: Evidence from Malaysia. *International Journal of Disclosure and Governance, 11*(4), 326–340.

Grofčíková, J., & Izáková, K. (2018). Corporate governance and firm performance in Slovakia. In *18th international scientific conference Globalization and its socio-economic consequences* (pp. 532–539). Rajecké Teplice.

Izáková, K., & Přečková, L. (2014). Predpokladané zmeny v corporate governance po zavedení Sloventnosti II. *Acta Aerarii Publici, 11*(1), 4–18.

Khanchel, I. (2007). Corporate governance: Measurement and determinant analysis. *Managerial Auditing Journal, 22*(8), 740–760.

Mardi, M., Sudiro, A., & Rahayu, M. (2017). The effect of good corporate governance and premium growth on the performance of insurance companies. *Journal of Finance and Banking Review, 2*(2), 1–7.

Millstein, I. M. (1998). *Corporate governance: Improving competitiveness and access to capital in global markets: A report to the OECD*. https://doi.org/10.1787/9789264162709-en.

Mizuno, M. (2010). Institutional investors, corporate governance and firm performance in Japan. *Pacific Economic Review, 15*(5), 653–665.

Musa, H., & Debnárová, L. (2014). The impact of corporate governance on selected areas of finance decision making. Management: Science and education. *Slovak Scientific Journal, 3*, 60–63.

Saeed, U., & Khurram, N. (2015). Factors influencing the financial performance of non-life insurance companies of Pakistan. *International Journal of Empirical Finance., 4*(6), 354–361.

Shleifer, A., & Vishny, R. W. (1986). Large shareholders and corporate control. *Journal of Political Economy, 94*(3, Part 1), 461–488.

Stroe, M. A. (2014). Insurances and consumer perception in the Romanian insurance market. *Procedia Economics and Finance, 15*, 1717–1723. https://doi.org/10.1016/S2212-5671(14)00646-7.

Škare, M., & Hasić, T. (2015). Corporate governance, firm performance and economic growth—theoretical analysis. *Journal of Business Economics and Management, 17*(1), 35–51.

Uddin, G. E., Oserei, K. M., Oladipo, O. E., & Ajayi, D. (2018). Industry competitiveness using firm-level data: A case study of the nigerian insurance sector. In N. Tsounis, & A. Vlachvei (Eds.), *Advances in panel data analysis in applied economic research. ICOAE 2017. Springer proceedings in business and economics*. Cham: Springer. https://doi.org/10.1007/978-3-319-70055-7_37.

Vo, D., & Phan, T. (2013). Corporate governance and firm performance: Empirical evidence from Vietnam. *Journal of Financial Economics, 78*, 210–226.

Vu, N. H., & Nguyen, T. (2017). *Impacts of corporate governance on firm performance. Empirical study of listed Singaporean companies*. [Online]. Lund University. Available: https://lup.lub.lu.se/student-papers/search/publication/8917364.

Wang, J. L., Jeng, V., & Peng, J. L. (2007). The impact of corporate governance structure on the efficiency performance of insurance companies in Taiwan. *The Geneva Papers, 32*, 264–282. https://doi.org/10.1057/palgrave.gpp.2510125.

Zahroh, N., & Hamidah, (2016). The role of corporate governance in firm performance. SHS Web of Conferences, *34*, (13003). https://doi.org/10.1051/shsconf/20173413003.

Chapter 2
Volatility of Education Aid and Female Education

Nihal Bayraktar

Abstract Positive contributions of females to economic growth cannot be denied and they can contribute more effectively to economic development if they get a better education. Thus, it is essential to explore the different ways of enhancing female education and reducing the gender gap. Such actions can be even more crucial in low-income countries where the need for higher economic growth is more pressing. The important point for these countries is that the scope and quality of education are highly dependent on foreign aid on education. This paper empirically investigates the link between schooling of female students and the volatility of foreign aid on education to better understand the impact of aid on female education and the ways of improving it. The results show that the share of female students increases with declining volatility of foreign aid in low-income countries. Another interesting finding is that the volatility of education aid also affects total students, but this effect is relatively weak when compared to female students only. The dataset covers the years 2002–2016 and 27 low-income countries from Africa and Asia.

Keywords Female education · Foreign aid on education · Volatility of aid · Low-income countries

JEL codes I25 · O15

2.1 Introduction

Economic contributions of females to development have been widely investigated in the literature, and it has been shown that when females have a better education, the quality of their contributions to economic growth improves significantly (Hill and King 1995; Klasen 2002; Boserup et al. 2013). Thus, it is important to investigate the

N. Bayraktar (✉)
Penn State University, 777 W., Harrisburg Pike Middletown, Harrisburg, PA 17057, USA
e-mail: nxb23@psu.edu

N. Tsounis and A. Vlachvei (eds.), *Advances in Cross-Section Data Methods in Applied Economic Research*, Springer Proceedings in Business and Economics,
https://doi.org/10.1007/978-3-030-38253-7_2

ways of improving female education outcomes, especially in low-income countries where the contributions of females to economic growth can be major (Bayraktar and Fofack 2018).

When compared to the other income groups, what is special in low-income countries is that the scope and the quality of education are highly dependent on foreign aid on education. Human capital and education indicators become worse with declining foreign aid in these countries (Easterly and Pfutze 2008; Asiama and Quartey 2009). Not only the level of foreign aid but also its volatility is expected to have an important impact on education outcomes (Agenor and Bayraktar 2018). Based on this expectation and given the importance of female education, this paper empirically investigates the link between schooling of female students and the volatility of foreign aid on education. The results show that the share of female students increases with declining volatility of foreign aid in low-income countries. Another interesting finding is that the volatility of education aid has a more dramatic impact on female students when compared to the impacts on total students.

The main data sources are the OECD's Creditor Reporting System Database for foreign aid on education, and the World Bank's World Development Indicators and Barro-Lee Database for additional variables. Due to the limited availability of data on education aid, the dataset covers the years 2002–2016. Since the importance of the volatility of foreign aid is tested in this paper, only low-income countries are included based on the availability of data on education indicators (27 low-income countries from Africa and Asia).

The econometric analysis in the paper is based on a regression specification where the share of female students in secondary education is the dependent variable. The volatility of foreign education aid is measured by calculating the rolling standard deviation of education aid in percent of GDP and per capita terms over 3-year overlapping sub-periods. The explanatory variables consist of four sets: the volatility measure of foreign education aid; economic development variables such as income per capita in real terms or the share of the population living in urban areas; the quality of education supplied (public expenditure on education and the ratio of students to teachers); health status (life expectancy at birth and mortality rate, under-five). The empirical methodology is panel least squares with time and fixed effects. The empirical analysis also includes results with total students to understand the specific impact of volatility of aid on female students.

2.2 Background and Graphical Analysis

In addition to the positive effects of the level of aid itself, the volatility of aid is expected to have a significant impact on education outcomes. Higher aid volatility increases uncertainty about returns to schooling on the decision to invest in human capital skills. Given that improved human capital has a positive impact on economic growth, as presented extensively in the literature, foreign aid volatility is also expected

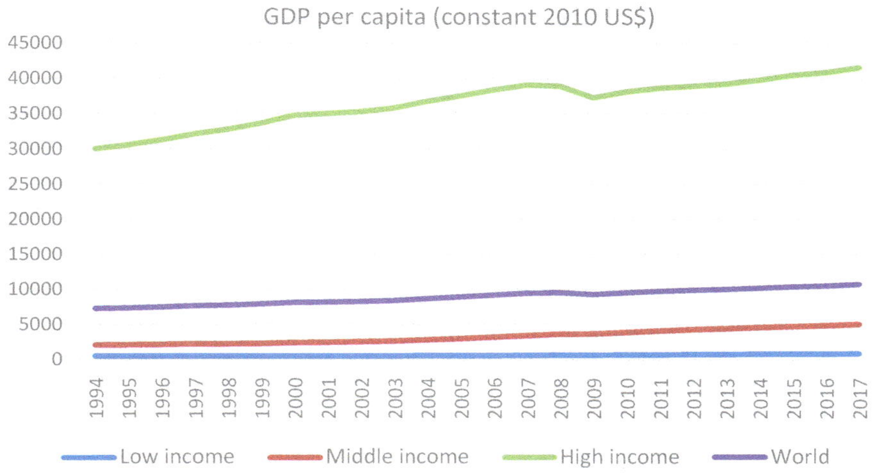

Fig. 2.1 Income levels in different groups of countries, 1994–2017. *Source* The World Bank's World Development Indicators

to negatively determine the rate of economic growth.[1] The link between foreign aid on education and female education outcomes will be investigated in the following section of the paper. In this section, as background information, empirical evidence on the existence of females in education and labor markets is presented for low-income economies and compared to other regions and income groups of the world.

In this section, countries are classified into income groups based on the World Bank's definition. Figure 2.1 presents real GDP per capita levels in the low-, middle- and high-income groups between 1994 and 2017. It can be seen in this figure that income levels are extremely low in the low-income group. It was only US$ 746 on average in constant 2010 US$ in 2017. In the same year, as a comparison, income was US$ 41,540 in the high-income group and US$ 4992 in the middle-income group on average. Such low-income levels in the low-income group clearly show their urgent need for foreign aid to support their economic activities, including education.

The share of females in the labor force in different income groups is shown in Fig. 2.2 to understand the role of women in these groups. Interestingly, the share is highest in the low-income group when compared to the world average as well as other income groups. Almost half of the labor force is female in the low-income group. On average, females comprised 46% of the labor force in 2017 in these countries. Also, the share has been slightly increasing in this group. In 2017, this share was only 37% in the middle-income group and 44% in the high-income group. In the same year, the world average was only 39%. One possible explanation for higher involvement of females in labor force in this group of countries would be the presence of extremely

[1]For a review of empirical evidence on the positive effect of human capital on development, and methodological issues in assessing that link, see Stevens and Weale (2004), Hanushek and Woessmann (2012), and Glewwe et al. (2014).

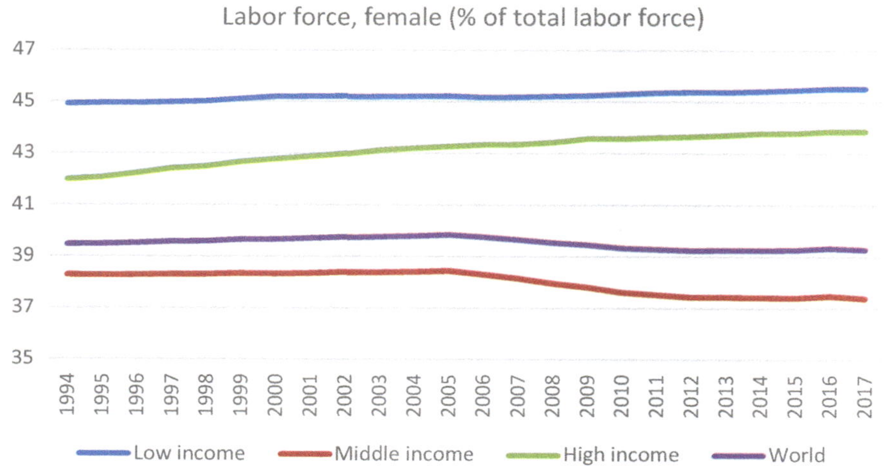

Fig. 2.2 Share of females in labor force, 1994–2017. *Source* The World Bank's World Development Indicators

low-income levels, which forces females to work to support their families in addition to male members. One interesting observation is that while the share of females in the labor force has been increasing in the high- and low-income groups, it has been declining on average in middle-income countries.

Such a high share of females in the labor force demonstrates the undeniable importance of the female workforce in low-income countries. Hence, it would not be wrong to expect that females' contributions to economic development will be more meaningful with improving human capital and education indicators. School enrollment of female students, a measure of education indicator, is presented at different education levels in Fig. 2.3 between 1998 and 2017. This variable is defined as the ratio of female children of official school age who are enrolled in school to the female population of the corresponding official school age. At the primary level, the share of female students enrolled in primary education to the female population of the corresponding official school age is high in each income group. While the share is close to 100% in the high-income group in recent years, it is close to 80%

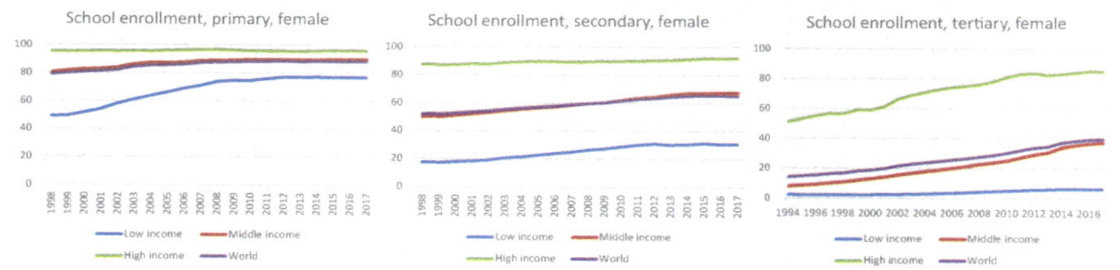

Fig. 2.3 School enrollment of females at different education levels, 1998–2017. *Source* The World Bank's World Development Indicators

in the low-income group, which corresponds to 30 percentage-points improvements in the rate when compared to its value in 1998. The gap across income groups starts getting larger when we consider school enrollment of female students in secondary education. While the share is again close to 100% in the high-income group and 70% in the middle-income group, it is only 30% in low-income countries. Even though there is a big improvement in school enrollment of females in secondary education in the low-income group, which increased from 18% in 1998 to 30% in 2017, the share is still not adequate to support a meaningful amount of human capital formation. Low-income countries still have a long way to go to reach the education level of female students in other income groups. When the level of tertiary education is considered, the share of females enrolled is even lower and its value is less than 10% in the low-income group. Given the fact that tertiary education is one of the most essential sources of advanced human capital accumulation, low-income countries fall significantly short of well-educated female students. Governments need to invest more in tertiary education to support a higher share of females so that they can contribute more to economic growth. In this process, the availability of foreign aid is expected to be a crucial determinant in low-income countries.

The comparison of the share of female students with the share of male students can be informative. Figure 2.4 shows the share of female students in total students in secondary education in different income groups. It should be noted that this variable is the dependent variable of the regression specifications that will be analyzed in the following sections. The share of female students is lowest in low-income countries, but it has been increasing significantly from 39 to 46% throughout the years. In the middle- and high-income groups, the shares of female and male students are almost equal and close to 50%.

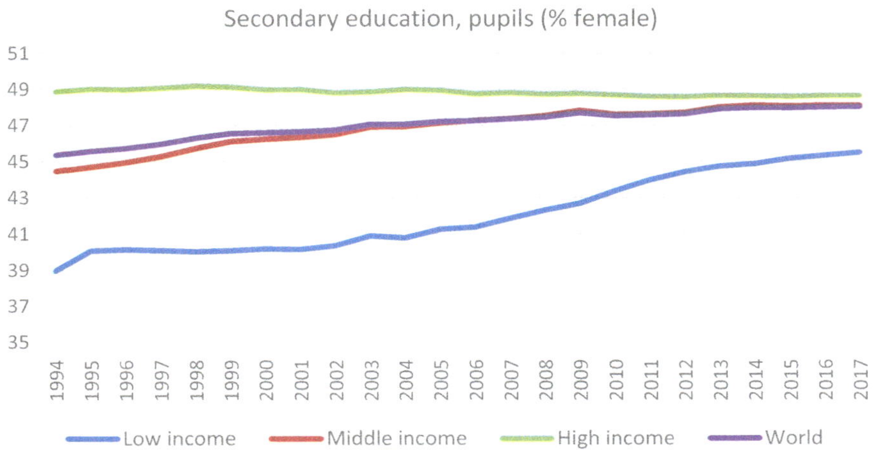

Fig. 2.4 Share of female students in secondary education, 1994–2017. *Source* The World Bank's World Development Indicators

Education outcomes can be also measured by the average years of education for males and females, as presented in Fig. 2.5. The gap between the advanced and other groups of countries is extremely large. In advanced economies, both males and females get close to 11 years of education and gender inequality is negligible. On the

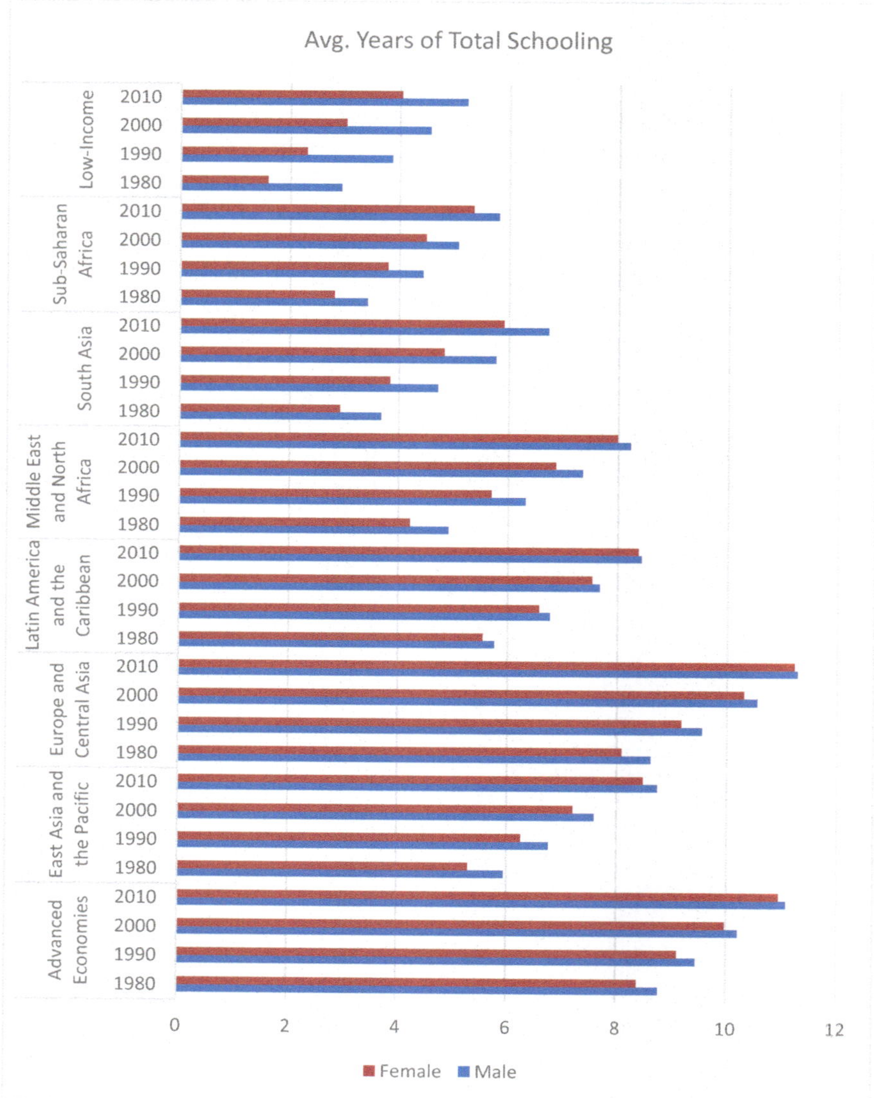

Fig. 2.5 Average years of total schooling for males and females, 1980–2010. *Source* Barro-Lee Database

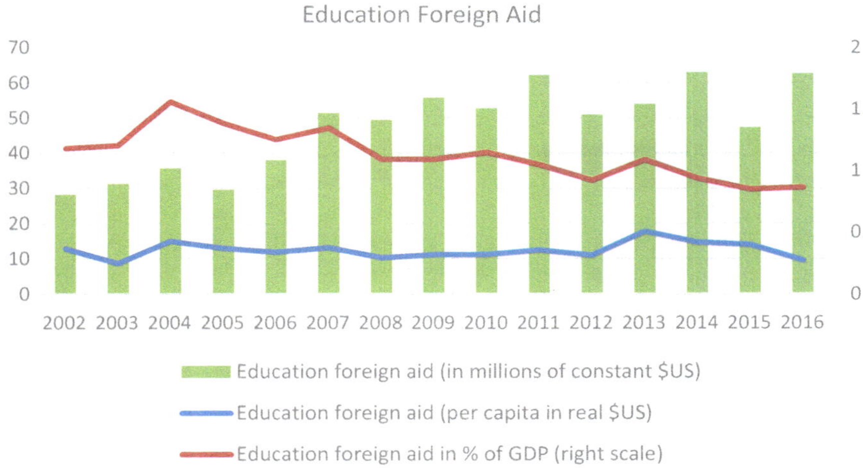

Fig. 2.6 Low-income countries: Education Foreign Aid, 2002–2016. *Source* OECD's Creditor Reporting System Database

other hand, in the low-income group, the years of total schooling was around 5 years in 2010 and the gender gap is largest when compared to other regions. However, it is encouraging to see that the years of schooling were doubled between 1980 and 2010 and the gap between males and females has been getting smaller, indicating significant improvements in the educational outcomes in the low-income group.

As indicated earlier, foreign aid on education plays a major role in low-income countries to improve education facilities, indicators, outcomes and the gender gap. Figure 2.6 shows trends in education foreign aid in real terms (total), in per capita terms (average) and in % of GDP (average) in low-income countries. Total education foreign aid flowing to low-income countries had an increasing trend until 2011, but it became flat on average in recent years. Despite its increasing and then constant trend, large fluctuations have been observed from year to year in the level of education aid. For example, it declined by 20% in 2015, but then it increased back again by more than 20% in 2016. In per capita terms, foreign aid on education has been constant at around US$ 13 in real terms. However, it fluctuates considerably around this value. In % of GDP, education foreign aid has been declining because it did not increase as quickly as rising GDP values in the low-income group. Similar to the per capita and total measures, the fluctuations are also observed from year to year in this measure of education aid. The impacts of such large fluctuations in education aid on education outcomes of females are investigated in more detail in the following sections.

2.3 Information on Data and Empirical Specification

This section gives information on regression data and introduces the regression specification and methodology. The main data sources are the OECD's Creditor Reporting System (CRS) Database for foreign aid on education and the World Bank's World Development Indicators and African Development Indicators databases. The dataset covers the years between 2002 and 2016 because data information on education aid is available from OECD databases during that period. In the study, only low-income countries are included because the importance of foreign aid for female education is tested. In addition to these criteria, the availability of variables has also determined the set of countries. With these restrictions, 27 countries low-income countries are included in the dataset. Most of these countries are from the Sub-Saharan Africa region. The list of countries included in the analysis is:

(SSA countries) Angola, Benin, Burkina Faso, Burundi, Chad, Djibouti, Guinea, Kenya, Lesotho, Madagascar, Mali, Mauritania, Mozambique, Rwanda, Senegal, Sudan, Tanzania, Togo, Uganda and Zambia;

(Non-SSA countries) Afghanistan, Bangladesh, Bhutan, Cambodia, Lao People's Democratic Republic, Myanmar, Nepal and Timor-Leste.

Following Agenor and Bayraktar (2018), the main regression specification is:

$$\begin{aligned}\mathrm{Fedu}_{\mathrm{it}} = {} & \alpha_0 + \alpha_1 x \mathrm{Vola}_{\mathrm{it}} + \alpha_2 x \mathrm{EconDev}_{\mathrm{it}} + \alpha_3 x \mathrm{Qual}_{\mathrm{it}} + \alpha_4 x \mathrm{Health}_{\mathrm{it}} \\ & + \mathrm{Time}_t + \mathrm{Country}_i + \varepsilon_{\mathrm{it},}\end{aligned}$$

where i represents countries and t represents time. The dependent variable, $\mathrm{Fedu}_{\mathrm{it}}$, is an education outcome for females in country i in period t.[2] The explanatory variables are classified in four different groups. Variable *Vola* measures the volatility of foreign education aid. EconDev stands for variables capturing economic development, for example, GDP per capita in real terms and the share of urban population (see Verner 2005). Qual captures the quality of education with government expenditure on education and the ratio of pupils to teachers (see Michaelowa 2001). *Health* represents health status of students with life expectancy at birth and mortality rate (see Behrman 1996). The vector of parameters is $\{\alpha_0, \alpha_1, \alpha_2, \alpha_3, \alpha_4\}$ and $\varepsilon_{\mathrm{it}}$ is error terms. $\mathrm{Time}_{\mathrm{t}}$ represents time effects and $\mathrm{Country}_{\mathrm{i}}$ represents country fixed effects. It should be noted that any variable measuring the quality of institutions or governance is not included in the specification because these variables were mostly constant during the time period covered in the analysis.

The dependent variable of the specification is the share of female students in secondary education school enrollment. Because its impact on economic efficiency is limited, primary education outcomes are not considered. Tertiary education outcomes are also excluded because of severe data limitations in low-income countries. Since we cover only low-income countries, secondary education outcomes are considered significant determinants of the quality of human capital. In the regressions analysis

[2]See Data Appendix for details on variables.

for total education outcomes, the dependent variable is the share of population in secondary education.

The volatility of foreign education aid is measured by the rolling standard deviation of education aid in percent of GDP over 3-year overlapping sub-periods, following Museru et al. (2014), Ebeke and Ehrhart (2011) and Bayraktar (2018). Foreign education aid in gross disbursements is downloaded from the OECD's CRS database (find more details in Clemens et al. 2004 and Neanidis and Varvarigos 2009). The expected sign of the volatility variable is negative. In the regression analysis, alternative measures of aid volatility are also considered, for example, the rolling standard deviation of education foreign aid in per capita terms. Because this alternative measure does not produce higher performance, they are not reported in this paper.

Government education expenditure is expected to be a significant determinant of education outcomes because more spending can improve the quality of education. In this analysis, it is measured in % of GDP. It should be noted that because education foreign aid has been already included in government education spending, only public education spending is included in the specification, not the level of education foreign aid. The expected link between public spending on education and education outcomes is positive.

It should be noted that the public education spending series may have incomplete data points in some countries. Such missing data information may raise uncertainty associated with data aggregation and negatively affect the possibility of making proper conclusions. In the literature, several techniques are suggested to estimate incomplete data points. In this analysis, the data imputation technique of expectation maximization is introduced (Dempster et al. 1977; Anderson et al. 1983; Rubin 1987; Ruud 1991; Honaker and King 2010; Awasthi and Bayraktar 2015). With this technique, as also described in Agenor and Bayraktar (2018), missing data points are estimated with the help of a predictive model that incorporates the available information, and any prior information on the data, as well as relationships between variables, included in the process. The imputation technique consists of a two-stage iterative method. In the first stage (expectation stage), a log-likelihood function for missing data points is formulated and their expectations are taken. In the second stage (maximization stage), the expected log-likelihood from the first stage is maximized. Before the application of imputations, all series used in the process is standardized to enhance the distributional features of the series. The data imputation technique of expectation maximization requires including different related variables as predictors of series that needs to be completed. In this paper, because the share of public education spending in GDP is the variable with missing data points, the candidates of predictors must be related to this variable. The predictors are also expected to be as complete as possible in terms of both time and cross-section dimensions. A government expenditure series from the World Bank's WDI is taken as the predictor because it is the most related to the education spending and at the same time its number of observations is mostly complete. After the imputation process, the education spending ratio has been transformed to its original scale. While extending the public education spending variable by using the available information for predicted values of missing years, it should be noted that its statistical features do not change. The already available data points in the variable are taken as they are and only the remaining data points are predicted.

Another indicator of education quality, the ratio of pupils to teachers, is included in the regression specification. The quality of education is expected to have a positive and significant impact on education outcomes. Because the higher the value of the ratio means that the lower the quality of education, the estimated coefficient is expected to have a negative sign.

It is expected that improving health indicators have a positive impact on education outcomes. In the analysis, life expectancy and the mortality rate, under-five capture the significance of health for improved education. Longer life expectancy and lower mortality rates indicate better health conditions and healthy pupils can have better education opportunities. Longer life expectancy also increases the value of education with higher expected returns. As a result, it is expected to see a positive link between life expectancy and secondary female education outcomes and a negative link between mortality rates and education outcomes.

The development level of countries can also determine education outcomes. Higher incomes are expected to increase the value of education and as a result improve education outcomes. In the analysis, two alternative measures of economic development are considered: GDP per capita in real terms and the share of urban population. Both of these variables are expected to have a positive effect on education outcomes due to increasing expected returns on education investment.

In the regression analysis, annual data are used.[3] Alternatively, longer-term averages could capture long-run relationships and smooth variables from fluctuations in business cycle frequencies. However, the use of annual data has been favored because, as discussed in more detail, for example, in Attanasio et al. (2000), Bond et al. (2010), and Bayraktar and Moreno Dodson (2015), the use of annual data can be more informative than that of averages in determining both short- and long-run relationships between variables: (i) it is not clear that averaging eliminates business cycle fluctuations; (ii) averaging of variables can lead to losing valuable information given in annual data; (iii) focusing only on long-run effects prevents the analysis of interesting short-run dynamics; (iv) given that different countries are combined in analysis, averaging may give up the possibility of considering cross-sectional heterogeneity in the estimated coefficients.

The regression specifications are estimated with panel least squares, including time and country dummies. Panel data methodologies enable corrections of omitted explanatory variables and biases in estimations. With this methodology, country-specific heterogeneity can be captured for, and other unobservable characteristics

[3]It should be noted that, in addition to annual data, both cross-section regressions and regressions with 5-year averages are also considered. Cross-section analysis including country averages could not capture the negative effect of the volatility of education foreign aid on education outcomes. This finding indicates that the time dimension is important to capture the link between the volatility of education aid and education outcomes. Given that the time period is short due to the limited availability of the detailed classification of foreign aid from the data sources, a sufficient number of observations could not be obtained with 5-year averages for robust panel regressions. Thus, these two results are not reported in this paper.

determining the relationship between the measure of education outcome and its determinants can be accounted for while estimating the regression specification. Country effects (fixed effects) can control country heterogeneities and reduce the risk of omitted variables and endogeneity bias (Verbeek 2008). The inclusion of fixed effects can also separate the unobservable characteristics of countries from the error term. Causality tests could not identify any dual causality issues and the causality moves from the right-hand side variables to education outcomes. No multicollinearity problem has been observed either.

It should be noted that an alternative regression methodology to capture endogeneity and heterogeneity issues would be generalized method of moments (GMM) suggested by Arellano and Bond (1991). This methodology eliminates fixed effects with first differences of variables and using the lagged values of explanatory variables as instruments. Nonetheless, as also covered in Coulombe and Tremblay (2006), GMM is not a valid technique in this paper due to the short cross-sectional and time dimensions of our panel dataset, which can exacerbate measurement errors in female or total schooling data.

2.4 Regression Results

In this section, empirical evidence on the link between the volatility of education aid and education outcomes of female students is presented by using panel data regressions for low-income countries. Before presenting the regression outcomes, a table presenting the level of education aid and female education in individual countries can be informative. Table 2.1 gives this information and shows the share of females in secondary education and foreign aid on education in the countries included in the regression analysis. Education aid is indeed high for many low-income countries as presented in the table. Thus, its volatility can have a significant impact on the education outcomes of students. The effect on female students is expected to be even more dramatic because the quality and the availability of education tends to decline with fluctuating foreign aid, and mostly male students can continue to get an education under these circumstances because most families tend to give more emphasis on education of male students over females due to gender inequality.

Before the presentation of the regression results, it would be also informative to see the simple relationship between the volatility of education aid and education outcomes for females. Figure 2.7 shows the link between the volatility of education aid and two of female education indicators (share of female students in primary and secondary education). Each dot in the graphs represents a country average between 2002 and 2016. The figure presents that the link is actually negative as expected. It means that as the volatility declines, the share of female students in education rises.

The regression results are presented in Table 2.2. The first four columns present the results for all low-income countries and the last four columns present the results for the SSA in this group. For each group, different regression specifications are estimated. It should be noted that the estimated coefficients are robust. Even after

Table 1. Education foreign aid and education outcomes at country level, 2002–2016 (averages)

	Share of females (secondary education)	Education aid (% of GDP)		Share of females (secondary education)	Education aid (% of GDP)
Angola	48.94	0.07	Senegal	45.31	1.17
Benin	36.97	0.73	Sudan	47.97	0.08
Burkina Faso	42.43	1.05	Tanzania	46.70	0.68
Burundi	43.88	1.34	Togo	35.95	0.63
Chad	28.48	0.22	Uganda	46.07	0.88
Djibouti	41.67	2.19	Zambia	46.36	0.64
Guinea	35.06	0.80	Afghanistan	29.43	1.70
Kenya	48.25	0.25	Bangladesh	51.87	0.27
Lesotho	56.87	0.63	Bhutan	49.09	0.96
Madagascar	49.43	0.84	Cambodia	44.98	0.55
Mali	39.25	1.10	Lao	44.41	0.73
Mauritania	45.91	0.83	Myanmar	50.40	0.11
Mozambique	45.10	1.42	Nepal	47.30	0.74
Rwanda	50.13	1.57	Timor-Leste	49.73	1.01
Average	**44.57**	**0.83**			

Source The World Bank's World Development indicators and OECD's Creditor Reporting System Database.

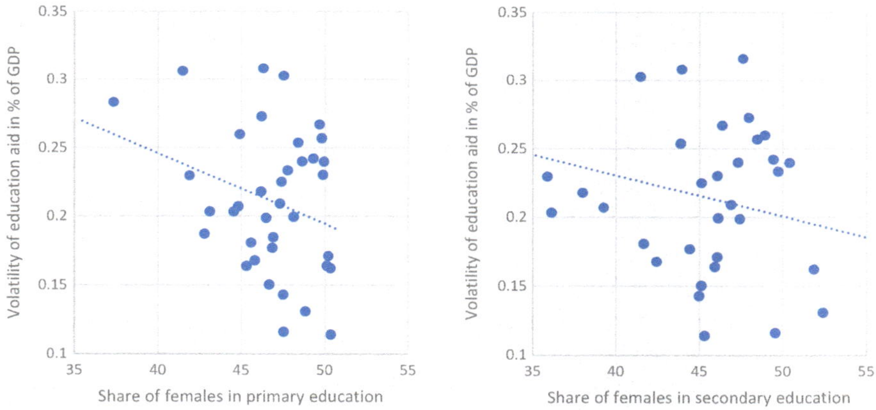

Fig. 2.7 Volatility of education foreign aid and share of female students, 2002–2016 (averages). *Source* Author's calculations based on data from the World Bank's World Development Indicators and OECD's Creditor Reporting System Database

Table 2.2 Regression results: female education outcome and volatility of education aid

Dependent variable: Number of students in secondary education in % of population				
All countries				
	(1)	(2)	(3)	(4)
Constant	−1.32 (−1.91)**	−9.16 (−2.61)***	−7.22 (−5.22)***	−4.13 (−3.18)***
Volatility of education aid (in % of GDP)	−2.19 (−5.11)***	−2.43 (−5.12)***	−1.99 (−3.14)***	−2.12 (−3.27)***
Public education spending (in % of GDP)	0.15 (2.95)***	0.16 (3.01)***	0.12 (2.55)***	0.11 (1.82)**
Life expectancy	…	…	0.26 (8.05)***	…
Mortality rate, under−five (per 1000 live births)	…	…	…	−0.05 (−9.12)***
Pupils/teachers ratio (in %)	−0.07 (−4.21)***	−0.08 (−5.22)***	−0.06 (−3.64)***	−0.06 (−3.11)***
Share of urban population (in %)	0.28 (10.13)***	…	0.21 (8.14)***	0.22 (7.13)***
ln(GDP per capita)	…	3.12 (8.12)***	…	…
Fixed and time effects included?	Yes	Yes	Yes	Yes
# of observations	297	290	297	297
# of countries	27	26	27	27
Adjusted *R*-squared	0.943	0.912	0.945	0.949
F-statistic	112.2	97.6	132.1	133.0
Only SSA countries				
	(5)	(6)	(7)	(8)
Constant	−4.06 (−2.55)***	−8.11 (−2.71)***	−7.11 (−6.12)***	−3.34 (−3.58)***
Volatility of education aid (in % of GDP)	−1.81 (−4.16)***	−1.91 (−3.19)**	−1.71 (−1.75)*	−1.32 (−1.89)*
Public education spending (in % of GDP)	0.14 (2.14)**	0.13 (2.23)**	0.12 (3.11)**	0.11 (2.23)**
Life expectancy	…	…	0.19 (9.13)***	…

(continued)

Table 2.2 (continued)

Mortality rate, under-five (per 1000 live births)	…	…	…	−0.06 (−7.44)***
Pupils/teachers ratio (in %)	−0.07 (−4.02)***	−0.12 (−7.21)***	−0.09 (−3.67)***	−0.04 (−3.12)***
Share of urban population (in %)	0.36 (9.14)***	…	0.18 (4.18)***	0.22 (4.23)***
ln(GDP per capita)	…	4.11 (8.12)***	…	…
Fixed and time effects included?	Yes	Yes	Yes	Yes
# of observations	221	214	221	221
# of countries	19	18	19	19
Adjusted *R*-squared	0.921	0.891	0.921	0.934
F-statistic	73.2	71.5	99.1	101.7
Dependent variable: Number of students in secondary education in % of population				
All countries				
	(9)	(10)	(11)	(12)
Constant	−1.58 (−149)	−11.39 (−3.89)***	−9.49 (−6.93)***	4.71 (3.88)***
Volatility of education aid (in % of GDP)	−1.18 (−4.02)***	−1.39 (−4.02)***	−0.45 (−1.64)*	−0.61 (−2.27)**
Public education spending (in % of GDP)	0.11 (2.73)***	0.17 (3.62)***	0.10 (2.85)***	0.06 (1.66)**
Life expectancy	…	…	0.19 (8.05)***	…
Mortality rate, under-five (per 1000 live births)	…	…	…	−0.03 (−8.36)***
Pupils/teachers ratio (in %)	−0.06 (−5.36)***	−0.08 (−6.63)***	−0.04 (−4.04)***	−0.04 (−3.45)***
Share of urban population (in %)	0.31 (12.64)***	…	0.17 (6.04)***	0.15 (5.32)***
ln(GDP per capita)	…	3.01 (7.65)***	…	…

(continued)

Table 2.2 (continued)

Fixed and time effects included?	Yes	Yes	Yes	Yes
# of observations	297	290	297	297
# of countries	27	26	27	27
Adjusted *R*-squared	0.911	0.889	0.928	0.929
F-statistic	102.3	81.2	124.9	127.0

Note Regression method is panel least squares with fixed and time effects. *T*-statistics are given in parenthesis. *stands for 10% significance; **stands for 5% significance; ***stands for 1% significance. All F-statistics are statistically significant at 1%

controlling for other possible determinants of education, such as public education spending and the quality of education, one of the common observations is the clear negative and significant effect of volatility of education aid on the educational outcome for female students. Higher volatility of education aid in percent of GDP, and lower shares of female students in secondary education. Most of the coefficients are highly significant at the 1% level. It means that higher volatility of aid raises uncertainty and lowers expected returns on education for students. This will be especially true for female students who earn relatively lower wages when they start to work after graduation.[4] Therefore, a declining share of female students in secondary education is observed.

The regression results show that stable foreign aid in education in low-income countries is expected to be important for higher human capital accumulation, which can lead to higher productivity and growth. In my dataset, the average share of education aid is around 1% of GDP for the low-income countries and it can rise up to 4.1%. Given these high contributions of education foreign aid, its stability gets even more important. Indeed, the estimation results indicate that a 1 percentage point higher volatility of education aid (in % of GDP) leads to almost 2 percentage points drop in the share of female students in secondary education.

The estimation results for the remaining control variables are as expected. Government education spending has a positive and significant impact on female education outcome. When the share of education spending in GDP rises by a 1 percentage point, the share of female students in secondary education gets higher by nearly 0.15 percentage points. Life expectancy raises the share of female students in secondary education thanks to improved health conditions and higher expected returns on education with lower life expectations. Likewise, increasing mortality rates lower the share of female students in secondary education due to declining health standards. The decreasing quality of education (higher pupil to teacher ratio) has a significant

[4] A report by International Labor Organization (2018) finds that globally women continue to be paid approximately 20 percent less than men.

and negative effect on female education due to crowded classrooms. Both increasing urban population and income have positive and significant effects on female education outcomes.

The results show that female students will be negatively affected by higher education aid volatility. However, it is also important to investigate the impact of aid volatility on education outcomes involving both male and female students to better evaluate the specific impact of volatility on female students. The last section of Table 2.2 (columns 9–12) presents results when the dependent variable is the ratio of the number of students in secondary education to the total population of the country, which is obtained from the World Development Indicators and African Development Indicators Databases of the World Bank. This dependent variable can capture the impact of aid volatility and other determinants of education on education outcomes for all students without classifying them as males and females. The estimated coefficients indicate that a 1 percentage point higher volatility of foreign aid in percent of GDP can lead to almost the same amount of drop in the share of students in secondary education. The findings support that the economic and statistical impact of aid volatility on total education outcome is significant and negative, but lower than the impact on specifically female students, indicating that unstable foreign aid has a stronger negative effect on female students due to gender inequality.

Overall, the estimation results highly support the significance of stable foreign education aid to contribute higher education for female students in low-income countries.

2.5 Conclusion

Educated females are essential to promote economic growth, especially in low-income countries where there is a high need for contributions from all segments of society. Interestingly, the share of females in the labor force is higher in the low-income group when compared to the other income groups. However, the issue is that their education indicators are inferior to the ones observed for males and the gender gap in education is wide in low-income countries. As these countries promote female education in addition to total education, higher growth rates are expected to be observed. The issue is that lower-income countries have limited resources to support public expenses and in this case the role of foreign aid on education gets even more important. Not only the level of foreign aid but also its stability determines its effectiveness in promoting female education in low-income countries. The main reason is that when education gets more limited with fluctuating foreign aid, generally male students can smoothly continue their education because families prefer supporting males over females in education due to higher expected returns on education investment for males, originating from gender inequality in payments in labor markets.

The empirical findings in the paper show that when the volatility of education aid gets larger, the share of females in secondary education declines. The regression results also show that the impact of the volatility of aid is stronger on females than on total students. These results support the importance of stable foreign aid on education to create better opportunities for females in education in low-income countries. Thus, donating countries should try to keep foreign aid on education as stable as possible if they want to improve the educational outcomes and reduce gender inequality in education in low-income countries to help their economic development.

Data Appendix—Variable Definitions and Sources

(*Note* Definitions are copied from the data sources)

Number of female and male students in secondary education: Secondary education, female and male pupils: Secondary education male and female pupils are the total number of pupils enrolled at secondary level in public and private schools. Source: World Bank's World Development Indicators (WDI); African Development Indicators (ADI).
School enrollment, secondary, female (% net): Net enrollment rate is the ratio of children of official school age who are enrolled in school to the population of the corresponding official school age. Secondary education completes the provision of basic education that began at the primary level, and aims at laying the foundations for lifelong learning and human development, by offering more subject- or skill-oriented instruction using more specialized teachers. Source: Data from WDI and ADI
Number of students in secondary education in % of population: Number of students in secondary education divided by total population from WDI
Education aid (gross disbursements): Education, total (gross disbursements) in current US dollars. Source: OECD's Creditor Reporting System (CRS)
Education aid (in % of GDP): Education aid (gross disbursements) divided by GDP from WDI (in %)
Volatility of education aid (in % of GDP): Rolling standard deviation of education aid in percent of GDP over 3-year overlapping sub-periods
Mortality rate, under-five (per 1000 live births): Under-five mortality rate is the probability per 1000 that a newborn baby will die before reaching age five, if subject to age-specific mortality rates of the specified year. Source: World Bank's WDI
Pupils/teachers ratio (in %): Pupil-teacher ratio, secondary: Secondary school pupil-teacher ratio is the average number of pupils per teacher in secondary school. Source: World Bank's WDI and ADI
GDPPC (in constant 2010 dollars): GDP per capita is gross domestic product divided by midyear population. GDP is the sum of gross value added by all resident producers in the economy plus any product taxes and minus any subsidies not included in the value of the products. It is calculated without making deductions for depreciation of fabricated assets or for depletion and degradation of natural resources. Data are in constant 2010 US dollars. Source: World Bank's WDI

Urban population (% of total): Urban population refers to people living in urban areas as defined by national statistical offices. The data are collected and smoothed by United Nations Population Division. Source: World Bank's WDI
Life expectancy: Life expectancy at birth indicates the number of years a newborn infant would live if prevailing patterns of mortality at the time of its birth were to stay the same throughout its life. Source: World Bank's WDI
Public education spending (in % of GDP): Government expenditure on education, total (% of GDP): General government expenditure on education (current, capital and transfers) is expressed as a percentage of GDP. It includes expenditure funded by transfers from international sources to government. General government usually refers to local, regional and central governments. Source: Authors' calculation with data from the World Bank's WDI and ADI.

References

Agenor, P.-R., & Bayraktar, N. (2018). *Aid volatility, human capital, and growth, unpublished paper*. United Kingdom: University of Manchester.

Anderson, A. B., Basilevsky, A., & Hum, D. P. J. (1983). Missing data: A review of the literature. In P. H. Rossi, J. D. Wright, & A. B. Anderson (Eds.), *Handbook of survey research*. Boston: Academic Press, Inc.

Arellano, M., & Bond, S. (1991). Some tests of specification for panel data: Monte Carlo evidence and an application to employment equations. *Review of Economic Studies, 58*(2), 277–297.

Asiama, J. P., & Quartey, P. (2009). Foreign aid and the human development indicators in Sub-Saharan Africa. *Journal of Developing Societies, 25*(1), 57–83.

Attanasio, O. P., Picci, L., & Scorcu, A. E. (2000). Saving, growth, and investment: A macroeconomic analysis using a panel of countries. *The Review of Economics and Statistics, 82*(2), 182–211.

Awasthi, R., & Bayraktar, N. (2015). Can tax simplification help lower tax corruption? *Eurasian Economic Review, 5*(2), 297–330.

Bayraktar, N. (2018). Effectiveness of public investment on growth in sub-Saharan Africa. *Eurasian Economic Review*, *9*(4), 421–457. (expected publication in 2019). https://doi.org/10.1007/s40822-018-0119-z.

Bayraktar, N., & Fofack, H. (2018). A model for gender analysis with informal production and financial sectors. *Journal of African Development, 20*(2), 1–20.

Bayraktar, N., & Moreno-Dodson, B. (2015). How can public spending help you grow? An empirical analysis for developing countries. *Bulletin of Economic Research, 67*(1), 30–64.

Behrman, J. R. (1996). The impact of health and nutrition on education. *The World Bank Research Observer, 11*(1), 23–37.

Bond, S., Leblebicioglu, A., & Schiantarelli, F. (2010). Capital accumulation and growth: A new look at the empirical evidence. *Journal of Applied Econometrics., 25*(7), 1073–1099.

Boserup, E., Tan, S. F., & Toulmin, C. (2013). *Woman's role in economic development*. Routledge.

Clemens, M.A., Radelet, S., Bhavnani, R., 2004. Counting chickens when they hatch: The short-term effect of aid on growth. *Center for Global Development working paper no. 44*.

Coulombe, S., & Tremblay, J.-F. (2006). Literacy and growth. *Topics in Macroeconomics., 6,* 1404.

Dempster, A. P., Laird, N. M., & Rubin, D. B. (1977). Maximum likelihood from incomplete data via the EM Algorithm. *Journal of the Royal Statistical Society Series B (Methodological), 39,* 289–309.

Easterly, W., & Pfutze, T. (2008). Where does the money go? Best and worst practices in foreign aid. *Journal of Economic Perspectives, 22*(2), 29–52.
Ebeke, C., & Ehrhart, H. (2011). Tax revenue instability in Sub-Saharan Africa: Consequences and remedies. *Journal of African Economies, 21*(1), 1–27.
Glewwe, P., Maiga, E., & Zheng, H. (2014). The contribution of education to economic growth: A review of the evidence, with special attention and an application to Sub-Saharan Africa. *World Development, 59*, 379–393.
Hanushek, E. A., & Woessmann, L. (2012). Do better schools lead to more growth? Cognitive skills, economic outcomes, and causation. *Journal of Economic Growth, 17*(4), 267–321.
Hill, M. A., & King, E. (1995). Women's education and economic well-being. *Feminist Economics, 1*(2), 21–46.
Honaker, J., & King, G. (2010). What to do about missing values in time series cross-section data. *American Journal of Political Science, 54*(3), 561–581.
International Labor Organization. (2018). *Global Wage Report 2018/19: What lies behind gender pay gaps*. Geneva: ILO.
Klasen, S. (2002). Low schooling for girls, slower growth for all? Cross-country evidence on the effect of gender inequality in education on economic development. *The World Bank Economic Review, 16*(3), 345–373.
Michaelowa, K. (2001). Primary education quality in francophone Sub-Saharan Africa: Determinants of learning achievement and efficiency considerations. *World Development, 29*(10), 1699–1716.
Museru, M., Toerien, F., & Gossel, S. (2014). The Impact of aid and public investment volatility on economic growth in Sub-Saharan Africa. *World Development, 57,* 138–147.
Neanidis, K. C., & Varvarigos, D. (2009). The allocation of volatile aid and economic growth: Theory and evidence. *European Journal of Political Economy, 25*(4), 447–462.
Rubin, D. B. (1987). *Multiple imputations for nonresponse in surveys*. New York: Wiley.
Ruud, P. A. (1991). Extentions of estimation methods using the EM Algorithm. *Journal of Econometrics, 49,* 305–341.
Stevens, P., & Weale, M. (2004). Education and economic growth. *International Handbook on the Economics of Education, 27*, 205–311.
Verbeek, M. (2008). *A Guide to Modern Econometrics* (3rd ed.). West Sussex: Wiley.
Verner, D. (2005). *What factors influence world literacy? Is Africa different?* World Bank Policy Research Working Paper No: 3496 (January).

Chapter 3
Quality Perceptions of Feta Cheese

Irene Kamenidou, Spyridon Mamalis, Stavros Pavlidis and Evangelia Zoi Bara

Abstract This study deals with the quality of feta cheese as perceived by 534 individuals 18–35 years of age. Additionally, differences were explored based on the area of residence (urban, semi-urban, and rural area) and gender. Data analysis included basic descriptive statistics, factor analysis, independent samples Kruskal–Wallis one-way ANOVA test and Mann–Whitney *U* test. Results revealed that the strongest quality indicators for consumers are taste, odor, color, and texture of feta cheese. Factor analysis provided with four quality dimensions treated as new variables used in hypothesis testing, namely quality assurance, core product characteristics, price and packaging, and marketing communication. The Mann–Whitney *U* test revealed that for all quality dimensions gender differences exist. As to the independent samples Kruskal–Wallis one-way ANOVA test, it indicated differences regarding consumers' area of residence and perceptions of quality, as regards the dimensions of quality assurance and marketing communication of feta cheese.

Keywords Feta cheese · Quality indicators · Greece · Consumer perceptions · Marketing

JEL Codes M37 · M38

I. Kamenidou (✉) · S. Mamalis · S. Pavlidis · E. Z. Bara
Department of Management Science and Technology School of Business and Economics, International Hellenic University, Kavala Campus, Agios Loukas, 65404 Kavala, Greece
e-mail: rkam@mst.ihu.gr

S. Mamalis
e-mail: mamalis@econ.auth.gr

S. Pavlidis
e-mail: stavrospavlides@yahoo.gr

E. Z. Bara
e-mail: evaeva13@hotmail.gr

N. Tsounis and A. Vlachvei (eds.), *Advances in Cross-Section Data Methods in Applied Economic Research*, Springer Proceedings in Business and Economics,
https://doi.org/10.1007/978-3-030-38253-7_3

3.1 Introduction

Product quality is recognized as a principal notion in building customer value and satisfaction and is defined in many ways (Ophuis and Van Trijp 1995). Its significance is recognized not only at a country's micro-level (comparative advantage of each business) but also at the macro-level, i.e., defining the national comparative advantage of enterprises (Steenkamp 1990).

Regarding the food industry and the concept of "food quality," there is no general agreement between the researchers of the term, nor how food quality can be measured (Acebrón and Dopico 2000). Thus, in the food industry "quality" has a variety of meanings, depending upon who is giving the definition, e.g., the food scientists, the industry, or the consumer (Cardello 1995). Even more, the same consumer will define "quality" differently which depends upon the product and the purchasing and consumption situation (Moskowitz 1995). Hence, when referring to consumer behavior towards food, food quality regards the individual consumer perspective of the concept since it is relative to his/her needs (Steenkamp 1986). Additionally, since consumers differ in their socioeconomic and demographic characteristics, they consider the quality of a food product differently due to their values and norms. Meaning that of interest is consumers' perceived quality which is reliant on the consumer's judgment (Ophuis and Van Trijp 1995). For so, consumers perceived quality is explored in food marketing (Hansen 2005), to understand food choice and preference (e.g., Machín et al. 2014; Steenkamp 1986). Additionally, perceived quality is examined because it affects food perceived value (Yonatan 2014), satisfaction (Namkung and Jang 2007), and loyalty (Hansen 2001).

Ophuis and Van Trijp (1995) postulate that consumers use quality indicators in order to form their perception of product quality. These indicators are quality cues, i.e., intrinsic and extrinsic (Olson and Jacoby 1972) and quality attributes (Steenkamp 1989). The intrinsic cues are associated with the physical product itself, while extrinsic cues are not part of the physical product but are related to it (Olson and Jacoby 1972). On the other hand, quality attributes can be observed only after consumption (Steenkamp 1989). Since food quality is a subjective matter for consumers and depends on the food product and the consumer's perception, it is needed to investigate the notion of food quality for each specific product researched.

Taking into mind the before mentioned, this paper deals with a Greek traditional product, namely, feta cheese, which is the national Greek cheese, and particularly deals with the quality perception of feta cheese of consumers belonging in the age group of 18–35 years old. Since previous research confirms that consumers' gender and place of residence impact on food consumption behavior (Guerrero et al. 2009; Bernués et al. 2003), this research explores differences of feta cheese quality perception based on these two demographic characteristics (i.e., gender and area of residence).

The outcomes of this research are of great importance for the people that are engaged in food marketing because, to our knowledge, no current study has been found that deals with the consumers' perception of feta cheese quality; the specific age group of 18–35 years of age; and consumers' gender or area of residence differences as regards the dimensions of feta cheese quality.

3.2 Feta Cheese

The ancestor of the Feta cheese is reported in Homer's Odyssey (9th to 8th B.C. century), and it was the cheese that was prepared by Cyclope Polyfimos (Tamime et al. 1996). According to Real Greek Feta (2017), production and consumption of cheese in ancient Greece are shown in the work of Aristoteles, Pythagoras, and ancient comedy writers. Anifantakis (1996) states that feta is a soft white cheese, ripened and kept in brine, while he also provides references to its Greek originality. Anifantakis and Moatsou (2006: 44) provide the standards regarding feta cheese: "Feta cheese is a soft cheese without rind with pure white color and slightly acid taste. It can be cut into slices, and the characteristic of its texture is the presence of a few mechanical openings. It is made of sheep's milk or from its mixtures with goat's milk, of which the latter must not exceed 30% of the total cheese milk. The cheese milk must be produced exclusively in the geographic areas of Macedonia, Thraki, Ipiros, Thessalia, Sterea Ellada, Peloponnissos, and Lesvos island. The use of condensed milk and the addition of milk powder, milk proteins concentrate, or caseinates in the cheese milk, as well as the use of colorings and preservatives, is forbidden. The maximum moisture must be 56 g 100 g–1 and the minimum fat-in-dry matter (FDM) 43 g 100 g–1. • The maturation period must be at least 60 days".

For the Greeks, feta cheese is a significant element in their diet; it is part of their culture, cultural values, gastronomy, and consumption routine. Anifantakis (1996: 50) refers that in Greece, the per capita consumption of feta cheese was annually more than 12 kg and is the highest in the world. Hughes et al. (1998) refer that according to the Greek Ministry of Agriculture, the per capita consumption of cheese (all types) in Greece, is 23 kg with an increasing tendency. In 2011 by the estimations of National Statistic Service of Greece (NSSG), the per capita consumption of cheese in Greece was 32.6 kg. In 2013, Greece had the highest per capita cheese consumption in Europe with 31 kg, exceeding France which was in the 2nd place with 26 kg (Relou 2015). According to the National Statistic Service of Greece, the per capita consumption of feta cheese from the year 2000–2011 was continuously increasing from 13 to 15 kg. According to ICAP (2016), there was an increase in domestic demand for Greek feta cheese. Specifically, consumption of feta cheese had a 4.3 increase rate for the years 2013/2012; 2.6 increase rate for 2014/2013 and 2.0 increase rate for the years 2015/2014. These facts confirm the significance of cheese and especially feta cheese consumption for the Greek people.

3.3 Literature Review

Various academic papers have been found regarding feta cheese. Some papers study the feta cheese production method (e.g., Angelopoulou et al. 2017; Valsamaki et al. 2000); while others studied its sensory attributes and expectancy with or without manipulating its ingredients or fat content (e.g., Rashidi et al. 2015; Hamad 2015; Karimi et al. 2012; Tsigkros et al. 2003; Heisserer and Chambers 1993). Additionally, research focused on implementation of quality control systems in feta production (Azar and Nejad 2009; Adamopoulos et al. 2001), quality certification, such as geographical identification (Anthopoulou and Goussios 2015; Vlachos 2013; Van Ittersum et al. 2007; Teuber 2011), or consumers' willingness to pay for PDO certification or other quality indicators of feta cheese (Krystallis and Chryssohoidis 2005; Taki and Drichoutis 2012). Furthermore, another area dealt with is the research of feta cheese in other countries (e.g., Kokthi et al. 2014) or positioning of feta in the market (Krystallis et al. 2004), or even the location effects in the production and marketing of the product (Vakrou et al. 1997).

While all the above studies that concern feta-cheese are very important in order to understand consumers' behavior as well as its market, a handful of studies focus on consumers' perception of quality indicators regarding the product. Additionally, no study was found that dealt with the comparison of quality perceptions between genders as well as the area of residence.

Cacciolatti et al. (2015) investigated perceptions on the purchase of Greek feta regarding 273 UK specialty food shoppers. They found that product knowledge, country of origin, perceived transactional value, consumers' life stage, and available income are the five critical factors affecting decision making. Kokthi et al. (2014) investigated.

Albanian consumers' preferences of a feta-type cheese and segmented consumers on this basis. Data analysis included Principal Component Analyses and k-Mean clustering to segment consumers. Five groups are identified: the best option buyer; the food safety buyer; the price-driven buyer; the experienced buyer; and the low-involved buyer. They found that the familiarity with the product characteristics, the consumption experience, and the relationship buyer–seller are the main moderators of the origin importance in the process of preference creation. De Souza Monteiro and Ventura Lucas (2001) found that for traditional cheeses, recognition as PDO, price, texture, and unit of sale are the main predictors of choice. Lastly, the only research that directly interests the focus of this paper is the one that was presented by the National Agricultural Research Foundation (NAGREF) and referred to a survey conducted by the Agricultural University of Athens in 1993. They found that consumers base their choice of cheese products on taste, purity, hygiene, nutritional value, price and trust towards the product (NAGREF 1999).

Gender differences have been studied also extensively regarding food choice and eating behavior, revealing that men and women choose and eat food differently (Arganini et al. 2012; Bellows et al. 2010; Wardle et al. 2004; Fagerli and Wandel 1999; Roos et al. 1998). However, no research was found as to the authors' knowledge regarding gender differences of cheese quality (and especially feta cheese), other aspects of quality indicators and food were researched. Some examples that fall in the categories of gender differences and food are studies on local foods (Gracia et al. 2012), organic food or natural food (Dickson-Spillmann et al. 2011; Tobler et al. 2011), and food price (Boek et al. 2012). Furthermore, studies were found concerning the country of origin effects (Hoffmann 2000), food likes and dislikes (Boek et al. 2012), environmental food issues (Schafer et al. 1993), packaging (Vila-López and Kuster-Boluda 2016), and traditional food products (Guerrero et al. 2009). The above issues constitute some of the subjects researched. In the same vein, area of residence and its impact on consumers' food preferences and quality has a fair share in academic research (Guerrero et al. 2009; Chambers et al. 2007; Fortomaris et al. 2006).

Since the literature review regarding feta cheese perceived quality by Greek consumers was not found, the authors considered that qualitative research should take place before proceeding to the field research in order to have an in-depth understanding of the perceptions of feta cheese quality that this specific age group holds.

3.4 Methodology

After an extensive literature review and depth interviews with six consumers (3 from each age group: 18–25 and 26–35 years old), 15 quality attributes and cues considered as important quality indicators derived regarding feta cheese. Since the population's age targeted was 18–35 years, to elicit answers through these ages, a web-based self-administered online questionnaire was utilized for data collection due to its advantages (Garton et al. 1999).

To collect the required data, a non-probability, mixed sampling method approach was utilized. Three criteria were applied for the respondents to be part of the final sample, i.e., to be 18–35 years old; be the ones in the household making the purchasing decisions regarding food and specifically cheese and eat feta cheese. By convenience sampling, researchers send Facebook messages and e-mails to friends and relatives that fell in the above criteria. Facebook and e-mail were considered as the only communication means since individuals in this age range have ease with these means of communication. In the messages sent, they were informed about the aim of the research (as a cover letter) and were sent the link of the questionnaire. They were requested to complete it and pass it on to people that fulfilled the sample criteria, employing snowball sampling as well.

The fifteen quality cues/attributes derived from in-depth interviews and literature review were used to measure consumers' perception of quality criteria regarding feta cheese (5-point Likert scale). From these fifteen quality indicators, two were quality attributes (taste and texture), and thirteen were quality cues (four intrinsic and nine extrinsic cues). Anonymity and confidentiality were maintained throughout the research, and the data collected for this study were not linked to the participants in any way. Data analysis included frequencies, percentages, means, factor and reliability analysis, normality statistics, Mann–Whitney U and independent samples Kruskal–Wallis one-way ANOVA (*k* samples) tests. In the Mann–Whitney U and independent samples Kruskal–Wallis one-way ANOVA tests performed, the gender and area of residence were the independent variables and the quality dimensions (derived from factor analysis) were the dependent variables. Accordingly, the statistical hypotheses based on the literature review and the findings of qualitative research were as follows:

Hypothesis No. 1:
H0: there are no difference between men and women and their perception of feta cheese quality ($\alpha = 0.05$)
H1: there are difference between men and women and their perception of feta cheese quality ($\alpha = 0.05$).

Hypothesis No. 2:
H0: there are no difference between area of residence and their perception of feta cheese quality ($\alpha = 0.05$)
H1: there are difference between area of residence and their perception of feta cheese quality ($\alpha = 0.05$).

3.5 Results and Discussion

3.5.1 Sample Profile

The total number of usable questionnaires was 534, with 65.2% being 18–25, and 34.8% being 26–35 years of age, with a mean age 24.5 years old. As to gender, 49.4% were males and 50.6% were females, revealing an almost equal representation of gender in the sample. Additionally, 73.6% were single; 24.5% married, and 1.9% divorced or widowed. The vast majority (85.2%) had secondary education, i.e., had finished the Lyceum. As to profession most of the sample (60.4%) fell into two categories: 41.0% were university students, and 19.4% were employees in the private sector. Moreover, 61.8% lives in the city (urban), 17.2% resides in towns (semi-urban), and 21.0% lives in villages (rural area). Lastly, participants' monthly net family income was categorized as 25.8% up to 600.0€; 33.5% from 600.1–1000.0 €; 32.6% from 1000.01–2000.0€; and lastly, 8.1% had income more than 2000.1 €.

Table 3.1 Perceived quality cues and attributes for feta cheese by sample

Quality attributes/cues of feta cheese	1	2	3	4	5	MS
1. Taste	1.7	2.3	8.7	34.3	53.1	4.35
2. Odor	2.6	4.3	10.2	37.9	45.0	4.18
3. Color	5.8	7.0	19.4	38.8	29.0	3.78
4. Texture	3.2	7.0	26.9	34.3	28.6	3.78
5. Geographical Identification (PDO/PGI) certification	4.2	8.4	32.6	30.2	24.7	3.63
6. Producer certification	5.3	12.1	27.9	30.9	23.9	3.56
7. Quality certification (Hasp, ISO, Agrocert)	5.3	12.2	28.3	29.5	24.8	3.56
8. Produced locally	5.6	15.4	31.3	27.5	20.2	3.41
9. The production country	8.6	15.2	27.2	28.3	20.6	3.37
10. Price	5.8	13.7	35.2	28.8	16.4	3.36
11. Organic cheese	6.2	15.0	35.5	25.2	18.0	3.34
12. Production details, e.g., fat content, calories	7.4	15.5	32.5	29.1	15.7	3.30
13. Brand name of feta	20.6	13.7	21.8	28.1	15.8	3.05
14. Package characteristics (material, reusable, etc.)	13.1	22.0	28.3	23.5	13.1	3.02
15. Advertisement, sales promotions, and product communication	22.8	17.2	30.7	19.7	9.6	2.76

3.5.2 *Feta Cheese Quality Perception*

Participants were asked to state their degree of agreement towards the before mentioned 15 quality cues and attributes of feta cheese (Table 3.1). These quality indicators were rated on a 5-point Likert scale, and reliability of the scale was calculated. Cronbach α of the total scale was $\alpha = 0.872$ ($n = 534$); being considered as satisfactory (Hair et al. 2010).

Results identified that regarding quality, consumers consider that the main attributes/cues that they perceive as quality indicators of feta cheese are its odor, taste, color, and texture; all concerning the core product itself.

3.5.3 *Factor Analysis*

Continuously, factor analysis with Principle Component Analysis (Varimax Rotation) was performed to decrease the quality variables in a smaller manageable set of items to perform further analysis. Factor analysis provided with four quality dimensions (KMO = 0.875; BTS = 2699.073; df = 105; $p = 0.000$), accounting for 65.8% of total variance (Table 3.2).

Table 3.2 Factor analysis of cheese quality items

	Variable	1	2	3	4
Factor 1: Quality assurance	Quality certification (Hasp, ISO, Agrocert)	0.786			
	Geographical Identification (PDO/PGI) certification	0.781			
	Producer certification	0.778			
	Organic cheese	0.752			
	Production details e.g. fat content, calories	0.739			
	Produced locally	0.624			
	The production country	0.511			
Factor 2: Core product characteristics	Taste		0.847		
	Odor		0.796		
	Color		0.654		
	Texture		0.636		
Factor 3: Price and packaging	Price			0.822	
	Package characteristics (material, reusable, etc.)			0.716	
Factor 4: Marketing communication	Brand name of feta				0.863
	Advertisement, communication sales promotions and product				0.854

The derived factors-dimensions were named "Quality assurance", "Core product characteristics", "Price and packaging", and "Marketing communication" for the first, second, third and fourth feta cheese quality dimensions, respectively, based on the variables that each dimension incorporates. Additionally, for each dimension, the Mean Factor Score (MFS) was calculated in order to proceed to further analysis.

3.5.4 Hypotheses Testing

3.5.4.1 Hypothesis No. 1

As regards the first hypothesis (referring to gender), normality test revealed that Kolmogorov–Smirnov statistics were in all cases $p < 0.05$, thus proceeding with non-parametric tests and specifically with independent samples Mann–Whitney U test

Table 3.3 Hypothesis test summary for gender and cheese quality dimensions with independent samples Mann–Whitney *U* test

Null Hypothesis	Mann–Whitney *U* test	Sig.	Decision
The distribution of MFS1 is the same across categories of gender	28826.0	0.000	Null hypothesis rejected
The distribution of MFS2 is the same across categories of gender	29652.0	0.001	Null hypothesis rejected
The distribution of MFS3 is the same across categories of gender	31954.5	0.043	Null hypothesis rejected
The distribution of MFS4 is the same across categories of gender	32138.5	0.047	Null hypothesis rejected

Table 3.4 Mann-Whitney U test between gender groups

Variable	Gender	p sig.	Median
Quality assurance	Males	0.000	3.29
	Females		3.62
Core product characteristics	Males	0.001	4.00
	Females		4.25
Price and packaging	Males	0.043	3.00
	Females		3.05
Marketing communication	Males	0.047	3.00
	Females		3.05

(Field 2009). Table 3.3 presents the results of the hypothesis testing with independent samples Mann–Whitney *U* test as regards gender differences.

Results reveal that in all cases men and women perceive the quality of feta cheese differently (Table 3.4).

Specifically, the Mann–Whitney test indicated that quality assurance of the product was rated higher as a feta cheese quality indicator for females (Mdn $= 3.62$) than for males (Mdn $= 3.29$), $U = 28826.0$, $p = 0.000$. The same test indicated that the core product characteristics were rated higher as a feta cheese quality indicator for females (Mdn $= 4.25$) than for males (Mdn $= 4.00$), $U = 29652.0$, $p = 0.001$. Furthermore, a Mann–Whitney test indicated that the price and packaging of the feta cheese was rated higher as a quality indicator for females (Mdn $= 3.05$) than for males (Mdn $= 3.00$), $U = 31{,}954.5$, $p = 0.043$. Lastly, the Mann–Whitney test indicated that the marketing communication techniques was rated higher as a feta cheese quality indicator for females (Mdn $= 3.05$) than for males (Mdn $= 3.00$), $U = 32138.5$, $p = 0.047$.

Table 3.5 Hypothesis test summary regarding the quality of feta cheese and area of residence with Independent samples Kruskal–Wallis one-way ANOVA for all groups (*p*-value)

Null Hypothesis	Median MSF	Kruskal–Wallis H Test	Sig. (*p*)	Decision
The distribution of MFS1 is the same across categories of the area of residence	3.43	8.625	0.013	Null hypothesis rejected
The distribution of MFS2 is the same across categories of the area of residence	4.00	2.350	0.309	Null hypothesis retained
The distribution of MFS3 is the same across categories of the area of residence	3.00	4.369	0.113	Null hypothesis retained
The distribution of MFS4 is the same across categories of the area of residence	3.00	14.191	0.001	Null hypothesis rejected

3.5.4.2 Hypothesis No. 2

Normality test revealed that Kolmogorov–Smirnov statistics were in all cases $p < 0.05$, thus proceeding with non-parametric tests and specifically with independent samples Kruskal–Wallis one-way ANOVA (*k* samples) test. Using the independent samples Kruskal–Wallis one-way ANOVA assessment, significant differences based on area of residence were found in two cases. Specifically, these cases refer to the quality perceptions of the MFS1, i.e., the Quality assurance dimension ($H(2) = 8.625$, $p = 0.013$) and MFS4, i.e., the Marketing communication dimension ($H(2) = 14.191$, $p = 0.001$), as shown in Table 3.5.

Kruskal–Wallis one-way ANOVA was followed by Mann–Whitney *U* test for two independent samples to investigate the specific differences between the area of residence and MSF1 and MSF2 (Table 3.6).

The Mann–Whitney *U* test indicated that the *Quality Assurance* dimension, was rated higher as a feta cheese quality indicator for the residents of cities (Mdn = 3.43) than those residing in the villages (Mdn = 3.29), $U = 15967.0$, $p = 0.035$. Additionally, this test indicated that the same quality dimension was rated higher as a feta cheese quality indicator for the residents of towns (Mdn = 3.62) than those residing in the villages (Mdn = 3.29), $U = 3987.5$, $p = 0.005$. Lastly, the Mann–Whitney test indicated that the *Marketing Communication Techniques* was rated higher as a feta cheese quality indicator for the residents of cities (Mdn = 3.00) than those residing in the villages (Mdn = 2.50), $U = 14315.5$, $p = 0.000$).

Table 3.6 Mann–Whitney *U* test between groups

Variable	Area of residence	Mann–Whitney *U* test	*P* sign	Median
Quality assurance	City (1)	13504.5	0.114	3.43
	Town (2)			3.62
	City (1)	15967.0	0.035	3.43
	Village (3)			3.29
	Town (2)	3987.5	0.005	3.62
	Village (3)			3.29
Marketing communication	City (1)	13264.0	0.061	3.00
	Town (2)			3.00
	City (1)	14315.5	0.000	3.00
	Village (3)			2.50
	Town (2)	4596.0	0.180	3.00
	Village (3)			2.50

3.6 Conclusions—Limitations and Recommendations

This research was designed to obtain knowledge of the quality indicators of feta cheese as perceived by individuals 18–35 years old ($N = 534$). It was realized on a three-fold basis: at first extended literature review was done followed by qualitative research and thirdly the field research was undertaken. The first two axons (literature review and qualitative research) produced 15 attributes and cues as quality indicators that were tested in order to measure the perceived quality of feta cheese. Results revealed that participants' top-quality indicators for feta cheese were odor, taste, color, and texture of feta. Additionally, the findings of this research confirm previous research that differences between gender and area of residence do exist as to food products. These findings, even though they cannot be directly compared with previous ones since prior research was not found tackling the same issues, they can be considered as significant, due to the fact that they provide insight of consumers' behavior towards a product that has been understudied from this point of view.

This research has some limitations, which even though there was a considerable effort to avoid them, unfortunately, this was not possible. First of all, this study implemented an online research approach due to economic and time restraints. This resulted in a non-probability sampling method, leading to the limitation of generalizability of results. Therefore, the sample was adequate for the aim and objectives of the study and generalizations cannot be made from the sample to the population. Consequently, future research could validate the outcomes of this study. Finally, it is essential that similar studies should be undertaken, having participants with a broader age range in order to build upon the current findings. Even though this study has the above limitations, its significance should be recognized, since it builds theoretically and practically in the academic cheese-product field.

Ethical approval There are no ethical issues involved in the processing of the questionnaire data used in the study. The necessary consents have been obtained by the persons involved and the anonymity of the participants has been secured. All procedures performed in studies involving human participants were in accordance with the ethical standards of the International Hellenic's University research committee and with the 1964 Helsinki declaration and its later amendments or comparable ethical standards.

References

Acebrón, L. B., & Dopico, D. C. (2000). The importance of intrinsic and extrinsic cues to expected and experienced quality: An empirical application for beef. *Food Quality and Preference, 11*(3), 229–238.

Adamopoulos, K. G., Goula, A. M., & Petropakis, H. J. (2001). Quality control during processing of feta cheese—NIR application. *Journal of Food Composition and Analysis, 14*(4), 431–440.

Angelopoulou, A., Alexandraki, V., Georgalaki, M., Anastasiou, R., Manolopoulou, E., Tsakalidou, E., & Papadimitriou, K. (2017). Production of probiotic Feta cheese using Propionibacterium freudenreichii subsp. shermanii as adjunct. *International Dairy Journal, 66*(3), 135–139.

Anifantakis, E. M., (1996) Traditional Feta cheese. In R. K. Robinson, & A. Y. Tamime (Eds.), *Feta and related cheeses* (pp. 49–69). CRC Press.

Anifantakis, E. M., & Moatsou, G. (2006). Feta and other Balkan cheeses. In A. Tamime (Eds.), *In Brined cheeses* (pp. 43–76). Oxford: Blackwell Publishing.

Anthopoulou, T., & Goussios, D. (2015). Activating territorial specificities under a national PDO cheese label. Cooperation of small dairy territories to promote local-placed Feta in Thessaly Region. http://www.prd.uth.gr/uploads/publications/2015/e0f45fcfa07ccca7debe19731e532b9055aaaf81.pdf.

Arganini, C., Saba, A., Comitato, R., Virgili, F., & Turrini, A. (2012). Gender differences in food choice and dietary intake in modern western societies. In J. Maddock (Ed.), *Public health-social and behavioral health* (pp. 83–102). IntechOpen. Chapter 4. ISBN 978-953-51-0620-3, https://doi.org/10.5772/37886 https://www.intechopen.com/books/public-health-social-and-behavioral-health/gender-differences-in-food-choice-and-dietary-intake-in-modern-western-societies.

Azar, M. T., & Nejad, L. R. (2009). The implementation of HACCP (Hazard Analysis Critical Control Point) to UF-FETA cheese production lines. *Research Journal of Biological Sciences, 4*(4), 388–394.

Bellows, A. C., Alcaraz, V. G., & Hallman, W. K. (2010). Gender and food, a study of attitudes in the USA towards organic, local, U.S. grown, and GM-free foods. *Appetite, 55*(3), 540–550.

Bernués, A., Olaizola, A., & Corcoran, K. (2003). Extrinsic attributes of red meat as indicators of quality in Europe: An application for market segmentation. *Food Quality and Preference, 14*(4), 265–276.

Boek, S., Bianco-Simeral, S., Chan, K., & Goto, K. (2012). Gender and race are significant determinants of students' food choices on a college campus. *Journal of Nutrition Education and Behavior, 44*(4), 372–378.

Cacciolatti, L. A., Garcia, C. C., & Kalantzakis, M. (2015). Traditional food products: The effect of consumers' characteristics, product knowledge, and perceived value on actual purchase. *Journal of International Food and Agribusiness Marketing, 27*(3), 155–176.

Cardello, A. V. (1995). Food quality: Relativity, context and consumer expectations. *Food Quality and Preference, 6*(3), 163–170.

Chambers, S., Lobb, A., Butler, L., Harvey, K., & Traill, W. B. (2007). Local, national and imported foods: A qualitative study. *Appetite, 49*(1), 208–2013.

de Souza Monteiro, M. D., & Ventura Lucas, R. M. (2001). Conjoint measurement of preferences for traditional cheeses in Lisbon. *British Food Journal, 103*(6), 414–424.
Dickson-Spillmann, M., Siegrist, M., & Keller, C. (2011). Attitudes toward chemicals are associated with preference for natural food. *Food Quality and Preference, 22*(1), 149–156.
Fagerli, R. A., & Wandel, M. (1999). Gender differences in opinions and practices with regard to a healthy diet. *Appetite, 32*(2), 171–190.
Field, A. (2009). *Discovering statistics using SPSS* (3rd ed.). London: SAGE Publications Ltd.
Fortomaris, P., Arsenos, G., Georgiadis, M., Banos, G., Stamataris, C., & Zygoyiannis, D. (2006). Effect of meat appearance on consumer preferences for pork chops in Greece and Cyprus. *Meat Science, 72*(4), 688–696.
Garton, L., Haythornthwaite, C., & Wellman, B. (1999). Studying on-line social networks. In S. Jones (Ed.), *Doing internet research: Critical issues and methods for examining the net* (pp. 75–105). Thousand Oaks, CA: Sage. Retrieved June 20, 2016, from http://qhr.sagepub.com/content/early/2014/09/10/1049732314549031.full.pdf+html.
Gracia, A., De Magistris, T., & Nayga, R. M., Jr. (2012). Importance of social influence in consumers' willingness to pay for local food: Are there gender differences? *Agribusiness, 28*(3), 361–371.
Guerrero, L., Guàrdia, M. D., Xicola, J., Verbeke, W., Vanhonacker, F., Zakowska-Biemans, S., et al. (2009). Consumer-driven definition of traditional food products and innovation in traditional foods. A qualitative cross-cultural study. *Appetite, 52*(2), 345–354.
Hair, J. F., Black, W. C., Babin, B. J., & Anderson, R. E. (2010). *Multivariate data analysis* (7th ed.). Englewood Cliffs: Prentice Hall.
Hamad, M. N. F. (2015). Comparative study between traditional Domiati cheese and recombined Feta cheese. *Indian Journal of Dairy Science, 68*(5), 442–452.
Hansen, T. (2001). Quality in the marketplace: A theoretical and empirical investigation. *European Management Journal, 19*(2), 203–211.
Hansen, T. (2005). Understanding consumer perception of food quality: The cases of shrimps and cheese. *British Food Journal, 107*(7), 500–525.
Heisserer, D. M., & Chambers, E. I. V. (1993). Determination of the sensory flavor attributes of aged natural cheese. *Journal of Sensory Studies, 8*(2), 121–132.
Hoffmann, R. (2000). Country of origin–a consumer perception perspective of fresh meat. *British food journal, 102*(3), 211–229.
Hughes, D., Hutchins, R., & Karathanassi, V. (1998). Purchase involvement methodology and product profiles: The case of cheese products in Greece. *British Food Journal, 100*(7), 343–350.
ICAP. (2016). An increase of total domestic cheese consumption is recorded the last years (In Greek). Press Release, Monday, 5th of December 2016. http://www.agrotypos.gr/images/stories/file/ICAP_PR_Dairy%20Products_Dec2016.pdf.
Karimi, R., Sohrabvandi, S., & Mortazavian, A. M. (2012). Review article: Sensory characteristics of probiotic cheese. *Comprehensive Reviews in Food Science and Food Safety, 11*(5), 437–452.
Kokthi, E., Gonzàles Limon, M., & Vàzques Bermudez, I. (2014). Analyzing Albanian consumer preferences for origin using cluster analyses (The case of cheese). *International Journal of Innovative Research in Science and Engineering, 2*(10), 718–729.
Krystallis, A., & Chryssohoidis, G. (2005). Consumers' willingness to pay for organic food: Factors that affect it and variation per organic product type. *British Food Journal, 107*(5), 320–343.
Krystallis, A., Papadopoulou, V., & Chryssochoidis, G. M. (2004). The positioning of Greek Feta Cheese in a local UK market Â-A major marketing strategy problem. *Agricultural Economics Review, 5*(2), 5–20.
Machín, L., Giménez, A., Vidal, L., & Ares, G. (2014). Influence of context on motives underlying food choice. *Journal of Sensory Studies, 29*(5), 313–324.
Moskowitz, H. R. (1995). Food quality: Conceptual and sensory aspects. *Food Quality and Preference, 6*(3), 157–162.
Namkung, Y., & Jang, S. C. (2007). Does food quality really matter in restaurants? Its impact on customer satisfaction and behavioral intentions. *Journal of Hospitality and Tourism Research, 31*(3), 387.

National Agricultural Research Foundation. (1999). *The Mediterranean products as Greek traditional products and the future of their support mechanisms*, Ministry of Agriculture (Eds.) In Greek.
Olson, J. C., & Jacoby, J. (1972). Cue utilization in the quality perception process. In M Venkate-San (Ed.), *Proceedings of the third annual conference of the association of consumer research* (pp. 167–79). Iowa City: Association for Consumer Research. http://acrwebsite.org/volumes/11997/volumes/sv02/SV-02.
Ophuis, P. A. O., & Van Trijp, H. C. (1995). Perceived quality: A market driven and consumer-oriented approach. *Food Quality and Preference, 6*(3), 177–183.
Rashidi, H., Mazaheri-Tehrani, M., Razavi, M. A., & Ghods-Rohani, M. (2015). Improving textural and sensory characteristics of low-fat UF Feta cheese made with fat replacers. *Journal of Agricultural Science and Technology, 17*(1), 121–132.
Real Greek Feta. (2017). *History of Feta*. Retrieved February, 2, 2017 from: http://www.realgreekfeta.gr/history-of-feta/.
Relou, E. (2015). *Greek are first in cheese consumption* (In Greek). Retrieved January, 16, 2017 from: http://www.ypaithros.gr/%CE%B5%CE%BB%CE%BB%CE%B7%CE%BD%CE%B9%CE%BA%CE%AE-%CF%80%CF%81%CF%89%CF%84%CE%B9%CE%AC-%CF%83%CF%84%CE%B7%CE%BD-%CE%BA%CE%B1%CF%84%CE%B1%CE%BD%CE%AC%CE%BB%CF%89%CF%83%CE%B7-%CF%84%CF%85%CF%81%CE%B9/.
Roos, E., Lahelma, E., Virtanen, M., Prättälä, R., & Pietinen, P. (1998). Gender, socioeconomic status and family status as determinants of food behaviour. *Social Science and Medicine, 46*(12), 1519–1529.
Schafer, E., Schafer, R. B., Bultena, G. L., & Hoiberg, E. O. (1993). Safety of the US food supply: Consumer concerns and behaviour. *Journal of Consumer Studies & Home Economics, 17*(2), 137–144.
Steenkamp, J. B. E. (1986). Perceived quality of food products and its relationship to consumer preferences: Theory and measurement. *Journal of Food Quality, 9*(6), 373.
Steenkamp, J. B. E. (1989). *Product quality: An investigation into the concept and how it is perceived by consumers*. https://research.wur.nl/en/publications/product-quality-an-investigation-into-the-concept-and-how-it-is-p.
Steenkamp, J. B. E. (1990). Conceptual model of the quality perception process. *Journal of Business Research, 21*(4), 309–333.
Taki, C., & Drichoutis, A. (2012). Willingness to pay (WTP) for feta cheese in a standardized packaging. In *Sustainable agriculture and food production: adaptations to a changing social, economic and institutional environment, 11th biannual conference of the Hellenic Association of Agricultural Economists*, (pp. 249–258). Thessaloniki, Greece, 26–27 November 2010. Hellenic Association of Agricultural Economists.
Tamime, A. Y., Dalgleisht, D. C., & Banks, W. (1996). Introduction, Chapter 1. In R. K. Robinson & A. Y. Tamime (Eds.), *Feta and Related Cheeses* (pp. 11–48). CRC Press.
Teuber, R. (2011). *The economics of geographically differentiated agri-food products: Theoretical considerations and empirical evidence* (Doctoral dissertation, Universitätsbibliothek Giessen). http://geb.unigiessen.de/geb/volltexte/2011/8105/pdf/TeuberRamona_2011_03_18.pdf.
Tobler, C., Visschers, V. H., & Siegrist, M. (2011). Eating green. Consumers' willingness to adopt ecological food consumption behaviors. *Appetite, 57*(3), 674–682.
Tsigkros, D., Folland, E., Moate, R., & Brennan, C. S. (2003). Feta cheese texture: The effect of caprine and ovine milk concentration. *International Journal of Dairy Technology, 56*(4), 223–236.
Vakrou, A., Fotopoulos, C., & Mattas, K. (1997, June). Location effects in the production and marketing of traditional Greek cheeses. In F Arfini & C. Mora (Eds.), *Typical and traditional products: Rural effect and agro-industrial problems, proceedings of the 52nd EAAE Seminar* (pp. 187–200). http://ageconsearch.umn.edu/bitstream/231173/2/Alexandra%20Vakrou,%20Christos%20Fotopoulos,%20Konstantinos%20Mattas%20(1997)%20Location%20effects%20in%20the%20production%20and%20marketing.pdf.

Valsamaki, K., Michaelidou, A., & Polychroniadou, A. (2000). Biogenic amine production in Feta cheese. *Food Chemistry, 71*(2), 259–266.
Van Ittersum, K., Meulenberg, M. T., Van Trijp, H., & Candel, M. J. (2007). Consumers' appreciation of regional certification labels: a Pan European study. *Journal of Agricultural Economics, 58*(1): 1–23. http://geb.unigiessen.de/geb/volltexte/2011/8105/pdf/TeuberRamona_2011_03_18.pdf.
Vila-López, N., & Kuster-Boluda, I. (2016). Adolescents' food packaging perceptions. Does gender matter when weight control and health motivations are considered? *Food Quality and Preference, 52,* 179–187.
Vlachos, I. P. (2013). Consumers' perceptions of food quality products: Greece's experiences. In M. Klopći, A. Kuipers & J.-F.., Hocquette (Eds.), *Consumer attitudes to food quality products* (pp. 247–259). Wageningen Academic Publishers.
Wardle, J., Haase, A. M., Steptoe, A., Nillapun, M., Jonwutiwes, K., & Bellisie, F. (2004). Gender differences in food choice: the contribution of health beliefs and dieting. *Annals of Behavioral Medicine, 27*(2), 107–116. https://doi.org/10.1207/s15324796abm2702_5.
Yonatan, M. (2014). *The relationship between consumers' attitude towards packaging attributes and perceived food quality, value and brand preference*. MBA dissertation, AAU- Addis Ababa University. http://etd.aau.edu.et/bitstream/123456789/5220/1/Yonatan%20Thesis.pdf.

Chapter 4
Risk-Neutral Densities and Their Application in the Piterbarg Framework

Alexis Levendis and Pierre Venter

Abstract In this paper, we consider two well-known interpolation schemes for the construction of the JSE Shareholder Weighted Top 40 implied volatility surface. We extend the Breeden and Litzenberger formula to the derivative pricing framework developed by Piterbarg post the 2007 financial crisis. Our results show that the statistical moments of the constructed risk-neutral densities are highly dependent on the choice of interpolation scheme. We show how the risk-neutral density surface can be used to price options and briefly describe how the statistical moments can be used to inform trading strategies.

4.1 Introduction

It is well-known in quantitative finance literature that the volatility of an underlying asset is not constant as initially proposed by Black and Scholes (1973). Instead, for different strikes on the same underlying contract, the volatility displays a smile shape which is so significant that it has been termed the "volatility smile". Practitioners soon realised that inversion of the Black and Scholes (1973) equation would lead to volatilities implied by market prices now known as "implied volatility". Nowadays, it is convention to quote option contracts by implied volatility.

Implied volatility is a forward-looking measure which contains rich information if a continuum of these volatilities is available at different strikes and maturity dates. Unfortunately, implied volatility data is usually sparse and it is necessary to infer values by making use of interpolation/extrapolation techniques. Dumas et al. (1998) and Gatheral (2004) proposed parameterisation techniques for implied volatility with respect to strike which will be explained in Sect. 4.2.

A. Levendis (✉) · P. Venter
College of Business and Economics, University of Johannesburg,
Johannesburg, South Africa

N. Tsounis and A. Vlachvei (eds.), *Advances in Cross-Section Data Methods in Applied Economic Research*, Springer Proceedings in Business and Economics,
https://doi.org/10.1007/978-3-030-38253-7_4

Breeden and Litzenberger (1978) show that the risk-neutral density function of an underlying asset based on the Black and Scholes (1973) valuation formula can be obtained from a call option price surface by differentiating the call option prices twice with respect to strike. This is only possible if the call option price surface exists at a variety of strikes and maturity dates. We show the importance of the chosen interpolation/extrapolation scheme to create the surface, since different techniques lead to different risk-neutral densities. The risk-neutral density is a powerful tool which can be used to inform trading strategies.

More sophisticated pricing models have been developed after lessons learned from the 2007 global financial crisis. One such model is proposed by Piterbarg (2010) where the author takes collateral into account when pricing derivatives. The literature regarding risk-neutral densities in the Black and Scholes (1973) framework is well developed. However, not much research has been done on risk-neutral densities in the Piterbarg (2010) framework. This paper attempts to bridge the gap. The rest of this paper is structured as follows: Sect. 4.2 introduces the interpolation/extrapolation schemes proposed by Dumas et al. (1998) and Gatheral (2004), respectively, Sect. 4.3 introduces the Breeden and Litzenberger (1978) formula for risk-neutral densities in the Black and Scholes (1973) framework which we extend to the Piterbarg (2010) framework by making use of the work done by von Boetticher (2017), Sect. 4.4 shows our numerical results applied to the JSE Shareholder Weighted Top 40 index as at 4 February 2019 and in Sect. 4.5 we conclude our findings.

4.2 Interpolation/Extrapolation Schemes

4.2.1 Dumas Quadratic Function

We define the implied volatility in the Black and Scholes (1973) framework by $\sigma_{BS}(K,\tau)$ where K is the strike and $\tau = T - t$ is the time to expiry. Dumas et al. (1998) proposed four equations for the shape of implied volatility:

$$\sigma_{BS}(K,\tau) = a_0, \tag{4.2.1}$$

$$\sigma_{BS}(K,\tau) = a_0 + a_1 K + a_2 K^2, \tag{4.2.2}$$

$$\sigma_{BS}(K,\tau) = a_0 + a_1 K + a_2 K^2 + a_3\tau + a_5 K\tau, \tag{4.2.3}$$

$$\sigma_{BS}(K,\tau) = a_0 + a_1 K + a_2 K^2 + a_3\tau + a_4\tau^2 + a_5 K\tau. \tag{4.2.4}$$

Equation (4.2.1) is the same constant volatility as in the Black and Scholes (1973) model. Equation (4.2.2) is a function of strike only, which means that the model is fit to each time to expiration separately. Equations (4.2.3) and (4.2.4) are functions of both the strike and time to expiry.

Dumas et al. (1998) conclude that model specifications with a time to maturity parameter perform the worst of all. Therefore, we only consider Eq. (4.2.2) at this stage and will explain how to model the term structure of implied volatility in due course.

Equation (4.2.2) can be calibrated to market implied volatilities by minimising the sum of square error terms as follows:

$$\min_{\{a_0,a_1,a_2\}} \sum_{i=1}^{N} (\sigma_{Dumas_i} - \sigma_{BS_i})^2,$$

where σ_{Dumas_i} is the estimated implied volatility for strike i using Eq. (4.2.2) proposed by Dumas et al. (1998) and N is the number of observed market implied volatilities.

4.2.2 *Gatheral SVI Parameterisation*

The stochastic volatility inspired (SVI) model introduced by Gatheral (2004) is a popular model among quantitative finance practitioners. The model attempts to explain the volatility smile by making use of only five parameters. The "raw" SVI model initially proposed by Gatheral (2004) takes the form:

$$w(x) = a + b\{\rho(x - m) + \sqrt{(x - m)^2 + \sigma^2}\}, \tag{4.2.5}$$

with left and right asymptotes:

$$w_{Left}(x) = a - b(1 - \rho)(x - m),$$

$$w_{Right}(x) = a + b(1 - \rho)(x - m),$$

where

- $x = \ln(\frac{K}{F_t})$ is the log-forward moneyness with forward price $F_t = S_t e^{r\tau}$, S_t being the spot price of the underlying at time t and r the unique risk-free interest rate in the Black–Scholes framework.
- w is the total implied variance defined as $w(K, \tau) = \sigma_{BS}^2(K, \tau)\tau$.

- a gives the overall level of variance.
- b gives the angle between the left and right asymptotes.
- σ determines how smooth the vertex is.
- ρ determines the orientation of the graph.
- m shifts the graph left or right.

The model is calibrated in a similar fashion to the model proposed by Dumas et al. (1998) by minimising the sum of square errors:

$$\min_{\{a,b,\rho,m,\sigma\}} \sum_{i=1}^{N} (\sigma_{SVI_i} - \sigma_{BS_i})^2,$$

where σ_{SVI_i} is the estimated implied volatility for strike i using the Gatheral (2004) parameterisation and N is the number of observed market implied volatilities.

Both of the interpolation schemes described above only deal with interpolation/ extrapolation in the strike (K) direction. Next, we show how to interpolate implied volatilities in the time to maturity (τ) direction.

4.2.3 Interpolating Time to Maturity

For each fixed time to maturity, the techniques proposed by Dumas et al. (1998) and Gatheral (2004) allow us to infer implied volatilities for a wide range of strikes. Option contracts typically only trade at a limited number of maturities, especially on the Johannesburg Stock Exchange (JSE) where options expire quarterly in March, June, September and December. It is therefore necessary to interpolate implied volatilities between sparse expiry dates in order for us to price contracts and obtain information regarding unknown expiries. We are interested in the work of Kahalé (2004) where the author shows that the no-arbitrage condition with respect to time to maturity (τ) holds if and only if the total implied variance $\sigma_{BS}^2(K, \tau)\tau$ is an increasing function of τ. We apply the method as shown in his paper:

- For each time to maturity $\tau \in [\tau_i, \tau_{i+1}]$ and each strike K, we calculate the implied volatility $\sigma_{BS}(K, \tau)$ so that $\sigma_{BS}^2(K, \tau)\tau$ is a linear interpolation of $\sigma_{BS}^2(K, \tau_i)\tau_i$ and $\sigma_{BS}^2(K, \tau_{i+1})\tau_{i+1}$.

Once an implied volatility surface has been constructed covering a wide range of strikes and times to expiration, the next step is to build a risk-neutral density surface which contains information about the underlying asset through statistical moments, i.e. mean, standard deviation or volatility, skewness and kurtosis. The next section reviews the work of Breeden and Litzenberger (1978) and extends their equation to the Piterbarg (2010) framework by making use of formulas derived by von Boetticher (2017).

4.3 Risk-Neutral Densities

The risk-neutral probability measure is crucial in quantitative finance as it allows us to price financial derivatives. The risk-neutral measure is not to be confused with the real-world probability measure. In fact, they can be vastly different since different investors require different risk premiums in the real world, whereas all investors are assumed to be insensitive to risk in the risk-neutral world (Hull (2008)). In the Black and Scholes (1973) framework, the assumption is that there exists a unique constant risk-free rate r which can be used to price a European option V_t at time t as:

$$V_t = e^{-r\tau} E[f(S_T)], \tag{4.3.1}$$

where $f(S_T)$ is the terminal payoff function of a contract with underlying stock price S_T at maturity date T.

In the case of a European call option, where:

$$\begin{aligned} f(S_T) &= \max(S_T - K, 0), \\ &= (S_T - K)^+, \end{aligned}$$

Equation (4.3.1) can be written as:

$$\begin{aligned} V_t &= e^{-r\tau} \int_{-\infty}^{\infty} (S_T - K)^+ p(S_T) dS_T, \\ &= e^{-r\tau} \int_{K}^{\infty} (S_T - K) p(S_T) dS_T, \end{aligned}$$

where $p(S_T)$ is the risk-neutral probability density function of the underlying S_T at maturity T. Note the use of the words "risk-neutral". The reason being that the stock drifts at the risk-free rate r in the Black and Scholes (1973) framework according to the stochastic differential equation:

$$dS_t = rS_t dt + \sigma_{BS} S_t dW_t, \tag{4.3.2}$$

where W_t is standard Brownian motion.

Breeden and Litzenberger (1978) show that the risk-neutral probability density function $p(S_T)$ can be obtained by differentiating call prices twice with respect to strike (K). The proof is shown below:

First differentiate the market call price with respect to the strike (K) using the Leibniz integral rule:

$$\frac{\partial V}{\partial K} = e^{-r\tau}\left\{\int_K^\infty -p(S_T)dS_T\right\},$$

$$\frac{\partial V}{\partial K} = e^{-r\tau}\left\{-(1 - \int_0^K p(S_T)dS_T)\right\},$$

$$\frac{\partial V}{\partial K} = e^{-r\tau}\left\{\int_0^K p(S_T)dS_T - 1\right\},$$

$$e^{r\tau}\frac{\partial V}{\partial K} = \left\{\int_0^K p(S_T)dS_T - 1\right\}.$$

Differentiate again with respect to the strike (K) and use the fundamental theorem of calculus to obtain the formula for the risk-neutral density function:

$$e^{r\tau}\frac{\partial^2 V}{\partial K^2} = p(K). \tag{4.3.3}$$

Given a call price surface at different strikes (K) and times to maturity (τ), Eq. (4.3.3) allows us to construct a risk-neutral density surface on the domain (K, τ). This surface contains information about the level of the underlying at different forward-looking times. The interpolation/extrapolation algorithm that we choose to adopt plays a significant role in the construction of the risk-neutral density. We will explain this further in Sect. 4.4.

The assumption of a unique constant risk-free rate proposed in the Black and Scholes (1973) model proved to be flawed after the 2007 global financial crisis. Borrowing and lending at the risk-free rate, ignoring the dynamics of the repo and collateral markets was a limiting assumption because "risk-free" no longer held true when Lehman Brothers defaulted. Piterbarg (2010) extended the Black and Scholes (1973) model by relaxing the assumption of a unique constant risk-free rate r and considered three different interest rates:

- r_F—the unsecured funding rate used to finance the derivative,
- r_C—the collateral rate paid on funds received,
- r_R^S—the rate gained in a repurchase agreement into which an underlying asset S is entered into.

The relationship between the three interest rates is given by $r_C \leq r_R^S \leq r_F$. Piterbarg (2010) shows that in the absence of collateral, discounting occurs off the funding curve and in the presence of collateral, we discount off the collateral curve. We will denote zero collateral by ZC and full collateral by FC. The formulas for a European call option in the Piterbarg (2010) framework and in the case of constant r_F and r_C are:

$$V_{ZC_t} = e^{-r_F\tau} E[(S_T - K)^+], \tag{4.3.4}$$

$$V_{FC_t} = e^{-r_C\tau} E[(S_T - K)^+]. \tag{4.3.5}$$

By using the same steps as in the proof of the Breeden and Litzenberger (1978) formula in the Black and Scholes (1973) framework, the formulas for the risk-neutral densities in the case of zero and full collateral in the Piterbarg (2010) framework are given by:

$$e^{r_F\tau} \frac{\partial^2 V_{ZC}}{\partial K^2} = p(K), \tag{4.3.6}$$

$$e^{r_C\tau} \frac{\partial^2 V_{FC}}{\partial K^2} = p(K). \tag{4.3.7}$$

Note that the term "risk-neutral" in the Piterbarg (2010) framework differs slightly compared to the Black and Scholes (1973) framework since the stock drifts at the repurchase rate r_R^S. In this case, we sell the underlying and agree to buy it back at a premium r_R^S, which leads to the following stochastic differential equation for the underlying:

$$dS_t = r_R^S S_t dt + \sigma_P S_t dW_t. \tag{4.3.8}$$

Hence, pricing occurs under the measure associated with the repurchase rate r_R^S. In Eq. (4.3.8), σ_P refers to the implied volatility in the Piterbarg (2010) framework which is a function of the strike (K) and the time to maturity (τ).

Levendis and Venter (2019) show that the implied volatility in the Piterbarg (2010) framework differs to the implied volatility in the Black and Scholes (1973) framework, which leads to different prices for European call options. For the remainder of this paper, we will consider the Piterbarg (2010) framework and follow the steps below in our numerical testing:

- Market implied volatilities will be calculated using the closed-form solution for European call options with zero collateral derived by von Boetticher (2017). Levendis and Venter (2019) show how this is done in their paper.
- The interpolation/extrapolation schemes proposed by Dumas et al. (1998) and Gatheral (2004) will be used to interpolate the market implied volatilities in the strike (K) direction and the method proposed by Kahalé (2004) will be used to interpolate in the time to maturity (τ) direction. We will create two implied volatility surfaces which we will then input into the Breeden and Litzenberger (1978) formula which we extended to the Piterbarg (2010) framework.

- From the constructed risk-neutral density surfaces, we will show how to price a binary option and we will tabulate the statistical moments including mean, volatility, skewness and kurtosis.

Our aim is to show that different interpolation/extrapolation algorithms lead to different statistical moments.

4.4 Numerical Results

4.4.1 Data

Data for the JSE Shareholder Weighted Top 40 Index as at 4 February 2019 was obtained from https://www.jse.co.za/downloadablefiles/equityderivatives/edmstats with spot $S_t = 10,279$. Further, we assume that $r_R^S = 5\%$ and $r_F = 9\%$. The market implied volatility data is shown graphically for options expiring in 33 days and 99 days. Note that the JSE Shareholder Weighted Top 40 Index is quoted in Rands.

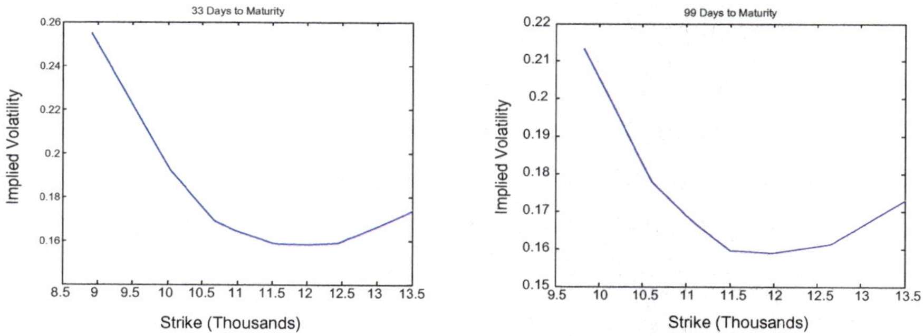

4.4.2 Constructing the Implied Volatility Surface

In this section, we show the interpolated/extrapolated implied volatility surfaces using the data in Sect. 4.4.1. First, the algorithm proposed by Dumas et al. (1998) making use of Kahalé (2004) for time to maturity (τ) and then the algorithm by Gatheral (2004) also utilising Kahalé (2004).

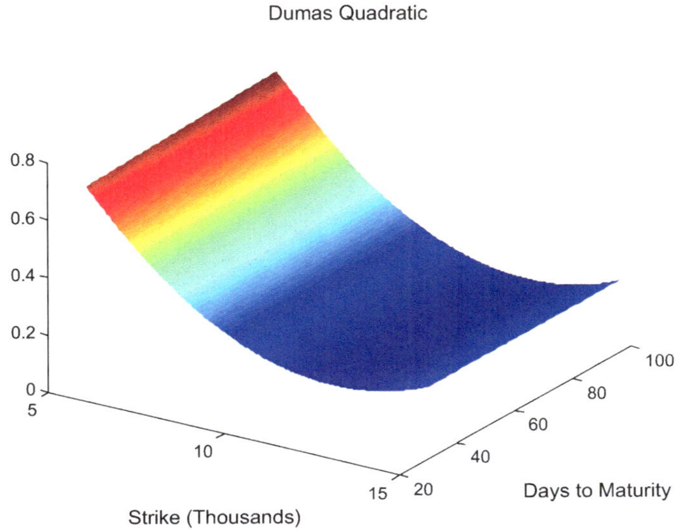

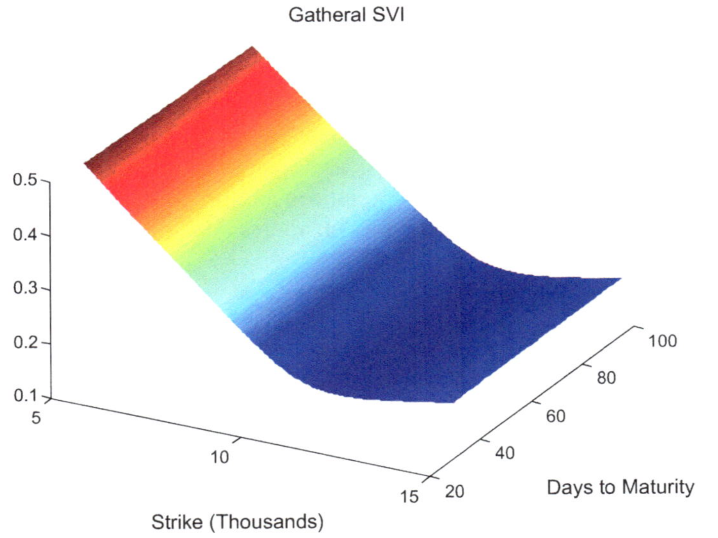

The two implied volatility surfaces differ in the wings (deep in the money and deep out of the money options). The 60-day volatility smile is shown below as an illustration.

Gatheral (2004) states that the total implied variance should increase linearly in the wings which are in line with our results shown above. The model proposed by Dumas et al. (1998) leads to much higher implied volatilities at the wings. Next, we construct the call price surface which we input into the Breeden and Litzenberger (1978) formula in order to obtain the risk-neutral densities.

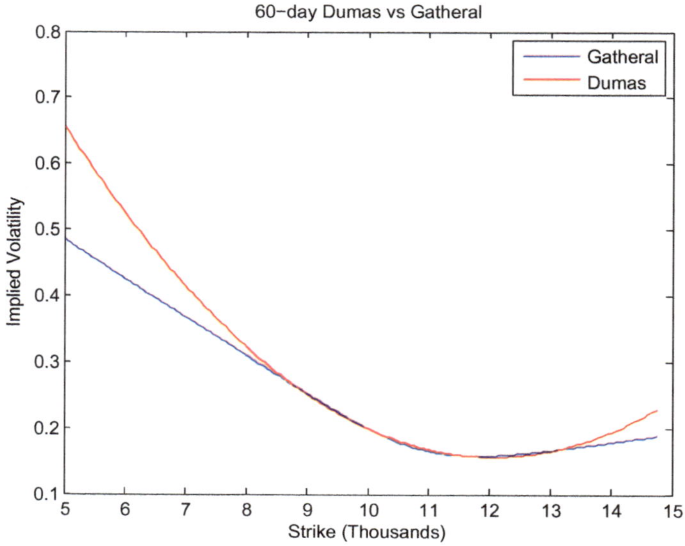

4.4.3 Constructing the Call Price Surface

This section shows the required formulas for construction of the call option surface. The implied volatilities from the constructed implied volatility surface in Sect. 4.4.2 can be substituted into the closed-form solutions for European call options derived by von Boetticher (2017). The solutions for zero collateral and full collateral European call options are shown below:

$$V_{ZC_t} = e^{-\int_t^T r_F(u)du}(S_t e^{\int_t^T r_R^S(u)du} N(d_1) - KN(d_2)), \tag{4.4.1}$$

$$V_{FC_t} = e^{-\int_t^T r_C(u)du}(S_t e^{\int_t^T r_R^S(u)du} N(d_1) - KN(d_2)), \tag{4.4.2}$$

where

$$d_1 = \frac{\ln(\frac{S_t}{K}) + \int_t^T r_R^S(u)du + \frac{1}{2}\sigma_P^2\tau}{\sigma_P\sqrt{\tau}},$$

$$d_2 = d_1 - \sigma_P\sqrt{\tau},$$

and $N(\cdot)$ denotes the standard normal distribution function.

The work of von Boetticher (2017) shows that a European call option that is fully collateralised is more expensive compared to a zero collateral call option. The interested reader is referred to Levendis and Venter (2019) where a recent study confirms the result.

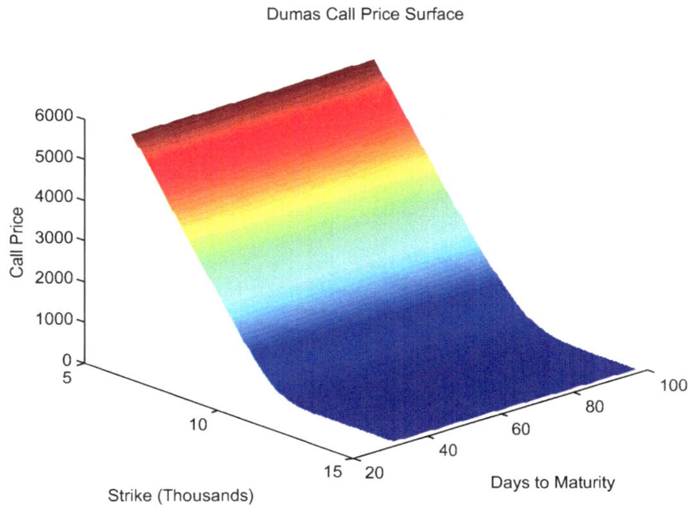

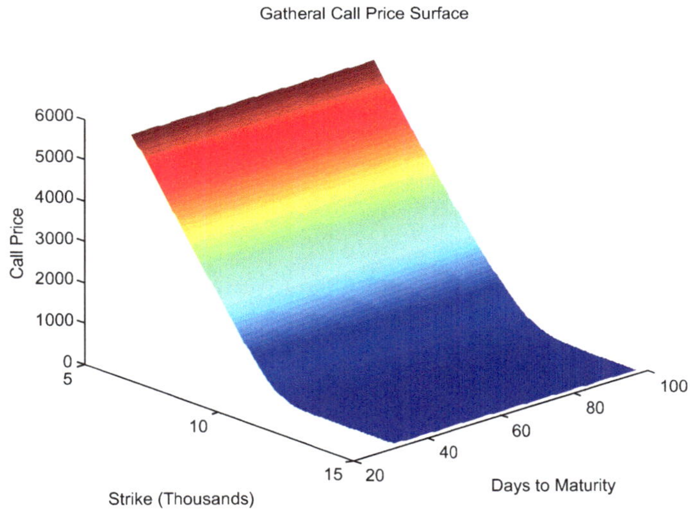

Using the constructed implied volatility surface by Dumas et al. (1998) or Gatheral (2004), the European call option surface for a zero collateral trade can be constructed by making use of Eq. (4.4.1). Two call option surfaces are shown below by making use of the respective interpolation/extrapolation schemes. In the next section, we introduce the risk-neutral density surface by using the call option surface as input into the Breeden and Litzenberger (1978) formula.

4.4.4 Constructing the Risk-Neutral Density Surface

In this section, we will show how to construct the risk-neutral density surface and discuss its use. The call option surface from Sect. 4.4.3 can be used as input into Eq. (4.3.6) in order to obtain the risk-neutral density surface in the Piterbarg (2010) framework. The two risk-neutral density surfaces using the "Dumas Call Price Surface" and "Gatheral Call Price Surface" from Sect. 4.4.3, respectively, are shown below:

Dumas Risk-Neutral Density

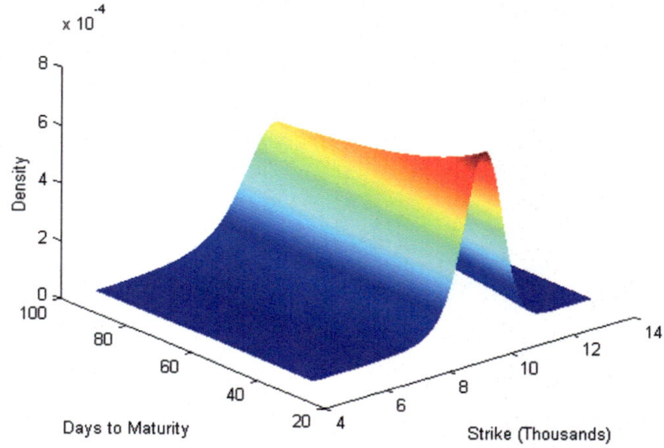

Gatheral Risk-Neutral Density

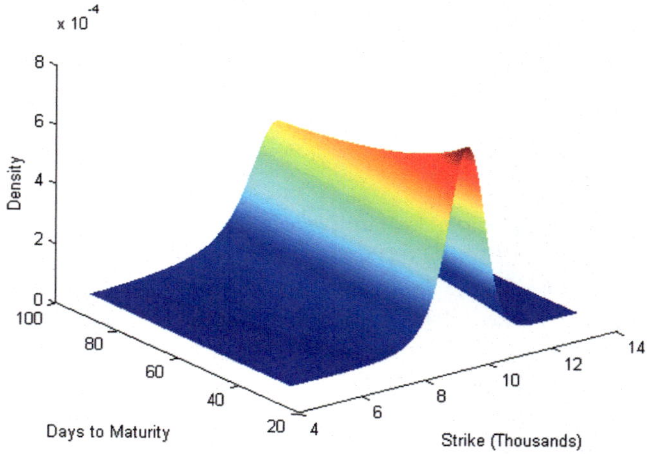

The risk-neutral density surface can be used to price options. Consider a binary option as an example that pays 1 if the underlying is above a certain strike K and 0 otherwise. Mathematically, this can be written as:

$$f(S_T) = \begin{cases} 1 & S_T > K, \\ 0 & S_T \leq K. \end{cases}$$

Then, if the trade has no collateral, the price of a binary option in the Piterbarg (2010) framework is given by:

$$\begin{aligned} V_t &= e^{-r_F \tau} E[f(S_T)], \\ &= e^{-r_F \tau} \int_{-\infty}^{\infty} f(S_T) p(S_T) dS_T, \\ &= e^{-r_F \tau} \int_{K}^{\infty} (1) p(S_T) dS_T. \end{aligned}$$

Here, $p(S_T)$ is known from the risk-neutral density surface. The table below shows the prices for zero collateral binary options with strike $K = 10,000$ expiring in 60 days and 90 days, respectively:

	60 day price	90 day price
Dumas surface	0.69982	0.69948
Gatheral surface	0.70892	0.70522

The table indicates that the price of a binary option is dependent on the choice of interpolation/extrapolation scheme.

The graphs below compare the distribution of the underlying 60 days and 90 days in advance by using the respective interpolation/extrapolation algorithms:

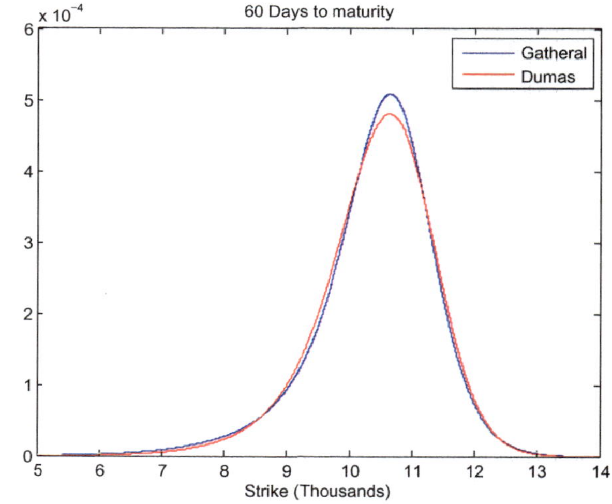

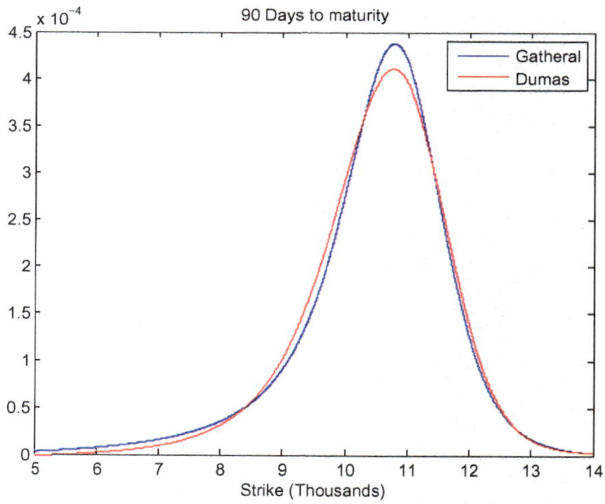

The graphs indicate that different interpolation/extrapolation choices lead to different risk-neutral densities. Below we tabulate the statistical moments obtained from the respective algorithms:

Moment	60 days Dumas	60 days Gatheral	90 days Dumas	90 days Gatheral
Mean	10,402	10,398	10,498	10,439
Volatility	1064	1032	1282	1397
Skewness	−2.41	−1.61	−2.20	−2.38
Kurtosis	22.16	12.60	18.27	16.62

The table shows that the mean and volatility of the underlying do not differ much when comparing the two algorithms, but the skewness and kurtosis show some deviation. In a recent study, Flint and Maré (2017) investigated a statistical moment trading strategy where their results were very promising. Their goal was to create a risk-neutral density surface weekly and based on the skewness or kurtosis, either hold the underlying or move to cash. If the skewness or kurtosis for the current week was higher compared to the previous week, then the investor would hold the underlying, else they would hold cash. Our results show that the choice of interpolation/extrapolation scheme could impact this trading strategy, especially if the trading strategy relies on the relative week-on-week movement in the skewness or kurtosis. We do not attempt to favour any interpolation/extrapolation algorithm because the choice of scheme will be unique to each problem.

4.5 Conclusion

In this paper, we investigated two interpolation/extrapolation schemes for implied volatility based on JSE Top 40 data as at 4 February 2019. We showed how to create a risk-neutral density surface in the Piterbarg (2010) framework from the implied volatility surface. The risk-neutral densities constructed from the Breeden and Litzenberger (1978) formula lead to an elegant and simple way to price options with non-complex payoff features. Another powerful feature is the forward-looking information contained in the densities as shown by Flint and Maré (2017).

Our results show that the choice of interpolation/extrapolation scheme has an impact on the statistical moments and also leads to different option prices. Each scheme has its own strengths and weaknesses regarding the complexity of implementation and accuracy. We do not attempt to favour a particular method, but merely point out that different techniques lead to different answers.

Areas for future research might include the implementation of the Ross (2015) recovery theorem as shown in a recent paper by Flint and Maré (2017), where the theorem provides a way in which real-world probabilities can be extracted.

References

Black, F., & Scholes, M. (1973). The pricing of options and corporate liabilities. *Journal of Political Economy, 81*(3), 637–654.

Breeden, D., & Litzenberger, R. H. (1978). Prices of state-contingent claims implicit in option prices. *Journal of Business, 51*, 621–651.

Dumas, B., Fleming J., & Whaley, R. E. (1998). Implied volatility functions: Empirical tests. *The Journal of FinanceIII*(6).

Flint, E., & Maré, E. (2017). Estimating option-implied distributions in illiquid markets and implementing the Ross recovery theorem. *South African Actuarial Journal, SAAJ, 2017*, 1–28.

Gatheral, J. (2004). A parsimonious arbitrage-free implied volatility parameterization with application to the valuation of volatility derivatives. *Presentation at Global Derivatives*.
Hull, J.C. (2008). *Options, futures and other derivatives* (7th ed.). Prentice Hall
Kahalé, N. (2004). An arbitrage-free interpolation of volatilities. *Risk, 17*(5), 102–106.
Levendis, A., & Venter, P. (2019). Implementation of local volatility in Piterbarg's framework. In *Paper submitted to international conference on applied economics 2019*.
Piterbarg, V. (2010). Funding beyond discounting: collateral agreements and derivatives pricing. *Risk Magazine, 23*(2), 97–102.
Ross, S. (2015). The recovery theorem. *The Journal of Finance, 70*(2), 615–648.
von Boetticher, S.T. (2017). The Piterbarg framework for option pricing. Ph.D. diss.

Chapter 5
Expected Shortfall Modelling of the CARBS Indices

Coenraad C.A. Labuschagne, Niel Oberholzer and Pierre J. Venter

Abstract The purpose of this study is to make use of time-varying volatility models to estimate expected shortfall (ES) for the CARBS indices and a global minimum variance portfolio (GMVP) constructed using the CARBS indices. The GARCH, GJR-GARCH and EGARCH models are considered. Furthermore, six different distributional assumptions are made regarding the error distribution. The evidence suggests that skewness and kurtosis are important factors to consider when modelling financial returns. Furthermore, it is also important to take leverage into account; asymmetric GARCH models produce the most reliable estimate for four out of six of the variables considered in this study. This is consistent with other findings in the literature.

5.1 Introduction

Recent changes in regulation following the GFC have forced financial modelling and risk management researchers and practitioners to alter their methods for measuring and reporting risk (Berggren 2017). Value at risk (VaR) is not a coherent risk measure because it does not adhere to the subadditivity principle. Therefore, a different approach is required when measuring and quantifying risk. This problem is considered in this paper.

The purpose of this study is to make use of time-varying volatility models to estimate expected shortfall (ES) for the CARBS indices and a global minimum variance portfolio (GMVP) constructed using the CARBS indices. As explained by

C. C.A. Labuschagne · N. Oberholzer · P. J. Venter (✉)
Department of Finance and Investment Management, University of Johannesburg, Auckland Park, Johannesburg 2006, South Africa
e-mail: pventer@uj.ac.za

C. C.A. Labuschagne
e-mail: ccalabuschagne@uj.ac.za

N. Oberholzer
e-mail: nielo@uj.ac.za

N. Tsounis and A. Vlachvei (eds.), *Advances in Cross-Section Data Methods in Applied Economic Research*, Springer Proceedings in Business and Economics,
https://doi.org/10.1007/978-3-030-38253-7_5

Hull (2012), ES is a coherent risk measure and, hence, adheres to the subadditivity property. ES provides an estimate of the expected loss conditional on the loss being greater than VaR (McNeil et al. 2005).

The error distribution assumed when estimating different GARCH family models is an important factor to consider when estimating ES. Conventional wisdom among financial researchers is that skewness and kurtosis are important factors when estimating risk measures. Therefore, the empirical analysis of this chapter aims to determine which GARCH model and error distribution produce the most reliable estimate of ES for the CARBS indices and the GMVP.

Another important factor to consider is the back-testing procedure that should be used to determine the accuracy of a model used to estimate ES. According to Danielsson (2011), back-testing ES is more challenging, because it is not as intuitive as back-testing VaR. In this study, the process outlined by McNeil and Frey (2000) is used to determine the accuracy of the different models and respective error distribution assumptions. This approach makes use of violation residuals. This is discussed in more detail in the methodology section.

The `rugarch R` package by Ghalanos (2014) is used to estimate the different models used in this chapter. The remainder of this paper is structured as follows: in the next section, the relevant and recent literature is discussed, thereafter the concept of ES and testing the accuracy of ES is discussed in depth in the methodology section, the empirical results are reported and interpreted, and finally, the main results and concluding remarks are summarised.

5.2 Literature Review

The application of GARCH models to tail risk measures is well documented in the literature. Because of recent changes in regulation, the focus has moved from VaR to the coherent risk measure, ES. Zakrisson and Solheim Karlsson (2016) compared different parametric estimation methods to determine whether complex methods are required for tail risk measurement of the S&P500 index. Six different GARCH models, two exponentially weighted moving average (EWMA) models and two different historical simulation models were used. Zakrisson and Solheim Karlsson (2016) conclude that the less complex EWMA models are the most reliable when estimating VaR and ES for the S&P500 index.

Forsgren (2016) estimated VaR and ES for commodities using GARCH, GJR-GARCH and EGARCH. In terms of error distributions, the normal and Student-*t* distributions were assumed to estimate VaR. ES was estimated by assuming that the violations of the estimated VaR follow the gneralised Pareto distribution. The results suggest that the GJR-GARCH and the Student-*t* distribution produce the most reliable estimate of the different risk measures. Finally, Forsgren (2016) suggests that different error distributions should be considered when measuring risk in commodity markets as an area for future research.

In a recent study, Berggren (2017) made use of time-varying volatility models and four different error distributional assumptions to estimate VaR and ES for the Swedish index OMSX30. The main findings indicate that the skewed Student-*t* distribution was the most reliable for most of the models estimated. Berggren (2017) suggests that further research is required to determine if the same results hold for equities, commodities and derivative instruments.

To account for long memory and asymmetry in financial time series, Walther (2017) estimated several GARCH family models to forecast VaR and ES for the Vietnamese VNI and HNXI indices. For the estimation of GARCH parameter, the Student-*t* and skewed Student-*t* distributions were assumed. The results show statistically significant signs of long memory in variance. Walther (2017) suggests that fractionally integrated GARCH models estimated assuming a skewed Student-*t* error distribution should be used for short trading positions. Finally, asymmetric power ARCH models estimated assuming a Student-*t* error distribution should be used for long trading positions.

In a similar study, Katzke and Garbers (2016) estimated VaR and ES for the eight main economic sectors of the JSE All Share Index. GARCH models that take the leverage effect and long memory into account were used. The Kupiec and dynamic quantile tests were used to test the accuracy of the estimated VaR and ES. The results indicate that the reliability of risk measures can be improved when long memory and asymmetry are accounted for when modelling financial returns.

Huang (2014) compared parametric, non-parametric and semi-parametric models to measure risk across different markets. Equities, gold, oil and bonds were included in the study. A new parametric model was presented, which includes an autoregressive moving average (ARMA) process to capture the effect of autocorrelation and the GJR-GARCH model to account for asymmetries. The model is estimated assuming a skewed GED distribution which captures the effect skewness and kurtosis in financial returns. The empirical analysis showed that the ARMA(1,1)-GJR-GARCH(1,1) model estimated assuming a skewed GED is the most reliable when estimating risk measures for the four markets. The methodology used in this chapter is discussed in the following section.

5.3 Methodology

5.3.1 Expected Shortfall

In this section, the concept of ES will be discussed more in depth. First, it is necessary to define a coherent risk measure. Consider the following definition from Hull (2012).

Definition 1 (*Coherent risk measure*) A risk measure is said to be coherent if it satisfies the following properties:

- *Monotonicity*: The risk measure of a portfolio that outperforms another in every state of the world should be less.
- *Translation invariance*: If an amount of cash K is added to a portfolio, its risk measure should decrease by K.
- *Homogeneity*: If the portfolio size is changed by a factor, while the relative amounts of different items in the portfolio remain unchanged, it should result in the risk measure being multiplied by the same factor.
- *Subadditivity*: Diversification benefits should be reflected by the risk measure, the risk of a portfolio is less than or equal to the risk of the individual assets included in the portfolio.

VaR does not adhere to the subadditivity property, and therefore, an alternative approach is required. Hence, ES is estimated in this chapter.

The concept of ES is described by the following definition from Danielsson (2011)

Definition 2 (*Expected shortfall*) Expected loss conditional on the loss being greater than VaR. For a loss L, ES is given by

$$ES_X = \frac{1}{1-X}\int_X^1 VaR_X(L). \tag{5.1}$$

If normality is assumed, and the return distribution has a mean μ and variance σ^2, McNeil et al. (2005) show that ES is given by the following formula

$$ES_X = -\mu - \sigma\frac{\phi\left(\Phi^{-1}(X)\right)}{1-X},$$

where ϕ is the standard normal density. As mentioned previously, volatility is very volatile over time. Therefore, the above equation takes the following form when a time-varying volatility model is used

$$ES_X = -\mu - \sigma_t\frac{\phi\left(\Phi^{-1}(X)\right)}{1-X},$$

where a GARCH process is used to model σ_t^2. In GARCH, GJR-GARCH and EGARCH.

In this chapter, the GARCH filtering approach is used to estimate ES for the CARBS indices and the GMVP. The three different GARCH family models are considered, GARCH, GJR-GARCH and EGARCH. In addition, both symmetric and skewed error distributions are assumed. Hence, the integral outlined in Definition 2 will be different for each respective error distribution assumption.

5.4 Error Distribution Assumptions

By using a similar approach to Narsoo (2016), different assumptions will be made regarding the error distribution of the mean model. Six different assumptions will be used for each model in this study, namely: normal, Student-t, generalised error distribution (GED), skewed normal, skewed Student's-t and the skewed GED. The different assumptions are discussed briefly below.

According to Peters (2001), skewness and kurtosis are important in financial modelling. Therefore, it is important to make use of a distribution that can model these two moments appropriately. As mentioned previously, univariate GARCH models are usually specified using a normal distribution. The density of the normal distribution is given by

$$f(z) = \frac{1}{\sqrt{2\pi}} \exp\left\{\frac{z^2}{2}\right\}, -\infty < z < \infty. \tag{5.2}$$

The log returns considered in this study show signs of leptokurtosis which cannot be captured by the normal distribution. An example of a model that is capable of capturing the effect of leptokurtosis is the Student-t distribution.

According to Peters (2001), the probability density function of the Student-t distribution is given by

$$f(z) = \frac{\Gamma(\frac{\nu+1}{2})}{\sqrt{\nu\pi}\,\Gamma(\frac{\nu}{2})}\left(1 + \frac{z^2}{\nu}\right)^{\frac{\nu+1}{2}}, -\infty < z < \infty,$$

where ν and Γ denote the shape parameter and the gamma function, respectively. Verhoeven and McAleer (2004) explain that the GED, similar to the Student-t distribution, also has one parameter (ν) to capture leptokurtosis. In addition, the GED is superior when it comes to capturing peaks, but not when capturing fat tails. According to Narsoo (2016), the density of the GED is given by,

$$f(z) = \nu \exp\left\{-\frac{1}{2\left|\frac{z}{\lambda\sigma}\right|}\right\}\left[2^{\frac{\nu+1}{\nu}}\Gamma(1/\nu\lambda\sigma)\right]^{-1}, -\infty < z < \infty,$$

where

$$\lambda = \left[\frac{\Gamma(1/\nu)}{2^{2/\nu}\Gamma(3/\nu)}\right].$$

The three symmetric error distributions considered in this study are illustrated (Fig. 5.1).

In the figure above, the shape parameter ν is set equal to 5 for the Student-t distribution, and 1.5 for the GED. The mean and standard deviation are set equal to 0

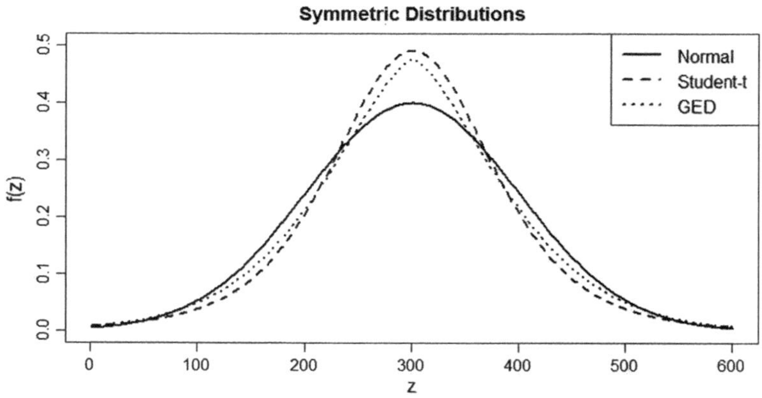

Fig. 5.1 Symmetric error distribution assumptions

and 1 respectively. It is clear that both the Student-t and the GED are able to capture the effect of leptokurtosis when compared to the normal distribution.

Financial return series are generally slightly skewed. The normal distribution and the distributions discussed above are symmetric about the mean, which might not be sufficient to capture extreme losses. Therefore, it is necessary to consider skewed error distributions. Kosapattarapim et al. (2012) show that the skewed normal distribution is given by

$$f(z) = \frac{1}{\sigma\pi} \exp\left\{\frac{-(z-\mu)^2}{2\sigma^2}\right\} \int_{-\infty}^{\xi\frac{z-\mu}{\sigma}} \exp\left\{\frac{t^2}{2}\right\} dt, -\infty < z < \infty,$$

where ξ, σ, and μ denote the shape of the density, the scale, and the location respectively. The integral above is evaluated numerically. Examples of the skewed normal distribution are plotted (Fig. 5.2).

The skewed normal distribution will not be able to capture the fat tails of financial returns. Therefore, it is necessary to specify the skewed Student-t distribution and the skewed GED. The density of the skewed Student-t distribution is given by (Kosapattarapim et al. 2012),

$$f(z) = \begin{cases} cd\left(1 + \frac{1}{\nu-2}\left(\frac{c(\frac{z-\mu}{\sigma})+b}{1-\xi}\right)^2\right)^{-\frac{\nu+1}{2}}, & \text{if } z < -\frac{b}{c} \\ cd\left(1 + \frac{1}{\nu-2}\left(\frac{c(\frac{z-\mu}{\sigma})+b}{1+\xi}\right)^2\right)^{-\frac{\nu+1}{2}}, & \text{if } z \geq -\frac{b}{c}, \end{cases}$$

where ν and ξ denote the shape and skewness parameter, respectively. Furthermore, the constants b, c and d are given by

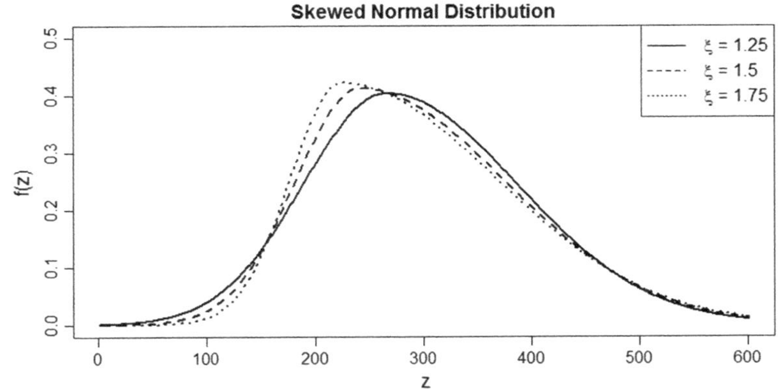

Fig. 5.2 Skewed normal distribution: different skewness parameters

$$b = 4\xi d\left(\frac{\nu-2}{\nu-1}\right)$$
$$c = 1 + 3\xi 2 - b^2$$
$$d = \frac{\Gamma\left(\frac{\nu+1}{2}\right)}{\sqrt{\pi(\nu-2)\Gamma\left(\frac{\nu}{2}\right)}}.$$

To show the effect of the shape and skewness parameters, examples of the skewed Student-t distribution are plotted (Figs. 5.3).

Finally, Kosapattarapim et al. (2012) show that the density of the skewed GED is given by,

$$f(z) = \nu[2\theta\Gamma(1/\nu)]^{-1}\exp\left\{\frac{|z-C|^{\nu}}{(1-\mathrm{sign}(z-C)\xi)^{\nu}\theta^{\nu}}\right\}, -\infty < z < \infty,$$

where

$$\theta = \Gamma(1/\nu)^{0.5}\Gamma(3/\nu)^{-0.5}F(\xi)^{-1}$$
$$C = 2\xi DF(\xi)^{-1}$$
$$F(\xi) = \sqrt{1+\xi^2-4D^2\xi^2}$$
$$D = \Gamma(2/\nu)\Gamma(1/\nu)^{0.5}\Gamma(3/\nu)^{-0.5},$$

and ν is the shape parameter, and ξ is the skewness parameter. Different cases of ν and ξ are illustrated in the figure (Figs. 5.4).

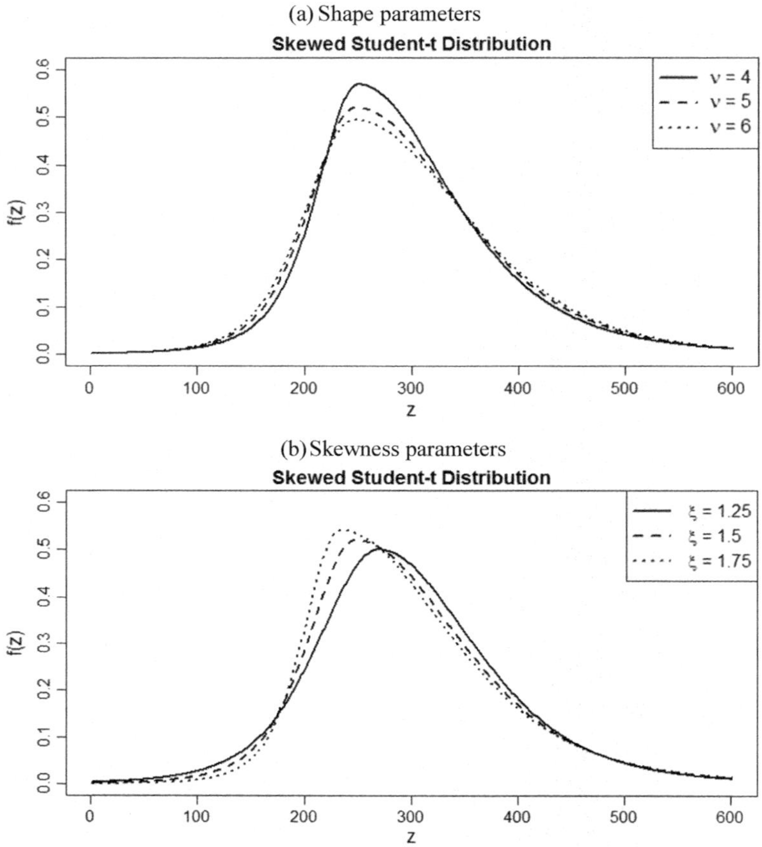

Fig. 5.3 Skewed Student-t distribution: different parameters

5.4.1 Expected Shortfall Performance Measure

As explained by Danielsson (2011), ES is more complicated to back-test when compared to VaR, because ES requires estimates of the tail expectation. Therefore, ES can only be compared to a model output while VaR can be compared to the actual return distribution. Hence, the method outlined by McNeil and Frey (2000) is used in this study.

The process works as follows, if risk measures and volatility are estimated, it is possible to form the following violation residuals,

$$\tilde{R}_{t+1} = \frac{\tilde{S}_{t+1}}{\tilde{\sigma}_{t+1}},$$

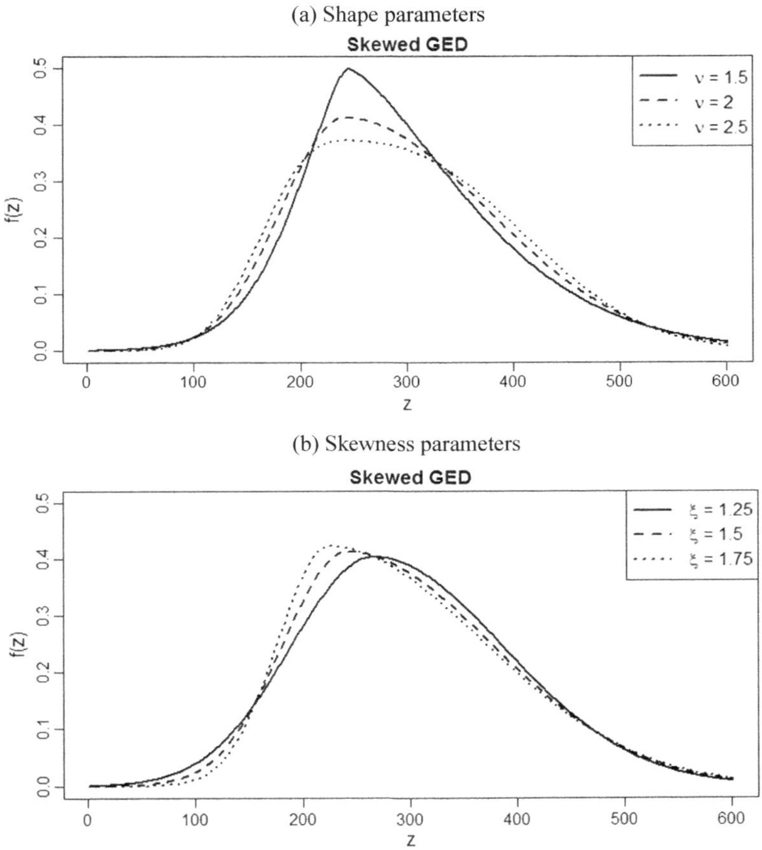

Fig. 5.4 Skewed GED: different parameters

where

$$\tilde{S}_{t+1} = (L_{t+1} - \tilde{ES}_X^{(t)})\tilde{I}_{t+1}.$$

In the above equation, $\tilde{\sigma}_{t+1}$ and $\tilde{ES}_X^{(t)}$ denote the one-step-ahead conditional variance and expected shortfall estimates, respectively. Moreover, L_t is an arbitrary loss process where $t \in \mathbb{Z}$, and $\tilde{I}_t$ is an indicator function that takes a value of one when the actual loss is greater than the one-step-ahead estimate of VaR, and zero otherwise.

As argued by McNeil et al. (2005), the equations above are expected to behave like realisations from identically and independently distributed variables from a zero mean distribution. To test for zero mean behaviour, a bootstrap test is used. The test is a one-sided t-test, and the null hypothesis is that the violation residuals are identically and independently distributed with mean zero (Ghalanos (2014)). Hence, the greater the p-value, the more reliable the model is for estimating expected shortfall.

Table 5.1 ES performance measure: symmetric error distributions

Return series	p-value	Model	Distribution
Canada	1	GARCH	Student-t
Australia	0.8264	GJR-GARCH	Student-t
Russia	0.3158	EGARCH	Student-t
Brazil	0.2508	GARCH	Student-t
South Africa	0.4250	EGARCH	Student-t
GMVP	0.7088	EGARCH	Student-t

5.5 Empirical Results

In this section, the ES performance measures of the best performing models are reported. This section will be divided into two subsections, the performance of the models estimated assuming a symmetric error distribution, thereafter, the models estimated assuming a skewed error distribution are considered.

5.5.1 *Symmetric Error Distributions*

The ES performance measure of the different models assuming a symmetric error distribution used to estimate ES in this study are reported (Table 5.1).

It is evident that the Student-t distribution is the most reliable when compared to the other symmetric error distributions used to calculate ES. Furthermore, the EGARCH model produces the most reliable estimate of ES for Russia, South Africa and the GMVP. The GARCH model is the most reliable for Canada and Brazil. The GJR-GARCH is the best performing model for Australia. Finally, the bootstrap test p-value indicates that all the models are appropriate for estimating ES. Skewness is not accounted for when using the above models. Therefore, the ES performance measure of the models estimated using skewed error distributions is considered in the next subsection.

5.5.2 *Skewed Error Distributions*

The bootstrap test p-values of the best performing models and error distribution assumptions are reported in the table (Table 5.2).

The empirical results indicate that the skewed Student-t distribution is the most reliable when estimating ES for the CARBS indices and the GMVP. This suggests that skewness and leptokurtosis are important factors to consider when modelling

Table 5.2 ES performance measure: skewed error distributions

Return series	p-value	Model	Distribution
Canada	1	GARCH	Skewed Student-t
Australia	0.9436	GJR-GARCH	Skewed Student-t
Russia	0.3931	EGARCH	Skewed Student-t
Brazil	0.2721	GARCH	Skewed Student-t
South Africa	0.7518	EGARCH	Skewed Student-t
GMVP	0.9168	EGARCH	Skewed Student-t

financial returns. This is consistent with the findings by Berggren (2017) and the findings in previous chapters.

With regard to the best fitting GARCH models, the standard GARCH model provides the most reliable estimate of ES for Canada and Brazil. Asymmetric GARCH models are required for all the other variables considered in this study. This is in line with the findings by Katzke and Garbers (2016). Furthermore, the bootstrap test p-value is greater for all the variables when a skewed error distribution is assumed, except for Canada. The p-value for Canada is the same when the different distributional assumptions are compared. The higher p-values imply that assuming a skewed error distribution leads to a more reliable estimate of ES.

5.6 Conclusion

Due to recent changes in regulation, a different approach is required for financial risk measurement. VaR is often criticised because it does not adhere to the subadditivity property, and is, therefore, not a coherent risk measure. Hence, the aim of this chapter was to estimate ES using the different time-varying volatility models used in previous chapters.

The GARCH, GJR-GARCH and EGARCH models were used along with the GARCH filtering approach to estimate ES. In addition, six different error distributions were assumed. The approach outlined by McNeil and Frey (2000) was used to measure the performance of the different models. This approach makes use of a bootstrap test. The greater the p-value, the more reliable the model is for estimating ES.

The empirical results indicated that the Student-t distribution assumption was superior to all the variables when the different symmetric error distributions are compared. Moreover, the skewed Student-t distribution assumption was the most reliable when a skewed error distribution was assumed. However, the empirical results show that the skewed error distribution assumption provided a more reliable estimate of ES when the different assumptions are compared to all the variables except Canada. This is consistent with the argument by Berggren (2017). The bootstrap test p-value for

Canada was the same when both Student-*t* and skewed Student-*t* error distributions were assumed.

The evidence suggests that skewness and kurtosis are important factors to consider when modelling financial returns. Furthermore, it is also important to take leverage into account; asymmetric GARCH models produced the most reliable estimate for four out of six of the variables considered in this study. This is consistent with other findings in the literature.

References

Berggren, E. (2017). Are GARCH models necessary for expected shortfall?

Danielsson, J. (2011). *Financial risk forecasting: The theory and practice of forecasting market risk with implementation in R and Matlab*. Wiley

Forsgren, J. (2016). *How low can you go? Quantitative risk measures in commodity markets.*

Ghalanos, A. (2014). *Rugarch: Univariate GARCH models* R package version 1.3-3.

Huang, X. (2014). *Analysing value at risk and expected shortfall methods: The use of parametric, non-parametric, and semi-parametric models.*

Hull, J. (2012). *Risk management and financial institutions* (3rd ed.). Wiley.

Katzke, N., & Garbers, C. (2016). Do long memory and and asymmetries matter when assessing downside return risk? *Investment Analysts Journal, 45*(3), 123–148.

Kosapattarapim, C., Lin, YX., & McCrae, M. (2012). Evaluating the volatility forecasting performance of best fitting GARCH models in emerging Asian stock markets.

McNeil, A. J., & Frey, R. (2000). Estimation of tail-related risk measures for heteroscedastic financial time series: An extreme value approach. *Journal of Empirical Finance*, *7*(3), 271–300.

McNeil, A., Embrechts, P. & Frey, R. (2005). *Quantitative risk management. Princeton Series in Finance* Princeton, 10.

Narsoo, J. (2016). Evaluation of GARCH-type models in volatility and value-at-risk forecasting: Evidences from USD/MUR exchange rates. *University of Mauritius Research Journal*, 22.

Peters, J. P. (2001). *Estimating and forecasting volatility of stock indices using asymmetric GARCH models and (Skewed) Student-t densities*. Belgium: University of Liege, Reprint.

Verhoeven, P., & McAleer, M. (2004). Fat tails and asymmetry in financial volatility models. *Mathematics and Computers in Simulation, 64*(3), 315–361.

Walther, T. (2017). Expected shortfall in the presence of asymmetry and long memory: An application to Vietnamese stock markets. *Pacific Accounting Review, 29*(2), 132–151.

Zakrisson, H., Solheim Karlsson, J. (2016). Practical estimation of value at risk and expected shortfall: Are complex methods really necessary?

Chapter 6
Social Benefits Versus Monetary and Multidimensional Poverty in Poland: Imputed Income Exercise

Jarosław Duda and Adam Szulc

Abstract In this study, an effect of the social benefits on monetary and multidimensional poverty in Poland is examined. The effect is evaluated by means of comparisons between actual and simulated poverty indices. The latter ones are based on incomes diminished by sums of the benefits. One of the main problems in research utilizing incomes derived from household surveys is the data quality, especially in extreme ranges of distributions. To cope this problems, the declared incomes are supplemented by imputed ones, estimated using the so-called hierarchical correlation reconstruction (HCR). This method allows estimation of the entire conditional income distribution on household welfare correlates. The poverty indices using both types of incomes differ substantially, especially for poverty depth, and those using imputed incomes seem to be more reliable. Supplementary, a strong demotivation effect of the benefits is obtained.

Keywords Monetary and multidimensional poverty · Social benefits · Income imputation

JEL Codes I32 · H53 · D31

6.1 Introduction

A standard method of evaluating impact of social benefits on poverty consists in comparing two values of poverty indices: calculated with the use of actual incomes and of incomes diminished by the benefits' values. Such a procedure is employed,

---

J. Duda (✉)
Jagiellonian University, Institute of Computer Science, Cracow, Poland
e-mail: dudaj@interia.pl

A. Szulc
Warsaw School of Economics, Institute of Statistics and Demography, Warsaw, Poland
e-mail: aszulc@sgh.waw.pl

N. Tsounis and A. Vlachvei (eds.), *Advances in Cross-Section Data Methods in Applied Economic Research*, Springer Proceedings in Business and Economics,
https://doi.org/10.1007/978-3-030-38253-7_6

for instance, in construction of Laeken index of social cohesion (see Atkinson et al 2002). This concept may be applied directly to income poverty; however, it needs a modification when multidimensional poverty is of interest. In the present research, a poverty indicator based on multidimensional household well-being is also included in the study. It captures household equivalent income, dwelling quality, household equipment and subjective evaluations of the material status. The indicator of well-being is defined using relative fuzzy sets approach (see Panek 2006); hence, it fits the interval [0, 1] (also within each dimension composing a multidimensional measure). An effect of subtracting some part of income is estimated using regressions of multidimensional well-being on incomes. The indices of poverty applied in the present study measure poverty incidence and depth.

One of the main problems appearing in research on incomes derived from household surveys is the data quality, especially in extreme ranges of distributions. While potential misestimation of highest incomes does not affect much the final results, the data errors in lowest incomes obviously flaw most of the results on poverty measurement. To overcome this problem, a new method of income imputation based on the so-called hierarchical correlation reconstruction is employed. The conditional probability distribution of declared income is predicted on endogenous variables by decomposing it into cumulant-like coefficients and predicting them with the least-squares linear regression. This predicted distribution is at first instance used for obtaining income expected values but can also be utilized to evaluate credibility of declared values, or to calculate variance and other moments for some further analysis. The set of exogenous variables (described in details in next section) is generally intended to capture household welfare indicators, usually non-monetary ones. There is a ground to find them more accurate and stable in time than monthly income declared by the households. The details of the estimation are described in Sects. 6.4 and 6.5. The same variables are used in the last part of the study, aimed at estimation of potential demotivation effect of receiving benefits, for both incomes and multidimensional well-being. This effect is estimated by means of matching estimation[1] in which receiving any benefits (except retirement and invalidity pensions) is a "treatment".

6.2 The Data

The individual data employed in this research come from the 2014 household budget survey (HBS) carried by Statistics Poland (GUS). The survey is generally based on the principles applied in the European Community Household Panel (European University Institute 2019). It encompasses information on household disposable income and its components, expenditures, assets, durables, dwelling conditions,

[1] See Heinrich et al. (2010) for technical details, and Smith and Todd (2005) and Brown et al. (2018) for a discussion.

demographic and socio-economic attributes and answers to subjective income questions. The yearly sample covers more than 37,000 households and 101,000 persons. The reference period of observation is one month. A two-stage sampling scheme is being applied. Information on income is collected at household level. Due to this limitation, information on social benefits refers to the households only, and it is impossible to estimate precisely number of persons receiving this type of transfer. More methodological details on Polish HBS may be found in household budget survey (2014).

At least, three sources of errors in income data may be pronounced. The first type affects mainly producer's (including farmers) households. A disposable income is calculated as a difference between the household revenues and spendings on productions. Overestimation of the latter ones is quite frequent and leads to underestimation of disposable incomes making them, in some cases, negative. Though negative disposable incomes constitute only about 0.3% of the whole sample, there is no reason to believe that the positive ones are free of such errors. The second type of error is caused by seasonality of the incomes, while the third one is due to intentional misreporting by the respondents (for instance, those receiving revenues from the grey economy). Assuming that income data in a middle of the distribution is relatively reliable and the relations between income and welfare correlates are stable, it is possible to reduce impact of the above-mentioned data errors by the imputation presented in Sects. 6.4 and 6.5.

The following variables are used to predict household income.

(1) Continuous or almost continuous:

- remaining equivalent cash at the end of the month
- shares of expenditures on luxury goods and for food
- household's head age.

(2) Discrete ordinal:

- household size
- number of children below 10 years of age and between 10 and 15 y. o. a.
- urbanization level of the living area
- type of residence (from largest cities to rural areas)
- number of cars in the household
- age of the newest car
- month of the query.

(3) Discrete categorical:

- main income source
- voivodship
- building type and its ownership type
- subjective evaluations of:
  - change in the material position
  - income sufficiency
  - level of satisfaction of needs for various types of consumption.

(4) Binary:

- household's head sex
- subjective evaluation whether the dwelling is too small or too large
- presence of persons:
  - with tertiary education
  - with the highest secondary education
  - unemployed
  - handicapped.

The model uses linear combinations of their features. The pairwise dependencies for all four continuous variables (including age) are displayed in Fig. 6.1. Their cumulant-like proprieties are used in linear combination for the prediction. To avoid arbitrary choice of the weights, all the remaining variables are treated as binary: split into 0/1 variables, as many as the number of distinct values, being 1 if the category agrees, 0 otherwise. The final coefficients are presented in Fig. 6.6.

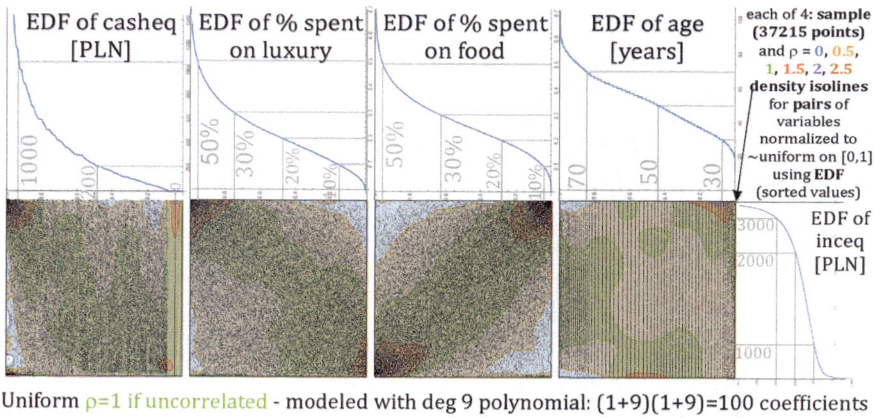

Fig. 6.1 Pairwise dependencies between 5 variables treated as continuous exogenous (inceq: equivalent income) on vertical axis to be predicted from endogenous variables on horizontal axes (casheq: equivalent remaining cash at the end of month). Each is normalized to nearly uniform marginal distribution—position can be seen as quantile, 0.5 as median, length e.g. 0.2 as 20% of population. Some of them have discreteness—corresponding to vertical dotted lines. Each of four $[0,1]^2$ presented diagrams contains 37,215 data points and isolines for their density (that would be $\rho \approx 1$ for independent variables)—estimated with HCR as polynomial $\sum_{ij=0}^{9} a_{ij} f_i(x_0) f_j(x_1)$ using 100 coefficients (mixed moments up to ninth). For example, for age, we can see that younger people have higher expected inceq, middle-age lower, older closer to median (lower variance)—we need at least second-order polynomial (f_2) of age to model such behaviour

6.3 Monetary and Multidimensinal Poverty Indicators

Monetary poverty is defined by means of equivalent (OECD 70/50 equivalence scales) monthly income. Multidimensional indicator covers also dwelling conditions (especially dwelling size and quality, presence of various appliances, neighbourhood), household equipment with durables and subjective evaluations of own material position. Each of those components was transformed into [0, 1] interval. Hence, at each dimension of well-being, households may be compared directly. The general idea of construction of fuzzy well-being indicator for i-th unit (here: household) is represented by the following equation[2]

$$f_i = f(y_i) = 1 - \frac{Y_{\max} - y_i}{Y_{\max} - Y_{\min}}$$

where y_i stands for well-being individual component, e.g. equivalent income, dwelling size or subjective income evaluation. In order to relax the impact of outliers, for continuous and almost continuous variables, minimum and maximum values were replaced by percentiles of rank 0.05 and 0.95, respectively, together with due censoring of y_{i}. More details as well as proposals of some more sophisticated fuzzy well-being indicators may be found in Panek (2006). In the aggregate well-being indicator, equivalent income receives (arbitrary) weight 0.4 while three remaining components 0.2. In the fuzzy set approach to poverty measurement, it is not necessary to set a poverty line. However, as multidimensional poverty is compared here with traditional monetary poverty, it was necessary to set poverty lines also for such a type of measure. People with well-being below the first quartile are considered poor while those below the first decile extremely poor. The head count ratio is an indicator of poverty incidence, while Dalton index is intended to measure poverty depth. Informally speaking, its value informs how poor the poor are. More formally, it is defined as a relative difference between the poverty line (z) and average well-being of the poor:

$$D = \frac{z - \overline{Y_P}}{z}$$

In Sect. 6.6, three types of poverty comparisons are made. The first one is a core of evaluation of the effect that social benefits have on poverty. Both above-mentioned types of poverty indices are calculated twice: using actual data and those based on incomes diminished by the social benefits. The second comparison is between monetary and multidimensional indices. Those exercises are then repeated using actual and imputed incomes.

---

[2]The ratio subtracted from the unity may be considered a fuzzy poverty indicator.

6.4 Some General Statistics

In Table 6.1, average values of benefits per equivalent unit are displayed. The largest part of the transfers is family benefits. However, due to low proportion of the recipients, the highest value per household of the recipients is observed in the case of unemployment benefits.

Concentration curves calculated for total sums of the benefits demonstrate definitely pro-poor distribution of those transfers (see Fig. 6.2). The distribution of the benefits is more favourable for the poorest when multidimensional well-being indicator instead of equivalent income is employed. This may suggest that policy makers' decisions are based on broad evaluations of potential recipients' material status, extending the current income (the more reason, the income declared for a household survey).

To estimate an impact of transfers on poverty, one can compare poverty indicators in the way described in the previous section, i.e. comparing the actual with the simulated ones. Simulation of changes in multidimensional poverty requires running regressions of multidimensional well-being indicator in lower ranges of distribution. Due to above-mentioned errors in income data, the observed shape of regression curves, especially in the lowest ranges of equivalent income distribution, is at least problematic. One could expect positive correlation between multidimensional well-being and equivalent income; however, this is not true below the first income decile.

Table 6.1 Benefits per equivalent unit by type, złoty per month, 2014

Type of benefit	Average benefit per household	
	All households	Recipient households[a]
Family benefits	25.87	160.28 (17.9%)
Unemployment benefits	5.88	263.36 (2.3%)
Social assistance	11.71	166.57 (7.5%)
Social rent	4.19	227.12 (1.9%)
Other	13.14	61.65 (21.3%)
Total	60.79	177.94 *(35.2%)*
As % of mean equivalent income	3.6%	13.0%
As % of poverty gap, threshold at first quartile of equivalent income	83.6%	

[a]In brackets proportions of the recipients

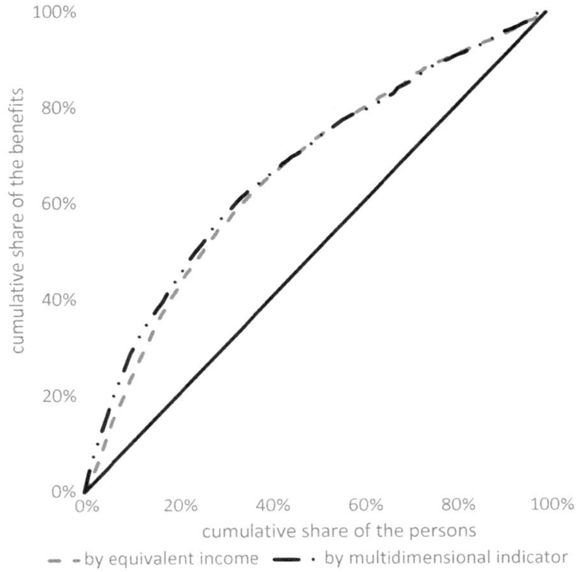

Fig. 6.2 Concentration curves for total sum of benefits, appointed by equivalent income and multidimensional (fuzzy) welfare indicator

Figure 6.3 displays the results of nonparametric Lowess estimation[3] of "fuzzy well being" on the equivalent income.

Due to a bizarre shape of the correlation some simulations on poverty indices reported in details in Sect. 6.6 yield nonsensical results: removing social benefits decreases multidimensional poverty gap. This problem does not appear when imputed incomes are employed. A shape of the correlation seems to be then more acceptable (negative correlation may be observed for very small portion of the observations, see Fig. 6.4) and all poverty indices increases due to removing the benefits.

6.5 Income Imputation: Normalization and Orthonormal Basis

When predictions are based on linear regression of exogenous variable as a linear combination of endogenous variables, large values in tails of distributions often have large unpredictable contributions to predicted value. To get more reasonable predictions, including nonlinear dependencies, we handle these issues by:

– transforming continuous variables to nearly uniform distribution on [0,1] like in copula theory, where value x corresponds to x-th quantile of the original variable,

[3]For details see Cleveland (1979).

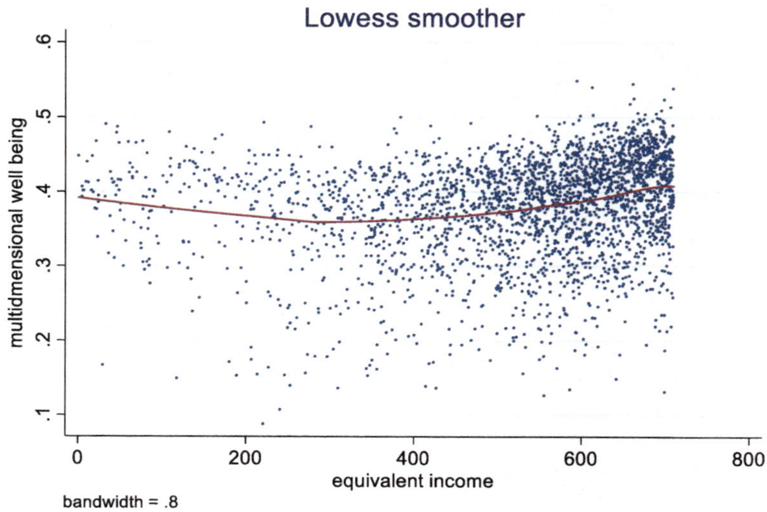

Fig. 6.3 Nonparametric estimation of multidimensional well-being indicator on declared equivalent incomes, non-negative below first income decile

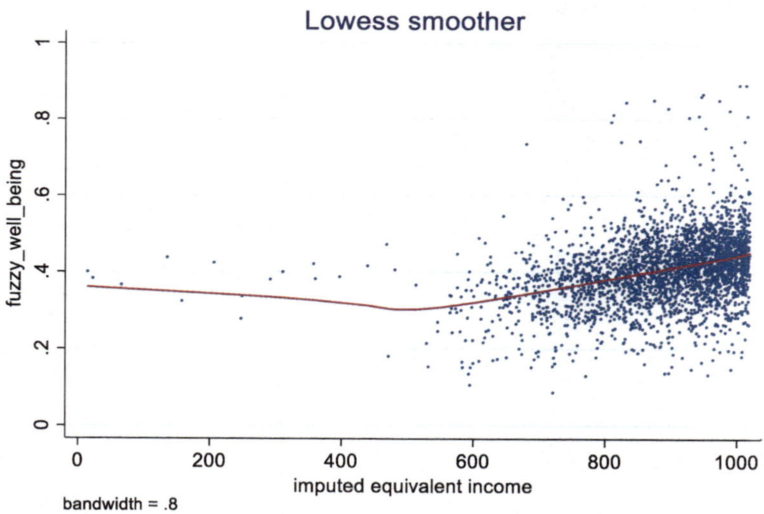

Fig. 6.4 Nonparametric estimation of multidimensional well-being indicator on imputed equivalent incomes, non-negative below first income decile

– instead of directly predicting the value, we directly predict the entire conditional probability distribution (based on the endogenous variables), then calculate expected value of such predicted probability distribution,
– to include nonlinearities in such prediction, we represent distribution in basis of orthonormal polynomials, having similar interpretation as corresponding cumulant.

A. *Normalization with empirical distribution function (EDF)*

Having $y^1, \ldots, y^n$ size n sample, we can normalize it with EDF by sorting the values—finding their order (bijection) $o : \{1 \ldots n\} \to \{1 \ldots n\}$ such that: $y^{o(1)} \leq y^{o(2)} \leq \ldots \leq y^{o(n)}$.

Hence, y^i is in $o^{-1}(i)$-th position of this order—wanting them to have nearly uniform distribution on [0, 1], a natural choice is $x^i = \frac{1}{n}\left(o^{-1}(i) - 1/2\right)$.

However, especially for discrete variables, many of them can have identical values, what needs a special treatment—there is no base to choose an order among equal values, all of them should be transformed into the same value x_i, naturally chosen as the centre of such range. We can see one such vertical line for casheq = 0 in Fig. 6.1 and age sample consisting only of vertical lines due to rounding to complete years.

Finally, the used generalized formula (working for both continuous and discrete variables) is:

$$x^i = \frac{\min\{k : y^{o(k)} = y^i\} + \max\{k : y^{o(k)} = y^i\} - 1}{2n}$$

We use this formula to normalize each variable of $\mathbf{y}^i = \left(y_i^0, \ldots, y_i^d\right)$: separately for each variable (lower index), getting $\mathbf{x}^i = \left(x_i^0, \ldots, x_i^d\right)$ for continuous variables having nearly uniform marginal distributions on [0, 1], with positions corresponding to quantiles of the original variable.

B. *Orthogonal polynomial basis and HCR*

Assuming (normalized) variable is from nearly uniform distributions on [0, 1], it is very convenient to represent its density with polynomial: $\rho(x) = \sum_j a_j f_j(x)$. Using orthonormal basis: $\int_0^1 f_i(x) f_j(x) dx = \delta_{ij}$, mean-square optimization leads to inexpensive estimation by just averaging: $a_j = \frac{1}{n}\sum_{i=1}^n f_j\left(x^i\right)$.

The first four of these polynomials (rescaled Legendre) are $f_0 = 1$ and f_1, f_2, f_3 correspondingly: $\sqrt{3}(2x - 1)$, $\sqrt{5}\left(6x^2 - 6x + 1\right)$, $\sqrt{7}\left(20x^3 - 30x^2 + 12x - 1\right)$, their plots are presented in Fig. 6.6.

As $\int_0^1 f_j(x) dx = 0$ for $j > 0$, density normalization needs $a_0 = 1$. The a_1 term shifts the expected value towards left or right. Positive a_2 increases the probability of extreme values—has analogous behaviour as variance. And so on: a_j coefficient has similar interpretation as j-th cumulant. Using degree m polynomial: $j = 0 \ldots m$ corresponds to modelling distribution using the first m moments, additionally directly getting density estimation from them.

We can also exploit statistical dependencies between two or more variables this way—by analogously modelling joint distribution on $[0, 1]^{d+1}$ using product basis: $\rho(\boldsymbol{x}) = \sum_{j=j_0 \ldots j_d} a_j f_{j_0}(x_0) \cdot \cdots \cdot f_{j_d}(x_d)$. This way a_j represents mixed cumulants—their dependencies between multiple variables. For a large number of variables, most of coordinates of used j should be 0—coefficients with single nonzero coordinate describe probability distribution of corresponding variable, with two nonzero describe pairwise dependencies and so on—getting hierarchical correlation reconstruction (HCR) of a given distribution.

We could directly use such modelled joint density $\rho(x_0 \ldots x_d)$ for credibility evaluation $(\Pr(x_0|x_1, \ldots, x_d))$ by just substituting $x_1 \ldots x_d$ and normalizing obtained polynomial of x_0 to integrate to 1. This way $f_{j_0}(x_0)$ is expressed as nearly a linear combination of various products of $f_j(x_k)$. However, this approach hardly handles discrete values—hence, there is finally used linear regression to directly optimize coefficients of such linear combination.

6.6 Prediction of the Income Distribution: Used Algorithm

The currently used algorithm optimizes coefficients with the least-squares regression (more details and evaluations can be found in Duda and Szulc 2018):

(1) All variables treated as continuous—including casheq having a large percentage of exactly 0 value and age obtaining 87 distinct discrete values—are normalized to nearly uniform marginal distribution using formula described in the previous section.

(2) All the remaining variables are treated as categorical and transformed into binary—thanks of it, weights of individual categories are optimized in further regression. For example, edu(cation) obtains 11 different values; hence, it is transformed into 11 binary variables: each being 1 if category agrees, 0 otherwise.

(3) Denote $v(y_1 \ldots y_d)$ as vector built of all features of endogenous variables (normalized or not) directly used for prediction as a linear combination—here, it has 223 coordinates visualized in Fig. 6. Its zeroth coordinate is fixed as 1 to get constant term (β_0) in further regressions. Then, for variables treated as continuous, it contains $f_j(x_k)$ for $j = 1$ up to a chosen degree, which is 9 here for all 4 variables treated this way (casheq, luxury, food, age)—getting $4 \times 9 = 36$ coordinates of v. It further contains all the remaining variables—categorical transformed into binary and the original binary variables—both using only 0 or 1 values.

(4) Build, e.g. $n \times 223$, matrix M with rows being applied $v\left(y_1^i \ldots y_d^i\right)$ function to all $i = 1 \ldots n$ data points.

(5) The least-square linear regression is used to infer $f_j(x_0)$ for $j = 1 \ldots m$ from $v(y_1 \ldots y_d)$ to predict density as degree m polynomial. For this purpose, build vectors $b^j = \left(f_j\left(x_0^i\right)\right)_{i=1 \ldots n}$ are built; then coefficient vectors β^j minimizing

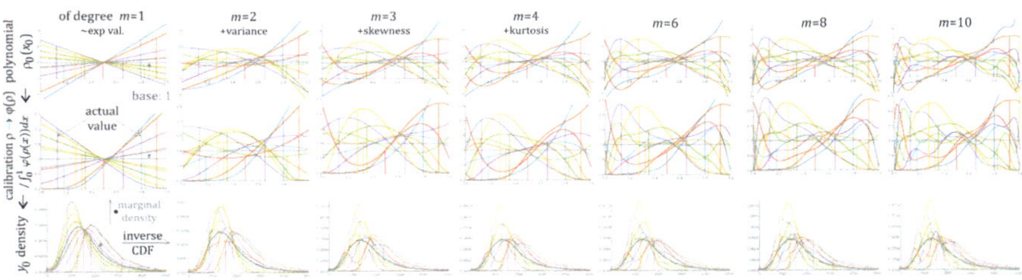

Fig. 6.5 Predictions of density for inceq based on the well-being correlates for 10 randomly chosen points (indicated by colours, the same in all plots). Column corresponds to used degree m polynomial predicting density—they are presented in the top row, together with the actual values as vertical lines of the same colour. Middle row: calibration to actual non-negative densities from such predictions, using function $\varphi(\rho) = \ln(1 + \exp(5\rho)/2)/5$ here, which was obtained by approximating division of density of actual values by density of all predicted values. Beside applying $\rho \to \phi(\rho)$, we need to divide by $\int_0^1 \varphi(\rho(x))$ to ensure integrating to 1. Bottom row: translating to predicted density of original variable ($x \to y$, removing normalization with EDF)—position on horizontal axis is obtained by using CDF^{-1}, on vertical by multiplying calibrated density by marginal density for a given point—presented as thick grey line, obtained from $\rho = 1$ base density while using no prediction

$\left\|M\beta^j - b^j\right\|^2$ are found. It can be realized with pseudoinverse and is implemented in many numerical libraries, e.g. as "LeastSquares[M, b]" in Wolfram Mathematica. Values of these final used coefficients are visualized in Fig. 6.6.

(6) Now predicted density is

$$\rho_0(x_0) = 1 + \sum_{j=1}^{m} a_j f_j(x_0) \quad \text{for} \quad a_j = v(y_1 \ldots y_d) \cdot \beta^j$$

(7) To prevent it from negative values, a type of calibration like presented in Fig. 6.5 is applied. For simplicity there can be used e.g. $\rho(x_0) = c \cdot \max(\rho_0(x_0), \varepsilon)$ for some chosen $\varepsilon \approx 0.1$ and $c = 1/\int_0^1 \max(\rho_0(x_0), \varepsilon)dx_0$ normalization to integrate to 1 (Fig. 6.6).

(8) To calculate predicted moments of the original variable (equivalent income), we assign $\rho\left(\frac{i-0.5}{n}\right)$ to i-th value of the order: $y_0^{o(i)}$. For example, predicted expected value is $\sum_{i=1}^{n} y_0^{o(i)} \rho\left(\frac{i-0.5}{n}\right)$.

6.7 Impact of The Social Transfers on Poverty

In this section, two values of poverty indices are compared: those calculated using the actual data and hypothetical ones, calculated after diminishing the incomes by sums of the benefits. The higher the difference, the stronger the effect of the transfers. This routine may be easily performed for income poverty. When a multidimensional

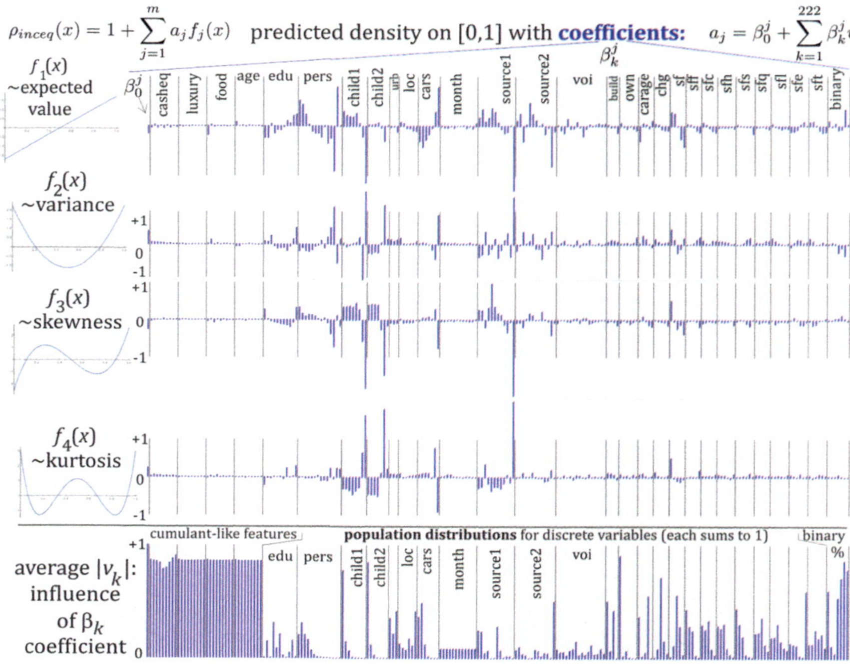

Fig. 6.6 Top: final 4 × 223 coefficients obtained by least-square regression (minimizing $\sum_i \|f_j(x_0^i) - a_j^2\|$) for predicting probability density of exogenous variable (equivalent income) based on features of endogenous variables—independently for coefficients corresponding to the expected value (f_1), variance (f_2), skewness (f_3) and kurtosis (f_4) of predicted normalized variable x_0. For endogenous variables treated as continuous (casheq, luxury, food, age), the used features are $f_j(x_l)$ for $j = 1 \ldots 9$ and $l = 1, 2, 3, 4$ describing j-th cumulant-like behaviour of l-th variable. The remaining variables are binary or discrete treated as binary: 0 or 1 for each appearing possibility. For example, in the first row, negative first coefficient for food connects their expected values—describes negative correlation, analogously for age, it is positive—they are correlated. Coefficients for voivodships (voi) describe individual corrections for each geographical region. Low statistics for some coefficients can lead to surprising behaviour, e.g. we can see reduction of equivalent income with the number of persons in the household (pers), with a surprising spike at the end—it corresponds to a single data point of 12 person household. Bottom: average $|v_k|$ describing average influence of β_k coefficient—it is fixed 1 for v_0, large nearly constant for cumulant-like coefficients of continuous variables (increasing their importance), for each binarized discrete variable, its contributions sum to 1: they describe proportions of such categories in the population, for binary variables, each is in [0, 1]

poverty is of interest, it is necessary to make first a prediction of changes in multidimensional well-being due to changes in income. For that purpose, a quadratic regression model was estimated. The poverty lines are set at: first decile (extreme poverty) and first quartile. The result of comparisons between the poverty indices is displayed in Table 6.2. All calculations were made twice: using actual incomes and imputed ones.

Table 6.2 Poverty indices before and after transfers

Poverty line and type of index	Poverty indices, in %					
	Actual incomes			Imputed incomes		
	Before	After	Difference	Before	After	Difference
Incidence						
Income poverty						
I decile	15.3	10.0	**5.3**	15.8	10.0	**5.8**
I quartile	29.0	25.0	**4.0**	28.7	25.0	**3.7**
Depth						
I decile	42.0	26.1	**15.9**	30.3	12.7	**17.6**
I quartile	38.0	27.8	**10.2**	28.0	17.2	**10.8**
Multidimensional poverty						
I decile	16.6	10.0	**6.6**	18.0	10.0	**8.0**
I quartile	33.7	25.0	**8.7**	33.2	25.0	**8.2**
Depth						
I decile	11.1	12.8	**−1.3**	18.6	12.6	**6.0**
I quartile	14.8	13.5	**1.3**	19.2	13.7	**5.5**

The strongest impact of the benefits may be observed for income poverty depth: it ranges from 10.2 to 17.6. It is much lower for income poverty incidence and ranges from 3.7 to 5.8. Generally, there are no substantial differences between monetary poverty indexes obtained with the use of actual and imputed incomes. Opposite relations between both types of poverty indices appear in the case of multidimensional poverty. Impact of the benefits on poverty incidence is higher than on poverty depth. Moreover, estimates of the effect are in most of the cases much higher for imputed incomes. This is especially true for the poverty depth. When the poverty line is set at the first decile, the effect obtained for actual incomes is negative! These unrealistic results do not surprise, considering the shapes of the multidimensional well-being curve on incomes (see Fig. 6.3). Moreover, the effect obtained for poverty gap when poverty line is set at the first quartile is surprisingly low. This result also may be attributed to the income data errors mentioned earlier. When imputed incomes are applied, the impact estimates are much more reliable. This confirms the importance of income imputation applied in the present study.

6.8 Testing the Behavioural Impact of the Benefits

Receiving "money for nothing" is likely to change the recipients' behaviour. Many pro-market economists (e.g. Murray 1984) argue for discouraging effect of such transfers and, consequently, their counter-productivity. To check this hypothesis empirically, average well-being of the recipients and non-recipients should be compared. Naturally, a simple difference between means would not yield a correct solution—due to self-selected sample of the recipients (they represent, by definition, least privileged group), the resulting estimator would be seriously downward biased. Matching estimation is one of the solutions to this problem: recipients are compared with non-recipients who are assumed to be identical in terms of various attributes correlated with well-being. If they are able to predict well-being perfectly, the identity postulate is satisfied: the only difference between units under comparison would be receiving or not receiving benefits. More formally, an unbiased estimator of the average effect of the "treatment" (here: receiving any social benefit) on household well-being Y is estimated as a difference between two expected values:

$$\hat{\tau} = E[Y(1)|D = 1] - E[Y(0)|D = 1]$$

where $D = 1$ means receiving a "treatment" and $Y(1/0)$ stands for a measure of well-being for "treated" (1) and control group (0). While the first term is observable, the second one has to be estimated by matching recipients with non-recipients on a set of correlates of well-being. $E[Y(0)|D = 1]$ may be interpreted as hypothetical well-being of recipients losing their benefits ("what would happened if …").

In Table 6.3, the estimates of the effect of receiving benefits, for equivalent income and for multidimensional well-being, are displayed. They are supplemented by simple differences between means of the recipients and non-recipients. As might be expected, the previous achieve much lower levels, both in terms of income (by 27%) and of multidimensional well-being (by 13%). The surprising result is a negative effect of the benefits obtained by matching estimation. This may be interpreted in two opposite ways. First, as a confirmation for a strong discouraging effect of the benefits in Poland. Second, as a serious downward bias of the estimates. The latter might be caused by omitted variables having an effect on well-being, for instance, of

Table 6.3 Comparisons between recipients and non-recipients by matching estimation: equivalent income and multidimensional indicator

Mean value estimate	Recipients	Non-recipients	Difference
Equivalent income			
Actual	1374	1884	**−510**
Adjusted			
1 match	1374	1615	**−241**
4 matches	1374	1572	**−198**
Multidimensional indicator			
Actual	0.542	0.620	**−0.078**
Adjusted			
1 match	0.542	0.549	**−0.007**
4 matches	0.542	0.549	**−0.007**

All estimates are significant below 0.01

psychological type (then unobservable). It is reasonable to assume that hard-working and/or talented persons are, on average, less likely to apply for social benefits. Hence, the persons that are assumed to be "identical" are in fact different, and those with lower such abilities are overrepresented among the recipients. To check this hypothesis, one more matching estimation was performed on the sub-sample of recipients. They were split into those below and above median value of the transfer. It seems to be reasonable to assume that unobservable abilities are much more equally distributed between both groups than in the first estimation. Hence, the problem of omitted variables becomes less important. The results[4] are consistent with the previous findings: the higher benefits received, the lower well-being. Therefore, a strong discouraging effect of the benefits is likely to be true. To be more precise, it is likely that some recipients quit their low paid and/or burdensome jobs after receiving the benefits. However, this hypothesis hardly can be examined without panel data providing pre- and post-transfer information. As a second best, predictions of salaries might be used for that purpose.

One more hypothetical explanation of a negative effect of the benefits might be added: as the benefits are means tested, the lower well-being of the recipients is an effect of self-selection, and the matching estimation was not sufficient to overcome it. Informally speaking, the set of variables on which recipients and non-recipients are matched has not enough "explanatory power" for well-being. However, a comparison of the effects for income and multidimensional well-being is not favourable for this hypothesis. Concentration curves (see Fig. 6.2) demonstrate that the benefits distribution is more advantageous for the poorest in terms of multidimensional well-being. Provided the above-mentioned hypothesis, this would suggest stronger effect for this type of measure rather than for income. This is not true, however, the effect for incomes stands for about 40% of the net difference, while for multidimensional well-being for 9% only.

6.9 Concluding Remarks

The general conclusions on the social benefits distribution in Poland definitely suggest their pro-poor shape, irrespectively to the well-being definition applied. This is confirmed both by concentration curves and by comparisons of post- and pre-transfer poverty indices. However, estimates of size of the effect are problematic due to income data errors (this is especially evident when multidimensional poverty depth is considered). To overcome this problem, a novel method of data imputation referred to as the hierarchical correlation reconstruction is employed. It is based on estimation of conditional income distribution on exogenous variables correlated to the household welfare. In the present study, only predictions of expected values were utilized to obtain alternative incomes; however, the method can yield also estimates of higher moments of distribution. Using imputed incomes instead of declared ones

[4]Available upon request.

yields much more reliable estimates of the benefits effects. It should be noted, however, that the obtained results do not take into consideration behavioural responses of the recipients. Matching estimation of the net differences between recipients and non-recipients suggests strong discouraging effect of the transfers.

Further, the study should focus on two issues. First, sensitivity of the results to the applied methods is worth to be checked. For instance, Szulc (2012) demonstrated that impact of the social assistance on poverty depends strongly on the poverty threshold. Also, the definition of multidimensional well-being is likely to have an effect on the final results. The second issue to be explored could take advantage of possibilities offered by the hierarchical correlation reconstruction, more precisely of estimates of higher moments of the income distribution. For instance, a variance may be employed for evaluation of credibility of declared incomes. In the present study, they were just replaced by estimates of expected values; however, it is possible to calculate the means of both types of incomes. Those with lower variance, i.e. with higher credibility, would receive higher weight.

References

Atkinson, T., Cantillon, B., Marlier, E., & Nolan, B. (2002). *Social indicators: The EU and social inclusion*. Oxford: Oxford University Press.

Brown, C., Ravallion, M., & van de Walle, D. (2018). A poor means test? Econometric targeting in Africa. *Journal of Development Economics, 134,* 109–124.

Cleveland, W. S. (1979). Robust locally weighted regression and smoothing scatterplots. *Journal of the American Statistical Association, 74,* 829–836.

Duda, J., & Szulc, A. (2018). Credibility evaluation of income data with hierarchical correlation reconstruction, arXiv: 1812.08040. https://arxiv.org/pdf/1812.08040.pdf.

European University Institute. (2019). European Community Household Panel https://www.eui.eu/Research/Library/ResearchGuides/Economics/Statistics/DataPortal/ECHP.

Household Budget Survey. (2014). *Statistics Poland*. Warsaw.

Heinrich, C., Maffioli, A., & Vázquez, G. (2010). *A primer for applying propensity-score matching. Impact-Evaluation Guidelines*. Washington, D.C., USA: Inter-American Development Bank.

Murray, C. (1984). *Losing ground: American social policy, 1950–1980*. New York: Basic Books.

Panek, T. (2006). Multidimensional fuzzy relative poverty dynamic measures in Poland. In A. Lemmi & G. Betti (Eds.), *Fuzzy set approach to multidimensional poverty measurement*. Springer.

Smith, J. A., & Todd, P. E. (2005). Does matching overcome LaLonde's critique of nonexperimental estimators? *Journal of Econometrics, 125,* 305–353.

Szulc, A. (2012). Social policy and poverty. Checking the efficiency of the social assistance system in poland. *Eastern European Economics, 50,* 66–92.

Chapter 7
R&D Cooperation Facilitates Cartel Formation

Jacek Prokop and Adam Karbowski

Abstract The objective of this research is to investigate the impact of R&D cooperation between firms on industry cartel formation. We consider process R&D investments aimed at reduction of the unit costs of manufacturing. These investments create positive externalities for the competitors. We assume that the competition between rival firms in the industry takes place according to the Stackelberg (quantity) leadership model. For simplicity, we focus on the duopoly symmetric case. Numerical analysis shows that closer cooperation between rivals at the R&D stage strengthens the incentives to create a cartel in the final product market, thus serious public policy concerns occur.

7.1 Introduction

The costs of research and development (R&D) in many industries have long exceeded the financial capabilities of individual firms (Galbraith 1952). Even the largest enterprises may not be able to develop and implement new technologies on their own (see, e.g., Kaiser 2002). This is the reason why enterprises undertake various forms of cooperation in research and innovation. Apart from the benefits arising from overcoming the cost barrier of conducting R&D, cooperation in R&D also helps avoid

---

The previous version of this paper is available online as the discussion paper: Prokop and Karbowski (2013) R&D Cooperation and Industry Cartelization. The Economics Discussion Paper Series, 2013–41, The Kiel Institute for the World Economy.

J. Prokop · A. Karbowski (✉)
Department of Business Economics, Warsaw School of Economics, Al. Niepodległości 162, 02-554 Warsaw, Poland
e-mail: adam.karbowski@sgh.waw.pl

J. Prokop
e-mail: jacek.prokop@sgh.waw.pl

N. Tsounis and A. Vlachvei (eds.), *Advances in Cross-Section Data Methods in Applied Economic Research*, Springer Proceedings in Business and Economics,
https://doi.org/10.1007/978-3-030-38253-7_7

unnecessary duplication of performed activities (d'Aspremont and Jacquemin 1988; Kamien et al. 1992). Acknowledging overall economic benefits of R&D cooperation, the European Commission has supported cooperation between firms in R&D (see, e.g., Geroski 1993; van Wegberg 1995; Cassiman 2000; Georghiou 2001; Barajas et al. 2012; Karbowski and Prokop 2018). Still, the question is whether the facilitation of cooperation between rival firms in R&D does not lead to reduction of competition in the industry, and, in particular, to the formation of a cartel in the product market. The latter would have negative effects on the consumer and total surplus in the industry.

The purpose of this research is to examine how R&D cooperation between rival firms influences the incentives to form a cartel in the product market. We consider a situation when the R&D investments, that precede the production process, reduce the unit costs of manufacturing, but at the same time generate positive externalities for competitors. We compare how various degrees of cooperation in R&D affects the incentives to form a cartel in the product market.

Similarly to the preceding literature on the topic, the analysis is based on a two-stage game with two firms as players.[1] In the first stage, the firms simultaneously decide on their R&D investments, and in the second stage, the firms meet in the product market (Prokop and Karbowski 2013).

Unlike the standard literature (cf., d'Aspremont and Jacquemin 1988; De Bondt and Veugelers 1991; Kamien et al. 1992), it has been assumed that under no cartel agreement, firms compete according to the Stackelberg leadership model. It is worth mentioning that unlike common beliefs and some stylized facts (cf., e.g., Bertilorenzi 2016) cartels are not necessarily formed among firms with fairly similar characteristics. The historically detected collisions show that the cartel members could substantially differ (cf., Karbowski and Prokop 2018). Clearly, that could be potentially an indication of asymmetric behavior.

For simplicity, in this paper, we focus on a duopoly case. Numerical analysis shows that closer cooperation at the R&D stage increases incentives for rival firms to form a cartel in the product market, thus serious antitrust policy concerns occur.

The paper is organized as follows. In the next section, the case of a noncooperative duopoly is analyzed, i.e., there is no cartel neither at the R&D stage nor in the final product market. In Sect. 7.3, we consider the conduct and performance of firms that formed a cartel in the product market and coordinated their R&D investments, i.e., they have fully cartelized the industry. Based on the comparison of the above two cases, the conclusions regarding the incentives for the firms to create a cartel are given in Sect. 7.4. Brief summary and concluding remarks close the paper.

---

[1]The models in the form of such games were introduced by d'Aspremont and Jacquemin (1988) and De Bondt and Veugelers (1991). They have been further developed by Kamien et al. (1992), Prokop and Karbowski (2018), Karbowski and Prokop (2018). See also our working paper, as a rough version of the present publication, i.e., Prokop and Karbowski (2013).

7.2 Stackelberg Competition

Consider an industry comprised of two firms, denoted 1 and 2. Firms manufacture q_1 and q_2 units of a homogeneous product, respectively. The inverse market demand for the product is given as a linear function:

$$p = a - bQ, \tag{7.1}$$

where p denotes the market price, $Q = q_1 + q_2$ is the volume of total production of the industry, while a and $b(a, b > 0)$ are given parameters.

Each of the firms is characterized by a linear function of the total manufacturing costs:

$$C_i(q_i, x_i, x_j) = (c - x_i - \beta x_j)q_i, \tag{7.2}$$

where $c(c < a)$ is a given parameter of an initial efficiency of firm i, x_i denotes the amount of R&D investments made by the firm i, and x_j denotes the amount of R&D investments made by the competitor. Parameter β $(0 \leq \beta \leq 1)$ determines the size of externalities, i.e., the benefits for a given firm obtained as a result of research undertaken by the competitor (see, e.g., Kamien and Zang 2000). Higher level of β means that the R&D investments made by one firm allow the competitor to reduce the manufacturing costs by a greater amount for free.

The costs of the R&D investments have a form of quadratic function:

$$\gamma \frac{x_i^2}{2}, \tag{7.3}$$

where $\gamma(\gamma > 0)$ is a given parameter.

The entry barriers to the industry are viewed as too high for new enterprises to enter.

We further assume that in this industry one firm, say firm 1, plays the role of the Stackelberg leader, and the other one, say firm 2, is the follower. Thus, firm 1 is the first to set the level of its supply (q_1), and firm 2, given the production level set by the leader, decides upon its own output level (q_2).

The game proceeds in two stages. At the first stage, both firms simultaneously and independently decide on their levels of R&D investments (x_i). These decisions affect the function of total manufacturing costs of each firm. At the second stage, the firms compete in the product market according to the Stackelberg leadership model.

Consider the profit of the follower firm at the second stage of the game for a given amount of R&D investments, x_1 and x_2:

$$\pi_2 = (a - bQ)q_2 - (c - x_2 - \beta x_1)q_2 - \gamma \frac{x_2^2}{2}. \tag{7.4}$$

For a given output level of the leader (q_1), the follower maximizes its own profit by setting the production level at:

$$q_2 = \frac{a - c + x_2 + \beta x_1}{2b} - \frac{1}{2}q_1. \tag{7.5}$$

Taking into account the follower's reaction given by (7.5), the leader maximizes its own profit, with a given size of research x_1 and x_2:

$$\pi_1 = (a - bQ)q_1 - (c - x_1 - \beta x_2)q_1 - \gamma\frac{x_1^2}{2}. \tag{7.6}$$

The optimal production volume of the leader is given by:

$$q_1 = \frac{a - c + (2 - \beta)x_1 + (2\beta - 1)x_2}{2b}. \tag{7.7}$$

Substituting (7.7) into (7.5), we obtain the optimal output level of the follower:

$$q_2 = \frac{a - c + (3\beta - 2)x_1 + (3 - 2\beta)x_2}{4b}. \tag{7.8}$$

The production levels q_1 and q_2 given by (7.7) and (7.8) constitute the Nash–Stackelberg equilibrium. After substituting (7.7) and (7.8) into the inverse demand function given by (7.1), we obtain the equilibrium market price of the final product:

$$p = \frac{a + 3c - (2 + \beta)x_1 - (2\beta + 1)x_2}{4}. \tag{7.9}$$

At the first stage of the game, when enterprises simultaneously choose the amount of R&D investments, x_1 and x_2, the profits of firms may be written as:

$$\pi_1 = \frac{1}{8b}[a - c + (2 - \beta)x_1 + (2\beta - 1)x_2]^2 - \gamma\frac{x_1^2}{2}, \tag{7.10}$$

$$\pi_2 = \frac{1}{16b}[a - c + (3\beta - 2)x_1 + (3 - 2\beta)x_2]^2 - \gamma\frac{x_2^2}{2}. \tag{7.11}$$

The Nash equilibrium strategies at the first stage of the game are found as a solution to the following system of two equations with two unknowns x_1 and x_2:

$$\frac{\partial\pi_1}{\partial x_1} = 0, \tag{7.12}$$

$$\frac{\partial\pi_2}{\partial x_2} = 0, \tag{7.13}$$

which takes the form of:

$$[a - c + (2 - \beta)x_1 + (2\beta - 1)x_2] - 4b\gamma x_1 = 0, \tag{7.14}$$

$$[a - c + (3\beta - 2)x_1 + (3 - 2\beta)x_2] - 8b\gamma x_2 = 0. \tag{7.15}$$

Under certain restrictions on the value of parameters a, b, c, γ and β, the above system has exactly one solution in the following form:

$$x_1 = \frac{(a - c)(2 - \beta)\big[2b\gamma - (1 - \beta)(3 - 2\beta)\big]}{[8b\gamma - (3 - 2\beta)^2 - 2(2 - \beta)^2\big]b\gamma + (3 - 2\beta)(2 - \beta)\big(1 - \beta^2\big)}, \tag{7.16}$$

$$x_2 = \frac{(a - c)(3 - 2\beta)\big[b\gamma - (1 - \beta)(2 - \beta)\big]}{[8b\gamma - (3 - 2\beta)^2 - 2(2 - \beta)^2\big]b\gamma + (3 - 2\beta)(2 - \beta)\big(1 - \beta^2\big)}. \tag{7.17}$$

Substituting (7.16) and (7.17) into (7.10) and (7.11), we obtain the equilibrium profits of the leader and the follower:

$$\pi_1 = \frac{(a - c)^2\gamma\big[2b\gamma - (1 - \beta)(3 - 2\beta)]^2\big[4b\gamma - (2 - \beta)^2]}{2[8b\gamma - (3 - 2\beta)^2 - 2(2 - \beta)^2\big]b\gamma + (3 - 2\beta)(2 - \beta)\big(1 - \beta^2\big)}. \tag{7.18}$$

$$\pi_2 = \frac{(a - c)^2\gamma\big[b\gamma - (1 - \beta)(2 - \beta)]^2\big[8b\gamma - (3 - 2\beta)^2]}{2[8b\gamma - (3 - 2\beta)^2 - 2(2 - \beta)^2\big]b\gamma + (3 - 2\beta)(2 - \beta)\big(1 - \beta^2\big)}. \tag{7.19}$$

Due to a relatively vague algebraic form of the above solutions, we turn to numerical analysis. We consider the case when four parameters of the model take the following values: $a = 100$, $b = 1$, $c = 10$, and $\gamma = 10$. The results of the calculations for various levels of parameter β are given in Table 7.1.

Using Table 7.1, let us consider the impact of parameter β, i.e. the extent of externalities in R&D, on the equilibrium behavior of firms. When the external benefits for a given firm resulting from the research undertaken by the rival are relatively small (parameter β is low), the R&D investments of each firm are relatively high and they decline with the growing scale of spillovers. It is not a surprise that the follower invests in R&D a smaller amount than the leader, because the latter derives relatively greater product market benefits. It is worth noticing that with the increase of β, the relative R&D effort of the leader in comparison to the follower increases; for $\beta = 0$, the ratio is approx. 4:3, and for $\beta = 1$ it becomes as much as 2:1.

When firms undertake R&D activities in a form of joint venture, the parameter β assumes the value of 1, which means the full internalization of spillovers (following Kamien and colleagues (1992), $\beta = 1$ means that RJV has been set up). Since, in this version of the game, the cooperation at the R&D stage does not lead to cooperation

Table 7.1 Stackelberg equilibrium for $a = 100, b = 1, c = 10, \gamma = 10$ and $\beta \in [0, 1]$

β	x_1	x_2	q_1	q_2	p	π_1	π_2
0.0	4.81132	3.39623	48.1132	22.6415	29.2453	1041.70	454.97
0.1	4.56580	3.19106	48.0611	22.7933	29.1456	1050.70	468.62
0.2	4.31940	2.98030	47.9934	22.9254	29.0812	1058.40	481.16
0.3	4.07222	2.76467	47.9085	23.0389	29.0526	1064.70	492.58
0.4	3.82440	2.54483	47.8050	23.1348	29.0602	1069.53	502.84
0.5	3.57616	2.32137	47.6821	23.2137	29.1042	1072.85	511.93
0.6	3.32772	2.09487	47.5389	23.2763	29.1848	1074.60	519.84
0.7	3.07936	1.86587	47.3748	23.3233	29.3019	1074.77	526.57
0.8	2.83136	1.63487	47.1893	23.3553	29.4554	1073.33	532.11
0.9	2.58402	1.40237	46.9822	23.3729	29.6449	1070.28	536.46
1.0	2.33766	1.16883	46.7532	23.3766	29.8701	1065.61	539.64

Source own calculations

in the product market, the decisions about the amount of R&D investments are made independently to maximize individual profits of each of the firms. At the same time, it should be noticed from Table 7.1 that R&D joint ventures lead to an overall decline in the efforts to reduce the costs of manufacturing.

Observe that leader's production level, q_1, decreases with the higher extent of spillovers, and it achieves its lowest value when firms form a joint venture. A reversed relationship takes place in the case of the follower: its production volume, q_2, increases with the higher amount of spillovers and achieves the largest value when the firms form a joint venture. The total market supply, $(q_1 + q_2)$, initially increases (for low values of the parameter β), and afterwards (for larger β) declines, and achieves its lowest value when the firms form a joint venture. This, in turn, influences the level of the market price, which becomes the highest when firms undertake R&D activities within a joint venture; thus the consumers will not be pleased with such behavior of producers.

The profits of individual firms, as it could have been expected, do not change in the same way for the leader and for the follower. On the one hand, the leader's profits initially go up with an increase in the parameter β, but when this parameter exceeds 0.7, the economic performance of the leader starts deteriorating. On the other hand, the follower's profits keep rising continuously, together with an increase of β, and they achieve their maximum when the firms form a joint venture. Thus, in the case of the Stackelberg competition, a joint venture is beneficial for the follower but less beneficial for the leader, who would rather limit the scale of spillovers.

Now, we move on to analyze the case of firms' cooperation within a cartel.

7.3 Full Cartelization of Industry

For the sake of comparison, we now consider a model proposed by d'Aspremont and Jacquemin (1988), in which the firms have formed a cartel both at the stage of R&D, and at the product market. We assume that the demand function as well as the cost functions of the firms are the same as in the previous section.

At the second stage of the game, the firms choose the production levels q_1 and q_2 to maximize their joint profit, given the amount of R&D investments, x_1 and x_2:

$$\pi = (a - bQ)Q - (c - x_1 - \beta x_2)q_1 - (c - x_2 - \beta x_1)q_2 - \gamma\frac{x_1^2}{2} - \gamma\frac{x_2^2}{2}. \quad (7.20)$$

At the symmetric equilibrium, i.e., $x_1 = x_2 = x$, the optimal production level of each firm in the cartel is:

$$q = q_1 = q_2 = \frac{a - c + (1 + \beta)x}{4b}. \quad (7.21)$$

Thus, after substituting (7.21) into the inverse demand function given by (7.1), we obtain the equilibrium price in the final product market as:

$$p = \frac{a + c - (1 + \beta)x}{2}. \quad (7.22)$$

At the first stage of the game, when firms simultaneously choose x_1 and x_2, their joint profit becomes:

$$\tilde{\pi} = \frac{1}{4b}[a - c + (1 + \beta)x]^2 - \gamma x^2. \quad (7.23)$$

When the firms cooperate within a cartel, both in the R&D activities and in the final product market, the symmetric equilibrium arises when the research investments of each of the firms are:

$$\tilde{x} = \frac{(a - c)(1 + \beta)}{4b\gamma - (1 + \beta)^2}. \quad (7.24)$$

and the production level of each of the firms, after substituting (7.24) into (7.21), is:

$$\tilde{q} = \tilde{q}_1 = \tilde{q}_2 = \frac{(a - c)\gamma}{4b\gamma - (1 + \beta)^2}. \quad (7.25)$$

From (7.23) it follows that the profit of each of the firms in the situation of full cartelization of industry becomes:

Table 7.2 Full cartelization equilibrium for $a = 100$, $b = 1$, $c = 10$, $\gamma = 10$, and $\beta \in [0, 1]$

β	$\tilde{x}$	$\tilde{q}_i$	p	$\tilde{\pi}_i$
0.0	2.30769	23.0769	53.8462	1038.46
0.1	2.55220	23.2019	53.5963	1044.08
0.2	2.80083	23.3402	53.3195	1050.31
0.3	3.05403	23.4926	53.0149	1057.17
0.4	3.31230	23.6593	52.6814	1064.67
0.5	3.57616	23.8411	52.3179	1072.85
0.6	3.84615	24.0385	51.9231	1081.73
0.7	4.12288	24.2522	51.4956	1091.35
0.8	4.40696	24.4831	51.0337	1101.74
0.9	4.69909	24.7321	50.5359	1112.94
1.0	5.00000	25.0000	50.0000	1125.00

Source own calculations

$$\tilde{\pi}_1 = \tilde{\pi}_2 = \frac{1}{2}\frac{(a-c)^2\gamma}{4b\gamma - (1+\beta)^2}. \tag{7.26}$$

For the sake of a comparison with the results obtained in the previous section, we continue our numerical analysis for the same parameter values, i.e., $a = 100$, $b = 1$, $c = 10$, and $\gamma = 10$. The results of the calculations for various levels of parameter β are presented in Table 7.2.

Using Table 7.2, let us consider the equilibrium behavior of firms, for various levels of the parameter β, i.e. the size of spillovers. In the case of full cartelization of the industry, together with the increase in the scale of R&D externalities, there is also an increase in research investments of individual firms aimed at the cost reduction of final product manufacturing. At the same time, we observe an increase in the supply of final products offered by each of the firms. That results in price reductions of the manufactured products when the amount of spillovers increases. Finally, the profits of each firm operating within a fully cartelized industry increase monotonically together with the growing extent of R&D externalities.

In a fully cartelized industry, the firms achieve the highest profits when R&D activities are performed within a joint venture, i.e., the parameter β assumes the value of 1, which means the full internalization of R&D spillovers.

7.4 Incentives for Cartelization

Comparing the results of Tables 7.1 and 7.2, we may draw final conclusions regarding the incentives for industry cartelization. When the benefits for an individual firm from the research performed by a rival are relatively low ($\beta < 0.5$), the profits gained by the Stackelberg leader (the second to last column in Table 7.1) are higher than the firm profits in a fully cartelized industry, i.e. when firms cooperate at the R&D stage and in the final product market (the last column in Table 7.2). Thus, when the level of spillovers is relatively low, the firm that may assume the role of the Stackelberg leader will not be interested in forming a cartel in this industry.

However, when the level of R&D spillovers is considerable ($\beta > 0.5$), the comparison of profits for the Stackelberg leader with the profits gained by a firm in the cartelized industry shows that none of the firms will have any incentives to stay outside of the cartel. Moreover, the firms earn the biggest profits when they coordinate their R&D investments and production quantities within a full industry cartel, and at the same time form an R&D joint venture in order to fully internalize the spillovers. As a result, it could be expected that R&D cooperation of firms raises the risk of industry cartelization. That creates a greater regulatory challenge for the antitrust authorities.

Thus the basic result of the above considerations is the conclusion that the tightening of cooperation at the R&D stage creates sufficient incentives for firms to fully cartelize the industry. It means that the buyers of the final products in this industry could be harmed. Joint efforts of the cartel participants to reduce manufacturing costs will contribute to lower market prices for the final products (second to last column in Table 7.2), nevertheless, the goods will be still much more expensive in comparison to prices when the firms compete according to the Stackelberg model. Hence, serious challenges for economic policy emerges.

European competition policy aims to differentiate (i) cooperation agreements that potentially reduce competition and harm consumers from (ii) cooperation agreements that are believed to promote innovation and competitiveness; hence the block exemption of R&D agreements was introduced[2] (Commission Regulation (EC) No 2659/2000):

Since cooperation in R&D helps promote the exchange of know-how and technologies, to facilitate technical and economic progress, and to rationalize the manufacture and use of products that benefit consumers, this regulation exempts not only agreements the primary object of which is R&D but also all agreements directly related to and necessary for the implementation of cooperation in R&D, provided that the combined market share of the parties does not exceed 25% of the relevant market.

Obviously, the R&D block exemption regulation is based on a large body of economic literature stating that in general interfirm R&D collaboration promotes firm innovation (provided that firms act competitively in the product market, cf., e.g., d'Aspremont and Jacquemin 1988; Kamien et al. 1992; Kaiser 2002; Becker and Dietz 2004). The provision that firms behave competitively in the product market seems critical to the assessment of the European exemption policy. If R&D cooperation strengthens firms' incentives to behave cooperatively in the product market

[2]The R&D block exemption regulation was further extended in 2010. European Commission *has considerably extended the scope of the R&D block exemption regulation, which now not only covers R&D activities carried out jointly but also so-called "paid-for research" agreements where one party finances the R&D activities carried out by the other party* (EC Press Release Database, Brussels, 14 December 2010).

(as suggested in this paper), the European block exemption regulation could be, at least to some extent, counterproductive (it may work in favor of collusion in the product market, and hence reduction rather than increase of the social welfare). In fact, the last prediction is supported by empirical evidence. Sovinsky and Helland (2012) in their original econometric study suggested that research cooperation may indeed serve (at least in part) a collusive function.

7.5 Conclusions

In this paper, we compared the performance of firms under various forms of R&D cooperation and for different types of behavior in the product market. The comparison shows that together with increasing size of R&D spillovers, the firm that becomes the Stackelberg leader in the final product market may earn lower profits than if it creates a full cartel with its rival in a given industry. Since the maximum level of spillovers is achieved when firms form an R&D joint venture, the incentives to create a full industry cartel are the strongest in this case. This result supports the thesis that R&D collaboration may, at least to some extent, serve a collusive function, thus serious antitrust policy concerns occur.

We should emphasize that in the standard models of oligopoly, in which the R&D stage is not considered, a cartel formed in the product market allows each of the firms to earn profits identical to the level gained by the Stackelberg leader. It means that in those models a firm is indifferent between behaving noncooperatively by playing the role of the Stackelberg leader or behaving cooperatively by forming a cartel with its rival. Thus, the incorporation of the R&D stage into the analysis of oligopoly generates qualitatively different results.

Among the directions of future research regarding the impact of R&D cooperation on the industry cartelization, other types of cost functions, and different forms of competition among firms could be studied. In addition, the comparative analysis might be extended to the case of potential mergers among the industry participants.

Acknowledgements This research was supported by National Science Centre, Poland (grant number UMO-2017/25/B/HS4/01632).

References

Barajas, A., Huergo, E., & Moreno, L. (2012). Measuring the economic impact of research joint ventures supported by the EU framework programme. *The Journal of Technology Transfer, 37,* 917–942.

Becker, W., & Dietz, J. (2004). R&D cooperation and innovation activities of firms—evidence for the German manufacturing industry. *Research Policy, 33,* 209–223.

Bertilorenzi, M. (2016). *The international aluminium cartel, 1886–1978.* New York: The Business and Politics of a Cooperative Industrial Institution, Routledge.

Cassiman, B. (2000). Research joint ventures and optimal R&D policy with asymmetric information. *International Journal of Industrial Organization, 18,* 283–314.

d'Aspremont, C., & Jacquemin, A. (1988). Cooperative and noncooperative R&D in duopoly with spillovers. *American Economic Review, 78,* 1133–1137.

De Bondt, R., & Veugelers, R. (1991). Strategic investment with spillovers. *European Journal of Political Economy, 7,* 345–366.

Galbraith, J. (1952). *American capitalism, the concept of countervailing power*. Boston: Houghton Mifflin Company.

Georghiou, L. (2001). Evolving frameworks for European collaboration in research and technology. *Research Policy, 30,* 891–903.

Geroski, P. (1993). Antitrust policy towards co-operative R&D ventures. *Oxford Review of Economic Policy, 9,* 58–71.

Kaiser, U. (2002). An empirical test of models explaining research expenditures and research cooperation: Evidence for the German service sector. *International Journal of Industrial Organization, 20,* 747–774.

Kamien, M., & Zang, I. (2000). Meet me halfway: Research joint ventures and absorptive capacity. *International Journal of Industrial Organization, 18,* 995–1012.

Kamien, M., Muller, E., & Zang, I. (1992). Research joint ventures and R&D cartels. *American Economic Review, 82,* 1293–1306.

Karbowski, A., & Prokop, J. (2018). R&D activities of enterprises, product market leadership, and collusion. *Proceedings of Rijeka Faculty of Economics: Journal of Economics and Business, 36,* 735–753.

Prokop, J., & Karbowski, A. (2013). R&D cooperation and industry cartelization. In *The economics discussion paper series, 2013–41*. The Kiel Institute for the World Economy.

Prokop, J., & Karbowski, A. (2018). R&D spillovers and cartelization of industries with differentiated products. *Journal of International Studies, 11,* 44–56.

Sovinsky, M., & Helland, E. (2012). Do research joint ventures serve a collusion function? In *Warwick economic research papers*, no 1030.

van Wegberg, M. (1995). Can R&D alliances facilitate the formation of a cartel? In *The example of the European IT industry*. Research Memoranda 004, Maastricht Research School of Economics of Technology and Organization.

Chapter 8
Greek Households After the 10-Year-Crisis: An Exploratory Research

Electra Pitoska and Evangelisti Paraskevi

Abstract The financial crisis has significantly affected the Greek economy for a decade, and, consequently, it has had a great impact on Greek households. The impacts of the crisis, ten years later, seemed to have shaped the Greek family environment, which has been directly affected by wider changes. To investigate the impact of the 10-year financial crisis and recession on Greek households, and the changes they have taken place in family lives, a survey was carried out, on subjects living in various Greek areas. The research is conclusive—descriptive and attempts to identify real facts in the daily lives and quality of life of Greek households. The survey demonstrated that, after the ten-year crisis, household incomes are not satisfactory for family members. Thus, a number of households, in view of price increase and purchasing power decline, have been forced to cut back on entertainment and travel spending. A great number of Greek people, particularly young, on account of financial problems and high unemployment rates, combined with the shrinking number of new job opportunities, have been forced to emigrate. In terms of the impact of crisis on psychological state, it is very disappointing that most people have been seriously affected, and, thus, are pessimist about prospects of future improvements. Remarkably, the research demonstrated a close relationship and correlation (dependent variables) between wage/pension cuts and spending cuts in various aspects of everyday life, and also highlighted people's inability to meet their obligations or basic needs.

Keywords Financial crisis · Greek households · Household incomes · Recessions

JEL Code H31

E. Pitoska (✉) · E. Paraskevi
School of Management & Economics, Department of Accounting & Finance, Western Macedonia University of Applied Sciences, Kozani, Greece
e-mail: ilpitoska@yahoo.gr

E. Paraskevi
e-mail: vivievagelis@hotmail.com

N. Tsounis and A. Vlachvei (eds.), *Advances in Cross-Section Data Methods in Applied Economic Research*, Springer Proceedings in Business and Economics,
https://doi.org/10.1007/978-3-030-38253-7_8

8.1 Crisis, Households and Everyday Life

The financial crisis has significantly affected the Greek economy for a decade, and, consequently, it has had a great impact on Greek households. The crisis, which had started in the USA, spread quickly both in developing countries, where economies had been rather unstable and also in developed prospering ones. Remarkably, the areas with the greatest financial problems—among others—were Latin America, the Caribbean, Europe and Central Asia (IEG 2010).

The crisis first struck the financial sector, in particular, the fragile banking system, and, subsequently, affected and upset all citizens' lives as autonomous natural persons. At first, banks banned business and household credit and raised interest rates. The impact was great on businesses, which had been striving to meet their obligations and were forced to redundancies, wage cuts and closures. A great number of people became redundant, incomes were reduced and most people were unable to meet obligations. The sharp drop in consumption has remained, triggering new business closures and causing new problems to banks, which have been cutting down loans until the situation improves (Savoyakis 2012).

For the last few years, the debt crisis in Greece has also generated a social crisis. The impacts of crisis, ten years later, seemed to have shaped the Greek family environment, which has been directly affected by wider changes. Typically, low-class families are more likely to be confronted with greater difficulties in their daily lives, due to a lack of material goods and their poor knowledge about which methods to apply to cope with any potential difficulties in a more drastic and rational way (Mendoza 2009). More specifically, nowadays, the problems faced by Greek families are rather complicated and multidimensional. Notably, for a vast number of families, lower incomes have been the reason which forced them to change lifestyles. Many have moved to low-rent neighborhoods or low-cost accommodation, and there are also cases of people who have moved back to parents' homes to reduce accommodation spending. In addition, a great number of families have also decided to emigrate in search of better living conditions (Papaioannou 2013; Children Ombudsman 2011–2012).

On account of the financial crisis and the consequent recession, Greek families have changed consumer habits, and, thus, search for bargains and discounts, low-priced goods and frequently carry out online purchases. In addition, they have significantly reduced the frequency of evening entertainment, whereas a considerable number never go out to restaurants, cinemas or pubs, but merely buy the basic essentials, and avoid purchases of unnecessary goods or use of credit cards. In addition, they have reduced summer holiday duration or have even stopped going on holidays. Many avoid social events and prefer staying at home to cut down spending, and also minimize traveling costs as their purchasing power has become low.

To overcome the impact of crisis, families have applied various strategies. Thus, the lower their budget, the greater the decline in food quantity and quality, and the greater the changes they have made in eating patterns; accordingly, many buy and consume substitutes or "second class" goods to survive (Mendoza 2009). Parents have reduced clothes and shoe purchases, especially for themselves, and frequently make forced cuts in healthcare and other expenses (Dornan 2010).

The impact of family financial distress is also evident in child and teenager behavior. As a result of the financial crisis, from 2010 to 2011, juvenile delinquency in Greece increased by 53.4% (Unicef 2017a). Remarkably, reduction or loss of family income, in case of unemployment, wage cuts or other reasons, have enhanced previously existing problems by causing conflicts, stress, negative attitudes, uncertainty as well as emotional withdrawal. Obviously, family crisis results in distressing interpersonal relationships and causes withdrawal, which destroys a family's daily life.

In addition, despite the fact it is hard to realize, normal life images and patterns have been constantly declining. It is worth noting that rates of abuse, exploitation and violence against children tend to be growing under conditions of financial pressure (Unicef 2017b). Remarkably, the socio-economic crisis, resulting in poverty, unemployment, emigration and social exclusion, apart from problems, such as alcoholism, drug abuse, and use of psychotropic substances, also tends to trigger aggression, violence, racism and xenophobia, and typically results in the so-called "social alienation" (Giudicelli 1984).

The financial crisis has also been observed to radically affect gender relationships. Apart from any inequalities in female employee salaries or career opportunities, the financial crisis has had a major impact on women, who are frequently more vulnerable to family responsibilities discrimination, and, consequently, redundancy and wage cuts, thus, making them victims of exploitation, inequity or sexual harassment in the workplace (Hossain and McGregor 2011).

The increase in unemployment rates during the financial crisis has had a negative effect on the psychological state of the unemployed, who suffer from depression, stress and lack of support, and have got problems communicating with other people; they also feel disappointed and socially excluded (Baldourd and Spyropoulou 2011).

Finally, Higher Education graduates who have been unable to find a job in Greece, are forced to emigrate, thus, depriving the country of a highly qualified potential, capable of contributing to growth and prosperity. Notably, the so-called constantly growing 'brain drain' in Greece has raised youth unemployment rates to 50%, according to surveys by the Hellenic Statistical Authority (ELSTAT 2014).

In conclusion, it is worth highlighting that surveys exploring the impacts of financial crises in various countries for the last decades, in attempt to define the citizens' quality of life, have underpinned a direct correlation between unemployment and morbidity, mortality, and depression rates (Giotakos et al. 2011).

8.2 Empirical Research

8.2.1 Research Methodology

To investigate the impact of the 10-year financial crisis and recession on Greek households, and the changes they have taken place in family lives, a survey was carried out, on subjects living in various Greek areas. The research is conclusive—descriptive and attempts to identify real facts in the daily lives and quality of life of Greek households.

The corpus of data was drawn from the analysis of a structured questionnaire based on the extant literature and is comprised of two parts. The first part includes the participants' demographic information (gender, age, educational status, occupation, family income, place of residence and marital status), whereas the second a set of closed-end and multiple-choice questions about the subjects' lifestyles during the financial crisis, surveying purchasing power and social life. The questionnaire was designed on Google Forms and was answered by 260 respondents via e-mail and social media (Facebook) from 20 July 2018 until 20 September 2018. The questionnaire results were analyzed using SPSS and Office Excel.

8.2.2 Research Results

The statistical analysis yielded the following results:

Of the 260 subjects, 66.4% are female and 33.6% male. 67.99% are aged up to 45 and 32.01% over 45. Most answers were given by subjects aged 36–45 (35.38%), whereas the fewest by those aged 66 and over (6.54%).

In terms of educational status, most respondents are Higher Education graduates (41.92%), whereas 30.38% Senior High school and post-secondary education graduates, followed by Vocational School (14.23%) and Junior high school graduates (7.69%). The lowest percentage (5.77%) comprises elementary education subjects. As far as professional status is concerned, most respondents are civil servants (25%), whereas 21.92% employees in private companies, and 8.85% pensioners. Only 4.23% are farmers, and 13.08% unemployed.

In terms of place of residence, 44.62% of the respondents live in cities, 43.07% in villages and 12.31% in small towns.

Most households are two- or three-membered (42.30%) and 45.53% four- or five-membered, whereas the number of very large families with many children is only 12 (4.61%). Finally, 11.53% are single-parent families.

In terms of income, 60.38% of the respondents stated that their incomes range from €601 to 1500, whereas 8.46% over €2001. However, there are also households with incomes of €600 or less (14.62%) (Fig. 8.1).

The majority of respondents (60.77%) are employees (public or private). Households with incomes mostly from business activity are estimated at 11.15%; of those,

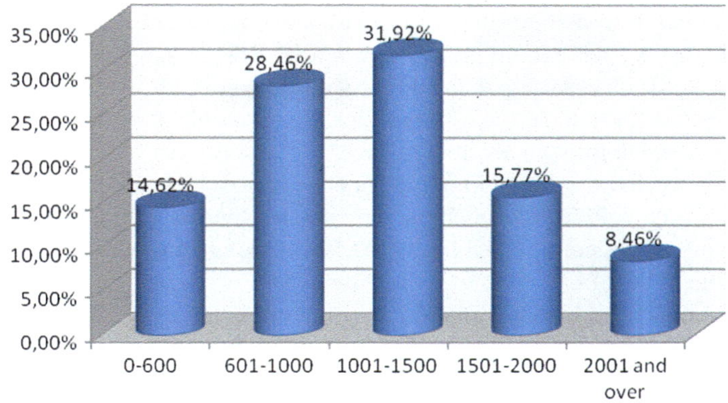

Fig. 8.1 Monthly family income in €

13.08% are pensioners and 4.6% farmers. Only 0.38% earn an income from ownership, whereas 5% are financially supported by relatives, and, finally, 1.92% live on state welfare benefits.

Fairly satisfied with financial status are 32.31% of the subjects, whereas 34.62% are less satisfied. In addition, 27.31% are completely dissatisfied and 1.54% very satisfied.

As regards changes in various aspects of life as a result of the crisis, it appears that an overwhelming majority (85%) has suffered wage or pension cuts, whereas 50.69% have lost their jobs. 53.46% of the respondents stated that payment was delayed, whereas 44.23% that there was no reduction in working hours.

Income changes during the crisis are significant, as incomes for 83.46% of the subjects were reduced, whereas for 10% they did not change. 5% did not answer and only 1.54% stated that incomes were raised (Fig. 8.2).

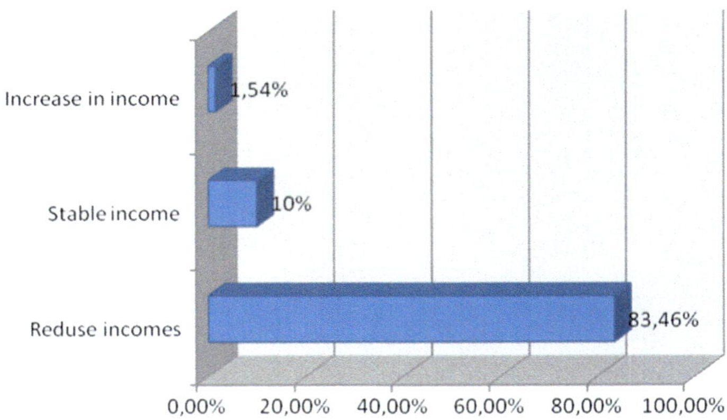

Fig. 8.2 Change in incomes

The analysis demonstrated that for 11.9% of the households, incomes cannot cover daily basic needs, and extra money is required. 48.1% of the participants stated that they had to cut back spending to meet obligations, in contrast to 36.5% who claimed that they were able to meet their obligations. Finally, only 3.5% answered that they have a comfortable life and are able to save.

It is also worth noting that about half of the researched subjects (52.3%) stated that their family includes one unemployed person, whereas 47.7% answered that all family members are employed. Finally, 90.5% of the unemployed do not receive an unemployment benefit.

As the financial crisis has forced many people to emigrate, a large number of people, particularly young, have been searching for a job in a different country, as low incomes, poor career prospects and scarce improvements in quality of life in Greece have been major problems. According to the survey results, 52.69% of the subjects have got relatives who are economic migrants.

In terms of meeting personal needs, the subjects answered that they find it difficult to pay for entertainment (64.61%), clothing (63.46%), household equipment (62.69), and electricity and water supply bills, rental and ownership charges (60%), heating (53.07%) and car fuel (50.76%). Nearly 50% of them find it difficult to pay monthly loan installments and mobile telephony bills. It is also noteworthy that most families (67.69%) have not cut back on food supply and education costs (41.92%).

As far as consumer habits are concerned, the survey demonstrated that a large percentage of the respondents have cut down on travel (85.38%), clothing (80%), entertainment (76.53%), heating (47.69%) and education expenditure (39.23%), whereas spending cuts on food do not demonstrate a significant decline, as only 32.69% of the respondents have reduced food supply costs (Fig. 8.3).

Most respondents could not afford holidays in the previous year, due to financial problems, whereas 36.54% had spent at least one week for the summer holidays.

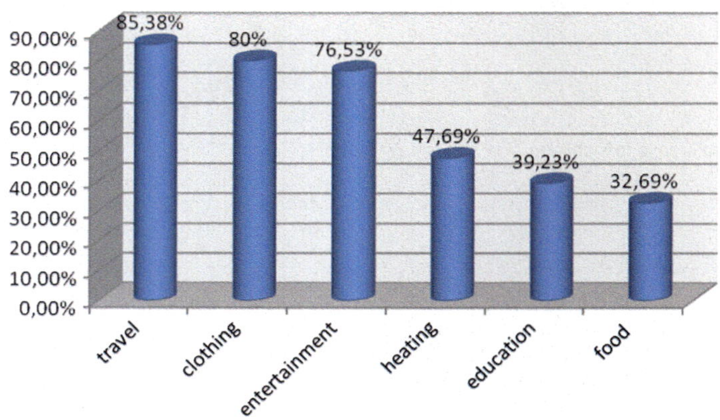

Fig. 8.3 Spending cuts

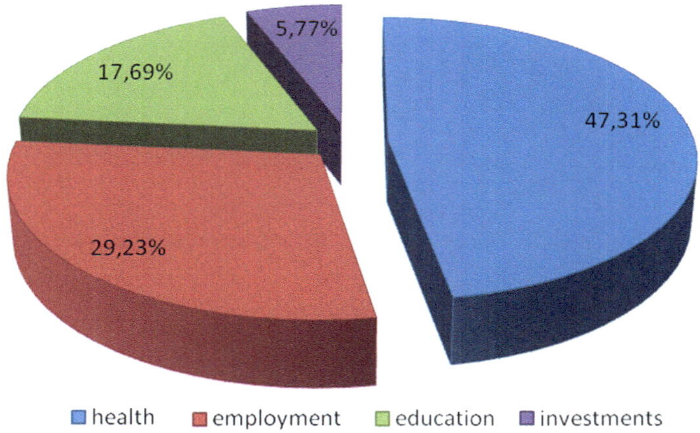

Fig. 8.4 State priorities

Remarkably, however, 63.46% of the subjects could not afford even one week—at least—for the summer holidays.

Healthcare is also crucial for Greek households; 24.21% of the respondents stated that a number of people have probably had difficulties in paying for medical care for themselves or another family member. In addition, 29.23% answered that they had not applied for healthcare, whereas 20% of the respondents had probably no difficulty in covering medical expenses. As regards the type of healthcare the respondents commonly prefer, 56.92% answered that they prefer the public to private healthcare services (39.62%).

Overall, the results demonstrated that special emphasis should be given to specific aspects of public life: health (47.31%), employment (29.23%), education (17.69%) and investments (5.77%) (Fig. 8.4).

A large percentage of the research subjects were pessimistic about the possibility of improvement in the near future; 80% of them are confident that there will be slight or no change in the future, and only 0.38% are optimistic about future improvement.

In addition, the crisis has affected the respondents' psychological state significantly (16.92%). Only 5% of them stated that they have remained unaffected by the impact of crisis, whereas a large percentage of 37.31% answered that the impact of crisis on their lives has been fairly significant.

8.2.3 Correlation Between Factors

Following the descriptive statistics, SPSS was used to investigate correlation between the various factors. The process involved hypothesis testing and x^2 statistics calculation. It is worth examining specific issues in terms of correlation between wage/pension and spending cuts in various aspects of everyday life. The following

Table 8.1 Correlation between food spending cuts and wage/pension cuts

Chi-square tests			
	Value	*df*	Asymptotic significance (two-sided)
Pearson chi-square	18.806[a]	3	0.000
Likelihood ratio	13.483	3	0.004
No. of valid cases	244		

[a]3 cells (37.5%) have expected counts less than 5. The minimum expected count is 0.45

tables demonstrate any possible correlations between wage/pension and spending cuts (in entertainment, travel, education, and heating). The analysis yielded a statistically significant correlation between wage/pension cuts and food supply (Table 8.1), entertainment (Table 8.2), travel (Table 8.3) and heating (Table 8.5), whereas no significant correlation was demonstrated in terms of spending cuts in education, as the respondents do not to tend to cut back on education costs (Table 8.4).

Table 8.2 Correlation between entertainment spending cuts and wage/pension cuts

Chi-square tests			
	Value	*df*	Asymptotic significance (two-sided)
Pearson chi-square	23.575[a]	3	0.000
Likelihood ratio	13.526	3	0.004
No. of valid cases	244		

[a]4 cells (50.0%) have expected counts less than 5. The minimum expected count is 0.36

Table 8.3 Correlation between travel spending cuts and wage/pension cuts

Chi-square tests			
	Value	*df*	Asymptotic significance (two-sided)
Pearson chi-square	15.203[a]	3	0.002
Likelihood ratio	9.563	3	0.023
No. of valid cases	244		

[a]4 cells (50.0%) have expected counts less than 5. The minimum expected count is 0.27

Table 8.4 Correlation between spending cuts in education and wage/pension cuts

Chi-square tests			
	Value	*df*	Asymptotic significance (two-sided)
Pearson chi-square	10.717[a]	3	0.013
Likelihood ratio	8.073	3	0.045
No. of valid cases	244		

[a]2 cells (25.0%) have expected counts less than 5. The minimum expected count is 1.08

Table 8.5 Correlation between spending cuts in heating and wage/pension cuts

Chi-square tests			
	Value	*df*	Asymptotic significance (two-sided)
Pearson chi-square	17.303[a]	3	0.001
Likelihood ratio	13.815	3	0.003
No. of valid cases	244		

[a]2 cells (25.0%) have expected counts less than 5. The minimum expected count is 0.81

In detail, data analysis demonstrated the following results:
According to hypothesis testing,

1. There are two research hypotheses:

H_0: *food spending cuts and wage/pension cuts are independent*
H_1: *food spending cuts and wage/pension cuts are dependent*

To carry out hypothesis testing, x^2 is calculated.
As $p < 0.01$, H_0 is rejected and H_1 is accepted; thus, there is a correlation between spending cuts in food and wage/pension cuts.

2. There are two research hypotheses:

H_0: *entertainment spending cuts and wage/pension cuts are independent*
H_1: *entertainment spending cuts and wage/pension cuts are dependent*

To carry out hypothesis testing, x^2 is calculated.
As $p < 0.01$, H_0 is rejected and H_1 is accepted; thus, there is a correlation between entertainment spending cuts and wage/pension cuts.

3. There are two research hypotheses:

H_0: *travel spending cuts and wage/pension cuts are independent*
H_1: *travel spending cuts and wage/pension cuts are dependent*

To carry out hypothesis testing, x^2 is calculated.
As $p < 0.01$, H_0 is rejected and H_1 is accepted; thus, there is a correlation between travel spending cuts and wage/pension cuts.

4. There are two research hypotheses:

H_0: *spending cuts in education and wage/pension cuts are independent*
H_1: *spending cuts in education and wage/pension cuts are dependent*

To carry out hypothesis testing, x^2 is calculated.
As $p > 0.01$, H_0 is accepted and H_1 is rejected; thus, there is no correlation between spending cuts in education and wage/pension cuts.

5. There are two research hypotheses:

H_0: *spending cuts in heating and wage/pension cuts are independent*
H_1: *spending cuts in heating and wage/pension cuts are dependent*

To carry out hypothesis testing, x^2 is calculated.

As $p < 0.01$, H_0 is rejected and H_1 is accepted; thus, there is a correlation between spending cuts in heating and wage/pension cuts.

Changes in incomes have also had an impact on the daily financial obligations of households; more specifically, they have deteriorated the respondents' financial status. The following tables demonstrate a correlation between changes in income and inability to pay for household equipment (Table 8.6), heating (Table 8.7), mobile telephony bills (Table 8.10), entertainment (Table 8.12). However, the analysis did not demonstrate spending cuts in fixed costs, such as car fuel (Table 8.8), bills (Table 8.9) and loan instalments (Table 8.11). The results are demonstrated in the following tables:

Table 8.6 Correlation between inability to pay for household equipment and changes in income

Chi-square tests

	Value	*df*	Asymptotic significance (two-sided)
Pearson chi-square	35.870[a]	9	0.000
Likelihood ratio	22.580	9	0.007
No. of valid cases	260		

[a]9 cells (56.3%) have expected counts less than 5. The minimum expected count is 0.15

Table 8.7 Correlation between inability to pay for heating and changes in income

Chi-square tests

	Value	*df*	Asymptotic significance (two-sided)
Pearson chi-square	38.112[a]	9	0.00
Likelihood ratio	25.911	9	0.002
No. of valid cases	260		

[a]9 cells (56.3%) have expected counts less than 5. The minimum expected count is 0.23

Table 8.8 Correlation between inability to pay for car fuel and changes in income

Chi-square tests

	Value	*df*	Asymptotic significance (two-sided)
Pearson chi-square	19.316[a]	9	0.023
Likelihood ratio	12.888	9	0.168
No. of valid cases	260		

[a]9 cells (56.3%) have expected counts less than 5. The minimum expected count is 0.15

Table 8.9 Correlation between inability to pay household bills and changes in income

Chi-square tests

	Value	*df*	Asymptotic significance (two-sided)
Pearson chi-square	20.323[a]	9	0.016
Likelihood ratio	16.617	9	0.055
No. of valid cases	260		

[a]9 cells (56.3%) have expected counts less than 5. The minimum expected count is 0.12

Table 8.10 Correlation between inability to pay mobile phone bills and changes in income

Chi-square tests

	Value	*df*	Asymptotic significance (two-sided)
Pearson chi-square	23.095[a]	9	0.006
Likelihood ratio	20.581	9	0.015
No. of valid cases	260		

[a]8 cells (50.0%) have expected counts less than 5. The minimum expected count is 0.18

Table 8.11 Correlation between inability to pay loan instalments and changes in income

Chi-square tests

	Value	*df*	Asymptotic significance (two-sided)
Pearson chi-square	15.932[a]	9	0.068
Likelihood ratio	12.873	9	0.168
No. of valid cases	260		

[a]9 cells (56.3%) have expected counts less than 5. The minimum expected count is 0.43

Table 8.12 Correlation between inability to pay for entertainment and changes in income

Chi-square tests

	Value	*df*	Asymptotic significance (two-sided)
Pearson chi-square	22.507[a]	9	0.007
Likelihood ratio	18.911	9	0.026
No. of valid cases	260		

[a]9 cells (56.3%) have expected counts less than 5. The minimum expected count is 0.12

6. There are two hypotheses:

H_0: *inability to pay for household equipment and changes in income are independent*
H_1: *inability to pay for household equipment and changes in income are dependent*

To carry out hypothesis testing, x^2 is calculated.

As $p < 0.01$, H_0 is rejected and H_1 is accepted; thus, there is a correlation between the inability to pay for household equipment and changes in income.

7. There are two hypotheses:

H_0: *inability to pay for heating and changes in income are independent*
H_1: *inability to pay for heating and changes in income are dependent*

To carry out hypothesis testing, x^2 is calculated.
As $p < 0.01$, H_0 is rejected and H_1 is accepted; thus, there is a correlation between the inability to pay for heating and changes in income.

8. There are two hypotheses:

H_0: *inability to pay for car fuel and changes in income are independent*
H_1: *inability to pay for car fuel and changes in income are dependent*

To carry out hypothesis testing, x^2 is calculated.
As $p > 0.01$, H_1 is accepted and H_0 is rejected; thus, there is no correlation between inability to pay for car fuel and changes in income.

9. There are two hypotheses:

H_0: *inability to pay household bills and changes in income are independent*
H_1: *inability to pay household bills and changes in income are dependent*

To carry out hypothesis testing, x^2 is calculated.
As $p > 0.01$, H_1 is rejected and H_0 is accepted; thus, there is no correlation between inability to pay household bills and changes in income.

10. There are two hypotheses:

H_0: *inability to pay mobile phone bills and changes in income are independent*
H_1: *inability to pay mobile phone bills and changes in income are dependent*

To carry out hypothesis testing, x^2 is calculated.
As $p < 0.01$, H_0 is rejected and H_1 is accepted; thus, there is a correlation between inability to pay mobile phone bills and changes in income.

11. There are two hypotheses:

H_0: *inability to pay loan instalments and changes in income are independent*
H_1: *inability to pay loan instalments and changes in income are dependent*

To carry out hypothesis testing, x^2 is calculated.
As $p > 0.01$, H_1 is rejected and H_0 is accepted; thus, there is no correlation between inability to pay loan instalments and changes in income.

12. There are two hypotheses:

H_0: *inability to pay for entertainment and changes in income are independent*

Table 8.13 Correlation between future improvement and impact on psychological state (crosstabs/tables = future Improvement by impact on psychological state)

Chi-square tests			
	Value	*df*	Asymptotic significance (two-sided)
Pearson chi-square	64.996[a]	16	0.000
Likelihood ratio	54.645	16	0.000
No. of valid cases	260		

[a] 13 cells (52.0%) have expected counts less than 5. The minimum expected count is 0.05

H_1: *inability to pay for entertainment and changes in income is dependent*

To carry out hypothesis testing, x^2 is calculated.

As $p < 0.01$, H_0 is rejected and H_1 is accepted; thus, there is a correlation between inability to pay for entertainment and changes in income.

Obviously, the Greek debt crisis and memoranda have had a psychological impact on the research respondents who feel pessimist about the future and do not seem to expect any improvements in future conditions. The following table (Table 8.13) demonstrates a correlation between the impact on the subjects' psychological state and future improvements.

13. There are two hypotheses:

H_0: *psychological state and expectations for future improvement are independent*
H_1: *psychological state and expectations for future improvement are dependent*

To carry out hypothesis testing, x^2 is calculated.

As $p < 0.01$, H_0 is rejected and H_1 is accepted; thus, there is a correlation between psychological state and optimistic expectations for future improvement.

8.3 Summary—Conclusions

The global financial crisis has had a negative impact on the Greek economy and, consequently, the Greek society and families. Overall, the debt crisis in Greece has led to reductions in welfare spending, a decline in household incomes, and an increase in unemployment rates.

The present survey demonstrated that, after the ten-year crisis, household incomes are not satisfactory for family members, as incomes of an overwhelming percentage (83.84%) of families have declined. Thus, a number of households, in view of price increase and purchasing power decline, have been forced to cut back on entertainment and travel spending. However, most respondents avoided spending cuts in basic essentials, such as food.

In addition, high unemployment rates are particularly worrying, as in 52.3% of the families there is at least one unemployed person, and an overwhelming majority (90.5%) do not receive an unemployment benefit. The crisis has resulted in a significant decline in job positions and a sharp increase in low-paid employment.

A great number of Greek people, particularly young, on account of financial problems and high unemployment rates, combined with the shrinking number of new job opportunities, have been forced to emigrate. As a result, 52.7% of Greek families have been separated from their relatives who attempted to restart a career in other countries.

As regards healthcare, the research results demonstrated that, overall, serious improvements should be made. It is worth noting that 24.3% of the Greek citizens are unable to pay for healthcare, which must become a state priority.

In terms of the impact of crisis on psychological state, it is very disappointing that most people have been seriously affected, and, thus, are a pessimist about prospects of future improvements. The analysis results demonstrated that 43.8% are confident that current conditions are going to be slightly changed, whereas for 48.5% the crisis has had a significant or fairly significant impact on their psychological state.

Remarkably, the research demonstrated a close relationship and correlation (dependent variables) between wage/pension cuts and spending cuts in various aspects of everyday life, and also highlighted people's inability to meet their obligations or basic needs.

Ethical Statement There are no ethical issues involved in the processing of the questionnaire data used in the study. The necessary consents have been obtained by the persons involved and the anonymity of the participants has been secured. Approval for the processing of the questionnaire data has been provided by the Ethics Committee of the University of Western Macedonia, Greece.

References

Baldourdos, D., & Spyropoulou, N. (2011). Portraits of poverty in Greece of the crisis. In A. Mouriki, D. Baldours, O. Papaliou, N. Spyropoulou, E. Fagadaki, & E. Fronimou (Eds.), *The social portrait of Greece 2012* (pp. 157–179). Athens: National Center for Social Research.

Child's Ombudsman. (2011–2012). The consequences of the crisis on student life: research by the adolescent counsel of the child advocate. In Retrieved on August 5, 2018, by http://www.0-18.gr/gia-megaloys/nea/oi-synepeies-tis-krisis-sti-zoi-ton-mathiton-ereyna-ton-efibon-symboylon-toy-synigoroy-toy-paidioy.

Dornan, P. (2010). *Understanding the impacts of crisis on children in developing countries: Young lives round 3 preliminary findings*. Oxford: Young Lives.

ELSTAT. (2014). Outgoing immigration. http://www.statistics.gr/el/statistics/-/publication/SPO15/2014.

Giotakos, O., Karampelas, D., & Kaikas, A. (2011). Impact of the economic crisis on mental health in Greece. *Psychiatry, 22,* 109–119.

Giudicelli, S. (1984). The concept of alienation, from theory to everyday practice. Posts (Vol. 6) website. http://www.theseis.com/index.php?Option=com_content&task=view&id=74&Itemid=29.

Hossain, N., & McGregor, J. A. (2011). A "lost generation"? Impacts of complex compound crises on children and young people. *Development Policy Review, 29*, 565–584. https://doi.org/10.1111/j.1467-7679.2011.00547.x.

Mendoza, R. (2009). *How economic shocks affect poor households and children.* Social and economic policy working briefs. Unicef Policy and Practice. UNICEF Retrieved May 22, 2011 from http://www.unicef.org/socialpolicy/files/How_economic_shocks_affect_final.pdf.

Papaioannou, G. (2013). Greece lost! Retrieved on August 10, 2018 by http://www.tovima.gr/politics/article/?aid=552790.

Savoyidaki, U. (2012). The 2011 debt crisis in Greece. In Graduate, Higher Technological Educational Institute of Crete. Retrieved from web site on 10/09/2018. http://nefeli.lib.teicrete.gr/browse/sdo/log/2012/SavoidakiOurania/attached-document-1375703391-968790-11369/SavoidakiOurania2012.pdf.

Unicef (2017a) *The situation of children in Greece 2017.* In Report on behalf of the Greek National Committee Unicef. Athens: Unicef.

Unicef (2017b) *Child well-being in rich countries a comparative overview* https://www.unicef-irc.org/publications/pdf/rc11_eng.pdf.

Chapter 9
Easy or Tough Coopetition? Perspective of Coopetitive Real Options Games

Elżbieta Rychłowska-Musiał

Abstract Cooperation between competing firms called coopetition has increasing relevance to business practice. However, firms and their managers who want to enjoy the benefits of coopetition are also aware of the risks that it entails. The key questions need to be answered: under which circumstances firms are willing to coopete and to keep the arrangement, what factors are decisive, and when benefits are most significant. In the paper, we are looking for answers to these questions on the basis of coopetitive real options games. We consider the case of two firms that can establish a coopetition arrangement to implement an investment project (each firm possesses a shared investment option). In the paper, we point out conditions under which coopetition between companies is easy, tough or impossible. The key factors are the project risk and the size of market shares. In particular, it is worth noting that for high-risk projects, the area of tough coopetition is larger than for low-risk projects. A large disproportion in market shares makes coopetition rather impossible.

Keywords Real options games · Investment option · Coopetition

JEL Codes L13 · L14 · G11

9.1 Introduction

Competition and cooperation are two basic forms of relationships between companies on the market. However, the main strategic challenge for many firms is not to choose between competition and cooperation, but to find a balance between them. Cooperation between competing firms called coopetition has increasing relevance to business practice. It is one of essential ways to create value and competitive advantage on a market. Value creation, which requires combining complementary resources and

E. Rychłowska-Musiał (✉)
Department of Applied Mathematics, Poznań University of Economics and Business, Poznań, Poland
e-mail: elzbieta.musial@ue.poznan.pl

N. Tsounis and A. Vlachvei (eds.), *Advances in Cross-Section Data Methods in Applied Economic Research*, Springer Proceedings in Business and Economics,
https://doi.org/10.1007/978-3-030-38253-7_9

unique competences of both partners and sharing its value, is a hallmark of coopetition. If pure competition is a zero-sum game between parties, where a single winner takes all, and cooperation is a positive-sum game, where both firms benefit and it is a win–win situation, then coopetition is a positive-sum game and it could be even a win–win–win situation, where the third beneficiary is a consumer (Walley 2007).

In general, previous studies have shown that coopetition between potential competitors really matters in their strategies and performance. However, the intensity of this impact depends on the characteristics of the sector in which firms operate. Previous studies suggested that coopetition occurs in knowledge-intensive sectors in which rival firms collaborate in creating interoperable solutions and standards, in sharing R&D costs and efforts, and in sharing risks. On the other hand, coopetition is not a necessary factor for success in sectors that are less knowledge-intensive, such as manufacturing (examples are given by Ritala 2012). However, systematic study of coopetition still requires many aspects to consider.

Strategies built on a coopetition arrangement are rarely stable (Das and Teng 2000). The coopetition agreement can be broken at any moment by any partner-rival. Managers of these partner-rival firms must create strategies and develop processes that are not fully controllable (Dagino and Padula 2002). Managers must also manage with different tensions arising on many levels (Fernandez et al. 2014).

So, one of the questions that managers face is: are there any chances to successfully complete the project under a coopetition agreement? And: how substantial is the risk that the partner will withdraw from the contract? How much will the firm benefit from this agreement? And if at all?

This is a business problem on one side and an academic challenge on another. One of the paths considered to face this problem in the field of academic research is the game theory approach. Nalebuff and Brandenburger (1996) were the first who proposed game theory to describe the interactive process of cooperation and competition. Next, a hybrid noncooperative–cooperative game model called a biform game was proposed by Brandenburger and Stuart (2007). And, as authors say, the biform model is a formalization of the idea that business strategies shape the competitive environment—and thereby the fortunes of the players. David Carfi (2010) proposed an analytical model of coopetitive games and its feasible solutions. Coopetitive games' applications to economics and finance were developed e.g. by Carfi and Schiliro (2012, 2013). Rychłowska-Musiał (2017) proposed the real options games approach to analyze a coopetition relationship.

The main aim of the paper has been built on the crucial managerial questions formulated in an academic way. The paper aims to provide a framework to analyze the proneness to coopetition between firms which market shares are substantially different or almost equal, benefits that rival-partner firms may achieve, and influence of crucial factors on firms' decisions/strategies. It addresses: (1) under which circumstances firms are willing to coopete, (2) what is the impact of the degree of asymmetry between companies and the risk of the project on the proneness to coopetition, (3) under which circumstances companies are willing to keep the cooperation agreement, and when they may be tempted to break it.

The paper also provides a contribution to the existing literature on real options and coopetitive games by combining these two areas in order to more suitable analysis of relationship between firms sharing an investment option.

9.2 Firms' Decisions and Payments

Let us assume that two parties A and B operate on a competitive market and each of them holds a real option to invest in a project. The project requires an investment outlay $I, I > 0$ (this may be both financial as well as non-financial contribution). The two competitors share the same investment opportunity, it is a *shared* option (Smit and Trigeorgis 2004). We assume that the lifetime of the investment project is infinite. The investment project generates a cash flow (Y_t), which evolves in accordance with the geometric Brownian motion, with drift α, $\alpha > 0$ and volatility σ, $\sigma > 0$ under the risk-neutral measure. A risk-free asset yields a constant rate of return r, δ is a convenience yield ($\delta > 0$) and it reflects an opportunity cost of delaying construction of the project, and instead keeping the option to invest alive. The present value of the project benefits is determined by the discounting and accumulating of its future cash flows. It is equal to $V(Y_0) = \frac{Y_0}{\delta}$ (Dixit and Pindyck 1994).

According to Dixit and Pindyck (1994) we assume the following links between model parameters:

$$\alpha + \delta = r + (r_m - r) \cdot \frac{\sigma \cdot \rho_m}{\sigma_m},$$

where r_m is the expected return on the market on which the financial asset perfectly correlated with Y_t is listed, σ_m is the standard deviation of r_m, and ρ_m is the correlation of this financial asset with the market portfolio.

When a firm is considering implementation of the project there are three basic strategies for it to choose from: *Wait*, *Invest*, or *Abandon*. The primary criterion for making investment decisions is the comparison between the investment option value, the benefits of instantaneous investment, and zero. However, in the case of the shared option, a firm has to include its rival's decision into its decision-making process. A firm has to take into account the way its investment decision affects competitors, and how it itself may be impacted by rival's reaction.

When both firms are active on a market there may be a market power asymmetry between them. Without any loss of generality, we will assume that firm A has u market share ($0.5 \leq u < 1$), firm B is left with $(1 - u)$ share. If only one of the firms decides to invest—it obtains the whole market. The firm which deferred its investment loses its market share in favor of the investing firm.

The logic of coopetition is that cooperation and competition merge together to form a new kind of strategic interdependence between firms, giving rise to a coopetitive system of value creation (Dagino and Padula 2002). With this type of agreement, firms can reach more customers, which would be impossible individually (e.g. Nike and Apple described by Rodrigues et al. 2009). Moreover, firms often need access to the others' firms know-how to collectively use this knowledge to produce benefits to them all (Liu 2013). Coopetitve agreement may also help firms avoid a cut-throat price war. Therefore, a coopetition agreement can cause enlarging the total market value ("market pie").

Coopetition can help firms combine complementary resources in developing new products and allow firms to reduce costs, risks and uncertainties associated with innovation or product development (Luo 2007, Gnyawali and Park 2009). Thus, another distinctive feature of coopetition in the paper will be cost sharing.

Therefore, we are going to consider three types of coopetition between firms:

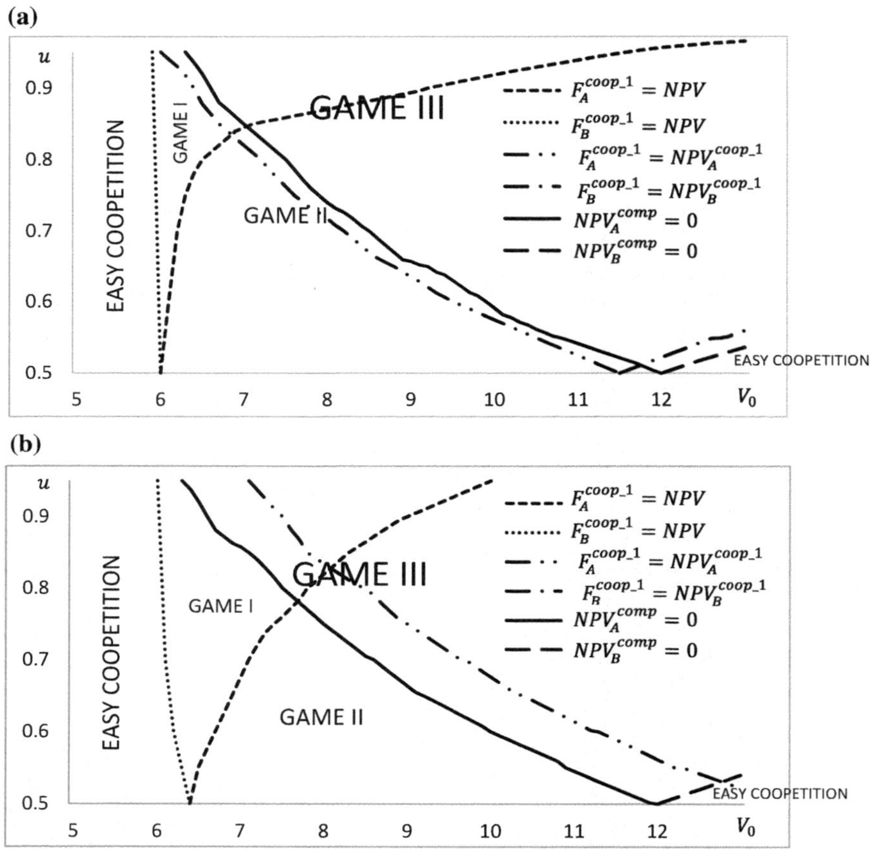

Fig. 9.1 Partial coopetition: market enlarging ($m = 1.2$), no cost-sharing ($n_A = 1,\ n_B = 1$). The impact of the degree of market enlarging on the proneness to coopetition. Scopes of easy, tough, or impossible coopetition. Ranges of coopetitive real options games between firms. Panel **a** low risk $\sigma = 20\%$, panel **b** high risk $\sigma = 60\%$

1. Partial coopetition (market enlarging)—the underlying market value is enlarged but both firms bear the whole costs of investment (coop_1),
2. Partial coopetition (costs sharing)—the underlying market value remains unchanged but firms share project expenditures in parts proportional to their market shares (coop_2),
3. Full coopetition—the underlying market value is enlarged and firms share project expenditures in parts proportional to their market shares (coop_3), and one case of pure competition,
4. Pure competition—the underlying market value remains unchanged and both firms bear the whole costs of investment (comp).

Because each of the firms has three basic strategies to choose from: *Wait*, *Invest*, or *Abandon*. Firms' choices lead to the following payments:

1. Firms *A* and *B* invest immediately and simultaneously. They may invest under a coopetition arrangement or on the basis of pure competition. The underlying market value may be enlarged or may remain unchanged. Firms share project benefits in parts proportional to their market shares. They may share project expenditures in parts proportional to their market shares or bear the whole costs. The payoff for each firm is the net present value of the project taking into account these enlarged and divided benefits and (possibly) reduced expenditures of the project:

$$\begin{aligned} \mathrm{NPV}_A^i &:= \mathrm{NPV}(u \cdot m \cdot Y_t)\big|_{t=0} = V(u \cdot m \cdot Y_0) - n_A \cdot I = u \cdot m \cdot V_0 - n_A \cdot I, \\ \mathrm{NPV}_B^i &:= \mathrm{NPV}((1-u) \cdot m \cdot Y_t)\big|_{t=0} = V((1-u) \cdot m \cdot Y_0) - n_B \cdot I \\ &= (1-u) \cdot m \cdot V_0 - n_B \cdot I, \end{aligned}$$

m—a cooperation mode multiple (a multiplier, which enlarged the underlying market value): $m \geq 1$ if $i =$ coop_1, coop_3, or $m = 1$ if $i =$ coop_2, comp.

n_A—a reduction factor of firm *A* investment expenditures: $n_A = u, 0 < u < 1$ if $i =$ coop_2, coop_3, or $n_A = 1$ if $i =$ coop_2, comp.

n_B—a reduction factor of firm *B* investment expenditures: $n_B = 1 - u, 0 < u < 1$ if $i =$ coop_2, coop_3, or $n_B = 1$ if $i =$ coop_2, comp.

2. Firm *A*(*B*) invest immediately and firm *B*(*A*) defers the investment project execution. Consequently, firm *A*(*B*) appropriates the whole market and bears all the investment expenditure, and firm *B*(*A*) is left with nothing. Payoff for firm *A*(*B*) is the net present value of the total project:

$$\mathrm{NPV} := \mathrm{NPV}(Y_t)|_{t=0} = V(Y_0) - I = V_0 - I,$$

and the payoff for firm *B*(*A*) is zero.
3. Firms *A* and *B* make (and keep) a coopetition agreement to defer the investment project execution and keep the investment option open. In this case, the payoff for

each of them is the call option value determined on the Black–Scholes–Merton formula (the underlying asset is the present value of the project determined with the use of an adequate part of (possibly enlarged) project benefits ($u \cdot m \cdot Y_t$ for firm A or $(1-u) \cdot m \cdot Y_t$ for firm B), and the exercise price is an adequate part of the investment expenditure ($n_A \cdot I$ for firm A or $n_B \cdot I$ for firm B):

$$F_A^i := F(u \cdot m \cdot Y_t)\big|_{t=0},$$

$$F_B^i := F((1-u) \cdot m \cdot Y_t)\big|_{t=0}.$$

$i =$ coop_1, coop_2, coop_3, comp.
m, n_A, n_B as in the previous case.

To visualize values of these payments and to analyse games, let us assume a base set of parameters: investment expenditure $I = 6$ (in monetary unit), expiration date $T = 2$ (years), risk free rate $r = 2.10\%$ (*YTM* of treasury bonds with maturity date equal to expiration date of investment option (DOS0321)), the expected percentage rate of change of project cash flows $\alpha = 1\%$ (own assumption), volatility of the project's benefits $\sigma = 20\%$ (low risk), $\sigma = 60\%$ (high risk), the expected return on the market $r_m = 8.38\%$ (rate of return on market index WIG 2016–2018), the standard deviation of r_m, $\sigma_m = 14.28\%$, the correlation of the asset with the market portfolio $\rho_m = 0.5$ (own assumption). Additionally we assume in the base case the firm A's market share is $u = 0.75$ (so 0.25 of the market pie is left for firm B). And the cooperation mode multiple $m = 1.2$ (according to Trigeorgis and Baldi 2017, a market value pie is enlarged by 20%). Assumptions about the parameters reflect a situation of a real company (a similar approach is used by authors of cited papers).

9.3 Analysis of Coopetitive Real Options Games

We consider a situation in which each of two companies possesses an investment option. The investment option is a shared one. Therefore, it is reasonable that they calculate values of their investment options and consider the benefits of possible cooperation during the implementation of the project.

Notice at first that for these values of the project benefits (V_0) for which $F_A^i <$ NPV$_A^i$ and $F_B^i <$ NPV$_B^i$, ($i =$ coop_1, coop_2, coop_3, comp) the optimal strategy for each firm is *Invest*.

However, when the option value exceeds the benefit of immediate investment, i.e. when $F_A^i >$ NPV$_A^i$ and $F_B^i >$ NPV$_B^i$, ($i =$ coop_1, coop_2, coop_3, comp) the classic concept of real options (ROA) recommends retaining the investment option and postponing the investment decision. However, the option game concept (ROG) indicates the weakness of such an approach and recommends considering jointly the decisions of both companies and their mutual influence on each other.

Table 9.1 Payoff matrix

		Firm *B*	
		Wait (W)	*Invest* (I)
Firm *A*	*Wait* (*W*)	$\left(F_A^i; F_B^i\right)$	(0; NPV)
	Invest (*I*)	(NPV; 0)	$\left(\mathrm{NPV}_A^{\mathrm{comp}}; \mathrm{NPV}_B^{\mathrm{comp}}\right)$

Remark $i =$ coop_1, coop_2, coop_3, comp
Source own study

Consider, therefore, the situation as a game option. Because firms can choose non-cooperative or cooperative strategies, we are dealing with a family of games. As Carfi (2010) has said: *any coopetitive game could be defined as a family of normal-form games* and *the examination of a coopetitive game should be equivalent to the examination of a whole family of normal-form games.*

Games considered in the paper have one general normal form presented in Table 9.1.

By establishing a coopetition arrangement, companies determine the type of game in which they participate.

Let us notice that when the value of the investment option for each firm exceeds the net present value of the project for the only investor, i.e. when $F_A^i > \mathrm{NPV}$ and $F_B^i > \mathrm{NPV}$, then the game described in Table 9.1 for each i ($i =$ coop_1, coop_2, coop_3, comp), has the only one unique Nash equilibrium in dominant strategies (W, W). Both players achieve the highest possible payoffs.

Thus, the project values at which $F_A^i > \mathrm{NPV}$ and $F_B^i > \mathrm{NPV}$ or $F_A^i < \mathrm{NPV}_A^i$ and $F_B^i < \mathrm{NPV}_B^i$ ($i =$ coop_1, coop_2, coop_3, comp) lead to a situation in which coopetition is a natural form of relationship between companies. There is no incentive to break the agreement. In these cases, we are going to talk about easy coopetition.

The analysis of the game indicates one more scope of the project values, at which coopetition is easy because there are no incentives to withdraw from the contract. This is the case when $\mathrm{NPV}_A^{\mathrm{comp}} > 0$ and $\mathrm{NPV}_B^{\mathrm{comp}} > 0$ simultaneously. Then the dominant strategy for firm A is the strategy *Invest*, and the B's best response to this A's strategy is the strategy *Invest*, as well. However, in this case, establishing cooperation in the implementation of the project and taking advantage of the benefits of coopetition is a better solution because $\mathrm{NPV}_A^{\mathrm{comp}} < \mathrm{NPV}_A^i$ and $\mathrm{NPV}_B^{\mathrm{comp}} < \mathrm{NPV}_B^i$, for $i =$ coop_1, coop_2, coop_3.

Therefore, taking into account the relationship between all values, we can talk about easy coopetition for these projects in which values meet the following conditions $F_A^i > \mathrm{NPV}$ and $F_B^i > \mathrm{NPV}$ ($i =$ coop_1, coop_2, coop_3, comp), or $\mathrm{NPV}_A^{\mathrm{comp}} > 0$ and $\mathrm{NPV}_B^{\mathrm{comp}} > 0$ simultaneously.

We can, therefore, formulate the first conclusion. There are two ranges of project values at which coopetition between firms is easy and there is no problem to keep an arrangement: when the project NPV for both companies (excluding the benefits of coopetition) is positive (very high-value projects) or if the value of the investment option is higher than benefits of instantaneous investment (even in the case of being the only investor). In both cases, there are dominant strategies for each party (*Invest* or *Wait*) and these dominant strategies give firms the highest possible payoffs. Their goals and interests are allied. This finding is in line with Liu's (2013) empirical observation that rivals cooperate when common interests are higher than private benefits, and compete on other occasions.

These "other occasions" in our model are investment projects, which present values that lead to relationships: $F_B^i < \text{NPV}$ ($i = \text{coop\_1}, \text{coop\_2}, \text{coop\_3}, \text{comp}$), and $\text{NPV}_B^{\text{comp}} < 0$ (B is the firm with smaller market shares). In this area, games between companies take different forms. In these games, dominant strategies may either not exist or lead to suboptimal payouts (often the worst possible). There are incentives to break the coopetition agreement. This is the area of though or impossible coopetition.

We can distinguish the following games (the general form of the payout matrix for each game is described in Table 9.1):

Game I. It occurs between firms if the present value of the project benefits (V_0) leads to the following relationships between the real option values and the net present value of the project: $\text{NPV}_A^i < 0 < \text{NPV} < F_A^i$ and $\text{NPV}_B^i < 0 < F_B^i < \text{NPV}$ ($i = \text{coop\_1}, \text{coop\_2}, \text{coop\_3}, \text{comp}$). Therefore, in such cases, a dominant strategy for firm A is *Wait*, and the B's best response is the strategy *Invest*. However, if they both invest, they both suffer losses. This is an area for negotiations between companies. Both parties should be interested in cooperation. Support for this cooperation may be other tools of game theory (Rychłowska-Musiał 2018). This is an area of tough coopetition between firms.

Game II. It ensue between firms if the present value of the project benefits (V_0) leads to the following relationships between the real option values and the net present values of the project: $\text{NPV}_A^i < 0 < F_A^i < \text{NPV}$ and $\text{NPV}_B^i < 0 < F_B^i < \text{NPV}$ ($i = \text{coop\_1}, \text{coop\_2}, \text{coop\_3}, \text{comp}$). There is no dominant strategy for any player in this game and a few equilibria. Without coordination, their decisions may lead to the strategy profile (I, I). Obviously (I, I) is the worst possible solution, since both A and B could be better off at strategy (W, W) getting positive payoffs instead of negative ones. This is an area of tough coopetition between firms and reasons for lose–lose situation. However, Liu (2013) revealed that fear of lose–lose situation was vital to drive firm cooperation. We are going to study this issue in the next section.

Game III. It occurs between firms if the present value of the project benefits (V_0) leads to the following relationships: $\text{NPV}_A^i > 0$ and $\text{NPV}_B^i < 0$ ($i = \text{coop}_1, \text{coop}_2, \text{coop}_3, \text{comp}$) (regardless of the relationship between the remaining values). Firm A gains benefits regardless if it is the only investor or both firms invest simultaneously on the market. Firm B bears losses or has to abandon the project. The dominant strategy for firm A is *Invest* and the B' best response is *Wait* what means *Abandon* in this case. It seems that from the perspective of market benefits, the dominant firm has no incentive to cooperate. In accordance with the criteria adopted in the study, coopetition is impossible in this case. As Liu (2013) empirically proved firms would never sacrifice their private benefits for common interests despite rich common benefits from cooperation with rivals.

9.4 Easy or Tough Coopetition. Ranges of Investment Project Values

The analysis in the previous section shows that the value of the project for the weaker company is the important determinant of easy, tough or impossible coopetition between firms. Therefore, the degree of asymmetry between firms market shares is going to be the key factor determining the type of relationship between firms. The second such factor is project risk, which affects the value of the project and the value of the investment option.

We will then carry out a sensitivity analysis that will answer the question of what is the impact of the degree of asymmetry between companies and the risk of the project on the willingness of companies to coopetition. We are going to consider three types of coopetition.

9.4.1 Partial Coopetition: Market Enlarging, no Costs Sharing

When firms benefit only from the market enlarging ($m = 1.2$, e.g. due to more customers or no price war) and there is no other agreements (e.g. investment expenditures sharing) their situation does not much differ from the case of pure competition ($m = 1$). In this case, we can only talk about the coordination of activities to achieve optimal payments (Fig. 9.1).

Compatible optimal strategies (easy coopetition) will only be taken for very low or very high-value project. For the majority of investment projects, strategies coordination will be either tough (Game I and Game II) or impossible (Game III). Note also that with large disparities in market shares, strategy coordination is either easy or impossible (Game III).

9.4.2 Partial Coopetition: Costs Sharing, no Market Enlarging

Cost-sharing is very beneficial for companies. As we can see in Fig. 9.2, the range of project values, for which the coopetition between companies is easy, is very wide. In the small scope of the project's value, we can talk about difficult coopetition, which requires additional solutions/mechanisms to ensure that both parties have the motivation to keep the contract. With the growing difference in market shares, the strategic importance of the weaker company is weakening. The dominant market firm has no incentives to initiate cooperation with a weaker partner. Similarly, to the previous case, when disparities in market shares are very large, coopetition is either

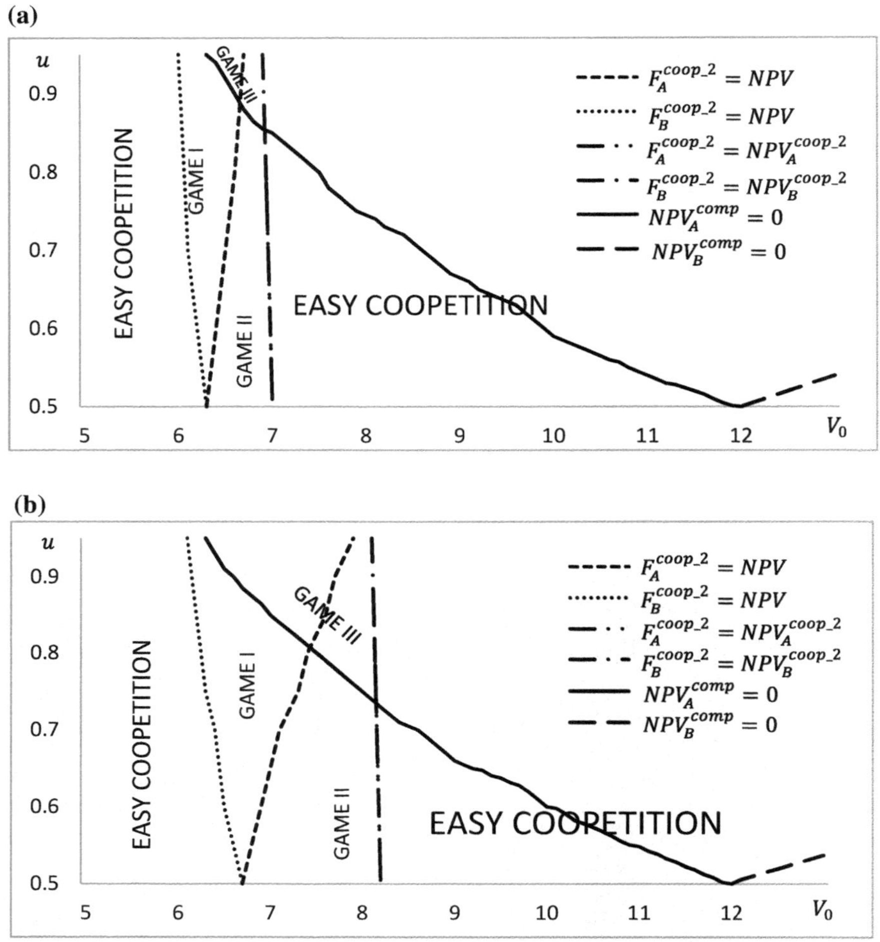

Fig. 9.2 Partial coopetition: Cost-sharing ($n_A = u, n_B = 1-u$), no market enlarging ($m = 1$). The impact of the degree of asymmetry between firms' market shares on the proneness to coopetition. Scopes of easy, tough, or impossible coopetition. Ranges of coopetitive real options games between firms. Panel **a** low risk $\sigma = 20\%$, panel **b** high risk $\sigma = 60\%$

easy or impossible (Game III). This result is consistent with the observations of Gast et al. (2017) who are researching small family firms discovered that coopetition among them (if it happens) tends to be cooperation-dominated.

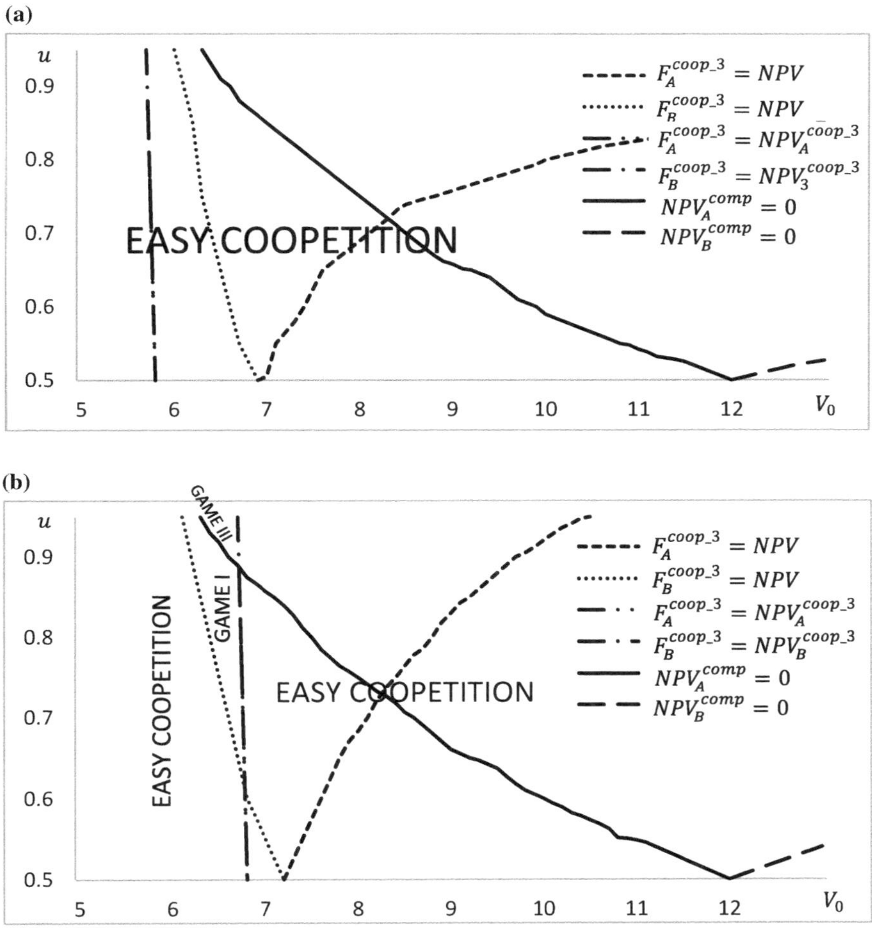

Fig. 9.3 Full coopetition: market enlarging ($m = 1.2$), costs sharing ($n_A = u, n_B = 1 - u$). The impact of the degree of asymmetry between firms' market shares on the proneness to coopetition. Scopes of easy, tough, or impossible coopetition. Ranges of coopetitive real options games between firms. Panel **a** low risk $\sigma = 20\%$, panel **b** high risk $\sigma = 60\%$

9.4.3 Full Coopetition: Market Enlarging, Costs Sharing

This is, of course, the most advantageous form of cooperation, which gives both rival-partners the greatest benefits. In this case, for low-risk projects, ($\sigma = 20\%$) there are conditions for easy coopetition for all project values, and it takes a form or sharing investment options ((W, W) strategy), or joint investment ((I, I) strategy).

If the investment project that is considered by firms is a high-risk project ($\sigma = 60\%$), there is a slight risk that the cooperation between partners may be difficult (for a small range of project values). And a very small risk that cooperation is impossible (in the case of very large disproportion between firms market shares) (Fig. 9.3).

9.5 Benefits of Coopetition

Benefits that the company can achieve as a result of coopetition determine its willingness to this form of cooperation. The tough coopetition is the area of the value of the project, where the lack of an agreement between companies puts them at risk. However, even reaching the agreement is not a guarantee of achieving benefits, because there are strong incentives that encourage both parties to break the contract and seek their own benefits at the expense of the other party.

We will determine the benefits that firms can get as a result of cooperation in areas identified as tough coopetition. We will examine the links between the benefits and the size of the firm's market share and the risk of the project. On this basis, we will try to answer the question, what factors may encourage companies to coopete.

Let's define benefits of coopetition (in the range of tough coopetition) as a percentage share of the difference between F_A^i (or F_B^i) (both firms keep an arrangement and keep their investment options) and $\mathrm{NPV}_A^{\mathrm{comp}}$ (or $\mathrm{NPV}_B^{\mathrm{comp}}$) (both firms invest without agreement—pure competition) in adequate firm's share of the present value of the project $u \cdot V_0$ (or $(1-u) \cdot V_0$) (Table 9.2):

$$\mathrm{Benefits}(A) = \frac{F_A^i - \mathrm{NPV}_A^{\mathrm{comp}}}{u \cdot V_0} \cdot 100\%,$$

$$\mathrm{Benefits}(B) = \frac{F_B^i - \mathrm{NPV}_B^{\mathrm{comp}}}{(1-u) \cdot V_0} \cdot 100\%, \quad (i = \mathrm{coop\_1}, \mathrm{coop\_2}, \mathrm{coop\_3})$$

Table 9.2 Benefits of tough coopetition

	F_A^i	F_B^i	$\mathrm{NPV}_A^{\mathrm{comp}}$	$\mathrm{NPV}_B^{\mathrm{comp}}$	Benefits(A)	Benefits(B)
$i = \mathrm{coop\_1}$	Sigma 20%					
$m = 1.2$	0.32	0.00	−1.31	−4.44	35%	283%
$n_A = 1$, $n_B = 1$	Sigma 60%					
$V_0 = 6.26$	0.98	0.05	−1.31	−4.44	49%	286%
$i = \mathrm{coop\_2}$	Sigma 20%					
$m = 1$	0.43	0.14	−1.31	−4.44	37%	292%
$n_A = u$, $n_B = 1-u$	Sigma 60%					
$V_0 = 6.26$	0.93	0.31	−1.31	−4.44	48%	303%

Remarks: F_A^i (F_B^i)—the investment option value in the case of i-type coopetition for firm A(B), ($i = \mathrm{coop\_1}, \mathrm{coop\_2}$, there is no tough coopetition for $i = \mathrm{coop\_3}$). $\mathrm{NPV}_A^{\mathrm{comp}}$ ($\mathrm{NPV}_B^{\mathrm{comp}}$)—the net present value of the project (benefits of instantaneous investment) in the case of pure competition for firm A(B). Values were calculated for $V_0 = 6.26$

If an investment project value qualifies it for the tough coopetition area, establishing coopetition agreements is advantageous for both companies. Both companies benefit if they establish cooperation and adhere to the terms of the contract. For both rival-partners, the benefits are all the greater, the greater the risk of the project. It may indicate that the greater the risk of the project, the more willing to cooperate are firms, due to the losses accompanying the *lose–lose* strategy.

A weaker company with small market share is benefiting more from the cooperative agreement. However, given the large disparity in market shares, as shown in Sect. 9.4, a stronger company has no incentive to negotiate terms of cooperation and coopetition is not possible.

9.6 Conclusions and Final Remarks

Increasing interdependence between firms operating on competitive markets and the growing necessity for common operations, expenditures and risk sharing, and strategic flexibility are roots of the growing importance of coopetition. Coopetition combines the advantages of both competition and cooperation. Firms and their managers who want to enjoy the benefits of coopetition are also aware of the risks that it entails. They want and need to know what are the chances to meet terms of contract by their partner, or how much will the firm benefit from the coopetition agreement. In the paper, we were looking for answers to these questions on the basis of coopetitive real options games. We considered the case of two firms that can establish a coopetition arrangement to implement an investment project for which they have no exclusivity. The relationships between firms were described as a family of coopetitive real options games.

The analyses carried out in the paper can be summarized in a few findings:

1. If there is no agreement between firms on the investment expenditures sharing, and they can only benefit from the market enlarging as a result of coordination of their strategies, achieving this coordination is almost always either difficult or impossible.
2. If the companies establish a coopetition agreement on sharing the expenditures of the investment project, for the majority of investment projects it will be easy to keep these findings, especially, if projects are low-risk ones or a coopetition agreement provides for the sharing of investment expenditures, and companies also benefit from the market enlarging. Then, none of the parties benefits from breaking of the agreement, there is no incentive to break it.

   The risk of breaking the coopetition arrangement arises if the net present value of the entire project is not much smaller or slightly higher than zero. Then the area of though coopetition appears. This area is all the larger, the higher the risk of the project. There is a temptation to break the agreement and achieve benefits at the expense of rival-partner firm. However, the higher the project risk, the greater

benefits are achieved by each firm by keeping coopetition agreement. The fear of lose–lose situation may encourage companies to keep their agreements.
3. Disproportion in market shares is also a factor affecting the firm's willingness to coopetition. If the difference in market shares is significant, the strategic position of a company with small market share is very weak and if coopetition between firms is not easy, it is impossible.

References

Brandenburger, A. M., & Nalebuff, B. J. (1996). *Co-opetition*. New York: Doubleday.
Brandenburger, A. M., & Stuart, H. (2007). Biform games. *Management Science, 53*(4), 537–549.
Carfi, D. (2010). *A model for coopetitive games* (p. 59633). No: MPRA paper.
Carfi, D., & Schiliro, D. (2012). *A model of coopetitive game for the environmental sustainability of a global green economy* (p. 38508). No: MPRA paper.
Carfi, D., & Schiliro, D. (2013). A model of coopetitive game and the Greek Crisis. *Contributions to Game Theory and Management, 6,* 35–62.
Dagnino, G. B., & Padula, G. (2002). Coopetition strategy. A new kind of interfirm dynamics for value creation, second annual conference. Stockholm: Innovative Research in Management, 9–11 May, 2002.
Das,T. K., & Teng, B. S. (2000). Instabilities of strategic alliances: An internal tensions perspective. *Organization Science, 11*(1), 77–101.
Dixit, A. K., & Pindyck, R. S. (1994). *Investment under uncertainty*. Princeton, New Jersey: Princeton University Press.
Fernandez, A. S., Le Roy, F., & Gnyawali, D. R. (2014). Sources and management of tension in co-opetition case evidence from telecommunications satellites manufacturing in Europe. *Industrial Marketing Management, 43,* 222–235.
Gast, J., Kallmünzer, A., Kraus, S., Gundolf, K., & Arnold, J. (2017). Coopetition of small- and medium-sized family enterprises: Insights from an IT business network. *International Journal of Entrepreneurship and Small Business.*
Gnyawali, D. R., & Park, R. (2009). Co-opetition and technological innovation in small and medium-sized enterprises: A multilevel conceptual model. *Journal of Small Business Management, 47*(3), 308–330.
Liu, R. (2013). Cooperation competition and coopetition in innovation communities. *Prometheus: Critical Studies in Innovation, 31*(2), 91–105.
Luo, Y. (2007). A coopetition perspective of global competition. *Journal of World Business, 42,* 129–144.
Ritala, P. (2012). Competition strategy—when is it succesful? *Empirical Evidence on Innovation and Market Performance, British Journal of Management, 23,* 307–324.
Rodrigues, F., Souza, V., & Leitao, J. (2009). *Strategic coopetition of global brands: A game theory approach to 'Nike +iPod Sport Kit' co-branding* (p. 16146). No: MPRA paper.
Rychłowska-Musiał, E. (2017). Value creation in a firm through coopetition. Real options games approach. In K. Jajuga, L. T. Orlowski & K. Staehr (Eds.), *Contemporary Trends and Challenges in Finance, proceedings from the 2nd wroclaw international conference in finance* (pp. 285–295). Springer Proceedings in Business and Economics, Springer.
Rychłowska-Musiał, E. (2018) Real options games between asymmetric firms on a competitive market. In N. Tsounis & A. Vlachvei (Eds.), *Advances in panel data analysis in applied economic research.* 2017 *International Conference on Applied Economics (ICOAE)* (pp. 299–310). Springer Proceedings in Business and Economics, Springer.
Smit, H. T. J., & Trigeorgis, L. (2004). *Strategic Investment. Real options and games*. Princeton and Oxford: Princeton University Press.

Trigeogris, L., & Baldi, F. (2017). Dynamic hybrid patent strategies: Fight or cooperate? Working paper.

Walley, K. (2007). Coopetition: An Introduction to the subject and an agenda for research. *International Studies of Management & Organization, 37*(2), 11–31.

Chapter 10
Corporate Governance and the Impact of Transferring the Owners' Registered Office to Tax Havens on the Future Financial Position of Slovak Companies

Michal Istok, Hussam Musa, Peter Kristofík and Lea Slampiakova

Abstract The purpose of this work is to examine the association between corporate governance and the financial decision-making process in the areas of tax planning and tax optimization. Specifically, the paper aims at analyzing the impact of moving the Slovak companies' registered office to a tax haven on their future financial position. We have performed statistical testing of selected bankruptcy indicators in Slovak companies. We have compared Altman Z′ score and Index IN05 between Slovak companies with ownership links to selected tax havens (2314) and Slovak companies with no ownership links to tax havens (157,480). For a deeper analysis we have divided tax havens into three categories, onshore, midshore and offshore jurisdictions and performed statistical testing between companies in each of these categories and companies with no ownership links to a tax haven. We have obtained the financial data of all Slovak companies from financial statements provided by Finstat and we have matched this data with the Bisnode database, which lists Slovak companies in tax havens. The results of our analysis showed statistically significant differences in the Altman Z-score as well as in the Index IN05 among the surveyed groups of enterprises. Specifically, businesses with no links to tax havens achieve an average of 55.3% better than the median values of the Altman Z-score and 32.8% higher than the median values of the Index IN05, which means that businesses with no links are on average in the so-called gray zone, whereas companies with tax haven links are on average in a zone where bankruptcy is more likely.

Keywords Altman Z-score · Corporate governance · Index IN05 · Slovak companies · Tax haven

JEL Codes M14

M. Istok · H. Musa · P. Kristofík · L. Slampiakova (✉)
Faculty of Economics, Matej Bel University in Banska Bystrica, Tajovskeho 10, 975 90 Banská Bystrica, Slovakia
e-mail: lea.slampiakova@umb.sk

N. Tsounis and A. Vlachvei (eds.), *Advances in Cross-Section Data Methods in Applied Economic Research*, Springer Proceedings in Business and Economics,
https://doi.org/10.1007/978-3-030-38253-7_10

10.1 Introduction

The phrase corporate governance can be considered a new phenomenon since it appeared in the last twenty years. Schleifer and Vishny (1997) claim that corporate governance deals with the ways in which suppliers of financial instruments to firms assure themselves of getting a return on their investment. The development of corporate governance was influenced by theories from a variety of fields including economics, finance, management, accounting, tax planning, and law. In recent years, the authors of numerous studies have researched the relationship between corporate governance and other aspects of financial management. In terms of the Slovak Republic, Musa et al. (2017) focused on the relationship of gender equality and corporate governance, and they confirmed the correlation between women on the board and the level of corporate governance. The correlation analysis between corporate governance and the financial decision-making process was examined by Musa et al. (2015) in the area of dividend policies and indebtedness.

In our paper, we have studied the financial decision-making process in the area of international tax planning, tax optimization and the future financial position of Slovak companies. Moreover, we have examined the impact of the transfer of the registered office of Slovak companies to tax havens on the selected prediction bankruptcy indicators (selected indicators of ex-ante financial analysis).

10.2 Theoretical Background

The controversial use of tax havens has already been researched by the academic community from different points of view. Tax havens allow companies to shift profit from a high tax jurisdiction to a low tax jurisdiction, most commonly via transfer pricing (Eden 2009). There's also typically a high degree of secrecy and an extremely low (sometimes even zero) rate of corporate income taxation. In general, by relocating the registered office to a tax haven, companies expect a variety of benefits mainly in the areas of ultimate beneficial owner anonymity, asset management, asset protection, flexible ownership arrangements and tax planning and tax optimization. Although it is difficult to identify the order of importance of the above-mentioned benefits by an external view, we can, based on available data, identify certain trends and selected financial flows and indicators.

The impact of corporate governance on the relationship between corporate tax avoidance and financial constraints was examined by Bayar et al. (2018). Their results suggest that tax avoidance in companies with poor corporate governance is associated with greater financial constraints and a greater likelihood of financial distress. However, in firms with strong corporate governance, they found that moving a company's registered office to a tax haven does not have a negative impact on financial constraints. Their results suggest that stronger governance mechanisms can help companies diminish the negative consequences of transferring their registered office to low tax jurisdictions. However, tax avoidance is a less useful source of gaining some extra financing instruments for constrained firms when they are plagued with potential agency problems and/or an opaque information environment. The impact of corporate governance on tax avoidance was empirically studied by Tandean and Winnie (2016). Their results show that while the audit committee has a positive effect on tax avoidance, the executive character, company size, institutional ownership and boards of commissioners have simultaneous effects on defining tax avoidance.

Therefore, there are two possible results that companies could achieve by moving their registered office to a tax haven in relation to their future financial situation. On one side, low tax jurisdictions can be used by companies to create a competitive advantage by reducing corporate funding costs or the cost of capital (Oxelheim et al 1998). Based on this statement, moving a company's office to a tax haven could improve their financial stability and improve their future financial performance measured by the bankruptcy indicator. On the other side, the predictive potential of bankruptcy prediction models is based on some significant factors, which include among others, values of net working capital, EBIT, retained earnings, total equity, cost interest and current assets. Companies could use tax havens to gain specific benefits by reducing the value of assets or shifting their profit. Such behavior was proven by numerous empirical studies. For instance, Godar's (2018) paper implies that a one-percent point decrease in the average foreign tax rate faced by companies reduces the reported profits by 4.8%. In the Slovak business environment, Ištok et al. (2018) proved that there is a statistically significant difference in reported values of land and structures after companies have moved to a tax haven. Most of the Slovak companies showed a decrease in the given area. Ištok and Kanderová (2019) carried out an analysis of the impact of the transferring of Slovak companies registered offices to tax havens on the interest expenses as a technique of profit shifting. Their study showed that Slovak companies usually use debt financing techniques, respectively, the interest deductible expenses for profit shifting to tax heavens. Our analysis tries to complete the tax haven puzzle by examining the future financial position of given Slovak companies.

Based on the above-mentioned studies we assume that transferring a company's registered office to a low tax jurisdiction will result in a worsening of the prediction bankruptcy indicators.

10.3 Methodology and Data

This article aims at assessing the likelihood of bankruptcy among Slovak companies located in tax havens in comparison with companies with no links to tax havens. There exist many bankruptcy models that are able to classify companies into prosperous ones, declining or at risk of bankruptcy, based on their financial data. The goal of these models is to achieve the highest accuracy. In terms of Slovak and Czech companies, model validations were made in several studies. While Delina and Packová (2013) as well as Lesáková and Gundová (2015) proved a higher accuracy of the Index

IN05 than the Altman Z-score, Gundová (2014) proved that the highest accuracy was achieved by the Ohlson model while the lowest accuracy was from the Index IN05. Based on the results of Gavurova et al. (2017), the Ohlson model should not be applicable within Slovak conditions as it reached the lowest bankruptcy prediction ability. They also proved that the Index IN05 is the most appropriate model for the Slovak business environment. Therefore, we have decided to analyze two indicators: The Altman Z-score, which is the most commonly used one worldwide, and the Index IN05.

- Altman 5-factor model is the most commonly used one worldwide. This model is based on the multidimensional discriminant analysis method and is the most successful one within the given methodology. Since we have examined not only companies traded on the capital markets, we have used revised the Altman model.
- Zones of discrimination for private firms are defined as:

  - $Z' > 2.9$ Safe zone
  - $1.23 < Z' < 2.9$ Gray Zone
  - $Z' < 1.23$ Distress zone

Altman Z' *score* = 0.717 * *Net working capital/Total assets* + 0.847 * *Retained earnings/Total assets* + 3.107 * *EBIT/Total assets* + 0.420 * *The capital/Outside capital* + 0.998 * *Turnover (sales)/Total equity.*

- Index IN05 is the model that has achieved the best accuracy within the conditions of the Czech and Slovak Republics.
- Zones of discrimination for private firms are defined as:

  - $Z' > 1.6$ Safe zone
  - $0.9 < Z' < 1.6$ Gray Zone
  - $Z' < 0.9$ Distress zone

IN05 = 0.13 * *Total equity/Outside capital* +0.04 * *EBIT/Cost interest* +9.97 * *EBIT/Total capital* +0.21 * *Total revenues/Total assets* +0.09 * *Current assets/(Current liabilities + Current bank loans).*

Firstly, we analyzed the Altman Z-score and the Index IN05 only for businesses with a link to a tax haven and without links to tax havens in general. Since there is a high variability with the data, we have focused on the median values of the indicators, not averages. To test statistically the significant difference between the selected indicators, the nonparametric Mann–Whitney test was used because the data did not meet the assumptions of the parametric *t*-tests. In order to broaden our study, we have also tested our assumptions in jurisdictions marked as tax havens which we divide into three categories:

(a) OFFSHORE JURISDICTIONS (OFF): Bahamas, Belize, Bermuda, British Virgin Islands, Gibraltar, Guernsey (United Kingdom), Jersey (United Kingdom), Cayman Islands, Marshall Islands, the Netherlands Antilles, Panama, Man Island, and Seychelles;

(b) MIDSHORE JURISDICTIONS (MID): Hong Kong, Cyprus, Malta, United Arab Emirates, United States of America;
(c) ONSHORE JURISDICTIONS (ON): Liechtenstein, Latvia, Luxembourg, Monaco, and the Netherlands.

The financial data of all Slovak companies was obtained from the financial statements' dataset provided by Finstat. The list of companies located in tax havens was obtained from the Bisnode database. Statistical processing was performed using statistical software SPSS.

In order to carry out a more detailed analysis of the future financial position of companies in lower tax jurisdictions, we have decided to categorize those jurisdictions. This approach was also used by some authors in analyzing the profit shifting behavior by testing multinational companies' ownership links to individual tax havens rather than to groups of them (e.g. Jánsky and Kokeš 2016). Similarly, Ištok et al. (2019) carried out a detailed study of given jurisdiction categories in the Slovak business environment where they examined the possible links between companies´ characterization criteria. Their results confirmed that there is a statistically significant relationship between the jurisdiction category (specifically onshore and midshore ones) and three parameters: the NACE sector, the size of share capital invested and ownership interests.

Classification of jurisdictions, respectively, tax havens, is the most common in both academic and professional literature to onshore and offshore ones. While the inclusion of jurisdictions in the offshore category is almost automatic (so-called pure tax havens), other jurisdictions are sometimes further divided between onshore and midshore. A separate midshore category list, e.g., Valencia (2013), which includes jurisdictions such as Hong Kong, United Arab Emirates or Malta and Cyprus. The main difference between onshore and midshore jurisdictions is mainly the cost of establishing and managing a foreign company (respectively corporate structure settings) and their usability (flexibility) for different levels of tax avoidance.

Offshore companies (jurisdictions) are primarily used to achieve anonymity of the ultimate beneficial owner (UBO), midshore companies mostly for tax optimization and tax planning and onshore companies for the purpose of asset protection, asset management and flexible arrangement of ownership relations. We have examined the Slovak companies whose owners reside in selected jurisdictions marked as tax havens (equity links—formation of international holdings).

10.4 Results and Discussion

The results of the analysis are structured into two complementary parts. The first one is focused on analyzing the bankruptcy prediction indicators between companies in tax havens in comparison to general companies in Slovakia (no ownership links to tax havens). The second one deals with a more detailed analysis of achieved results among companies in three different types of low tax jurisdictions and those with no links.

10.4.1 Bankruptcy Prediction Indicators Analysis (Altman Z-Score and Index IN05)

Based on the empirical studies which proved that companies usually transfer their registered offices to lower tax jurisdictions in order to reduce the reported profits and/or to reduce the reported values of land and structures (Godar 2018; Ištok et al. 2018; Ištok a Kanderová 2019) we assume that companies in tax havens will show worsened bankruptcy prediction indicators. There is data available for 160,693 Slovak companies since we have excluded companies that reported incorrect data (missing values of factors needed for the calculation of such indicators). In addition, we have also excluded companies where at least one of the indicators was showing an outlier (2%), which could distort the results of statistical tests. We have data available for 2314 companies with ownership links to tax havens, due to matching the data provided by Bisnode with the data available at Finstat. We reduced the large difference between the number of companies with links (2314) and without links to tax havens (157,480) by conducting a random selection of 5% of the ordinary companies (7874). We have statistically tested and compared the selected indicators. The base descriptive statistics of the Altman Z-score and Index IN05 are shown in Table 10.1.

Due to the extremely high variability of the given indicators, the arithmetic average has a low reporting ability, so we have focused on median values in the evaluation with respect to the diameter. In the case of both predictive indicators (Altman Z-score and Index IN05), the higher their value, the lower the probability of bankruptcy in the near future. In our sample of companies analyzed, the median value of both indicators is lower for companies that are located in jurisdictions marked as tax havens. Specifically, to determine if there are statistically significant differences between groups of companies with links and without links to tax havens, we performed the Mann–Whitney Test. We determined the significance level at 5%. The test results are shown in Table 10.2.

The nonparametric Mann–Whitney test showed a statistically significant difference in values as both the Altman Z-score indicator and the Index IN05. This confirms our assumption that companies that have moved or established their headquarters in

Table 10.1 Descriptive characteristics of bankruptcy prediction indicators

Altman Z-score		With links	With no links	Index 05		With links	With no links
N	Valid	2314	7874	*N*	Valid	2314	7874
	Missing	0	0		Missing	0	0
Mean		2.6273	−0.7265	Mean		218.2296	−3.8757
Median		1.0411	2.3317	Median		0.8391	1.2481
Std. Deviation		60.00130	57.82690	Std. Deviation		384.09560	4987.57420

Source Own processing by the software SPSS

Table 10.2 Mann–Whitney test (bankruptcy prediction indicators)

Rank					Test statistics[a]		
		N	Mean rank	Sum of ranks		Altman *Z*-score	Index 05
Altman *Z*-score	With links	2314	4477.78	10316816.50	Mann–Whitney U	7661456.500	8456877.500
	With no links	7874	5268.49	41484114.50	Wilcoxon W	10316816.50	11112237.50
	Total	10,175			*Z*	−11.363	−4.923
Index 05	With links	2314	4823.02	11112237.50	Asymp. Sig. (2-tailed)	0.000	0.000
	With no links	7874	5165.57	40658162.50			
	Total	10,175					

[a]Grouping variable: company links to tax heaven
Source Own processing by the software SPSS

low tax jurisdictions have a less stable financial position and thus a greater risk of bankruptcy in the near future.

Given the fact that individual low tax jurisdictions have different conditions for the establishment and subsequent operation of a company, it is clear that businesses choose the jurisdiction of their operation for various reasons. In general, jurisdictions can be divided into onshore, midshore, and offshore. For a more detailed picture of the impact of tax avoidance on predictive indicators, we conducted statistical testing of the significance in values between companies in different categories of jurisdictions and businesses that are not linked to tax havens. We assume that the most significant differences will be in onshore and midshore jurisdictions, as offshore is primarily used to acquire owner anonymity. However, onshore and midshore jurisdictions also offer tax optimization and asset protection. The basic descriptive statistics of enterprises in each category of jurisdiction is shown in Table 10.3.

Most businesses are located in midshore jurisdictions, with businesses in this category reaching the lowest median of both indicators. The Altman *Z*-score is at 0.8, which is a "distress zone" where there is a high risk of bankruptcy over the next two years. The Index IN05 reached 0.72, which is also a zone where the company does not generate value and is likely to go bankrupt. Offshore jurisdictions are in the bankruptcy zone on the basis of the Altman model, but based on the Index IN05 they are in a zone with an uncertain future financial situation. The best results are reported by enterprises in the onshore zone which have achieved in both indicators results for which they are included in the gray zone. The Kruskal–Wallis Test was used to test the statistical significance of the differences in the indicators (Table 10.4).

Since the *p*-value is less than our 5% significance level, it is clear that there are statistically significant differences between the different groups of companies according to the jurisdiction in which they have a registered office for both bankruptcy

Table 10.3 Descriptive characteristics of indicators in given categories of jurisdictions

Jurisdiction			Altman *Z*-score	Index 05
ON	*N*	Valid	977	977
		Missing	0	0
	Mean		8.1698	259.1600
	Median		1.3561	0.9755
	Std. Deviation		247.65920	5249.81890
MID	*N*	Valid	1020	1020
		Missing	0	0
	Mean		36.6849	260.8971
	Median		0.8036	0.7211
	Std. Deviation		495.01550	5462.03410
OFF	*N*	Valid	317	317
		Missing	0	0
	Mean		55.1173	36.6974
	Median		0.9787	1.0512
	Std. Deviation		548.38120	446.04560

Source Own processing by the software SPSS

Table 10.4 Kruskal–Wallis test (bankruptcy prediction indicators)

Rank				Test statistics[a]		
		N	Mean rank		Altman *Z*-score	Index 05
Altman *Z*-score	with no links	7874	5268.49	Kruskal–Wallis H	130.495	31.316
	OFF	317	4651.07	D*f*	3.00	3.00
	MID	1020	4294.02	Asymp. Sig.	0000	0000
	ON	977	4671.81			
		N	Mean rank			
Index 05	with no links	7874	5165.57			
	OFF	317	4974.57			
	MID	1020	4627.17			
	ON	977	5033.11			

[a]Kruskal–Wallis test
[b]Grouping variable: company jurisdiction
Source Own processing by the software SPSS

prediction indicators. The Mann–Whitney Test was used to determine specifically between which groups of companies there are statistically significant differences. Since in the execution of this test the first kind of error often occurs, it is recommended (Field 2005) to implement Bonferroni's correction. The first kind of error is a state where we reject the null hypothesis of equality of mean values in a set even if it is true. Since we divide businesses into four independent files, using Bonferroni's correction, the original 5% significance level is reduced to 0.83%.

Based on the post hoc test, it is clear that there are statistically significant differences between the Altman Z-score, which do not have links to tax havens and each category of enterprise in each low tax jurisdiction. However, according to Gavurova et al. (2017) the Index IN05 achieves a significantly higher probability of a correct prediction of the future financial situation in the Slovak Republic. At the same time, statistically significant differences between the values of this indicator were achieved only among the group of enterprises in midshore jurisdictions (Table 10.5).

Our results confirm that the countries listed by Bisnode in the midshore category provide businesses with the greatest opportunities for tax optimization and relief. In other words, businesses that have moved or established their headquarters in midshore jurisdictions are using tax optimization and asset protection options in a way that ultimately affects their likely future financial situation.

Table 10.5 Mann–Whitney test (bankruptcy prediction indicators among each category of jurisdictions)

Test statistics[a]

Jurisdiction		Altman *Z*-score	Index 05
With no links—OFF	Mann–Whitney U	1098471.50	1200946.50
	Wilcoxon W	1148874.50	1251349.50
	Z	−3623	−1.129
	Asymp. Sig. (2-tailed)	0.00	0.26
With no links—MID	Mann–Whitney U	3249065.50	3591959.00
	Wilcoxon W	3769775.50	4112669.00
	Z	−9.94	−5.48
	Asymp. Sig. (2-tailed)	0.00	0.00
With no links—ON	Mann–Whitney U	3392659.50	37426343.00
	Wilcoxon W	3870412.50	4220396.00
	Z	−6.03	−1.36
	Asymp. Sig. (2-tailed)	0.00	0.17

[a]Grouping variable: company links to tax haven
Source Own processing by the software SPSS

10.5 Discussion

The issue of tax havens is currently a commonly discussed topic in the academic and professional spheres. The use of tax havens provides businesses with benefits that, on the one hand, can offer a competitive advantage (Oxelheim et al. 1998), but on the other hand it also provides scope for activities that can cause financial difficulties in the case of weak corporate governance (Bayar et al. 2018). From ex-ante analysis, respectively, the ability to predict the development of the company's financial situation is based on an assessment of the results achieved by the company at present and allows for a better picture of business behavior in practice and its likely future financial situation. Specifically, the Altman *Z*-score. The Index IN05 includes indicators that link results from asset management, tax planning, profit reporting, and the use of debt finance instruments. Previous research in the Slovak Republic pointed to a tendency for greater use of debt (Ištok and Kanderová 2019), asset value reduction (Ištok et al. 2018) and a reduction in reported earnings (Godar 2018). Our research has complemented the "tax haven puzzle" with information that companies based in low tax jurisdictions achieve statistically significantly worse results in the predictive indicators than Slovak businesses with no ownership links to tax havens. The biggest differences are in the case of midshore jurisdictions, which we also expected at the beginning of the analysis due to the fact that midshore jurisdictions (especially Cyprus) are most often used by Slovak companies because of the relatively low costs needed to set up and manage the company and the possible use of relatively intense profit-shifting techniques.

Based on our research to date, this article is the first to look at the impact of moving a company headquarters to tax havens on predictive indicators. Since it would be appropriate to focus further research on a more detailed examination of the issue, it would be interesting to find out the differences between the median values of the selected indicators in companies divided by sector as well as company size.

10.6 Conclusion

The aim of the article was to explore the association between corporate governance and the financial decision-making process in the areas of international tax planning and optimization. In particular, the work focuses on analyzing the impact of establishing a business in low tax jurisdictions on the value of predictive indicators, Altman *Z*-score and Index IN05. We examined 2314 businesses in tax havens, with 317 of them offshore, 1020 in midshore and 977 in onshore jurisdictions. We compared the given categories of businesses with classical Slovak companies that have no ownership links to tax havens. In order to make our files comparable in size, we made a random selection of 5% (7874) from the given data (157,480).

In the case of the Altman *Z*-score, there are statistically significant differences between each of our tax haven categories and businesses with no links to tax havens.

The best result is achieved by the indicator in the enterprise group with no links to tax havens (2.33), which means that companies are in a gray zone when their future financial situation is uncertain. The median index of businesses in onshore jurisdictions is significantly lower, but the businesses are still in the so-called gray zone, although close to the lower values of the interval. However, companies based in midshore and offshore jurisdictions have a lower median value (0.80 and 0.98), which puts them in a high probability of bankruptcy in the next two years.

The Index IN05 indicator has slightly different results. Significant differences are only between businesses in midshore jurisdictions that are known to have the largest tax and businesses with no links to tax havens. In particular, the highest indicator values are achieved by businesses with no links to tax havens (1.25), which classify them into zones with an undefined future financial situation. Enterprises in the onshore and offshore jurisdictions have achieved similar indicator median values (0.98 and 1.05), which also rank them in the so-called "offshore" jurisdictions gray zone. Businesses in midshore jurisdictions (0.72) have achieved the worst performance of the indicator, thus risking potential bankruptcy over the next two years.

Acknowledgements This work has been supported by the Scientific Grant Agency of Slovak Republic under project VEGA No. 1/0749/18. Research on the application of corporate governance principles in companies in Slovakia.

References

Bayar, O., Huseynov, F., & Sardarli, S. (2018). Corporate governance, tax avoidance, and financial constraints. *Financial Management, 47*(3), 651–677. https://doi.org/10.1111/fima.12208.

Delina, R., & Packová, M. (2013). Validation of bankruptcy prediction models in the Slovak environment. *E&M Economics and management, 16*(3), 101–112.

Eden, L. (2009). Taxes, transfer pricing and the multinational enterprise. In A. M. Rugman (Ed.), *The Oxford handbook of international business* (2nd ed., pp. 557–590). Oxford: Oxford University Press. https://doi.org/10.1093/oxfordhb/9780199234257.003.0021.

Gavurova, B., Packova, M., Misankova, M., & Smrcka, L. (2017). Predictive potential and risks of selected bancruptcy prediction models in the Slovak business environment. *Journal of Business Economics and Management, 18*(6), 1156–1173. https://doi.org/10.3846/16111699.2017.1400461.

Godar, S. (2018). Tax haven investors and corporate profitability-evidence of profit shifting by German-based affiliates. In *IES Working Papers 36/2018, IES FSV*. Charles University.

Gundova, P. (2014). Verification of the selected prediction methods in Slovak companies. *Acta Academica Karviniensia, 14*(4), 26–38. https://doi.org/10.25142/aak.2014.065.

Istok, M., & Kanderova, M. (2019). Interest expenses as a technique of profit shifted used by Slovak Companies. In *Hradec Economic days 2019* (pp. 292–305), University of Hradec Hralové. ISSN 2464-6067.

Istok, M., Kanderova, M., & Kristofik, P., (2018). The impact of moving the owners´ registered office to tax havens on the reported values of land and stuctures. In *Interantional Scientific Conference Managing and Modelling of Financial Risks* (pp. 195–204). Ostrava. ISSN 2464-6989.

Istok, M., Kanderova, M., Kristofik, P., & Scerba, K. (2019). International corporate structuring of slovak companies using tax havens. *Journal of Competitiveness, 11*(1), 22–40. https://doi.org/10.7441/joc.2019.01.02.

Jánsky, P., & Kokeš, O. (2016). Profit-shifting from Czech multinational companies to European tax havens. *Applied Economics Letters, 23*(16), 1130–1133. https://doi.org/10.1080/13504851.2015.1137543.
Lesáková, Ľ., & Gundová, P. (2015). Modification of financial health prediction model for Slovak companies, *Journal of Economics and Social Research, 16*(1), 14–24. ISSN 1335–7069.
Musa, M., Debnárová, L., Musová, Z., & Krištofík, P. (2017). Gender equality and corporate governance in Slovakia. *E&M Economics and management*, *XX*(1), 98–110. https://dx.doi.org/10.15240/tul/001/2017-1-007.
Musa, M., Musová, Z., & Debnárová, L. (2015). Responsibility in the corporate governance framework and financial decision making proces. *Procedia Economics and Finance, 23,* 1023–1029. https://doi.org/10.1016/S2212-5671(15)00371-8.
Oxelheim, L., Stonehill, A., Randoy, T., Vikkula, K., Dullum, K., B., & Modén, K. M. (1998). *Corporate strategies to internationalise the cost of capital* (pp. 334). Copenhaugen Business School Press. ISBN 9788716132710.
Shleifer, A., & Vishny, R. W. (1997). A survey of corporate governance. *The Journal of Finance*, *52*(2), 737–783. https://www.jstor.org/stable/2329497.
Tandean, V. A., & Winnie, W. (2016). The effect of good corporate governance on tax avoidance: an empirical study on manufacturing companies listed in IDX period 2010–2013. *Asian Journal of Accounting Research*, *1*(1), 28–38. https://doi.org/10.1108/AJAR-2016-01-01-B004.
Valencia, M. (2013). Storm survivors. The Economist. Available at https://www.economist.com/special-report/2013/02/16/storm-survivors.

Chapter 11
Temporary Incapacity for Work in the Context of Legislative Changes in Sickness Insurance in the Czech Republic

Ivana Košturíková

Abstract The aim of the paper is to evaluate the impact of legislative changes in the area of sickness insurance on temporary incapacity for work in the Czech Republic. Temporary incapacity for work is presented by their indicators (number of new cases of TIW per 100 insured persons, average duration of one case of TIW and average percentage of TIW). Using regression analysis, the development of individual indicators in the following years based on knowledge of the development of indicators in the years 2000–2017 is estimated. The research results are captured using trend line which displays the possible development in the Czech Republic in the following years. Regression equation presents an approximation of the entered values where the coefficients are determined by the method of least squares, so that the sum of squared deviations of the original values from obtained model would be minimum. The R^2 index expresses the degree of reliability of the calculated estimate of the development. There was a rapid decline in the number of cases of incapacity for work, which stopped in 2013, when the values of this indicator slowly pick up an increasing trend. The average percentage of temporary incapacity for work was similar in the same course. On the other hand, the average duration of one case of TIW gradually increased from 28 days to 42.6 days.

Keywords Temporary incapacity for work · Employee · Social security · Sickness insurance · Sickness benefits

JEL Codes I13 · I18 · J17

I. Košturíková (✉)
Department of Finance and Accounting, School of Business Administration in Karviná, Silesian University in Opava, Univerzitní Nám 1934/3, 733 40 Karviná, Czech Republic
e-mail: kosturikova@opf.slu.cz

N. Tsounis and A. Vlachvei (eds.), *Advances in Cross-Section Data Methods in Applied Economic Research*, Springer Proceedings in Business and Economics,
https://doi.org/10.1007/978-3-030-38253-7_11

11.1 Introduction

The sickness insurance system is intended for employed persons who are provided with cash sickness insurance benefits in the event of loss of income in cases of temporary incapacity for work due to illness, accident, quarantine, family member care, pregnancy and maternity or child care.

A significant research in the area of sickness insurance has been performed in the Scandinavian countries, especially in Sweden and Norway, where not only the historical development of the Swedish social insurance system and its reform has been researched (Edebalk 2009), but also the processes of reforming sickness insurance in Norway and Sweden has been compared (Hagelung and Bryngelson 2014). Ståhl et al. (2011) researched the effect of changes in the Swedish sickness insurance system on the return to work with a special focus on work ability assessments, and Larsson (2006) is engaged in the interactions between unemployment and sickness insurance. A similar research was performed by Hall (2011). Hägglund (2013) also researched the impact of changes in the Swedish sickness insurance system on incapacity for work, respectively, on the employees' return to work.

The impact of reforms in the sickness insurance system was also researched in Germany by Ziebarth and Karlsson (2014); one of the areas of research was the matter how the increase of sickness benefits affects a duration of incapacity for work.

Besides other things, the Act no. 187/2006 Coll., on sickness insurance was approved as a part of the reform of public finances. This Act became effective 1 January 2009 and provides a comprehensive adjustment of the sickness insurance for all persons who are participated in this insurance. During 2008, there were made the adjustments in sickness insurance three times, and the aim of these legislative changes was to increase the motivation of employees and employers to reduce disproportionately high incapacity for work.

The aim of the paper is to evaluate the impact of legislative changes in the area of sickness insurance on temporary incapacity for work (TIW) in the Czech Republic, which is presented by the main indicators, the number of new cases of TIW per 100 insured persons, the average duration of one case of TIW and the average percentage of TIW.

11.2 Sickness Insurance in the Czech Republic

Sickness insurance is a part of social security, and its task is to insure people participating in this system by the insurance benefits at law intended social events in order to reduce or completely eliminate the effects of these events (Sirovátka 1997).

11.2.1 Balance of Sickness Insurance

There were changes in the sphere of sickness insurance lately because revenues generated from the sickness insurance to the state budget was not enough to cover expenses to pecuniary sickness benefits, which are paid from insurance revenues (Krebs).

As we can see in t2007he following figure, there has been a decrease in expenditures on sickness benefits since 2004, which was caused partly by changes in the structure of sickness benefits and partly by reducing rates. In 2008, there were further changes in sickness benefits within the stabilization of public finances, which included new four percentage rates depending on the duration of incapacity for work, and sickness benefits have been provided since the fourth day of the incapacity for work. Based on the findings of the constitutional court, sickness benefits were provided again amounting to 60% for the first three days since 30 June 2008 and then amounting to 25% since 1 September of this year. The result was a significant increase in the ratio of sickness insurance income and expenditure on sickness benefits. In 2009, there was another reduction in insurance rates (decrease of 2.1 pp), which caused a significant decline in insurance income. The graph shows that the sickness insurance system showed a deficit in that year, but the situation in the following year turned, and this trend still continues. The reasons for decrease of expenditures are the payment of refund of wages by employers and also decrease of number of temporary incapacity for work (TIW) (Fig. 11.1).

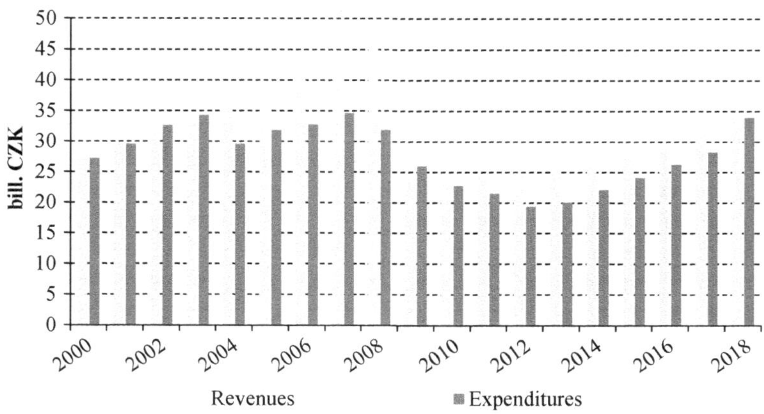

Fig. 11.1 Balance of sickness insurance in the CR (in bill. CZK). *Source* Own processing according to MLSA (2017) and CSSA (2018)

11.2.2 Legislative Regulation

In the Czech Republic, since 1 January 2009, sickness insurance has been regulated by Act no. 187/2006 Coll., on sickness insurance, as amended. It is a comprehensive adjustment of sickness insurance, which includes both the group of persons participating in sickness insurance, their entitlements from this insurance and the determination of the amount of provided benefits, health assessment for the purposes of sickness insurance and the organization of sickness insurance and management in this insurance.

Sickness insurance as part of social insurance is obligatory for a majority of Czech citizens—i.e. they are required by law to pay this insurance (Tröster 2005). Compulsory participants of the sickness insurance are employees, who receive or could receive wages or salaries from employers, regardless of the type of employment relationship, as opposed to self-employed persons whose participation in sickness insurance is voluntary Gregorová and Galvas (2000).

Participation in sickness insurance commences on the date of entry into employment and expires on the date of termination of employment (Ženíškova and Přib 2011). According Novotný (2013), the law laid down the conditions for participation in the sickness insurance system together with the subsequent claim for payment of benefits, and these include:

- the performance of gainful employment on the territory of the Czech Republic,
- the minimum level of agreed income, i.e. the applicable income,
- an assessable income in an amount higher than CZK 10,000 for employees under contracts for performed work (CPW).

Table 11.1 shows the development of applicable income, which constitutes mandatory participation in sickness insurance.

The amount of the insurance is calculated as a percentage of the assessment base for the relevant period. As for employees, the insurance as a percentage of social security and state employment policy is partly paid by the employee himself and partly by the employer from the gross wage. In order to provide wage compensation, amounting to half of the salary, during the first period of incapacitation the insurance rate was reduced by 1% point in 2009 and 2010. The premium rate for both employers and self-employed persons for sickness insurance has been set at 2.3% of the assessment base since 2011. From 1 July 2019, the so-called waiting period is cancelled, and employees' wages are paid for the first three days. Therefore, the

Table 11.1 Development of applicable income for sickness insurance

Period	Applicable income
2009–2011	2 000 CZK
2012–2018	2 500 CZK
2019	3 000 CZK

Source Own processing according to MLSA (https://www.mpsv.cz/cs/7)

Table 11.2 Development of sickness insurance rates

Person	2009–2010 (%)	2011–06/2019 (%)	From 1. 7. 2019 (%)
Employee	0.0	0.0	0.0
Foreign employee	1.4	2.3	2.1
Employer	2.3	2.3	2.1
Self-employed	1.4	2.3	2.1

Source Own processing according to MLSA (https://www.mpsv.cz/cs/7)

employer's sickness insurance rate is reduced to 2.1%. The rate of sickness insurance premiums for foreign employees and self-employed persons is reduced by 0.2% in view of uniformity in rates. Table 11.2 shows the development of sickness insurance rates by payers.

11.2.3 Sickness Benefits

The sickness insurance system of benefits comprises four benefits, namely sickness benefit, attendance allowance, maternity benefit and pregnancy and maternity compensation benefit. With the changes in total expenditure on sickness insurance, there was a change in the structure of these expenditures by the benefit type (Fig. 11.2). The most significant change was the decrease in sickness benefit expenditure, which led to a reduction in its share of total sickness insurance expenditure, thereby increasing the share of other benefits. Expenditure on sickness benefits accounted for 67.2% of

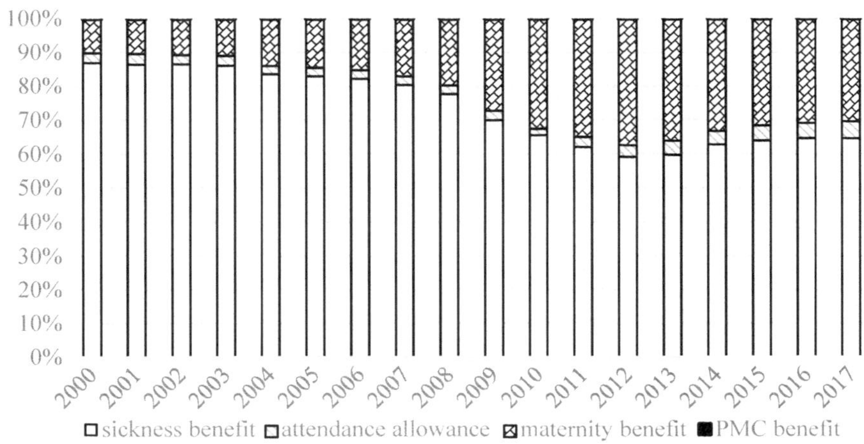

Fig. 11.2 Percentage distribution of expenditure on individual sickness insurance benefits. *Source* Own processing according to CSO data (https://www.czso.cz/)

total sickness insurance expenditure in 2017. In 2000, the share of sickness benefit expenditure was 19.7 pp higher. The data for 2018 have not been published yet.

Since 1993, when the above-mentioned Act on social security insurance and contribution to the state employment policy came into force, there have been many changes in the calculation of sickness benefits. The amount of these benefits started to be counted from the gross income of employees attained in the previous calendar quarter, and at the same time, the rates for the calculation of benefits were reduced. In 1999, the reduction limits were introduced, of which sickness benefits are subsequently calculated.

Since 1 January 2009, a new Act no. 187/2006 Coll., of sickness insurance has become effective and brought a radical transformation in sickness insurance and sickness benefits in particular. Among the most significant changes related to the new legal regulation are in particular:

- payment of refund of wages or salary during the first 14 days,
- payment of sickness benefits only from the 15th calendar day of incapacity for work,
- sickness insurance for all insured persons (other than members of the armed forces and safety brigades, persons in custody and convicted persons) is already performed only by social security administrations district offices.

Since 1 January 2011, changes occurred in the payment of sickness benefits by amendment to Act, which were provided from the 22nd day of incapacity for work. This situation was in force to 31 December 2013, and then, it returned to its original duration, i.e. those sickness benefits are again provided from the 15th day until the end of TIW, but not more than 380 calendar days from the beginning of TIW.

Another significant change occurred 1 January 2012, ever since the amendment of the Labour Code introduced a participation in sickness insurance for employees who practise their jobs under CPW at the agreed income higher than CZK 10,000 (Hulec 2012). Since that time these employees have also been entitled to sickness

Table 11.3 Changes in sickness benefits in the years 2009–2018

Year	Provision of benefits	
	Period	Daily rate (%)
2009	From 15th to 30th day	60
	From 31st to 60th day	66
	From the 61st day	72
2010	From the 15th day	60
2011–2013	From the 22nd day	60
2014–2017	From the 15th day	60
2018	From 15th to 30th day	60
	From 31st to 60th day	66
	From the 61st day	72

Source Own processing according to MLSA (2017)

benefits, if certain conditions are met. Changes in the provision of sickness benefits in 2009–2018 are shown in Table 11.3.

11.3 Temporary Incapacity for Work in the Czech Republic

The reason for the above-described changes in sickness insurance was too high income solidarity, insufficient control mechanisms and, unfortunately, widespread abuse of the system. Although the state of health of the population demonstrably improved in the Czech Republic, there was not any reduction of incapacity for work of employees. The main indicators of the development of temporary incapacity for work include:

- new notified cases of TIW per 100 sickness-insured persons (SIPs),
- average duration of one case of TIW (days),
- average percentage of TIW.

The simplest indicator of incapacity for work, reflecting the frequency of incapacity, is the number of newly reported incapacity for work. The overall incidence rate of incapacity for work has a long-term downward trend. A more comprehensive indicator of incapacity for work compared to a mere nominal number of newly reported cases is the number of calendar days of incapacity for work per one newly reported case (Eq. 11.1), which reflects the actual impact of incapacity for work on the use of the working time fund (weight of average incapacity for work over time).

$$\text{average duration of 1 TIW case} = \frac{\text{number of calendar days of TIW}}{\text{number of cases of TIW}} \tag{11.1}$$

The aggregate indicator is the average percentage of incapacity for work, which takes account of the number of new cases of incapacity for work and their duration in relation to the number of sickness-insured persons and the calendar fund (Eq. 11.2). It expresses the percentage of the total length of incapacity for work on the calendar fund of sickness-insured persons in the given period.

$$\frac{\text{average percentage of TIW} = \text{number of calendar days of TIW} \times 100}{\text{number of sickness insured persons} \times \text{number of calendar days}} \tag{11.2}$$

Changes in payment of sickness benefits, including the fact that the benefits were paid from the 22nd day of temporary incapacity for work (and also their lower percentage level), had a significant effect on the insured person's decision about the origin of their incapacity for work.

11.3.1 Methodology

The impact of legislative changes in the area of sickness insurance on temporary incapacity for work in the Czech Republic will be presented using selected TIW indicators. Using regression analysis, the development of individual indicators (regressands) in the following years based on knowledge of the development of indicators in the years 2000–2017 (regressors) will be estimated.

The research results will be captured using trend line which will display the possible development based on the data in the various regions of the Czech Republic in the following years. Regression equation presents an approximation of the entered values where the coefficients are determined by the method of least squares, so that the sum of squared deviations of the original values from the obtained model would be minimum. The R^2 index expresses the degree of reliability of the calculated estimate of the development.

11.3.2 Results and Discussion

Legislative changes in the sickness insurance influenced significantly the development of all indicators of temporary incapacity for work in the Czech Republic. These changes are reflected noticeably in indicators such as the number of new cases of TIW per 100 sickness-insured persons, the average duration of one case of TIW and the average percentage of TIW.

Number of new cases of TIW per 100 sickness-insured persons. There was a decrease in the number of new cases of temporary incapacity for work in the last decade; the significant drop in the number of new cases of TIW occurred in 2004 due to the aforementioned change in the construction of sickness benefits and cut rates. Further, the significant decrease occurred in 2009, when the new sickness insurance legislation came into force. The decline did not stop until 2013, when the values of this indicator began to slowly pick up an increasing tendency as shown in Fig. 11.3.

Given that there was another legislative change in sickness insurance, when the waiting period was abolished, we can expect further growth of this indicator as confirmed by the regression equation with a high degree of reliability R^2.

Average duration of TIW. The relative index of the average duration of incapacity for work has a completely opposite development. This indicator is also a more appropriate tool for comparing the intensity of incapacity of work. In the period 2007–2014, the average duration of one case of temporary incapacity for work increased from 34.6 days to 45.8 days, i.e. about 11 days (Fig. 11.4), with the highest value reached in 2012 (46.1 days).

In the following years, there was a slight decline to 42.6 days in 2017, but it can be expected (based on regression analysis, the reliability 0.9351) that the duration of TIW will not be changed significantly in the following years.

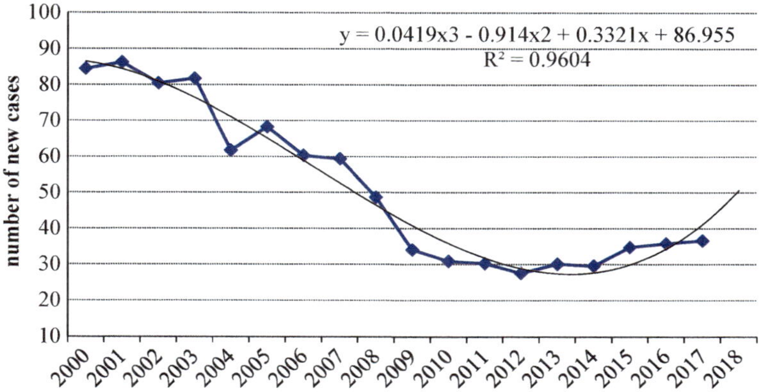

Fig. 11.3 Development of the number of new cases of TIW per 100 SIPs in the Czech Republic. *Source* Own processing according to CSO data (https://www.czso.cz/)

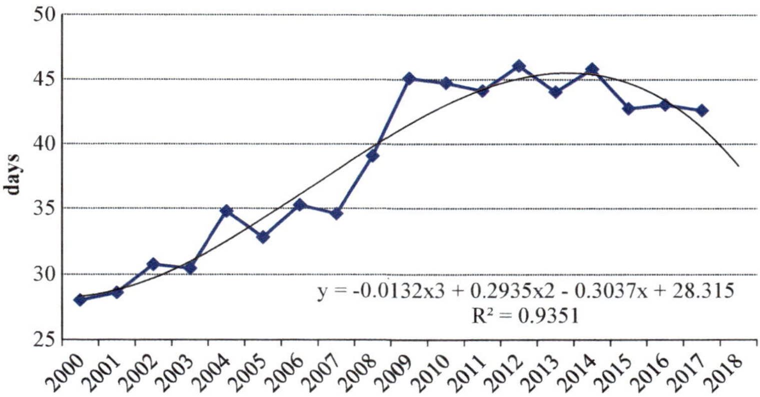

Fig. 11.4 Development of duration of TIW in the Czech Republic. *Source* Own processing according to CSO data (https://www.czso.cz/)

Average percentage of TIW. The maximum value of the average percentage of temporary incapacity for work (6.8%) was reached in 2003 (Fig. 11.5). In the context of gradual legislative changes involving stricter drawing of sickness benefits, since 2004, the indicator's values have been gradually declining to almost half of its initial level (to 3.5% in 2012). This indicator takes account of both the total number of incapacities for work (how often people get into TIW) and the average duration of one case of TIW (how long they remain in one). Starting in 2013, there was a change coming perhaps from the fact that the set of insured persons accustomed to stricter legislative conditions of sickness benefits drawing and value of the indicator began to rise again. In 2015, it exceeded 4% and reached 4.3% in 2017.

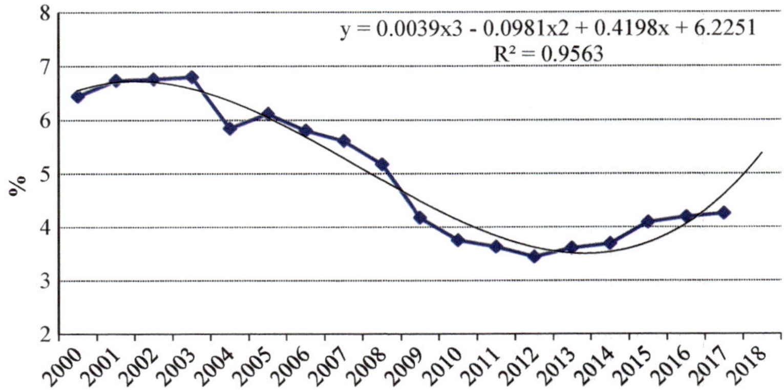

Fig. 11.5 Development of the average percentage of TIW in the Czech Republic. *Source* own processing according to CSO data (https://www.czso.cz/)

11.4 Conclusion

This paper determines the legislative changes in sickness insurance and their impact on temporary incapacity for work in the Czech Republic using an elementary research method R^2 index. Since 2009, there has been a lot of changes in the regulation of sickness insurance. The new law strengthened the safeguards against abuse of the system (waiting period, compensation for wage), ensured a more proportionate amount of sickness insurance benefits and involved employers in the development of temporary incapacity of work.

It was found that legislative changes in sickness insurance significantly influenced the development of all indicators of temporary incapacity for work in individual regions. These changes are reflected most markedly in the indicators of the number of new cases of TIW per 100 insured persons, the average duration of one case of TIW and the average percentage of TIW.

In 2009, there was a rapid decline in the number of cases of incapacity for work, which stopped in 2013, when the values of this indicator slowly pick up an increasing trend.

On the other hand, the average duration of one case of TIW gradually increased, when the highest value of this indicator was reached in 2012. Between 2000 and 2017, the average duration of one case of TIW increased from 28 days to 42.6 days (by almost 15 days).

Since 2005, there has been a downward trend in the average percentage of incapacity for work, which has been strongly exacerbated by legislative changes in 2009. The downward trend of this indicator continued until 2012. However, in the following years there was a gradual increase to its average value of 4.3.

Comparative indicators affecting different aspects of incapacity for work show that there have been significant changes recently. The question is whether the approved cancellation of the waiting period will have a significant impact on the current trend of temporary incapacity for work. It can be assumed that the country's economic situation is also important. The Czech economy has been growing in recent years, reflecting, among other things, wage growth and a low unemployment rate. Due to labour shortages, wages will also increase this year. This fundamental research can also become the basis for further, thorough exploration of the issue, where more sophisticated methods could already be used.

Acknowledgements This research was financially supported by the Ministry of Education, Youth and Sports within the Institutional Support for Long-term Development of a Research Organization in 2019.

References

Act no. 187/2006 Coll., on sickness insurance, as amended.

Act no. 589/1992 Coll., the social security insurance and contribution to the state employment policy, as amended.

CSSA. (2018). *Výroční zpráva 2017*. (online]. Available from: https://www.cssz.cz/NR/rdonlyres/796E4EB2-7F45-4ECB-8502-C3235B0CAD75/0/VZ_2017.pdf. Accessed March 22, 2019.

Edebalk, P. G. (2009). Emloyers and sickness insurance. *Scandinavian Journal of History, 34*(1), 49–68.

Gregorová, Z., & Galvas, M. (2000). *Sociální zabezpečení* (2nd ed.). Brno: Masarykova univerzita.

Hagelung, A., & Bryngelson, A. (2014). Change and resilience in welfare state policy: The politics of sickness insurance in Norway and Sweden. *Social Policy and Administration, 48*(3), 300–318.

Hägglund, P. (2013). Do time limits in the sickness insurance system increase return to work? *Empirical Economics, 45*(1), 567–582.

Hall, C. (2011). Do interactions between unemployment insurance and sickness insurance affect transitions to employment? *LABOUR Review of Labour Economics and Industrial Relations, 25*(4), 447–467.

Hulec, V. (2012). Okruh pojištěných osob od 1: ledna 2012. *Národní pojištění, 43*(2), 11–13.

Krebs, V. (2007). *Sociální politika* (4th ed.). Praha: ASPI.

Larsson, L. (2006). Sick of being unemployed? Interactions between unemployment and sickness insurance. *Scandinavian Journal of Economics, 108*(1), 97–113.

MLSA. (2017). *Analýza vývoje nemocenského pojištění*. (online). Available from: https://www.mpsv.cz/files/clanky/32895/Analyza_vyvoje_nemocenskeho_pojisteni_2017.pdf. Accessed March 22, 2019.

Novotný, T. (2013). Nemocenské pojištění zaměstnanců činných na základě dohody o provedení práce. *Národní pojištění, 44*(4), 18–21.

Sirovátka, T. (1997). *Sociální zabezpečení*. Brno: Masarykova univerzita.

Ståhl, Ch., Svensson, T., Petersson, G., & Ekberg, K. (2011). Swedish rehabilitation professionals' perspectives on work ability assessments in a changing sickness insurance system. *Disability and Rehabilitation, 33*(15–16), 1373–1382.

Tröster, P. (2005). *Právo sociálního zabezpečení* (3rd ed.). Praha: C. H. Beck.

Ženíšková, M., & Přib, J. (2011). *Zákon o nemocenském pojištění s komentářem a příklady od 1. 1. 2011* (4th ed.). Praha: ANAG.

Ziebarth, N. R., Karlsson, M. (2014). The effects of expanding the generosity of the statutory sickness insurance system. *Journal of Applied Econometrics, 29*(2), 208–230.

Chapter 12
Analysis of Website Performance Dependence on Global Brand Value

Lubica Gajanova, Anna Krizanova and George Lăzăroiu

Abstract Brands are a contemporary phenomenon, and their significance goes far beyond the mere effort of a manufacturer to distinguish himself from a competing product or service. Over the last decades, brands have become a symbol of quality and value they represent. Among other things, they managed to gain considerable control over the consumer behaviour of many people. That is why companies realize that it is important to create a brand equity and continue to build the created value in today's competition. Different aspects are involved in the measurement of brand value and its financial valuation. In this paper, we focused only on the composed valuation methods, where the total brand value consists of gross financial value and the quantification of soft marketing factors as well. The aim of this contribution is to answer the research question if there are some website metrics, which affect the brand value determined in this way. For answering this issue, hypotheses expressing the existence of a statistical dependence of basic website metrics on the brand value have been identified. Based on statistical testing of established hypotheses, we have confirmed the existence of website metric with greater impact on brand value.

Keywords Global brand · Corporate website · Statistical dependence · Content marketing

JEL Codes M31 · M37

L. Gajanova (✉) · A. Krizanova
University of Zilina, Zilina, Slovak Republic
e-mail: lubica.gajanova@fpedas.uniza.sk

A. Krizanova
e-mail: anna.krizanova@fpedas.uniza.sk

G. Lăzăroiu
The Cognitive Labor Institute, New York, USA
e-mail: lazaroiu@aa-er.org

Spiru Haret University, Bucharest, Romania

N. Tsounis and A. Vlachvei (eds.), *Advances in Cross-Section Data Methods in Applied Economic Research*, Springer Proceedings in Business and Economics,
https://doi.org/10.1007/978-3-030-38253-7_12

12.1 Introduction

If a brand value is already created, it is important to know how to build it further so that the value is not reduced or lost over time. The brand value should be cared through various marketing activities that will continue to support it. The concept of branding is defined by a number of authors, but it is difficult to find a clear definition. In spite of the different explanations of the term, it is possible to say that branding is related to the brand and is sometimes referred to as brand management, thanks to which brand value can be increased. Marketing communication also contributes to building brand value. If its individual instruments are correctly chosen, it is possible to increase the brand value by communication, including by new forms of marketing communication. New forms of marketing communication are associated with the development of technology, online communication, the Internet and social media at the beginning of the twenty-first century. New media are experiencing high development, offering new information opportunities, and marketers should use new media either by replacing traditional media or by adding them (Vysekalova 2012; Abakumova and Primierova 2018). She considers the company's Web presentation to be a new medium as well.

As part of the science project APVV "Integrated model of management support for building and managing the brand value in the specific conditions of the Slovak Republic", we investigated the factors that affect the brand value. The aim of the research was to verify if there is the statistically significant relationship between brand value and basic website metrics. It was achieved through the application of the correlation analysis. Because the correlation analysis provides just only the information about the strength and direction of a relationship between two continuous variables, subsequently, it was used the regression analysis. Regression analysis is a type of statistical evaluation that enables description of relationships among the dependent and the independent variables and the estimation the values of the dependent variables from the observed values of the independent variables. (Schneider et al. 2010; Singh and Rao 2018) The analysis of the research results confirmed that the companies should focus on a certain basic website metrics, which enhance the brand value.

12.2 Literature Review

The concept of brand equity has emerged in the eighties of the twentieth century. This has made the brand more important in the company's marketing strategy (Kicová et al. 2018). Brand equity expresses the commercial value that derives from consumer perception of the brand name of a particular product or service, rather than from the product or service itself. The brand's added value is mainly created by how consumers think, feel and behave in relation to a brand. The brand value is, therefore, an intangible asset with a psychological and financial value for the company (Kotler 2007). Brand equity is derived from the overall brand image created by the totality of brand associations, perceived by customers (Michell et al. 2001). Aaker (1991) defines brand equity as a set of brand assets and liabilities linked to a brand, its name and symbol that add to or subtract from the value provided by a product or service to a firm and/or to that firm's customers. The brand equity is given by how customers are loyal to it, how well the brand is known, how large it is the quality and how are products identified with it from the consumer's perspective (Machková 2006; Janoskova and Krizanova 2017; Nadanyiova and Kicova 2017). Kotler and Keller (2007) also talk about the differences in brand equity. These are determined by how customers know the brand. Thus, they mean all thoughts, feelings, ideas, experiences and beliefs associated with the brand. Brands must then strive to create associations that are strong, favourable and unique to the customer. Marketing should, therefore, strongly focus on delivering the right product experience to customers who build themselves a desirable knowledge structure about the brand.

From the above, three basic approaches are distinguished in the definition of brand equity: asset perspective, customer perspective and comprehensive perspective (Mahmood 2017; Kicova and Nadanyiova 2017). But, in general, brand equity also altered the perception of brand value by demonstrating that a brand is not only a tactical aid to generate short-term sales, but also a strategic support to a business strategy that will add long-term value to the organization (Aaker 2016). Brand value reflects the present value of all the equity in the future. There are several ways to measure brand value. These methods are based on the above-mentioned division of approaches to the definition of brand equity (Janoskova and Kral 2018; Misankova et al. 2017; Kramarova and Svabova 2016). Since a brand value is a multidimensional concept, multiple measurements may increase the diagnostic power of research, and the likelihood that company's management should better understand the factors affecting branding. Combined respectively composite methods of evaluation use simultaneously financial and behavioural approach to attempt to eliminate the shortcomings of the other techniques (Nadányiová and Klieštiková 2017). From research conducted by de Chernatony (2009), which was based both on the study of literature and on consultations with the world's leading brand advisors, the brand's success requires an assessment using a combination of different dimensions. In principle, this research has concluded that it is necessary to apply enterprise-based (economic) criteria as well as customer-based criteria. The concept emphasized by the author is the need for a more balanced view of internal and external brand issues.

12.3 Methodology

For the purposes of this paper, we focused on combined value valuation method by Interbrand, specifically Best Global Brands 2018. Interbrand was the first company to have its methodology certified as compliant with the requirements of ISO 10668 (requirements for monetary brand valuation) and has played a key role in the development of the standard itself. There are three key components to all of valuations: an analysis of the financial performance of the branded products or services, of the role the brand plays in purchase decisions and of the brand's competitive strength. Financial analysis measures the overall financial return to an organization's investors, or its economic profit (Weissova and Durica 2016; Kollar et al. 2015; Valaskova et al. 2018). Economic profit is the after-tax operating profit of the brand, minus a charge for the capital used to generate the brand's revenue and margins (Emerling and Wojcik-Jurkiewicz 2018). Role of brand measures the portion of the purchase decision attributable to the brand as opposed to other factors (e.g. purchase drivers such as price, convenience or product features). The Role of Brand Index (RBI) quantifies this as a percentage. RBI determinations for Best Global Brands derive, depending on the brand, from one of three methods: primary research, a review of historical roles of brands for companies in that industry or expert panel assessment. Brand strength measures the ability of the brand to create loyalty and, therefore, sustainable demand and profit into the future. Brand strength analysis is based on an evaluation across ten factors that Interbrand believes to constitute a strong brand. Performance in these areas is judged relative to other brands in the industry and relative to other world-class brands. The brand strength analysis delivers an insightful snapshot of the strengths and weaknesses of the brand and is used to generate a road map of activities to grow the brand's strength and value into the future (Interbrand 2019). Brand strengths are based on both internal dimensions (Clarity, Commitment, Governance, Responsiveness) and external dimensions (Authenticity, Relevance, Differentiation, Consistency, Presence, Engagement Roll 2015).

The brand is essentially a summary of how we perceive the business. It depends on what their promotion raises in you, what you hear about it from the people you trust, on personal experience with their products, services, packaging, customer support and last but not least their website. Přikrylová and Jahodová (2010) state that communication in the form of corporate websites can be considered as the basic and most widely used way of communication on the Internet. External audience-oriented company Web presentations have become a common tool for corporate marketing communication to inform the current and potential customers and other interest groups, build relationships with various target groups and create an environment for two-way communication (Siekelova 2015). According to Jakovic and Galetic (2014), the marketing and business activities offered on the company's website have a significant impact on its commercial success. Fahmy and Ghoneim (2016) report that consumers make purchases of products or services through business websites, minimizing their waiting and planning time and maximizing their enjoyment. Nowadays, more customers are now making their purchases through the website, so McMahan et al. (2009) report that the perceived image and usability of a business website directly affect customers' purchasing goals. Zamazalová (2010) lays down metrics for websites based on the goals a business wants to achieve:

- Visits—expresses the traffic of the company website or average number of visits for the reporting period,
- Unique visits—expresses the unique visit rate of the company website or their number for the reporting period based on IP addresses and cookie,
- Page views—expresses the number of pages viewed over the reporting period,

- View time—expresses the time spent on a visitor's website,
- Pages per visit—expresses how many pieces of webpages a particular user or group of users views on a single website.

We have found the necessary information of this nature through SimilarWeb. SimilarWeb's database is one of the largest in the world. SimilarWeb acquires data from tens of millions of users per month from more than 200 countries, giving its analysis a global dimension and the ability to compare geographic locations. It also monitors traffic on mobile applications. It emphasizes the accuracy of traffic data that it can distinguish between days. SimilarWeb robot adds panel information by analyzing more than one billion Web pages per month. The data is analyzed in content, assigned to categories and subcategories and marked with characteristics describing the Web content.

As part of our analysis, we tracked these website metrics: visits (monthly visits in millions), view time (average visit duration in seconds), pages per visit and page views. SimilarWeb calculates a visit (session) for a website if a visitor accesses one or more pages. Subsequent page views are included in the same visit until the user is inactive for more than 30 min. If a user becomes active again after 30 min, that counts as a new visit. A new session will also start at midnight. SimilarWeb calculates average visit duration based on the time elapsed between the first and last page view per visit (visits are closed after 30 min of inactivity). SimilarWeb calculates pages per visit by dividing the total number of page views by the total number of visitors. A page view is an instance of a page being loaded or reloaded in a browser (Similarweb 2019).

Based on the delimitation of the theoretical backgrounds and taking into account the science project APVV "Integrated model of management support for building and managing the brand value in the specific conditions of the Slovak Republic", we identified a research problem as follows: Are there some website metrics, which affect the brand value?

12.4 Results

To answer the research question, we have identified hypotheses expressing the existence of a statistical dependence of brand value on website performance. In Table 12.1, there are data about the first twenty brands according to the Best Global Brands 2018 by Interbrand along with the basic measurement data of their website performance according to SimilarWeb.

Subsequent statistical testing was performed from all brands in the above ranking. The regression and correlation analysis can be used to investigate the dependencies of mass phenomena expressed by quantitative variables.

Table 12.1 Interbrand Best Global Brands 2018

Website	Brand value in thousands	Monthly visits in millions	Average visit duration in seconds	Pages per visit	Page views in millions
apple.com	214,480	498.42	198	3.45	1719.549
google.com	155,506	63,100	586	8.56	540,136
amazon.com	100,764	2480	351	8.03	19,914.4
microsoft.com	92,715	735.93	245	3.58	2634.6294
coca-cola.com	66,341	3.24	192	4.93	15.9732
samsung.com	59,890	926.11	164	2.1	1944.831
toyota.com	53,404	11.72	251	5.07	59.4204
mercedes-benz.com	48,601	3.58	236	5.57	19.9406
facebook.com	45,168	21,180	673	10.49	222,178.2
mcdonalds.com	43,417	28.14	94	2.07	58.2498
intel.com	43,293	39.65	222	3.55	140.7575
ibm.com	42,972	40.24	235	4.38	176.2512
bmw.de	41,006	2.34	320	10.59	24.7806
disney.com	39,874	11.34	210	4.29	48.6486
cisco.com	34,575	32.33	388	5.81	187.8373
ge.com	32,757	4.24	389	6.22	26.3728
nike.com	30,120	61.91	268	6.98	432.1318
louisvuitton.com	28,152	8.36	267	8.14	68.0504
oracle.com	26,133	51.28	286	4.72	242.0416
honda.com	23,682	8.94	231	4.4	39.336

12.4.1 Monthly Visits Dependence on Global Brand Value

A correlation analysis whose role is to detect and measure the strength of (linear) dependence between a pair of quantitative variables (brand value and monthly visits) is shown in Table 12.2.

In Table 12.2, there are information about level of correlation coefficient and test of statistical significance of correlation coefficient. Correlation coefficient, namely Pearson correlation, is 0.484 that belongs to the interval $0.3 \leq r < 0.8$, which means the moderate dependence. Based on the comparison of the significance level (0.05) with the *P*-value (Sig. 2-tailed), the null hypothesis is rejected, so the correlation is statistically significant, and the variables are dependent.

Based on the existence of statistical dependence, it is appropriate to perform a regression analysis because its role is to model the existing dependency, *i. j.*, and find a functional relationship by which one variable varies depending on another variable, see Table 12.3.

Table 12.2 Correlation analysis of brand value and monthly visits

		Brand value	Monthly visits
Brand value	Pearson correlation	1	0.484[a]
	Sig. (2-tailed)		0.000
	N	100	100
Monthly visits	Pearson correlation	0.484[a]	1
	Sig. (2-tailed)	0.000	
	N	100	100

[a]Correlation is significant at the 0.01 level (2-tailed)

Table 12.3 Regression analysis of brand value and monthly visits

R	*R* square	Adjusted *R* square	Std. error of the estimate
0.484	0.234	0.227	26089.499

ANOVA

	Sum of squares	*df*	Mean square	*F*	Sig.
Regression	20432945920.098	1	20432945920.098	30.019	0.000
Residual	66704871429.692	98	680661953.364		
Total	87137817349.790	99			

The independent variable is monthly visits

Coefficients

	Unstandardized coefficients		Standardized coefficients	*t*	Sig.
	B	Std. error	Beta		
Monthly visits	2.166	0.395	0.484	5.479	0.000
(Constant)	18150.457	26340.430		6.890	0.000

ANOVA is a test of the significance of the model as a whole. It tests whether this type of regression was correctly selected and whether the whole model is statistically significant. Based on the comparison of the significance level (0.05) with the *P*-value (Sig.), the null hypothesis is rejected, so the model is statistically significant. Table 12.3 also contains the information about the coefficients of the resulting regression line and test their statistical significance as well. The *p*-value of the coefficient significance test in the model (Sig.) is lower than the significance level (0.05), so both coefficients of the regression line are statistically significant. The regression line with its equation is shown in Fig. 12.1.

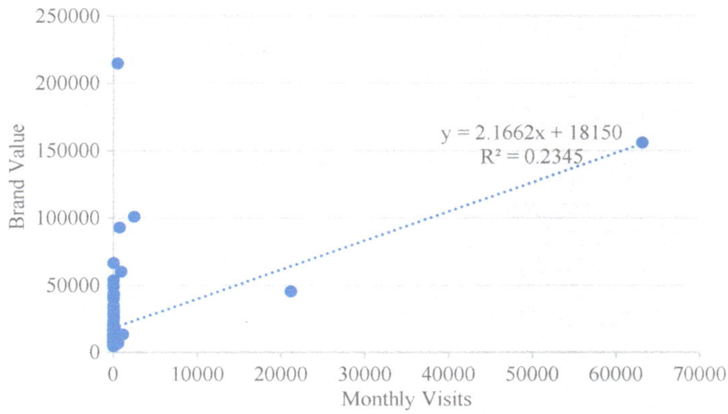

Fig. 12.1 Regression line of brand value and monthly visits

12.4.2 Average Visit Duration Dependence on Global Brand Value

A correlation analysis whose role is to detect and measure the strength of (linear) dependence between a pair of quantitative variables (brand value and average visit duration) is shown in Table 12.4.

In Table 12.4, there are information about level of correlation coefficient and test of statistical significance of correlation coefficient. Correlation coefficient, namely Pearson correlation, is 0.203 that belongs to the interval $0.1 \leq r < 0.3$, which means the low dependence. Based on the comparison of the significance level (0.05) with the *P*-value (Sig. 2-tailed), the null hypothesis is rejected, so the correlation is statistically significant, and the variables are dependent.

Table 12.4 Correlation analysis of brand value and average visit duration

		Brand value	Average visit duration
Brand value	Pearson correlation	1	0.203[a]
	Sig. (2-tailed)		0.043
	N	100	100
Average visit duration	Pearson correlation	0.203[a]	1
	Sig. (2-tailed)	0.043	
	N	100	100

[a]Correlation is significant at the 0.05 level (2-tailed)

Table 12.5 Regression analysis of brand value and average visit duration

R	*R* square	Adjusted *R* square	Std. error of the estimate
0.203	0.041	0.032	29196.241

The independent variable is average visit duration

ANOVA

	Sum of squares	*df*	Mean square	*F*	Sig.
Regression	3600606926.125	1	3600606926.125	4.224	0.043
Residual	83537210423.665	98	852420514.527		
Total	87137817349.790	99			

The independent variable is average visit duration

Coefficients

	Unstandardized coefficients		Standardized coefficients	*t*	Sig.
	B	Std. error	Beta		
Average visit duration	45.009	21.900	0.203	2.055	0.043
(Constant)	9581.801	5914.466		1.620	0.108

Based on the existence of statistical dependence, it is appropriate to perform a regression analysis because its role is to model the existing dependency, *i. j.*, and find a functional relationship by which one variable varies depending on another variable, see Table 12.5.

ANOVA is a test of the significance of the model as a whole. It tests whether this type of regression was correctly selected and whether the whole model is statistically significant. Based on the comparison of the significance level (0.05) with the *P*-value (Sig.), the null hypothesis is rejected, so the model is statistically significant. Table 12.5 also contains the information about the coefficients of the resulting regression line and test their statistical significance as well. The *p*-value of the coefficient significance test in the model (Sig.) is lower than the significance level (0.05) just only by regression coefficient, so the constant of the regression line is not statistically significant.

12.4.3 Pages Per Visit Dependence on Global Brand Value

A correlation analysis whose role is to detect and measure the strength of (linear) dependence between a pair of quantitative variables (brand value and pages per visit) is shown in Table 12.6.

In Table 12.6, there are information about level of correlation coefficient and test of statistical significance of correlation coefficient. Correlation coefficient, namely Pearson correlation, is only 0.045. It means that there is no dependence. Based on the non-existence of statistical dependence, it is not appropriate to perform a regression analysis.

Table 12.6 Correlation analysis of brand value and pages per visit

		Brand value	Pages per visit
Brand value	Pearson correlation	1	0.045
	Sig. (2-tailed)		0.657
	N	100	100
Pages per visit	Pearson correlation	0.045	1
	Sig. (2-tailed)	0.657	
	N	100	100

12.4.4 Page Views Dependence on Global Brand Value

A correlation analysis whose role is to detect and measure the strength of (linear) dependence between a pair of quantitative variables (brand value and page views) is shown in Table 12.7.

In Table 12.7, there are information about level of correlation coefficient and test of statistical significance of correlation coefficient. Correlation coefficient, namely Pearson correlation, is 0.472 that belongs to the interval $0.3 \leq r < 0.8$, which means the moderate dependence. Based on the comparison of the significance level (0.05) with the *P*-value (Sig. 2-tailed), the null hypothesis is rejected, so the correlation is statistically significant, and the variables are dependent.

Based on the existence of statistical dependence, it is appropriate to perform a regression analysis because its role is to model the existing dependency, *i. j.*, and find a functional relationship by which one variable varies depending on another variable, see Table 12.8.

ANOVA is a test of the significance of the model as a whole. It tests whether this type of regression was correctly selected and whether the whole model is statistically significant. Based on the comparison of the significance level (0.05) with the

Table 12.7 Correlation analysis of brand value and page views

		Brand value	Page views
Brand value	Pearson correlation	1	0.472[a]
	Sig. (2-tailed)		0.000
	N	100	100
Page views	Pearson correlation	0.472[a]	1
	Sig. (2-tailed)	0.000	
	N	100	100

[a]Correlation is significant at the 0.01 level (2-tailed)

Table 12.8 Regression analysis of brand value and page views

R	*R* square	Adjusted *R* square	Std. error of the estimate
0.472	0.223	0.215	26283.547

The independent variable is page views

ANOVA

	Sum of squares	*df*	Mean square	*F*	Sig.
Regression	19436984346.470	1	19436984346.470	28.136	0.000
Residual	67700833003.320	98	690824826.564		
Total	87137817349.790	99			

The independent variable is page views

Coefficients

	Unstandardized coefficients		Standardized coefficients	*t*	Sig.
	B	Std. error	Beta		
Page views	0.241	0.045	0.472	5.304	0.000
(Constant)	18195.594	2654.136		6.856	0.000

P-value (Sig.), the null hypothesis is rejected, so the model is statistically significant. Table 12.8 also contains the information about the coefficients of the resulting regression line and test their statistical significance as well. The *p*-value of the coefficient significance test in the model (Sig.) is lower than the significance level (0.05), so both coefficients of the regression line are statistically significant. The regression line with its equation is shown in Fig. 12.2.

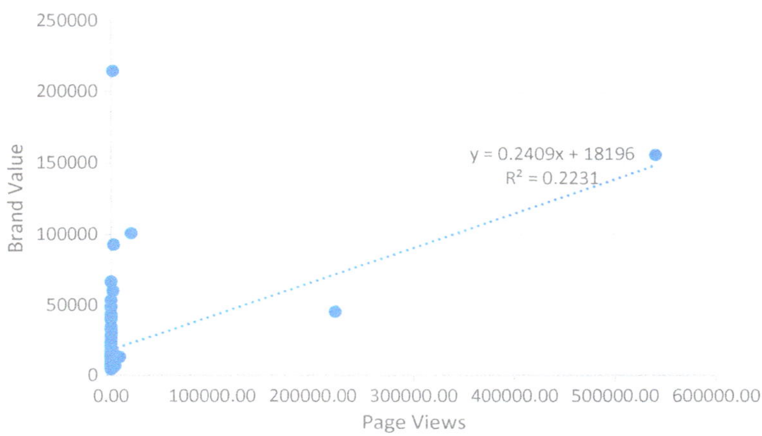

Fig. 12.2 Regression line of brand value and page views

12.5 Conclusions

The value of the brand includes an important tool for competitiveness and, at the same time, the ability of the brand to withstand environmental change (Kliestik et al. 2018; Gyalog et al. 2017). Through comprehensive values, the brand must be distinguished and defined against the competition (Gudgin et al. 2018) Branding is about signals, which create associations. The signals are used by people to determine what the brand means to them. Brand signals are a brand presentation whose role is to evoke feelings, create brand ideas and enable the gathering of experience. This includes websites as well. The aim of this contribution is to answer the research question if there are some website metrics, which affect the brand value.

The first surveyed website metrics was the monthly visits. Based on the results, we can say that there is a statistically significant dependence between the variables, brand value and monthly visits. Correlation coefficient is at the level 0.484, which means the moderate dependence. Based on the existence of statistical dependence, it a regression analysis to find a functional relationship between surveyed variables was performed. The relationship is given by the equation $y = 2.1662x + 18{,}150$. The significance of the model as a whole as well as the significance of the coefficients of the regression line was statistically confirmed. The second surveyed website metrics was the average visit duration. Based on the results, we can say that there is a statistically significant dependence between the variables, brand value and average visit duration. Correlation coefficient is at the level 0.203, which means the low dependence. Based on the existence of statistical dependence, it a regression analysis to find a functional relationship between surveyed variables was performed. The significance of the model as a whole was statistically confirmed. But, this is not the case with the significance of the coefficients of the regression line. The third surveyed website metrics was the pages per visit. Based on the results, we can say that there is no statistically significant dependence between the variables, brand value and pages per visit. The last surveyed website metrics was the page views. Based on the results, we can say that there is a statistically significant dependence between the variables, brand value and page views. Correlation coefficient is at the level 0.472, which means the moderate dependence. Based on the existence of statistical dependence, it a regression analysis to find a functional relationship between surveyed variables was performed. The relationship is given by the equation $y = 0.2409x + 18{,}196$. The significance of the model as a whole as well as the significance of the coefficients of the regression line was statistically confirmed.

The analysis of the research results confirmed that the companies should focus on a certain basic website metric, which enhances the brand value at mostly level. Specifically, it is monthly visits. Enterprises should focus on activities to raise precisely this indicator. As recent surveys show, it is possible to increase website traffic through content marketing. Organizations that have strategic approach to managing content are seeing benefits. According to 2018 Content Management and Strategy Survey, in the top five there are inter alia extended reach of content (57%), improved ability to provide the right content to the right person at the right time (50%) and enhanced customer experiences due to improved interactions (45%) (Content Marketing Institute 2018). A quality content marketing strategy can become a tool to differentiate from competitors. By regularly adding new content in different forms, you will gain new visitors, keep the original ones and also improve your position in the search engines. In this way, you will surpass your competitors by not only adding value in the eyes of visitors or customers, but Internet browsers will also take you to the top.

The more content you create and add to your website, the more attention it gets. Content is the key to make your site more visible. However, the quality of the content is essential (Stefko et al. 2016). Not only visitors and readers who like to share quality and engaging content, but also search engines like Google will appreciate it. Even if you create content as a priority for the reader, you need to remember the search engine. It also has certain preferences, such as the occurrence of a keyword in an article, H1 tags and so on. If you think of these preferences when creating content, you will be rewarded with organic traffic. Organic traffic represents visitors who searched for the keyword on which your content is targeted. We can say that this is exactly your target audience. So, with high quality, regular, relevant and targeted content, you can attract a large number of potential clients to your website.

Acknowledgements This contribution is a partial output of the project APVV-15-0505: Integrated Model of Management Support for Building and Managing the Brand Value in the Specific Conditions of the Slovak Republic.

References

Aaker, D. A. (1991). *Managing brand equity* (p. 299). New York: The Free Press.

Aaker, D. (2016). *Brand equity versus brand value: What's the difference?* Aaker on Brands. https://www.prophet.com/2016/09/brand-equity-vs-brand-value/.

Abakumova, J., & Primierova, O. (2018). Globalization, growth and inequality: Testing causality and asymmetries. *Ekonomicko-manazerske spektrum., 12*(2), 83–95.

Content Marketing Institute. (2018). *Content management and strategy survey.* https://contentmarketinginstitute.com/wp-content/uploads/2018/05/2018-content-management-strategy-survey-research.pdf.

De Chernatony, L. (2009). *Znacka: od vize k vyssim ziskum* (p. 352). Brno: Computer Press.

Emerling, I., & Wojcik-Jurkiewicz, M. (2018). The risk associated with the replacement of traditional budget with performance budgeting in the public finance sector management. *Ekonomicko-manazerske spektrum., 12*(1), 55–63.

Fahmy, M. M., & Ghoneim, A. I. (2016). The impact of interactivity on advertising effectiveness of corporate websites: a mediated moderation model. *International Journal of Marketing Studies., 8*(5), 41–55.

Gudgin, G., Coutts, K., Gibson, N., & Buchanan, J. (2018). The macro-economic impact of Brexit: using the CBR macro-economic model of the UK economy (UKMOD). *Journal of Self-Governance and Management Economics., 6*(2), 7–49.

Gyalog, G., Olah, J., Békefi, E., Lukácsik, M., & Popp, J. (2017). Constraining factors in Hungarian carp farming: An econometric perspective. *Sustainability, 9,* 2111.

Interbrand. (2019). Methodology. https://www.interbrand.com/best-brands/best-global-brands/methodology/.

Jakovic, B., & Galetic, F. (2014). Marketing and commercial activities offered on Croatian five-star hotel web sites. *Procedia Engineering, 69,* 112–120.

Janoskova, K., & Kral, P. (2018). A comprehensive literature review of international brand valuation methods. In *Proceedings of International scientific conference Globalization and its socio-economic consequences* (pp. 577–583). PRC: Rajecke Teplice.

Janoskova, K., & Krizanova, A. (2017). Comparison of selected internationally recognized brand valuation methods. *Oeconomia Copernicana, 8*(1), 99–110.

Kicova, E., & Nadanyiova, M. (2017). Brand as a tool of company's strategic marketing in practice. In *Proceedings of ESE International Conference on Sports, Health and Management* (pp. 29–34). PRC: Madrid.

Kicova, E., Kral, P., & Janoskova, K. (2018). Proposal for brands communication strategy developed on customer segmentation based on psychological factors and decision-making speed in purchasing. *Economics and Culture., 15*(1), 5–14.

Kliestik, T., Kovacova, M., Podhorska, I., & Kliestikova, J. (2018). Searching for key sources of goodwill creation as new global managerial challenge. *Polish Journal of Management Studies, 17*(1), 144–154.

Kollar, B., Weissova, I., & Siekelova, A. (2015). Comparative analysis of theoretical aspects in credit risk models. In *International Conference on Applied Economics* (pp. 331–338). PRC: Kazan.

Kotler, P. (2007). *Moderní marketing* (p. 1041). Praha: Grada.

Kotler, P., & Keller, K. L. (2007). *Marketing management* (p. 788). Praha: Grada.

Kramarova, K., & Svabova, L. (2016). Selected issues of brand valuation. *Podniková ekonomika a manažment, 2,* 49–63.

Mahmood, S. M. F. (2017). Evaluating the impact of brand equity and price variance upon consumers buying behavior: An empirical analysis on Bangladesh. *International Journal of Entrepreneurship and Development Studies, 5*(2), 111–127.

Machková, H. (2006). *Mezinárodní marketing* (p. 205). Praha: Grada.

McMahan, C., Hovland, R., & McMillan, S. J. (2009). Online Marketing communications: Exploring online consumer behavior by examining gender differences and interactivity within internet advertising. *Journal of Interactive Advertising, 10*(1), 61–76.

Michell, P., King, J., & Reast, J. B. (2001). Values related to industrial products. *Industrial Marketing Management, 30*(5), 415–425.

Misankova, M., Kiestikova, J., & Krizanova, A. (2017). Some remarks to specifics of brand valuation in Slovakia. In *Proceedings of the 29th international academic conference* (pp. 73–81). PRC: Rome.

Nadanyiova, M., & Kicova, E. (2017). Mobile marketing of banking entities as a brand value enhancing tool and its perception from the perspective of consumers' generations X, Y, Z. In *Proceedings of International Scientific Conference on Marketing Identity: Online Rules* (pp. 184–193). PRC: Smolenice.

Nadanyiova, M., & Kliestikova, J. (2017). Brand value and the factors affecting it. *In International Conference on Applied Economics* (pp. 391–402). PRC: Coventry.

Přikrylová, J., & Jahodová, H. (2010). *Moderní marketingová komunikace* (p. 320). Praha: Grada.

Roll, M. (2015). *Asian brand strategy (revised and updated): Building and sustaining strong global brands in Asia* (p. 339). Palgrave, Macmillan.

Similarweb. (2019). Knowledge center. https://support.similarweb.com/hc/en-us.

Singh, S. K., & Rao, D. T. (2018). Is monetary policy symmetrical in its effect on sectoral output? *Economics, Management, and Financial Markets, 13*(1), 11–31.

Schneider, A., Hommel, G., & Blettner, M. (2010). Linear regression analysis. *Deutsches Ärzteblatt International, 107*(44), 776–782.

Siekelova, A. (2015). The role of the receivables management in conditions of globalization. In *International Scientific Conference on Globalization and its Socio-Economic Consequences* (pp. 686–690). PRC: Rajecke Teplice.

Stefko, R., Fedorko, R., & Bacik, R. (2016). Website content quality in terms of perceived image of higher education institution. *Polish Journal of Management Studies., 13*(2), 153–163.
Valaskova, K., Kliestik, T., & Kovacova, M. (2018). Management of financial risks in Slovak enterprises using regression analysis. *Oeconomia Copernicana, 9*(1), 105–121.
Vysekalová, J. (2012). *Psychologie reklamy* (p. 324). Praha: Grada.
Weissova, I., & Durica, M. (2016). The possibility of using prediction models for monitoring the financial health of Slovak companies. In *International Scientific Conference on Managing and Modelling of Financial Risks Location* (pp. 1062–1070). PRC: Ostrava.
Zamazalová, J. (2010). *Marketing* (p. 528). Praha: C. H. Beck.

Chapter 13
Impact of R&D Cartelization with Endogenous Product Differentiation

Bartlomiej Wisnicki

Abstract We analyze the multistage model of a duopoly in which firms decide on the level of product differentiation, R&D investment and production. The decision of differentiation is strongly related to the cost-reducing technology spillover. We find that there is a positive relationship between the level of substitution and R&D investment, which transfers into higher production and lower market price. The critical aspect of the paper is the welfare analysis of the cartelization in the market. We show that cooperation in R&D investment coordinates high investment with closer substitution, and it increases both firms profits and consumer welfare. Moreover, from the consumers' perspective, the total monopolization of the market is more efficient scenario than a fully competitive one. Hence, the gains from coordinated joint research far outlast the possible loss from monopolization of the market.

Keywords R&D spillovers · Horizontal differentiation · Market cartelization

13.1 Introduction

The impact of research and development on the economic progress of an enterprise is a non-debatable issue in the current economic world. Nowadays, there are even several examples of firms in which R&D investment highly exceeds their financial possibilities. Thus, some form of joint activity among the firms is required to achieve an economically reasonable level of investment and production, cf. (Kaiser 2002).

The impact of antitrust policies and joint R&D procedures is a constant topic of the debate in economic and policy forums. Since 1980, the three centers of economic regulation (European Commission, FTC and MITI) changed their courses on actively banning such form of cooperation, seeing the benefits that lie from having a joint research center between firms, cf. (Horváth 2002). A joint research center is an

B. Wisnicki (✉)
Department of Business Economics, Warsaw School of Economics,
al. Niepodleglosci 162, 02-554 Warsaw, Poland
e-mail: bwisni@sgh.waw.pl

N. Tsounis and A. Vlachvei (eds.), *Advances in Cross-Section Data Methods in Applied Economic Research*, Springer Proceedings in Business and Economics,
https://doi.org/10.1007/978-3-030-38253-7_13

alternative form to a merger of companies, cf. (Davidson and Deneckere 1984). However, this form is deemed by the antitrust agencies as providing a significantly harmful effect for consumers, due to market monopolization, cf. (van Wegberg 1995).

In this paper, we investigate the effects of horizontal R&D cooperation on the heterogeneous market. The horizontal cooperation is a way of know-how sharing by two equal (in terms of size or capacities) firms operating on the same market while remaining competition, cf. (Kamien et al. 1992; Belderbos et al. 2004). The idea of such an agreement being beneficial for the firms is that R&D activity is associated with increasing marginal cost, thus making it efficient to split tasks between two or more units, cf. (Camagni 1993; Becker and Dietz 2004).

The purpose of the research is to examine how R&D cooperation impacts a market in which goods are horizontally diversified. Therefore, we will be able to compare the situation of the cooperation in R&D with a fully competitive scenario as well as a monopolized market. The existing literature finds that for a significant amount of technological spillover between firms, the cooperation in R&D provides a better situation for consumers as well as firms, cf. (d'Aspremont and Jacquemin 1988; De Bondt and Veugelers 1991; Kamien et al. 1992). However, for a limited spillover of technologies, the R&D cooperation makes the consumers worse off than in the case when firms choose their investment decision non-cooperatively. The research also revealed a positive relation between spillover ratio and firms' profits as well as consumer surplus.

We propose an extension to the model of (d'Aspremont and Jacquemin 1988) later developed by Kamien et al. (1992) by adding a heterogeneity of the product. Thus, we analyze a Cournot duopoly in which firms decide first how close they are from each other in terms of substitutability, then they made simultaneous decisions concerning their level of R&D investment and then production. The addition of a decision concerning the scale of product heterogeneity allows us to study the effect of cooperation on horizontal differentiation of goods as well as its impact on the consumers. Hence, we add a new stage to the game: before other strategic decisions are being made, firms decide on how apart from each other their products are, as in the horizontal differentiation way that can be related to the Hotelling model, cf. (Hotelling 1990). We assume that this decision maximizes their joint profit – this can be associated with a simplified form of obtaining Hotelling competition result of profit-maximizing differentiation.

We set a trade-off between a decision of product differentiation and spillover ratio. Thus, we assume that if the products are close substitutes, they can generate a significant cost reduction from each other's investment in R&D. Hence, the decision of differentiation can be modeled as a decision of choosing an optimal level of spillover.[1] The goods horizontal differentiation and spillover ratio are linked by

[1] For modeling reasons (mainly having a similar cost function that in original works), we assume that firms decide on the level of spillover and that level is transformed into substitution ratio by function h. However, as the economic context and real possibility seems more plausible in assuming that firms decide on the scope of differentiation, we will refer to that decision process in that manner.

a continuous function h with parameter α that allows to modify the easiness of differentiation for a given level of closeness of technologies.

We find that the optimal level of spillover ratio from the firms' perspective, contrary to original research, is below the perfect spillover level. If differentiating between each other's products is very limited, the optimal strategy is to disregard the gains from spillovers and operate on two separate markets. For some easiness of differentiation, there can be an equilibrium when firms decide on the positive but not complete level of substitutability of the offered products. Moreover, the easier it is to differentiate from one another, the higher the level of spillover is set by the firms.

As in the original papers, we analyze the welfare implications of cooperation in the R&D investment and full market monopolization.[2] Similarly to the result of the homogeneous market, we find that R&D cooperation is beneficial both to firms and to the consumers. However, contrary to (d'Aspremont and Jacquemin 1988), we find that the cooperation in R&D is beneficial to both market parties for any tested parametrization. It is because firms want to coordinate high investment with a high level of spillover which significantly lowers the market price.

Another critical point of our findings is that full monopolization, in any analyzed scenario, is a better alternative than a fully competitive one regarding the total welfare. Moreover, it is only slightly worse than the R&D cooperation from the perspective of consumers and total welfare. This result comes from the fact that monopolization stimulates more R&D investment and increases its efficiency from the cost-reduction perspective and thus allows firms to lower the market price while remaining a positive margin.

The relationship between product differentiation and R&D research has been examined in economic literature. Dixit (1979), Singh and Vives (1984), Lin and Saggi (2002), Cefis et al. (2009) are just some prominent examples of the contemporary theoretical and empirical investigation of this relation. The analysis focused mainly on finding the interrelationship of product differentiation, R&D investment in a competitive scenario. The emphasis in the research was mainly placed on differentiation strategies and entry barriers in an innovative market. Symeonidis (2003) compares Bertrand and Cournot competition for different levels of exogenous technology spillover and horizontal market differentiation. Harter (1993) looks at the horizontal location model in a context of R&D investment and looks for entry barriers. Park (2001) analyzes a vertical market differentiation with R&D investment and examines the impact of subsidies on the market. The first notion of heterogeneous products and R&D investment was examined by Piga and Poyago-Theotoky (2005). They propose a three-stage game with the location, R&D investment and price stage. They find that, for the high cost of differentiation, there is a perfect differentiation equilibrium. They also find a positive relationship between product differentiation and R&D activity.

The remaining unsolved issue is the examination of the impact of cartelization on the industry with R&D spillover in which products are differentiated. It is an

[2] In that case, it is a situation of a monopolist operating on two horizontally differentiated markets with two separate (but not entirely due for spillover) production facilities.

especially important research question concerning antitrust policies in the aspect of innovative industries. Prokop and Karbowski (2018) analyzes the Stackelberg model with technology spillover and exogenous differentiation. Thus, the link between the decision of horizontal differentiation and R&D investment in cooperative scenarios has not been researched. The paper is trying to fill the gap in this area.

The article is structured as follows. Section 13.2 describes the basic model of Cournot duopoly with endogenous differentiation and R&D investment. The model is then solved for a given parametrization. In Sect. 13.3, we analyze two cooperative scenarios: the R&D investment cooperation and full market monopolization in terms of welfare comparisons. Section 13.4 concludes.

13.2 The Model of Duopoly

We examine a model of a two-firm, Cournot-type competition, in which firms compete by producing each a single heterogeneous good. The goods are horizontally differentiated; hence, they remain substitutes for each other. Therefore, the inverse demand function of a firm 1 is

$$p_1 = a - h(\beta)q_2 - q_1, \tag{13.1}$$

where a is a demand function parameter, q_1 and q_2 are the produced quantities of firms 1 and 2 and $h : [0, 1] \to [0, 1]$ is a function of substitutability between the goods. Its argument $\beta \in [0, 1]$ is the technology spillover parameter between the firms, which is described below. The function h links the technology spillover into the substitution of the goods from the perspective of a consumer. We assume that firms are identical in the sense of production technology and demand, to the extent of their heterogeneity in the offered product. Thus, the inverse demand function of firm 2 is symmetrical to the one in the formula 13.1.

Firms incur a linear cost of production $c < a$, which can be lowered by R&D investment. We denote by x_i the investment in R&D of firm i, which is described in monetary terms. Moreover, the investment of the firms can impact the production cost of each other due to technology spillover. This phenomenon is captured by the parameter $\beta \in [0, 1]$ which states what proportion of one firm investment can be transferred to its competitor. The cost of R&D investment is quadratic with parameter $\gamma > 0$. The cost function of firm 1 is then (with symmetrical one for firm 2):

$$c_1 = q_1 (c - \beta x_2 - x_1) + \frac{\gamma x_1^2}{2}. \tag{13.2}$$

Hence, the firm 1 profit is then given by the following formula

$$\pi_1 = (a - c - h(\beta)q_2 - q_1 + \beta x_2 + x_1)\, q_1 - \frac{\gamma x_1^2}{2}, \tag{13.3}$$

with an analogous one for firm 2.

The game has the following dynamics:

1. Firms decide upon the spillover ratio β which corresponds to product differentiation $h(\beta)$;
2. Firms choose their level of R&D investment x_i;
3. Firms choose their level of production q_i;
4. The market prices are obtained, and firms receive their profits.

Each firm is informed about the action of its opponent after each stage. At stages 2–3, firms decide simultaneously about the level of R&D investment and the quantity produced. At stage 1, the decision is mutual: firms decide on the level of substitution to maximize their joint profit.

The function h transforms the decision of how much the products should differ from the technological perspective into their substitutability from the consumers' perspective. While firms would like to obtain a monopoly power and the products not to be easily substituted for one another, there is a trade-off of technological advantage from closely related goods that come from cost-reducing spillover. Thus, for $\beta = 0$, there is no spillover effect, but firms can perfectly distinct their products and become monopolists. On the other hand, if $\beta = 1$, the game transforms into a classic Cournot homogeneous competition from the standpoint of market demand with complete spillover, representing a situation of two firms supplying a homogeneous good and having a joint research unit. The choice of β does not bear any cost or restraints. Hence, function h provides a limit of possible product differentiation for a given level of technological closeness.[3]

Mathematically, h should be a monotonic function transforming the interval $[0, 1]$ into itself. In the following analysis, we will use the function $h(\beta) = \beta^\alpha$ as an example of such a function. While satisfying the above requirements, it has relatively simple form that can trace whether high differentiation, so low level of $h(\beta)$, is achieved for relatively close technologies (that happens if $\alpha > 1$, we will denote the possibility of differentiation as "easy") or whether firms cannot differentiate their product from the opponents without losing a substantial part of the spillover effect (so when $\alpha < 1$, the differentiation is "difficult").

The game is solved using backward induction. The resulted solution is a subgame perfect Nash equilibrium. The equilibrium then takes the form of a tuple including decision about the optimal spillover level β, the R&D investment amount x_i for given β and the amount of the good produced given x_i and β for $i = 1, 2$. As the game is symmetric, we focus only on a symmetric equilibrium of the game. Moreover, we only allow for pure strategies to be played.

[3] We can, without a loss in generality, reverse this logic and state that firms choose how distinct their products are and given that they will try to obtain as much spillover as possible. Both principles would lead to the same conclusions.

13.2.1 Optimal Production Level

Going through backward induction, we start solving the model by finding the optimal levels of production, given a level of spillover β and R&D investment levels x_1, x_2. We find that by separately optimizing the firms' profits with respect to their amount of production. The optimal production is then:

$$q_i^*(x_i, x_{-i}, \beta) = \frac{\beta^\alpha (a - c + \beta x_i + x_{-i}) - 2\,(a - c + \beta x_{-i} + x_i)}{\beta^{2\alpha} - 4}, \tag{13.4}$$

where $i = 1, 2$ and subscript $-i$ refers to the opponent of i. We can see that the level of firm's optimal production increases with the R&D investment, both its own as well as its opponent's. Moreover, as it is the case in the (d'Aspremont and Jacquemin 1988) and in the standard Cournot model, the levels of production are strategic substitutes.

An increase in the spillover effect level β does not constitute a straightforward response in the equilibrium production. For identical levels of firms' R&D investment, if the diversification is easy, the production lowers with the level of the spillover. It means that the substitution effect, generated by $h(\beta)$, dominates the cost-lowering one that comes from the technology spillover.

13.2.2 Optimal R&D Investment Level

Knowing the equilibrium production function $q_i^*(x_i, x_{-i}, \beta)$ from the formula 13.4, firms decide separately on the optimal level of R&D investment. Their equilibrium decision, x_i^* for firm $i = 1, 2$, is then a function of β and model parameters:

$$x_i^*(\beta) = \frac{2(a - c)\left(\beta^{1+\alpha} - 2\right)}{\beta^\alpha\left(\gamma\beta^\alpha\left(\beta^\alpha + 2\right) - 2\left(\beta^2 + \beta + 2\gamma\right)\right) + 4(\beta - 2\gamma + 1)}. \tag{13.5}$$

For $\alpha \geq 1$ (so when differentiation is easy), the R&D investments are, contrary to production levels, strategic complements. However, if the differentiation is difficult, the increase in opponent's investment may not cause a positive reaction in that area. For a given $\alpha < 1$ and for low levels of β, it might be possible that the investment levels are strategic substitutes. This relation comes from the fact that the increase of opponent's investment forces firms to raise their production in a linear way, which leads to a lower market price. Moreover, the increase of opponent's investment, due to the spillover effect, already lowers the firm's production cost. As the investment cost is quadratic, it might be more profitable to decrease the level of investment as a response to opponent's increase in R&D spending. It is especially true for the case of high product differentiation, where the price effect, as well as spillover, is small.

13.2.3 Optimal Level of Product Differentiation

At the beginning of the game, firms decide cooperatively on the level of product differentiation. That is, they determine the level of β in a way that maximizes their joint profit. This decision comes with a trade-off. On the one hand, higher β lowers their production cost for given R&D investment through spillover effects. On the other hand, high β constraints their ability to differentiate the products which are reflected in the offered price.

We were, unfortunately, unable to obtain an exact analytic form of optimal spillover variable for the general specification of the parameters. However, we were able to obtain some general results, summarized, by the following proposition:

Proposition 1 *If $\alpha \leq 1$, the optimal level of spillover ratio β^* is equal to 0. If $\alpha > 1$, the optimal level of spillover ratio β^* is higher than 0.*

If it is difficult to differentiate products, then firms would not like to engage in technology exchange through spillovers. Instead, the optimal situation is when they produce maximally differentiated products and obtain monopoly profits. However, if firms can easily make their products distinct from each other, they allow some level of spillover in order to lower their production cost. This comes from the fact that while the increase in β leads to a linear reduction in production cost as well as sublinear (for $\alpha > 1$) or superlinear (for $\alpha < 1$) price increase. Thus, the intuition is that the optimal level of β should be then weakly increasing with the level of α (if differentiation is easy), which is in line with the following numerical simulations.

13.2.4 Numerical Results

To obtain exact solution of the model, we assume that the parameters take the following form: $a = 1$, $c = 1/2$, $\gamma = 1/2$.[4] This parametrization would lead to the monopoly price of 2/3 with monopoly production of 1/3. We gathered the results from numerical simulations into the following statements.

Statement 1 *The optimal level of β^* is weakly increasing in α. If $\alpha > 1$, $\beta^*(\alpha)$ is strictly increasing.*

As we can see in Fig. 13.1, for $\alpha > 1$, the optimal level of spillover ratio β^* is strictly increasing in α. This increase, apart from the initial level, is marginally decreasing. Thus, as the ability to differentiate for a given level of spillover is higher, firms are more willing to accept the closeness of their products. At the limit, as $\alpha \to \infty$, $\beta^* \to 1$.

[4]It shall be noted, that while there is no general proof to that statement, the following results are robust to the changes in the listed parameters' values.

Fig. 13.1 The optimal level of spillover β^* for different values of differentiation constraint parameter α

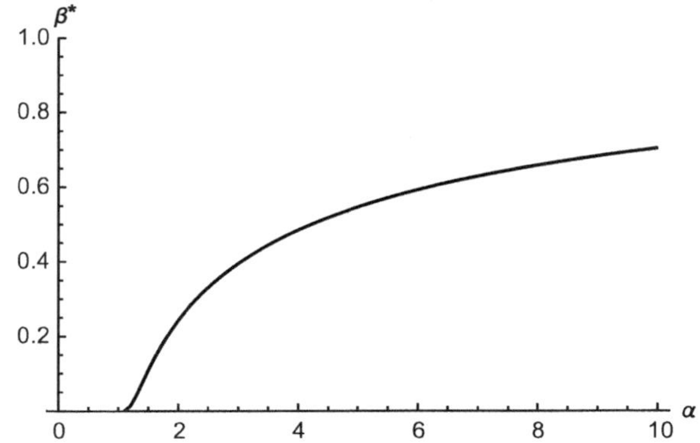

Fig. 13.2 R&D investment of a single firm in the equilibrium for different values of α

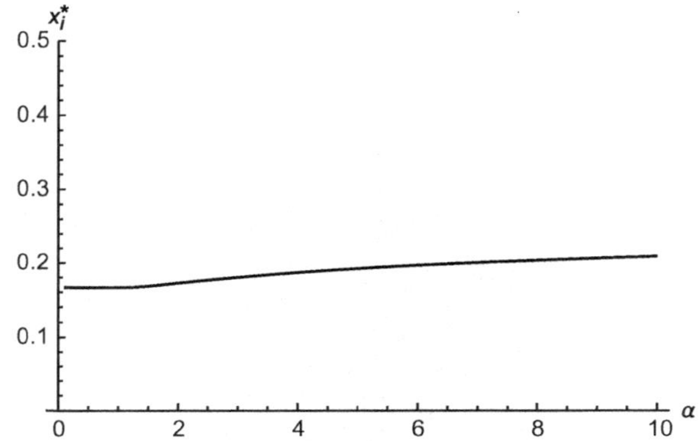

Statement 2 *The level of firm's R&D investment in the equilibrium* x_i^* *is weakly increasing in* α *and strictly increasing for* $\alpha > 1$.
The amount of firm's production in the equilibrium q_i^* *is weakly increasing in* α *and strictly increasing for* $\alpha > 1$.
The equilibrium price in the equilibrium is weakly decreasing in α *and strictly decreasing for* $\alpha > 1$.

The other decision variables of firms: R&D investment and production level are also weakly increasing in α. If $\alpha < 1$, due to no spillover, the optimal levels of x_i^* and q_i^* are the same for any value of the parameter. Thus, with higher spillover ratio that comes from higher values of β^*, the firms will commit to higher R&D investment. However, because of lower differentiation of products, they need to engage in a fiercer competition by increasing their production over the monopoly level.

It shall be noted that for the given parametrization, the increase in R&D investment and quantity produced due to increase in α (if the differentiation is easy) has a steady, linear property as we can see in Fig. 13.2. The rates of increase of these variables are not very significant, in comparison with the reaction of the optimal level of spillover. As α increases from 1 to 10, the optimal level of R&D spending and

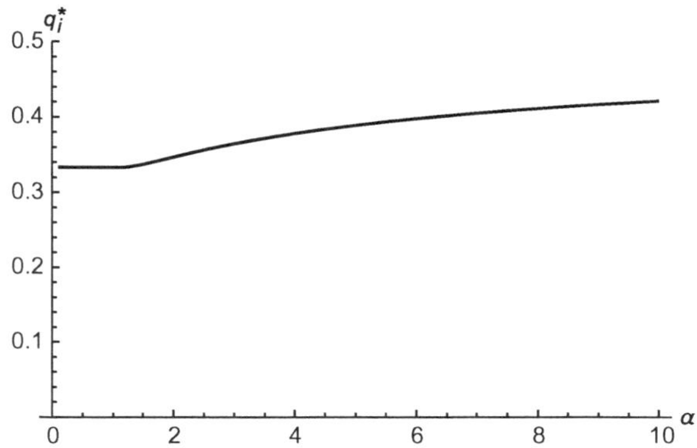

Fig. 13.3 Production of a single firm in the equilibrium for different values of α

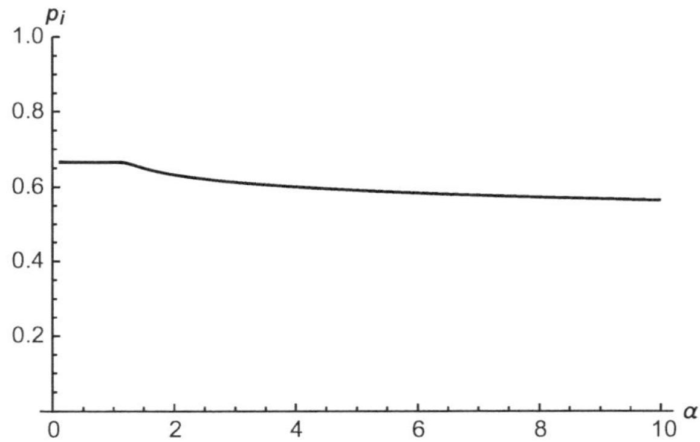

Fig. 13.4 The equilibrium price for a good of a single firm for different values of α

production amount increase for about 25.1% and 26.4%, respectively in an almost linear fashion. The linearity comes from the fact that, while higher α (and thus, a higher level of spillover) lowers the production cost linearly, it also lowers the price in a sublinear fashion (for $\alpha > 1$). Hence, the product of these two forces leads to a modest increase in decision variables due to an increase of α.

The equilibrium price, as it is depicted in Fig. 13.4, is strictly decreasing in α if the differentiation is easy for firms. The decrease is stronger than the increase in production from Fig. 13.3. It follows from the fact that the price of firm's i product depends linearly on the quantity of it produced but also for higher values of α, the optimal level of spillover increases, which makes the goods closer substitutes. Thus, the higher impact of the quantity increase of the opponent makes, by joint force, the market price fall more rapidly than the increase in the quantity of the product itself.

Although the increase in α lowers the price for the firm's i product, the single firm's profit is increasing with the value of the parameter, as it is shown in Fig. 13.5. It is due to the higher quantity produced (the total revenue is increasing with α) as well as cost reduction as a result of a higher technology spillover.

Fig. 13.5 The equilibrium profit of a single firm for different values of α

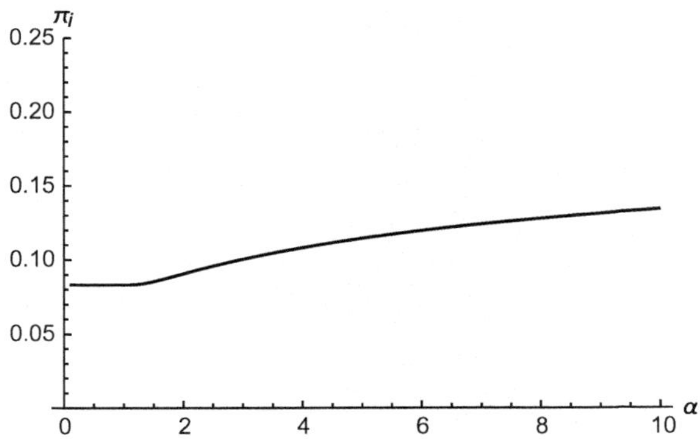

Fig. 13.6 The total welfare in equilibrium for different values of α

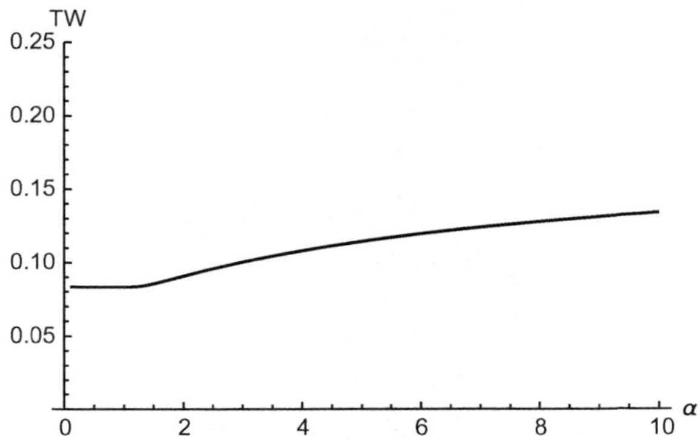

From the welfare perspective, it might be interesting to see how differentiation constraint affects consumers. We define the consumer surplus CS as follows:

$$CS = \frac{(a - p_i)^2}{2}. \tag{13.6}$$

The consumer surplus is taken from the standard formula of single-good demand–supply analysis. Hence, it does not consider any effect of a multiproduct market, particularly the benefit of having a broad area of products. Thus, the only variable that affects the consumer surplus is the price. The definition was chosen for its simplicity but also because the market price for a single good captures the spillover and differentiation effects into a single number. Also, the price is decreasing with α, which makes consumer surplus positively related to the market homogeneity. Thus, including the fact of a wider variety of product due to product differentiation would not change this relation.

The total welfare, being the sum of consumer surplus and firms' profits, is also increasing with the easiness of differentiation as it is shown in Fig. 13.6. Therefore, it is in both firms' and consumers' interest to allow firms to differentiate their product.

It allows for higher spillover, lowering the production cost, which translates into a higher supply of product and thus lower prices.

The effects of differentiation constraint α on firms' profits, consumer surplus and total welfare are summarized in the following statement.

Statement 3 *The single firm profit in equilibrium is weakly increasing in α. If $\alpha > 1$, the profit is strictly increasing.*
The consumer welfare is weakly increasing in α. If $\alpha > 1$, the consumer welfare is strictly increasing.
The total welfare is weakly increasing in α. If $\alpha > 1$, the total welfare is strictly increasing.

13.3 Market Cartelization

We now investigate the impact of a partial or total cartelization of the markets in the presented setting. As in (d'Aspremont and Jacquemin 1988), we will consider two types of cartelization: the collective decision in R&D investment (leaving the competition in the production stage) and full monopolization (in R&D investment and production). Since the differentiation decision is already assumed a cooperative one, we do not impose any changes on that from the baseline analysis standpoint. Hence, we can investigate how the market equilibrium changes in response to making competition less fierce in such a market structure and how will it affect consumers and total welfare. For language simplicity, we will denote the base model as a fully competitive one, although it shall be noted that the optimal level of spillover is not decided upon competitively.

13.3.1 Cooperation in the R&D Investment

We now allow firms to choose the level of R&D investment at period 2 in a cooperative manner, that is, in such a way that maximizes their joint profits. Thus, knowing the optimal production function from the formula 13.4, they choose x_1 and x_2 to maximize the sum of their profits for a given value of β. The optimal investment x_i^{CX} is then

$$x_i^{CX}(\beta) = \frac{2(a-c)(1+\beta)}{\gamma\beta^{2\alpha} + 4\gamma\beta^{\alpha} - 2(2+\beta)\beta + 4\gamma - 2}. \tag{13.7}$$

The comparison between the optimal level of R&D investment in the base model, given by Eq. 13.5 and the one with the cartel at the investment stage is given by the following proposition.

Proposition 2 *If the differentiation is easy (so $\alpha > 1$), the optimal level of investment is higher in the game with R&D investment cooperation than in competitive scenario for any value of spillover ratio β.*

If it is easy to differentiate, allowing firms to decide on R&D investment jointly will lead to higher spending in that area. For $\alpha < 1$, so when it is difficult to differentiate, the difference is ambiguous. It shall be noted that from the Proposition 1, at least in the base model, there is no spillover if α is not higher than 1. Thus, in that case, firms act as monopolists on the separate market and have no economic interaction. Therefore, if firms can coordinate their actions on R&D, they can boost each others decision in that regard. In comparison with (d'Aspremont and Jacquemin 1988), this relation is independent from the value of β.

The optimal level of spillover ratio β^{CX} for the model with R&D cartel has similar properties as in the fully competitive scenario. This finding is summarized in the following proposition.

Proposition 3 *If $\alpha \leq 1$, the optimal level of spillover ratio β^{CX} in the game with R&D cooperation is equal to 0. If $\alpha > 1$, the optimal level of spillover ratio β^{CX} is higher than 0.*

Thus, as in the fully competitive scenario, firms will cut any form of market interaction if the differentiation is difficult in exchange for being a monopolist without any technology spillover benefits.

Given the same parametrization as in the base model, we can compare the optimal values of β between scenarios. The following statement provides an impact of cartelization on product differentiation.

Statement 4 *If the differentiation is easy (so $\alpha > 1$), $\beta^{CX} > \beta^*$.*

Hence, if the cooperation in R&D is possible, firms decide on the spillover ratio that is higher than the one in the case of no cooperation. This comes as an implication of higher investment in R&D: if firms coordinate on higher investment, they want to gain cost greater cost reduction by increasing their spillover ratio. Figure 13.7 shows a comparison between the two optimal spillover ratios.

The increase in spillover ratio transfers into higher spending (as stated in Proposition 2) as well as higher production. As the coordination itself makes the investment higher, the increase in spillover ratio uplifts the values of R&D spending to even higher values as it is shown in Fig. 13.8. A very high boost to investment leads consequently to increased production, depicted in Fig. 13.9. Furthermore, the cooperation in R&D makes the values of this decision variables more influenced by the changes in differentiation constraint parameter α.

The following statement summarizes the impact of cooperation in R&D investment on welfare.

Statement 5 *If differentiation is easy (so $\alpha > 1$):*

- *Single firm profit is higher in the case of R&D cooperation than in full competition. Moreover, it is increasing in α.*

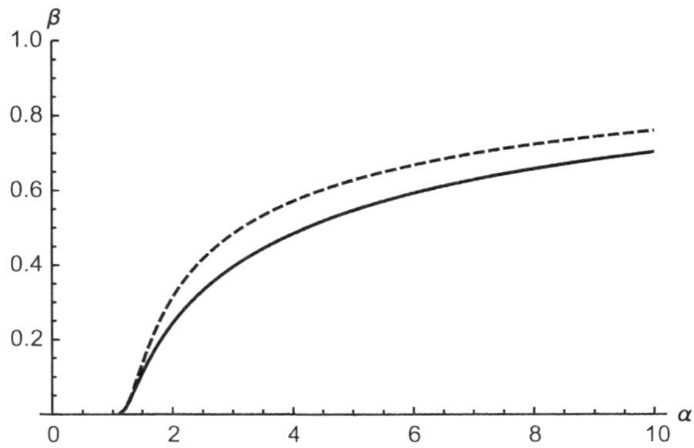

Fig. 13.7 Optimal level of spillover for the full competition model (solid line) and R&D cooperation (dashed line) for different values of α

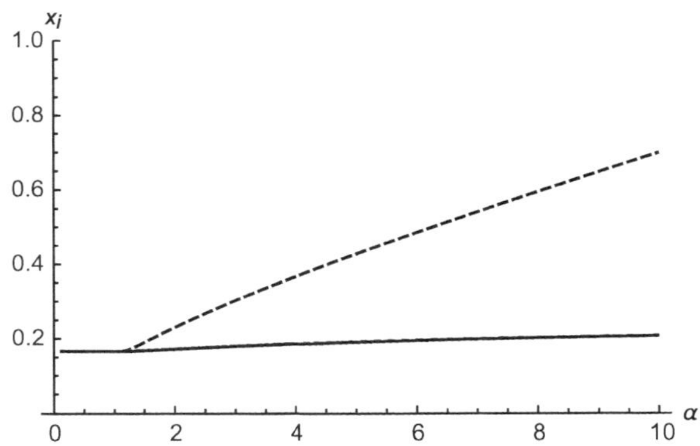

Fig. 13.8 R&D investment of a single firm in the equilibrium in the full competitive scenario (solid line) and R&D cooperation (dashed line) for different values of α

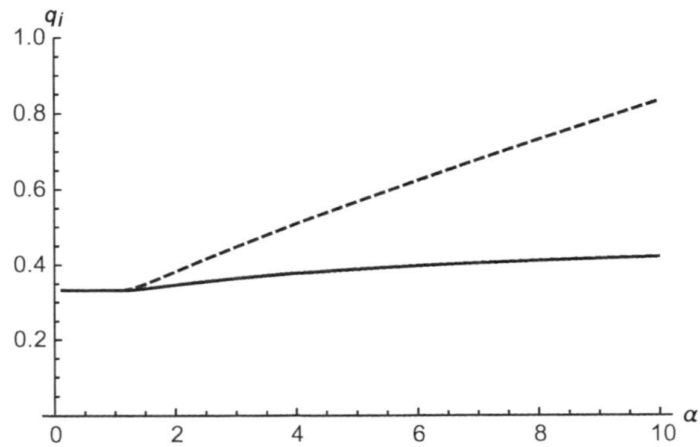

Fig. 13.9 Production of a single firm in the equilibrium in the full competitive scenario (solid line) and R&D cooperation (dashed line) for different values of α

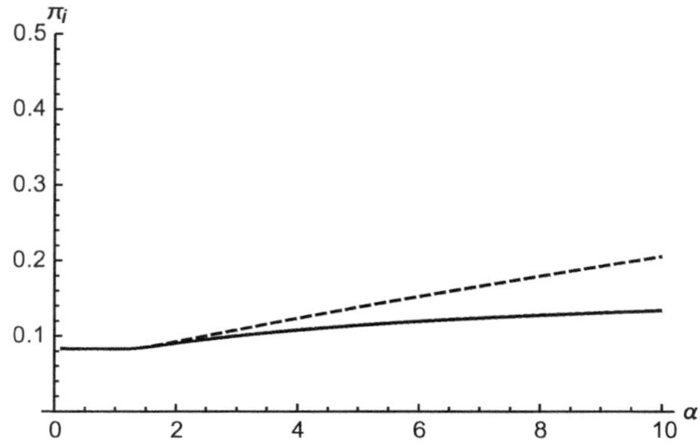

Fig. 13.10 Single firm's profit in the equilibrium in the full competitive scenario (solid line) and R&D cooperation (dashed line) for different values of α

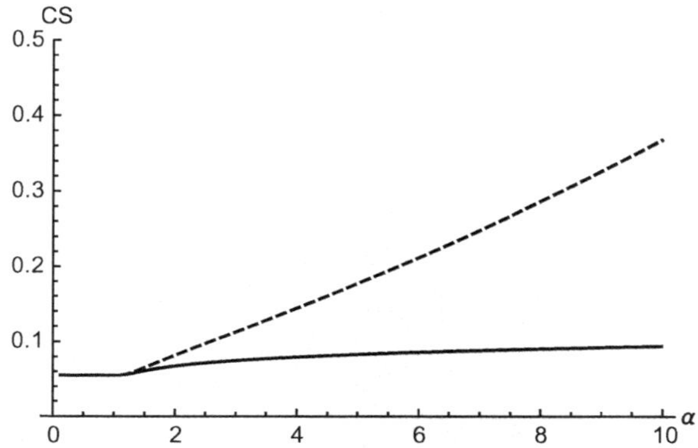

Fig. 13.11 Consumer surplus in the equilibrium in the full competitive scenario (solid line) and R&D cooperation (dashed line) for different values of α

- *Consumer surplus is higher in the case of R&D cooperation than in full competition. Moreover, it is increasing in α.*
- *Total welfare is higher in the case of R&D cooperation than in full competition. Moreover, it is increasing in α.*

Intuitively, coordinating on R&D investment makes both firms better off in terms of their profits, as it is shown in Fig. 13.10. The coordinated increase in R&D investment and higher spillover ratio transfers into significant lowering of production cost. The closer substitutability lowers the price for the firm's product, but higher production compensates for that in terms of revenue. The easier it is for firms to differentiate their product, the higher the profit: while an increase in spillover, as a result of higher α, makes the competition stronger, the cost reduction is significant enough to compensate for that.

Because the market price goes down as a result of an increase in production, as well as in spillover ratio (due to lower differentiation), the consumer surplus rises when firms attempt to coordinate investment levels in R&D as it is depicted in Fig. 13.11. Thus, the total welfare, being the sum of firms' profits and consumer surplus, is also higher in the case of R&D cooperation than in full competition as it is increasing with the easiness of differentiation between firms.

13.3.2 Full Cartel

Similarly to (d'Aspremont and Jacquemin 1988), we will also examine the scenario in which both R&D investment and production are decided on cooperatively. Therefore, all the strategic variables are chosen as if firms were acting like a monopolist on two linked markets with two production and R&D facilities. Moving through the backward induction, the optimal level of production q_i^{FC} of a single firm is then:

$$q_i^{FC}(x,\beta) = \frac{a - c + \beta x + x}{2\left(\beta^{\alpha} + 1\right)}, \tag{13.8}$$

where x is a R&D spending of a single firm[5] and β is the chosen beforehand optimal level of spillover. For the given level of β and $x_1 = x_2 = x$, the quantity produced under full competition is higher than under full cooperation iff $x(1+\beta) > a - c$.

The R&D investment in the case of full cooperation is subject to the same rules as in the R&D cooperation scenario. The optimal level of spending x_i^{FC} of a single firm for a given value of technology spillover ratio is then

$$x_i^{FC}(\beta) = \frac{(1+\beta)(a-c)}{2\gamma\beta^{\alpha} - \beta^2 - 2\beta + 2\gamma - 1}. \tag{13.9}$$

For the given value of β, the order between $x_i^*(\beta)$, $x_i^{CX}(\beta)$ and $x_i^{FC}(\beta)$ is ambiguous and strongly depends on value of parameters.

Investigating further the case of full cooperation, we find that, similar to two previous cases, the optimal level of spillover is increasing with the easiness of differentiation as it is stated in the following proposition.

Proposition 4 *If $\alpha \le 1$, the optimal level of spillover ratio β^{FC} in the game with R&D cartel is equal to 0. If $\alpha > 1$, the optimal level of spillover ratio β^{FC} is higher than 0.*

For the same parametrization as in the previous scenarios, we find that the optimal level of spillover is highest in this scenario. This finding is summarized in the following statement.

Statement 6 *For $\alpha > 1$, the optimal level of spillover in the full cooperation scenario is higher than in any other two cases, so $\beta^{FC} > \beta^{CX} > \beta^*$.*

---

[5] Note that since the marginal cost of R&D investment is increasing, it is optimal to allocate the total R&D investment between the firms equally.

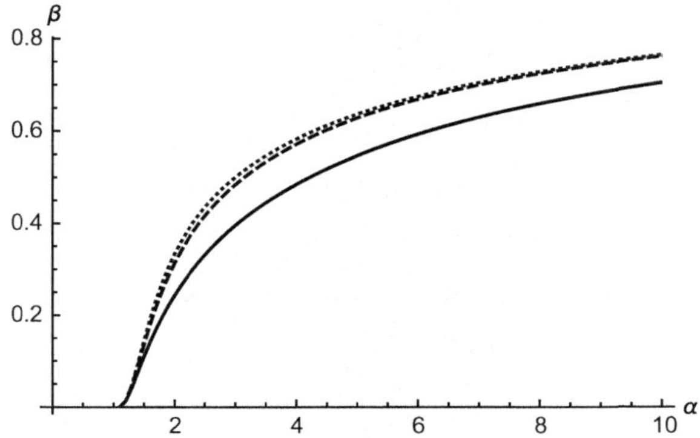

Fig. 13.12 Optimal level of spillover for the full competition model (solid line), R&D cooperation (dashed line) and full cooperation (dotted line) for different values of α

In the case of a monopoly operating on two markets with two production and R&D facilities, it chooses to have a very high ratio of spillover. It partially comes from the fact that having control over the production level, firms in full cooperation are not as much troubled by the closeness of their products for consumers. As numerical simulations in Fig. 13.12 show, the optimal level of spillover ratio (and thus the corresponding level of substitutability between their products) is just a bit higher than in the case of cooperation in only R&D investment. As in the case of two previous scenarios, the optimal level of spillover is increasing in α (if the differentiation is easy) in a marginally decreasing manner. The highest difference between β^{FC} and β^{XC} is obtained at $\alpha = 2.8$.

The optimal values of decision variables in case of full cooperation equilibrium, as our numerical simulations suggest, are very closely related to the values in the case of only R&D cooperation. They also fall under the same relationship with parameter α. The following statement summarizes the relation between decision variables in the three analyzed scenarios.

Statement 7 *If* $\alpha > 1$ *(so differentiation is easy):*

- *The R&D investment is subject to the following relation:* $x^{FC} > x^{CX} > x^*$.
- *The production is subject to the following relation:* $q^{CX} > q^{FC} > q^*$.

Thus, even if the markets are monopolized, due to a high level of R&D investment and thus cost reduction, the production level under full cooperation is higher than under fully competitive scenario. From the equilibrium outcome standpoint, a fully cooperative case does not differ a lot from the case of cooperation in only R&D cooperation—it presents with a bit higher investment in R&D and a little lower production with more spillover effect.

As intuition suggests, the single firm profit is higher if it is part of a full cooperative scenario than in any case when there is competition at any stage of the game. However, the difference obtained by numerical simulations between full cooperation and cooperation in only R&D investment is insignificant—at the highest point with respect to α, it amounted for only 0.16% increase in profits.

The consumer surplus, due to lower production and thus higher price (which is not suppressed by a bit higher differentiation), is lower for full cooperation scenario than in the case when only R&D investment is coordinated. This results in total welfare being highest in the scenario of cooperation in only R&D investment, but the case of full cooperation is a not much worse one from the perspective of total welfare: performed numerical simulations suggest that in the worst case, the total welfare would drop for 1.8% due to cooperation in production (assuming cooperation in R&D investment). The formal statement of the relation of welfare values for the three scenarios is given below.

Statement 8 *Given that* $\alpha > 1$*:*

- *The single firm's profit is subject to the following relation:* $\pi_i^{FC} > \pi_i^{CX} > \pi^*$.
- *The consumer surplus is subject to the following relation:* $CS^{XC} > CS^{FC} > CS^*$.
- *The total welfare is subject to the following relation:* $TW^{XC} > TW^{FC} > TW^*$.

13.4 Conclusion

The paper examines the impact of R&D cooperation and full monopolization on product differentiation, R&D investment and production levels. In our three-stage game, firms want to differentiate the product in order to gain more monopoly power, while the closer substitutes their products are, the more they can gain from technology spillover. We find a positive relationship between the level of differentiation and R&D investment. Thus, the easier it is for firms to differentiate, the more they will invest in R&D, to reduce the negative impact of differentiation on cost-reducing spillover that transfers into production increase and thus price reduction. The results are consistent with the similar model of horizontal differentiation with R&D investment of (Piga and Poyago-Theotoky 2005).

The key aspect of the paper comes from the investigation of welfare analysis in two cooperation scenarios, R&D cooperation and full market monopolization. We find that allowing firms to coordinate their R&D investment leads to a significantly lower market differentiation (which transfers into a higher level of spillover) and much higher investment in R&D. This allows firms to increase their profits due to significant cost reduction but also allows them to increase production which implies a lower market price for consumers and thus increase in consumer surplus.

What is an especially significant finding is that the full monopolistic outcome outlasts in terms of consumer surplus and total welfare the fully competitive scenario. While the firms can coordinate the production process to obtain more monopoly power, the coordination in R&D surpasses that effect. Moreover, the welfare results from full monopolization are very close to the ones from cooperation in only R&D investment. Hence, as the results show, the restrictions on R&D cooperation that can be made by the antitrust agencies for fear of market cartelization are not justified by the theoretical model as the lack of coordinated R&D investment does the consumers more harm than market monopolization.

Although the presented model gives theoretical insight into the welfare implications of coordinated activity with endogenous differentiation and R&D investment, the presented research is just a first step into an examination of this relationship. A more general investigation of possible cost functions and their parametrizations is necessary to determine the paper conclusions in a more throughout manner. Moreover, the decision of spillover ratio (which translates into differentiation level) can be examined as an outcome of competitive decision-making. The increase of heterogeneity between firms and the increase in the number of competitors might also serve as an inspiring generalization. Thus, we think that by the paper, we allow much more extensive research concerning the implications of R&D cooperation on market differentiation.

Appendix

Proof of Proposition 1

The profit of the firm i, given the optimal reactions of production and R&D investment, is:

$$\pi_i(\beta) = \frac{\gamma(a-c)^2\left(\beta^\alpha\left(\gamma\beta^{3\alpha} - 2\beta^\alpha\left(\beta^2+4\gamma\right)+8\beta\right)+16\gamma-8\right)}{\left(2\gamma\beta^{2\alpha}+\gamma\beta^{3\alpha}-2\beta^\alpha\left(\beta^2+\beta+2\gamma\right)+4\beta-8\gamma+4\right)^2}, \tag{13.10}$$

while, if $\beta = 0$, the profit function is then

$$\pi_i(\beta = 0) = \frac{\gamma(a-c)^2}{4\gamma-2}. \tag{13.11}$$

Assuming $0 < c < a$ and $\alpha \leq 1$, the profit from the formula 13.10 is always lower than if $\beta = 0$.

For $\alpha > 1$, the profit for $\beta > 0$ is always higher than the one for $\beta = 0$.

Proof of Proposition 2

To proof Proposition 2 we need to state that the optimal level of firm's investment x_i^* from formula 13.5 is higher than x_i^{CX} from the formula 13.7. It can be shown, after some calculations, that it is the case for $\alpha > 1$.

Proof of Proposition 3

The profit of firm i in the R&D investment cooperation scenario, for the given optimal level of R&D investment function and best response in terms of production, is

$$\pi_i^{CX}(\beta) = \frac{\gamma(a-c)^2}{\gamma\beta^{2\alpha} + 4\gamma\beta^{\alpha} - 2(\beta+2)\beta + 4\gamma - 2}. \tag{13.12}$$

If $\beta = 0$, the above formula is then the same as in formula 13.4. It can be seen that if $\alpha \leq 1$, the profit is highest when $\beta = 0$, while if $\alpha > 1$ the profit for $\beta > 0$ will be always higher than if $\beta = 0$.

Proof of Proposition 4

The profit of the firm i in the fully cooperative scenario, for the given optimal level of R&D investment function and production, is

$$\pi_i^{FC}(\beta) = \frac{\gamma(a-c)^2}{4\gamma\beta^{\alpha} - 2(\beta+2)\beta + 4\gamma - 2}. \tag{13.13}$$

As in Propositions 1 and 3, for $\alpha \leq 1$, the firm's profit is highest if $\beta = 0$, while for $\alpha > 1$, it is always higher for $\beta > 0$.

References

Becker, W., & Dietz, J. (2004). R&D cooperation and innovation activities of firmsevidence for the german manufacturing industry. *Research Policy*, *33*(2), 209–223.

Belderbos, R., Carree, M., & Lokshin, B. (2004). Cooperative R&D and firm performance. *Research Policy*, *33*(10), 1477–1492.

Camagni, R. (1993). Inter-firm industrial networks: The costs and benefits of cooperative behaviour. *Journal of Industry Studies*, *1*(1), 1–15.

Cefis, E., Rosenkranz, S., & Weitzel, U. (2009). Effects of coordinated strategies on product and process R&D. *Journal of Economics*, *96*(3), 193–222.

d'Aspremont, C., & Jacquemin, A. (1988). Cooperative and noncooperative R&D in duopoly with spillovers. *The American Economic Review*, *78*(5), 1133–1137.

Davidson, C., & Deneckere, R. (1984). Horizontal mergers and collusive behavior. *International Journal of Industrial Organization*, *2*(2), 117–132.

De Bondt, R., & Veugelers, R. (1991). Strategic investment with spillovers. *European Journal of Political Economy*, *7*(3), 345–366.

Dixit, A. (1979). A model of duopoly suggesting a theory of entry barriers. *Journal Reprints Antitrust Law and Economics*, *10*, 399.

Harter, J. F. (1993). Differentiated products with R&D. *The Journal of Industrial Economics*, 19–28.

Horváth, R. (2002). *Cooperation in research and development*, Universitat Autònoma de Barcelona.

Hotelling, H. (1990). Stability in competition, In *The collected economics articles of harold hotelling* (pp. 50–63). Springer.

Kaiser, U. (2002). An empirical test of models explaining research expenditures and research cooperation: evidence for the german service sector. *International Journal of Industrial Organization*, *20*(6), 747–774.

Kamien, M. I., Muller, E. & Zang, I. (1992). Research joint ventures and R&D cartels. *The American Economic Review*, 1293–1306.

Lin, P., & Saggi, K. (2002). Product differentiation, process R&D, and the nature of market competition. *European Economic Review*, *46*(1), 201–211.

Park, J.-H. (2001). Strategic R&D policy under vertically differentiated oligopoly. *Canadian Journal of Economics*, 967–987.
Piga, C., & Poyago-Theotoky, J. (2005). Endogenous R&D spillovers and locational choice. *Regional science and urban economics*, *35*(2), 127–139.
Prokop, J., & Karbowski, A. (2018). *R&D spillovers and cartelization of industries with differentiated products*, ZBW.
Singh, N., & Vives, X. (1984). *Price and quantity competition in a differentiated duopoly.*
Symeonidis, G. (2003). Comparing cournot and bertrand equilibria in a differentiated duopoly with product R&D. *International Journal of Industrial Organization*, *21*(1), 39–55.
van Wegberg, M. (1995). Can R&D alliances facilitate the formation of a cartel? the example of the European it industry.

Chapter 14
Online Popularity of Luxury Brands and Its Impact on the Brand Value

Margareta Nadanyiova, Pavol Durana and Gheorghe H. Popescu

Abstract Currently, there are many luxury brands on the market. Many brands have found that luxury contributes to their competitiveness, and most consumers have a positive attitude towards luxury brands. Along with the growing interest in luxury brands, luxury company managers strive to increase brand value in accordance with the key characteristics of exclusivity and uniqueness, which are a prerequisite for luxury. The aim of this article is to define the theoretical basis of online communication and brand value from the viewpoint of domestic (Slovak) and foreign authors. This includes a regression and correlation analyses focused on investigating the dependence between the online popularity (represented by website traffic, social media audience and social media engagement) and brand value of luxury goods. The basic sources of research were secondary data obtained from worldwide surveys in the form of rankings published by Interbrand, annual reports of companies and published professional publications. General scientific methods were applied for the processing of the data, as well as mathematical–statistical methods to evaluate the data collated from the results of regression and correlation analyses and test the linear independence. The results of analyses show that the web traffic and brand value are linearly dependent; specifically, it is medium-strong direct linear dependence. Therefore, the web traffic has a direct effect on brand value of luxury goods. Conversely, the brand value of luxury brands is not primarily dependent on the level of social media audience and social media engagement.

Keywords Luxury brands · Brand value · Online communication · Website traffic · Social media audience · Social media engagement

M. Nadanyiova (✉) · P. Durana
Faculty of Operation and Economics of Transport and Communications, Department of Economics, University of Zilina, Univerzitna 1, 010 26 Zilina, Slovak Republic
e-mail: margareta.nadanyiova@fpedas.uniza.sk

G. H. Popescu
Center for Applied Macroeconomic Analysis, at AAER, New York, USA

Dimitrie Cantemir Christian University, Bucharest, Romania

N. Tsounis and A. Vlachvei (eds.), *Advances in Cross-Section Data Methods in Applied Economic Research*, Springer Proceedings in Business and Economics,
https://doi.org/10.1007/978-3-030-38253-7_14

14.1 Introduction

Luxury goods are not just about exceptional design and processing quality. The essential role lies in the brand value of luxury goods. The strong brand value is one of the most valuable assets of the company and also a very effective tool in a competitive battle. It is very complicated and costly to get customers who are faithful to another established brand, especially in the case of luxury goods.

The aim of this article is to define the theoretical basis of online communication and brand value from the viewpoint of domestic (Slovak) and foreign authors. This includes a regression and correlation analyses focused on investigating the dependence between the online popularity (represented by website traffic, social media audience and social media engagement) and brand value of luxury goods. The basic sources of research were secondary data obtained from worldwide surveys in the form of rankings published by Interbrand, annual reports of companies and published professional publications. General scientific methods were applied for the processing of the data, as well as mathematical–statistical methods to evaluate the data collated from the results of regression and correlation analyses and test the linear independence. The results of analyses show that the web traffic and brand value are linearly dependent; specifically, it is medium-strong direct linear dependence. Therefore, the web traffic has a direct effect on brand value of luxury goods. Conversely, the brand value of luxury brands is not primarily dependent on the level of social media audience and social media engagement.

14.2 Literature Review

The issue of the brand value has been researched and analyzed by many foreign and domestic authors and remains actual.

According to Aaker (2003), the brand value is a set of assets or liabilities linked to a brand's name and symbol that adds to or subtracts from the value provided by a product or service. However, in addition to these standard items, the value of the brand and the company is also made up of extensive intellectual property, goodwill and last but not least, the price of brands that they have in their portfolio.

Leek and Christodoulides (2012) define brand value as the value of goods and services, as well as added value (functional and emotional) from the brand.

The brand value is often magnetizable because companies invest substantial funding in the creation and management of a brand (Rodrigues and Martines 2016; Tringh et al. 2016). As a result, this effort leads to increased sales of branded production. Mostly, this element is referred to as the added value of products or services, which is based on how consumers perceive a brand in its price, market share or the profit rate that the brand produces (Wang and Tzeng 2012).

Chevalier and Mazzalovo (2008) mention four major categories of luxury brand values that are ranked in order of intensity. First is elitism that represents the social dimension of luxury, its role is to show social success or it is a simulator of this success. Product quality and high prices are also significant features (Kliestikova et al. 2018). Third are personal emotional elements typical for luxury brands, such as hedonism. Finally, it includes the brand power, which stems from past decisions and relates to brand reputation and uniqueness.

According to Wiedmann et al. (2009), the perception of luxury brand value by customers and the motives of consumption of luxury goods are not tied solely to a range of social factors that include status, success, diversity and human desire for recognition and respect. It also depends on the financial, functional and individual brand aspects. The financial dimension of luxury value addresses direct monetary aspects such as price, resale cost, discount and investment, and refers to the value of the product as expressed in financial units. The functional dimension of luxury value refers to product benefits and basic utilities such as quality, uniqueness, usability, reliability and durability. The individual dimension of luxury value focuses on a customer's personal orientation towards luxury consumption and addresses personal matters such as materialism. The social dimension of luxury value refers to the perceived utility individuals acquire with products recognized within their own social group, such as conspicuousness and prestige value, that may significantly affect the evaluation and propensity to purchase or consume luxury brands. Although these value dimensions operate independently, they interact with each other and have various influences on individual luxury value perceptions and behaviours that can be used to further identify and segment different types of luxury consumers (Lizbetinova et al. 2016; Lord 2018).

Online marketing, so-called digital marketing, is one of the most widely used areas of marketing communication, which is not only for luxury goods (Kicova et al. 2018; Krizanova et al. 2013). It is formed very quickly depending on current market requirements (Drugău-Constantin 2018). It is a modern way to offer customers a product that suits their needs (Kmecova 2018). Nothing can predict sales and future growth for a luxury brand quite as well as its currently popularity online. Digital marketing has gradually become an integral part of business activities in various business sectors, including luxury brands.

Prikrylova and Jahodova (2010) characterize digital marketing as a modern communication tool with a number of platforms that provide fast communication with the ability to target and personalize the content.

Busalim (2017) analyzes the development of social commerce (s-commerce) and underlines the understanding of social networking users as a key competitive advantage for companies seeking to create a customer-oriented business.

Shareef et al. (2019) examine the value of advertising and consumer attitudes towards advertising. The aim of his research is to identify a source exception from a credibility perspective in order to create an advertising value and a positive attitude towards ads posted on social network Facebook.

E-marketing, as an emerging strategic tool, plays an important role in bringing buyers and sellers to the digital environment (Stefanikova et al. 2015; Stefko et al. 2015).

Digital marketing offers a number of tools that are differentiated by their goals. The most widely used tools of digital communication are (Prirylova and Jahodova 2010):

- Web Optimization;
- Online Public Relations;
- Search Engine Optimization (SEO);
- Pay Per Click (PPC);
- Google Company Profile;
- Advertising Campaigns;
- Blogs and Vlogs;
- Email Marketing;
- Social Networks (Facebook, Instagram, Twitter, YouTube and so on);
- Banners;
- Viral Marketing.

14.3 Methods

As part of the science project APVV—Slovak abbreviation of Slovak Research and Development Agency, our study "Integrated model of management support for building and managing the brand value in the specific conditions of the Slovak Republic", we investigated online popularity of brands and its impact on brand value. We focused on the world's most valuable brands, based on Best Global Brands 2018 Rankings published by Interbrand (Nadanyiova and Kliestikova 2018).

The brand value is affected by many factors, such as costs, incomes, customer preferences, marketing communication and so on.

Varying marketing trends, rapid digital development and evolving consumer preferences are creating a new competitive landscape where traditional tools of marketing communication are under threat (Bikar and Sedliacikova 2018; Jurkovic et al. 2016). And just online popularity of brand can increase sales and its brand value. That is the reason why we have analyzed how the best global brands are ranking online and how this fact affects their brand value.

Our survey focused on the field of luxury brands. Luxury brands are increasingly embracing a multichannel sales approach and transforming their brand websites into mobile-optimized e-commerce sites with rich editorial content (Kicova et al. 2018; Kliestikova et al. 2017). Winning luxury brands are those offering a seamlessly high-end experience to customers across all channels and devices.

Luxury brands are also seamlessly leveraging the new digital influencers on Instagram, Facebook, YouTube and so on. These allow luxury brands to participate in social conversations online and to establish genuine consumer connections with untapped consumer segments.

As mentioned, we started with ranking from Interbrand of the Best Global Brands 2018 focusing on luxury brands.

The current market is supported by many luxury brands. A luxury brand represents a very exclusive brand that is almost the only one in its product category, and it may seem like a very selective symbol of rarity, refinement and good taste (Sadaf et al. 2018; Valaskova et al. 2018; Vetrakova et al. 2018). Along with the growing interest in luxury brands, luxury company managers strive to balance the demand for their goods on the global market without compromising the key characteristics of exclusivity and uniqueness, which are a necessary prerequisite for luxury (Weissova et al. 2015).

The online popularity is represented by website traffic, social media audience and social media engagement.

Website traffic is estimated based on Similar Web data for 2018, using the primary brand domain.

Social media audience is calculated based on Rival IQ reports for each brand. It represents the sum of Facebook fans, Instagram followers, Twitter followers, YouTube subscribers and Google Plus followers.

Social media engagement is calculated based on Rival IQ reports for each brand. It represents the total number of engagement actions across all tracked social channels, combining comments, likes and shares.

Our sample included nine of the most valuable global luxury brands based on the previously mentioned worldwide survey published by Interbrand. We assessed the impact of online popularity (represented by website traffic, social media audience and social media engagement) on the brand value set for the year 2018. In our study, the consistency of input data played a key role in the methodical approach for quantifying brand value (The 15 Most Popular Luxury Brands Online in 2019 2019; Best Global Brands 2018 Rankings 2019).

Table 14.1 shows the world's most valuable luxury brands with information about their rank, brand value, change in brand value, website traffic, social media audience and social media engagement (Nadanyiova and Kliestikova 2018).

Table 14.1 The world's most valuable luxury brands 2018

Rank	Brand	Change in brand value	Brand value ($B)	Web traffic	Social media audience	Social media engagement
18	Louis Vuitton	+23%	28.15	7,700,000	56,886,821	7,400,000
23	Chanel	NEW	20.01	4,270,000	67,499,041	2,591,803
32	Hermès	+15%	16.37	1,770,000	10,356,812	1,380,000
39	Gucci	+30%	12.94	9,440,000	54,144,179	13,600,000
67	Cartier	+1%	7.65	1,280,000	12,279,311	314,015
83	Tiffany & Co.	+5%	5.64	2,130,000	20,874,200	801,000
91	Dior	+14%	5.22	2,910,000	48,306,113	6,290,000
94	Burberry	−3%	4.99	2,790,000	43,329,468	1,485,372
95	Prada	+2%	4.81	1,530,000	23,934,422	2,186,210

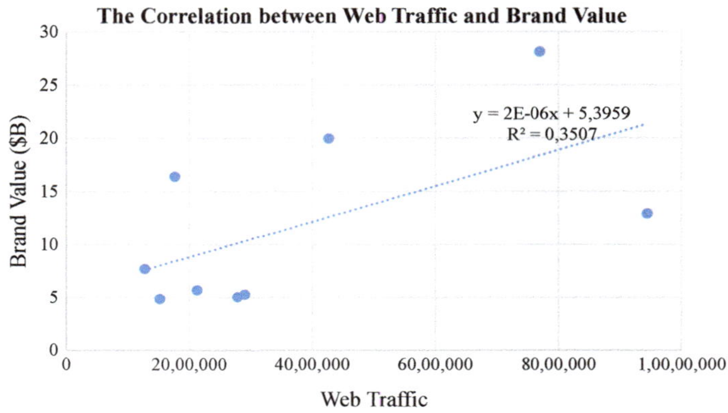

Fig. 14.1 The correlation between web traffic and brand value

Figure 14.1 shows a graphical representation (scatter plot) of the relationship between website traffic and brand value, which we tried to express by means of a linear function (Nadanyiova and Kliestikova 2018).

Figure 14.2 shows a graphical representation (scatter plot) of the relationship between social media audience and brand value, which we tried to express by means of a linear function (Nadanyiova and Kliestikova 2018).

Figure 14.3 shows a graphical representation (scatter plot) of the relationship between social media engagement and brand value, which we tried to express by means of a linear function (Nadanyiova and Kliestikova 2018).

In all cases, we evaluated the relationship between independently variable (individually—website traffic, social media audience, social media engagement) and brand value using the Pearson correlation coefficient (PCC), which is a measure of the linear dependence (correlation) between two variables, x and y (Nadanyiova and Kliestikova 2018):

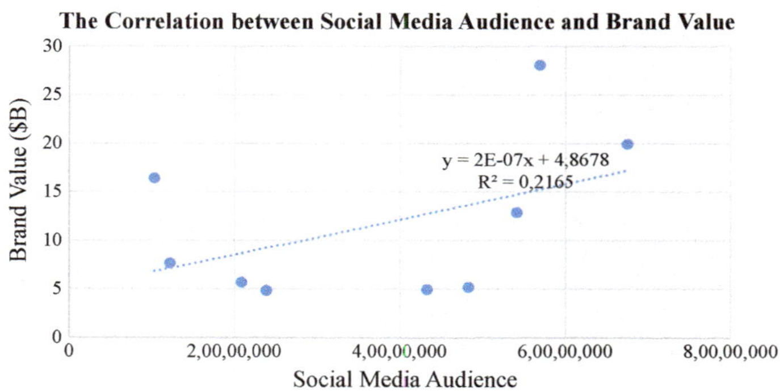

Fig. 14.2 The correlation between social media audience and brand value

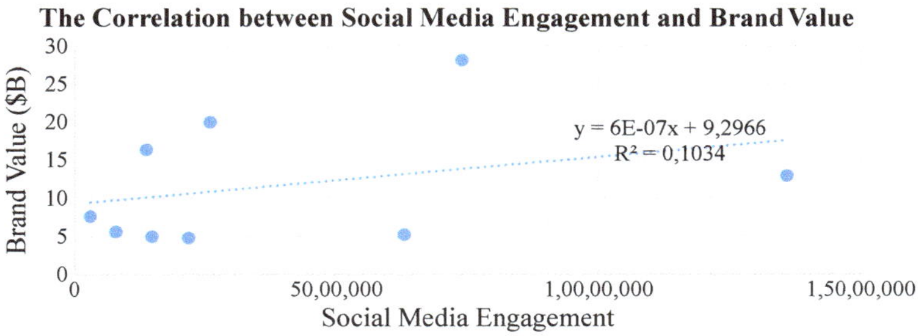

Fig. 14.3 The correlation between social media engagement and brand value

$$R = \frac{cov(x, y)}{s_x * s_y} = \frac{\overline{xy} - \bar{x} - *\bar{y}}{\sqrt{\overline{x^2} - \bar{x}^2} * \sqrt{\overline{y^2} - \bar{y}^2}} \quad (1)$$

14.4 Results

Table 14.2 shows the results of our regression and correlation analysis, which we performed using Data Analysis in Excel (Nadanyiova and Kliestikova 2018).

The PPC value as a measure of the linear dependence (correlation) between web traffic and brand value is 0.592197434, which means that the web traffic and brand value are linearly dependent; specifically, it is medium-strong direct linear dependence.

The PPC value as a measure of the linear dependence (correlation) between social media audience and brand value is 0.465260012, which means that the social media audience and brand value are linearly dependent; specifically, it is medium-strong direct linear dependence.

The PPC value as a measure of the linear dependence (correlation) between social media engagement and brand value is 0.321528274 m which means that the social media engagement and brand value are linearly dependent; specifically, it is medium-strong direct linear dependence.

However, it is necessary to verify whether examined parameters in all cases are indeed linear dependent or not. For verification, we use the test of linear independence (Nadanyiova and Kliestikova 2018).

We evaluated the degree of causal dependence between the web traffic and brand value by applying a coefficient of determination, which is defined as the square of the correlation coefficient R. The value of the coefficient of determination, in this case, is $R^2 = 0.3507$, which means that 35.07% of the variance brand value is explained by a linear relationship with web traffic (regression line). Up to 64.93% of the variability brand value can be explained by other causes, such as a linear relationship between the web traffic and brand value.

Table 14.2 Summary output of regression statistics

Regression statistics

	Brand value ($B)	Web traffic	Social media audience	Social media engagement
Brand value ($B)	1			
Web traffic	0.592197434	1		
Social media audience	0.465260012	0.706958019	1	
Social media engagement	0.321528274	0.904068913	0.595320231	1

Analysis of variance

	df	SS	MS	*F*	Significance *F*
Regression	3	330.9545732	110.3181911	2.511811599	0.172801
Residual	5	219.5988568	43.91977135		
Total	8	550.55343			

	Coefficients	Standard error	*t* stat	*P*-value	Lower 95%	Upper 95%	Lower 90,0%	Upper 90,0%
Intercept	3.044	4.825	0.631	0.556	−9.359	15.447	−6.679	12.766
Web traffic	4.741E-06	2.168E-06	2.187	0.080	−8.3E-07	1.031E-05	3.73E-07	9.11E-06
Social media audience	−3.788E-09	1.592E-07	−0.024	0.982	−4.1E-07	4.056	−3.247E-07	3.171E-07
Social media engagement	−2.238E-06	1.274E-06	−1.756	0.139	−5.5E-06	1.0378	−4.806E-06	3.296E-07

Next, we evaluated the degree of causal dependence between the social media audience and brand value by applying a coefficient of determination. The value of the coefficient of determination, in this case, is $R^2 = 0.2165$, which means that 21.65% of the variance brand value is explained by a linear relationship with social media audience (regression line). Up to 78.35% of the variability brand value can be explained by other causes, such as a linear relationship between the social media audience and brand value.

Finally, we evaluated the degree of causal dependence between the social media engagement and brand value by applying a coefficient of determination. The value of the coefficient of determination, in this case, is $R^2 = 0.1034$, which means that 10.34% of the variance brand value is explained by a linear relationship with social media engagement (regression line). Up to 89.66% of the variability brand value can be explained by other causes, such as a linear relationship between the social media engagement and brand value.

The test of linear independence includes the following steps (Nadanyiova and Kliestikova 2018):

1. Determination of the null hypothesis:

$$H_0 : R = 0 \tag{2}$$

   The correlation coefficient is considered to be null, so the variables are linearly independent.
2. Determination of the alternative hypothesis:

$$H_1 : R \neq 0 \tag{3}$$

   The correlation coefficient is significantly different from zero. Thus, the variables are linearly dependent.
3. Selection of the significance level

$$\alpha = 0, 1 \tag{4}$$

4. Application of the test criteria:

$$T = R \cdot \sqrt{\frac{n-2}{1-R^2}} \tag{5}$$

   The test criteria in the case of causal dependence between the web traffic and brand value are 1.9444.

   The test criteria in the case of causal dependence between the social media audience and brand value are 1.3906.

   The test criteria in the case of causal dependence between the social media engagement and brand value are 0.8984.

5. Critical field of the test:

$$|T| \geq t_{\alpha}(n-2) \tag{6}$$

where $t_{\alpha}(n-2)$ is the critical value of the t-distribution at the significance level α with $n-2$ degrees of freedom, to be 1.8946.

6. Decision:

In the case of causal dependence verification between the web traffic and brand value, the inequality applies, so we do not accept the hypothesis H_0, we accept the hypothesis H_1. Therefore, the correlation coefficient is significantly different from zero and the variables are linearly dependent. It means, that the correlation between web traffic and brand value exists (Nadanyiova and Kliestikova 2018).

In the case of causal dependence verification between the social media audience and brand value as well as in the case of causal dependence verification between the social media engagement and brand value, the inequality does not apply, so we do not reject the hypothesis H_0. Therefore, the correlation coefficient is zero and the variables are linearly independent. PCC values in these two cases are thus not statistically significant and were due to random sampling. It means if we choose another sample, the correlation will not be confirmed (Nadanyiova and Kliestikova 2018).

14.5 Conclusion

Our results indicate that the brand values included in our analyses were directly determined by web traffic but not by social media audience and social media engagement. The brand value of luxury brands is therefore significantly dependent on the web traffic. Conversely, the brand value of luxury brands is not primarily dependent on the level of social media audience and social media engagement (Nadanyiova and Kliestikova 2018).

Innovation in digital and online retail, evolving consumer tastes and preferences are creating a new competitive landscape for luxury goods. Although the term luxury good does not necessarily refer to the goods' quality, they are generally expected to be high-end goods in terms of quality and price which differentiate them from mainstream products.

Therefore, building and managing the brand value of luxury goods as well as common represents an important process. Due to the growing competition, this process requires its efficient operation and uses well-targeted promotion with use online communication tools. It is the brand value that gives the consumer perception of the brand.

Effective brand value management allows to create a brand that is different from others. Based on its value, the brand improves customer loyalty and also helps to determine positioning, as it is essential for the brand to reach consumer awareness (Nadanyiova and Kliestikova 2018).

The issue of online communication and its impact on the brand value has the potential for deeper research in the future—both qualitatively and quantitatively. To obtain statistical relevance, it would be appropriate to investigate the findings of qualitative research quantitatively. A further qualitative investigation would be appropriate for expanding knowledge and comparing the impact of online communication on brand value in other industries, possibly exploring the impact of other communication tools on brand value and their comparison.

Acknowledgements This paper is an outcome of the science project APVV-15-0505: Integrated model of management support for building and managing the brand value in the specific conditions of the Slovak Republic.

References

Aaker, D. A. (2003). *Brand building*. Brno: Computer Press.

Best Global Brands 2018 Rankings. (2019). Interbrand. Available from: https://www.interbrand.com/best-brands/best-global-brands/2018/ranking/. Accessed April 10, 2019.

Bikar, M., & Sedliacikova, M. (2018). The change of the trajectory towards growing economy: The evidence from Russia. *Ekonomicko-manazerske spektrum, 12*(2), 26–36.

Busalim, A. H. (2017). Factors influencing customer engagement in social commerce websites: A systematic literature review. *Journal of Theoretical and Applied Electronic Commerce Research, 14*(2), 1–14.

Chevalier, M., & Mazzalovo, G. (2008). *Luxury brand management a world of privilege*. Singapore: Saik Wah Press.

Drugău-Constantin, A. (2018). Emotional and cognitive reactions to marketing stimuli: Mechanisms underlying judgments and decision making in behavioral and consumer neuroscience. *Economics, Management, and Financial Markets, 13*(4), 46–50.

Jurkovic, M., Kalina, T., Sosedova, J., & Tvrda, E. (2016). Globalisation of the LNG trade in Caspian region. In *Globalization and its socio-economic consequences* (pp. 793–799). Slovak Republic, Rajecke Teplice.

Kicova, E., Bartosova, V., & Moravcikova, D. (2018a). SEO as a powerful brand building tool in online environment. In *8th ESE International Conference on Sports, Health and Management* (pp. 210–214). France, Paris.

Kicova, E., Kral, P., & Janoskova, K. (2018b). Proposal for brands communication strategy developed on customer segmentation based on psychological factors and decision-making speed in purchasing: Case of the automotive industry. *Economics and Culture, 15*(1), 5–14.

Kliestikova, J., Krizanova, A., Corejova, T., Kral, P., & Spuchlakova, E. (2018). Subsidies to increase remote pollution? *Science and Engineering Ethics, 24*(2), 755–767.

Kliestikova, J., Misankova, M., & Moravcikova, D. (2017). Convergences and divergences in perceived value sources of sport brands. In *Proceedings of 7th ESE International Conference on Sports, Health and Management* (pp. 66–70). Spain, Madrid.

Kmecova, I. (2018). The processes of managing human resources and using management methods and techniques in management practice. *Ekonomicko-Manazerske Spektrum, 12*(1), 44–54.

Krizanova, A., Majerova, J., Kliestik, T., & Majercak, P. (2013). Theoretical aspects of brand building in seafood industry. *Nase More, 60*(5–6), 105–112.

Leek, S., & Christodoulides, G. (2012). A framework of brand value in B2B markets: The contributing role of functional and emotional components. *Industrial Marketing Management, 41,* 106–114.

Lizbetinova, L., Weberova, D., & Starchon, P. (2016). The importance and influence of country-of-origin on consumer brand perception. In *Proceedings of 28th International Business-Information-Management-Association Conference* (pp. 1710–1722). Spain, Seville.

Lord, C. (2018). The UK and European 'centre formation' from 1950 to Brexit. *Geopolitics, History, and International Relations, 10*(1), 46–78.

Nadanyiova, M., & Kliestikova, J. (2018). Brand value and the factors affecting it. In N. Tsounis & A. Vlachvei (Eds.) *Advances in panel data analysis in applied economic research.* 2017 International Conference on Applied Economics (ICOAE), Springer Proceedings in Business and Economics (pp. 391–401). Switzerland: Springer International Publishing.

Prikrylova, J., & Jahodova, H. (2010). *Modern marketing communication.* Praha: Grada Publishing.

Rodrigues, P., & Martines, F. V. (2016). Perceptual and behavioural dimensions: Measuring brand equity consumer based. *Journal of Fashion Marketing and Management, 20*(4), 507–519.

Stefanikova, L., Rypakova, M., & Moravcikova, K. (2015). The impact of competitive intelligence on sustainable growth of the enterprises. *Procedia Economics and Finance, 26,* 209–214.

Stefko, R., Fedorko, R., & Bacik, R. (2015). The role of e-marketing tools in constructing the image of a higher education institution. *Procedia Social and Behavioral Sciences, 175,* 431–438.

Sadaf, R., Olah, J., Popp, J., & Mate, D. (2018). An investigation of the influence of the worldwide governance and competitiveness on accounting fraud cases: A cross-country perspective. *Sustainability, 10,* 588.

Shareef, M. A., et al. (2019). Social media marketing: Comparative effect of advertisement sources. *Journal of Retailing and Consumer Services, 46,* 58–69.

The 15 Most Popular Luxury Brands Online in 2019. (2019). *Luxe digital.* Available from: https://luxe.digital/digital-luxury-ranking/most-popular-luxury-brands/. Accessed April 10, 2019.

Tringh, G., Romaniuk, J., & Tanusondjaja, A. (2016). Benchmarking buyer behavior towards new brands. *Marketing Letters, 27*(4), 743–752.

Valaskova, K., Kliestikova, J., & Krizanova, A. (2018). Consumer perception of private label products: An empirical research. *Journal of Competitiveness, 10*(3), 149–163.

Vetrakova, M., Hitka, M., Potkany, M., et al. (2018). Corporate sustainability in the process of employee recruitment through social networks in conditions of Slovak small and medium enterprises. *Sustainability, 10,* 1670.

Wang, Y. L., & Tzeng, G. H. (2012). Brand marketing for creating brand value based on a MCDM model combining DEMATEL with ANP and VIKTOR methods. *Expert Systems with Applications, 39*(5), 5600–5615.

Weissova, I., Kollar, B., & Siekelova, A. (2015). Rating as a useful tool for credit risk measurement. *Procedia Economics and Finance, 26,* 278–285.

Wiedmann, K. P., et al. (2009). Value-based segmentation of luxury consumption behavior. *Psychology and Marketing, 26*(7), 625–651.

Chapter 15
Denaro … vil Denaro! When Sparafucile Would Not Gain, Whoever the Dead!

Angela Besana

Abstract Independent foundations are grant-makers whose aim is to engage citizens and communities and develop and improve their quality of life according to the vision of the founder. The founder can be an individual, a family, a patron whose legacy is matched with needs of a community and a territory… when alive and/or when dead. The founder can be an artist and the artist, as philanthropist, is a very recent topic and issue in the economics of American foundations and not-for-profit organizations (Aspen Institute, 2018). Though a small portion of all US foundations, these endowments are growing in number and grant-making and they represent a potential force shaping cultural philanthropy, old and contemporary art heritage, creative industries and education. With a strong advocacy for community betterment, they can be both operating and grant-making. The aim of this paper is to highlight the role of American artist-endowed foundations, trusts and associations in contemporary times, both of them supporting community development and, foremost, culture: from education to heritage, from visual arts to performing ones and above all, music education. The methodology includes the analysis of mission statements, Web sites and 990 Forms, and a cluster analysis of 2016s accounting data of a sample of the biggest USA artists-endowed foundations. Thanks to cluster analysis, economic performances, fundraising and fund-giving are highlighted together with a 'concentration ratio' for their being involved either in the education of specific arts (music, visual, performing, etc.) or in arts next to community welfare and other not-for-profit issues.

Keywords Artist-endowed foundation · Education · Music · Economics · Cluster

JEL Codes L31 · Z11

I greatly thank my father for music education and suggestions about *Belcanto* in America.

A. Besana (✉)
IULM University, Milan, Italy
e-mail: angela.besana@iulm.it

N. Tsounis and A. Vlachvei (eds.), *Advances in Cross-Section Data Methods in Applied Economic Research*, Springer Proceedings in Business and Economics,
https://doi.org/10.1007/978-3-030-38253-7_15

15.1 The Artist-Endowed Foundation: When Money is Not Guilty

Sparafucile is a famous role in Verdi's *Rigoletto*. Used to kill people as a hired killer, a skillful job for money, he meets Rigoletto when the 'vil scellerato' is desperate and he calls for vengeance. Sparafucile will fulfill with the business Rigoletto has committed him to. As a matter of fact, Sparafucile is foreseen to gain from having killed the Duca of Mantua… though the dead will not exactly be the Duca…but Rigoletto's daughter! Sparafucile is a win-win among Verdi's roles. Who would object? He will have to share money only with his sister Maddalena, who *profited by* the Duca (… *il vostro gioco, mel credete, so apprezzar…*).

Well, money is not always guilty as regards artists' commitments.

During their life and with legacy after their death, artists commit themselves to support and supplement public and private resources for growth of local communities, arts education, battle against inequalities, poverty and other injustice they perhaps coped with at the very beginning of their careers.

Artists become sponsors, ambassadors, patrons… friends of multiple and good causes. In the American landscape, they can give birth to artist-endowed foundations, trusts, family foundations, societies and associations, whose aims can be the above mentioned and the whole community betterment.

US independent foundations are grant-makers whose aim is to engage citizens and communities and develop and improve their quality of life according to the vision of the founder. The founder can be an individual, a family, a patron whose legacy is matched with needs of a community and a territory… when alive and/or when dead.

The founder can also be an artist and the artist as philanthropist is a very recent topic and issue in the economics of American foundations and not-for-profit organizations (Aspen Institute, 2018). Though a small portion of all US foundations, these endowments are growing in number and grant-making and they represent a potential force shaping cultural philanthropy, old and contemporary art heritage, creative industries and education.

The aim of this paper is to highlight the role of American artist-endowed foundations and not-for-profits like trusts and associations in contemporary times, both of them supporting community development and, foremost, culture: from education to heritage, from visual arts to performing ones and above all, music education.

The methodology includes the analysis of mission statements, Web sites and 990 Forms, and a cluster analysis of 2016s accounting data of a sample of the biggest USA artists-endowed foundations. Thanks to cluster analysis, economic performances, fundraising and fund-giving are highlighted together with a concentration ratio for their being involved either in the education of specific arts (music, visual, performing, etc.) or in arts next to community welfare and other not-for-profit issues.

15.2 The Economics of Art Education in North America. The Economics of Artists... When Alive and When Dead

Art education is well spread in American schools, universities and life-long learning programs. Arts are taught in public and private schools and fundraising can supplement school budgets for any kind of art education, from visual to performing arts. Art education is today an issue for parents, who combine their efforts in order to maximize resources for music education in public schools. At the same time, grant-makers like corporate foundations, independent, family and community ones, they are all friends and supporters of music education and performances in schools, theaters, symphony orchestras and opera houses (Elpus and Grisé 2019; Besana and Esposito 2019; Negley 2017; Besana and Esposito 2017; Fermanich 2011).

Art education *does shape* artists who can grow in the star system in America and out of America. Besides, America had always welcome artists from abroad and, as several artists gained from their careers, they left legacies for art education in America (Arturo Toscanini with his legacies in New York, for example), too.

As a consequence, art education can be supported by living artists (alive... and not *starving*! According to Smith 1759), parents, family foundations, public administrations and several nonprofits, which provide money, civic engagement, volunteering and social capital (Ma and Konrath 2018). Art education can be supported by artists' legacies, foundations, trusts, associations, societies... auctions of their memorabilia, too. Music education takes place in schools, universities, performing organizations like symphony orchestras and opera houses, all of them, where they can afford multiple resources from different stakeholders, artist-endowed foundations among them.

Artist foundation is not only referred to a dead artist but also to living ones. They can take care of their singing traditions and America song like Hampsong Foundation. They can take care of their study end exhibition and they support higher education like the Graham Gund Charitable Trust. They can be independent foundations. They can be family foundation like the Alden and Vada Dow Fund, Alden B. Dow family foundation for culture, education and community betterment, primarily in the midland Michigan region. Art education can be one focus for their operating and grant-making. Nevertheless, other issues can be issues and goals: animal welfare, editorial cartooning, supporting specific university programs like graphic design, social services, medical research... the range of not-for-profit goals they deliver funds to, is only increasing. *Branching* of this growth is multiple for markets, issues and goals.

Where are roots of these not-for-profit *Denaro*? Their roots are in art assets as charitable use assets. They are in financial assets, which can grant investment income. Their roots are in communities where they connect with multiple stakeholders (Esposito and Besana 2018; Essig 2014). Contributions and gifts are *branched* to multiple goals. Contributions and grants can be resources from and for the same communities, at the same time, thanks to a revenue diversification these nonprofits emphasize, in order to confront contemporary and financial uncertainties (Berrett and Holliday 2018; Kim 2017; Shea and Hamilton 2015).

According to the Study Report Supplement 2018 of the Aspen Institute, artist as a philanthropist, 207 foundations report contributions, gifts and grants for $90.17 million in 2015. Some of them are operating (study and exhibition) foundations, as they manage exhibitions, collections of house museums, galleries. 79% of their grant-making is for arts and culture. Grants of artworks to institutions like museums, they are a best practice, too. The non-arts and culture interests of artist-endowed foundations include medical research and services, higher education, human services, social action, HIV/AIDS research, environment, community improvement, religious institutions and animal welfare (Vincent 2018).

As a matter of fact, if these foundations enable the growth of local communities, they commit themselves to a *multitasking grant*, whose focus is not only on art education but also on higher education as a whole, next to other priorities like medical research in the same education programmes and life-long learning… These foundations refer to dreams of their founders and these dreams do not only include arts, but also the community betterment, the end of poverty, the battle against inequality and discrimination, so that grants are acknowledged to areas where a whole philanthropy network is able to promote the culture of giving, well coherent with a mature marketing and communication strategy, which includes social media and their *tam-tam*, in order to spread information about their operating and their grant-making (Besana et al. 2018). Their philanthropy can be both multitasking and multi-fund-given, as they can link with several stakeholders on several issues thanks to conventional and unconventional communication strategies, tools and media. As a matter of fact, they rely on governance, who is not only founded on family lines but it also and at the same time, includes connected fundraisers and trusts.

15.3 Performances of the Multitasking Philanthropy of American Artist Foundations

The sample includes 100 US biggest artist-endowed foundations according to 2015s data for charitable purpose disbursements (from the highest to 200.000$), as they were classified and ranked in the 2018s Study Report Supplement of Aspen Institute.

The sample was investigated for available 2016s 990 Forms at GuideStar Database. As 990 Forms were not available for 100 US biggest artist-endowed foundations in April 2019, the sample was summed up with data for nor-for-profit organizations related to 'music education' in USA, from foundations to trusts for available 990 Forms. 65 Forms were collected with useful data.

Forms of this sample are investigated for the following accounting lines of fiscal year 2016: contributions and grants received, program service revenue, investment income, total revenues, contributions, gifts and grants paid, total expenses, total assets, net assets and investments.

Investments are one main asset of the biggest foundations like Jerome, the Atlantic, Joan Mitchell, De Kooning, Block Herb, Cornell Memorial, Helen Frankenthaler, Judd, etc., and they include state government obligations, corporate stocks and bonds, mortgage loans and other investments like interests, receivable or accrued investment incomes. Besides, most of these foundations sell artworks, which can be most of their endowments. As a consequence, resources of these foundations derive of investment income, sales of assets and contributions and grants they receive, too. Program service revenues can be very few: for sure, they are accounted when the foundation is operating (next to grant-making) with ticketing of concerts, exhibitions, music education, royalties, sales of catalogues, permissions and licenses, entry fees for house museums, etc. With very few fundraising expenses, they can afford contributions (paid) for amounts, which can be more than revenues.

For each foundation and artist-endowed organization of the sample, following ratios are firstly calculated: contributions and grant received/total revenues, investment income/total revenues, grants paid/total expenses, investments/total assets, net assets/total assets. grants/total revenues or total expenses, they both give evidence of the philanthropic role for all resources, the foundation is able to collect and deliver to multitasking projects: what and how much the foundation can support local communities, from very specific needs as regards art education to community betterment as a whole. If investments/total assets are an estimate of the involvement in financial markets, investment income/total revenues refer to financial revenues. Net assets/total assets give evidence of financial soundness and solvency.

For each foundation and organization, according to mission statements, a ratio is labeling for 1 the concentration on one goal (arts, music and creative industries) and for 0 the charitable purpose for multitasking grants next to art education: scholarships, projects (from Asian languages fellowships to editorial cartooning), social sciences, medical research, residency programs and production grants for filmmakers, mental health, environmental conservation and community betterment.

Secondly, *k*-means clustering (normal mixture) with JUMP Statistical Software of these economic and concentration ratios allows to separate and to classify two main groups.

Average performances can be read in Table 15.1 of final cluster centers. Composition of clusters can be read in Table 15.2.

The analysis was further implemented with the analysis of Web sites and reports of every foundation, in order to appreciate their engagement and involvement for culture, creative industries and any other goal like community betterment. An outlier is a cluster itself and it was here excluded from comments.

The most crowded cluster is the *ArtistFORartist*, which collects foundations and organizations whose main goal is study and exhibition of an art. If investments are not the main assets, the investment income cannot be the main revenue. Contributions (received) derive of artists themselves, artists' family (when the artist is dead),

Table 15.1 2016's average economic performances of US artist-endowed foundations and organizations. Cluster means %

Clusters	*Artists for artists*—38 foundations	*Artists for communities*—26 foundations
Contributions received/total revenues	41.87	10.04
Investment income/total revenues	26.49	45.33
Grants paid/total expenses	21.67	67.02
Investments/total assets	34.03	70.17
Net assets/total assets	97.19	96.92
Concentration ratio for granted industry	1	0

Source Elaboration with JUMP statistics software

Table 15.2 Composition of clusters

Cluster *artists for artists*	500 Capp Street Foundation, Aaron Copland Fund, Adolph and Esther, Gottlieb Foundation, Al Held Foundation, Anonimo Foundation, Clinton Hill Allen Tran Foundation, Copland House, De Kooning Foundation, Defeo Foundation, Degrazia Foundation, Diebenkorn Foundation, Eames House Preservation Foundation, Easton Foundation, Education Through Music, Falcon Charitable Foundation, Frederick Hammersly Foundation, Frelynghuysen Morris Foundation, Graham Foundation, Hampsong Foundation, Helen Frankenthaler Foundation, Heliker Lahotan Foundation, Hockney Foundation, Joan Mitchell Foundation, Judd Foundation, Kazt Alez Foundation, Kelley Foundation, Kogelnik Foundation, Lachaise Foundation, Nancy Graves Foundation, National Association for Music Education, Ohio Music Education, One Million Years Foundation, Oratorio Society for Queens, Renee And Chaim Gross Foundation, Roy Lichtenstein Foundation, Sam Francis Foundation, Seaword Johnson Atelier, Tennessee Music Education
Cluster *artists for communities*	Al Hirschfeld Foundation, Alden and Vada Dow Fund, Blakemore Foundation, Block Herb Foundation, Camargo Foundation, Dr. Seuss Foundation, Edith C Blum Foundation, Elizabeth Ireland Graves Charitable Trust, Ezra Jack Keats Foundation, Gensler Family Foundation, Gertrud and Bernoudy Fund, Jerome Foundation, John Burton Harter Foundation, Johnson Art and Education Foundation, Joseph and Robert Cornell Memorial Foundation, Keith Haring Foundation, Kelly Foundation, Lantz Foundation, Low Road Foundation, Robert Mapplethorpe Foundation, Ruth H Bohan Foundation, Sansom Foundation, The Atlantic Foundation, The Hoie Charitable Foundation, The Viola Fund, Wolf Kahn and Emily Mason Foundation

Source Own

grants of supporters, other grant-makers and communities, etc. Works of art are the main assets, which can be sold in order to collect resources for a specific industry, from painting to film-making, from photo-making to cartooning, from sculpturing to performing arts. Grants paid are more than one-fifth of expenses and net assets are evidence of a mature solvency. This cluster includes foundations and nonprofits for music education. For example, the Hampsong Foundation and the National Association for music education: being the focus of either a living artist (Thomas Hampson) or a national brand and organization for the specific education, song, music, *bel-canto*, opera, musical and their spreading in America, they are all fulfilled by solvent organizations, with the trust of (contributions) artists, citizens, families, foundations, trusts and other grant-makers.

The cluster *ArtistFORcommunity* relies on investments as the main assets and investment income as the main revenue. These foundations and organizations collect 10% of their revenues as contributions. Thanks to these grants and investment income they can deliver grants for more than 67% of their expenses to multitasking goals. At the same time, they are solvent, for sure. This cluster includes Jerome and the Atlantic Foundations, the biggest investors of the sample.

The analysis clearly separated two kinds of artist-endowed foundations: one is relying on works of arts as assets and it is granting the same arts (education) with resources in order to focus on a legacy of a visual or performing artist; the other one is relying on works of arts and investments, so that diversified revenues (together with contributions received) can be available for multitasking goals in the same community.

15.4 Conclusion

Artist-endowed foundations are a recent phenomenon to be investigated in America. They play a key role in emphasizing an artist's legacy and, at the same time, in addressing community needs, and build endowments to ensure that grants are available to support the community as a whole. Furthermore, they are involved in the strategic development of culture and heritage.

From a marketing and communication point of view, relationship marketing is a key strategy in order to develop multiple relations with fund-givers, sponsors, artists, community administrations and promote initiatives, thanks to social media, too.

Then, the paper has also analyzed economic performances and concentration ratios of these foundations, so that they can be confirmed as a fundamental node and link of the philanthropy tree of contemporary communities for education of a specific art or for the growth and betterment of the community as a whole. As the cluster analysis confirmed, two poles are differently collecting resources and granting arts and any other education (medical research included) together with legacies against poverty, inequalities, etc.

Further research will explore a bigger sample in order to estimate the concentration ratio in different creative industries (visual, performing, movie and the entertainment), and it will explore how much these foundations connect with other grantmakers like community and corporate ones. It will be useful to better understand how much these foundations nurture their *roots* with other foundations and how much they network for multiple fund-giving in their communities.

While writing, the Indiana University School of Arts announced a $20 million gift from alumni Sidney and Lois Eskenazi. The largest gift in the school history, will build an endowment for scholarships for painting, fellowships, visiting artists and scholars, research funding, equipment, facilities and other projects. The commitment of Eskenazi couple was already founded on a $15 million gift in 2016, together with the donation of a collection of nearly a 100 works of art.

Further research will also investigate how much these artist-endowed foundations and gifts can implement and support art education in American schools and universities, as they are multipliers of resources, assets, projects and *shaping* of contemporary artists.

References

Berrett, J. L., & Holliday, B. S. (2018). The effect of revenue diversification on output creation in nonprofit organizations: A resource dependence perspective. *VOLUNTAS: International Journal of Voluntary and Nonprofit Organizations, 29,* 1190–1201.

Besana, A., & Esposito, A. (2019). Fundraising, social media and tourism in American symphony orchestras and opera houses. *Business Economics, 15,* 1–8.

Besana, A., Bagnasco, A., Esposito, A., & Calzolari, A. (2018). It's a matter of attention: The marketing of theatres in the age of social media. *International Journal of Arts Management, 20*(3), 20–37.

Besana, A., & Esposito, A. (2017). Economics, marketing and performances of US classical music: Journey in together to de promise land. In N. Tsounis, & A. Vlachvei (Eds.), *Advances in panel data analysis in applied economic research. ICOAE 2017* (pp. 161–173). Springer Proceedings in Business and Economics.

Esposito, A., & Besana, A. (2018). US community foundations: Building a generous society in challenging times. *Journal of Nonprofit and Public Sector Marketing, 30,* 200.

Elpus, K., & Grisé, A. (2019). Music booster groups: Alleviating or exacerbating funding inequality in American public school music education? *Journal of Research in Music Education, 67*(1), 6–22.

Essig, L. (2014). Arts incubators: A typology. *The Journal of Arts Management, Law, and Society, 44,* 169–180.

Fermanich, M. L. (2011). Money for music education: A district analysis of the how, what, and where of pending for music education. *Journal of Education Finance, 37,* 130–149.

Kim, M. (2017). The relationship of nonprofits' financial health to program outcomes: Empirical evidence from nonprofit arts organizations. *Nonprofit and Voluntary Sector Quarterly, 46*(3), 1–24.

Ma, J., & Konrath, S. (2018). A century of nonprofit studies: Scaling the knowledge of the field. *VOLUNTAS: International Journal of Voluntary and Nonprofit Organizations, 29,* 1139–1158.

Negley, B. (2017). The ford foundation symphony orchestra program. *Journal of Musicological Research, 36*(2), 115–142.

Shea, M., & Hamilton, R. D. (2015). Who determines how nonprofits confront uncertainty? *Nonprofit Management and Leadership, 25*(4), 383–401.

Smith A (1759) (1976) The theory of moral sentiments. Clarendon Press: Oxford.

Vincent, C.J. (2018). *The artists as philanthropist. Strengthening the next generation of artist-endowed foundations. A study of the emerging artist-endowed foundation field in the U.S. Study report supplement 2018*. The Aspen Institute: Washington, DC.

Chapter 16
Impact of Tax Simplification on Tax Efficiency

Nihal Bayraktar

Abstract Tax simplification always has been on the agenda of policymakers to increase the efficiency of tax systems. Less complex taxes can contribute to higher tax revenues with minimum negative distortions to economies. Therefore, the link between tax simplification and tax efficiency is even more relevant now for policy-makers in the era of high government budget deficits. The aim of this paper is to explain the empirical study of this important link in a panel setting, which is considerably limited in the literature. The findings of the paper place numerical values on the impact of tax simplification on the effectiveness of tax collection systems. Tax efficiency is measured by tax efforts which are introduced through two alternative measures: a traditional regression approach and a stochastic frontier analysis. Tax simplification is measured by *Time to Comply* and *Number of Payments* from the "Doing Business Database". The paper investigates both direct and indirect links between tax simplification and efforts. The indirect link, introducing a kind of transmission mechanism, works through changing values of tax corruption associated with adjustments in tax complexity. The tax corruption indicator is generated from the Enterprise Surveys Database. The panel dataset includes 104 developed and developing countries and covers the years from 2002 to 2016.

Keywords Tax efficiency · Tax policies · Tax corruption · Tax simplification

JEL Codes D73 · H2 · H20 · E62 · O23

16.1 Introduction

Tax simplification always has been on the agenda of policymakers to increase the efficiency of tax systems and tax compliance burdens for taxpayers. Simpler tax laws contribute towards a more efficient administration with less discretion and lead to greater efficiencies in tax collection. There is also an idea that less complex tax

N. Bayraktar (✉)
Economics, Penn State University, Middletown, Harrisburg, PA 17057, USA
e-mail: nxb23@psu.edu

N. Tsounis and A. Vlachvei (eds.), *Advances in Cross-Section Data Methods in Applied Economic Research*, Springer Proceedings in Business and Economics,
https://doi.org/10.1007/978-3-030-38253-7_16

systems can also contribute to higher tax revenues. Especially, lower tax corruption associated with simpler tax systems is expected to yield higher revenues which are extremely important for policymakers in the era of high government budget deficits. Another attraction towards less complex tax systems for policymakers is that it provides ways of increasing tax revenues with minimum negative distortions to their economies. Therefore, tax simplification can be a better and less distortionary alternative to higher tax rates or larger tax bases to increase revenue.

In the literature, the impact of tax simplification on tax systems has been extensively investigated. However, one missing point is that most of these studies are theoretical. Empirical studies, especially on cross-country analysis, have been extremely limited. In my best knowledge, there is no cross-country empirical study investigating the impact of tax simplification on the efficiency of tax systems. Given the importance of tax simplification for the healthier work of tax systems, the aim of this paper is to find empirical evidence of the link between tax simplification and tax effectiveness, which is measured by tax efforts, in a cross-country setting.

In addition to the direct link between tax efficiency and simplification, the paper also investigates the indirect link, introducing a type of transmission mechanism, which works through lower tax corruption associated with simpler tax systems. A less complex tax system is shown to be empirically associated with lower corruption in tax administration (Awasthi and Bayraktar 2015). It is predicted that the combined effect of a 10% reduction in both the number of payments and the time to comply with tax requirements can lower tax corruption by 9.64%. This paper extends these findings in order to relate tax simplification to tax efficiency through the tax corruption mechanism.

The outcomes of this paper place numerical values on the impact of tax simplification on the efficiency of tax collection systems and have useful policy implications. This way, the importance of efficient and corruption-free tax administration for higher tax revenues can be better appreciated.

The paper continues with a short literature review. Information on data and variables follows the literature review. Regression specifications, methodology, regression results and robustness checks are available in Sects. 16.4 and 16.5 concludes.

16.2 Literature Review

Figure 16.1 summarizes the aim of this paper. Complex tax systems are expected to have a direct negative impact on tax efficiency, which is measured by tax efforts. Such complex tax systems can also lower tax revenues indirectly through increasing tax corruption in the tax collection process.

The literature on the *direct* impact of complexity of taxes on tax effectiveness, revenues, cost, and administration can be grouped into three categories. One set of papers, mostly covering theoretical models, focuses on increasing tax costs due to complex tax systems (see, for example, Quandt 1983; Alm et al. 1992; Heyndels and

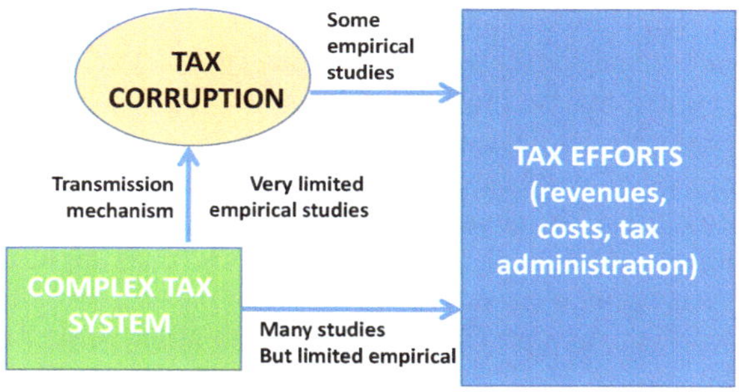

Fig. 16.1 Direct and indirect link between tax simplification and tax efforts

Smolders 1995; Paul 1997; Alm 1999; Cuccia and Carnes 2001; Evans 2003; Dean 2005; Oliver and Bartley 2005; Picciotto 2007; Mulder et al. 2009; Saad 2009). There are also theoretical papers specifically focusing on the issue of how complex taxes can lower tax revenues. The examples of such studies are Milliron (1985), Mills (1996), Spilker et al. (1999), Forest and Sheffrin (2002), Kirchler et al. (2006), Richardson (2006), and Slemrod (2007), and Marcuss et al. (2013). The third category includes some controversial studies, claiming that tax complexity can lead to higher taxes, especially in the advanced economies (Scotchmer 1989; White et al. 1990).

In terms of the indirect link through tax corruption, there are several papers on the impact of corruption on tax revenues in the literature. Tanzi and Davoodi (1997) investigate the impact of general corruption on growth and public finance. Friedman et al. (2000) study the determinants of unofficial activities, which lower tax revenues, in 69 countries and identify general corruption as one of the determinants. Crandall and Bodin (2005) and Imam and Jacobs (2007) conclude that general corruption has a negative effect on tax revenues. Even though it is not necessarily tax-related, the study by Fisman and Gatti (2006) can be useful to understand the impact of corruption. They, using firm-level data from 61 countries, find a positive link between corruption and time spent with bureaucrats. While all these papers study the impacts of general corruption, Purohit (2007) investigates corruption in tax administration.

In the literature, there are also papers on the effects of the complexity of taxes on tax corruption. Dos Santos (1995), Tanzi (1998), and Keen (2003) identified through two possible sources of tax corruption: (1) Complex tax systems: Tax auditors can collect bribes from taxpayers by taking advantage of complex rules or unclear laws, regulations, and procedures. The taxpayer may choose to bribe the tax auditor to evade taxes. (2) Time-consuming and costly appealing: the taxpayer may choose to bribe to get things done. Complex declaration forms, high costs of compliance, and intricate compliance procedures. Lambsdorff (2006) recommends that reform should avoid complicated rules and those that are difficult to administer, and should design individual incentives to promote honest decision making. Obwona and Muwonge (2002) and Kasimbazi (2003) find tax complexity and lack of transparency leads to tax corruption in Uganda. Only cross-country study on tax corruption and tax complexity belong to Awasthi and Bayraktar (2015). They present a positive link between tax simplification and lower corruption.

The contributions of the paper to this literature: (1) It introduces empirical analysis in a panel setting with cross-country and time-series dimensions. In this way, the results can have broader applications. (2) Tax efficiency is captured by two measures of tax efforts, instead of using actual tax revenues as a simple substitute. Tax efforts are calculated based on the gap between actual tax revenues and tax capacities of countries. The advantage of using tax effort variables instead of actual taxes is that efforts give better information on how tax simplification helps countries to reach their optimal tax collection. (3) The paper also defines a transmission mechanism working through tax corruption to identify the link between tax simplification and tax efforts.

16.3 Information on Data and Measures of Tax Effort, Tax Complexity, and Tax Corruption

Because the aim of this paper is to empirically study the direct and indirect impacts of tax complexity on tax efficiency, we need to define the possible measures of tax effort, tax complexity, and tax corruption. These variables are calculated with a panel dataset. The main databases are the World Bank's World Development Indicators, Doing Business Indicators, and Enterprise Surveys. We include 104 developed and developing countries from different regions of the world. The dataset covers the years from 2002 to 2016.

How to measure tax efficiency?: Tax efficiency of countries can be calculated using economic measures of taxes (tax space). In this paper, two types of tax effort variables are calculated to measure tax efficiency. While the first measure is the traditional regression approach, the second method introduces stochastic frontier analysis for robustness checks. It should be noted that Cyan et al. (2012) compare these two alternative methodologies to compute the tax effort series of countries. After comprehensive comparison analysis, they conclude that the results obtained from these two methodologies produce highly-correlated, similar tax effort series.

The first method involves two steps (some examples of the papers using this approach are Bayraktar et al. 2016; Tanzi and Davoodi 1997; Bird et al. 2004):

(1) In the first step, **predicted tax** revenues of a country (approximation for **tax capacity**) are empirically estimated taking into account its specific economic, demographic, and institutional features, which all change through time. We will use the specification introduced in Bayraktar et al. (2012).

$$\begin{aligned}\text{TAX/GDP}_{\text{it}} = {} & \alpha_0 + \alpha_1 \cdot \text{GDPPC}_{\text{it}} + \alpha_2 \cdot \text{DEMOG}_{\text{it}} \\ & + \alpha_3 \cdot \text{TRADE}_{\text{it}} + \alpha_4 \cdot \text{AGR}_{\text{it}} \\ & + \alpha_5 \cdot \text{GOVERNANCE QUALITY}_{\text{it}} + \varepsilon \end{aligned} \tag{16.1}$$

TAX/GDP is total taxes in percent of GDP. GDPPC stands for real GDP per capita. DEMOG stands for a demographic variable, such as age dependency ratio. TRADE is trade openness and equals exports plus imports in percent of GDP. AGR is agriculture value-added in percentage of GDP. GOVERNANCE QUALITY stands for corruption index. The estimated coefficients of this equation predict tax capacity. The regression methodology is an OLS for panel datasets. We include both regional and time dummies. No endogeneity or dual causality problem has been identified. The regression result indicates that countries with higher income, lower age dependency, more trade openness, lower agricultural production, and higher institutional quality (lower corruption) tend to collect higher taxes. The estimated coefficients are as follows: $\text{TAX/GDP}_{\text{it}} = 32.1 + 2.14x\ \text{GDPPC}_{\text{it}} - 0.1x\ \text{Age dependency}_{\text{it}} + 0.01x\ \text{TRADE}_{\text{it}} - 0.23x\ \text{AGR}_{\text{it}} - 0.557x\ \text{CORRUPTION}_{\text{it}}$. All coefficients are statistically significant at the 1% level, except the last one which is significant at the 10% level. It should be noted that the definition is robust to alternative specifications, including shadow economy, general consumption, or population growth (for details, see Bayraktar et al. 2012).

(2) After this first step, tax efforts are defined as the ratio of actual tax collection to predicted tax revenue (tax capacity) from the first step.

Figure 16.2 presents the relationship between actual tax collection and taxable capacity (country averages over 1994–2016). It can be seen that predicted tax revenues are positively correlated with actual tax collection, meaning that higher collection tends to be associated with higher tax capacity. The countries taking place above the 45° line are the ones with a high tax effort (actual taxes are higher than predicted taxes). Given the values of their macroeconomic and demographic indicators, they seem to do well in terms of tax collection. On the other hand, the countries located below the 45° line are the ones collecting taxes below their tax capacity (low effort) and they have room for improvements in their tax collection efforts.

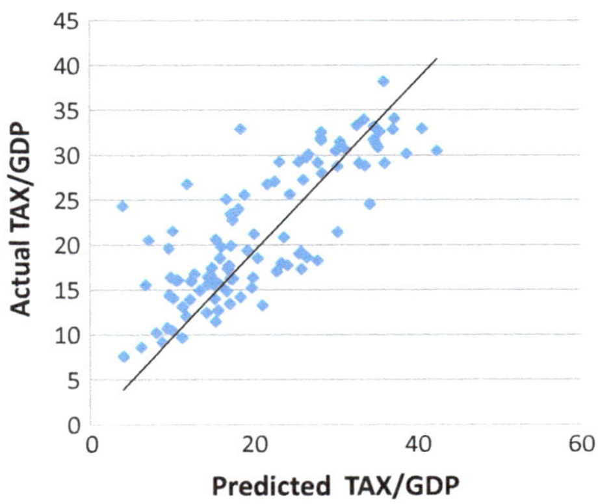

Fig. 16.2 Tax capacity and actual taxes, 2002–16

The second method calculating the alternative measure of tax efforts involves stochastic frontier analysis. Some examples of the papers used this method to calculate tax efforts are: Pitt and Lee (1981), Battese (1992), Battese and Coelli (1992), Alfirman (2003), and Pessino and Fenochietto (2010). Detailed information on this measure of tax efforts is included in the robustness check section of the regression results.

How to measure tax complexity?: One important reason for a limited number of empirical studies on tax simplification is the difficulty of measuring this variable (Binh and Evans 2014). It is important to define tax complexity indicators, considering international comparisons overtime. The only viable option available for cross-country analysis is to use series from the Doing Business Database (DB) created by the World Bank Group. DB Reports measure the ease of doing business in each country by using 10 indicators, including one on complying with the tax system (Paying Taxes). Two of the variables in the "Paying Taxes" set are *Time to Comply* and *Number of Payments*. The premise is that the lower the time taken to comply with the tax system is and the fewer the number of payments is, the easier for businesses to comply with their taxpaying obligations. Based on definitions and the methodology of collecting data around them, it appears that for the purposes of this paper, these two variables, Time to Comply (TAXTIME) and Number of Payments (TAXPAY), are the best-suited measures of "tax simplicity" in a panel setting (see, for example, Lawless 2013; Awasthi and Bayraktar 2014). TAXTIME is defined as a collection of all information and data needed to calculate tax liability and filling out the declaration forms. Existence of special tax concessions or exemptions can increase TAXTIME. TAXPAY is a good measure of the ease of payment procedures of taxes. The DB indicators have been criticized as they are not considered the most robust of measures. However, it should be noted that they are the only available data that provide an objective, world-wide comparison of indicators of the complexity or simplicity of tax regimes. DB reports have recently been reviewed by an independent panel constituted by the President of the World Bank (Independent Panel Report 2013, p. 40). Even though the independent panel report criticizes Time to Comply (TAXTIME) due to its subjectivity, they agree (as does the ITD) that this indicator is a good, useful measure of the compliance burden of a tax system. The Panel has recommended that the Number of Payments (TAXPAY) measures must be dropped or modified, as the number of times a firm needs to make payments may not represent simplicity or lower compliance burdens, in their view. On this, my view is a bit different; I believe the indicator is a useful measure of simplicity.

How to measure tax corruption?: An indicator of tax corruption has been empirically generated by Awasthi and Bayraktar (2014), using the World Bank's Enterprise Surveys (ES), which cover 130,000 firms from 138 countries. Each ES is a firm-level survey of a representative sample of an economy's private sector. The surveys cover a broad range of business environment topics including access to finance, corruption, infrastructure, crime, competition, and performance measures. The number of firms interviewed is large and it includes firms with different characteristics. Thus, firms included in the ES Database can represent the average position of countries. In these surveys, the response rates on tax corruption are reasonably large in many countries.

In the questionnaire administered by the Enterprise Surveys, the following questions are asked about corruption in tax administration:

- "J3 question" from the survey: over the last 12 months, was this establishment visited or inspected by tax officials?
- "J5 question" from the survey: in any of these inspections or meetings was a gift or informal payment expected or requested?

Based on the response, the measure of percent of firms giving gifts to tax officials is computed. More specifically, for each country, the tax corruption indicator is defined as the ratio of the number of "yes" answers to "J5 question" to the total number of "yes" answers to "J3 question". This is a direct measure of corruption in tax administrations.

A problem with ES is that it does not cover every country and is not available each year. Data imputation technique of expectation maximization is used to predict missing years of tax corruption series (after extension, statistical features of the series do not change). This technique estimates missing data points with the help of a predictive model that incorporates the available information, and any prior information on the data, as well as relationships between variables, included in the process. In this technique, a general corruption index is picked as the predictor because it is the most related to the tax corruption ratio and at the same time their numbers of observations are mostly complete.

Sample Selection: Because the rest of the variables are easier to obtain, the main criteria for sample selection is the availability of meaningful tax corruption data. Survey data can be objective and cultural perception issues can play an important role in how firms define bribery or corruption in their countries. To eliminate negative impacts of such cross-country cultural differences, some countries are eliminated if their tax corruption ratio is unexpectedly high or low.[1] We deleted countries after comparing two country rankings: (1) Tax corruption ratio from ES; (2) Bribery index from the Global Competitiveness Index Database. If the difference between the two rankings for any country is larger than 70, it is excluded. After this elimination process, 104 countries from different regions and income groups remain in the dataset. The sample period is 2002–2016. Tax efforts and tax simplification series are calculated for these countries for the same time period. Table 16.1 shows country averages of main variables in each country. Tables 16.8, 16.9 and 16.10 give further information on descriptive statistics and correlation matrixes as well as data definitions and sources.

16.4 Regression Results

Direct Link Between Tax Complexity and Tax Efforts: In this sub-section, the direct effect of tax simplification on tax efforts is examined. Figure 16.3 shows the positive link between these two variables. It indicates that the value of tax efforts

[1] Details are available in Awasthi and Bayraktar (2014).

Table 16.1 County averages: tax corruption, tax efforts, and tax simplification (2002–2016)

	Tax corruption (demand for bribery % of total tax visits)	Tax payments (number per year)	Tax Time (hours per year)	Tax effort (actual tax/tax capacity)		Tax corruption (demand for bribery % of total tax visits)	Tax payments (number per year)	Tax time (hours per year)	Tax effort (actual tax/tax capacity)
Albania	47.8	44	364	0.77	Lebanon	24.5	19	180	0.87
Angola	18.9	30	276	0.84	Lesotho	4.2	33	379	1.26
Armenia	33.6	40	527	0.78	Ijberia	62.5	33	155	0.55
Azerbaijan	50.8	25	491	0.89	U thuania	18.3	12	170	0.83
Bahamas	12.4	18	58	0.78	Macedonia, FYR	23.1	37	150	1.07
Bangladesh	59.6	20	335	0.64	Madagascar	9.9	24	241	0.62
Belarus	14.3	79	773	1.06	Malawi	12.7	25	247	0.67
Belize	6.2	37	147	0.91	Mali	25.7	55	270	1.02
Benin	19.1	56	270	1.03	Mauri tania	43.1	37	696	0.81
Bhutan	3.3	19	274	0.91	Mauritius	1.2	8	160	0.73
Bosnia and Herzegovina	39.3	52	401	1.22	Mexico	6.8	15	454	0.83
Botswana	6.5	34	145	0.98	Moldova	39.7	48	224	1.12
Brazil	9.7	9	820	1.62	Mongolia	12.9	41	197	1.92
Bulgaria	26.7	18	567	1.04	Montenegro	6.4	67	359	0.91
Burkina Faso	17.8	45	270	0.88	Mozambique	10.6	37	230	0.82
Burundi	26.8	30	193	0.95	Namibia	2.7	37	333	1.11

(continued)

Table 16.1 (continued)

	Tax corruption (demand for bribery % of total tax visits)	Tax payments (number per year)	Tax Time (hours per year)	Tax effort (actual tax/tax capacity)		Tax corruption (demand for bribery % of total tax visits)	Tax payments (number per year)	Tax time (hours per year)	Tax effort (actual tax/tax capacity)
Cambodia	72.1	41	157	1.14	Nepal	14.5	34	365	1.29
Cameroon	40.2	44	651	0.93	Niger	15.4	41	270	0.81
Cape Verde	5.3	38	186	1.03	Nigeria	26.8	38	1003	0.82
Central African Republic	20.9	56	499	0.71	Pakistan	56.0	47	562	0.83
Chad	19.6	54	732	0.69	Panama	4.7	53	486	0.89
Chile	2.3	8	310	0.96	Paraguay	24.3	34	345	1.11
China	19.1	17	533	1.02	Peru	5.0	9	372	0.93
Congo, Dem. Rep.	48.8	32	322	1.14	Philippines	23.9	46	195	0.82
Congo	20.7	60	606	0.72	Poland	24.4	33	362	1.07
Costa Rica	2.0	36	304	1.11	Romania	22.9	95	205	0.96
Cote d'Ivoire	19.6	64	270	0.80	Russia	34.4	8	342	0.91
Croatia	25.1	31	196	1.01	Rwanda	6.6	22	152	0.86
Czech Republic	29.4	12	670	1.01	Samoa	17.7	37	224	0.79
Dominica	13.9	37	127	0.81	Senegal	14.5	59	674	0.97
Ecuador	4.2	8	624	0.81	Serbia	20.1	66	279	1.03

(continued)

Table 16.1 (continued)

	Tax corruption (demand for bribery % of total tax visits)	Tax payments (number per year)	Tax Time (hours per year)	Tax effort (actual tax/tax capacity)		Tax corruption (demand for bribery % of total tax visits)	Tax payments (number per year)	Tax time (hours per year)	Tax effort (actual tax/tax capacity)
Egypt	28.5	33	517	0.86	Sierra Leone	9.3	30	375	0.92
Gabon	13.4	26	488	0.87	Slovak Republic	26.2	29	273	0.94
Gambia, The	12.8	50	376	0.71	Slovenia	23.0	20	260	1.05
Ghana	21.5	33	251	1.07	South Africa	2.1	9	250	1.08
Greece	60.8	12	231	0.97	Sri Lanka	4.0	62	251	0.80
Guatemala	4.6	28	341	0.81	St. Lucia	5.15	32	82	0.71
Guinea	57.3	57	419	0.82	St. Vincent and the Grenadines	2.90	36	100	0.72
Guinea-Bissau	25.2	46	208	0.61	Swaziland	3.6	33	105	1.32
Honduras	4.2	47	291	1.38	Tanzania	19.7	48	172	0.91
Hungary	13.5	13	310	1.23	Timor-Leste	3.08	13	438	0.76
India	60.2	49	260	1.15	Togo	8.4	50	270	1.10
Indonesia	28.3	51	332	0.76	Trinidad and Tobago	7.8	40	210	1.33
Iraq	32.1	13	312	0.75	Turkey	19.0	11	231	0.74
Jamaica	4.6	64	404	1.46	Uganda	11.4	31	210	0.76
Jordan	0.5	26	141	1.06	Ukraine	41.4	118	1115	1.24

(continued)

Table 16.1 (continued)

	Tax corruption (demand for bribery % of total tax visits)	Tax payments (number per year)	Tax Time (hours per year)	Tax effort (actual tax/tax capacity)		Tax corruption (demand for bribery % of total tax visits)	Tax payments (number per year)	Tax time (hours per year)	Tax effort (actual tax/tax capacity)
Kazakhstan	43.6	8	243	1.12	Uruguay	0.8	49	320	1.36
Kenya	37.0	41	389	1.13	Vanuatu	5.0	31	120	0.81
Kosovo	0.9	33	163	0.92	Vietnam	36.6	32	986	1.72
Kyrgyz Republic	63.4	64	205	0.78	Yemen	44.8	44	248	0.49
Lao PDR	28.8	34	487	1.50	Zambia	8.7	38	183	0.90
Latvia	21.1	9	288	0.70	Zimbabwe	10.6	50	242	1.37

Source Authors' calculations based on series from the World Bank's ES and DB databases

Fig. 16.3 Tax effort and tax simplification (country averages, 2002–2016)

gets higher, as tax systems get simpler, i.e., lower number of tax payments or less time spent on complying with taxes.

This relationship between tax complexity and tax efforts can be better determined in regression analysis. We estimate tax efforts with the following regression specification:

$$\begin{aligned} \text{TAXEFFORT}_{\text{it}} = {} & \alpha_0 + \alpha_1 \cdot \text{GDPPC}_{\text{it}} + \alpha_2 \cdot \text{SHADOWECONOMY}_{\text{it}} \\ & + \alpha_3 \cdot \text{TRADE}_{\text{it}} + \alpha_4 \cdot \text{AGR}_{\text{it}} \\ & + \alpha_5 \cdot \text{GOVERNANCEQUALITY}_{\text{it}} + \alpha_6 \cdot \text{INFLATION}_{\text{it}} \\ & + \alpha_7 \cdot \text{TAXCOMPLEXITY}_{\text{it}} + \varepsilon \end{aligned} \tag{16.2}$$

TAX EFFORT is measured as described in the previous section of the paper. GDPPC is a real GDP per capita. Higher income countries tend to collect more taxes as a percentage of GDP. Thus, it is expected that GDP per capita will have a positive and significant impact on tax efforts (Bahl 1971; Fox et al. 2005; Piancastelli 2001).

SHADOW ECONOMY is the share of shadow economy in GDP. A smaller shadow economy with less widespread informal economic activities outside the tax base improves tax efforts because formal workers and economic activities remain inside the tax base (Bird et al. 2004; Davoodi and Grigorian 2007). The shadow economy variable used in this chapter includes all market-based legal production of goods and services that are deliberately concealed from public authorities for any of the following reasons: (1) to avoid payment of income, value-added, or other taxes, (2) to avoid payment of social security contributions, (3) to avoid having to meet certain legal labor market standards, such as minimum wages, maximum working hours, safety standards, etc., and (4) to avoid complying with certain administrative procedures, such as completing statistical questionnaires or other administrative forms (see Schneider et al. 2010).

TRADE is the total exports and imports of a country in percent of GDP. Trade openness is one of the variables commonly considered as an important determinant of taxation (Rodrik 1998; Piancastelli 2001; Norregaard and Khan 2007; Aizenman and JinJarak 2009). The dynamic of international trade may have two opposite effects on tax efforts. On the one hand, higher trade openness is expected to lower taxes collected on imports and exports; thus, it may have a negative impact on tax and total fiscal revenue (Keen and Mansour 2010). On the other hand, given that higher trade openness is associated with higher economic growth rates, open economies usually tend to grow faster; and as a result, more taxes can be collected, and tax efforts improve (Alonso and Garcimartin 2011). It is therefore expected that the second effect dominates over the first and trade openness has a positive impact on tax efforts.

AGR is the share of agricultural production in GDP. Given that it is relatively harder to tax the agricultural sector, it is expected that a higher share of agriculture value added to GDP, results in a lower tax effort due to a smaller tax base (Leuthold 1991; Piancastelli 2001). Thus, the expected sign of the agriculture value-added ratio to GDP is negative.

INFLATION is the inflation rate based on the consumer price index. It measures macroeconomic stability of countries and expected to have a negative effect on tax efforts.

GOVERNANCE QUALITY stands for bureaucracy quality index or corruption index. Institutional and governance quality is considered as one of the most essential factors in determining tax revenue collections (Tanzi and Davoodi 1997; Ghura 1998; Abed and Gupta 2002; Bird et al. 2004, 2006; Gupta 2007; Aizenman and JinJarak 2009). Countries can present higher tax efforts when the tax administration is more effective. In this regard, the bureaucracy quality and corruption index, which is a possible variable to measure institutional and governance quality, is expected to have a significant impact on tax efforts. Lower index values indicate a more efficient bureaucracy and lower corruption. With this definition, we expect tax efforts to drop with increasing index values, meaning negative estimated coefficients of these variables.

TAX COMPLEXITY is measured by TAXPAY or TAXTIME as defined in the previous section.

The regression methodology is an ordinary least square (OLS) for panel datasets. One potential problem in using this methodology is the possible endogeneity and/or dual causality problem associated with institutional variables and tax efforts. Higher tax efforts usually lead to improved governance, while improved governance can further improve tax efforts. I run Hausman endogeneity tests to understand whether any statistically significant endogeneity problem is observed. Such a problem could lead to inconsistencies in estimated coefficients if a panel least squared technique was used for regression analyses. The null hypothesis of exogeneity is failed to reject, indicating the absence of a significant endogeneity problem. I also ran dual granger causality tests between the tax revenue ratio and the independent variables. The F-statistics of the test indicate that there is no causality from tax revenues to the independent variables, so we do not observe any dual causality in our sample. In the absence of any endogeneity or dual causality problems, the panel OLS method is used to estimate the coefficients of the regression specification.

In Table 16.2, the estimated coefficient of TAXPAY is 2.5 and significant at 5%. The estimated coefficient of TAXTIME is 2.1 and significant at 1%. The rest of the explanatory variables are significant and have the expected signs. After obtaining the estimated coefficients, different simulations are run to understand the economic significance of the tax simplification variables on tax corruption. The empirical specification given in Eq. (16.2) is a powerful predictor of significant gains in increasing tax efforts through tax simplification. This can be confirmed with different simulations measuring the economic significance of tax simplification for tax efforts. In the simulations, it is asked how much the tax effort ratio is expected to increase if the complexity of tax systems is reduced, corresponding to the lower values of TAXPAY and TAXTIME. For the simulations, the predicted values of the tax effort ratio are computed for different values of the tax simplification variables, as well as the control variables. While calculating the predicted values of tax efforts, the estimated

Table 16.2 Impact of tax simplification on tax efforts, 2002–2016

Dependent variable: tax effort (actual tax/tax capacity in %)								
	(1)		(2)		(3)		(4)	
Constant	27.4	(21.1)***	28.5	(23.6)***	29.1	(25.1)***	28.5	(23.6)***
Tax simplification								
Time spent for Tax (TAXTIME)	2.1	(2.5)***	–		2.2	(2.3)***	2.1	(2.3)***
No. of tax payments (TAXPAY)	–		2.5	(2.0)**	3.2	(1.9)**	3.3	(1.9)**
Control variables								
GDP per capita (constant)	2.1	(10.7)***	2.3	(10.2)***	2.5	(10.7)***	2.4	(9.5)***
Inflation rate	−1.8	(−6.4)***	−2	(−5.7)***	−2.1	(−6.5)***	−2.1	(−6.3)***
Trade openness (% of GDP)	0.01	(1.7)*	0.01	(2.4)***	0.01	(2.3)**	0.01	(2.1)**
Agriculture value added (% of GDP)	−0.2	(−8.1)***	−0.2	(−8.4)***	−0.26	(−8.7)***	−0.2	(−8.8)***
Size of shadow economy (% of GDP)	−0.1	(−2.9)***	−0.2	(−3.1)***	−0.15	(−3.4)***	−0.2	(−3.3)***
CORRUPTION INDEX	−0.6	(−2.4)***	−0.7	(−2.3)***	−0.6	(−2.5)***	–	
BUREAUCRACY INDEX	–		–		–		−0.4	(−2.2)**
OBS adjusted R^2	874 0.659		874 0.659		874 0.660		874 0.659	

Note The estimation technique is panel OLS with regional and time dummies. *t*-statistics are reported in parenthesis. *Indicates 10% significance level, **indicates 5% significance level, and ***indicates 1% significance level. The estimated coefficients of GDP per capita are multiplied by 10,000. The dependent variable in each panel is tax effort (actual tax/tax capacity in %). See Table 16.10 for the definitions of the variables. We also include both regional and time dummies. The time dummies are annual coefficients of tax simplification variables and the control variables are taken from the empirical specifications of Table 16.2. The predicted values of improvements in the tax simplification variables are also computed using the same estimated coefficients from the regression outcomes presented in Table 16.2, keeping the values of all other variables in the specifications constant.

When we run simulations with numerical examples as described above, the results show that a 10% decline in TAXPAY is expected to lead to around a 3.7% increase in the tax effort ratio. Similarly, a 10% cut in TAXTIME leads to a 4.7% increase in tax efforts. When we simulate the combined effects of a 10% drop in both TAXPAY and TAXTIME (coefficients are from Eq. (16.3) in Table 16.2), we observe an 8.3% higher tax effort ratio.

Estimation of the Link between Tax Complexity and Tax Corruption (First Step of Indirect Link Between Tax Efforts and Tax Simplification): In this section, we use specifications from Awasthi and Bayraktar (2014). The simple link between tax complexity variables and tax corruption is presented in Fig. 16.4. It is positive and indicates that tax simplification lowers tax corruption. Variables are calculated as defined in the previous sections.

Based on the literature on general corruption, the empirical specification for tax corruption is:

$$\begin{aligned}\text{Tax corruption}_{\text{it}} = {} & \beta_0 + \beta_1 \cdot \log(\text{tax simplification}_{\text{it}}) + \beta_2 \cdot \text{bureaucracy quality}_{\text{it}} \\ & + \beta_3 \cdot \text{democratic ademocratic } n \text{ specification is : ablesk} \\ & \text{between corruption and alate level tion, and} \\ & \text{nal regression specifications, aticcountability}_{\text{it}} \\ & + \beta_4 \cdot \text{government effectiveness}_{\text{it}} + \beta_5 \cdot \text{burden of government}_{\text{it}} \\ & + \beta_6 \cdot \text{rule of law}_{\text{it}} + \text{country fixed effects} \\ & + \text{time fixed effects} + \varepsilon_{\text{it}} \end{aligned} \tag{16.3}$$

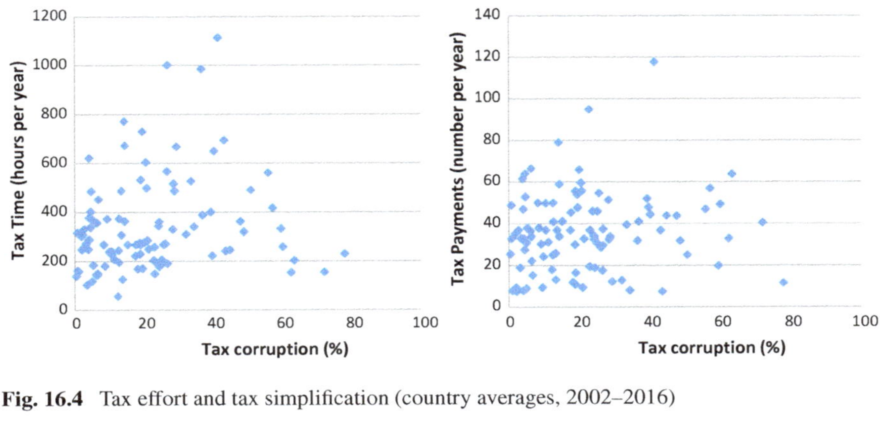

Fig. 16.4 Tax effort and tax simplification (country averages, 2002–2016)

Two tax simplification variables are TAXTIME and TAXPAY. Bureaucracy quality (BUREAUC) is taken from the International Country Risk Guide Database and it is defined as: "Institutional strength and quality of the bureaucracy is a shock absorber that tends to minimize revisions of policy when governments change." It is an index number between 1 and 6, where 6 corresponds to the highest quality. Thus the expected sign of the estimated coefficient is negative. Democratic Accountability (DEMOC) is also from the International Country Risk Guide Database. The database defines the series as: "A measure of, not just whether there are free and fair elections, but how responsive government is to its people. The less responsive it is, the more likely it will fall. Even democratically elected governments can delude themselves into thinking they know what is best for the people, regardless of clear indications to the contrary from the people." The series consists of index numbers taking a value between 1 and 6. 6 represents the highest democratic accountability. Its sign is expected to be negative.

Hausman endogeneity tests are run to understand whether any statistically significant endogeneity problem is observed. Such a problem may lead to inconsistencies in estimated coefficients if a panel least squared technique is used for regression analyses. The null hypothesis of exogeneity is rejected, indicating the presence of an endogeneity problem which is most probably caused by omitted variables. For consistent estimation coefficients, that problem has to be corrected. The Generalized Method of Moments (GMM) is one of the most commonly used regression techniques to handle endogeneity problems (Arellano and Bond 1991; Arellano and Bover 1995; and Blundell and Bond 1998). This methodology requires introduction of instrumental variables. In the regression analyses below, instrumental variables are defined as the first lagged values of the right-hand-side variables of the benchmark regression specification.

Table 16.4 shows selected estimation results of Eq. (16.3) from Table 16.3 of Awasthi and Bayraktar (2015). In this table, the regress results show the clear significant positive effect of tax simplification on tax corruption. The estimated coefficients of tax corruption are both economically and statistically significant. The simulation results based on these estimated coefficients are given in Table 16.5. A 10% drop in the number of tax payments lowers tax corruption by 3.9% when we use the first specification in Table 16.4. The drop in tax corruption is even higher at 5.9% when we have a 10% cut in time to comply with taxes, based on results presented in Eq. (16.2) in Table 16.4. The combined effect of a 10% cut in both TAXPAY and TAXTIME is even more dramatic and gets close to −9.1%.

Estimation of the Link between Tax Efforts and Tax Corruption (Second Step of Indirect Link Between Tax Efforts and Tax Simplification): In Fig. 16.5, we see the negative relationship between tax efforts and tax corruption, as expected. Higher tax corruption lowers tax efforts.

We use a regression specification similar to the one used in the direct link regressions [Eq. (16.2)]. The only difference is that instead of tax simplification, we have tax corruption now:

$$\text{TAX EFFORT}_{\text{it}} = \alpha_0 + \alpha_1 \cdot \text{GDPPC}_{\text{it}} + \alpha_2 \cdot \text{SHADOW ECONOMY}_{\text{it}}$$

Table 16.3 Simulations: impact of tax simplification on tax efforts (in percentage terms)

	10% drop in tax payments	10% drop in tax time	10% drop in tax payments and tax time
Equation (16.1) from Table 16.2	3.655	–	–
Equation (16.2) from Table 16.2	–	4.744	–
Equation (16.3) from Table 16.2	3.112	5.211	8.323

Source Authors' calculation

Table 16.4 Impact of tax simplification on tax corruption

Dependent variable: tax corruption	(1)	(2)	(3)
Constant term	22.675	10.644	10.676
	(5.663)***	(1.418)	(1.323)
Tax simplification			
Log(tax payments)	2.451 (2.444)***		2.611 (2.011)**
Log(tax time)		2.316 (1.876)*	5.317 (1.872)*
Political and political institution determinants of corruption			
Bureaucracy quality (higher better quality)	−0.772 (−1.881)*	−0.556 (−1.703)*	−0.555 (−1.799)*
Democratic accountability (higher better)	−1.543 (−2.937)***	−1.298 (−2.429)**	−1.298 (−2.418)**
Judicial and bureaucratic determinants of corruption			
Rule of Law (higher better)	−6.775 (−6.449)***	−6.492 (−6.296)***	−6.495 (−6.041)***
No. of observations	856	847	847
J-statistics	3.131	2.527	3.261
Arellano-bond serial correlation test AR(1)	0.224	0.229	0.231
Arellano-bond serial correlation test AR(2)	0.832	0.851	0.891
Jarque–Bera normality test	1.421	1.419	1.487

Note The results are taken from Awasthi and Bayraktar (2015) Table 16.3. The estimation method is a panel—GMM. Annual data are used. *t*-statistics are given in parenthesis. *indicates 10% significance level, **indicates 5% significance level, and ***indicates 1% significance level. These significance levels are equal to one minus the probability of rejecting the null hypothesis of zero coefficients. J-test is for the overidentification problem where $H0$: there is no overidentification problem. For serial correlation z-tests, $H0$ is "there is no serial correlation"; and for normality test, $H0$ is "normal distribution"

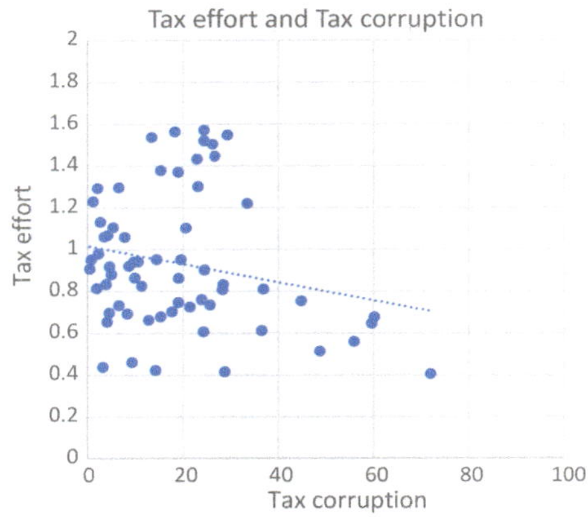

Fig. 16.5 Tax effort and tax corruption (country averages; 2002–2016)

$$
\begin{aligned}
&+\alpha_3 \cdot \mathrm{TRADE}_{\mathrm{it}} + \alpha_4 \cdot \mathrm{AGR}_{\mathrm{it}} \\
&+\alpha_5 \cdot \mathrm{GOVERNANCE\ QUALITY}_{\mathrm{it}} + \alpha_6 \cdot \mathrm{INFLATION}_{\mathrm{it}} \\
&+\alpha_7 \cdot \mathrm{TAX\ CORRUPTION}_{\mathrm{it}} + \varepsilon \qquad (16.4)
\end{aligned}
$$

The equation is again estimated using a panel OLS with regional and year effects. In Table 16.6, the estimated coefficient of tax corruption is −0.7 and significant at 5%. The estimated coefficients of other control variables are similar to the results presented in Table 16.2. Given that both tax efforts and tax corruption is in percentage terms, a 5% drop in tax corruption is expected to lead to a 3.5% increase in tax efforts. In the first step analysis of the indirect link from Table 16.5, we calculated that we need to cut TAXPAY or TAXTIME by around 10% to obtain a 5% drop in tax corruption on average which can lead to a 3.5% rise in tax efforts based on the results in Table 16.6. This calculation means that a 10% drop in tax simplification can indirectly lead to 3.5% points in higher tax efforts.

Summary of results: Figure 16.6 summarizes the outcomes of the direct and indirect empirical analysis. When we use the model investigating the direct link between tax

Table 16.5 Simulations: impact of tax simplification on tax corruption (in percentage terms)

	10% drop in tax payments	10% drop in tax time	10% drop in tax payments and tax time
Equation (16.1) from Table 16.4	−3.912	–	–
Equation (16.2) from Table 16.4	–	−5.913	–
Equation (16.3) from Table 16.4	−3.213	−5.911	−9.124

Source Authors' calculation

Table 16.6 Impact of tax corruption on tax corruption, 2002–2016

Dependent variable: tax effort (actual tax/tax capacity in %)				
	(1)		(2)	
Constant	15.4	(7.1)***	13.5	(5.6)***
Tax corruption	−0.7	(1.9)**	−0.8	(2.0)**
GDP per capita (constant)	2.2	(11.7)***	2.2	(9.1)***
Inflation rate	−1.7	(−5.4)***	−1.8	(−6.3)***
Trade openness (% of GDP)	0.01	(1.6)*	0.01	(1.8)*
Agriculture value added (% of GDP)	−0.2	(−7.1)***	−0.2	(−6.8)***
Size of shadow economy (% of GDP)	−0.1	(−2.6)***	−0.1	(−2.7)***
Corruption index	−0.5	(−2.2)**	–	
Bureaucracy index	–		−0.5	(−2.5)***
OBS	871		871	
Adjusted R^2	0.722		0.767	

Note The estimation technique is panel OLS with regional and time dummies. *t*-statistics are reported in parenthesis. See Table 16.2 note for further details
*Indicates 10% significance level
**Indicates 5% significance level
***Indicates 1% significance level

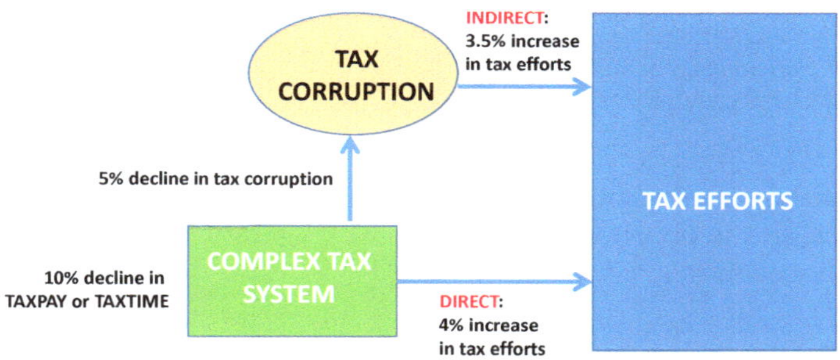

Fig. 16.6 Summary chart on tax efforts and tax simplification

simplification and tax efforts, it is estimated that a 10% cut in tax complexity variables increases the tax effort ratio by 4% on average. On the other hand, when we use the indirect model with tax corruption as a transmission mechanism, the impact of the same amount of tax simplification leads to slightly lower increase in tax efforts (3.5% rise).

Robustness check: In the literature, alternative ways of measuring tax efforts are introduced. Fenochietto and Pessino (2013) present a useful overview of alternative models for tax capacity and effort estimations. Alternative to the traditional regression method, we also use one of the most commonly used methods, i.e. stochastic

Table 16.7 Robustness check with alternative tax effort measure

Dependent variable: new measure of tax effort with stochastic frontier analysis				
	(1)		(2)	
Constant	17.5	(18.6)***	9.7	(6.5)***
Tax simplification				
Time spent for tax (taxtime)	2	(2.6)***	–	
No. of tax payments (taxpay)	2.9	(2.4)***	–	
Tax corruption				
Tax corruption	–		−0.7	(2.8)***
Control variables				
GDP per capita (constant)	2.1	(8.7)***	2.3	(6.1)***
Inflation rate	−1.9	(−4.1)***	−1.6	(−8.3)***
Trade openness (% of GDP)	0.01	(1.7)*	0.01	(1.8)*
Agriculture value added (% of GDP)	−0.3	(−5.1)***	−0.2	(−6.1)***
Size of shadow economy (% of GDP)	−0.1	(−2.8)***	−0.2	(−2.9)***
Bureaucracy index	−0.5	(−1.8)*	−0.4	(−2.1)**
OBS	874		871	
Adjusted R^2	0.691		0.651	

Note The estimation technique is panel OLS with regional and time dummies. *t*-statistics are reported in parenthesis. See Table 16.2 note for further details
*Indicates 10% significance level
**Indicates 5% significance level
***Indicates 1% significance level

frontier analysis method, to check the robustness of the regression results to alternative measures of tax efforts. For this alternative measure, I slightly modified the regression specification given in Eq. (16.1).

$$\begin{aligned}\text{TAX/GDP}_{\text{it}} = {} & \alpha_0 + \alpha_1 \cdot \text{GDPPC}_{\text{it}} + \alpha_2 \cdot \text{DEMOG}_{\text{it}} + \alpha_3 \cdot \text{TRADE}_{\text{it}} \\ & + \alpha_4 \cdot \text{AGR}_{\text{it}} + \alpha_5 \cdot \text{GOVERNANCE QUALITY}_{\text{it}} + v_{\text{it}} - u_{\text{it}}.\end{aligned}$$

In this modified equation, we introduce $v_{\text{it}} - u_{\text{it}}$ which is a composite error term, incorporating both the normally distributed random shock v_{it} and the positive inefficiency term u_{it}, reflecting observable heterogeneity (for more information, see, for example, Jondrow et al. 1982; Langford and Ohlenburg 2015). One interpretation of u_{it} can be a lack of tax effort. After estimating v_{it} and u_{it}, the stochastic frontier (tax capacity) is given by $\alpha_0 + \alpha_1 \cdot \text{GDPPC}_{\text{it}} + \alpha_2 \cdot \text{DEMOG}_{\text{it}} + \alpha_3 \cdot \text{TRADE}_{\text{it}} + \alpha_4 \cdot \text{AGR}_{\text{it}} + \alpha_5 \cdot \text{GOVERNANCE QUALITY}_{\text{it}} + v_{\text{it}}$. This frontier specifies the highest tax to GDP ratio country *i* could achieve in year *t*, in the absence of any inefficiency. The parameters of the stochastic frontier and u_{it} are estimated simultaneously, using maximum likelihood. u_{it} is estimated in a random-effects framework.

After generating tax capacity through the stochastic frontier equation, tax effort is again defined as the ratio of actual taxes to tax capacity. Then, we estimate Eqs. (16.2) and (16.4) for direct and indirect links, successively, to find the impact of tax simplification or tax corruption on the new definition of tax efforts. The regression technique is again a panel OLS with regional and time dummies.

Because the correlation coefficient between the initial measure and the new measure of tax efforts is high at 0.83, the estimation results are expected to be similar. The selected regression results with the new measure of tax efforts are presented in Table 16.7. When we compare the results presented in Tables 16.2 and 16.6 with the findings in Table 16.7, it can be seen that the estimated coefficients are robust to the new definition of tax efforts. The estimated coefficients of tax simplification variables and tax corruption variables are slightly lower with the new measure but significant at the 1% level. After simulating changes in tax efforts with these new estimated coefficients, we conclude that the direct impact of a 10% cut in TAXPAY or TAXTIME is a 3.3% increase in the tax effort ratio. The indirect effect of a 10% lower tax complexity, working through lower tax corruption, is a 3.5% rise in the tax effort ratio.

16.5 Conclusion

The empirical outcomes show that tax simplification (lower number of tax payments or less time spent on complying with taxes) can help governments raise their tax efforts. On average the expected impact is around 3.5% higher tax efforts with a 10% cut in tax complexity. This paper helps us better understand the overall impact of tax simplification on tax efficiency directly as well as indirectly, working through the tax corruption mechanism. The outcomes of the paper can have useful policy implications. These outcomes can place numerical values on possible impacts of tax simplification on efficiency of tax collection systems. Governments are in need of higher tax revenues to balance their deficits, and at the same time, they need to concern about market distortions and pick their methods to raise taxes accordingly. The empirical results show that tax simplification can provide such desired outcomes. The issue is that many tax systems are extremely complex and it requires a lot of legislative changes to simplify them. Therefore, it is not easy to implement. However, if they accomplish it, the result of tax revenues and tax efforts is expected to be highly positive.

Appendix

See Tables 16.8, 16.9 and 16.10.

Table 16.8 Descriptive statistics (2002–16)

	Tax revenue in % of GDP	GDP per capita	Age dependency ratio	Trade openness	Agriculture value added (in % of GDP)	Bureaucracy quality index	Corruption index	Size of shadow economy (in % of GDP)
Mean	22.74	10211.41	62.94	87.11	15.28	−5.33	−5.78	31.95
Standard deviation	11.14	15096.08	18.48	54.95	13.76	3.05	2.61	13.06
Minimum	1.63	118.64	24.68	0.31	0.00	−10.00	−10.00	8.10
Maximum	63.48	87716.73	117.43	562.06	65.86	−1.00	−1.00	68.30
Count	1182	1143	1156	1134	1123	1087	1056	1098
	BURDEN = Burden of government regulation	BUREAUC = Bureaucracy quality	DEMOC = Democratic accountability	EFFECTIVE = Government Effectiveness	RULE = Rule of Law	TAX CORRUP = Tax corruption rate	TAXPAY = Tax Payments (number per year)	TAXTIME = Tax time (hours per year)
Mean	3.218	1.981	4.079	−0.350	−0.399	22.047	36	344
Standard deviation	0.579	0.988	1.494	0.662	0.704	18.741	21	119
Minimum	1.847	0.000	0.000	−1.877	−1.924	0.398	6	58
Maximum	5.297	4.000	6.000	1.263	1.367	81.667	147	1585
Count	839	1230	1230	1064	1069	1107	882	873

Table 16.9 Correlation matrix (2002–16)

	Fiscal revenue in % of GDP	Tax revenue in % of GDP	GDP per capita	Age dependency ratio	Trade openness	Agriculture value added (in % of GDP)	Bureaucracy Quality Index	Corruption index	Size of shadow economy (in % of GDP)
Tax revenue in % of GDP	0.90	1.00							
GDP per capita	0.65	0.64	1.00						
Age dependency ratio	−0.46	−0.49	−0.25	1.00					
Trade openness	0.16	0.14	0.21	−0.29	1.00				
Agriculture value added (in % of GDP)	−0.61	−0.57	−0.34	0.36	−0.30	1.00			
Bureaucracy quality index	−0.46	−0.46	−0.45	−0.39	0.05	−0.33	1.00		
Corruption index	−0.42	−0.40	−0.40	−0.22	0.01	−0.40	0.83	1.00	
Size of shadow economy (in % of GDP)	−0.14	−0.06	−0.38	0.42	−0.27	0.38	−0.38	−0.31	1.00

(continued)

Table 16.9 (continued)

	BURDEN	BUREAUC	DEMOC	EFFECTIVE	RULE TAX CORRUP		TAXPAY	TAXTIME
Burden	1.00							
Bureauc	0.65	1.00						
Democ	0.59	0.31	1.00					
Effective	0.52	0.64	0.56	1.00				
Rule	0.10	0.24	0.31	0.41	1.00			
Tax corrup	−0.14	−0.16	−0.22	−0.26	−0.31	1.00		
Taxpay	0.07	−0.16	−0.08	−0.32	−0.29	0.13	1.00	
Taxtime	−0.09	−0.10	−0.23	−0.19	−0.25	0.17	0.32	1.00

Note: *BURDEN* Burden of government regulation; *BUREAUC* Bureaucracy quality; *DEMOC* Democratic accountability; *EFFECTIVE* Government effectiveness; *RULE* Rule of law; *TAX CORRUP* Tax corruption rate; *TAXPAY* Tax payments (number per year); *TAXTIME* Tax time (hours per year)

Table 16.10 Variable definitions and sources

Variables	Description	Source
Tax revenue in % of GDP	Series is calculated using data series from GFS and WDI. In WDI the series that are used to calculate tax revenue including social security contribution is tax revenue (GC.TAX.TOTL.GD.ZS) and social contributions (GC.REV.SOCL.ZS) when available Tax revenue refers to compulsory transfers to the general government for public purposes (when general data not available, we have used central government data). Certain compulsory transfers such as fines, penalties, and most social security contributions are excluded. Refunds and corrections of erroneously collected tax revenue are treated as negative revenue. Social contributions include social security contributions by employees, employers, and self-employed individuals, and other contributions whose source cannot be determined. They also include actual or imputed contributions to social insurance schemes operated by governments	WDI (2018) and GFS (2018)
GDP per capita	Constant in 2010 US$	WDI (2018)
Age dependency ratio	Age dependency ratio (in %) is the ratio of dependents–people younger than 15 or older than 64—to the working-age population–those ages 15–64	WDI (2018)
Trade openness	Series: trade (% of GDP) (NE.TRD.GNFS.ZS). Trade is the sum of exports and imports of goods and services measured as a share of gross domestic product	WDI (2018)
Agriculture value added (in % of GDP)	Series: agriculture, value added (% of GDP) (NV.AGR.TOTL.ZS). Cultivation of crops and livestock production. Value added is the net output of a sector after adding up all outputs and subtracting intermediate inputs. It is calculated without making deductions for depreciation of fabricated assets or depletion and degradation of natural resources. The origin of value added is determined by the international standard industrial classification (ISIC), revision 3. Note: For VAB countries, gross value added at factor cost is used as the denominator	WDI (2018)

(continued)

Table 16.10 (continued)

Variables	Description	Source
Bureaucracy quality index	The institutional strength and quality of the bureaucracy is a shock absorber that tends to minimize revisions of policy when governments change. The original score ranges from 1 to 4. High points are given to countries where the bureaucracy has the strength and expertise to govern without drastic changes in policy or interruptions in government services. The score is recalculated to -10 to -1 where low points are countries with strength bureaucracy and high points are countries with weak bureaucracy	ICRG (2018)
Corruption index	The assessment of corruption refers to the political system. Corruption index ranges from 1 to 6. High points are given to low corruption countries and low points are given to high corruption countries. The scores are recalculated to -10 to -1 where low points mean low corruption and high points mean high corruption	ICRG (2018)
Size of shadow economy	The shadow economy includes all market-based legal production of goods and services that are deliberately concealed from public authorities for any of the following reasons: (1) to avoid payment of income, value-added or other taxes, (2) to avoid payment of social security contributions, (3) to avoid having to meet certain legal labor market standards, such as minimum wages, maximum working hours, safety standards, etc., and (4) to avoid complying with certain administrative procedures, such as completing statistical questionnaires or other administrative forms	Hassan and Schneider (2016)

References

Aizenman, J., & JinJarak, Y. (2009). Globalisation and developing countries—A shrinking tax base? *Journal of Development Studies, 45*(5), 653–671.

Alfirman, L. (2003). *Estimating stochastic frontier tax potential: Can Indonesian local governments increase tax revenues under decentralization?* Department of Economics, University of Colorado at Boulder, Colorado. Working Paper No. 03–19 (November).

Alm, J. (1999). Tax compliance and administration. *Public Administration and Public Policy, 72,* 741–768.

Alm, J., Jackson, B., & Mckee, M. (1992). Institutional uncertainty and taxpayer compliance. *The American Economic Review, 82*(4), 1018–1026.

Alonso, J. A., & Garcimartín, C. (2011). *Does aid hinder tax efforts? More evidence*. CREDIT Research Paper No. 11/04. Nottingham: Centre for Research in Economic Development and International Trade, University of Nottingham.

Arellano, Manuel, & Bond, Stephen. (1991). Some tests of specification for panel data: Monte Carlo evidence and an application to employment equations. *Review of Economic Studies, 58*(2), 277–297.

Arellano, Manuel, & Bover, Olympia. (1995). Another look at the instrumental variables estimation of error-components models. *Journal of Econometrics, 68,* 29–51.

Awasthi, R., & Bayraktar, N. (2014). *Can tax simplification help lower tax corruption?* WB Working Paper No: WPS6988.

Awasthi, R., & Bayraktar, N. (2015). Can tax simplification help lower tax corruption? *Eurasian Economic Review, 5,* 297–330.

Bahl, Roy. (1971). A regression approach to tax effort and tax ratio analysis. *International Monetary Fund Staff Paper, 18,* 570–612.

Battese, G. E. (1992). Frontier production functions and technical efficiencies: A survey of empirical applications in agricultural economics. *Agricultural Economics, 7*(3–4), 185–208.

Battese, G. E., & Coelli, T. J. (1992). Frontier production functions, technical efficiency and panel data: With application to paddy farmers in India. *Journal of Productivity Analysis, 3*(1–2), 153–169.

Bayraktar, N., Le, T. M., & Moreno-Dodson, B. (2012). *Tax capacity and tax effort: Extended cross-country analysis from 1994 to 2009*. World Bank Working Paper No: 6252.

Bayraktar, N., Moreno-Dodson, B., & Le, T. M. (2016). Tax revenues and tax efforts across the world. In M. Erdogdu & B. Christiansen (Eds.), *Handbook of research on public finance in Europe and MENA region (Chap. 4)* (pp. 48–95). Hershey, Pennsylvania: IGI Global.

Binh, T. N., & Evans, C. (2014). Towards the development of a tax system complexity index. *Fiscal Studies, 35*(3), 341–370.

Bird, R. M., Martinez-Vazquez, J., & Torgler, B. (2004). *Societal institutions and tax efforts in developing countries*. Working Paper 04–06. Andrew young School of Policy Studies, Georgia State University: Georgia, Atlanta.

Bird, R. M., Martinez-Vazquez, J., & Torgler, B. (2006). Societal institutions and tax efforts in developing countries. International Tax Program, University of Toronto. No: 04011.

Blundell, Richard, & Bond, Stephen. (1998). Initial conditions and moment restrictions in dynamic panel data models. *Journal of Econometrics, 87,* 115–143.

Crandall, W., & Bodin, J.P. (2005). *Revenue administration reform in Middle Eastern countries, 1994–2004*. Working Paper No. 203. International Monetary Fund: Washington, DC.

Cuccia, A. D., & Carnes, G. A. (2001). A closer look at the relation between tax complexity and tax equity perceptions. *Journal of Economic Psychology, 22*(2), 113–140.

Cyan, M., Martinez-Vazquez, J., & Vulovic, V. (2012). *Measuring tax effort: How much does the Estimation Approach Matter?* International Center for Public Policy, Andrew Young School of Policy Studies, Georgia State University (September).

Davoodi, H. R., & Grigorian, D.A. (2007). *Tax potential versus tax effort: A crosscountry analysis of Armenia's stubbornly low tax collection*. IMF Working Paper No: WP/07/106 (May 2007).
Dean, S. A. (2005). Attractive complexity: Tax deregulation, the check-the-box election, and the future of tax simplification. *Hofstra L. Rev., 34,* 405.
Evans, C. (2003). Studying the studies: An overview of recent research into taxation operating costs. *eJournal of Tax Research, 1*(1), 64–92.
Fenochietto, R., & Pessino, C. (2013). *Understanding countries' tax effort*. International Monetary Fund Working Paper WP/13/244.
Fisman, R. J., & Roberta, G. (2006). Bargaining for bribes: The role of institutions. In S. Rose Ackerman (Ed.), *International Handbook on the Economics of Corruption*. Edward Elgar Publishing, Inc.: Northampton.
Forest, A., & Sheffrin, S. M. (2002). Complexity and compliance: An empirical investigation. *National Tax Journal, 55*(1), 75–88.
Fox, W. F., & Gurley, Tami. (2005). An exploration of tax patterns around the world. *Tax Notes International: Special Reports, 37*(9), 793–807.
Friedman, Eric, Johnson, Simon, Kaufmann, Daniel, & Zoido-Lobaton, Pablo. (2000). Dodging the grabbing hand: The determinants of unofficial activity in 69 countries. *Journal of Public Economics, 76*(3), 459–493.
Ghura, D. (1998). Tax revenue in Sub-Saharan Africa: Effects of economic policies and corruption. IMF Working Paper, No: WP/98/135 (September 1998).
Gupta, A. S. (2007). Determinants of tax revenue efforts in developing countries. IMF Working Paper, No: WP/07/184 (July).
Hassan, M., & Schneider, F. (2016). *Size and development of the shadow economies of 157 countries worldwide: Updated and new measures from 1999 to 2013*. IZA DP No. 10281.
Heyndels, B., & Smolders, C. (1995). Tax complexity and fiscal illusion. *Public Choice, 85*(1), 127–141.
Imam, P. A., & Jacobs, D. F. (2007). *Effect of corruption on tax revenues in the middle east*. IMF Working Paper No: WP/07/270 (November).
Independent Panel. (2013). *Independent panel review of the doing business report* (June 2013). World Bank: Washington D.C. (http://www.dbrpanel.org/sites/dbrpanel/files/doing-business-review-panelreport.pdf).
Jondrow, J., Lovell, C. A. K., Materov, I. S., & Schmidt, P. (1982). On the estimation of technical efficiency in the stochastic frontier production model. *Journal of Econometrics, 19*(2/3), 233–238.
Kasimbazi, Emmanuel. (2003). *Taxpayers rights and obligations: Analysis of implementation and enforcement mechanisms in Uganda*. Copenhagen: Danish Institute for International Studies.
Keen, M. (2003). *Changing customs: Challenges and strategies for the reform of customs administrations*. International Monetary Fund: Washington, DC.
Keen, Michael, & Mansour, Mario. (2010). Revenue mobilisation in Sub-Saharan Africa: challenges from globalisation I—Trade reform. *Development Policy Review, 28*(September), 553–571.
Kirchler, E., Niemirowski, A., & Wearing, A. (2006). Shared subjective views, intent to cooperate and tax compliance: Similarities between Australian taxpayers and tax officers. *Journal of Economic Psychology, 27*(4), 502–517.
Lambsdorff, Johann Graf. (2006). Causes and consequences of corruption: What do we know from a cross section of countries? In Susan Rose-Ackerman (Ed.), *international handbook on the economics of corruption*. Northampton: Edward Elgar Publishing, Inc.
Langford, B., & Ohlenburg, T. (2015). *Tax revenue potential and effort*. International Growth Centre Working Paper.
Lawless, Martina. (2013). Do complicated tax systems prevent foreign direct investment? *Economica, 80,* 1–22.
Leuthold, Jane H. (1991). Tax Shares in developing countries: A panel study. *Journal of Development Economics, 35,* 173–185.

Marcuss, Rosemary, Contos, George, Guyton, John, Langetieg, Patrick, Lerman, Allen, Nelson, Susan, et al. (2013). Income taxes and compliance costs: How are they related? *National Tax Journal, 66*(4), p833.

Milliron, V. C. (1985). A behavioral study of the meaning and influence of tax complexity. *Journal of Accounting Research, 23*(2), 794–816.

Mills, L. F. (1996). Corporate tax compliance and financial reporting. *National Tax Journal, 49,* 421–436.

Mulder, L. B., Verboon, P., & De Cremer, D. (2009). Sanctions and moral judgments: The moderating effect of sanction severity and trust in authorities. *European Journal of Social Psychology, 39*(2), 255–269.

Norregaard, J., & Khan, T. S. (2007). *Tax policy: Recent trends and coming challenges.* IMF Working Paper, No: WP/07/274 (December 2007).

Obwona, M., & Muwonge, A. (2002). *The efficiency and effectiveness of the revenue administration in Uganda.* Report developed for the Taxation, aid and democracy project (draft). Institute for International Studies (IIS), Copenhagen.

Oliver, T., & Bartley, S. (2005). Tax system complexity and compliance costs—Some theoretical considerations. *Economic Roundup, Winter, 2005,* 53–68.

Paul, D. L. (1997). Sources of tax complexity: How much simplicity can fundamental tax reform achieve. *NCL Review, 76,* 151.

Pessino, C., & Fenochietto, R. (2010). Determining countries tax effort. *Hacienda Publica Española / Revista de Economía, 195*(4), 65–87.

Piancastelli, M. (2001). *Measuring the tax effort of developed and developing countries: Cross country panel data analysis—1985/95.* Texto Para Discussao No: 818 (September 2001).

Picciotto, S. (2007). Constructing compliance: Game playing, tax law, and the regulatory state. *Law and Policy, 29*(1), 11–30.

Pitt, M. M., & Lee, L.-F. (1981). The measurement and sources of technical inefficiency in the indonesian weaving industry. *Journal of Development Economics, 9,* 43–64.

Purohit, M. C. (2007). Corruption in tax administration. In A. Shah (Ed.), *Performance, accountability and combating corruption.* Washington, D.C.: International Bank for Reconstruction and Development/The World Bank.

Quandt, R. E. (1983). Complexity in regulation. *Journal of Public Economics, 22*(2), 199–214.

Richardson, G. (2006). Determinants of tax evasion: A cross-country investigation. *Journal of International Accounting, Auditing and Taxation, 15*(2), 150–169.

Rodrik, Dani. (1998). Why do more open economies have bigger governments? *Journal of Political Economy, 106*(5), 997–1032.

Saad, N. (2009). Fairness perceptions and compliance behaviour: The case of salaried taxpayers in Malaysia after implementation of the self-assessment system. *eJournal of Tax Research, 8,* 32–63.

Santos, D., & Sergio, P. (1995). *Corruption in tax administration.* Presented at the Twenty-Ninth Annual Assembly of the CIAT, Lima, Peru, March 29, 1995.

Schneider, F., Buehn, A., & Montenegro, C. E. (2010). *Shadow economies all over the world: new estimates for 162 countries from 1999 to 2007.* World Bank Policy Research Working Paper No: 5356 (July 2010).

Scotchmer, S. (1989). The effect of tax advisors on tax compliance. In J. A. Roth & J. T. Scholz (Eds.), *Taxpayer compliance: Social science perspectives* (Vol. 2, pp. 182–199). USA: University of Pennsylvania Press.

Slemrod, J. (2007). Cheating ourselves: The economics of tax evasion. *The Journal of Economic Perspectives, 21*(1), 25–48.

Spilker, B. C., Worsham, R. G., & Prawitt, D. F. (1999). Tax professionals' interpretations of ambiguity in compliance and planning decision contexts. *The Journal of the American Taxation Association, 21*(2), 75–89.

Tanzi, V. (1998). *Corruption around the world: Causes, consequences, scope, and cures*. IMF Working Paper No. 98/63 (May).

Tanzi, V., & Davoodi, H. (1997). *Corruption, public investment, and growth*. Washington, DC: IMF.

White, R., Curatola, A., & Samson, W. (1990). A behavioral study investigating the effect of knowledge of income tax laws and tax policy on individual perceptions of federal income tax fairness. *Advances in Taxation, 3,* 165–185.

Chapter 17
Public Investment and Monetary Poverty in the Department of Puno

River Huaquisto-Ramos, Polan Franbalt Ferró-Gonzales, Ana Lucia Ferró-Gonzáles and Vicente Alanoca-Arocutipa

Abstract This study analyzes the effect of public investment on monetary poverty in the department of Puno, Peru, during the period 2004–2015. According to the results obtained from the econometric estimations, it has been shown that public investment has positive effects in the reduction of monetary poverty; since on average for every 100 million soles executed in the previous period in investment projects public in the department of Puno, the poverty indicator will be reduced by 4.45%; evidence has also been found that public social investment has contributed the most to reducing poverty. On the other hand, it was found that public investment projects in sanitation, transportation, agriculture and energy were those that have contributed the most in reducing poverty.

Keywords Budget · Monetary poverty · Public investment

JEL Codes H54 · H61

17.1 Introduction

The economic growth of Peru, during the period 2004–2015, was on average 5.8% per year (INEI 2018), stemming from a substantial increase in revenue, which translated into a remarkable growth of the economic resources, to transfer to the subnational

R. Huaquisto-Ramos
CONSPROY S.A.C, Puno, Peru

P. F. Ferró-Gonzales (✉)
Economic Engineering Faculty, Universidad Nacional del Altiplano, Peru. Av. Ejercito N° 321, P.O. Box 291 Puno, Peru
e-mail: polanf@unap.edu.pe

A. L. Ferró-Gonzáles
Universidad Privada San Carlos, Puno, Peru

V. Alanoca-Arocutipa
Social Sciences Faculty, Universidad Nacional del Altiplano, Puno, Peru

N. Tsounis and A. Vlachvei (eds.), *Advances in Cross-Section Data Methods in Applied Economic Research*, Springer Proceedings in Business and Economics,
https://doi.org/10.1007/978-3-030-38253-7_17

governments greater resources. This has allowed to promote public investment[1] with greater intensity in order to improve infrastructure and basic services in the department of Puno, since the regional government and local governments together had a budget for public investment of 48–1218 million soles[2] between 2004 and 2015, managing to execute 39 to 735 million soles (increase in more than 1780%) during the study period, with an average annual execution of 500 million soles and an average annual execution progress of 64% (Ministerio de Economia y Finanzas 2018).

Although it is true that public investment in recent years has presented significant growth, however, this does not seem to be reflected in the socioeconomic indicators. It is the case of monetary poverty[3], which during the same period shows a decrease from 58.7 to 21.8% in Peru, and in the department of Puno, it has only decreased from 78.3 to 34.1%, a statistic that is still above the national figure (21.8%), and 11 of the 13 provinces that constitutes the department have an incidence of poverty greater than 40%, the province with the highest incidence is Moho with 64.6%, and the lowest incidence is San Román with 18.9%. Therefore, the question arises: What effect does public investment have on monetary poverty in the department of Puno?

Therefore, the research aims to analyze the effect of public investment on monetary poverty in the department of Puno; since public investment is considered as a driver of development, mainly through the conditions, it provides for private investment which is the true determining factor of socioeconomic development (Máttar 2015).

Likewise, public investment increases the capital endowment, and the production possibilities frontier provides public goods, generates complementary investment (for private investment) and is a key variable for poverty reduction through its effect on aggregate demand and employment (Máttar 2015).

17.2 Literature Review

The article does not intend to study the correlation between public investment and the growth of the gross domestic product (GDP), since this phenomenon has already been widely investigated. Therefore, we focus our analysis on the poverty reduction

[1] Public investment is understood as any expenditure of public resources destined to create, increase, improve or replenish the stock of physical capital of public origin destined to create, increase, improve or replace stocks of physical capital in the public domain, with the object of expanding the country's capacity to provide services and produce goods (Ponce 2013).

[2] 01 USD = 3.35 PEN Soles (S/) approx.

[3] The National Institute of Statistics and Informatics (INEI) considers people who live in households whose per capita spending is insufficient to acquire a basic basket of food and not food (housing, clothing, education, health, transport, etc.) as poor money. Those who integrate households whose per capita expenditures are below the cost of the basic food basket are extremely poor. The INEI to measure the incidence of poverty uses the monetary approach. According to this notion of poverty, all people living in private households are considered poor, whose per capita expenditure valued monetarily does not exceed the threshold of the poverty line which is set at S/ 315.00 for 2015 (this figure varies for every year).

effect that should be generated as a result of an increase in the volume of public investment in the department of Puno.

In the international arena, the first work developed by Herrera and Roubaud (2002) showed that access to public services (electricity, drinking water and toilets) not only significantly reduces the probability of falling into a situation of "permanent poverty", but also increases the probability that households can get out of the poverty trap. They also argue that a larger size of the household and a higher proportion of young children, as well as a poor endowment of human capital (educational level) and physical (housing and access to public services), are other risk factors associated with the poverty.

However, Mehmood and Sadiq (2010), using the error correction model and Johnson's cointegration test, demonstrated that there is an inverse relationship between poverty and government spending, and that this relationship is long-term. To say, in the face of increases in public spending, reductions in the poverty indicator are expected.

Otherwise, Saavedra (2012) found, based on the results of econometric estimations, that the variable Gross Domestic Product (GDP) continues to be the main mechanism to reduce poverty, but that investment in irrigation works, road infrastructure and concessions they also have significant effects on poverty.

Likewise, Fort and Parades (2015) showed that "… the components of irrigation, roads, telecommunications and producer support programs have a significant effect on the reduction of rural poverty, and that this is manifested mainly through improvements in agricultural productivity. Likewise, the strengthening of human capital and investments in connectivity and access to markets are also relevant, with an impact that is manifested through changes in income and the composition of rural employment."

The analysis of the dynamics of poverty can describe how the severity of poverty or the depth of deprivation changes over time. It can show at what stage an individual enters or leaves poverty or deprivation and for how long it remains poor or not. It can allow policymakers to address the problems of poverty and focus better on the chronically poor (Kim 2019).

Studies in Peru, there is a work developed by Quiñones Huayna (2016), who reveals that following the reforms implemented in the 1990s, economic growth was promoted and low inflation contributed to the reduction of poverty in the country; and that this economic growth has allowed a substantial increase in revenue, which translated into a notable growth in ordinary resources, the canon and the Municipal Compensation Fund (FONCOMUN) that benefited subnational governments, as well as the increase in public salaries, elements that also helped reduce poverty. The author also showed that poverty grows significantly with an increase in its lag and falls before an increase in public spending per capita.

However, Ponce Sono (2013) has shown that social public investment has had a variation over time, explained by the dynamism of investment that has intensified over the years, and that, in the case of public investment in economic infrastructure, this has also presented a greater variation over time, which would indicate that this type of investment has been intensive, focused mainly on the construction and rehabilitation of roads and roads. On the other hand, the author argues that public investment is in a process of greater momentum in the use of public resources. However, the process of fiscal decentralization would have allowed the regions of the country to have increased their public resources to a great extent, presenting in turn balances due to the low execution in investment projects derived from the weak spending capacity of some regions, which could properly channel their resources in favor of their population.

The foregoing is supported by the Contraloría General de la República y Apoyo Consultoría (2014), in its document "Estudio del Proceso de Descentralización en el Perú," found that, as a result of the decentralization process between 2005 and 2012, the budget managed by the regional governments of the country would have increased by 143%; likewise, local governments handled 183% more budget in 2012 than in 2007.

17.3 Theoretical Foundations of the Relationship Between Public Investment and Poverty

17.3.1 Monetary Poverty

The National Institute of Statistics and Informatics of Peru, INEI, considers as poor money people who live in households whose per capita spending is insufficient to acquire a basic basket of food and not food (housing, clothing, education, health, transportation, etc.). Extremely poor are those who integrate households whose per capita expenditures are below the cost of the basic food basket (see Fig. 17.1).

The National Institute of Statistics and Informatics of Peru to measure the incidence of poverty uses the monetary approach. According to this notion of poverty, all persons living in private households, whose per capita expenditure valued monetarily, does not exceed the poverty line threshold, are considered poor.

Foster, Greer and Thorbecke (cited in Camones 2015), from now on FGT (by the initials of the surnames of the authors), state that in order to measure the monetary poverty, three indices are estimated. The first refers to the incidence of poverty[4] (FGT_0), which represents the proportion of the poor or extreme poor as a percentage of the total population. In other words, it determines the proportion of the population whose consumption is below the value of the poverty line or the value of the extreme poverty line, as the case may be. This measure of poverty does not take into account the magnitude of the gap that separates spending from the poor from the poverty line, nor does it consider the way in which spending is distributed among the poor. Therefore, it is complemented by measurements of the poverty gap index (FGT_1), which measures the average insufficiency of the poor's consumption with respect to

[4]For purposes of the present investigation, the first index, that is, incidence of poverty FGT_0, has been considered.

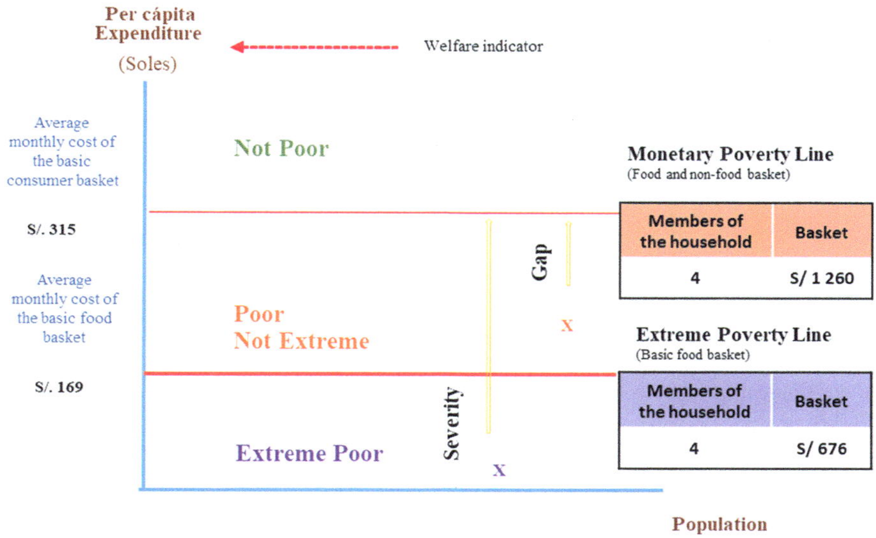

Fig. 17.1 Measurement of monetary poverty in Puno and Peru. *Source* INEI (2016)

the poverty line, taking into account the proportion of the poor population in the total population and by the severity of poverty (FGT_2), which measures inequality among the poor.

17.3.2 Relationship Between Public Investment and Poverty

Adams (1985) points out that the theory of public expenditure turns out to be a theory of adjustment between the ratio of expenditure made by the public and private sectors, whether the state allocates resources in sectors in which the private sector does not participate, At the same time, it considers the distribution of the necessary resources to all the sectors that are part of it. Regarding the latter, depending on the resources available to the state, spending will have to be allocated to sectors where basic needs are met (i.e., education, health, sanitation, transportation, among others), which is necessary to lay the foundations for the sustainable economic development of a country.

On the other hand, Wilhelm and Fiestas (2005) argue that public spending can generate an internal stimulus that promotes economic growth and that, moreover, can allow people who qualify as poor to the various productive activities in the economy, and that, they can improve their income and have an opportunity to escape poverty. The impact will depend on the allocation of public spending by the central government, since it may be more focused on generating greater economic growth than on reducing poverty levels. If poverty levels are to be reduced, spending should be focused on improving the provision of productive infrastructure (for example, in transport, electricity or irrigation infrastructure), since the lack of these assets can be the main constraint for the population which has the option to improve their income. In parallel, it is also important to consider the participation of the private sector through the different investment modalities, such as public–private partnerships (PPP) and works for taxes (OxI), since it complements the efforts of the state to provide better infrastructure and services public.

It is necessary to mention the main characteristics that distinguish decentralization processes, which basically seek to promote greater administrative and economic deconcentration at the national level, and whose main objective is the development of the regions and, therefore, the generation of greater well-being, avoiding unequal growth at the subnational level.

In the same way, for Saavedra (2012) investments in infrastructure directly affect the reduction of poverty (see Fig. 17.2), but also indirectly since investment generates economic growth, and the latter impacts on the fall of poverty. poverty. Also, there are other variables, macro and microeconomic, that also influence the economic growth of a country; Therefore, it is not enough to explain the fall in poverty only with investment, whether public or private. The author argues that since not all the other variables that influence economic growth are known, the variables GDP and investment in infrastructure are chosen as variables that can explain the fall in poverty. Finally, there are microeconomic variables such as cultural, geographical or specific shocks to each region that impact on the incidence of poverty.

According to the World Bank (n/d), the effects of investment in transport infrastructure on the welfare of the population are manifested in three aspects: economic opportunity, social security and urban empowerment. First, public investment in transportation provides greater economic opportunities for the population by generating access to new markets, facilitating job opportunities and reducing transportation costs for people, which means an increase in real wages. Second, access to social security is increased, understood as the possibility of accessing schools, health centers and other public services. Likewise, investment in roads and highways impacts the rating, since by allowing the transport of new inputs and products. In the same way, investments in the agricultural sector and energy have an impact on poverty through productive activities.

In addition, for the Comptroller General of the Republic of Peru (CGRP) investment in educational infrastructure has significant monetary and nonmonetary effects,

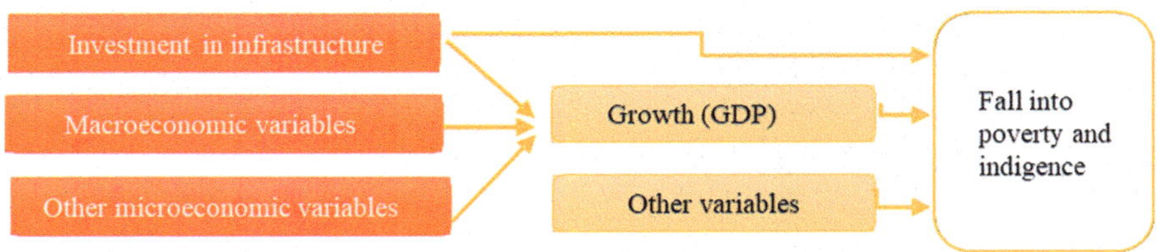

Fig. 17.2 Variables that influence poverty. *Source* Saavedra (2012)

individually and collectively. Likewise, increasing access to potable water service and improving the quality of this service contribute to reducing the incidence of diseases such as diarrhea. According to the Organization for Economic Cooperation and Development (OECD), close to 10% of the global burden of disease could be prevented through water, sanitation and hygiene interventions. Access to drinking water and sanitation services indirectly impacts the reduction of chronic malnutrition, the achievement of the students' learning objectives and the increase in the productivity of the people, significantly affecting the reduction of poverty (Contraloría General de la República del Perú 2016).

On the other hand, for the CGRP, the adequate provision of health infrastructure reduces the incidence and severity of diseases due to a better offer of medical services. This generates benefits in terms of productivity because they reduce the costs associated with the treatment of diseases and increase the time available for productive activities. In addition, greater nutrition and better health also determine intellectual conditions that entail greater creativity for work, which results in greater productivity.

17.4 Method and Data

The data collection was based on secondary sources, through the Portal of Economic Transparency of the Ministry of Economy and Finance of Peru (MEF) and the National Institute of Statistics and Informatics of Peru (INEI). The economic variables (annual) considered in this research are monetary poverty expressed in percentage terms and public investment at the accrual level; both variables have been analyzed based on the year 2010 = 100. Regarding public investment, this has been grouped into: total public investment executed (i.e., the sum of all the investments executed in public investment projects), public economic investment (transport, agriculture and energy) and social public investment (health education and sanitation), classification considered taking as reference the works of Arpi (2015), Huamaní (2016). In addition, monetary poverty has been correlated with public investment executed in four important sectors: transport, sanitation, agriculture and energy.

In general terms, the present investigation is of a quantitative nature, and the research methods used were correlational and explanatory. The first method is intended to know the relationship or degree of association that exists between two or more concepts, categories or variables in a particular sample or context; sometimes only the relationship between two variables is analyzed, but they are often located in the study links between three, four or more variables; the second method goes beyond the description of concepts or phenomena or the establishment of relationships between concepts; that is, they are aimed at responding to the causes of events and physical or social phenomena. As the name implies, his interest is focused on explaining why a phenomenon occurs, and under what conditions, it manifests or why two or more variables are related (Hernandez Sampieri et al. 2010).

The proposed model basically has the function of determining and explaining the behavior of the variations of the monetary poverty (PM) indicator, as a consequence of the public investment variable, that is, explaining the variations of the indicator of the variable of PM, due to variations in the execution of public investment in the department of Puno, specifically the Puno regional government and local governments (district and provincial municipalities).

Economic model: Monetary poverty $= f$ (public investment)

$$\mathrm{PM}_t = f(\mathrm{Inv}P_t) \tag{17.1}$$

From function (17.1), the following regression models have been proposed:

$$\mathrm{PM}_t = \beta_0 + \beta_1 \mathrm{Inv}pT_{t-1} + u_t \tag{17.2}$$

$$\mathrm{PM}_t = \alpha_0 + \alpha_1 \mathrm{InvpEcon}_{t-1} + \alpha_2 \mathrm{InvpSoc}_{t-1} + u_t \tag{17.3}$$

$$\mathrm{PM}_t = \gamma_0 + \gamma_1 \mathrm{Transp}_{t-1} + \gamma_2 \mathrm{Saneam}_{t-1} + \gamma_3 \mathrm{Agropec}_{t-1} + \gamma_4 \mathrm{Energ\acute{i}}a_{t-1} + u_t \tag{17.4}$$

where

PM_t	Departmental monetary poverty (%).
InvpT_{t-1}	Total public investment (S/) at the accrual level.
$\mathrm{InvpEcon}_{t-1}$	Economic public investment (S/) at the accrual level.
$\mathrm{InvpSoc}_{t-1}$	Public social investment (S/) at the accrual level.
Transp_{t-1}	Public investment in transportation projects (S/) at the accrual level.
Saneam_{t-1}	Public investment in sanitation projects (S/) at the accrual level.
$\mathrm{Agropec}_{t-1}$	Public investment in agricultural projects (S/) at the accrual level.
$\mathrm{Energ\acute{i}}\,a_{t-1}$	Public investment in energy projects (S/) at the accrual level.
$\beta_0, \alpha_0, \gamma_0$	Intercept of the models.
β_1	Regression coefficient of the variable InvpT on PM.
α_1	Regression coefficient of the variable InvpEcon on PM.
α_2	Regression coefficient of the variable InvpSoc on PM.
γ_1	Regression coefficient of the variable Transp on PM.
γ_2	Regression coefficient of the variable Saneam on PM.
γ_3	Regression coefficient of the variable Agropec on PM.
γ_4	Regression coefficient of the variable energy on PM.
u_t	Stochastic variable (which is different for each equation).
t	Time (Annual).

The estimation was carried out using the ordinary least squares (OLS) technique and subsequently subjected to an econometric evaluation by submitting them to a series of statistical tests such as the relevance test of the estimated coefficients (t), joint test (F), model goodness of fit (coefficient of determination, R2), Durbin–Watson and Breusch–Godfrey self-correlation test, Ramsey RESET model specification error test, White heteroscedasticity test, error normality (Jarque–Bera) and stability test of the model through the sum of normalized residuals CUSUM and CUSUM square.

17.5 Results and Discussion

17.5.1 Dynamic Evolution of Public Investment in the Department of Puno

It has been shown that the budget allocated for public investment in the department of Puno, during the period 2004–2015, showed a growing trend, from 48 to 1218 million soles, increasing by more than 2425% with an average annual budget of 800 million soles (Fig. 17.3). In this period, the subnational governments executed 39 million soles in 2004 and 735 million soles in 2015 (18 times than the one executed in 2004) (Fig. 17.4). This conjuncture of the growth of resources for public investment is reinforced by Ponce Sono (2013), who found that public investment is in a process

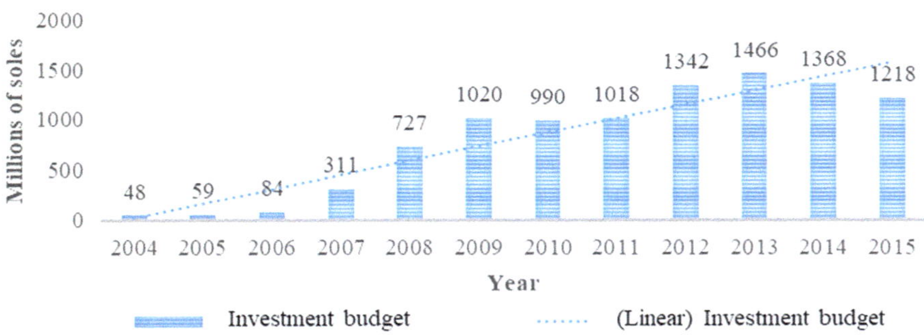

Fig. 17.3 Evolution of the budget for public investment in the department of Puno, 2004–2015. *Source* Own elaboration based on MEF data

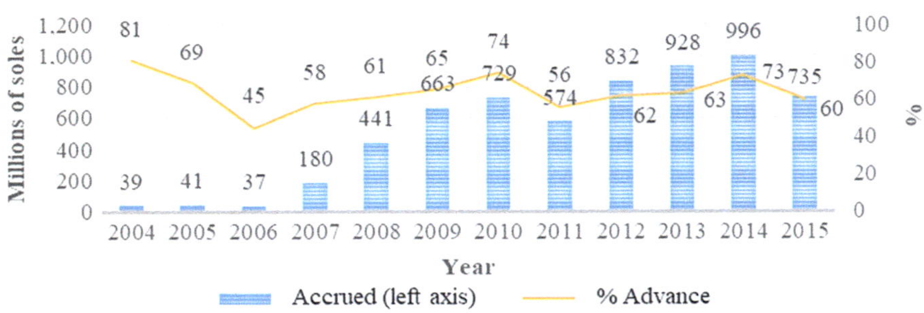

Fig. 17.4 Evolution of the budgetary execution of public investment in the department of Puno, 2004–2015. *Source* Own elaboration based on MEF data

of greater momentum in the use of public resources, as part of the decentralization process. Likewise, the Contraloría General de la República y Apoyo Consultoría (2014) argues that between 2005 and 2012, the budget managed by the regional governments of the country has increased by 143%, and the local governments handled 183% more budget in 2012 than in 2007, all as a result of the decentralization process.

It has also been found that the main items that financed spending on investment projects of the Puno regional government were the ordinary resources (RO) and the canon (CANON) mainly, items that during the period 2004–2015 maintained a growing trend, with a fall of the line of canon as of 2012 (see Fig. 17.5). During the study period, 39% (1130 million soles) of the investment expenses were financed with a canon and 35% (1028 million soles) with the ordinary resources item. On the other hand, in the case of local governments during the period 2007–2015, the resources that financed the expenditure on investment projects were mainly the canon, ordinary resources and FONCOMUN as shown in Fig. 17.6, plus observe that the evolution of the canon and ordinary resources was ascending and sustained compared to the FONCOMUN that maintained a stable behavior. However, during 2007–2015, close to 50% of public investment was financed by canon and 21% and 20% by ordinary resources and FONCOMUN, respectively.

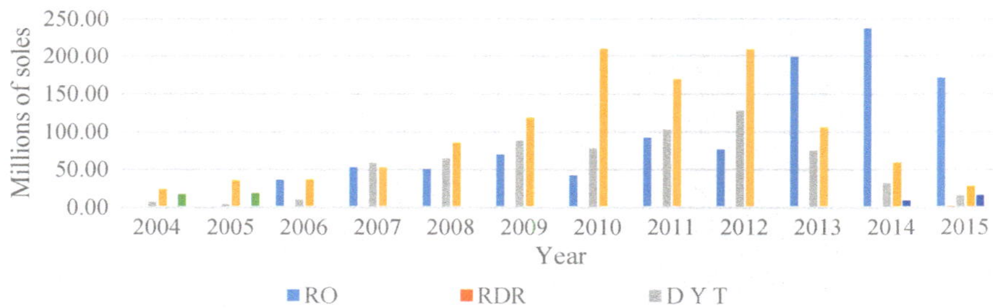

Fig. 17.5 Evolution of the sources of financing of public investment of the Puno regional government, according to headings, 2004–2015. RO: ordinary resources; RDR: resources directly collected; D Y T: donations and transfers. *Source* Own elaboration based on MEF data

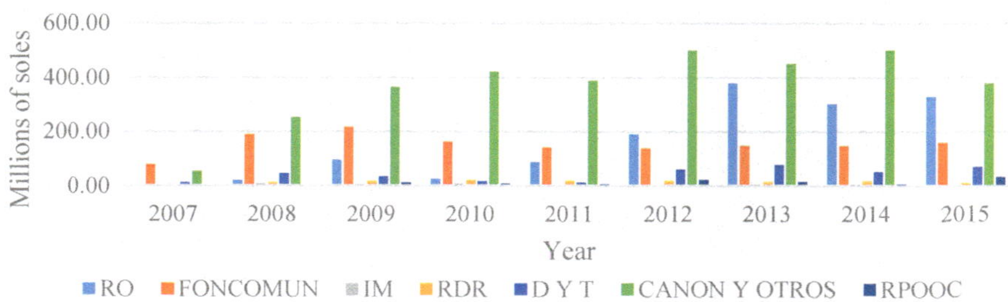

Fig. 17.6 Evolution of sources of financing of public investment of local governments, according to items, 2007–2015. *Source* Own elaboration based on MEF data

Quiñones Huayna (2016) argued that the reforms implemented in the 90s were the starting point of the drive for economic growth and low inflation that contributed to the reduction of poverty in the country, and that, economic growth has allowed for a substantial increase in revenue, which translated into a notable growth in ordinary resources, the canon and the FONCOMUN that ended up benefiting subnational governments, elements that have also helped to reduce poverty.

In summary, the evidence shown has validated the hypothesis that the resources for public investment of the subnational governments (GRP and GL) of the department of Puno have been increasing, as a result of the process of decentralization and budgetary collection of the state, mainly ordinary resources, canon and FONCOMUN.

However, certain limitations still persist in the execution stage. Such is the case that during 2004–2015, the Puno regional government reached, on average, an execution rate of 0.60, a ratio below the average of the country's regional governments (0.65), and the local governments reached an average implementation rate of as low as 0.67. However, the low level of the execution rate is attributable to the strong increase in public resources that the department of Puno has been receiving, generating that the execution of public investment has not been able to keep pace with the growth of its revenues.

17.5.2 Effects of Public Investment on Poverty

An inverse relationship has been found between the poverty variable and public investment, which is consistent with economic theory and the revised background. Table 17.1 shows that, in contrast to increases in public investment, the poverty indicator decreases. This is reinforced by Mehmood and Sadiq (2010), who, in his study, demonstrated the existence of an inverse relationship between poverty and government spending.

From the results of the first econometric model, it has been found that, on average, for every 100 million additional soles executed in the previous period in public investment projects in the department of Puno, the poverty indicator falls to 4.45%, and the results found were very similar to those found by Huamaní (2016), who points out that for every one hundred million soles executed in the previous period in public investment projects, it translates into a reduction of poverty of 3.02%, keeping everything else constant.

However, from the second estimated model, it can be inferred that both types of public investment (economic and social) have contributed to reducing poverty; however, the investments made in social investment projects (education, sanitation and health) had a greater impact on the reduction of monetary poverty than investments made in economic investment projects (transport, agriculture and energy), since the effects (estimated with a negative sign) on poverty were 0.09 and 0.03 percentage points, respectively.

From the third model, it can be concluded that the public investments, according to functions, that have contributed the most in reducing poverty in the department of

Table 17.1 Results of the effect of public investment on poverty

	Modelo lineal		Modelo lineal		Modelo lineal	
Variable[a]	1		2		3	
	Coef.	tc	Coef. tc		Coef.	tc
C	74.50101 (0.0000)	19.47196	73.14505 (0.0000)	19.26574	72.74270 (0.0000)	12.073
INVPT	−0.044516 (0.0001)	−6.666650				
INVPECON			−0.027618 (0.2855)	−1.144437		
INVPSOC			−0.091621 (0.0063)	−3.668918		
TRANSP					−0.036254 (0.8286)	−0.226
SANEAM					−0.151148 (0.1461)	−1.669
AGROPEC					−0.053764	−1.669
ENERGIA					(0.8794)–0.020803 (0.9302)	−0.091
S.E.	SI		SI		SI	
R^2	0.831600		0.870260		0.866000	
R^2 Ajustado	0.812889		0.837826		0.776666	
F estadistico	44.44422 (0.000092)		26.83099 (0.000283)		9.693990 (0.008657)	
D.W.	1.428897		1.424932		1.544840	

Source Self-made
Note The results were estimated in the EViews software
S.E. Expected sign
(…) *p*-value
[a]All the explanatory variables are expressed in millions

Puno, were the sanitation, transportation, agricultural and energy projects, although these last three were not individually significant, but that together (statistical *F*) are significant; that is, the complementarity between public investment projects in transportation, agriculture and energy would have greater effects on the reduction of poverty in the department of Puno.

17.5.3 Discussion of Results

With the results found in the research, the existence of an inverse relationship between poverty and public investment has been evidenced, consistent with the results found by Máttar (2015), Mehmood and Sadiq (2010), Quiñones Huayna (2016) and Saavedra (2012). However, Huamaní (2016) found an inverse relationship between the variables under study, but that this was not significant, and that, its explanation would be in the low levels of budget execution reached by both the regional government and the local governments[5] of the department of Puno. On the other hand, the author had already demonstrated the existence of problems in the execution of investments, such as the lack of quality in investment projects, acts of corruption, limited capacities of authorities and officials and problems of transparency in participatory processes.

On the other hand, it has also been found that the sectors that have contributed the most to reducing poverty levels were investments in sanitation (0.15%), transportation (0.04%) agriculture (0.05%) and energy (0.02%); however, it has also been shown that the magnitude and direction of the estimated effects show the degree of complementarity between investments of a productive nature, since it would have a direct impact on the income of the families and thus be able to leave the situation of the poor. Along this line, there is a series of coincidences with authors such as Fort and Parades (2015) where they found that the components of irrigation, roads, telecommunications and producer support programs have a significant effect on the reduction of rural poverty, and that, this manifests itself through improvements in agricultural productivity added mainly. On the other hand, Camones (2015) finds similar results where it states that budget execution in the transport and irrigation sectors has a positive impact in reducing poverty, and that, these were chosen because of the direct impact they can have on the productivity of the population.

In summary, we have demonstrated the existence of an inverse relationship between poverty and public investment, and that, when public investment is divided into economic and social, the latter was the largest contributor in reducing poverty levels; this situation would be explained mainly by the priority and importance given by local governments (municipalities) to sanitation projects (water and sewage). On the other hand, when an analysis was made of public investment at the level of sectors (functions), it was found that complementarity between investments, especially productive investment (transport, agriculture and energy), would have a greater impact in reducing poverty levels. However, Saavedra (2012) argued that it would not be enough to explain the reduction of poverty levels only with public and/or private investment.

17.6 Conclusions

During the 2004–2015, public investment in the department of Puno has presented an increasing behavior, product of the process of decentralization and increases in the ordinary resources, FONCOMUN and canon mainly; thus, the subnational governments (Puno regional government and local governments) had a budget for public

[5]Jorge Luis Urquia, Vice President of the Network of Urban and Rural Municipalities of Peru (REMURPE), points out that behind the low level of budgetary execution is the issue of resource transfers by the Central Government, which generally makes them mid-year and when the execution stage is entered, there is no longer time to execute these budget increases, therefore the level of execution falls significantly; He also mentions that only for the legal terms to tender the work would it take at least three months to start the work.

investment of 48 to 1218 million soles, increasing by more than 2425%, managing to execute 39 million soles in 2004 and 735 million soles in 2015 (18 times the one executed in 2004), with an average annual execution of 500 million soles and an annual execution rate of 64%. Although the resources for public investment have increased, certain limitations still persist in the execution stage; since during the study period, the Puno regional government reached on average an execution rate of 0.60, a ratio below the average of the regional governments of the country (0.65), and the local governments reached on average an execution rate of only 0.67.

According to the results of the econometric estimation, it has been determined that monetary poverty decreases in the face of an increase in spending on public investment, results that are consistent with economic theory and the revised background; in terms of magnitudes, it was found that, on average for every 100 million soles executed in a previous period in public investment projects in the department of Puno, the poverty indicator falls to 4.45%. On the other hand, it was also evident that public social investment has contributed the most in reducing poverty compared to public economic investment, since the effects (estimated with a negative sign) on poverty were 0.09 and 0.03 percentage points, respectively. It was also found that the sanitation, transportation, agricultural and energy investment projects contributed the most to reducing poverty; although these last three (individually) were not statistically significant, overall they are significant, i.e., the complementarity of public investment, especially in transportation, agriculture and energy, would have greater effects on the reduction of poverty in the department of Puno. Finally, it can be affirmed that public investment is an instrument that helps in the reduction of monetary poverty and has greater importance since it is a variable that the government controls.

References

Adams, H. C. (1985). *The Theory of Public Expenditures*. Retrieved from https://www.jstor.org/stable/2485646.

Arpi, R. (2015). Perú, 2004–2013: Inversión Pública en Infraestructura, Crecimiento Y Desarrollo Regional—Informe Final Proyecto Mediano CIES-IDRC-DFATD-Fundación M. J. Bustamante 2014. *CIES*. Retrieved from https://www.cies.org.pe/sites/default/files/investigaciones/inversion_publica_en_infraestructura_crecimiento_y_desarrollo_regional_arpi_una.pdf.

Bank, W. (n.d.). *Notas técnicas N° 1 : Nexos entre el transporte y la reducción de la pobreza*. Retrieved from http://siteresources.worldbank.org/INTPRS1/Resources/383606-1205334112622/4768783-1205337105916/trtn0119.pdf.

Camones, L. (2015). *Impacto del Gasto en Infraestructura Productiva en la Reducción de la Pobreza: Análisis a Nivel de Gobiernos Locales* (pp. 55–58). Retrieved from http://tesis.pucp.edu.pe/repositorio/bitstream/handle/123456789/7242/CAMONES_GARCIA_LUIS_ALBERTO_IMPACTO.pdf?sequence=1&isAllowed=y.

Contraloría General de la República del Perú. (2016). *Efectividad de la inversión pública a nivel regional y local durante el periodo 2009 al 2014. 2*, 1–189. Retrieved from http://doc.contraloria.gob.pe/estudios-especiales/estudio/2016/Estudio_Inversion_Publica.pdf.

Contraloría General de la República y Apoyo Consultoría. (2014). *Estudio del proceso de descentralización en el Perú*. 418. https://doi.org/10.1002/jpln.201100407.

Fort, R., & Parades, H. (2015). Inversión pública y descentralización: sus efectos sobre la probreza rural en la ultima década. *Documento de Investigación*. https://doi.org/10.1017/CBO9781107415324.004.

Hernandez Sampieri, R., Fernandez Collado, C., Baptista Lucio, M., & Del P. (2010). *Metodolodía de la investigación*.

Herrera, J., & Roubaud, F. (2002). Dinámica de la pobreza urbana en el Perú y en Madagascar 1997–1999: un análisis sobre datos de panelDynamique de la pauvreté urbaine au Pérou et à Madagascar 1997-1999 : une analyse sur données de panelUrban Poverty Dynamics in Peru and Madagascar 1997–19. *Bulletin de l'Institut Français d'études Andines, 31*(3), 495–552. https://doi.org/10.4000/bifea.6688.

Huamaní, A. (2016). Inversión pública y sus implicancias en el desarrollo socioeconómico en el. *Revista de Investigaciones Altoandinas—Journal of High Andean Research, 18*(3), 337–354. https://doi.org/10.18271/ria.2016.223.

INEI. (2016). *Evolucion de la Pobreza Monetaria 2009–2015. Peru.* https://doi.org/10.1017/CBO9781107415324.004.

INEI. (2018). *Series Nacionales; Cuentas nacionales, Producto Bruto Interno*.

Kim, H. (2019). Beyond monetary poverty analysis: the dynamics of multidimensional child poverty in developing countries. *Social Indicators Research, 141*(3), 1107–1136. https://doi.org/10.1007/s11205-018-1878-3.

Máttar, J. (2015). *Inversión pública: contribución al crecimiento, productividad y competitividad*. Retrieved from http://www.mef.gob.pe/contenidos/inv_publica/docs/eventos-taller/SEMINARIO_INTERNACIONAL/files/06Julio/1-Inversion-publica-y-su-contribucion-al-crecimiento-economico_Jorge-Mattar.pdf.

Mehmood, R., & Sadiq, S. (2010). The relationship between government expenditure and poverty: A cointegration analysis. *Romanian Journal of Fiscal Policy, 1*(1), 29–37. Retrieved from https://www.econstor.eu/handle/10419/59799.

Ministerio de Economia y Finanzas. (2018). *Reportes de ejecución y avance presupuestal 2004–2015*.

Ponce Sono, S. S. (2013). Inversión pública y desarrollo económico regional. *Pontificia Universidad Católica Del Perú*. Retrieved from http://tesis.pucp.edu.pe/repositorio/handle/123456789/4837.

Quiñones Huayna, N. M. (2016). Efectos del gasto publico sobre la pobreza monetaria en el Perù: 2004–2012. *Pontificia Universidad Católica Del Perú*. Retrieved from http://tesis.pucp.edu.pe/repositorio/handle/20.500.12404/7147.

Saavedra, E. (2012). *Infraestructura y pobreza en Chile*. Retrieved from http://www.sociedadpoliticaspublicas.cl/archivos/CBLOQUET/Panel_Otros_Temas_de_Politicas_Publicas/InfraestructurayPobrezaenChile.pdf.

Wilhelm, V., & Fiestas, I. (2005). Exploring the link between public spending and poverty reduction lessons from the 90s. *World Bank Institute*, 42 p. Retrieved from http://unpan1.un.org/intradoc/groups/public/documents/apcity/unpan028789.pdf.

Chapter 18
Does Reforming the Benchmark Policy Rate Really Work? The Analysis of Monetary Policy Transmission in Indonesia

Ahmad Danu Prasetyo

Abstract We conduct a VAR model to analyze the effectiveness of transmission of monetary policy aftermath the implementation of the new policy rate in Indonesia. We include variables that proxy five channels of the monetary policy transmission, i.e., the inflation, the exchange rate, the asset price, and the credit channel. The result of the study shows that the change of the monetary policy regime does make an impact through the transmission channels. Furthermore, the impulse of the intertemporal gap of policy rate would increase the government bond yield, expected inflation, and investment credit rate in the short term. On the opposite, it will depreciate the stock index and the domestic exchange rates. However, the response of the impulse will be diminished over the long-term period; except for investment credit rate, the impulse will persist for the long term.

Keywords Monetary policy transmission · Change of policy rate · Interest pass-through · Bank of Indonesia

JEL Codes E52 · E58

18.1 Introduction

The policy interest rate is one key instrument for central banks to influence other economic indicators. It becomes the benchmark for any other interest rates, especially in the banking sector. Different countries have different policy interest rates. The most common are the overnight lending rate, discount rate, and repurchase rate (of different maturities). Central banks use the policy interest rate to perform contractive or expansive monetary policy. A rise in interest rates is commonly used to prevent high inflation, currency depreciation, excessive credit growth, or capital outflows. On the opposite, by cutting interest rates, a central bank might be seeking to boost

A. D. Prasetyo (✉)
Institut Teknologi Bandung, Ganesha st. No. 10, Bandung 40132, Indonesia
e-mail: ahmad.danu@sbm-itb.ac.id

N. Tsounis and A. Vlachvei (eds.), *Advances in Cross-Section Data Methods in Applied Economic Research*, Springer Proceedings in Business and Economics,
https://doi.org/10.1007/978-3-030-38253-7_18

economic activity by fostering credit expansion or currency depreciation to gain competitiveness.

However, some lag may apply; it might need time for the banking sector and other markets to adjust their behavior along with the changes in policy rates. Sometimes, due to poor monetary policy transmissions, the desired effect never happened. At this moment, the central banks may consider changing its policy rates regime to improve the effectiveness of the transmission.

Since August 19, 2016, Bank of Indonesia (BI) has officially implemented the 7-day repo rate replacing the BI rate—that was a discount rate—as the policy rate for Indonesian banks. Other than Indonesia, a similar policy has been implemented in at least 14 countries, including India, Sweden, Republic of South Africa, Turkey, Saudi Arabia, UAE, and Thailand, each with different underlying assets and tenors. The new policy rate was believed to have greater impacts on the money market, banking industry, and real sector compared to the previous reference rate. This is because it refers to monetary instruments actively traded daily between BI and the banking sector and has a strong correlation with the operational targets of monetary policy (BI 2016a, b).

There are three effects expected from this policy, i.e., (1) to strengthen the monetary policy signal, (2) to increase the monetary policy transmission effectivity through banking and money market interest rates, and (3) to broaden the money market, especially in the interbanking transaction and interest structure development (BI 2016b). BI used both rates as references in the transition period, April to August 2016 to avoid shocks in the market.

Triugroho et al. (2014) explained that the interest rates in Indonesia are relatively higher compared to its neighbors and other developing countries, especially the lending rates. This further restricts the growth of the business and real sectors. BI as monetary authority has taken several ways to push the banks to decrease their lending rates such as reporting obligation of the basic lending rates and interest subsidies for SMEs. However, the stickiness was persisted (Trinugroho et al. 2014). Switching policy rate to the 7-day repo rate was the latest attempt that is expected to help the interest rate to decrease.

Despite the high expectations on the new benchmark rate, however, the mechanisms of the transmission effect are still blurred, especially when it is linked to the government bonds as the underlying assets. Whether this policy will affect the inflation targeting framework pursued by BI is also remained unclear. In addition, the effectiveness of the monetary transmission towards the lending rate was also doubted. A report says that there is no improvement in lending rates a month after the new regime was implemented (Tempo.co, 8 September 2016). This indicates that lending rates might be sticky. Therefore, the long-term effect of this new policy rate regime needs to be measured and evaluated.

18.2 Literature Review

The effectiveness of monetary policy transmission is one of the interesting and important topics in monetary economics. The policy implication needs to be measured from time to time due to the dynamics of economic conditions. One of the main references is proposed by Taylor (1993) that explained the role of central bank in setting the interest rates should correspond to the inflation and output gap; this then known as Taylor rule.

$$i_t = \pi_t + r_t^* + \alpha_\pi \left(\pi_t - \pi_t^*\right) + \alpha_Y (y_t - y_t)$$

where i_t is the target policy rate, r_t^* is the equilibrium real interest rate, π_t is the inflation rate, π_t^* is the expected inflation rate, y_t is the real GDP, and y_t is the potential output.

In addition to Taylor rule, Mishkin (1995) elaborated the monetary policy transmission mechanism through several channels, i.e., the interest rate, the exchange rate, the asset price, and the credit channel. The interest rate channel works based on the Keynesian model that dictates that a contractionary monetary policy would lead to a rise in real interest rates. This would further increase the cost of capital, declining investment spending, and then reducing the aggregate output. The exchange rate channel works in an open economy where the contractionary monetary policy would increase the real interest rate. Subsequently, this would cause the value of domestic currency increase compared to the value of other currency, which would decrease the net export and in turn would decrease the aggregate output. The asset price channel is related to the demand for the asset. The contractionary monetary policy would increase the interest rate. This then would increase the required rate of return of the asset, which would decrease the asset prices. The decrease in asset prices would decrease consumer wealth. They would be restrained to consume, leading to a decrease in output. Through the credit channel, the contractionary monetary policy would decrease the demand for banking deposit. This would cause a decrease in bank reserve. In turn, banks would increase its lending interest rate, which would decrease the amount of borrowing.

One way to measure the effectiveness of monetary policy transmission is by measuring the interest rate pass-through; it measures the impact of changes in the central bank's benchmark rate on other interest rates. Previous research shows asymmetric interest rate adjustment on the benchmark rate in banking and money market. In Malaysia, interest pass-through adjustment was more significant in a loose monetary policy that it was in tight monetary policy (Zulkhibri 2012). In opposite, Das (2015) empirically prove that lending rate adjustment was faster in tight monetary policy.

Several works of literature explore the interest pass-through during a financial crisis. Humala (2005) explained that a financial crisis could change the effectivity and adaptability of lending rates in response to changes in benchmark rates in Argentina. Aristei and Gallo (2014) found that there is a decreasing pass-through of the lending rate from interest rates in money markets during the financial crisis, especially for households and non-financial institutions. They argued that the lending rates for non-financial institutions were more vulnerable to fluctuation in the market rather than the lending rates for households. Liu et al. (2017) explore the impact of the global financial crisis on the interest rate pass-through for several types of lending rates in Australia. They found that there is a shifting behavior on how the banks adjust their lending rates as the markup spreads go up and the interest rate pass-through decreases.

Chandra and Unsal (2014) explained that global economic conditions were the main factors that affect the interest rate change in Asia. However, the monetary policy transmission was still effective since it was done through short-term interest rate arrangement; even though the effectiveness of this policy deteriorated at the capital inflow periods. Oppositely, Fan et al. (2011) argued that the benchmark rate only has a low impact on the low inflation rate. In addition, it does not have any significant impact on current or future real output in China; it was the money supply that has a significant impact on inflation and real output.

18.3 Methodology

As mentioned earlier, the monetary policy transfer mechanism would go through five channels, i.e., interest rate, exchange rate, asset prices, credit, and expected inflation. However, these variables would be interdependent to each other. In addition, there may be a lag in the transmission of the monetary policy, which may vary across the variables.

In this study, we collect monthly data of BI rate, 7-day reverse repo rate, inflation rate, government's bond yield, stock index, investment credit rate, lending rate, and the working capital credit rate to measure the effectiveness of the monetary policy transmission in the normal economic situation. The data were collected from January 2014 to September 2018 to avoid the economic shock in 2013, except for BI rate and 7-day reverse repo rate which are ended and started on August 2016, respectively.

The common method for measuring the interest rate pass-through is by using a vector autoregression model (VAR) that captures the interperiod interrelationship of the variables. However, the use of the VAR method requires the variables not to be co-integrated to each other (Engle and Granger 1987). In the case of co-integration exists among the variables, we will use the vector error correction model (VECM) that extends the VAR model for co-integrated variables.

18.4 Result and Analysis

18.4.1 Descriptive Analysis

One of the main objectives of the central bank in determining the policy rate is to affect the expected inflation rate. We do an exponential smoothing method to estimate the value of expected inflation based on the year-on-year inflation data. As there are several exponential smoothing methods that could be used for estimation, we do backtesting for each method by comparing the estimated values with the actual values of inflation by using *t*-test. From Table 18.1, even though all estimation methods indicate that *t*-values and probabilities are statistically insignificant, we choose to use the double exponential smoothing method since it has the lowest *t*-values and higher probability means that the expected inflation values have the most similar distribution with the actual value. By using this method, the values of expected inflation (EXP_INF) rates were ranged between 2.21 percent and 9.64 percent during the analysis period.

We use Jakarta Interbank Spot Dollar Rate (JISDOR) as the unit of analysis for the exchange rate. This rate serves as a reference rate for exchange rate transactions in the banking system in Indonesia. It is announced by the central bank every working day at 10 AM. The values were determined by using the weighted average of all USD transactions that were done between 8 AM to 9.45 AM on a respective day. In our data collection, the value of the JISDOR ranged between IDR 11427 and IDR 14414 per USD with average and standard deviation at IDR 13155 and IDR 795.67 per USD, respectively.

The asset channeling is proxied by two instruments. We include a monthly average of 10-year government bonds' yields (BYIELD) as a measure for bond assets and the composite index of the Indonesian Stock Exchange (SINDEX) as a measure for stock assets. The government bond yields ranged from 6.30% to 9.62%, with average and standard deviation at 7.66% and 0.75% respectively, whereas the stock composite index was varied between 4223.91 and 6605.63, with average and standard deviation at 5290.87 and 569.89, respectively.

Even though in the monetary transmission channels proposed by Mishkin (1995) the credit channel and interest channel would work separately, due to high correlation, the investment credit rate (as a proxy the lending rate of the credit channel) and interbank interest rate (that proxy the interest rate) cannot be put together in one

Table 18.1 Selection of exponential smoothing method for expected inflation

Method	*t*-value	Probability
Single	−0.1719	0.8639
Double	−0.0049	0.9961
Holt-winters no seasonal	−0.2413	0.8098
Holt-winters additive	0.0241	0.9808
Holt-winters multiplicative	−0.0152	0.9879

equation. We prefer to include investment credit rate since in this research we would like to know the impact of the policy rate of the central bank towards the real sector instead of the financial sector. The investment credit rate (INVCRRATE) values are taken from the average investment credit rates offered by commercial banks in Indonesia. It was varied between 10.29% and 12.39% within the analysis period. The average of investment credit rates is 11.56% with a standard deviation at 0.70%.

Another endogenous variable included in the analysis is the intertemporal difference of the policy rate (DPOLICY). As explained in the background, the Bank of Indonesia changed its policy rate from the BI rate to a repo rate in the mid of August 2016. Even though there are gaps between the values of the two policy rates due to the different characteristics, the intertemporal changes of those two rates are similar. This can be seen from the data of the two rates in the transition period April to July 2016. For example, in May 2016, the Bank of Indonesia decided to keep the BI rate at 6.75%, similar to the value in April 2016. At the same time, the repo rate was kept at 5.5%. Likewise, when the central bank decreased the BI rate by 25 bp in the next month, the repo rate was also decreased by the same value. Taking this similarity, we combine the two policy rates into one variable by considering the intertemporal differences.

In addition, we also include one dummy variable as an exogenous variable, REGIME, that indicates the different regime periods of the policy rates. The period when the BI rate is taken as the policy rate is noted as 0, while the period when the repo rate is taken as the policy rate is noted as 1.

The descriptive statistics of the variables employed in this study is shown in Table 18.2.

Table 18.2 Descriptive analysis of variables

	Mean	Maximum	Minimum	Std. Dev.	Note
Endogenous					
EXP_INF	4.7481	9.6402	2.2121	1.8654	Double exponential smoothing
JISDOR	13155.2900	14868.7400	11427.0500	795.6696	USD to IDR
BYIELD	7.6586	9.6240	6.2980	0.7553	In percentage
SINDEX	5290.8710	6605.6300	4223.9100	569.8901	
INVCRRATE	11.5591	12.3900	10.2900	0.7048	In percentage
DPOLICY	−0.0132	0.6250	−0.2500	0.1469	In percentage
Exogenous					
REGIME	0.4561	1	0	0.5025	Dummy

18.4.2 Policy Interest Pass-Through Towards Lending Rate

The first step in the vector regression is to find out whether the residuals of common variables are stationary or not. By using Levin, Lin and Chu t-test we found that the probability of the t-value is lower than 5%, meaning that there is enough evidence to reject the hypothesis that there is unit root in the variables. This result allows us to proceed to use VAR without having to take the differenced values nor checking the existence of co-integrating variables. However, prior to VAR measurement, we first need to examine the lag order should be assigned to the model. Based on the Schwarz Information Criterion, we obtain that 1 month is the optimal lag that would minimize the value of the SIC.

The preliminary analysis of causality between the endogenous variables shows that the intertemporal gap of the policy rates Granger causes the exchange rates and the investment credit rates, whereas exchange rates and expected inflations were also granger cause investment credit rates. On the other hand, investment credit rates along with government bond yields granger cause the stock index (Table 18.3).

We further analyze the causalities between the variables by using the VAR model. The result shows that nothing is significantly affecting DPOLICY except for its lagged value. On the other hand, there is not enough evidence to prove that it was directly affecting other variables except for the exchange rates. However, the indirect effect towards investment credit rate might still happen since there are recursive causalities between the exchange rate and investment credit rate. In addition, there is not enough evidence to accept the hypothesis that the change of the monetary policy regime does make an impact through the transmission channels.

The magnitude of the coefficient shows that there is a positive relationship between DPOLICY and JISDOR, which indicate that every time BI increases the policy rate, then the domestic currency will weaken against USD in the following month. This will lead to a decrease in the investment credit rate that causes the exchange rate rebounds to half of its decreased amount.

In order to understand the long-term impact of the intertemporal gap of the policy rate, we further analyze the impulse–response graphs of DPOLICY towards other variables. As shown in Fig. 18.1, the impulse of DPOLICY would increase the government bond yield, expected inflation, and investment credit rate in the short term. On the opposite, it will depreciate the stock index and the domestic exchange rates. However, the response of the impulse will be diminished over the long-term period; except for investment credit rate, the impulse will persist for the long term.

We also test the residuals of VAR to indicate the existence of serial correlation in the model. The autocorrelation LM test yields that the probability of LM Statistic is lower than 10% significance level. This would indicate that there is no serial autocorrelation between residuals in the model.

Table 18.3 Result of vector autoregression model

	DPOLICY		JISDOR		EXP_INF		BYIELD		INVCRRATE		SINDEX	
DPOLICY (−1)	0.2681	*	439.5941	*	−0.1853		0.3182		0.0542		176.8587	
JISDOR (−1)	0.0000		1.0116	***	−0.0001		0.0001		−0.0000	***	−0.0507	
EXP_INF (−1)	0.0076		0.4633		0.7747	***	0.0242		0.0108	**	−9.2745	
BYIELD (−1)	0.0612		−51.9481		0.3536		0.7434	***	0.0137		−176.3890	**
INVCRRATE (−1)	−0.1163		211.8237	*	0.4047		0.2373		0.9718	***	– 136.6076	
SINDEX (−1)	0.0001		0.1716		0.0006		0.0000		0.0000		0.5912	***
C	0.7886		−3091.4960		−7.9480		−2.0875		0.7398		5824.0510	***
REGIME	−0.0946		55.7472		0.0158		0.0864		0.0048		4.3732	
R^2	0.2449		0.9286		0.7717		0.7959		0.9957		0.9356	
Adj. R^2	0.1300		0.9177		0.7370		0.7648		0.9950		0.9258	

Note The numbers showed in the table are coefficients of the lagged variables
*, **, *** Indicates the 1%, 5%, and 10% significance level respectively

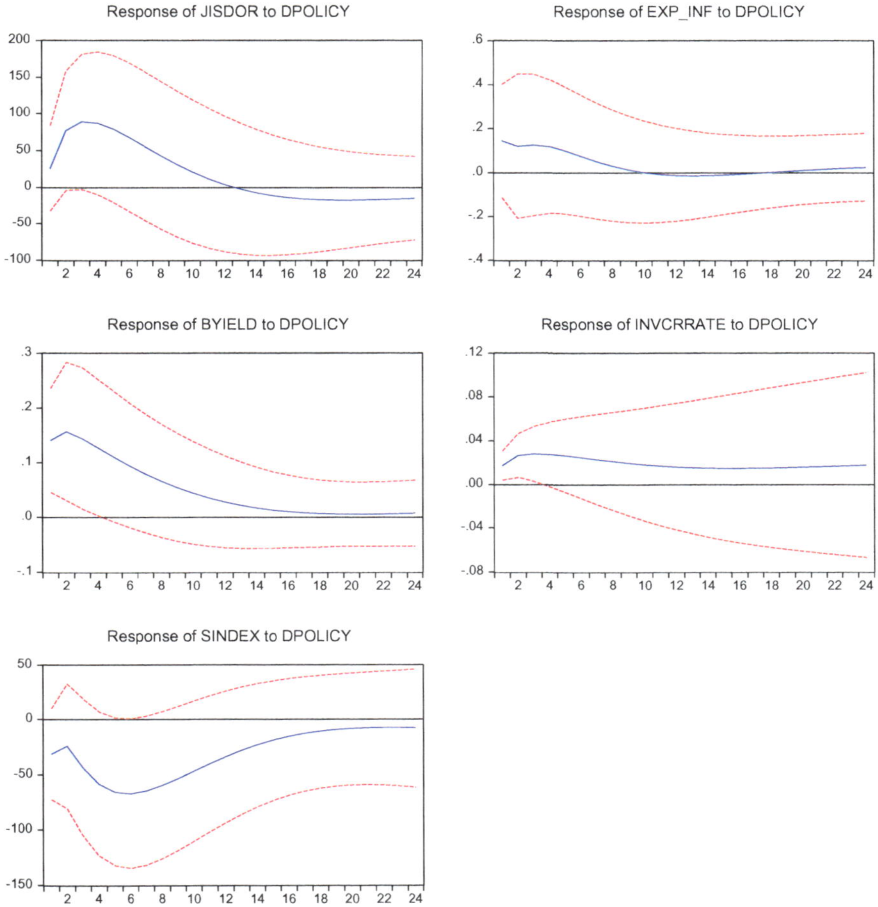

Fig. 18.1 Response to Cholesky one S.D. Innovations ±2 S.E

18.4.3 Robustness Test

For robustness test, we replicate the same methodology by using another variable. We use working capital credit rates (WCCRRATE) that are usually given in shorter maturity compared to the investment credit rate. Similar to the previous model, the LLC unit root test shows that there is no unit root for the variables, while the lag order also shows that 1 month is the optimal lag based on SIC (Table 18.4).

The result of VAR of the second model is pretty much similar to the first one, where the intertemporal gap of the policy rate would only directly affect the exchange rate. However, there might be indirect effect towards the WCCRRATE through the exchange rate channel. When BI increases the policy rate, the domestic currency

Table 18.4 Result for robustness test by replacing INVCRRATE with WCCRRATE

	DPOLICY		JISDOR		EXP_INF		BYIELD		WCCRRATE		SINDEX	
DPOLICY (−1)	0.2820	*	436.5457	*	−0.1911		0.3387		0.0070		169.5375	
JISDOR (−1)	0.0000		1.0085	***	−0.0001		0.0001		−0.0001	***	−0.0518	
EXP_INF (−1)	0.0060		2.2045		0.7780	***	0.0249		0.0132	**	−9.8858	
BYIELD (−1)	0.0548		−43.4814		0.3698		0.7494	***	0.0561	*	−180.4792	***
WCCRRATE (−1)	−0.0873		203.4116	*	0.3885		0.2754		0.9549	***	−149.6268	*
SINDEX (−1)	0.0001		0.1735		0.0006		0.0000		0.0001		0.5855	***
C	0.4373		−3122.1920		−8.0055		−2.8411		0.4611		6122.8580	***
REGIME	−0.0977		104.4230		0.1088		0.1871		−0.0218		−44.8993	
R^2	0.2333		0.9293		0.7721		0.8000		0.9952		0.9373	
Adj. R^2	0.1166		0.9185		0.7374		0.7695		0.9945		0.9278	

Note The numbers showed in the table are coefficients of the lagged variables
*, **, *** Indicates the 1%, 5%, and 10% significance level respectively

will be depreciated against USD in the following month. Later, the working capital credit rate will be decreased, that leads to an increase of the exchange rate since there is positive relationship between WCCRRATE in the previous month with JISDOR. Strengthening the finding in the previous model, it seemed that there is no significant impact of the change of monetary policy regime towards all variables.

18.4.4 Discussion

This result confirms the ineffectiveness of monetary policy transmission in Indonesia. Changing the monetary regime did not necessarily make any difference. The impulse–response graph indicates that the impact of the policy rate set by BI would only work temporarily on the expected inflation. However, against all reservations, the policy rate indeed has an indirect impact of towards lending rate; and it might persist for long term. This should diminish the sticky price argument of the lending rate in Indonesia.

However, there is a need to keep monitoring and analyze the credit channel due to disintermediation and asymmetric information problem in the banking sector in Indonesia. (Warjiyo 2004). The open market operation done by the central bank seemed to be an effective panacea to overcome the problem. Nevertheless, a thorough examination and prudent regulations must be conducted to solve the root cause of this acute problem in the banking system.

18.5 Conclusion

To increase the monetary policy transmission effectivity through banking and money market interest rates, the Bank of Indonesia switches their policy rate from previously a discount rate to a repo rate. We conduct a VAR model to analyze the effectiveness of transmission of monetary policy aftermath the implementation of the new policy rate. We include variables that proxy five channels of the monetary policy transmission, i.e., the inflation, the exchange rate, the asset price, and the credit channel. The monthly data set was taken from April 2014 until September 2018.

The result of the study shows that the change of the monetary policy regime does make an impact through the transmission channels. Furthermore, the impulse of the intertemporal gap of policy rate would increase the government bond yield, expected inflation and investment credit rate in the short term. On the opposite, it will depreciate the stock index and the domestic exchange rates. However, the response of the impulse will be diminished over the long-term period; except for investment credit rate, the impulse will persist for the long term.

Appendix 1: Summary of Unit Root Analysis

Series: SINDEX, BYIELD, JISDOR, EXP_INF, INVCRRATE, DPOLICY				
Exogenous variables: individual effects, individual linear trends				
Automatic selection of maximum lags				
Automatic lag length selection based on SIC: 0–1				
Newey–West automatic bandwidth selection and Bartlett kernel				
Method	Statistic	Prob.**	Cross-sections	Obs
Null: unit root (assumes common unit root process)				
Levin, Lin and Chu t	−3.46852	0.0003	6	331
Null: unit root (assumes individual unit root process)				
Im, Pesaran and Shin W-stat	−2.53322	0.0057	6	331
ADF—Fisher Chi-square	33.6282	0.0008	6	331
PP—Fisher Chi-square	27.6821	0.0062	6	332

**Probabilities for Fisher tests are computed using an asymptotic Chi-square distribution. All other tests assume asymptotic normality

Appendix 2: Summary of Lag Measurement in the Model

Endogenous variables: DPOLICY JISDOR EXP_INF BYIELD INVCRRATE SINDEX

Exogenous variables: C

Included observations: 51

Lag	LogL	SC
0	−875.3298	34.78922
1	−594.0700	26.53484*
2	−554.6387	27.76392
3	−520.2615	29.19120
4	−472.0084	30.07433

*Indicate the selected lagging period

Appendix 3: Granger Cause Analysis

Null hypothesis	F-statistic	Prob.	
JISDOR does not granger cause DPOLICY	0.0209	0.8855	
DPOLICY does not granger cause JISDOR	4.0782	0.0485	**
EXP_INF does not granger cause DPOLICY	0.0960	0.7579	
DPOLICY does not granger cause EXP_INF	0.0240	0.8774	
BYIELD does not granger cause DPOLICY	0.6356	0.4289	
DPOLICY does not granger cause BYIELD	0.2945	0.5896	
INVCRRATE does not granger cause DPOLICY	1.3283	0.2545	
DPOLICY does not granger cause INVCRRATE	3.7543	0.0582	*
SINDEX does not granger cause DPOLICY	1.4112	0.2404	
DPOLICY does not granger cause SINDEX	0.0015	0.9693	
EXP_INF does not granger cause JISDOR	0.0007	0.9785	
JISDOR does not granger cause EXP_INF	1.2525	0.2681	
BYIELD does not granger cause JISDOR	1.2860	0.2619	
JISDOR does not granger cause BYIELD	0.0421	0.8383	
INVCRRATE does not granger cause JISDOR	0.2261	0.6364	
JISDOR does not granger cause INVCRRATE	15.2333	0.0003	***
SINDEX does not granger cause JISDOR	3.4771	0.0680	*
JISDOR does not granger cause SINDEX	0.1178	0.7328	
BYIELD does not granger cause EXP_INF	0.5329	0.4686	
EXP_INF does not granger cause BYIELD	0.9163	0.3428	
INVCRRATE does not granger cause EXP_INF	1.9219	0.1717	
EXP_INF does not granger cause INVCRRATE	7.4612	0.0086	***
SINDEX does not granger cause EXP_INF	0.2122	0.6470	
EXP_INF does not granger cause SINDEX	1.4939	0.2272	
INVCRRATE does not granger cause BYIELD	1.4227	0.2385	
BYIELD does not granger cause INVCRRATE	0.0028	0.9584	
SINDEX does not granger cause BYIELD	0.0436	0.8355	
BYIELD does not granger cause SINDEX	6.2683	0.0155	**
SINDEX does not granger cause INVCRRATE	0.2236	0.6384	
INVCRRATE does not granger cause SINDEX	4.7316	0.0343	**

Appendix 4: VAR Residual Serial Correlation LM Test

Null Hypothesis: no serial correlation at lag order h
Included observations: 54

Lags	LM-stat	Prob.
1	50.04437	0.0600

Probs from chi-square with 36 df

References

Aristei, D., & Gallo, M. (2014). Interest rate pass-through in the euro area during the financial crisis: a multivariate regime-switching approach. *Journal of Policy Modeling*. https://doi.org/10.1016/j.jpolmod.2013.12.002.

Bank Indonesia. (2016a). Penjelasan BI 7-day reverse repo rate. Retrieved September 24, 2016 from http://www.bi.go.id/id/moneter/bi-7day-RR/penjelasan/Contents/Default.aspx (in Indonesian language).

Bank Indonesia. (2016b). Menjawab Pertanyaan Seputar BI rate dan BI 7-day repo rate. Retrieved September 24, 2016 from http://www.bi.go.id/id/ruang-media/siaran-pers/Documents/FAQ%20BI%207-day%20Repo%20Rate_ver2.pdf (in Indonesian language).

Chandra, S. J., & Unsal, D. F. (2014). The effectiveness of monetary policy transmission under capital inflows: evidence from Asia. *Borsa Istanbul Review*. https://doi.org/10.1016/j.bir.2014.03.002.

Das, S. (2015). *Monetary policy in India: Transmission to bank interest rates*. In IMF Working Paper, International Monetary Fund. Retrieved October 15, 2017 from https://www.imf.org/external/pubs/ft/wp/2015/wp15129.pdf.

Engle, R. F., & Granger, C. W. (1987). Co-integration and error correction: representation, estimation, and testing. *Econometrica, 55*(2), 251–276. https://doi.org/10.2307/1913236.

Fan, L., Yu, Y., & Zhang, C. (2011). An empirical evaluation of China's monetary policies. *Journal of Macroeconomics, 33*, 358–371. https://doi.org/10.1016/j.jmacro.2010.11.003.

Humala, A. (2005). Interest rate pass-through and financial crises: Do switching regimes matter? The case of Argentina. *Applied Financial Economics, 15*(2), 77–94. https://doi.org/10.1080/0960310042000297908.

Liu, M. H., Margaritis, D., & Qiao, Z. (2016). The global financial crisis and retail interest pass-through in Australia. In *Review of Pacific Basin financial markets and policies, 19*(4). https://doi.org/10.1142/s0219091516500260.

Mishkin, Frederic S. (1995). Symposium on the monetary transmission mechanism. *Journal of Economic Perspectives, 9*(4), 3–10.

Taylor, J. B. (1993). Discretion versus policy rules in practice. *Carnegie-Rochester Conference Series on Public Policy, 39*, 195–214. https://doi.org/10.1016/0167-2231(93)90009-L.

Tempo.co (8 September 2016) *7 Day Repo Rate tidak ampuh turunkan bunga kredit*. Retrieved September 24, 2016 from https://m.tempo.co/read/news/2016/09/08/090802689/7-day-repo-rate-tak-ampuh-turunkan-bunga-kredit. (in Indonesian language).

Trinugroho, I., Agusman, A., & Tarazi, A. (2014). Why have bank interest margins been so high in Indonesia since the 1997/1998 financial crisis? *Research in International Business and Finance, 32,* 139–158. https://doi.org/10.1016/j.ribaf.2014.04.001.

Warjiyo, Perry (2004). *Mekanisme Transmisi Kebijakan Moneter di Indonesia*, Seri Kebanksentralan No. 11, Jakarta:Pusat Pendidikan dan Studi Kebanksentralan, Bank Indonesia (in Indonesian Language).

Zulkhibri, M. (2012). Policy rate pass-through and the adjustment of retail interest rates: Empirical evidence from Malaysian financial institutions. *Journal of Asian Economics, 23,* 409–422. https://doi.org/10.1016/j.asieco.2012.04.001.

Chapter 19
Quo Vadis Brand Management? Specifics in Brand Value Sources Across Markets

Jana Kliestikova, Maria Kovacova, Judit Olah and Elvira Nica

Abstract Although national economies are more and more interdependent due to the accelerating globalization, contemporary managerial practice indicates the trend of localization and adaptation to intercultural specifics of markets. Thus, the incorporation of sociological theories into the traditional managerial patterns is going to be an imperative of optimal market performance. This statement is valid also for the practice of brand management. In accordance with previously mentioned, the aim of this paper is to identify specifics in brand value sources across markets on the case study of Slovak Republic creating so a platform for future research of relevant disparities in cross-cultural brand value sources. The data used in the presented study were obtained by our own survey carried out on the sample of 2000 respondents (Slovak citizens older than 15 years). The given data have been statistically evaluated by the factor analysis supported by implementation of KMO test, Barlett's test of sphericity and calculation of Cronbach's Alpha for brand value sources in general as well as for the example of brands characterized by habitual buying behaviour. It has been found that (1) there are four groups of brand value sources in general as well as in case of selected product category but (2) the ranking of these groups in scope of their perception as brand value sources is different. Therefore, we state that the issue

J. Kliestikova (✉) · M. Kovacova
Faculty of Operation and Economics of Transport and Communications, Department of Economics, University of Zilina, Univerzitna 1, 010 26 Zilina, Slovak Republic
e-mail: jana.kliestikova@fpedas.uniza.sk

M. Kovacova
e-mail: maria.kovacova@fpedas.uniza.sk

J. Olah
Faculty of Economics and Business, Institute of Applied Informatics and Logistics, University of Debrecen, Böszörményi út 138, 4032 Debrecen, Hungary
e-mail: olah.judit@econ.unideb.hu

E. Nica
Center for Human Resources and Labor Studies at AAER, New York City, USA
e-mail: popescu_elvira@yahoo.com

The Bucharest University of Economic Studies, Piata Romana 6, 010374 Bucharest, Romania

N. Tsounis and A. Vlachvei (eds.), *Advances in Cross-Section Data Methods in Applied Economic Research*, Springer Proceedings in Business and Economics,
https://doi.org/10.1007/978-3-030-38253-7_19

of cross-cultural specifics in perceived brand value sources is relevant for effective brand management in times of finding ways to brand's long life.

Keywords Brand · Brand value · Brand value sources · Psychografic specifics · Buying behaviour

JEL Code M31

19.1 Introduction

Most schools of brand management are built on rational and prescriptive approaches. Despite this fact, from the strategy-derived dimensions, approaches to brand management are surprisingly heterogeneous, with no one school diverging from the dominating pattern (Nadanyiova et al. 2015). Thus, contemporary brand research faces to the trend of fragmentation of scientific literature (Krizanova et al. 2018; Tartaglione et al. 2019). The existence of coherent scientific schools focused on key issues of interest is more exception than normal state, and there are many partial topics which are not elaborated in mutual context. Aime et al. (2018) verify this state by the usage of the prism of institutional isomorphism to highlight four distinct periods that show that the brand management system has gradually imposed itself on the Western world and managed to adapt to an ever-changing environment.

Moreover, they show that in the current digital age, the brand management system is now torn between two opposing directions: the brand manager should act as both absolute expert and galvanic facilitator, and the brand management system needs to reinvent itself once again. Possible way of this reinvention is the renaissance of sociocultural basis of brand management. It is because nowadays, it has been abandoned from traditional marketing sense of branding in favour of its financial aspects and calculation of brand value in its hard financial nature (Majercak et al. 2013; Mehrpouya and Willmott 2018).

The shift of the brand value concept from its traditional, marketing, to alternative, financial, prospective has caused the transition from the research focused on brand value sources perception by consumers (*ex ante* approach) to brand value evaluation by company (*ex post* approach)—i.e. the attention has been paid not to ask "why" but to ask "how". Radulescu and Hudea (2018) assume that the value of a powerful brand lies in its capacity to decrypt the consumers' preference and fidelity. Moreover, there is observable and also other phenomenon—dominant brand value source schism as a conflict between "quality" and "image" shifted to other dimension (Mala and Bencikova 2018). Traditionally, this schism is considered as a consequence of bipolar construction of world economies during the twentieth century (Valaskova and Krizanova 2008; Nadanyiova 2013; Okuneviciute Neverauskiene and Pranskeviciute 2018).

Thus, according to Pitra and Zauskova (2014), image has been connected with brand value building in western brand schools while quality has been unified with brand schools from eastern (nowadays also so-called transforming) economies. In contrast to the traditional schism between western image concept and eastern quality concept of brand value from the regional point of view, it highlighted the existence of such a schism even across markets from product point of view (Krizanova et al. 2015; Parobek et al. 2016; Kicova and Nadanyiova 2017). Akdeniz and Calantone (2017) focused on the examination of the impact of a quality perception gap on brand performance and its moderating role in the relationship between marketing-mix signals and performance on the example of US automotive industry. Similarly, Tatoglu et al. (2018) have developed the theory of brand value sources diversity among emerging markets highlighting the aspect of cross-product variability of brand value sources. Unfortunately, contemporary research does not take into consideration the penetration of regional and product categories with the intention to modify traditional managerial approaches with respect to specific brand value sources. So, the aim of this paper is to fulfil this gap and to identify specifics in brand value sources across markets on the case study of Slovak Republic creating so a platform for future research of relevant disparities in cross-cultural brand value sources.

Referring to the quadratic typology of purchasing behaviour, depending on the degree of engagement and differentiation and the national sociocultural profile of the Slovak Republic, it is possible to identify as a relevant type of buying behaviour the so-called habitual buying behaviour characterized by a low engagement in obtaining additional information about products and few differences between brands (Bracinikova and Matusinska 2017; Peters 2017). Thus, a suitable product for examining the internal variability of subjectively perceived sources of brand value in the conditions of the specific market of the Slovak Republic is beverages. Despite in general, it is not possible to examine them without regarding intra-group variability, and such an approach does not have the requisite explanatory power to meet the goal set by us. Based on the above, we chose the subcategory: non-alcoholic flavoured which has been highlighted as representative for habitual buying behaviour also by Yang and Yang (2019). Su and Tong (2015) explore the personalities of brands and their relationship to brand equity using Aaker's methodology, and they have showed that not all brand personality dimensions have the same influence in increasing the value of a sportswear brand from a consumer perspective, some dimensions being more efficient than others. These authors merely state diversity without determining the order of importance of the individual attributes (Gajanova et al. 2019).

19.2 Methods and Data

From the methodological point of view in the study, not only primary but also secondary data are used. Primary data were collected via a questionnaire survey. The questionnaire survey was conducted using the method computer-assisted web interviewing (CAWI) by an external agency in the year 2018 on a sample of 2000 respondents. The main surveyed population was the population of the Slovak Republic aged over 15 years (acquiring legal personality according to valid Slovak legislation). The reason for such a limitation was the requirement to ensure the autonomy of purchasing decisions and the real mirroring of the value of the brand in the economic behaviour of the Slovak population. The structure of the surveyed sample was socio-demographically representative.

Secondary data consist of the values of the sociocultural profiles of the countries according to Geert Hofstede. From the viewpoint of usability in economic sciences, Hsu et al. (2013) indicate precisely the sociological model of cultural specifics, Hofstede model of sociocultural dimensions, as the most appropriate. This model was created in the 80s of the twentieth century. The reliability and validity of this model were verified in the context of current global change by Basnakova et al. (2016). It defines the sociocultural profiles of the countries using six basic attributes, namely (1) power distance; (2) individualism; (3) masculinity; (4) uncertainty avoidance; (5) long-term orientation and (6) indulgence. Mazanec et al. (2015) use this model to generally state the impact of the sociocultural profile of consumers on their purchasing behaviour. The impact of national specifics on perceived brand value is stated using this model by Hur et al. (2015). However, their findings are only of a general nature, and the issue of detecting the impact of individual sociocultural profile attributes on the value of the brand is not specified in their research. The Slovak Republic acquires values outside the range values of the scale 0–100 (which are an indicator of the ambiguity of characteristics of dimensions of sociocultural profiles and, therefore, their usability in the context of marketing practice is low) in dimensions "power distance" (100), "masculinity" (100) and a "long-term orientation" (77)—above average values and in dimension "indulgence" (28) below average values (Hofstede 2018) (see Fig. 19.1).

In the context of these findings and in the light of the marketing implications of the questionnaire survey formulated by Sobocinska (2017), we have compiled a questionnaire and filled the brand value sources (imageries, attitudes, attributes and benefits) with each relevant component. These are summarized in Table 19.1.

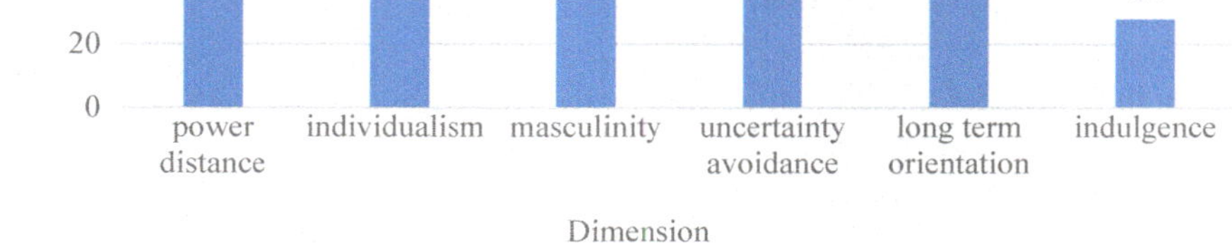

Fig. 19.1 Dimensions of Slovak sociocultural profile according to Hofstede

Table 19.1 Brand value sources and components

Brand value sources	Components of brand value sources	Code	
		Generally	Non-flavoured beverages
Imageries	Happiness	1	1
	Expectations	2	2
	Certainty	3	4
	Satisfaction	16	3
	Positive associations	17	5
Attitudes	I aim to buy branded products	4	6
	I am interested in branded products on a regular basis	5	7
	Branded products attract my attention because I consider them better	6	8
	Branded products attract my attention because I consider them more prestigious	7	9
Attributes	Quality	8	10
	Creativity of ad	9	11
	Popularity	10	12
	Available	18	13
	Innovative	19	14
Benefits	It makes me happier	11	15
	It increases my social status	12	16
	It makes it easier for me to get friends	13	17
	It attracts the attention of others	14	18
	It belongs to my lifestyle	15	19

Customer comparison of subjectively perceived brand value sources in general and in the category of non-alcoholic flavoured (based on the so-called Likert's scale) was statistically evaluated using factor analysis. Factor analysis is a multidimensional statistical method aimed at creating new unobservable variables, the so-called factors, which reduce and simplify the original number of data while retaining a substantial portion of the information (Agarwal et al. 2018; Smith and Stirling 2018). The linear combination of factors approximates the original observation, capturing the hidden relationships between the original variables (Stefko et al. 2016). In the last decades, the use of this method has grown in the sphere of social sciences, mainly through the development of information technology and the reduction in subjective interventions (Stefko et al. 2015; Lipovetsky 2017). The starting point for this analysis is the definition of the statistical model and the determination of rational assumptions (Cygler and Sroka 2017).

To determine the factors, it is necessary first to examine the dependencies between the original variables using the covariance or correlation matrix. The condition for performing the data reduction is the correlation of the original variables resulting from the matrix and the assumption that found correlation arises due to the existence of a smaller number of undetected hidden variables, the so-called factors. Consequently, it is possible on the basis of mutual relationships to diversify the original variables into subgroups where variables within one group correlate more than with the variables of the other groups (Jinho and Havin 2017).

We assume that x is a p-dimensional random vector of the considered variables with a vector of mean values μ, a covariance matrix $C(X) = \Sigma$ and a correlation matrix of simple correlation coefficients $P(X) = P$. One of the basic assumptions of factor analysis is the existence of R common background factors $F_1, F_2, \ldots, F_R$, trying to have them as little as possible, preferably less than p. The p-dimensional random vector consists of the j-observable random variables X_j, $J = 1, 2, \ldots, p$, which can be expressed by equation (Eq. 19.1) as follows:

$$X_j = \mu_j + \gamma_{j1} F_1 + \gamma_{j2} F_2 + \ldots + \gamma_{jR} F_R + \varepsilon_j, \quad (19.1)$$

where $\varepsilon_1, \varepsilon_2, \ldots, \varepsilon_p$ are p stochastic error terms referred to as specific factors. If we write this in matrix, we get the equation (Eq. 19.2):

$$x = \mu + \Gamma f + \varepsilon, \quad (19.2)$$

where Γ is a matrix of factors loadings type pR; f is R-member vector of common factors, and ε is p-member vector of specific factors. Factors loadings can be considered as regression coefficients p of observed variables on R non-observable factors, and when certain conditions of solution are met, they are also covariance between the original and the new variables.

Factors loadings can be interpreted as the contribution of the r-factor of the j-specified variable, when the same units of measurement are used. To determine the adequacy of the statistical sample, we use the Kaiser–Meyer–Olkin (KMO) test (Eq. 19.3)

$$\text{KMO} = \frac{\sum\limits_{j \neq j'}^{p} \sum\limits_{j \neq j'}^{p} r^2(x_j, x_{j\prime})}{\sum\limits_{j \neq j'}^{p} \sum\limits_{j \neq j'}^{p} r^2(x_j, x_{j'}) + \sum\limits_{j \neq j'}^{p} \sum\limits_{j \neq j'}^{p} r^2(x_j, x_{j'} \cdot \text{other } x)} \quad (19.3)$$

where $r^2(x_j, x_{j'})$ are simple correlation coefficients, and $r^2(x_j, x_{j'} \cdot \text{other } x)$ are partial correlation coefficients under the condition of statically constant remaining $p - 2$ variables. $(x_1, x_2, \ldots, x_{j-1}, x_{j+1}, \ldots, x_{j'-1}, x_{j'+1}, x_p)$. The adequacy of a statistical sample can be determined when the resulting test value is greater than 0.6.

Barlett's test of sphericity is used to determine the degree of dependence between variables. Its resulting value should be less than 0.05. The intrinsic consistency of the factors is verified by the so-called Cronbach's Alpha.

Based on the results of factor analysis, we are able to determine the order between the individual brand value sources in general and the category of non-alcoholic flavoured beverages. We compare the observed ranking and formulate the conclusions that can be used in the practice of building and managing brand value across products and markets.

19.3 Results and Discussion

Kaiser–Meyer–Olkin (KMO) test indicated the sampling adequacy (>0.6) in both cases. In the case of examination of the brand value sources, it has generally reached a value of 0.975 and, in the case of non-alcoholic flavoured beverages, 0.934. Barlett's test of sphericity also identified the dependence between variables (<0.05) by acquiring the resulting value at 0.00 in both cases. In both cases, we have demonstrated the relevance of four relevant factors (see Fig. 19.2).

The testimonial value of factor analysis in the case of the brand value sources, in general, has reached a value of 65.422% (see Table 19.2).

Individual components of brand value sources, in general, have been verified their grouping within individual brand value sources based on factor analysis—i.e. ***imageries*** with Cronbach's Alpha value 0.875, ***attitudes*** with Cronbach's Alpha value 0.863, ***attributes*** with Cronbach's Alpha value 0.802 and ***benefits*** with Cronbach's Alpha value 0.808.

In the case of the brand value sources examination, in general, it has been shown to include the component (1) "creativity of ad" (code 10) into a group of factors "imageries" resp. "benefits" and (2) "it belongs to my lifestyle" (code 15) into a group

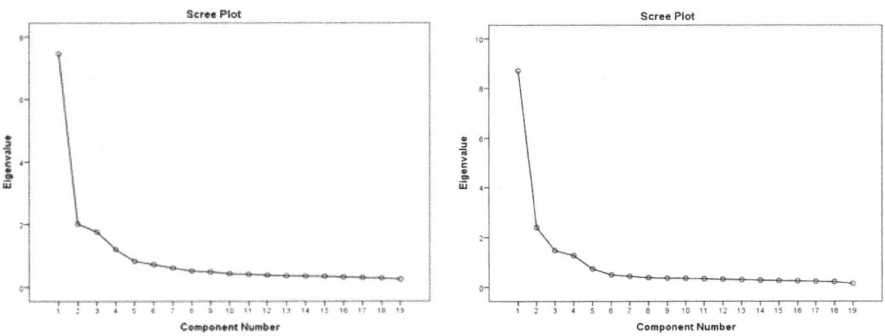

Fig. 19.2 Scree plots of general brand value sources factor analysis (left) and non-alcoholic flavoured beverages brand value sources factor analysis (right)

Table 19.2 Total variance explained—general brand value sources

Code	Initial eigenvalues			Extraction sums of squared loadings			Rotation sums of squared loadings		
	Total	% of variance	Cumulative (%)	Total	% of variance	Cumulative (%)	Total	% of variance	Cumulative (%)
1	7.331	38.587	38.587	7.331	38.587	38.587	3.520	18.524	18.524
2	2.154	11.339	49.926	2.154	11.339	49.926	3.078	16.201	34.726
3	1.664	8.757	58.683	1.664	8.757	58.683	2.950	15.527	50.253
4	1.281	6.740	65.422	1.281	6.740	**65.422**	2.882	15.170	**65.422**
5	0.871	4.585	70.007						
6	0.713	3.752	73.759						
7	0.563	2.962	76.721						
8	0.489	2.575	79.296						
9	0.473	2.487	81.783						
10	0.447	2.351	84.134						
11	0.422	2.219	86.353						
12	0.379	1.995	88.348						
13	0.364	1.916	90.264						
14	0.357	1.877	92.141						
15	0.334	1.759	93.900						
16	0.329	1.731	95.632						
17	0.312	1.641	97.272						
18	0.277	1.458	98.731						
19	0.241	1.269	100.000						

Table 19.3 Rotated component matrix—general brand value sources

Code	Brand value source			
	Imageries	Attitudes	Benefits	Attributes
1	0.771			
2	0.753			
3	0.751			
4		0.832		
5		0.796		
6		0.700		
7		0.682		
8				0.676
9			**0.435**	**0.614**
10				0.717
11			0.430	
12			0.792	
13			0.770	
14			0.773	
15		**0.550**	**0.528**	
16	0.795			
17	0.738			
18				0.727
19				0.728

of factors "attitudes" resp. "imageries" as a variation. For more detailed information, see Table 19.3.

We have found that there are some discrepancies from our original assumptions. All the brand value sources have been relevant for the factor analysis but their clustering into factors needs further analysis. It is mainly in case of attributes: (1) satisfaction; (2) positive associations; (3) available and (4) innovative. In all these cases, the clustering has been different as we have originally expected. For more detailed information, see Table 19.1 again.

On the basis of the rotated component matrix, it is possible to create a ranking of general brand value sources depending on their impact on consumers subjectively perceived brand value. This order is as follows: (1) imageries; (2) attitudes; (3) benefits and (4) attributes (see Table 19.4).

The testimonial value of factor analysis in the case of the brand value sources of non-alcoholic flavoured beverages has reached a value of 72,931% (see Table 19.5).

Individual components of brand value sources of non-alcoholic flavoured beverages have been verified their grouping within individual brand value sources based on factor analysis—i.e. ***imageries*** with Cronbach's Alpha value 0.913, ***attitudes*** with

Table 19.4 General brand value sources

Factors	F_1	F_2	F_3	F_4
	Imageries	Attitudes	Benefits	Attributes
No. of items	5	4	5	5
Cronbach's Alpha	0.875	0.863	0.808	0.802
% of variance	38.587	11.339	8.757	6.740

Cronbach's Alpha value 0.904, ***attributes*** with Cronbach's Alpha value 0.847 and ***benefits*** with Cronbach's Alpha value 0.874.

It has been shown that the inclusion of these components is variant: (1) "branded products attract my attention because I consider them more prestigious" (code 9) into a group of factors "benefits" resp. "attitudes"; (2) "quality" (code 10) into a group of factors "imageries" resp. "attributes"; (3) "it makes me happier" (code 15) into a group of factors "imageries" resp. "benefits". For more detailed information, see Table 19.6.

On the basis of rotated component matrix, it is possible to create a ranking of non-alcoholic flavoured beverages brand value sources depending on their impact on consumers subjectively perceived brand value. This order is as follows: (1) imageries; (2) benefits; (3) attributes and (4) attitudes (see Table 19.7).

Based on the above mentioned, we can conclude that the clustering of brand value components into four main factors has been proved but realized analysis as well as the variation of brand value sources ranking. In both cases, imageries are the most relevant brand value source but the relevancy of other factors varies. This explains the exceptions to the applicability of the theory of the need to take into account the specificities of the national sociocultural profiles that arise in practice. We have found that the order of importance of brand sources is different and reflects the specificity of the branded product category. For more detailed information, see Table 19.8.

On the example of non-alcoholic flavoured beverages, it is possible to illustrate the possible reason for failing brand management. This applies not only to the selected product category but also to the brand of other products that, from the point of view of the purchasing behaviour mechanism, belong to a shopping behaviour based on the so-called habitual buying behaviour characterized by a low engagement in obtaining additional information about products and few differences between brands. It can be stated that proving the diversity in the order of brand value sources between the selected product characterized by such a mechanism and the order of brand value sources, in general, implies the need to supplement the current state of knowledge about the specifics perceiving the importance of brand value sources across all the product categories. Such knowledge will contribute to modifying the current concept of irrationality in consumer behaviour with impacts on brand management theory and practice in such a way that on the platform, the specificity of national sociocultural profiles will create a construct of priority for individual brand value sources (assuming that the priority of components within them will be unchanged as this reflects national sociocultural specificities in full).

Table 19.5 Total variance explained—non-alcoholic flavoured beverages brand value sources

Code	Initial eigenvalues			Extraction sums of squared loadings			Rotation sums of squared loadings		
	Total	% of variance	Cumulative (%)	Total	% of variance	Cumulative (%)	Total	% of variance	Cumulative (%)
1	8.699	45.783	45.783	8.699	45.783	45.783	3.986	20.980	20.980
2	2.405	12.660	58.443	2.405	12.660	58.443	3.892	20.486	41.465
3	1.477	7.771	66.215	1.477	7.771	66.215	3.018	15.883	57.349
4	1.276	6.716	72.931	1.276	6.716	**72.931**	2.961	15.582	**72.931**
5	0.734	3.862	76.792						
6	0.499	2.627	79.419						
7	0.441	2.321	81.739						
8	0.380	2.002	83.741						
9	0.366	1.925	85.666						
10	0.357	1.880	87.546						
11	0.337	1.775	89.322						
12	0.322	1.693	91.014						
13	0.302	1.587	92.601						
14	0.283	1.490	94.092						
15	0.261	1.376	95.468						
16	0.252	1.325	96.793						
17	0.237	1.249	98.042						
18	0.222	1.168	99.209						
19	0.150	0.791	100.000						

Table 19.6 Rotated component matrix—non-alcoholic flavoured beverages brand value sources

Code	Brand value source			
	Imageries	Benefits	Attributes	Attitudes
1	0.810			
2	0.767			
3	0.817			
4	0.793			
5	0.756			
6				0.808
7				0.735
8				0.794
9		**0.422**		**0.662**
10	**0.402**		**0.597**	
11			0.749	
12			0.793	
13			0.750	
14			0.673	
15	**0.401**	**0.591**		
16		0.887		
17		0.886		
18		0.843		
19		0.625		

Table 19.7 Non-alcoholic flavoured beverages brand value sources

Factors	F_1	F_2	F_3	F_4
	Imageries	Benefits	Attributes	Attitudes
No. of items	5	5	5	4
Cronbach's Alpha	0.913	0.874	0.847	0.904
% of variance	45.783	12.660	7.771	6.716

Table 19.8 Ranking of groups of components according to their importance in brand value perception in general and in case of non-alcoholic flavoured beverages

Rank	Brands	
	In general	Non-alcoholic flavoured beverages
1	Imageries	Imageries
2	Attitudes	Benefits
3	Benefits	Attributes
4	Attributes	Attitudes

19.4 Conclusion

The need to provide revision of traditional strategic concepts with emphasis on behavioural approach has been the leading motive to provide analysis of consumer's perception of brand value sources. The data used in the presented study were obtained by our own survey carried out on the sample of 2000 respondents (citizens of the Slovak Republic older than 15 years). We have statistically evaluated the given data by the factor analysis supported by implementation of KMO test, Barlett's test of sphericity and calculation of Cronbach's Alpha for relevant brand value sources, in general, as well as for brands of non-alcoholic flavoured beverages. We have proved the clustering of brand value components into four main factors, but on the other hand, realized analysis has proven also the variation of brand value sources ranking. In both cases, imageries are the most relevant brand value source but the relevancy of other factors varies. In the case of brand value sources, in general, the ranking follows with attitudes, benefits and attributes while in case of brand value sources of non-alcoholic flavoured beverages the ranking follows with benefits, attributes and attitudes. This explains the exceptions in the applicability of the theory of the need to take into account the specificities of the national sociocultural profiles that arise in practice. We have also found that the order of importance of brand sources is different and reflects the specificity of the branded product category. We have also found that there are some discrepancies from our original assumptions. In case of brand value sources, in general, all the brand value sources have been relevant for the factor analysis but their clustering into factors needs further analysis. It is mainly in case of attributes: (1) satisfaction; (2) positive associations; (3) available and (4) innovative. In all these cases, the clustering has been different as we have originally expected. The implications of these findings in managerial practice are wide. First of all, they present a valuable source of relevant information for brand managers, and they are anticipated to enhance and deepen the understanding of previous practice as well. So, they must strive to understand and provide relevant content to consumers, responding to rapidly changing consumer demands and expectations. Overall, these findings help to understand the complexity of internal and external factors motivating consumers to interact with brand, generating added value for their consumers. This is useful within marketing practices. However, there are still many issues that should be analysed in scientific literature. The main one is the critical discussion of findings in scope of generational approach to consumers as this trend in brand management has been set by contemporary scientific literature, and its importance has been identified as significant.

Acknowledgements This paper is an outcome of the science project APVV-15-0505: Integrated model of management support for building and managing the brand value in the specific conditions of the Slovak Republic.

References

Akdeniz, M. B., & Calantone, R. J. (2017). A longitudinal examination of the impact of quality perception gap on brand performance in the US Automotive Industry. *Marketing Letters, 28*(1), 43–57.

Agarwal, N., Kwan, P., & Paul, D. (2018). Merger and acquisition pricing using agent based modelling. *Economics, Management, and Financial Markets, 13*(1), 84–99.

Aime, I., Berger-Remy, F., & Laporte, M. E. (2018). Lessons from nearly a century of the brand management system. *Journal of Historical Research in Marketing, 10*(4), 420–450.

Basnakova, J., Brezina, I., & Masaryk, R. (2016). Dimensions of culture, the case of Slovakia as an outlier in Hofstede's research. *Ceskoslovenska Psychologie, 60*(1), 13–25.

Bracinikova, V., & Matusinska, K. (2017). Marketing mix of financial services from the customers' perspective. *Forum Scientiae Oeconomia, 5*(4), 35–48.

Cygler, J., & Sroka, W. (2017). Coopetition disadvantages: The case of the high tech companies. *Inzinerine Ekonomika-Engineering Economics, 28*(5), 494–504.

Gajanova, L., Nadanyiova, M., & Moravcikova, D. (2019). The use of demographic and psychographic segmentation to creating marketing strategy of brand loyalty. *Scientific Annals of Economics and Business, 66*(1), 65–84.

Hofstede G (2018) Geert Hofstede dimensions of national culture. Available at https://geert-hofstede.com/national-culture.html. Accessed May 12, 2018.

Hsu, S. Y., Woodside, A. G., & Marshall, R. (2013). Critical tests of multiple theories of cultures' consequences, comparing the usefulness of models by Hofstede, Inglehart and Baker, Schwartz, Steenkamp, as well as GDP and distance for explaining overseas tourism behaviour. *Journal of Travel Research, 52*(6), 679–704.

Hur, W. M., Kang, S., & Kim, M. (2015). The moderating role of Hofstede's cultural dimensions in the customer-brand relationship in China and India. *Cross Cultural Management, 22*(3), 487–508.

Jinho, C., & Havin, L. (2017). An analysis of factor influencing sporting goods consumption through qualitative method, focus on women's sports participants. *Advanced Science Letters, 23*(3), 1682–1685.

Kicova, E., & Nadanyiova, M. (2017). Brand as a tool of company's strategic marketing in practice. *Lecture Notes in Management Science, 73,* 29–34.

Krizanova, A., Gajanova, L., & Nadanyiova, M. (2018). Design of a CRM level and performance measurement model. *Sustainability, 10*(7), 2567.

Krizanova, A., Masarova, G., Stefanikova, L., & Rypakova, M. (2015). Building a brand in the context of sustainable development. *AEBMR-Advances in Economics Business and Management Research, 3,* 79–84.

Lipovetsky, S. (2017). Factor analysis by limited scales, which factors to analyze? *Journal of Modern Applied Statistical Methods, 16*(1), 233–245.

Majercak, P., Kliestik, T., Masarova, G., Buc, D., & Majercakova, E. (2013). System approach of logistic costs optimization solution in supply chain. *Nase More, 60*(5–6), 95–98.

Mala, D., & Bencikova, D. (2018). Innovations of a green product. *Ekonomicko-manazerske spectrum, 12*(1), 64–74.

Mazanec, J. A., Crotts, J. C., Gursoy, D., & Lu, L. (2015). Homogeneity versus heterogeneity of cultural values: An item-response theoretical approach applying Hofstede's cultural dimensions in a single nation. *Tourism Management, 48,* 299–304.

Mehrpouya, A., & Willmott, H. (2018). Making a niche: The marketization of management research and the rise of "knowledge branding". *Journal of Management Studies, 55*(4), 728–734.

Nadanyiova, M. (2013). The possibility of introducing the CRM system in railway company Cargo Slovakia. In *Proceedings of 17th International Conference on Transport Means* (pp. 87–92). Kaunas, Lithuania: Kaunas University of Technology, October 24–25, 2013.

Nadanyiova, M., Kicova, E., & Rypakova, M. (2015). Green marketing and its exploitation in Slovak companies. *Procedia —Economics and Finance, 26,* 219–226.

Okuneviciute Neverauskiene, L., & Pranskeviciute, I. (2018). Overcoming paradox for social enterprise definition: Case of Lithuania. *Ekonomicko-manazerske spectrum, 12*(1), 104–118.
Parobek, J., Palus, H., Kalamarova, M., Loucanova, E., Supin, M., Krizanova, A., et al. (2016). Energy utilization of renewable resources in the European Union—cluster analysis approach. *BioResources, 11*(1), 984–995.
Pitra, Z., & Zauskova, A. (2014). Communication in knowledge transfer management. *Communication Today, 5*(2), 50–65.
Peters, M. A. (2017). Ecopolitical philosophy, education and grassroots democracy, the 'return' of Murray Bookchin (and John Dewey?). *Geopolitics, History, and International Relations, 9*(2), 7–14.
Radulescu, C., & Hudea, O. S. (2018). Econometric modelling of the consumer's behaviour in order to develop brand management policies. *Economic Research-Ekonomska Istrazivanja, 31*(1), 576–591.
Smith, A., & Stirling, A. (2018). Innovation, sustainability and democracy: An analysis of grassroots contributions. *Journal of Self-Governance and Management Economics, 6*(1), 64–97.
Sobocinska, M. (2017). Marketing research in film and television production management. *Forum Scientiae Oeconomia, 5*(SI1), 71–78.
Stefko, R., Fedorko, R., & Bacik, R. (2016). Website content quality in terms of perceived image of higher education institution. *Polish Journal of Management Studies, 13*(2), 153–163.
Stefko, R., Fedorko, R., & Bacik, R. (2015). The role of e-marketing tools in constructing the image of a higher education institution. *Procedia Social and Behavioral Sciences, 175,* 431–438.
Su, J., & Tong, X. (2015). Brand personality and brand equity, evidence from the sportswear industry. *Journal of Product and Brand Management, 24*(2), 124–133.
Tartaglione, A. M., Cavacece, Y., Russo, G., & Granata, G. (2019). A systematic mapping study on customer loyalty and brand management. *Administrative Sciences, 9*(1), 8.
Tatoglu, E., Sahadev, S., & Demirbag, M. (2018). Brand management practices in emerging country firms—exploring the patterns of variation and its impact on firm performance. *Journal for East European Management Studies, 23*(3), 447–473.
Valaskova, M., & Krizanova, A. (2008). The passenger satisfaction survey in the regional integrated public transport system. *Promet-Traffic & Transportation, 20*(6), 401–404.
Yang, C. Y., & Yang, C. H. (2019). The impact of sustainable environmental management in the food and beverage industry on customer loyalty: A view of brand attitude. *Ekoloji, 28*(107), 965–972.

Chapter 20
Are We Spending Our Scarce R&D Resources Adequately? Analyzing the Efficiency of EU's Regional Innovation Systems

Thomas Baumert and Cristián Gutiérrez

Abstract The purpose of this article is to measure the efficiency of regional innovation systems (RIS) of the European Union (EU-14) between 2000 and 2010 based on the Data Envelopment Analysis. To measure the efficiency, we used 29 input variables synthesized in 5 factors or composite indicators. The output is reflected by patents and scientific publications. The results obtained highlight that only a few European RIS are situated on or near the efficiency frontier and most regions present very low efficiency levels. We detected a broad dispersion in terms of efficiency, although the tendency over time is a reduction of the dispersion reflecting a process of convergence. Moreover, the results reveal that an important possible cause of the inefficiencies is a problem of scale rather than technical inefficiency.

Keywords Efficiency · Regional innovation systems · DEA · Scale efficiency

JEL O32 · R58 · C61

20.1 Introduction

The economics of innovation, driven mainly—though not exclusively—by the so-called 'evolutionary approach,' has made an important effort in analyzing the allocation of resources towards the generation of scientific and technological knowledge. In doing so, it has stressed the importance not only of the agents intervening in the innovation process, but also the interactions between them, the institutional framework in which they interact and the policies aimed to favor them. In conjunction with growth economics, it has also been possible to solidly establish that the innovations derived

T. Baumert (✉)
Economics and History, ESIC Business & Marketing Madrid, Madrid, Spain
e-mail: thomasbaumert@esic.edu

C. Gutiérrez
Economics, Depto. Tecnologías de Gestión, Facultad Tecnológica, Univ. de Santiago de Chile, Santiago, Chile

N. Tsounis and A. Vlachvei (eds.), *Advances in Cross-Section Data Methods in Applied Economic Research*, Springer Proceedings in Business and Economics,
https://doi.org/10.1007/978-3-030-38253-7_20

from new knowledge constitute the central fundament of economic development.[1] A result of this paradigm is the widespread social belief regarding the convenience of government support towards science and technology (S&T); and, among politicians, the need for maintaining a broad set of economic and political instruments aimed at assisting R&D activities without any apparent limit in expenditure.

Accordingly, only seldom have economists of innovation or the makers of S&T policies analyzed in depth the possible limits of resource-assignment in the generation of knowledge. In general, it has been assumed that any level of R&D expenditure is pertinent insofar as it will always have a positive effect on economic development.

This notwithstanding, the matter of efficiency used to be a central question in the discussions of economists regarding innovation. Schumpeter (1942) already referred to it when emphasizing the role carried out by innovation in the long-run economic expansion, allowing the multiplication of a level of production given a limited volume of resources. At the same time, the neoclassical authors—who might be considered pioneers in the economics of innovation—also highlighted efficiency-related aspects.

Our purpose in this article is to embed the efficiency analysis into the evolutionist theory of the economics of innovation and the systemic approach. In fact, the efficiency is one of the driving forces behind the evolutionary path of competitiveness because those firms, regions or countries that are able to adapt themselves to the new circumstances will be more successful and efficient and therefore increase their possibilities of surviving during the competitive struggle between enterprises or regions. More specifically, our work aims to measure the efficiency level reached by RIS of the European Union (EU-14) during the production of knowledge (patents and scientific publications). In order to approach the matter of efficiency of the regional innovation systems from an empirical standpoint, we combine two multivariate analysis techniques. The first one (Factor Analysis), is used to create the combined input variables that allow us to describe in a synthetic way the complexity of the regional innovation systems.[2] The second technique (Data Envelopment Analysis), is used to build the efficiency frontier and determine the relative position of each of the regional systems with reference to it, and also permits the study of the causes of their inefficiency. This last aspect allows us to draw some relevant conclusions and suggestions for the design of innovation policies.

The existing studies[3] offer only some description of the detected efficiency indexes and only one of them tries to explain to a certain extent the causes of the inefficiency. Also, none of them except one analyses the possible potential for improvement. On the other hand, none of the studies used such many input factors based on a systemic approach. In this study, we use 29 input variables while in the twelve identified studies only one to seven variables were used. In fact, for several of these studies,

[1] Including the concept of 'new combinations' (Schumpeter 1911, Chap. 2), which Schumpeter would later include in his description of the 'process of creative destruction' (Schumpeter 1942, Chap. 7).

[2] Following the conceptual approach proposed by Buesa et al. (2007, 2010).

[3] Fritsch (2004), Fritsch and Slavtchev (2007, 2010), Zabala-Iturriagagoitía et al. (2008), Broekel (2008), Broekel and Meder (2008), Chen et al. (2011), Bosco and Brugnoli (2011), Badiola-Sánchez and Coto-Millán (2012), Niu et al. (2013), Kaihua and Mingting (2014).

the efficiency index was just an intermediate result to analyze other aspects such as the level of competitiveness or commercial success. Moreover, some studies used very debatable output indicators as the GDP per capita or the growth of regional employment. Concluding this study implies a significant methodological advance and can be considered as novel within the international literature. However, the analysis of the efficiency is still a new field, our paper is just one step forwards and many future improvements are still required.

20.2 Measuring Efficiency: The Basic Concepts

Several authors have challenged the task of defining and measuring the efficiency of activities related to the production of goods and services. Among them, the most noted are Koopmans (1951) and Debreu (1951), although it was Farrell (1957) who, relying on the works of the former two authors, prepared the ground of modern efficiency measurement. Following those authors, a global efficiency coefficient will be calculated, which is the correct approach when the microeconomic instrument of reference is the production function. This coefficient will be decomposed by the *pure technical efficiency*: which refers to the optimal employment of the inputs related to the output production. In the case of an *output orientation*, it refers to the maximum output that can be obtained given a certain level of input. There will also be the *scale efficiency:* which indicates whether the decision-making unit (DMU) operates on an optimal scale or not.

The purpose of this study is to measure the global technical efficiency[4] which consists of estimating production frontiers in such a way that the most efficient regions are the references and shape the form to the frontier of efficiency. The leading regions will have a normalized efficiency coefficient or level of 100, while the non-efficient units will be calculated (or 'positioned') in relation to their distance in percentage with the most efficient ones. In other words, they receive a lower score reflecting their (in) efficiency (as a percentage) regarding the frontier.

We followed the non-parametric DEA approach to measure the technical efficiency of the innovative results of the European regions regarding the use of resources during the innovation process for a timespan reaching from 2000 to 2010 (cross-section analysis) by means of a DEA, as this method has certain advantages in analyzing the efficiency of RIS (Niu et al. 2013: 149). The results thus obtained will allow us to establish which regions make a more efficient use of their innovation-oriented resources and quantify the inefficiency of the other regions.

[4]Which is the most commonly used methodology; although a few authors use non-frontier methods such as the construction of productivity indexes and other related econometric models.

20.3 Dataset and Methodology

20.3.1 Variables and Dataset

Opting for a holistic approach (using composite indicators) and using the DEA method—in which no specific functional form of the production function of innovations is going to be specified—implies that the selection of variables acquires special relevance. The variables employed in the model are 29 input and 2 output indicators that reflect the most significant and/or available information referring to regional innovation systems (see Fig. 20.1), which have been successfully employed in previous studies (Buesa et al. 2007).

The use of patents as a proxy for innovation output has been extensively debated in the literature,[5] confronting their advantages and disadvantages, with the former always by far outweighing the latter. Besides, there is also a pragmatic reason, namely the assignment of patents to the region where the research, design or engineering activity has in fact taken place, thus overcoming the so-called 'headquarter effect' (Eurostat 2011, Chap. 2). However, this does not mean that we ignore the fact that an important part of the research output of the regional innovation systems, especially those of scientific research is left out of analysis including only patents. To solve this problem, we include the scientific publications[6] in our analysis taking advantage of fact that the Data Envelopment Analysis allows us to simultaneously estimate the efficiency with two or more outputs.

The data employed in the empirical part of the paper correspond to the IAIF-RIS(EU) database[7] that basically contains data obtained from Eurostat's REGIO. It should be noted, that for some cases and for specific years REGIO does not offer data. In those, we have taken the missing values from the corresponding National Statistics Offices. Only rarely, have missing values been estimated according to the common procedure. Consequently, the initial database consists of a panel with 60

[5]See, among others, Scherer (1965), Schmookler (1966), Pavitt (1985), Mansfield (1986), Griliches (1990), Trajtenberg (1990), Archibugi (1992), Schmoch (1999), European Commission (2001: 38), Smith (2005: 158–160), Rondé and Hussler (2005: 1156), Hu and Mathews (2005: 1470) and Li (2009: 345). Regarding the time lag between R&D-input and patent application, we consider it to be nearly contemporaneous, a decision that seems to fit the results recently obtained by Wang and Hagedoorn (2014).

[6]The literature also recognizes certain problems associated with the use of publications as output variables. On the one hand, there is the language bias, in the sense that most publications in the most prestigious scientific journals are published in the English language, generating a bias towards researchers whose native language is this. Another criticism is that many publications are written by multiple authors, often from different regions or countries, and it is almost impossible to distinguish the individual contribution to the publication. However, both problems lose strength at the regional level within a country, since language bias affects all regions equally, as does the problem of co-authorship. This last problem was treated using the complete counting method (see Winkler 2014). Therefore, we have chosen to use this variable in the study. Regarding the time lag between R&D-input and scientific publication, we consider it to be nearly contemporaneous too.

[7]Employed, among others, by Buesa et al. (2007, 2010).

variables by 1452 cases (132 regions for 11 years). After revising the database and applying the factor analysis and its statistical tests 31 variables were used to identify and characterize the regional innovation systems (see Fig. 20.1). Those variables refer to the region's economic and population size, human resources, its sophistication of demand (wealth), the R&D efforts (both in economic and personnel terms), the propensity to patent[8] and other aspects related to the economic environment. On

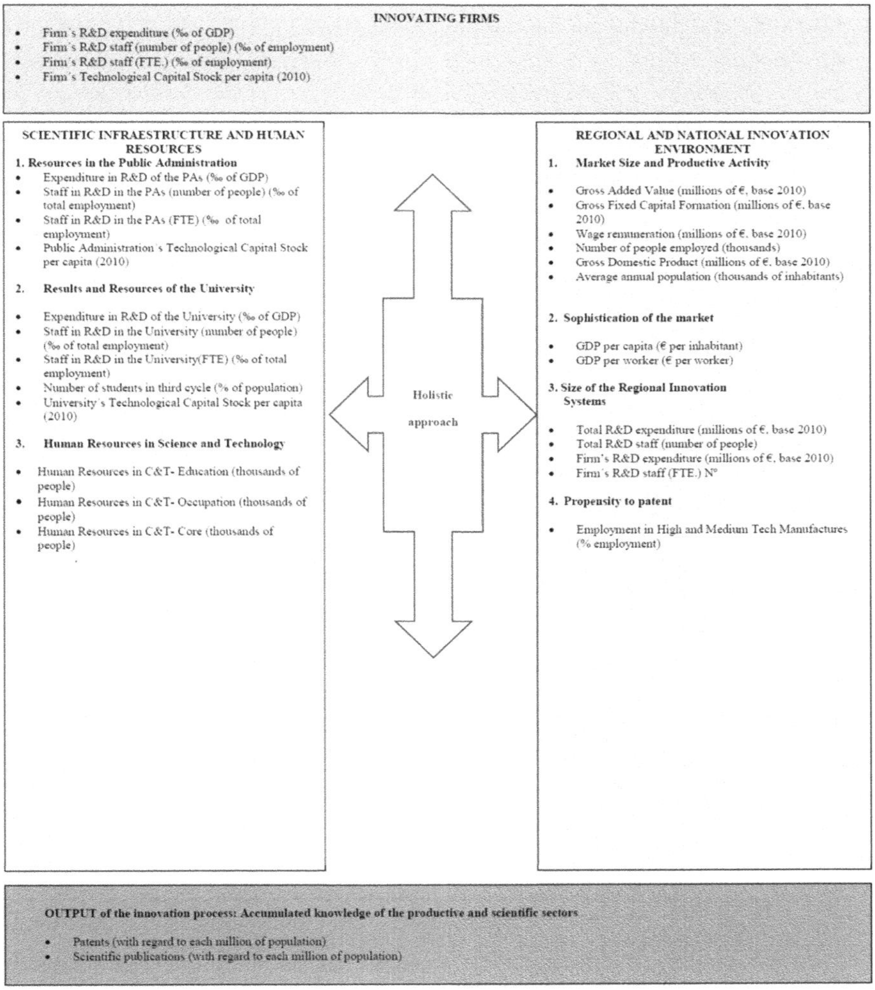

Fig. 20.1 Variables and indicators regarding regional innovation systems (own elaboration)

[8]Using Regional Employment in High-Medium Tech Manufactures (% of employment) as proxy.

the other side, regarding large several aspects considered as important by the 'systemic approach' no (statistical) data are available. In fact, no homogeneous publicly available data exist on aspects as the quality and quantity of technical infrastructures, R&D and innovation policies or institutional settings.

Another important limitation of the empirical research in the case of the regional innovation system is the limited availability of information that is equally measured for all the 132 European regions on the most appropriate level and moreover, those standardized indicators should be available for the whole period (11 years). Although our objective was to use a regional delimitation based on the region's autonomy in the design and implementation of innovation policies, we had to work for some countries with other levels due to the absence of data. In fact, for some countries, no regional level data were available so we opted to use the national level data as in the case of Ireland, Denmark and Luxembourg. The NUTS level used for each country and the final used RIS (132) as DMU is presented in Fig. 20.2.

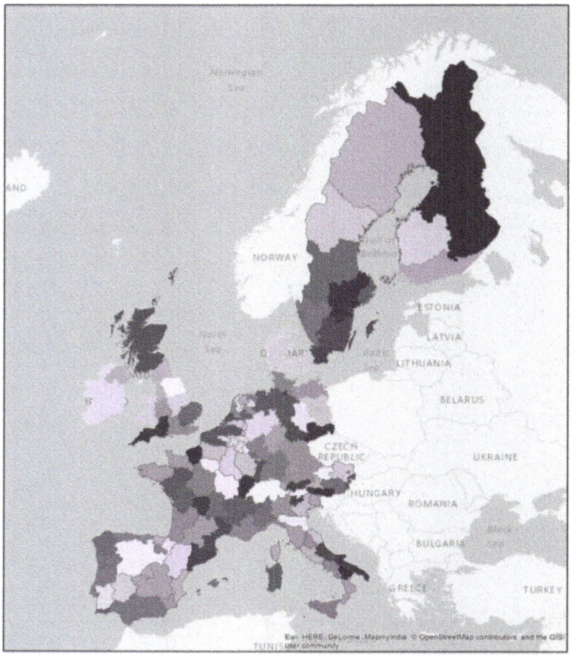

Fig. 20.2 Regional innovations systems in Europe (own elaboration)

20.3.2 Synthesizing the Elements of the Regional Innovation Systems in the European Union: Factor Analysis

As discussed before, regional innovation systems are complex realities composed by multiple actors whose institutional configuration can be very diverse and its interactions. This implies that, for a correct representation of these systems, a great variety of indicators is required.[9] As has been explained above, in the present case we are working with 29 input variables and two output variables (patents and publications) from the initial dataset with 60 variables. However, the set of input variables can be summarized in a smaller number of 'abstract', synthetic variables—called factors—which can be clearly identified with the elements that compose the RIS, while retaining most of the information (in terms of variance) contained in the original dataset. The use of the statistical technique of factor analysis turns out to be very appropriate for the study of such multidimensional economic realities as innovation systems,[10] as it does not only group together related variables taking into account their interaction but also considers at the same time the correlations with all the rest of the variables outside the specific factor. More specifically, the factorial scores are calculated using not only the correlations among the variables within each factor but also the correlations with all other variables/factors of the model. In this way, it implicitly measures somehow the interaction or interdependency between the subsystems. The relevance of these interactions in measuring an innovation system is pointed out, among others, by Niosi (2002).

The validation or quality of the factor analysis is based on the statistical tests and the inherent logic of the discovered factors. The different tests to confirm the quality of our factor analysis are all satisfying.[11] Moreover, the communalities (correlation of each variable regarding the set of the other variables making up this factor) of the variables are relatively high, most of them well above 0.75, which guarantees the reliability of the composite indicators, and indicates the high degree of preservation of their variance. The five factors obtained retain over 87% of the original variance, that is, there is scarcely a 13% loss of information originally contained in the variables. The second and maybe the most important criterion to judge the outcome of a factor analysis is that the extracted factors are consistent and interpretable in accordance with the theoretical or conceptual framework of the study, in our case, the regional innovation system. In other words, factor analysis is only useful if the results can be

[9]It should be noted, that using factors instead of a set of individual variables makes possible matters of collinearity irrelevant.

[10]Additionally, the working with factors as explanatory variables of an econometric model has a series of statistical advantages—such as the a priori maximization of orthogonally between factors when rotating them by the Varimax method, thus minimizing the possible collinearity between them—which have been detailed in previous studies (Buesa et al. 2007, 2010) and econometric manuals (Hair et al. 1999: 152).

[11]Thus, the Kaiser–Meyer–Olkin (KMO) test, which is based on the study of the partial correlation coefficients, gives a value a 0.8, within the upper limit of the recommended value of 0.6–0.8. Also, the Barlett Sphericity test, which tests for the null hypothesis that the correlation matrix is the identity matrix, is rejected at the 99% level.

interpreted correctly from a theoretical point of view. And such interpretation is only possible if simultaneously: (1) the included variables belong to the same component or subsystem of the overall regional innovation system; (2) the variables belonging to a certain subsystem are in only one factor; and (3) if each factor can be labeled with a 'name' which, without any reservation, clearly expresses its whole content.

On the other hand, comparing Fig. 20.1 and Table 20.1, it can be highlighted that the classification of the variables in five factors (based on the real correlations between the variables) doesn't differ from the initially a priori classification of Fig. 20.1 in which the variables were grouped by the theoretical arguments of the innovation system approach. We consider that the appropriateness of the model with five factors is supported by several facts, among others that our five factors (see Table 20.1) accomplish the three requirements mentioned above.

The composition of the factors and their interpretation ('names') and respective retained variance are given in Fig. 20.3. It should be observed that the resulting factors essentially coincide with the main determinants of a regional innovation system obtained by Buesa et al. (2010). Summing up, we can conclude that the factor analysis results in a coherent reduction of the original dataset, which fulfill all statistical and conceptual criteria and conveniently synthesize the main elements that constitute the European Union's regional innovation system. Thus, they seem suitable for further employment as independent variables in the study of the innovative efficiency of the European regions.

20.3.3 Data Envelopment Analysis

Once the five factors, which appropriately reflect the main elements of regional innovation systems, have been conveniently transformed,[12] we relate them with the output variable of the regional innovation systems (number of patents and publications—considering only technical fields—per capita) to analyze the efficiency in each year of period 2000–2010. Considering that—like in most real situations of economic analysis—we do not precisely know what the knowledge production function in terms of efficiency looks like. The Data Envelopment Analysis (DEA) allows the efficiency frontier to be drawn without the need for assuming a specific functional form under quite unrestrictive assumptions. This frontier is approached or estimated using the available data in which the frontier is drawn by the regions with the highest output level given a certain level of input (output orientation). It is not possible to draw the 'real' frontier which, in fact, is unknown but this approximation allows us to obtain a valid and quite useful measure of the *relative* level of efficiency of each singular case. For that reason, the DEA is the fundamental technique within the non-parametric approaches and has been much employed in microeconomic studies aimed to control and evaluate diverse units and actions of the public and private sector.

[12] As factor scores are calculated to follow a $N(0; 1)$ distribution, we use a linear transformation converting them into $N(4; 1)$ distributions in order to avoid any negative values in the input variables.

Table 20.1 Matrix of rotated components (own elaboration)

	Component				
	1	2	3	4	5
Wages (millions €2010)	0.977				
GAV (millions €2010)	0.976				
GDP (millions €2010)	0.975				
Number of people employed (thousand)	0.975				
Human resources in C&T—occupation (thousand)	0.969				
Annual average population (thousand)	0.964				
Human resources in C&T—core (thousand)	0.962				
Human resources in C&T—education (thousands of people)	0.950				
Gross fixed capital formation (millions €2010)	0.945				
Total R&D staff N°	0.900				
Total expenditure R&D (millions €2010)	0.860				
Firms R&D staff N°	0.851				
Firms R&D expenditures (millions €2010)	0.818				
Firms R&D staff (HC) ‰ employment		0.881			
Firms R&D expenditures (‰ GDP)		0.877			
Firms R&D staff (HC) ‰ employment		0.861			
Stock of technological capital firms per capita (€2010)		0.852			
Regional employment hi-medium tech manufactures (% of employment)		0.587			
Universities R&D staff (HC) ‰ employment			0.909		
Universities R&D staff (FTE) ‰ employment			0.893		
Universities R&D expenditures (‰ GDP)			0.860		
Regional 3rd cycle students (% population)			0.833		
Stock of technological capital universities per capita (€2010)			0.829		
Public administration R&D staff (FTE) ‰ employment				0.944	
Public administration R&D staff (HC) ‰ employment				0.924	
Public administration R&D expenditures (‰ GDP)				0.921	
Stock of technological capital Public Administration per capita (€2010)				0.901	
GDP per worker (€2010)					0.799
GDP per capita (€2010)					0.793

Fig. 20.3 The factorial model (own elaboration)

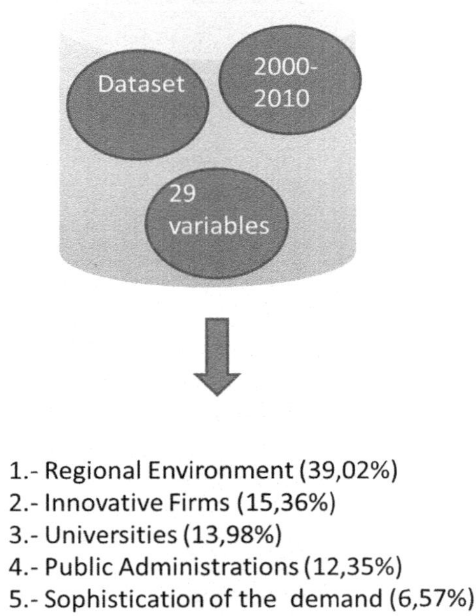

There are two different models that can be implemented in the application of the technique: the model originally proposed by Charnes et al. (1978) (CCR model), which assumes *constant returns of scale* in the production function; and the modified version of this model proposed by Banker et al. (1984) (BCC model), that includes the possibility to consider *the efficiency of scale*. The model employed in the present work is the CCR one, as our aim is to make a comparative study among *all* the regions that compose the European Union and not only among those which present innovation systems with similar scale. However, we have also employed the BCC model as an instrument to calculate a measure of the efficiency of scale[13]: the coefficient between the CCR and the BCC model (multiplied by hundred), offers an index of the scale efficiency which indicates if a region is operating—or not—on its optimum scale. Accordingly, the inefficiencies of scale would be the result either of a region already operating on the stretch of the production function with decreasing returns to scale; or because it is still situated in the section of increasing returns of scale.[14]

The formulation of the DEA is based on a mathematical program that for each DMU—that is, for each RIS—calculates, from a perspective of input-reduction or from output-increase an index of pure technical efficiency. In the present paper, we have opted for an input orientation where the indexes reflect the reduction of the inputs that would be necessary for a region to become efficient.[15] The DEA also

[13]Comparing the efficiency level between those groups of regions with a similar input level.

[14]Or, in other words, because it is not situated on the section of constant returns of scale.

[15]The DEA analysis has been calculated using rDEA package for *R*.

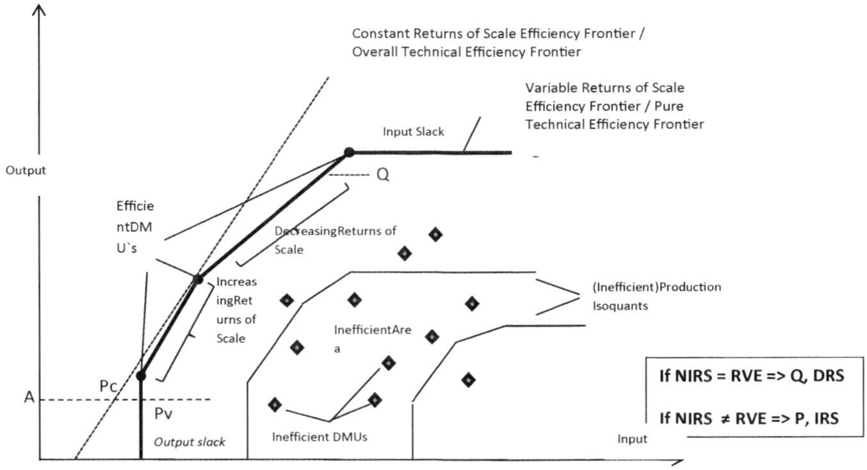

Fig. 20.4 Constant and variable returns of scale (Santin 2009)

allows other relevant information to be obtained: the volumes of input that a region could save by reaching a same output level (or the volume of output that a region could generate additionally, given a certain input) would it operate efficiently.[16]

These concepts are presented in Fig. 20.4, which illustrates different efficiency frontiers (isoquants) that can be estimated under constant and variables returns of scale, following the DEA-CCR model. This graph shows that the efficiency of a production unit *P*, under an input-orientation and constant returns to scale, is given by $ET^{I}_{CRS} = APv/AP$. Taking into consideration these two measures, the scale efficiency (SE) is equal to $SE^{I} = APc/APv$. When calculating some scale-inefficient units like P or *Q* are situated in the section of increasing returns to scale (*P*) or decreasing returns to scale (*Q*), an additional mathematical program must be computed if the scale returns are not increasing (NIRS). Thus, when NIRS = RVE, there are decreasing returns to scale; and when NIRS $\neq$ RVE, the returns to scale are considered constant (Santin 2009).

Summing it up, the aim of the DEA is to draw an evolving (hyper) plane that includes the efficient regions (and its linear combinations), that situates below it all inefficient units. As the envelopment plane represents the efficiency frontier, the distance of each region regarding this envelopment plane gives a value of its relative[17]

[16]The efficiency indexes present a measurement of radial efficiency, while these additional efficiencies, denominated slacks, provide a measure of the non-radial efficiency.

[17]It should be borne in mind, that DEA will measure a DMU's performance regarding its peers but—as it only very slowly converges to 'absolute' efficiency—not regarding the 'theoretical maximum' (Bhat et al. 2001: 32). However, we may assume that, given that some of the world's most innovation-efficient regions might be among the European ones, the 'maximum efficiency' might not be too far away from the one calculated in the present paper.

(in)efficiency that will be of one (100) if the region is situated on the border and less than one (100) if it is situated below it.

20.4 Results

Before developing the traditional DEA, we applied the super efficiency technique (Simar 2003; Banker and Chang 2006) with the objective to detect outliers in our dataset. The basic idea of this technique is that in the linear mathematical program used by DEA, each DMU is excluded from its own optimization, thus allowing some efficiency scores to reach values greater than one (100). The results of super-efficiency detect four regions that show super efficiency ratings in all the years of the series: Baden-Württemberg in Germany, Etelä-Suomi in Finland, Groningen in the Netherlands and Östra Mellansverige in Sweden. However, the only region with super efficiency ratings that would recommend its exclusion from the series is Noord-Brabant in the Netherlands, which in 2001, 2002, and 2003 obtained super efficiency scores higher than 2. Despite this, it was decided not to exclude this region from this dataset since more than an outlier is a region of high industrial development with a strong propensity to patent where one of the largest technology companies in the world as Philips is based and is entirely appropriate to consider it a benchmark to European level.

20.4.1 The Main Results in Terms of Efficiency Scores

In Tables 20.2, 20.3 and 20.4 we reflect the results for the efficiency scores for the years 2000, 2005 and 2010 using, as explained, the scientific publications and patents like outputs.

Calculating the efficiency using the two outputs separately (last two columns in Tables 20.2, 20.3 and 20.4 for the year 2010) is possible to divide the leading regions into three distinct groups. The leading technological regions (basically driven by patents) headed by Baden-Württemberg, Etelä-Suomi, Noord-Brabant, and Voralberg; secondly, the leading scientific regions (driven by publications) such as Groningen, Östra-Mellansverige, Övre-Norrland and Wien. A third group is formed by those regions that are jointly efficient (as well in patent and publications) such as Sydsverige, Stockholm and Bayern. One thing that should be emphasized is that the leading regions in some field are pushed to greater overall efficiency when considering the complementary field. For example, Baden-Württemberg and Etelä-Suomi, technology leaders in eight years have been global leaders (patents and publications) in 11 years.

Table 20.2 Efficiencies scores: Years 2000, 2005 and 2010 (0.6 till 1.0 in TE 2010) (own elaboration, using rDEA package from *R*)

		2000	2005	2010		
Regions	Countiy	TE	TE	TE	Tech E	Scient E
Baden-Württemberg	Germany	**1.000**	**1.000**	**1.000**	**1.000**	0.495
Eteä-Suomi (NUTS 2006)	Finland	**1.000**	**1.000**	**1.000**	0.998	0.646
Groningen	Nertherlands	**1.000**	**1.000**	**1.000**	0.161	**1.000**
Östra Mellansverige	Sweden	**1.000**	**1.000**	**1.000**	0.494	**1.000**
Övre Norrland	Sweden	**1.000**	0.994	**1.000**	0.310	**1.000**
Stockholm	Sweden	0.962	0.992	**1.000**	0.737	0.788
Vorarlberg	Austria	0.714	0.982	**1.000**	**1.000**	0.014
Sydsverige	Sweden	**1.000**	**1.000**	0.991	0.618	0.706
Noord-Brabant	Nertherlands	**1.000**	**1.000**	0.939	0.863	0.305
Bayern	Germany	0.912	0.873	0.913	0.786	0.473
Wien	Austria	**1.000**	0.912	0.869	0.215	0.869
Berlin	Germany	0.777	0.762	0.764	0.393	0.610
Nordrhein-Westfalen	Germany	0.751	0.816	0.749	0.592	0.319
Gelderland	Nertherlands	0.558	0.532	0.744	0.279	0.688
London	UK	0.813	0.726	0.705	0.228	0.569
Noord-Holland	Nertherlands	0.770	0.815	0.683	0.232	0.641
Denmark	Denmark	0.684	0.658	0.675	0.385	0.567
Utrecht	Nertherlands	**1.000**	**1.000**	0.672	0.333	0.567
Tirol	Austria	0.691	0.716	0.665	0.353	0.509
Vlaams Gewest	Belgium	0.648	0.724	0.656	0.283	0.582
Zuid-Holland	Nertherlands	0.681	0.643	0.649	0.300	0.583
Hessen	Germany	0.724	0.697	0.628	0.457	0.405
Rhône-Alpes	France	0.512	0.566	0.614	0.421	0.396
Länsi-Suomi	Finland	0.585	0.564	0.608	0.423	0.426
Scotland	UK	0.805	0.618	0.603	0.157	0.603
Västsverige	Sweden	0.825	0.838	0.603	0.432	0.380

The annual mean values are between 0.41 (2006) and 0.45 (2004) and the results are very heterogeneous with SD between minimum score 0.23 (2008) and 0.26 (2001), although the tendency over time is a reduction of the dispersion reflecting a process of convergence in terms of efficiency.

We used two ways of analyzing the level of dispersion among the regions of a specific country in 2010. The first is the calculation of distance of the values between

Table 20.3 Efficiencies scores: Years 2000, 2005 and 2010 (from average 0.41 till 0.6 in TE 2010) (own elaboration, using rDEA package from *R*)

		2000	2005	2010		
Regions	Country	TE	TE	TE	Tech E	Scient E
Île de France	France	0.588	0.586	0.595	0.367	0.462
Bremen	Germany	0.491	0.569	0.593	0.170	0.593
Rheinland-Pfalz	Germany	0.567	0.667	0.588	0.522	0.262
Pohjois- ja Itä-Suomi	Finland	0.628	0.553	0.588	0.269	0.576
Région de Bruxelles-Capitale/Brussels Ho	Belgium	0.806	0.718	0.584	0.240	0.516
Steiermark	Austria	0.650	0.556	0.578	0.366	0.444
Limburg (NL)	Nertherlands	0.460	0.544	0.578	0.254	0.503
Emilia-Romagna	Italy	0.650	0.693	0.567	0.273	0.481
South East (England)	UK	0.903	0.626	0.560	0.261	0.498
Centro (PT)	Portugal	0.230	0.374	0.532	0.024	0.532
Oberösterreich	Austria	0.344	0.382	0.532	0.482	0.152
Provincia Autonoma Trento	Italy	0.456	0.604	0.529	0.118	0.502
Comunidad Foral de Navarra	Spain	0.433	0.464	0.526	0.209	0.496
East of England	UK	0.934	0.643	0.526	0.209	0.487
Friuli-Venezia Giulia	Italy	0.568	0.572	0.516	0.290	0.425
Sachsen	Germany	0.411	0.458	0.512	0.293	0.474
Toscana	Italy	0.548	0.584	0.502	0.187	0.474
Alsace	France	0.454	0.495	0.490	0.309	0.360
North East (England)	UK	0.655	0.514	0.485	0.105	0.485
Salzburg	Austria	0.336	0.423	0.485	0.312	0.359
Niedersachsen	Germany	0.446	0.470	0.484	0.358	0.342
Saarland	Germany	0.481	0.516	0.474	0.302	0.355
Mecklenburg-Vorpommern	Germany	0.322	0.424	0.470	0.143	0.470
Overijs sel	Nertherlands	0.345	0.423	0.460	0.245	0.387
Thüringen	Germany	0.326	0.379	0.459	0.307	0.393
Hamburg	Germany	0.689	0.687	0.453	0.311	0.321
Wales	UK	0.577	0.427	0.450	0.083	0.450
Lombardia	Italy	0.472	0.498	0.450	0.245	0.369
Yorkshire and The Humber	UK	0.644	0.540	0.448	0.114	0.448
Norte	Portugal	0.154	0.265	0.447	0.022	0.447
Midi-Pyrénées	France	0.288	0.330	0.439	0.200	0.401
South West (England)	UK	0.588	0.451	0.437	0.196	0.389
Lazio	Italy	0.502	0.490	0.433	0.099	0.419

(continued)

Table 20.3 (continued)

		2000	2005	2010		
Regions	Country	TE	TE	TE	Tech E	Scient E
Schleswig-Holstein	Germany	0.516	0.428	0.431	0.283	0.294
Cataluña	Spain	0.379	0.422	0.422	0.128	0.404
Lisboa	Portugal	0.209	0.296	0.420	0.025	0.420
Aragón	Spain	0.350	0.419	0.416	0.107	0.401
Ireland	Ireland	0.353	0.390	0.412	0.128	0.383
East Midlands (England)	UK	0.643	0.466	0.410	0.153	0.395

the most efficient and least efficient region in a specific country. It should be noted that the greatest difference is observed for those countries with at least one very efficient region (Austria, Germany, Netherlands, Sweden and Finland). The second way to analyze the dispersion is to divide for each country its highest regional efficiency score with the lowest. In this case, the biggest differences in 2010 (Table 20.5) are observed in Italy (with the most efficient region being almost 30 times more efficient than the lowest), followed by Finland and Germany with a multiplier of 11 and 9, respectively.

About the efficiency distributions, applying normality test is easy to demonstrate that these are not normal, so using kernel density functions can reveal important features that would otherwise be hidden. This nonparametric approach requires the choice of a method to 'smooth' the data. In this paper, the kernel smoothing method has been chosen as this is one of the most commonly used in this type of work.[18] One of the advantages of kernel density functions is that they do not impose a priori functional forms on the distribution of data. We applied the kernel, and in particular estimating a Gaussian kernel with optimum bandwidth. Further, the differences among the European RIS and the dynamic perspective of the distribution of efficiency can be analyzed using stochastic kernel estimations that consider the probability of moving between any two levels in the range of values. A stochastic kernel is therefore conceptually equivalent to a transition matrix with the number of intervals tending to infinity (Quah 1993, 1996). The stochastic kernel can be approximated by estimating the density function of the distribution at a particular time $t + k$, conditioned by the values corresponding to a previous time t. For this, a nonparametric estimation of the joint density function of the distribution at times t and $t + k$ is carried out. Figure 20.5 shows the stochastic kernels estimated from the efficiency for time period of 11 years ($t = 2000$ and $t + k = 2010$). In this graph it is possible to appreciate a group of leading regions whose behavior is clearly different from the rest of the regions.

[18]As indicated by Tortosa-Ausina et al. (2005), authors such as Walter and Blum (1979) or Terrell and Scott (1992) note that virtually all non-parametric algorithms are asymptotically kernel methods (Suárez and de Jorge 2008).

Table 20.4 Efficiencies scores: Years 2000, 2005 and 2010 (below 0.41 in TE 2010) (own elaboration, using rDEA package from *R*)

		2000	2005	2010		
Regions	Country	TE	TE	TE	Tech E	Scient E
Veneto	Italy	0.401	0.470	0.407	0.203	0.338
Umbria	Italy	0.485	0.482	0.404	0.074	0.404
Northern Ireland	UK	0.573	0.466	0.389	0.052	0.389
Picardie	France	0.371	0.347	0.384	0.135	0.335
North West (England)	UK	0.529	0.429	0.381	0.118	0.376
Liguria	Italy	0.489	0.461	0.370	0.150	0.327
Luxembourg	Luxembourg	0.362	0.472	0.366	0.215	0.191
Piemonte	Italy	0.332	0.379	0.358	0.192	0.286
Languedoc-Roussillon	France	0.355	0.343	0.354	0.130	0.335
Comunidad de Madrid	Spain	0.388	0.379	0.351	0.105	0.337
Provence-Alpes-Côte d'Azur	France	0.269	0.326	0.348	0.208	0.270
Galicia	Spain	0.278	0.337	0.347	0.028	0.347
Bretagne	France	0.273	0.347	0.342	0.221	0.241
West Midlands (England)	UK	0.480	0.365	0.339	0.144	0.313
Principado de Asturias	Spain	0.284	0.329	0.336	0.028	0.336
Aquitaine	France	0.328	0.313	0.334	0.132	0.300
Cantabria	Spain	0.362	0.377	0.333	0.054	0.333
Marche	Italy	0.355	0.390	0.332	0.168	0.288
Abruzzo	Italy	0.457	0.378	0.331	0.071	0.331
Franche-Comté	France	0.255	0.282	0.320	0.242	0.205
Comunidad Valenciana	Spain	0.298	0.332	0.309	0.053	0.309
Région Wallonne	Belgium	0.316	0.331	0.307	0.195	0.215
Brandenburg	Germany	0.179	0.281	0.303	0.220	0.160
Algarve	Portugal	0.206	0.416	0.291	0.012	0.291
Norra Mellansverige	Sweden	0.279	0.251	0.281	0.238	0.119
Pais Vasco	Spain	0.211	0.220	0.269	0.130	0.224
Auvergne	France	0.166	0.167	0.268	0.268	0.000
Småland med öarna	Sweden	0.186	0.259	0.260	0.214	0.108
Haute-Normandie	France	0.212	0.239	0.258	0.206	0.135
Región de Murcia	Spain	0.234	0.290	0.257	0.043	0.257
Sardegna	France	0.285	0.299	0.255	0.028	0.255
Pays de la Loire	France	0.172	0.211	0.248	0.156	0.190
Centre	France	0.218	0.243	0.247	0.164	0.167
Niederösterreich	Austria	0.194	0.280	0.247	0.243	0.017

(continued)

Table 20.4 (continued)

		2000	2005	2010		
Regions	Country	TE	TE	TE	Tech E	Scient E
Campania	Italy	0.243	0.262	0.245	0.029	0.245
Andalucia	Spain	0.210	0.243	0.240	0.028	0.240
Castilla y León	Spain	0.201	0.251	0.233	0.021	0.233
Sicilia	Italy	0.193	0.216	0.228	0.024	0.228
Molise	Italy	0.174	0.236	0.227	0.011	0.227
Bourgogne	France	0.246	0.232	0.226	0.119	0.186
Lorraine	France	0.283	0.242	0.225	0.093	0.210
Provincia Autonoma Bolzano-Bozen	Italy	0.148	0.195	0.224	0.210	0.052
La Rioja	Spain	0.199	0.232	0.221	0.051	0.207
Mellersta Norrland	Sweden	0.258	0.235	0.221	0.163	0.145
Limousin	France	0.125	0.191	0.220	0.132	0.169
Poitou-Charentes	France	0.205	0.202	0.213	0.088	0.189
Nord—Pas-de-Calais	France	0.188	0.185	0.209	0.086	0.190
Canarias (ES)	Spain	0.160	0.182	0.201	0.008	0.201
Puglia	Italy	0.176	0.217	0.196	0.033	0.196
Basse-Normandie	France	0.186	0.173	0.195	0.115	0.152
Calabria	Italy	0.160	0.194	0.193	0.013	0.193
Extremadura	Spain	0.142	0.219	0.180	0.009	0.180
Champagne-Ardenne	France	0.178	0.174	0.165	0.111	0.116
Castilla-la Mancha	Spain	0.086	0.146	0.153	0.021	0.150
Illes Balears	Spain	0.168	0.197	0.152	0.028	0.148
Kärnten	Austria	0.162	0.218	0.151	0.137	0.050
Burgenland	Austria	0.120	0.120	0.147	0.147	0.000
Alentejo	Portugal	0.045	0.096	0.142	0.013	0.142
Friesland (NL)	Nertherlands	0.087	0.117	0.129	0.129	0.000
Corse	France	0.154	0.162	0.126	0.008	0.126
Drenthe	Nertherlands	0.148	0.120	0.114	0.114	0.000
Flevoland	Nertherlands	0.205	0.125	0.111	0.111	0.000
Zeeland	Nertherlands	0.112	0.096	0.105	0.105	0.000
Sachsen-Anhalt	Germany	0.093	0.105	0.104	0.104	0.000
Åland	Finland	0.275	0.013	0.093	0.087	0.024
Valle d'Aosta/Vallée d'Aoste	Italy	0.131	0.171	0.091	0.091	0.000
Basilicata	Italy	0.007	0.025	0.019	0.018	0.002

Table 20.5 Dispersion of efficiencies, year 2010 (own elaboration)

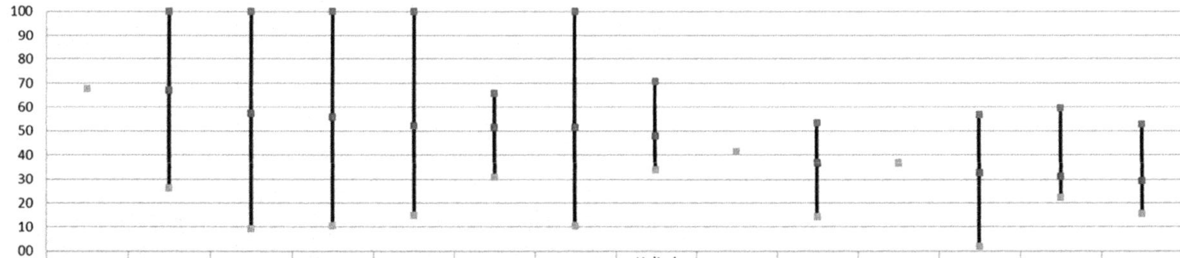

	Denmark	Sweden	Finland	Germany	Austria	Belgium	Netherlands	United Kingdom	Ireland	Portugal	Luxembourg	Italy	France	Spain
EI Maximum	68	100	100	100	100	66	100	71	41	53	37	57	60	53
EI Average	68	67	57	56	52	52	52	48	41	37	37	33	31	29
EI Minimum	68	26	09	10	15	31	11	34	41	14	37	02	22	15

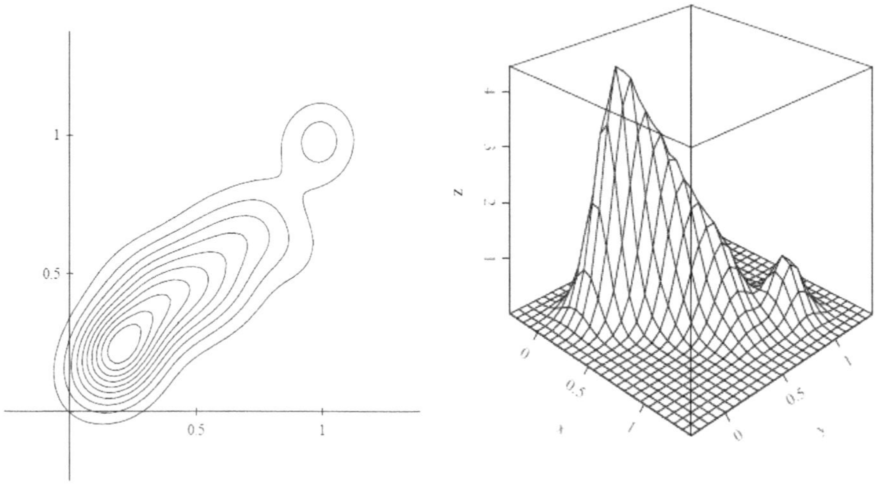

Fig. 20.5 Stochastic Kernel Efficiency for 2000–2010 period (*x* axis–*y* axis, respectively) in two (left) and three dimensions (right) (own elaboration using software Xtremes 4.1)

20.4.2 Changes Are the Efficiency Score Over Time; Convergence and Divergence

The inequality inefficiency was calculated for each of the models using the Gini index. This is, in fact, a concentration index is widely used in calculations of income inequality and takes values between 0 and 1, being 1 extreme inequality, only one is the most efficient, and 0 means total equality (all are equally efficient). The calculations were made for the years 2000, 2005 and 2010 and indicate that the Gini indexes are respectively 0.38, 0.34 and 0.33, showing a reduction of the inequality. Despite this process of convergence, the high level of heterogeneity (between and within countries) persists in the efficiency scores among European RIS. This heterogeneity is visualized in Table 20.5 for the year 2010.

Using the stochastic kernels again, we analyzed the evolution of the efficiencies distribution considering three years of our sample: 2000, 2005 and 2010. In Fig. 20.6, the stochastic kernels are estimated from the data of two years, 2000 and 2010, and then add the comparisons 2000–2005 and 2005–2010. This shows a convergence and a concentration process and displacement of the lines of level of the efficiency toward more values since the curves tend to concentrate reducing the group of leading regions as the comparisons are made between the greater years of the period. The in-depth analysis of the temporal dynamics and convergence goes beyond the scope of this paper.

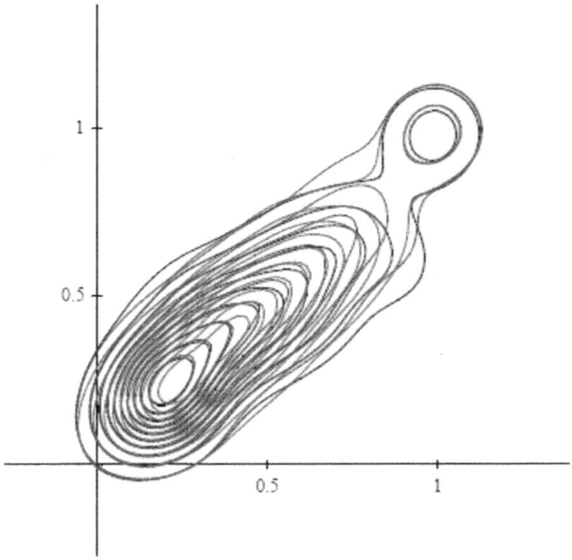

Fig. 20.6 Evaluation for periods of process of improvement of the efficiency in European RIS: 2000–2010 (black line), 2000–2005 (red line) and 2005–2010 (green line) (own elaboration using software Xtremes 4.1)

20.4.3 Scale Versus Technical Inefficiencies

Finally, the estimation of an index of scale efficiency for RIS as well as the test for returns to scale using bootstrap (Simar and Wilson 2002) reveals that much of the estimated inefficiencies in our model are caused by a dimension problem. Technical efficiency is high in many regions but its scale efficiencies[19] are very far from the frontier. This result highlights the fact that inefficiency maintains some relation with the need to reach a critical mass of economic and institutional resources of each region for the development of its innovation activities.

As mentioned above, the assumption of constant returns to scale, while useful for the determination of efficiency scores, is unrealistic. Therefore, in contrast to this hypothesis, we will try to confirm the greater relevance of scale problems in total inefficiency. We wish to test whether the technology set T from which our observations are sampled exhibits constant returns to scale (CRS). Formally, we

[19]In the case of the technical inefficiency it's about the technical capabilities of the regional agents to use their resources efficiently while in the case of scale advantages it is about the impact of the dimension of the regional innovation system on its efficiency. In fact, it analyzes what would happen with the efficiency of the regions with a similar input if they would have the same scale as the leading regions.

wish to test the hypothesis that the technology exhibits constant returns to scale (H_0) against the alternative (H_1), that it is variable returns to scale (VRS). If we reject H_0 then we can test if the technology set is decreasing returns to scale.

In accordance with Bogetoft and Otto (2011: 183): "If the hypothesis is true, then the efficiencies calculated from the VRS technology are the same as the efficiencies calculated from the CRS technology. If there is not CRS, then at least one of the efficiencies will be different; i.e., CRS efficiency will be smaller than VRS efficiency. One way to examine this is to see whether the scale efficiency,

$$\mathrm{SE}^k = \frac{E^k_{\mathrm{CRS}}}{E^k_{\mathrm{VRS}}}; \text{ with } k = 1, \ldots, K \tag{20.1}$$

is equal to 1 for all DMUs, meaning that the technology is CRS, or whether there is at least one firm where it is less than 1, meaning that the technology is VRS. For a given set of observations of K DMUs, we must therefore reject the hypothesis if at least one of the estimated SE has a value less than 1. However, as the connection between the technology set and the scale efficiencies is an uncertain or stochastic connection, we must reject the hypothesis if at least one of the estimated SE has a value significantly less than 1, i.e. if one of the estimated SE is less than a critical value."

We used the statistic defined by Bogetoft and Otto (2011),[20] but as we do not know the distribution of this statistic under H_0, therefore, we cannot calculate a critical value directly. One way to address this lack of distributional knowledge is to use a bootstrap method.

The results by each year are presented in the Table 20.6.

Applying the test with DRS as H_0 we rejected the null hypothesis at 95% of confidence and T (technology) would exhibit increasing returns to scale confirming the scale problems.

[20] In accordance with Bogetoft and Otto (2011: 183): "Instead of looking at the scale efficiencies individually, we could look at the test statistic $S^1 = \frac{1}{K}\sum_{k=1}^{K}\frac{E^k_{\mathrm{CRS}}}{E^k_{\mathrm{VRS}}}$; or the one that we are going to use in the following:

$S = \frac{\sum_{k=1}^{K} E^k_{\mathrm{CRS}}}{\sum_{k=1}^{K} E^k_{\mathrm{VRS}}}$; If the H_0 is true, then S will be close to 1, and if the alternative is true, then $S <$ 1. As $S \leq 1$ by construction, we will reject H_0 if S is significantly smaller than 1. We therefore seek a critical threshold for the statistic S; if it is smaller than this value, then we will reject the hypothesis. Thus, we seek a critical value c_α that will determine whether we reject H_0, the hypothesis of constant returns to scale, if $S < c_\alpha$ and Pr $(S < c_\alpha / H_0) = \alpha$ where α is the size of the test, typically 5% (α = 0.05). The size of the test, α is the probability of rejecting the hypothesis even though it is true (This is a type I error.)".

Table 20.6 Test of return to scale (own elaboration)

	2000	2001	2002	2003	2004	2005	2006	2007	2008	2009	2010
C_α	0.58	0.53	0.63	0.70	0.59	0.60	0.69	0.74	0.71	0.71	0.69
S	0.44	0.42	0.42	0.44	0.45	0.44	0.42	0.44	0.44	0.44	0.43
Test 5%	Reject H_0	Reject H_0	Reject H_0	Reject H_0	Reject H_0	Reject H_0	Reject H_0	Reject H_0	Reject H_0	Reject H_0	Reject H_0
Type *I* error	0.03	0.02	0.02	0.00	0.02	0.01	0.00	0.00	0.00	0.00	0.00

20.5 Conclusions

We start our study from the neoclassical and Schumpeterian framework of the economics of innovation using a holistic view in which all agents and organizations do interact and complement each other and add value to their mutual activities. Therefore, we decided to measure the efficiency of the RIS using a broad number of input variables (29) reflecting the broadest number of agents and factors as possible with the available statistical information. In this paper, we have explored the methods to measure the efficiency in which economic and institutional resources are used to obtain technologies useful to produce goods and services, as well as new scientific knowledge. The adopted approach is also linked to the evolutionary framework of this area of economic research, leaving the regional innovation systems in the center of the study, to calculate the level of innovative efficiency achieved by 132 regions from 14 countries belonging to the European Union. This is critically important as "the technical efficiency of a region largely reflects its ability to transform innovative investment into innovative output (and thereby transforming itself...) the key to this region to gain competitive advantage" (Chen and Guan 2012: 356).

The efficiency analysis carried out by the DEA technique allowed us to establish the efficient frontier by identifying those regions that maximize (minimize in an input orientation) the input/output relationship. In relation to this frontier, the DEA places the other regions by measuring their efficiency as a distance (in percentage) with respect to this border. The results obtained by this procedure allow us to point out, firstly, that only a few European regions are located on or very close to the efficiency frontier, with many regions obtaining systematically low efficiency scores. The dispersion of these levels of efficiency is very broad both within and between countries. Moreover, the differences in efficiency with which regions allocate their resources to innovation are a common feature of all multiregional nations, regardless of their level of income. In addition, RISs that are on or near the frontier belong to countries whose GDPs per capita are above the European average. On the other side, in all countries whose GDPs per capita are below the European average, the regions show efficiency levels below 20% of the frontier. Despite this, the tendency over time is a reduction of the dispersion reflecting a process of convergence in terms of efficiency.

The estimation of an index of scale efficiency for SRI as well as the test for returns to scale reveals that much of the estimated inefficiencies in our model are caused by a dimension problem. Technical efficiency is high in many regions, but its scale efficiencies are very far from the frontier. It points to the fact that inefficiency maintains some relation with the need to reach a critical mass of economic and institutional resources of each region for the development of its innovation activities. This last result should be considered by those responsible for designing and implementing innovation policies, aiming to economize resources employed with the highest possible returns. In other words, not any objective nor any actor is equally efficient developing R&D activities. According to this, there is no room for homogenous or 'coffee for all' policies; if not rather for 'tailor-made' innovation policies (see

Tödtling and Trippl 2005) implementing an improved personalized mix of science and technology instruments and R&D (see Chen and Guan 2012: 368), because at the end innovation activities differ strongly between regions in terms of their structural and institutional development.

Finally, the results support, to a certain extent, the organization of European R&D policy around two poles: one of promoting excellence through the Framework Program which would reward efficiency; And the other that of strengthening regional innovation systems through regional policy which would go in favor of critical mass and thus reduce the scale inefficiency.

References

Archibugi, D. (1992). Patenting as an indicator of technological innovation: A review. *Science and Public Policy, 19,* 357–368.

Badiola-Sánchez, A., & Coto-Millán, P. (2012). Determinants of technical efficiency and technological innovation of European regions in the period 2002–2006. *Journal of Business Management and Applied Economics, 5.*

Banker, R., Charnes, A., & Cooper, W. W. (1984). Some models for estimating technical and scale inefficiencies in data envelopment analysis. *Management Science, 30*(9), 1078–1092.

Banker, R., & Chang, H. (2006). The Super-efficiency procedure for outlier identification, not for ranking efficient units. *European Journal of Operational Research, 175,* 1311–1320.

Bhat, R., Verma, B. B., & Reuben, E. (2001). *Hospital efficiency and data envelopment analysis.* Ahmedabad: Indian Institute of Management.

Bogetoft, P., & Otto, L. (2011). *Benchmarking with DEA*. SFA and R: Springer.

Bosco, M. G., Brugnoli, A. (2011). Regional efficiency, innovation and productivity. In Cached, RSA conference proceedings, Pécs.

Broekel, T. (2008). From average to the frontier: A nonparametric frontier approach to the analysis of externalities and regional innovation performance. In *Papers in evolutionary economic geography* (pp. 04). Utrecht University.

Broekel, T., & Meder, A. (2008). The bright and dark side of cooperation for regional innovation performance. In *Jena economic research papers* (pp. 053). Jena, Germany.

Buesa, M., Martínez Pellitero, M., Baumert, T., & Heijs, J. (2007). Novel applications of existing econometric instruments to analyse regional innovation systems: The Spanish case. In J. Suriñach, R. Moreno & E. Vayá, *Knowledge externalities, innovation clusters and regional development* (pp. 155–75). Cheltenham: Edward Elgar.

Buesa, M., Heijs, J., & Baumert, T. (2010). The determinants of regional innovation in Europe: A combined factorial and regression knowledge production function approach. *Research Policy, 39*(6), 722–735.

Charnes, A., Cooper, W. W., & Rhodes, E. (1978). Measuring the efficiency of decision making units. *European Journal of Operational Research, 2,* 429–444.

Chen, C. P., Hu, J. L., & Yang, C. H. (2011). An international comparison of R&D efficiency of multiple innovative outputs: The role of the national innovation system innovation: Management. *Policy and Practice, 13*(3), 341–360.

Chen, K., & Guan, J. (2012). Measuring the efficiency of China's regional innovation system: Application of network data envelopment analysis (DEA). *Regional Studies, 46*(3), 355–377.

Debreu, G. (1951). The coefficient of resource utilization. *Econometrica, 19*(3), 273–292.

European Commission. (2001). *Recherche et développement: statistiques annuelles*. Luxembourg.

Eurostat. (2011). *Eurostat yearbook 2011, Europe in figures*. Belgium.

Farrell, M. J. (1957). The measurement of efficiency productive. *Journal of the Royal Statistical Society, Series A (General), 120*(III), 253–66.
Fritsch, M. (2004). Cooperation and the efficiency of regional R&D activities. *Cambridge Journal of Economics, 28,* 829–846.
Fritsch, M., & Slavtchev, V. (2007). *How does agglomeration affect the efficiency of regional innovation systems?*. Kiel: Workshop Agglomeration and growth in knowledge based societies.
Fritsch, M., & Slavtchev, V. (2010). How does industry specialization affect the efficiency of regional innovation systems? *The Annals of Regional Science, 45*(1), 87–108.
Griliches, Z. (1990). Patent Statistics as economic Indicators: A Survey. *Journal of Economic Literature, 28,* 1661–1707.
Hair, J. F., Anderson, R., Tatham, R. & Black. (1999). *Análisis multivariante de datos'*. Madrid.
Hu, M. C., & Mathews, J. A. (2005). National innovative capacity in East Asia. *Research Policy, 34*(9), 1322–1349.
Kaihua, C., & Minting, K. (2014). Staged efficiency and its determinants of regional innovation systems: A two-step analytical procedure. *The Annals of Regional Science, 52*(2), 627–657.
Koopmans, T. C. (1951). An analysis of production as an efficient combination of activities. In T. C. Koopmans (Ed.), *Activity analysis of production and allocation* (pp. 33–97). New York: Jhon Wiley and Sons Inc.
Li, X. (2009). China's regional innovation capacity in transition: An empirical approach. *Research Policy, 38*(2), 338–357.
Mansfield, E. (1986). Patents and innovation: An empirical study. *Management Science, 32*(2), 173–181.
Niosi, Jorge. (2002). National systems of innovations are "x-efficient" (and x-effective): Why some are slow learners. *Research Policy, 31*(2), 291–302.
Niu, D., Wang, R., Zhang, X., & Song, W. (2013). Comparative studies on efficiency of China's regional innovation system on the basis of cooperation measurement model. *Journal of Emerging Trends in Economics and Management Sciences, 4*(2), 147–157.
Pavitt, K. (1985). Patent statistics as indicators of innovative activities: Possibilities and problems. *Scientometrics, 7*(1-2), 77–99.
Quah, D. T. (1993). Empirical cross-section dynamics in economic growth. *European Economic Review, 37,* 426–434.
Quah, D. T. (1996). Empirics for economics growth and convergence. *European Economic Review, 40,* 1353–1375.
Rondé, P. & Hussler, C. (2005). Innovation in regions: What does it really matter? *Research Policy, 34*(8), 1150–72.
Santín, D. (2009). La Medición de la Eficiencia en el Sector Público. Técnicas Cuantitativas. http://www.sefin.fortaleza.ce.gov.br/apresentacoes/gerados/apresentacoes_madri/UD_EFICIENCIA_DANIEL_SANTIN.pdf.
Scherer, F. M. (1965). Firm size, market structure, opportunity and output patented inventions. *The American Economic Review, 55*(5), 1097–1125.
Schmoch, U. 1999. Eignen sich Patente als Innovationsindikatoren?. In: *Patentschutz und Innovation in Geschichte und Gegenwart*. In Frankfurt am Main et al: R. Boch.
Schmookler, J. (1966). *Invention and economic growth*. Cambridge Mass: Harvard University Press.
Schumpeter, J. A. (1911). *Theorie der wirtschaftlichen Entwicklung*. Leipzig: Duncker-Humboldt.
Schumpeter, J. A. (1942). *Capitalism, socialism and democracy*. Nueva York: Harper & Brothers.
Simar, L., & Wilson, P. (2002). Non-parametric tests of returns to scale. *European Journal of Operational Research, 139,* 115–132.
Simar, L. (2003). Detecting outliers in frontier models: A simple approach. *Journal of Productivity Analysis, 20,* 391–424.
Smith, K. (2005). Measuring innovation. In J. Fagerberg, D. Mowery & R. Nelson (Eds), *The oxford handbook of innovation* (pp. 148–77). New York: Oxford.
Suárez, C. & de Jorge, J. (2008). Efficiency convergence processes and effects of regulation in the nonspecialized retail sector in Spain. *The Annals of Reg Science.*

Terrell, G. R., & Scott, W. (1992). Variable kernel density estimation. *Annals of Statistics, 20*(3), 1236–1265.

Tödtling, F., & Trippl, M. (2005). One size fits All? Towards a differentiated regional innovation policy approach. *Research Policy, 34,* 1203–1219.

Tortosa-Ausina, E., Perez, F., Mas, T., & Goerlich, F. J. (2005). Growth and covergence profile in the Spanish provinces 1965–1997. *J Reg Sci, 45*(1), 147–182.

Trajtenberg, M. (1990). *Patents as indicators of Innovation.In Economic Analysis of Product Innovation?* MA: Cambridge.

Walter, G., & Blum, J. (1979). Probability density estimation using delta sequences. *Annals of Statistics, 7*(2), 328–340.

Wang, N., & Hagedoorn, J. (forthcoming—2014 online). The lag structure of the relationship between patenting and internal R&D revisited. *Research Policy* http://dx.doi.org/10.1016/j.respol.2014.03.010.

Winkler, W. E. (2014). Matching and record linkage. *WIREs Computational Statistics, 6*(5), 313–325.

Chapter 21
Volatility Modelling and Trading Volume of the CARS Equity Indices

Niel Oberholzer and Chalté Venter

Abstract In this study, the effect and significance of new information on the volatility of different markets (developed vs. emerging) are considered. The effect of new information on volatility is tested in a GARCH framework. Data for four commodity-based equity markets is used for the analysis. The Akaike and Schwarz information criterion are used to the fitted univariate GARCH models, and the root-mean-square error and mean absolute error are used to compare the forecasting performance. Empirical results show that new information (trading volume) does improve forward-looking estimates of volatility. There is not a significant difference in terms of the effect of new information in volatility modelling when developed and emerging markets are considered.

Keywords GARCH · Forecasting · Trading volume · Asymmetry

21.1 Introduction

In this paper, the significance of new information and the effect it will have on the volatility of different commodity-based equity markets (developed vs emerging) will be analysed. According to Mohr (2016), an external shock which affects market prices may stem from several sources. Demand and supply shocks could affect prices (and therefore volatility) of commodities which will be reflected in share prices. Currency shocks, owing to either global developments affecting a major currency (such as the dollar), or political and economic developments affecting the exchange rate of a country, or set of countries, could also impact share prices. Even if the value of a currency does not react to economic policy shifts, data releases or political developments, these news events may still have an impact on equity market prices (Koop 2005).

N. Oberholzer (✉) · C. Venter
Department of Finance and Investment Management, University of Johannesburg, Auckland Park, Johannesburg 2006, South Africa
e-mail: nielo@uj.ac.za

N. Tsounis and A. Vlachvei (eds.), *Advances in Cross-Section Data Methods in Applied Economic Research*, Springer Proceedings in Business and Economics,
https://doi.org/10.1007/978-3-030-38253-7_21

In this study, commodity-based equity markets will be used. Therefore, four of the CARBS (Canada, Australia, Russia, Brazil and South Africa) countries will be used in this study, namely Canada, Australia, Russia and South Africa (CARS). Brazil is excluded from this study as there is no trading volume data available for Brazil. Trading volume is used as a proxy for new information; this is consistent with the study by Chen et al. (2001). The reason for using this group of countries is because it includes both developed and emerging markets. The CARBS countries are known as the main exporting countries of commodities. These four countries are used to determine what effect new information and shocks will have on volatility of the different commodity-based equity markets (emerging and developed) and whether the impact of new information is significant when explaining the variation in different market prices. This will be formally tested in this study by making use of of different univariate heteroskedasticity models.

Research focussing on the efficient-market hypothesis (EMH) has been extensive. According to Bodie et al. (2010), the EMH is based on the premise that all the information which is available in the equity markets is reflected in financial share prices. When new information reaches the market, share prices appear to adjust rapidly (Reilly and Brown 2006). Therefore, it can be said that all information regarding a particular share is reflected by its current price (Reilly and Brown 2006). Bailey (2005) stated that a capital market is efficient if all relevant information determining share prices are entirely and properly reflected in the market.

Distinguishing between efficient markets brought about from past and current information, or market efficiency brought about from past and current information, information expectation is important. According to Caporin et al. (2013), if price changes are properly estimated, they must be unforecastable, which means that if expectations and new information are accurately included in price changes, price changes have to be unforecastable. Lo and MacKinlay (1988) argued that in an informationally efficient market, price changes must be unforecastable if they are accurately anticipated. This interpretation of Lo and MacKinlay (1988) was also argued in earlier works by Samuelson (1965). Samuelson (1965) also stated that in order for asset prices to be efficient, the price has to reflect all available information.

A similar method to Chen et al. (2001) will be applied in this study to determine the significance of new information when modelling and forecasting volatility. Chen et al. (2001) used Granger causality tests to study the causal relationship between market returns and trading volumes. The authors found that there was a positive relationship between trading volumes and price changes. Chen et al. (2001) also made use of GARCH and EGARCH models to determine the effect that trading volume will have on volatility. The EGARCH(1,1) model was used to determine equity market return volatility. The results showed that the representation of the returns in the data of the share indices was reflected properly. In addition, trading volume gives some information about the share indices of the returns processes and that after including simultaneous and lagged volume effects (which were used as proxies for the flow of information), the persistence in volatility was still present. Chen et al. (2001) found that there is much more to be learnt about the equity market by exploring the combined dynamics of share prices and trading volume (Chen et al. 2001).

In this study, the work by Chen et al. (2001) is extended by making use of GARCH, EGARCH and GJR-GARCH models. These models will be applied to determine whether the forecasting ability of the model will improve when trading volume is included. Autoregressive conditional heteroskedasticity (ARCH) and generalised autoregressive conditional heteroskedasticity (GARCH) models have been used in financial volatility modelling for decades to predict and examine the extent of errors in a model (Engle 2001). The volatility modelling section in this study is based on similar studies by Chen et al. (2001), and Kalu and Chinwe (2014). The Akaike information criterion (AIC) and Schwarz information criterion (SIC) of the GARCH, GJR-GARCH and EGARCH models will be compared to determine the best-fitting univariate GARCH family model in this study. The information criterion will also be used to compare models that include trading volume to the standard GARCH model specification. Finally, forecast performance metrics of the different models will be used to determine the most reliable forecasting model. In the following section, the recent and relevant literature will be discussed.

21.2 Literature Review

The CARBS (Canada, Australia, Russia, Brazil and South Africa) countries are known to be amongst the main exporting countries of commodities. However, there has not been much financial research published that focusses on the CARBS countries. Labuschagne et al. (2017a) forecast volatility and value-at-risk (VaR) of the CARBS indices using GARCH models. The log returns of the CARBS indices are used in this study to estimate the portfolio weights of a global minimum variance portfolio (GMVP). It was shown that the statistical characteristics of the indices and the GMVP appear to be in line with the stylised facts of financial time series. Labuschagne et al. (2017b) also found that volatility clustering is present and that the data of the return series is not normally distributed.

ARCH and GARCH models have been used in financial volatility modelling for the past few decades to predict and examine the extent of errors in a model (Engle 2001). In order to do this, the volatility of the model is modelled as an autoregressive conditional heteroskedasticity(ARCH) model and a generalised autoregressive conditional heteroskedasticity(GARCH) model, which is an extension of an ARCH model (Engle 2001).

Labuschagne et al. (2017c) used different univariate and multivariate GARCH models to determine the optimal parameters of the models when applied to the CARBS equity indices. The authors argued that it is impractical to make the assumption that volatility of financial returns is continuous. The symmetric GARCH model and asymmetric GJR-GARCH and EGARCH models were used to determine the best-fit model by making use of AIC and BIC. The authors concluded that the volatility of the CARBS indices is best explained by the EGARCH model.

Oberholzer and Venter (2015) used univariate GARCH models, such as the GJR-GARCH and EGARCH models, to examine the variations in day-to-day volatility of five indices on the Johannesburg Stock Exchange (JSE). The period between 2007 and the onset of the 2009 financial crisis was used, and the market price volatilities were compared for the periods before and after the crisis in order to determine whether there was any difference in the behaviour of volatility. The authors found that the best-fit model was the GJR-GARCH model for most of the indices.

Oberholzer and von Boetticher (2015) used the South African rand and five major JSE-indices to determine what the inter-market relationship is between them. The authors used a constant conditional correlation (CCC) GARCH model to determine whether there are spillover effects present, and what the significance of shocks will be in the market. Oberholzer and von Boetticher (2015) concluded that the rand fluctuates more if shocks enter the market when comparing it to the JSE/FTSEs All-Share Index, Top40 Index and the Midcap Index, but fluctuates less if shocks enter the market when comparing it to the JSE/FTSEs Small Cap Index and the Fledgling Index.

The studies mentioned above made use of univariate and multivariate GARCH models to model volatility of financial assets. However, volatility forecasting was not performed. The best-fit model was determined by making use of AIC, SIC or BIC. In the next section, literature about ARCH and GARCH volatility forecasting will be discussed.

Aydemir (2002) began by stating that over the past few years; volatility modelling has been an active research topic; and the significance of volatility in financial markets is the inspiration. Aydemir (2002) further explained that, for a simple risk measurement in asset pricing models, volatility approximations are often used. The development of numerous types of models ensued, with these models being utilised to reflect the different stylised facts of financial time series. The most common and well-known models used in financial modelling are the autoregressive moving average (ARMA), ARCH and stochastic volatility (SV) models (Aydemir 2002). An important characteristic of ARCH models is their ability to explain the trend for volatility clustering in financial data (Aydemir 2002). In other words, the trend for big movements in prices must be followed by big random movements, and the same applies for minor movements (Aydemir 2002).

Marcucci (2005) made a comparison between different GARCH models and their capability to forecast financial time series volatility from a daily basis to a monthly basis. Markov regime-switching GARCH (MRS-GARCH) models were examined in this study as it accounts for the unnecessary persistence which is frequently found in GARCH models. With the MRS-GARCH models, the parameters are allowed to change between a low and a high volatility regime (Marcucci 2005). The empirical results show that the MRS-GARCH models outperform the regular GARCH models when forecasting volatility over short time periods. However, the asymmetric GARCH models are better when forecasting volatility over long time periods.

Peters (2001) conducted a study on four GARCH models and examined the forecasting ability of each of them. The GARCH models that were used were GARCH, EGARCH, GJR-GARCH and APARCH models. Peters (2001) used two European share indices, the FTSE 100 and DAX 30. It was found that when asymmetric GARCH models were used and fat tails were accounted for in the conditional variance, there was an overall improvement of the estimation (Peters 2001). However, it was also found that the forecasting ability of the GJR and APARCH models was better than the asymmetric GARCH model. Finally, Peters (2001) concluded that improved forecast performance was not precisely perceived when non-normal distributions were used.

In this study GARCH, EGARCH and GJR-GARCH models will be used to determine whether the forecasting ability of the model will improve when trading volume, which is a proxy for new information, is taken into account. In the next section of the literature review, similar studies by Chen et al. (2001) and Sabiruzzaman et al. (2010) will be discussed.

Chen et al. (2001) used Granger causality tests to study the causal relationship between equity market returns and trading volumes. The authors found that there was a positive relationship between trading volume and price changes. Furthermore, it was also established that returns caused trading volume and to a smaller degree, trading volume caused returns when the Granger causality test was performed. Chen et al. (2001) also made use of GARCH and EGARCH models to determine the effect that trading volume will have on volatility. Chen et al. (2001) argued that there are benefits to using EGARCH models over GARCH models; this is mainly due to the non-negativity constraints required for the GARCH model. Another reason for the argument is that the symmetric GARCH model does not capture the negative asymmetry which is present in financial time series. The EGARCH(1,1) model was used to determine asset return volatility. The results show that the representation of the returns in the data of the share indices is reflected properly. In addition, trading volume gives some information about the share indices of the returns processes, and that after including simultaneous and lagged volume effects (which were used as proxies for the flow of information), the persistence in volatility was still present. Chen et al. (2001) concluded by stating that there is much more to be learnt about the equity market by exploring the combined dynamics of share prices and trading volume (Chen et al. 2001).

Sabiruzzaman et al. (2010) described volatility as a sign of uncertainty, which will have an impact on monetary policy, management of risk and investment decisions. The focus of this study is the volatility of trading volume. The daily trading volume index of Hong Kong was examined to determine the flow of volatility. The authors made use of GARCH and GJR-GARCH models to model the volatility of trading volume and found that the GJR-GARCH model is more reliable due to the fact that it takes asymmetries into account.

In a recent study, Kalu and Chinwe (2014) made use of univariate GARCH models to estimate the relationship between the conditional variance and trading volume of the Nigerian equity market. The authors also tested whether the inclusion of trading volume as an independent variable reduces volatility persistence. The results showed that there is a statistically significant positive relationship between trading volume and volatility. Furthermore, volatility persistence does not decrease when trading volume is accounted for.

The volatility modelling section in this study is based on similar studies by Chen et al. (2001), and Kalu and Chinwe (2014). In order to determine the best-fit univariate GARCH family model, the AIC and SIC of the GARCH, GJR-GARCH and EGARCH models will be compared. The information criterion will also be used to compare models that include trading volume to the standard GARCH model specification. Finally, forecast performance metrics of the different models will be used to determine the most reliable forecasting model.

21.3 Methodology

21.3.1 Data Specification

In this study, daily high, low and closing prices of the TSX Composite Index (Canada), ASX 200 Index (Australia), Micex Index (Russia) and JSE All-Share Index (South Africa) are used. The data is for a time period of four years from January 2013 to December 2016. Index data is used, as this will give a better reflection of the market as a whole (Sreedharan 2004). The data was acquired from Thomson Reuters Datastream databank. In this chapter, only the closing prices and trading volume of the different indices will be analysed.

21.3.2 Volatility Modelling

In this subsection, the volatility models used to test the significance of new information are briefly discussed. When it comes to the topic of volatility modelling in finance, most financial researchers agree that the generalised autoregressive conditional heteroscedasticity (GARCH) model is the most widely used and accepted approach.

According to Francq and Zakoïan (2012), most GARCH models are formulated as follows:

$$r_t = \mu + \varepsilon_t \tag{21.1}$$

where r_t is the logarithmic return, μ is the conditional expectation of the returns, and ε_t is the error term ($\varepsilon_t \sim \mathcal{N}(0, \sigma_t^2)$). Different GARCH processes are assumed for σ_t^2. In this study, the analysis by Chen et al. (2001) is extended to include three different GARCH models: the symmetric GARCH model, the Glosten, Jagannathan and Runkle (GJR) GARCH model, and the exponential GARCH (EGARCH) model.

According to Asteriou and Hall (2015), the symmetric GARCH model is specified as follows:

$$\sigma_t^2 = \omega + \theta\varepsilon_{t-1}^2 + \varphi\sigma_{t-1}^2.$$

Table 21.1 GARCH models including trading volume

Model	Specification
GARCH	$\sigma_t^2 = \omega + \theta\varepsilon_{t-1}^2 + \varphi\sigma_{t-1}^2 + \chi V_t$
GJR-GARCH	$\sigma_t^2 = \omega + \theta\varepsilon_{t-1}^2 + \varphi\sigma_{t-1}^2 + \vartheta 1_{\{\varepsilon_t<0\}} + \chi V_t$
EGARCH	$\ln\sigma_t^2 = \omega + \theta\frac{\varepsilon_{t-1}}{\sigma_{t-1}} + \varphi\ln\sigma_t^2 + \vartheta\left\lvert\frac{\varepsilon_{t-1}}{\sigma_{t-1}}\right\rvert + \chi V_t$

When using the GJR-GARCH model, an additional term is included to capture the effect of positive and negative news (Alexander 2008). The conditional variance equation of the GJR-GARCH model is given by:

$$\sigma_t^2 = \omega + \theta\varepsilon_{t-1}^2 + \varphi\sigma_{t-1}^2 + \vartheta 1_{\{\varepsilon_t<0\}}.$$

Finally, Asteriou and Hall (2015) show that the variance equation of the EGARCH model is given by:

$$\ln\sigma_t^2 = \omega + \theta\frac{\varepsilon_{t-1}}{\sigma_{t-1}} + \varphi\ln\sigma_t^2 + \vartheta\left|\frac{\varepsilon_{t-1}}{\sigma_{t-1}}\right|.$$

In this study, by making use of a similar approach to Chen et al. (2001), conditional variance equations as specified above are slightly modified to include trading volume (V_t) as an explanatory variable, which is a proxy for new information. The variable V_t is defined as follows:

$$V_t = \frac{CV_t}{CV_{t-1}}$$

where CV_t is the closing volume traded on day t. This is consistent with Kalu and Chinwe (2014). This gives an indication of the significance of new information when modelling volatility. The variance equations are given in Table 21.1. The mean equation (21.1) remains the same.

The empirical results are presented in the next section.

21.4 Empirical Results

In this section, the different models that are used in this study will be discussed, and the empirical results will be interpreted. This section is divided into two subsections. Firstly, the preliminary data analysis is performed. Thereafter, volatility models, such as GARCH, GJR-GARCH and EGARCH, will be used to determine the significance of new information and volatility forecasting.

21.4.1 Preliminary Data Analysis

21.4.1.1 Equity Indices

In this section, the different stylised facts of financial time series will be formally tested and discussed. When modelling financial time series, Cont (2007) described the following stylised facts of financial time series which appear to often occur in different markets and instruments over a period of time:

1. Excess volatility, where volatility seems to fluctuate over time.
2. Fatter tails or leptokurtosis shown by the return series.
3. The return series shows no signs of autocorrelation.
4. Autocorrelation is present in the squared return series.
5. Volatility clustering, where big movements in the return series will be followed by big movements and small movements in the return series will be followed by small movements (Brooks 2014).
6. The conditional expectation of returns tends to be close to zero.

As shown by the line graphs, in Fig. 21.1, all the indices seem to exhibit trends. It can also be seen that both the Russian and South African indices have an upward trend.

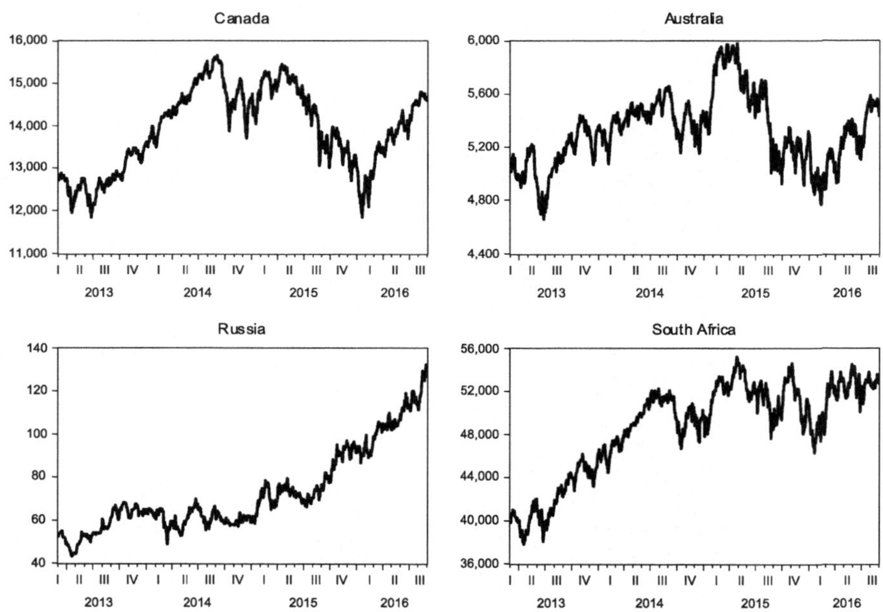

Fig. 21.1 Line graphs of logged closing prices. *Source* Thomson Reuters Datastream and Eview

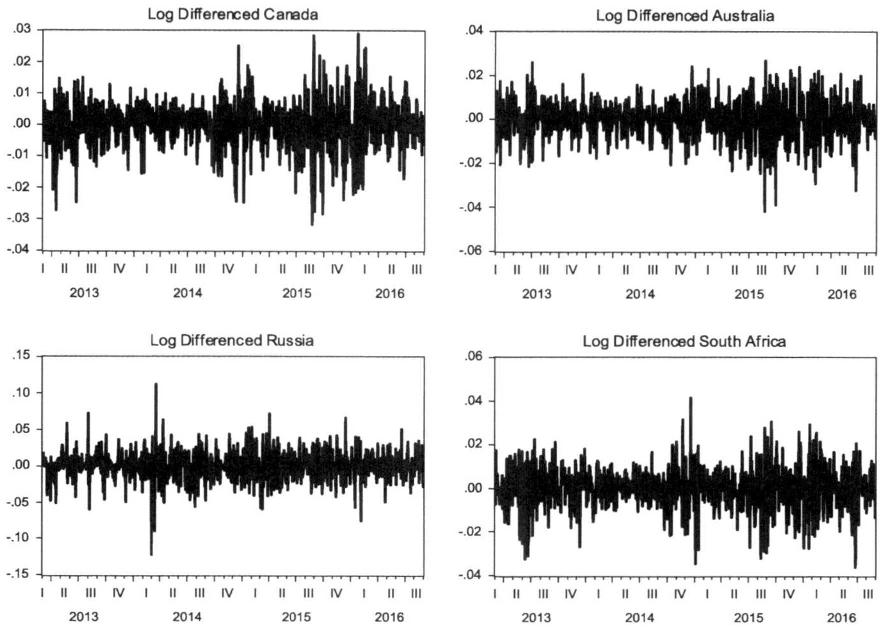

Fig. 21.2 Line graphs of log returns. *Source* Thomson Reuters Datastream and Eviews

The log returns depicted in Fig. 21.2 show that the indices appear to be mean reverting and that the mean is approximately equal to zero. In addition, there appear to be signs of volatility clustering during a number of periods. Volatility clustering is known to be a common occurrence in financial time series data. Gujarati (2003) described volatility clustering as periods where share prices or indices show extensive growth for a period of time which will then be followed by periods where the growth seems to decline or stagnate.

In this study, volatility clustering will be formally tested in the sections that follow. However, the presence of volatility clustering and the mean of each return series being approximately equal to zero are consistent with the stylised facts mentioned previously.

The histograms of the different indices are plotted below.

The histograms of the log returns of the indices in Fig. 21.3 show signs of fat tails when compared to the normal distribution. The normal distributions are indicated by the red bell curves, and it can, therefore, be seen that the log return series display higher peaks at the means. This is indicative of fat tails, also known as leptokurtosis. Danielsson (2011) explained that financial returns often show signs of leptokurtosis; this is also consistent with the stylised facts mentioned by Cont (2007).

According to Loy et al. (2016), a quantile-quantile plot also referred to as a QQ plot is another method of comparing the distribution to the normal distribution. This is also referred to as a normal probability plot. It shows how the data is distributed

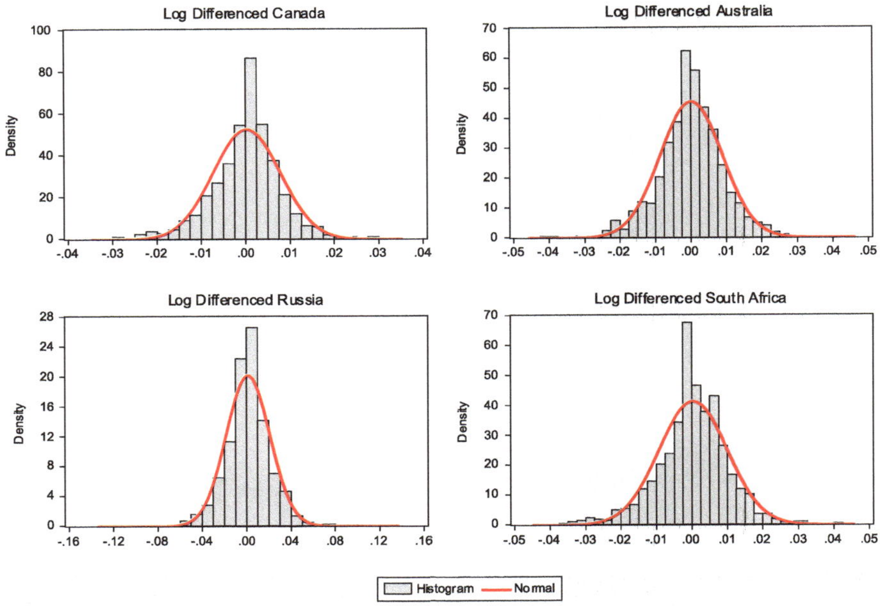

Fig. 21.3 Histograms of log returns. *Source* Thomson Reuters Datastream and Eviews

against the normal distribution. When data is normally distributed, most of the observations should lie on a straight line (Loy et al. 2016). For data which is non-normally distributed, the data points will deviate from the straight line, and there will also be some outliers in the data set (Loy et al. 2016).

The QQ plots in Fig. 21.4 show signs of non-normality as the data points deviate from the straight line. This confirms the results obtained in Fig. 21.3.

In order to summarise the statistical properties of the data set, descriptive statistics will be used. According to Wegner (2010), a data set of random variables can be explained by three characteristics. The first characteristic is measures of location, which includes the mean, median and mode. The second characteristic is measures of dispersion, which includes the variance and standard deviation of the data set and gives more information on how the data is distributed around the mean. The third characteristic is the measure of skewness which identifies the shape of the data around the mean and the kurtosis which measures the peak of how the data is distributed (Wegner 2010). The descriptive statistics for the data sets are summarised in Table 21.2.

From the descriptive statistics, Table 21.1, it can be observed that the means for the return series are all close to zero and the standard deviations of the return series are also close to zero. Small standard deviations indicate that data points are clustered close to the mean. The return series are negatively skewed, which show that the data values are clustered to the right of the mean (Kim 2013). The kurtosis values of

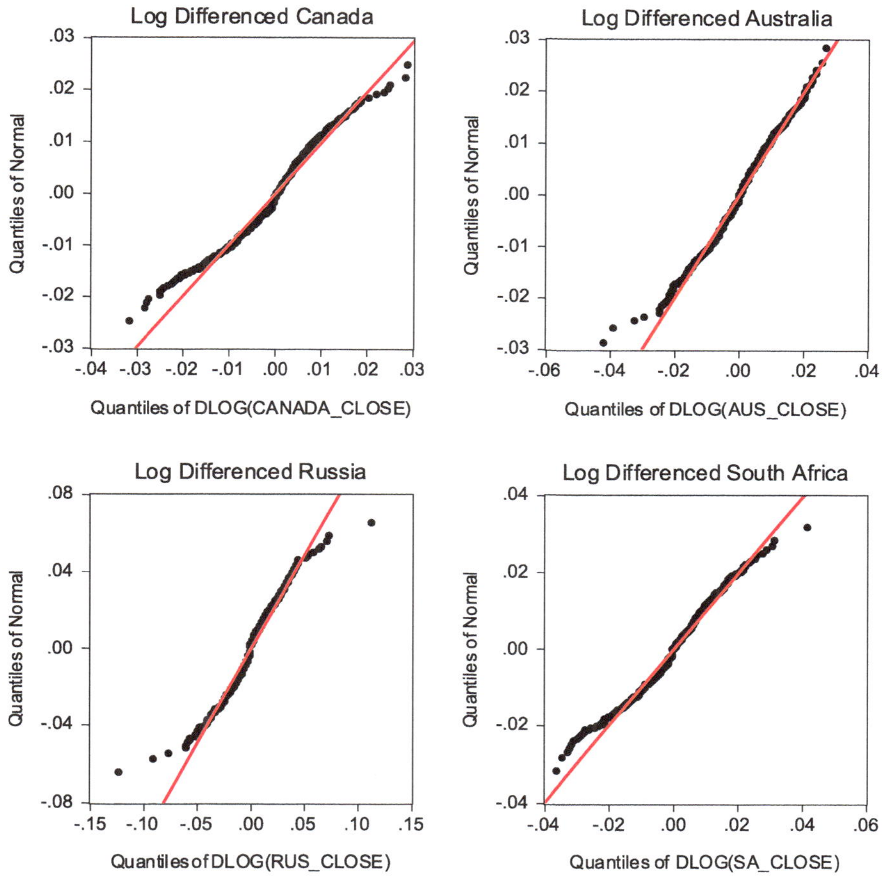

Fig. 21.4 QQ plots of log returns. *Source* Thomson Reuters Datastream and Eviews

the data series are all above three, indicating that the return series are leptokurtic and hence have high peaks at the mean. This confirms the results obtained from the graphical analysis. Finally, the Jarque–Bera test statistics show that the return series are not normally distributed, which confirms previous expectations.

Danielsson (2011) explained that return series do not show signs of autocorrelation. Gujarati (2003) defined autocorrelation as correlation which exists between a time series and previous lags of itself. According to Brooks (2014), autocorrelation represents the extent to which a given time series is similar to the lagged version of that time series. A positively correlated time series is said to be anticipated and probabilistic, because future prices are subject to present, as well as, historical prices (Brooks 2014).

The autocorrelation functions of the returns series are plotted in Fig. 21.5.

Table 21.2 Descriptive statistics (log returns)

	Canada	Australia	Russia	South Africa
Mean	0.0001	1.00E−04	0.001	0.0003
Median	0.0006	0.0003	0	0.0002
Maximum	0.029	0.0268	0.1124	0.0416
Minimum	−0.0317	−0.0418	−0.1227	−0.0362
Std. Dev.	0.0076	0.0088	0.0197	0.0097
Skewness	−0.3897	−0.3066	−0.1995	−0.2931
Kurtosis	4.864	4.3025	6.774	4.4094
Jarque–Bera	155.2925	78.843	547.8845	88.6378
Probability	0	0	0	0
Sum	0.1335	0.066	0.8839	0.273
Sum Sq. Dev.	0.0525	0.0703	0.3557	0.0849
Observations	913	913	913	913

Source Thomson Reuters Datastream and Eviews

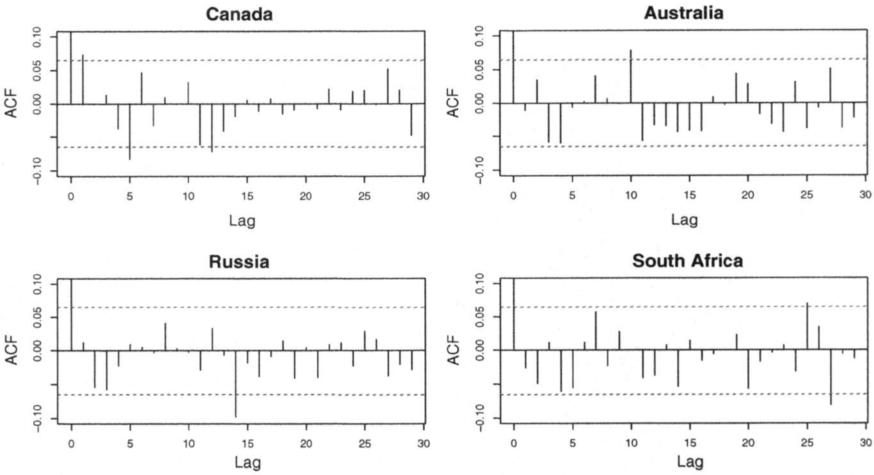

Fig. 21.5 Autocorrelation functions of log returns. *Source* Thomson Reuters Datastream and R

There does not seem to be any significant signs of autocorrelation. Therefore, the data looks stationary. However visual methods can be subjective and, therefore, formal tests, such as the Augmented Dickey–Fuller (ADF) and Phillips–Perron (PP) unit root tests are performed.

The ADF and PP tests are used to determine whether a unit root is present in the logged index, as the order of integration is important when a regression analysis is performed (Lütkepohl et al. 2004). According to Tsay (2005), stationarity is the basis of time series data. Most time series data is assumed to be stationary. A stationary

Table 21.3 Augmented Dickey–Fuller test

	Canada	Australia	Russia	South Africa
Intercept (level)	−1.7462	−2.6853	0.3427	−2.0923
Trend and intercept (level)	−1.7502	−2.7009	−1.7819	−2.8916
Intercept (1st dif)	−27.9001*	−30.3513*	−30.4792*	−30.6669*
Trend and intercept (1st dif)	−27.8872*	−30.3364*	−30.5232*	−30.6616*

*Indicates significance at a 1% level
Source Thomson Reuters Datastream and Eviews

Table 21.4 Phillips–Perron test

	Canada	Australia	Russia	South Africa
Intercept (level)	−1.8400	−2.6336	0.7229	−1.9861
Trend and intercept (level)	−1.8536	−2.6493	−1.5069	−2.7246
Intercept (1st dif)	−27.8547*	−30.3735*	−30.7098*	−30.9091*
Trend and intercept (1st dif)	−27.8413*	−30.3581*	−30.8535*	−30.9117*

*Indicates significance at a 1% level
Source Thomson Reuters Datastream and Eviews

process can be defined as a process where the mean, variance and autocorrelation properties do not vary over time (Asteriou and Hall 2015).

The results are reported in Tables 21.3 and 21.4.

The results obtained for the ADF and PP tests above, Tables 21.2 and 21.3 respectively, show that when an intercept is included, all the variables are non-stationary at level. However, when the variables are differenced once, they are stationary at a one per cent level of significance.

21.4.1.2 Trading Volume

In Fig. 21.6, the trading volume for each country is represented.

Figure 21.6 shows that the trading volume for each country appears to revert to a long-term mean. The volatilities of the volume series appear to show signs of clustering. The histograms of trading volume for each country are specified and are illustrated in Fig. 21.7.

Trading volume series of the CARS countries have fat tails when compared with their normal distributions. This indicates that trading volume is highly peaked around the means and not normally distributed.

Next, the autocorrelation functions of trading volume for each country are shown in Fig. 21.8.

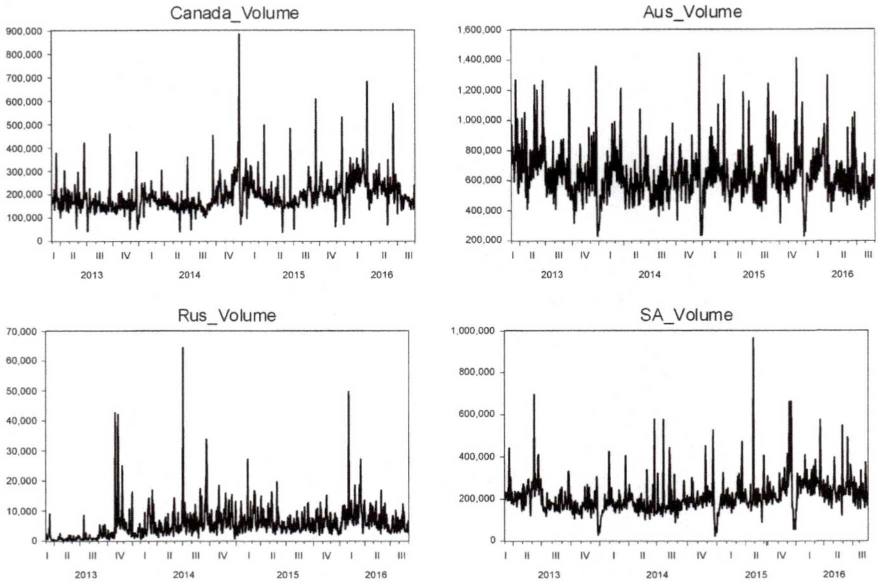

Fig. 21.6 Line graphs of trading volume. *Source* Thomson Reuters Datastream and Eviews

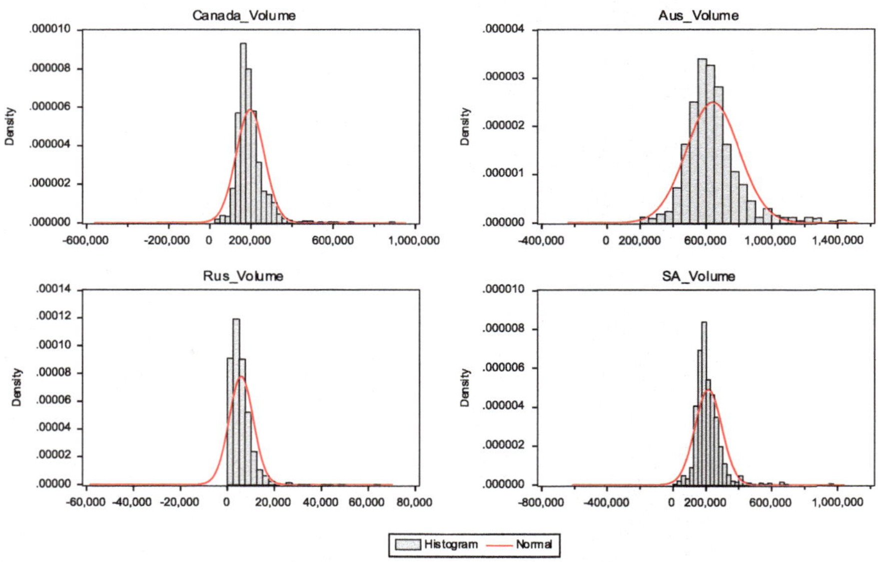

Fig. 21.7 Histograms of trading volume. *Source* Thomson Reuters Datastream and Eviews

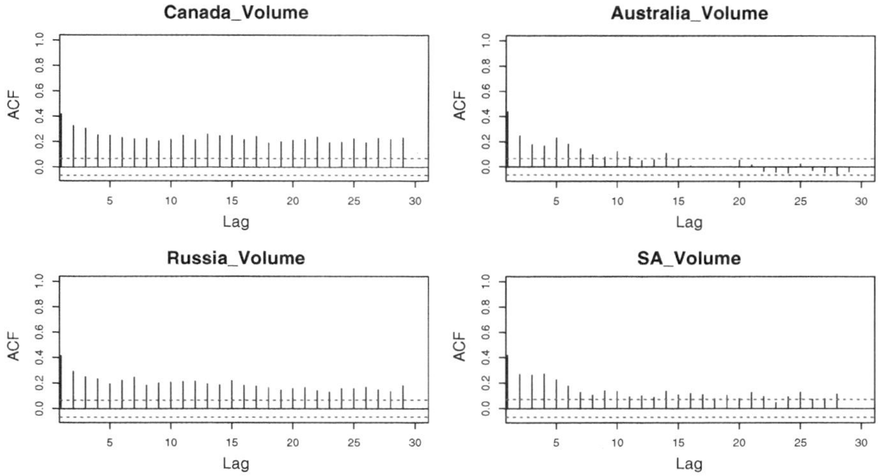

Fig. 21.8 Autocorrelation functions of trading volume. *Source* Thomson Reuters Datastream and R

Table 21.5 Augmented Dickey–Fuller test (trading volume)

	Canada	Australia	Russia	South Africa
Intercept (level)	−18.6181*	−8.1146*	−11.6345*	−19.0265*
Trend and intercept (level)	−20.1158*	−8.2086*	−20.1576*	−19.8832*

*Indicates significance at a 1% level
Source Thomson Reuters Datastream and Eviews

Table 21.6 Phillips–Perron test (trading volume)

	Canada	Australia	Russia	South Africa
Intercept (level)	−24.0316*	−20.9750*	−22.1451*	−21.1375*
Trend and intercept (level)	−24.0257*	−20.9764*	−21.7608*	−21.2047*

*Indicates significance at a 1% level
Source Thomson Reuters Datastream and Eviews

It does not appear that significant signs of autocorrelation are present. However, as mentioned previously, visual techniques are subjective and formal tests, such as the ADF and PP tests will be performed to determine whether trading volume is stationary.

In Tables 21.5 and 21.6, ADF and PP tests were used to determine whether trading volume is stationary and whether there is unit root present.

The results above indicate that trading volume of all countries is stationary at the 1% level of significance when both the ADF and PP test are considered.

21.4.2 Volatility Modelling

In this section, by making use of an approach similar to Chen et al. (2001) and Kalu and Chinwe (2014), different univariate GARCH models are applied to the CARS countries to determine the best fitting model based on different information criteria. In addition, the forecasting performance of the models is compared to models which include trading volume. This is based on the work by Chen et al. (2001).

21.4.3 GARCH Parameters

Asteriou and Hall (2015) explained that in order to fit univariate GARCH parameters, it is necessary to determine whether ARCH effects (volatility clustering) are present. The ARCH Lagrange multiplier (LM) test is reported in Table 21.7.

The ARCH LM test indicates that ARCH effects are present for all the variables considered, except Russia. Therefore, Russia is excluded from the analysis that follows. The GARCH parameters are reported in Table 21.8.

According to Alexander (2008), if the θ parameter in the GARCH(1,1) model is relatively large (i.e greater than 0.1), then it implies that the market is sensitive to market shocks. This is the case for Canada. Furthermore, the coefficient of the lagged volatility (φ) is a measure of volatility persistence (Alexander 2008). This

Table 21.7 ARCH LM test

Country	F-statistic	Obs*R-squared
Canada	29.5061**	28.6098**
Australia	33.6958***	32.5307***
Russia	0.0408	0.0409
SA	4.4609***	4.4466***

*(**) [***]: Statistically significant at a 10(5)[1]% level
Source Thomson Reuters Datastream and Eviews

Table 21.8 GARCH(1,1) parameters

	Canada	Australia	South Africa
μ	0.0003	0.0001	0.0006*
ω	2.35E−06***	1.41E−06***	2.80E−06***
θ	0.1354***	0.0581***	0.0855***
φ	0.8258***	0.9233***	0.8883***
AIC	−7.0894	−6.6877	−6.4913
SIC	−7.0677	−6.666	−6.4671

*(**) [***]: Statistically significant at a 10(5)[1]% level
Source Thomson Reuters Datastream and Eviews

Table 21.9 GJR-GARCH(1,1) parameters

	Canada	Australia	South Africa
μ	0.0001	0	0.0001
ω	1.21E−06***	1.42E−06***	3.61E−06***
θ	−0.0399***	−0.0124	−0.0117
φ	0.9215***	0.9381***	0.8771***
ϑ	0.1777***	0.1075***	0.1958***
AIC	−7.0894	−6.6877	−6.4913
SIC	−7.0677	−6.666	−6.4671

*(**) [***]: Statistically significant at a 10(5)[1]% level
Source Thomson Reuters Datastream and Eviews

Table 21.10 EGARCH(1,1) parameters

	Canada	Australia	South Africa
μ	0.0001	−0.0001	−0.0005***
ω	−0.1995	−0.1643	−0.1157
θ	0.0081	0.0456***	−0.0319***
φ	0.9807***	0.9866***	0.9839***
ϑ	−0.142***	−0.1107***	−0.1261***
AIC	−7.1609	−6.7468	−6.568
SIC	−7.1337	−6.7198	−6.5378

*(**) [***]: Statistically significant at a 10(5)[1]% level
Source: Thomson Reuters Datastream and Eviews

suggests that shocks to the Australian market will take a long time to die out. The GJR-GARCH parameters are reported in Table 21.9.

As explained in Chapter Two, the GJR-GARCH model modifies the symmetric GARCH model by including an indicator function (dummy variable) to capture the effect of bad news. According to Asteriou and Hall (2015), if the coefficient of the dummy variable (ϑ) is positive, it implies that bad news will lead to a greater rise in volatility when compared to good news; this is also known as the leverage effect. The ϑ coefficient is positive and statistically significant at a 1% level for all the countries considered. The EGARCH parameters are illustrated in Table 21.10.

Alexander (2008) explained that the EGARCH model was introduced to address the non-negativity constraints imposed on univariate GARCH models. Therefore, the natural logarithm of the conditional variance is the dependent variable, which ensures that the conditional variance is always positive. Furthermore, according to Brooks (2014), if ϑ in the EGARCH model is negative, and statistically significant, it indicates signs of the leverage effect. This is the case for the three markets considered (at a 1% level of significance).

According to Brooks (2014), information criteria can be used to determine the best-fitting model. The best-fitting model is the one which minimises the information criteria. In this case, the AIC and SIC indicate that the EGARCH model is the best

Table 21.11 GARCH(1,1) parameters (including trading volume)

	Canada	Australia	South Africa
μ	0.0005**	0.0007***	0.0007**
ω	9.34E−06	6.82E−06	0.00000318
θ	0.2445***	0.2038***	0.0829***
φ	0.5999***	0.7173***	0.8836***
χ	2.61E−05***	6.69E−058**	0.0000473***
AIC	−7.1175	−6.7449	−6.5242
SIC	−7.0903	−6.7179	−6.494

*(**) [***]: Statistically significant at a 10(5)[1]% level
Source Thomson Reuters Datastream and Eviews

Table 21.12 GJR-GARCH(1,1) parameters (including trading volume)

	Canada	Australia	South Africa
μ	0.0004*	0	0.0002
ω	1.55E−06***	1.33E−06***	3.55E−06***
θ	−0.0297***	0.0157	0.0054
φ	0.9064***	0.9234***	0.8716***
ϑ	0.1552***	0.0797***	0.1671***
χ	0.0000199	4.61E−05	4.78E−05
AIC	−7.182	−6.7539	−6.5597
SIC	−7.1494	−6.7214	−6.5234

*(**) [***]: Statistically significant at a 10(5)[1]% level
Source: Thomson Reuters Datastream and Eviews

Table 21.13 EGARCH(1,1) parameters (including trading volume)

	Canada	Australia	South Africa
μ	0	0.0003***	0
ω	−0.13563	0.100344	−0.12129
θ	−0.0354***	0.9922***	0.0037
φ	0.9838***	0	0.9873***
ϑ	−0.1126***	1.5689***	−0.1304***
χ	1.5757***	−0.0006***	0.6773***
AIC	−7.257	−6.7594	−6.5882
SIC	−7.2244	0	−6.5519

*(**) [***]: Statistically significant at a 10(5)[1]% level
Source: Thomson Reuters Datastream and Eviews

fit. Tables 21.11, 21.12 and 21.13 illustrate the univariate GARCH parameters when trading volume is included as a variance regressor.

The estimated parameters show that there is a statistically significant (at a 1% level) positive relationship between the conditional volatility and trading volume, which is consistent with the findings by Kalu and Chinwe (2014) and Chen et al.

(2001). Furthermore, when the information criteria of the models which include trading volume are considered, the EGARCH model is the best fit. Finally, when the AIC and SIC of all the models (including and excluding trading volume) are compared, the AIC and SIC show that the EGARCH model which includes trading volume is the best fit.

21.4.4 Forecasting Performance

The forecasting performance metrics are reported in Tables 21.14 and 21.15.

The forecast performance metrics show that the symmetric GARCH model is the most reliable when trading volume is not included as a variance regressor. Moreover, when trading volume is included as a variance regressor, the asymmetric models (GJR-GARCH and EGARCH models) outperform the symmetric GARCH model in most cases. Finally, when the RMSE and MAE of the models which include trading volume are compared to the standard GARCH models, the models which include trading volume are more reliable. This suggests that new information (trading volume) does improve forward-looking estimates of volatility. There is not a significant difference in terms of the effect of new information in volatility modelling when developed and emerging markets are considered.

Table 21.14 GARCH forecasting performance

	GARCH		GJR-GARCH		EGARCH	
	RMSE	MAE	RMSE	MAE	RMSE	MAE
Canada	0.00773	0.005644*	0.00773	0.00567	0.007725*	0.00566
Australia	0.008916*	0.006738*	0.00892	0.00675	0.00892	0.00675
South Africa	0.009836*	0.007294*	0.00984	0.00731	0.00987	0.00737

*Denotes the best performing model according to the RMSE or MAE
Source Thomson Reuters Datastream and Eviews

Table 21.15 GARCH forecasting performance (including trading volume)

	GARCH		GJR-GARCH		EGARCH	
	RMSE	MAE	RMSE	MAE	RMSE	MAE
Canada	0.00773	0.00564	0.00773	0.00564	0.007725*	0.005649*
Australia	0.00894	0.00673	0.008916*	0.00674	0.00892	0.006733*
South Africa	0.00984	0.007293*	0.009835*	0.00731	0.00984	0.00731

*Denotes the best performing model according to the RMSE or MAE
Source Thomson Reuters Datastream and Eviews

21.5 Conclusion

In this study, the effect and significance of new information on the volatility of different markets (developed vs. emerging) were analysed. The effect of new information on volatility was tested in a GARCH framework. A similar approach to Chen et al. (2001) was used in this study. GARCH models which included trading volume as an explanatory variable, which is a proxy of information flow, were used to forecast volatility. This gave an indication of whether trading volume (flow of information) is significant when forecasting volatility.

In this study, the work by Chen et al. (2001) was extended by making use of GARCH, EGARCH and GJR-GARCH models. These models were applied to determine whether the forecasting ability of the model would improve when trading volume was included. The volatility modelling in this study was based on similar studies by Chen et al. (2001), and Kalu and Chinwe (2014). The AIC and SIC of the GARCH, GJR-GARCH and EGARCH models were compared to determine the best-fitting univariate GARCH family model. The information criterion was also used to compare models which included trading volume to the standard GARCH model specification. Finally, forecast performance metrics of the different models were used to determine the most reliable forecasting model.

The ARCH LM test indicated that ARCH effects were present for all the variables considered, except Russia. Therefore, Russia was excluded from the analysis that followed. According to Alexander (2008), if the θ parameter in the GARCH(1,1) model is relatively large (i.e greater than 0.1), then it implies that the market is sensitive to market shocks. This was the case for Canada. Furthermore, the coefficient of the lagged volatility φ is a measure of volatility persistence (Alexander 2008). This suggested that shocks to the Australian market would take a long time to die out.

According to Asteriou and Hall (2015), if the coefficient of the dummy variable (λ) is positive, it implies that bad news will lead to a greater rise in volatility when compared to good news; this is also known as the leverage effect. The ϑ coefficient was positive and statistically significant at a one per cent level for all the countries when a GJR-GARCH model was considered. According to Brooks (2014), if ϑ in the EGARCH model is negative and statistically significant, it, therefore, indicated signs of the leverage effect. This was the case for the three markets considered (at a 1% level of significance).

According to Brooks (2014), information criteria can be used to determine the best-fitting model. The best-fitting model is the one which minimises the information criteria. In this case, the AIC and SIC indicated that the EGARCH model was the best fit.

When trading volume was included as a variance regressor, the estimated parameters showed that there was a statistically significant (at a 1% level) positive relationship between the conditional volatility and trading volume. This was consistent with the findings by Kalu and Chinwe (2014) and Chen et al. (2001). Furthermore, when the information criteria of the models which included trading volume were considered, the EGARCH model was the best fit. Finally, when the AIC and SIC of all the models (including and excluding trading volume) were compared, the AIC and SIC showed that the EGARCH model which included trading volume was the best fit.

The forecast performance metrics showed that the symmetric GARCH model was the most reliable when trading volume was not included as a variance regressor. Moreover, when trading volume was included as a variance regressor, the asymmetric models (GJR-GARCH and EGARCH models) outperformed the symmetric GARCH model in most cases. Finally, when the RMSE and MAE of the models which included trading volume were compared to the standard GARCH models, the models which included trading volume were more reliable. This indicated that new information (trading volume) does improve forward-looking estimates of volatility.

A shortcoming of this study was that only four countries were used to compare developed and emerging markets. However, the focus was on commodity exporting countries. Therefore, an area for future research might involve a similar analysis based on greater variety equity indices. Furthermore, the spillover of shocks in the commodity markets to equity markets should also be considered.

References

Alexander, C. (2008). *Practical financial econometrics*. Chichester: Wiley.

Asteriou, D., & Hall, S. G. (2015). *Applied econometrics*. Macmillan International Higher Education.

Aydemir, A. B. (2002). Volatility modelling in finance. *Forecasting Volatility in the Financial Markets, 1*.

Bailey, R. E. (2005). *The economics of financial markets*. New York: Cambridge University Press.

Bodie, Z., Kane, A., & Marcus, A. J. (2010). *Essentials of investments* (9th ed.). New York: McGraw-Hill.

Brooks, C. (2014). *Introductory econometrics for finance*. Cambridge, MA: Cambridge University Press.

Caporin, M., Ranaldo, A., & De Magistris, P. S. (2013). On the predictability of stock prices: A case for high and low prices. *Journal of Banking & Finance, 37*(12), 5132–5146.

Chen, G. M., Firth, M., & Rui, O. M. (2001). The dynamic relation between stock returns, trading volume, and volatility. *Financial Review, 36*(3), 153–174.

Cont, R. (2007). Volatility clustering in financial markets: Empirical facts and agent-based models. In *Long memory in economics* (pp. 289–309). Berlin, Heidelberg: Springer.

Danielsson, J. (2011). *Financial risk forecasting: The theory and practice of forecasting market risk with implementation in R and Matlab*. Hoboken: Wiley.

Engle, R. (2001). GARCH 101: The use of ARCH/GARCH models in applied econometrics. *Journal of Economic Perspectives, 15*(4), 157–168.

Francq, C., & Zakoïan, J. M. (2012). Strict stationarity testing and estimation of explosive and stationary generalized autoregressive conditional heteroscedasticity models. *Econometrica, 80*(2), 821–861.

Gujarati, D. N. (2003). *Basic econometrics*. New York: McGraw-Hill.

Kalu, E. O., & Chinwe, O. C. (2014). The relationship between stock returns volatility and trading volume in Nigeria. *Business Systems & Economics, 4*(2), 115–125.

Kim, H. Y. (2013). Statistical notes for clinical researchers: Assessing normal distribution (2) using skewness and kurtosis. *Restorative Dentistry & Endodontics, 38*(1), 52–54.

Koop, G. M. (2005). *Analysis of financial data*. London: Wiley.
Labuschagne, C. C., Oberholzer, N., & Venter, P. J. (2017a, July). A mean-variance analysis of the global minimum variance portfolio constructed using the CARBS indices.In *International Conference on Applied Economics* (pp. 55–68). Cham: Springer.
Labuschagne, C. C., Oberholzer, N., & Venter, P. J. (2017b, July). Value-at-risk forecasting of the CARBS Indices. In *International Conference on Applied Economics* (pp. 85–94). Cham: Springer.
Labuschagne, C. C., Oberholzer, N., & Venter, P. J. (2017c, July). Univariate and multivariate GARCH models applied to the CARBS indices. In *International Conference on Applied Economics* (pp. 69–83). Cham: Springer.
Lo, A., & MacKinlay, A. (1988). Stock market prices do not follow random walks: Evidence from a simple specification test. *The Review of Financial Studies, 1*, 41–66.
Loy, A., Follett, L., & Hofmann, H. (2016). Variations of Q-Q Plots: The Power of Our Eyes!. *The American Statistician, 70*(2), 202–214.
Lütkepohl, H., Krätzig, M., & Phillips, P. C. (Eds.). (2004). *Applied time series econometrics*. Cambridge University Press.
Marcucci, J. (2005). Forecasting stock market volatility with regime-switching GARCH models. *Studies in Nonlinear Dynamics & Econometrics, 9*(4).
Mohr, P. (2016). *Economic indicators*. Pretoria: Unisa Press.
Oberholzer, N., & Venter, P. (2015). Univariate GARCH models applied to the JSE/FTSE stock indices. *Procedia Economics and Finance, 24*, 491–500.
Oberholzer, N., & von Boetticher, S. T. (2015). Volatility spill-over between the JSE/FTSE indices and the South African Rand. *Procedia Economics and Finance, 24*, 501–510.
Peters, J. P. (2001). *Estimating and forecasting volatility of stock indices using asymmetric GARCH models and (Skewed) Student-t densities* (Vol. 3, pp. 19–34.). Preprint, University of Liege, Belgium.
Reilly, F. K., & Brown, K. C. (2006). *Investment analysis and portfolio management*. New York: South-Western Cengage Learning.
Sabiruzzaman, M., Huq, M. M., Beg, R. A., & Anwar, S. (2010). Modeling and forecasting trading volume index: GARCH versus TGARCH approach. *The Quarterly Review of Economics and Finance, 50*(2), 141–145.
Samuelson, P. A. (1965). Proof that properly anticipated prices fluctuate randomly. *IMR; Industrial Management Review (pre-1986), 6*(2), 41–49.
Sreedharan, N. J. (2004). *A vector error correction model (VECM) of stockmarket returns*. Hobart: University of Tasmania.
Tsay, R. S. (2005). *Analysis of financial time series*. Hoboken, NJ: Wiley.
Wegner, T. (2010). *Applied business statistics: Methods and excel-based applications*. Cape Town: Juta and Company Ltd.

Chapter 22
Relationship Between Competitive Strategies of Small and Medium-Sized Polish International New Ventures and Their Market Performance: Cluster Analysis Approach

Tomasz Sikora and Ewa Baranowska-Prokop

Abstract The main goal of this paper is to analyze the relationship between competitive strategies and market performance for Polish small and medium-sized international new ventures (INVs). Three dimensions used for classification of strategies are: standardization–adaptation of products, differentiated versus nondifferentiated products and selling products to the whole market, to selected segments, or to a niche only. The applied research method is statistical analysis (SPSS) of data obtained from questionnaire distributed in 2018 (mixed mode: CATI + CAWI method) to respondents from representative sample of 297 Polish INVs. The relationship between variables related to strategies and market performance measures shows weak correlations in line with the hypotheses: positive correlations with increasing adaptation, positive correlations with increasing differentiation, positive correlations with broadening vision of the market. Cluster analysis made it possible to identify a disadvantageous mix of strategies: The strongest product standardization combined with the weakest product differentiation together with addressing commercial efforts to niche markets led to the lowest results on all market performance measures. A non-segmentation approach led to the best results in 3 out of 4 market performance measures.

Keywords International new ventures · Strategy · Market performance

JEL Codes L11 · L14 · L17

T. Sikora (✉) · E. Baranowska-Prokop
Institute of International Management and Marketing, Warsaw School of Economics, Al. Niepodległości 162, 02-554 Warsaw, Poland
e-mail: tomasz.sikora@sgh.waw.pl

E. Baranowska-Prokop
e-mail: ebarano@sgh.waw.pl

N. Tsounis and A. Vlachvei (eds.), *Advances in Cross-Section Data Methods in Applied Economic Research*, Springer Proceedings in Business and Economics,
https://doi.org/10.1007/978-3-030-38253-7_22

22.1 Introduction

Internationalization of the firm in turbulent era of globalization is complex in its character. Research on this phenomenon requires provision for a number of variables explaining its specificity and nature. In the traditional models, the firm is perceived as an autonomous entity and the analysis is concentrated on its inner resources: size, knowledge, managerial skills, urge for internationalization, financial assets, etc. The more modern approach tends to concentrate on inter-organizational network and it emphasizes the search for relations in business network system. In the present article, we are taking the first approach, i.e., traditional division into small and medium-sized companies. We investigate their approach to applied competitive strategies and achieved financial results as well as other results (e.g., export sales dynamics and self-assessed market success).

According to literature review findings, in case of INVs—the strategic choice is bipolar in its character. Gassmann and Keupp (2007) indicated that early internationalizing firms should rather concentrate on homogeneous offers, and also Gabrielsson et al. (2012) suggested standardized strategies. Following Madsen and Servais (1997) recommendations, the other strategic choice is strong adaptation and adjustment to specific customer requirements. The basic strategic dilemma in international markets operations, i.e., standardization versus adaptation, is also crucial for INV's market strategy. It should also be stressed that scope and character of standardization is changing along with growing scope and scale of firms' activities (Gabrielsson 2005). Moreover, Knight and Cavusgil (2005) have proved that consistent implementation of adopted competitive strategy is a decisive factor for market success.

The research on Polish INVs is dated back to late 1990s, e.g., Nowakowski (1999), Gorynia (2007), Duliniec (2011), Kowalik and Baranowska-Prokop (2013), Baranowska-Prokop and Sikora (2014), Danik and Kowalik (2015). It has focused on various strategic and functional aspects of their operation. Sikora and Baranowska-Prokop (2018) proved the lack of coherent pattern of correlations between the degree of internationalization measured by simple indices (number of foreign markets, foreign market entry strategy, competences in doing business internationally, etc.) and success perceived by Polish INV's managerial staff. The only positive relationship (in two out of three samples) has been observed for "international competences of executive board" and success in foreign markets. This observation led the authors to further investigate the relationship between financial results and competitive strategies in aspects other than international orientation.

22.2 Research Method

This research has been based on a survey conducted in January–February 2018 with respondents from a sample of 297 Polish INVs. Applied method was (CATI and CAWI or mixed mode interview) targeted at the managerial staff of manufacturing enterprises employing 10–49 and 50–249 people (i.e., small and medium-sized enterprises). The sample was selected by a random stratified statistical sampling method allowing for generalization. The analysis included only the firms that started international activities after 1997 and within three years of their inception achieved the level of at least 25% of revenues coming from the exports. They came into being not a result of two firms' merger or as a foreign enterprise subsidiary.

The sampling base or gross sample (8750 firms) was the Central Statistical Office (GUS) database. The small enterprises accounted for 49.2% of the sample ($N = 146$) and the medium-sized ones—for 50.8% ($N = 151$). Response rate was relatively high—78.4%.

22.3 Research Hypotheses

As a result of literature review (e.g., Doole and Lowe 2001) and previous research the following hypothesis has been formulated:

H1: There is a positive relationship between the degree of product adaptation (to the needs of local customers) and the market performance of enterprises.

The second dimension of strategic choice is product differentiation (i.e., positive images for brands and products, better than those of competitors and not easily substitutable).

It was Porter (1998) who extensively presented the advantages of product and brand differentiation and warned about the danger of "strategic clutter".

Apart from differentiation, another viable strategic option was cost and price leadership, but this aspect has not been analyzed in this study, and we concentrate on the managerial decision regarding the extent of product differentiation.

Following Porter's recommendations concerning market-winning strategies and the benefits of differentiation we may formulate the following hypothesis:

H2. There is a positive relationship between the degree of product differentiation and the market performance of enterprises.

The third dimension of strategic choice is the segmentation of the market.

The segmentation strategy requires selection of one of the three options:

natural segmentation (the whole market is considered as the target and no specific actions or modifications of products, prices, promotion or distribution strategies are taken related to any specific group of customers),
proper segmentation (selecting several segments of customers and adapting marketing actions concerning products, prices, promotion and/or distribution to specific needs of customers within chosen segments),
niche strategy (selecting one segment of customers and concentrating all efforts to satisfy their requirements).

Not having data about specificity of particular markets and the degree of heterogeneity of customer's preferences nor detailed information about the resources of companies in our sample (besides the number of employees) we prefer to formulate the following non-directional hypothesis:

H3: There is a significant relationship between the choice of segmentation strategy and market performance of enterprises.

22.4 Interpretation of the Results

The three independent variables reflecting companies' strategic choices (or dimensions) are:

- selling standardized products versus products adapted to specific needs of particular clients,
- selling differentiated versus nondifferentiated products,
- not segmenting (natural segmentation, i.e., considering the whole market as a target) or segmenting the market with two options taken into account, i.e., selling products to several selected segments of customers and finally, selling products to one segment of customers (or to a market niche).

The standardization–adaptation and differentiation–nondifferentiation variables have been measured on 5-point Likert-type scales with the values from 1 to 5. The variable reflecting various segmentation options has been measured as a 3-point ordinal variable with the values increasing in the direction of broader vision of the target market (1—niche, 2—several selected segments and 3—the whole market as target.

The distribution of the strategic choice variables is presented in Tables 22.1, 22.2, 22.3.

The large majority of respondents declared that at least half of their product range was adapted to the needs of local customers.

Table 22.1 Export product strategy: standardization versus adaptation

	Frequency	Percent
The whole range of products is standardized (1)	46	15.5
Most of the product range is standardized	51	17.2
Half standardized–half adapted	72	24.2
Most of the product range is adapted	73	24.6
The whole range of products is adapted (5)	55	18.5
Total	297	100.0

Source Own elaboration

Table 22.2 Export strategy: products differentiated versus nondifferentiated

	Frequency	Percent
The whole range of products is undifferentiated (1)	46	15.5
Most of the product range is undifferentiated	87	29.3
Half undifferentiated–half differentiated	99	33.3
Most of the product range is differentiated	57	19.2
The whole range of products is differentiated (5)	8	2.7
Total	297	100.0

Source Own elaboration

Table 22.3 Segmentation strategy: the whole market, selected segments, niche

	Frequency	Percent
Niche	73	24.6
Selected segments	114	38.4
The whole market	110	37.0
Total	297	100.0

Source Own elaboration

The percentages for differentiation are visibly smaller than for the adaptation. If adaptation is required on given markets, firms which adapt their products, but do not have very strong images and brands, appear as nondifferentiated in the crowd of similar products. Respondents from some companies also declared that only a part of their product range was sold under their own brands. The remaining part was sold either under their clients' brands or as "anonymous" products. Therefore, sticking a label with customer's brand is considered to be product adaptation, and not differentiation. That is an explanation for partial product differentiation within a given company and for the lower percentages related to product differentiation than to adaptation. And inversely, products may be differentiated, but not adapted to specific local markets, e.g., evergreen products of strong brands may have the same composition and appearance worldwide.

The niche strategy was the least popular one. The strategies of segmenting the market and of not segmenting (natural segmentation) appear as almost equally popular.

Analysis of relationships between the size of enterprises and the three above-presented strategies reveals that there are no significant differences, i.e., each type of strategy enjoys similar popularity regardless of the fact that the firms are small or medium-sized ones. For segmentation strategy, it may be somewhat surprising, because—logically—niche strategy seems better adapted to smaller firms than to the bigger ones and the former should be over-represented in this group, what was not the case. Correlations between internationalization indices (share of exports in total sales, number of export markets, etc.) and the three analyzed strategic dimensions are also not significant.

As far as the relationship between the three strategies is concerned, the strategy of adaptation is moderately correlated with the strategy of differentiation (Kendall's tau-b = 0.4; $p < 0.0001$). The scope of segmentation is uncorrelated with differentiation and very weakly correlated with adaptation (Kendall's tau-b = 0.11; $p =$ 0.024).

The dependent variables reflect companies' market success. Since it is difficult to obtain precise figures about profits and profit-dependent indices, descriptive questions about market performance and achieved success had to be applied.

Distribution of the dependent variables is shown in Tables 22.4, 22.5, 22.6, 22.7.

Declaration about financial results (Table 22.4) was measured on a 5-point Likert-type scale with values from 1 (substantial financial loss) to 5 (substantial profit).

No respondents declared heavy losses and most of firms have been "moderately" profitable.

Export sales dynamics has also been measured on a 5-point Likert-type scale with values from 1 to 5.

Most of respondents declared an increase in export sales from a year earlier by one-digit per cent figure. Similarly, coded data for export sales dynamics concerning previous years are not presented here, but have been used for a composite measure of three-year export performance.

A composite measure of export sales performance has been elaborated as follows: Respondents' declarations about export dynamics for 3 periods between 2014

Table 22.4 Profit/loss declarations for 2017 compared to 2016

		Frequency	Percent	Valid percent
Valid	Small loss (2)	4	1.3	1.4
	Result close to zero	21	7.1	7.5
	Small profit	221	74.4	78.9
	Substantial profit (5)	34	11.4	12.1
	Total	280	94.3	100.0
Missing	System	17	5.7	
Total		297	100.0	

Source Own elaboration

Table 22.5 Export sales dynamics in 2017 compared to 2016

	Frequency	Percent
Substantial decrease (by 2-digit %) (1)	2	0.7
Decrease (by 1-digit %)	6	2.0
No change	56	18.9
Increase (by 1-digit %)	217	73.1
Substantial increase (by 2-digit %) (5)	16	5.4
Total	297	100.0

Source Own elaboration

Table 22.6 Three-year export sales evolution (2014–2017)

		Frequency	Percent
Valid	7	1	0.3
	8	5	1.7
	9	24	8.1
	10	27	9.1
	11	42	14.1
	12	180	60.6
	13	9	3.0
	14	6	2.0
	15	3	1.0
	Total	297	100.0

Source Own elaboration

Table 22.7 Perceived success compared to competitors

	Frequency	Percent
Rather not (2)	21	7.1
Comparably	103	34.7
Rather yes	140	47.1
Absolutely yes (5)	33	11.1
Total	297	100.0

Source Own elaboration

and 2017 were aggregated in the way that companies declaring 3 strong consecutive contractions of export sales by 2-digit percentage got the figure "3" (strong export sales decrease is coded as "1" in Table 22.5 and if strong export sales contraction was also registered in years 2014/2015 and 2015/2016, the final figure for such firms was "3") and to those firms whose export sales grew yearly by 2-digit percentage in 2014/2015, 2015/2016 and 2016/2017—the figure "15" was attributed (as a consequence of coding strong export sales growth as "5"). The aggregated measure of three-year export sales change is presented in Table 22.6.

The distribution of values for this variable indicates good export performance for the majority of analyzed firms (because export sales stagnation for three consecutive periods would be marked as "9" as a consequence of coding yearly stagnation in exports as "3", see Table 22.5).

The last measure of the market performance (on a 5-point Likert-type scale) was the most qualitative one and was based on one question concerning self-evaluation of achieved success compared to competitors (Table 22.7).

No respondents declared "decisive failure" and relatively few felt having done slightly worse than competitors. At the opposite end, those who declared having substantially outperformed their competitors have not been very numerous either.

Correlations between the dependent variables are shown in Table 22.8.

Table 22.8 Correlations between measures of market performance

Kendall's tau_b		Profit/loss declarations for 2017 compared to 2016	Export sales dynamics in 2017 compared to 2016	Three-year export sales evolution (2014–2017)
Profit/loss declarations for 2017 compared to 2016	Correlation coefficient	1.000	**0.315****	**0.363****
	Sig. (2-tailed)		0.000	0.000
	N	280	280	280
Export sales dynamics in 2017 compared to 2016	Correlation coefficient	**0.315****	1.000	**0.705****
	Sig. (2-tailed)	0.000		0.000
	N	280	297	297
Three-year export sales evolution (2014–2017)	Correlation coefficient	**0.363****	**0.705****	1.000
	Sig. (2-tailed)	0.000	0.000	
	N	280	297	297
Perceived success compared to competitors	Correlation coefficient	**0.269****	**0.311****	**0.283****
	Sig. (2-tailed)	0.000	0.000	0.000
	N	280	297	297

**Correlation is significant at the 0.01 level (2-tailed)
Source Own elaboration

For the measures of market performance based on financial results and export sales dynamics moderate to strong correlations can be observed. Evaluation of company's success related to competitors shows consistently the weakest, but still positive and significant correlations with other measures.

The relationship between the size of enterprises and market performance measures reveals that in 3 out of 4 cases there were no significant differences. In the case of export sales, dynamics in 2017 compared to 2016 some measures show no significant differences (like chi-square), some other measures (like linear-by-linear association) indicated slightly better results of medium-sized firms.

Correlations between independent (strategies) and dependent (market performance) variables presented in Table 22.9 apply to all three hypotheses.

In all but one case correlations are positive and significant. In all but one case when correlations are significant they are very weak and only one of them, between the type of segmentation strategy and profit/loss declarations for 2016/2017, can be considered as weak.

Specifically, for segmentation options three positive significant correlations with market performance measures mean that the broader vision of the market, the better market performance. This relationship holds also in subsamples of small and medium-sized enterprises when analyzed separately (although in one out

Table 22.9 Correlations between measures of strategies and of market performance

Kendall's tau_b		Export product strategy: standardization versus adaptation	Export strategy: products undifferentiated versus differentiated	Segmentation: niche, selected segments, the whole market
Profit/loss declarations for 2017 compared to 2016	Correlation coefficient	**0.157****	**0.136***	**0.218****
	Sig. (2-tailed)	0.003	0.010	0.000
	N	280	280	280
Export sales dynamics in 2017 compared to 2016	Correlation coefficient	**0.154****	**0.109***	**0.151****
	Sig. (2-tailed)	0.002	0.034	0.005
	N	297	297	297
Three-year export sales evolution (2014–2017)	Correlation coefficient	**0.136****	**0.126***	**0.140****
	Sig. (2-tailed)	0.005	0.011	0.006
	N	297	297	297
Perceived success compared to competitors	Correlation coefficient	**0.114***	**0.127***	**0.080**
	Sig. (2-tailed)	0.020	0.011	0.123
	N	297	297	297

**Correlation is significant at the 0.01 level (2-tailed)
*Correlation is significant at the 0.05 level (2-tailed)
Source Own elaboration

of three market performance measures correlations or differences measured by Kruskal-Wallis test are not significant).

Therefore, although from statistical point of view the hypotheses are confirmed (the relationship is significant for H3 and—if hypothesized—it is in an expected direction for H1 and H2), the weakness of relationships makes implications of our findings for management practice not obvious.

It has to be noted, however, that we have mostly successful and developing firms in our sample. It is a disadvantage of randomly drawn samples, because apart from periods of recessions and crises substantial majority of enterprises is profitable or successful. Therefore, it is difficult on the basis of such samples to make recommendations about how to avoid failure.

Weak linear relationships suggest the need to apply other statistical methods. Cluster analysis could be an option. It may lead to a discovery of specific links between strategic options, which may be more contrastingly related to market performance.

The results based on two-step clustering are presented in the following tables. The analysis includes three variables representing strategic choices. The distance measure is log-likelihood and the clustering criterion is BIC (or Schwarz's Bayesian criterion)—default options in the SPSS software.

As the result of clustering procedure, six segments have been obtained and there was no significant difference between the size of enterprises and the attribution to clusters (Table 22.10).

The Silhouette measure of cohesion and separation (a measure of how similar an object is to its own cluster [cohesion] compared to other clusters [separation]) equals 0.5 and is exactly on the border between "fair" and "good" value. Although clusters are not equal in size the share of none of them falls below 10%.

Tables 22.11, 22.12, 22.13 show the distribution of enterprises between strategies and clusters.

Clusters 4, 2 and 1 include product adapters and clusters 6, 5 and 3—standardizers.

Cluster 2 includes firms focusing mostly on differentiation while cluster 6 is constituted by firms whose products are mostly undifferentiated and easily substitutable.

Niche strategy is the main strategic choice for firms in clusters 1 and 6, segmenting the market—for firms in clusters 2 and 3, whereas looking large and targeting the whole market is the choice for firms in clusters 4 and 5.

Evaluation of relationship between clusters and market performance measures is presented in Tables 22.14 and 22.15.

The results of the Kruskal-Wallis test show that for each of market performance measures there is at least one significant difference between clusters. Robust tests of equality of means (Welch test and Brown-Forsythe test) lead to the same conclusion.

Table 22.10 Cross tabulation two-step cluster number * enterprises size

Count		Enterprises size		Total
		Small enterprises	Medium-sized enterprises	
Two-step: cluster number	1	26	35	61 (20.5%)
	2	22	16	38 (12.8%)
	3	26	22	48 (16.2%)
	4	21	31	52 (17.5%)
	5	29	29	58 (19.5%)
	6	22	18	40 (13.5%)
Total		146	151	297 (100%)

Chi-square tests

	Value	df	Asymptotic significance (2-sided)
Pearson chi-square	4.849[a]	5	0.435
Likelihood ratio	4.869	5	0.432
Linear-by-linear association	0.299	1	0.585
N of valid cases	297		

[a]0 cells (0.0%) have expected count less than 5. The minimum expected count is 18.68

Source Own elaboration

Table 22.11 Cross tabulation export product strategy: standardization versus adaptation * two-step cluster number

Export product strategy: standardization versus adaptation	Two-step cluster number						Total
	1	2	3	4	5	6	
The whole range of products is standardized	0	0	0	0	15	31	46
Most of the product range is standardized	2	0	23	0	19	7	51
Half standardized–half adapted	18	3	25	0	24	2	72
Most of the product range is adapted	25	21	0	27	0	0	73
The whole range of products is adapted	16	14	0	25	0	0	55
Total	61	38	48	52	58	40	297

Source Own elaboration

Table 22.12 Cross tabulation export strategy: products differentiated versus undifferentiated * two-step cluster number

Export strategy: products Differentiated versus undifferentiated	Two-step cluster number						Total
	1	2	3	4	5	6	
The whole range of products is undifferentiated	4	0	0	5	11	26	46
Most of the product range is undifferentiated	15	0	27	12	23	10	87
Half undifferentiated–half differentiated	27	0	20	24	24	4	99
Most of the product range is differentiated	15	30	1	11	0	0	57
The whole range of products is differentiated	0	8	0	0	0	0	8
Total	61	38	48	52	58	40	297

Source Own elaboration

Table 22.13 Cross tabulation segmentation: the whole market, selected segments, niche * two-step cluster number

Segmentation: the whole market, selected segments, niche	Two-step cluster number						Total
	1	2	3	4	5	6	
Niche	42	0	0	0	0	31	73
Selected segments	19	38	48	0	0	9	114
The whole market	0	0	0	52	58	0	110
Total	61	38	48	52	58	40	297

Source Own elaboration

The visualization of these differences is based on ranks obtained for the Kruskal-Wallis test (Table 22.15; the higher the rank, the higher frequencies at the top levels of the scales measuring market performance, i.e., the better market performance) and on figures showing average achievement reached by representatives of particular clusters on measures of market performance (Figs. 22.1, 22.2, 22.3 and 22.4).

Table 22.14 Test statistics[a,b] *t* for the relationship between market performance and clusters

	Profit/loss declarations for 2017 compared to 2016	Export sales dynamics in 2017 compared to 2016	Three-year export sales evolution (2014–2017)	Perceived success compared to competitors
Chi-square	31.251	18.304	14.491	11.079
df	5	5	5	5
Asymp. sig.	0.000	0.003	0.013	0.050

[a]Kruskal-Wallis Test
[b]Grouping Variable: Two-Step Cluster Number
Source Own elaboration

It is clearly visible, that cluster 6 has the mean rank of the lowest values on every market performance measure and clusters 4 and 5 are the best in all but one case (success compared to competitors).

Figures 22.1, 22.2, 22.3 and 22.4 show the relationships between clusters and market performance measures in a more visible way with means (range of the scales in Figs. 22.1, 22.2 and 22.4 is between 1 and 5 and range of the scale in Fig. 22.3 is between 3 and 15).

The most disadvantageous combination of options relative to the three analyzed strategies is visible on the example of firms belonging to cluster 6: The strongest product standardization combined with the weakest product differentiation together with addressing commercial efforts to niche markets lead to the lowest results on all market performance measures. It should be noted that the means are still above midpoints of the scales measuring market performance. This indicates that even in this cluster the majority of firms were profitable and successful. However, most of firms from the category "profits close to zero" belong to this cluster (more than in all other clusters combined) and none of them declared having achieved "substantial" profit.

Another interesting finding is that the niche strategy did not put all companies at disadvantage. The majority of firms from cluster 1 have also declared this strategy. But unlike firms from cluster 6, they rely more on strong adaptation and moderate differentiation.

It should also be noted that the conservative tests of differences do not allow, in most cases, to consider results obtained by firms as significantly worse or better when comparisons are done between clusters 1–5.

The winning combinations of strategic options are presented in clusters 4 and 5. Strong adaptation, moderate differentiation and addressing products to the whole market are a recipe for success in the case of companies belonging to cluster 4. Strong standardization, weak differentiation, but also a broad vision of the market led to success of companies in cluster 5.

Interestingly, strong product differentiation strategy applied by firms from cluster 2 together with strong adaptation was not a guarantee for the best results. Notwithstanding respondents from this cluster showed the highest level of satisfaction when

Table 22.15 Ranks of clusters (Kruskal-Wallis test)

	Two-step cluster number	*N*	Mean rank
Profit/loss declarations for 2017 compared to 2016	1	57	142.72
	2	37	146.86
	3	43	130.69
	4	49	161.90
	5	55	152.12
	6	39	98.77
	Total	280	
Export sales dynamics in 2017 compared to 2016	1	61	155.52
	2	38	150.39
	3	48	142.13
	4	52	160.75
	5	58	162.73
	6	40	110.80
	Total	297	
Three-year export sales evolution (2014–2017)	1	61	156.56
	2	38	151.80
	3	48	137.14
	4	52	161.10
	5	58	163.23
	6	40	112.69
	Total	297	
Perceived success compared to competitors	1	61	146.98
	2	38	172.28
	3	48	133.26
	4	52	151.12
	5	58	163.84
	6	40	124.58
	Total	297	

Source Own elaboration

comparing their firms' success to competitors. Maybe they are pulled down by their somewhat restricted vision of the market, i.e., addressing products to selected segments of customers?

As far as the position of firms in cluster 3 is concerned, they are in general slightly below firms from cluster 2. They share with them the segmented vision of the market, but they differ by relying more on product standardization and less on adaptation and differentiation.

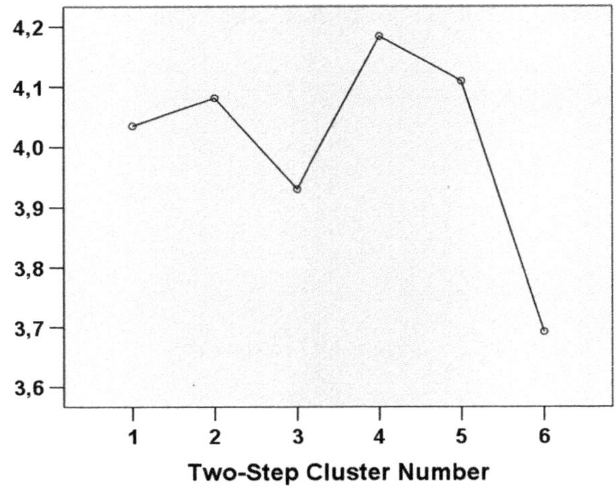

Fig. 22.1 Mean of profit/loss declarations for 2017 compared to 2016. *Source* Own elaboration

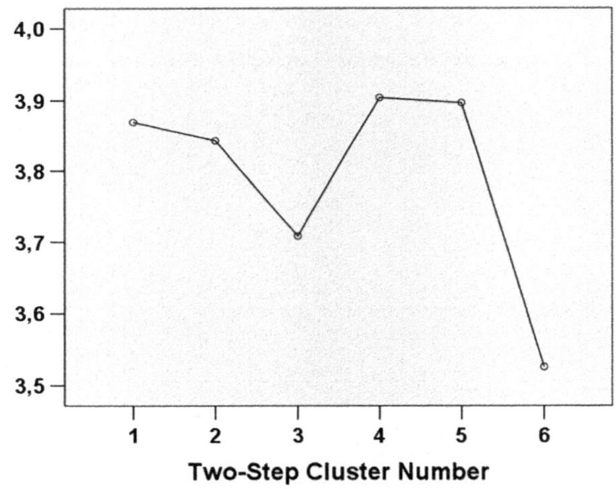

Fig. 22.2 Mean of export sales dynamics in 2017 compared to 2016. *Source* Own elaboration

Finally, taking into account the results of correlation and cluster analysis, we may conclude that the weak correlations are reflected in cluster specificities: The product adaptation and product differentiation contribute to success in the market competition, but the major drive for the success was a non-segmented approach to the markets.

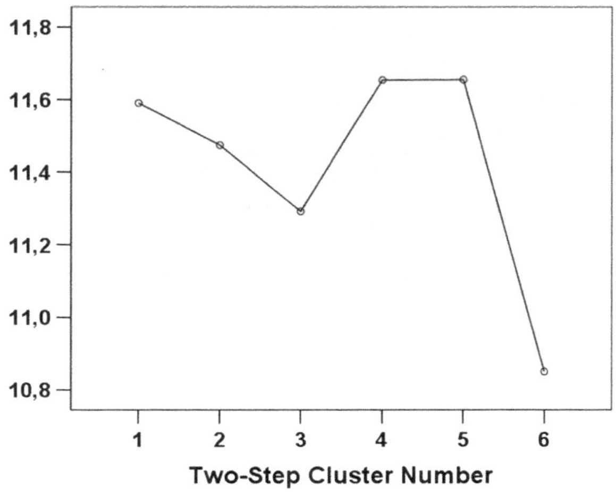

Fig. 22.3 Mean of three-year export sales evolution (2014–2017). *Source* Own elaboration

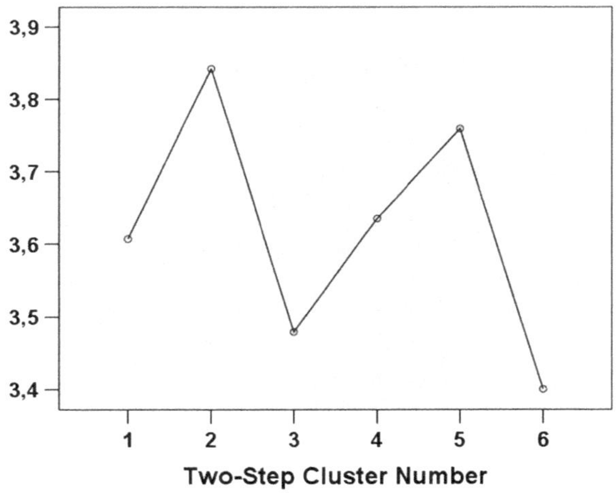

Fig. 22.4 Mean of perceived success compared to competitors. *Source* Own elaboration

22.5 Conclusions and Recommendations

The relationships between variables linked to strategies and market performance measures show weak correlations in line with hypotheses: positive correlations with increasing adaptation, positive correlations with increasing differentiation, positive correlations with broadening vision of the market (in the sequence: niche strategy, segmented approach, non-segmented approach).

The strong managerial recommendation based on our study is that a disadvantageous combination of strategies leading to the worst results in all market performance measures includes the strongest product standardization and the weakest product differentiation together with addressing commercial efforts to niche markets (firms in cluster 6).

A non-segmentation (or natural segmentation) approach led to the best results in almost all market performance measures (firms in clusters 4 and 5).

However, since differences between other combinations of strategies were small, we may consider that the performance of firms applying niche strategies did not produce significantly worse results when these firms relied on product adaptation and moderate differentiation (firms in cluster 1).

As far as the future research is concerned, a more in-depth analysis should be recommended on:

- detailed forms of product adaptation and differentiation,
- cost and price leadership as an element of market strategy.

Acknowledgements This research was supported by the National Science Centre, Poland; grant: "The entrepreneurial marketing concept and accelerated internationalization of new ventures. Antecedents, elements and outcomes", no. 2015/19/B/HS4/01728.

References

Baranowska-Prokop, E., & Sikora, T. (2014). Relationship between competitive strategies and the success perception of Polish born globals. *International Journal of Management and Economics* (43), 94–113.

Danik, L., & Kowalik, I. (2015). Success factors and development barriers perceived by the Polish born global companies. Empirical study results. *Journal of East European Management Studies, 20*(3), 360–390.

Doole, I., & Lowe, R. (2001). *International marketing strategy. Analysis, development and implementation*. London: Thomson Learning.

Duliniec, E. (2011). Koncepcje przedsiębiorstw wcześnie umiędzynarodowionych. Rozważania terminologiczne. *Gospodarka Narodowa* (1–2), 63–80.

Gabrielsson, M. (2005). Branding strategies of born globals. *Journal of International Entrepreneurship, 3*(3), 199–222.

Gabrielsson, P., Gabrielsson, M., & Seppälä, T. (2012). Marketing strategies for foreign expansion of companies originating in small and open economies: The consequences of strategic fit and performance. *Journal of International Marketing, 20*(2), 25–48.

Gassmann, O., & Keupp, M. M. (2007). The competitive advantage of early and rapidly internationalizing SMEs in the biotechnology industry: A knowledge-based view. *Journal of World Business, 42*(3), 350–366.

Gorynia, M. (2007). *Strategie zagranicznej ekspansji przedsiębiorstw*. Warszawa: PWE.

Knight, G. A., & Cavusgil, S. T. (2005). A taxonomy of born global firms. *Management International Review, 45*(3), 15–35.

Kowalik, I., & Baranowska-Prokop, E. (2013). Determinanty powstawania i motywy ekspansji polskich przedsiębiorstw wcześnie umiędzynarodowionych. *Gospodarka Narodowa, 4,* 41–64.

Madsen, T. K., & Servais, P. (1997). The internationalization of born globals: An evolutionary process? *International Business Review, 6*(6), 561–583.

Nowakowski, M. (1999). *Wprowadzenie do zarządzania międzynarodowego*. Warszawa: Difin.

Porter, M. E. (1998). *Competitive strategy. Techniques for analysing industries and competitors (with a new introduction)*. New York: The Free Press.

Sikora, T., & Baranowska-Prokop, E. (2018). Internationalization indices and success perception of Polish born globals. In: N. Tsounis & A. Vlachvei (Eds.), *Advances in time series data methods in applied economic research. ICOAE 2018*. Springer, Cham: Springer Proceedings in Business and Economics.

Chapter 23
Exploring Consumers' Orientation Toward Fast Food Consumption in Greece

Spyridon Mamalis, Ifigeneia Mylona, Irene (Eirini) Kamenidou and Stavros Pavlidis

Abstract This research explores the various factors that affect customers' choice of fast food consumption in the era of economic crisis by conducting field research in the wider Thessaloniki area of Greece. The sample consisted of 236 participants, of which, 195 were fast food customers. Data was collected with a questionnaire and selected via the mall intercept personal interview technique. Respondents reported that *easy and quick solution*, *saturation with tasty food at low cost*, and *variety of food* are the most critical factors for their choice. Factor analysis decreased the 19 variables to three dimensions used for customer segmentation, producing three clusters, i.e., the *out of necessity*, the *fast food lovers*, and the *rational customers*.

Keywords Fast food restaurants · Thessaloniki · Franchising · Consumers · Marketing research

JEL Codes M31 · L83

23.1 Introduction

The fast food quick service type is traced back to antiquity wherein Ancient Greece and Rome people bought prepared food from the *thermopolia* (thermo = hot in Greek and polia = shops, i.e., where hot food is sold) in the *agora* (market). The thermopolia

S. Mamalis · I. Mylona · I. Kamenidou (✉) · S. Pavlidis
Department of Management Science and Technology, School of Business and Economics, International Hellenic University, Kavala Campus, Agios Loukas, 65404 Kavala, Greece
e-mail: rkam@mst.ihu.gr

S. Mamalis
e-mail: mamalis@econ.auth.gr

I. Mylona
e-mail: imylona@mst.ihu.gr

S. Pavlidis
e-mail: stavrospavlides@yahoo.gr

N. Tsounis and A. Vlachvei (eds.), *Advances in Cross-Section Data Methods in Applied Economic Research*, Springer Proceedings in Business and Economics,
https://doi.org/10.1007/978-3-030-38253-7_23

are recorded as far back as 79 A.D., (at most), as the ruins of a thermopolium discovered in Pompeii revealed which was buried from the explosion of Vesuvius volcano eruption (Daley 2019; Berry 2011). Additionally, some of the thermopolia had back rooms, thus, as speculated had the role of dining rooms (Berry 2011).

Later on, in the twentieth century, the first fast food company was founded in 1922 in the USA (Recordati 2015), and its concept spread worldwide. The Technomic Foodservice Segment Time Series (2004, cited in Austen et al. 2005) reports that only in the US fast food retail sales from 1975 to 2004 has increased by 900%. Even more, fast food consumption has increased intensively after 1980s (Harnack and French 2003) and is considered as a popular away from home, delivery or pick up food which is quick, usually reasonably priced and inexpensive substitute to home-cooked food (Goyal and Singh 2007; Bowman and Vinyard 2004). Lob-Corzilius (2007) claims, in his study, that the low cost of fast food is an appealing food option, even more for people with low income, while Moreland et al. (2002, p. 26) point out that fast food restaurants are located usually, near or in, the "low-medium and medium-wealth neighborhoods."

As for the Greek reality and according to Mamalis (2004, p. 15) "Fast food restaurants cater to patrons who generally order at a cashier or select items from a food bar and pay in advance. The latter includes the main branded fast foods, such as burgers, pizzas, and chicken, as well as the traditional Greek takeaways that include souvlaki, mpougatsa (pies) and sandwiches, along with other ethnic foods mainly Italian, Chinese and Indian." Souvlaki is the traditional Greek food with meat (Farajian et al. 2011); and was introduced in Athens after World War II (Matalas and Yannakoulia 2000). Excluding the Greek traditional fast food, the western type fast food restaurants (burgers) dynamically appeared in the Greek market in the early 1990s (ICAP 2002).

While the fast food industry is growing all over the world (Wibowo and Tielung 2016; Tong and Wong 2016; Goyal and Singh 2007; Park 2004), in Greece due to the economic crisis that the country is undergoing, this industry has taken the downfall since 2009 (ICAP 2012, 2018; Giannarou 2013).

Under these conditions in the Greek economy, this study explores customer motivation to consume fast food and to segment customers based on their motivation. As there is limited research in Greece about factors that affect consumers' preferences in fast food, the study is focusing on this area trying to offer some insight regarding consumers' behavior and attitudes.

This research fills the following gap. While fast food restaurants and fast food consumption have been extensively studied all over the world, the fast food industry in Greece has been understudied. Specifically, the studies that the researchers have found (and do not refer to health issues/fat-calorie intake) are before the economic crises, whereas the industry at that time bloomed or the consequences of the crisis on the industry did not yet shown (e.g., Botonaki and Mattas 2010; Mamalis 2004, 2009; Mamalis et al. 2005, 2006).

23.2 The Fast Food Industry in Greece

According to ICAP (2015), the Greek domestic market regarding fast food restaurants followed an upward trend during the period 1992–2008, with an average annual growth rate of 15.1%. From 2009 and onward, a continuing decline in the fast food market is reported. Specifically, in 2009, it decreased by 3.9% compared to 2008. The downward trend continued in 2010, with market size declining by 3.7% compared with the previous year. Furthermore, in 2011, the market declined by 11.1%, in 2012, the decrease was 18.1%, while in 2013, the reduction rate stood to 7.9%.

In 2013/2012, the value of the total market was further decreased by an additional 8%. The category of burger dropped by 9.8%, pizza category by 11.9%, while the category of snack-sandwich stores decreased by 3.3% (Businessenergy.gr, 2015). In 2013, in a research conducted in 11 fast food companies in Greece, there was a reduction of 11.6% in the assets of the companies (https://www.euro2day.gr). In 2014, there was a growth of 3% in the Greek fast food market (https://bizexperts.gr, 2017). Lastly, as concerns the fast food category, in the previous years, the burger category was the "king" in the fast food market, holding a 36.5% in 2008 (ICAP 2008). Though, after the crisis condition of the country, the traditional souvlaki has taken the leadership position of the domestic fast food market (Tsakiri 2016).

23.3 Literature Review

There is an abundance of research referring to fast food restaurants all over the world, focusing on different aspects and points of views. Thus, fast food consumption is one area of study (Ghoochani et al. 2018; Bassett et al. 2008; Park 2004), attitudes and perceptions, (Ghoochani et al. 2018; Goyal and Singh 2007), accessibility and marketing strategies (Thornton et al. 2009; Kara et al. 1995), and consumers values (Botonaki and Mattas 2010; Schroder and McEachern 2005). The above studies are considered only a few of the issues studied, with a great interest being calorie, fat intake and the obesity-"healthy" dimension of fast food consumption (Alsabieh et al. 2019; Niemeier et al. 2006; Bowman et al. 2004; Paeratakul et al. 2003). Lastly, motivation for eating fast food is relatively less frequent studied (Biyiri et al. 2018; Ebadi et al. 2018).

As regards fast food restaurants and fast food consumption, various studies have been found that refer to Greece, mainly focusing on health–nutrition–obesity issues (Grammatikopoulou et al. 2019; Tambalis et al. 2018), or service marketing (Mamalis 2009; Mamalis et al. 2005). While as regards fast food consumption motivation, as is the focus of this research, few studies have been detected by the authors (Botonaki and Mattas 2010; Mamalis 2009; Mamalis et al. 2006).

Botonaki and Mattas (2010) examined how personal values (using Schwartz theory of values) are associated with convenience food consumption on a sample ($N = 729$; 18+) that was responsible for food purchasing and preparation in the family.

They found that convenience food consumption (in restaurants or fast food outlets) was associated with motivations to seek new experiences, act independently, and enhance their interests.

Mamalis (2009) in his research ($n = 400$) identified six dimensions in determining consumer choice of fast food restaurants, which are critical for business success, namely (a) adaptation to locality, (b) service, (c) facilities, (d) food quality, (e) place to be, and (g) sales incentive program.

Mamalis et al. (2006) explored the role of culture in the formation of consumer perceptions toward fast food restaurants in Greece. They employed a six-factor questionnaire of consumer perceptions toward fast food restaurants (i.e., adaptation to locality, service, facilities, food quality, place to be, and sales incentive program), and exploring their influence in customers' overall image, as well as satisfaction and loyalty. They found that adaptation to locality was the most significant factor in the formation of store image as well as in predicting satisfaction and loyalty.

23.4 Methodology of the Study

A quantitative research method was used for the collection of data. A structured questionnaire was designed and via mall intercept personal interviews, 236 citizens of the urban planning complex of Thessaloniki participated. The questionnaire used for the survey consisted of 23 closed-type questions. Only the ones that are in line with the aim and objectives of the study are presented, thus referring to fast food consumption, fast food restaurant visit and the frequency of the visit, and socioeconomic and demographic characteristics. The answers for the multi-item questions were given on a five-point Likert scale (5 = completely agree, down to 1 = completely disagree). The statistical program Statistical Package for Social Sciences (SPSS) was used for the analysis of the data.

23.5 Results

23.5.1 Sample Profile

Regarding gender, 63.6% of the sample was women, and 36.4% were men. In addition, 26.7% of the participants belong to the age group 18–24, 29.7% to the group 25–34, another 19.1% was between 25 and 44, and 24.6% of them were between 45 and 55 years old. In terms of the educational level of the participants, the largest percentage was secondary school graduates (40.7%), 22% had a university or a master's degree, and only 11% were students. In terms of occupation, most of the participants worked in the private sector (30.1%), 16.5% were businesspeople, 14.8% worked in public sector, and 38.6% were dependent on others (students, home keepers, unemployed). Additionally, as regards net family monthly income, the majority of the sample fell in two categories: 400–1000 € (46.6%) and 1000–2000 € per month (41.5%). Regarding the marital status, 34.8% of the sample was single, 50.8% was married, 14.4% was divorced or widowers. Lastly, 34% of the sample lived in Eastern Thessaloniki, 30% of the sample in the municipality of Thessaloniki, 23.7% in Western Thessaloniki, and only 11.9% in the suburbs.

23.5.2 *Fast Food Consumption*

From the initial sample of 236 respondents, 82.6% (n = 195) eat at fast food type of restaurants and 17.4% (n = 41) do not. The three main reasons for avoiding fast food consumption, as stated by participants were the safety of food, with mean score (MS) MS = 4.79; children should not get used to this kind of food (MS = 4.61) and are considered as unhealthy and "plastic food" (MS = 4.59). On the other hand, the main reasons for eating fast food (Table 23.1) are the quick and easy solution

Table 23.1 Reasons for consuming fast food (%)

I eat fast food because…/it is/it has a/an/…	1	2	3	4	5	MS
Easy and quick solution	0.0	1.0	4.6	32.8	61.5	4.55
Saturation with tasty food at low cost	2.1	5.1	6.7	45.1	41.0	4.18
Variety of food	0.0	4.1	16.9	39.0	40.0	4.15
Eat at a comfortable environment	0.0	1.5	14.9	52.3	31.3	4.13
For all social classes	0.0	4.1	12.3	55.4	28.2	4.08
Good taste	0.5	3.6	16.9	49.7	29.2	4.04
For all financial classes	0.0	3.1	17.4	58.5	21.0	3.97
For all ages	0.0	7.7	14.4	52.3	25.6	3.96
I spend a lot of time out of home	0.0	15.4	10.8	38.5	35.4	3.94
Covers all type of taste requirements	0.0	9.2	24.6	38.5	27.7	3.85
I like the fast foods' environment	2.6	4.1	22.6	55.4	15.4	3.77
My children want to eat fast food	0.5	4.7	39.6	32.3	22.9	3.72
Staff respects its customers	0.0	9.2	31.8	48.2	10.8	3.61
I cannot or do not like to cook	2.6	21.0	29.7	40.0	6.7	3.27
Good quality	2.6	22.6	26.7	43.1	5.1	3.26
My friends do so too	5.6	25.1	30.3	28.2	10.8	3.13
Safe to eat	5.6	25.6	31.8	32.8	4.1	3.04
Adds to my "prestige" and "social image"	10.3	36.4	26.2	20.5	6.7	2.77
Healthy food	7.2	39.0	29.2	24.1	0.5	2.72

Table 23.2 Frequency of consuming and visiting fast food restaurants

Frequency of dining	Frequency	Percentage
At least once per day	4	2.1
1–2 times per week	51	26.2
3–4 times per week	26	13.3
4–5 times per week	17	8.7
Once per week	47	24.1
Once per fortnight	21	10.8
Once per month	17	8.7
Less than once per month	12	6.2
Total	195	100.0

(MS = 4.55), saturation feeling with tasty food at low cost (MS = 4.18), and food variety (4.15).

Furthermore, as regards frequency of eating at fast food restaurants, the largest percentage (26.2%) dines 1–2 times a week, while the smallest percentage (2.1%) dines at least once a day. Moreover, we can argue that obviously 74.3% of the sample dines at a fast food restaurant at least once a week (Table 23.2).

23.5.3 Factor Analysis

Principle component factor analysis was conducted with varimax rotation in order to produce a smaller set of variables for further analysis. Three factors derived from the analysis (KMO = 0.815; BTS = 1651.513; df = 66; sign $p = 0.000$), explaining 72.9% of total variance (TVE), while seven items were discarded due to loading to at least two factors, and one was discarded due to low communality. Thus, the final items in the factor analysis were 11, providing with a three-dimension solution for further analysis (segmentation based on motivation dimensions). The three dimensions were named as: *good food quality, fast food for all, and convenient and value for money food.* Table 23.3 presents each factor dimension, the items that are consisted of, the TVE of each factor, Cronbach α of factor, as well as its mean factor score (MFS), which is used in segmentation analysis.

23.5.4 Segmentation Analysis

The derived factors and specifically their MFS was used in segmentation analysis using hierarchical cluster analysis in order to investigate the number of groups that should be formed based on participants motivation to eat fast food at fast food restaurants. Table 23.4 presents the derived consumers' segments based on motives for fast

Table 23.3 Factor analysis of independent variables with varimax rotation

Variables	Component		
	1	2	3
F1: Good food quality. Eigenvalue = 5.065; TVE = 32.6; α = 0.921; MFS = 3.01 (StD = 0.86)			
Good quality	0.910		
Safe to eat	0.908		
Healthy food	0.868		
I cannot or do not like to cook	0.861		
Adds to my prestige and social image	0.715		
F2: Fast food for all. Eigenvalue = 2.379; TVE = 20.7; α = 0.866; MFS = 4.00 (StD = 0.68)			
For all social classes		0.890	
For all financial classes		0.853	
For all ages		0.827	
F3: Convenient and value for money food; Eigenvalue = 1.041; TVE = 19.6; α = 0.805; MFS = 4.12 (StD = 0.66)			
Easy and quick solution			0.872
Saturation with tasty food at low cost			0.838
Covers all type of taste requirements			0.645

Table 23.4 Final cluster centers

Variables	Cluster			ANOVA	
	1	2	3	*F*	Sig.
Good food quality	2.46	3.79	2.39	163.722	0.000
Fast food for all	3.24	4.21	4.26	58.399	0.000
Convenient and value for money food	3.27	4.53	4.18	120.308	0.000

food consumption. As ANOVA results reveal, all groups are significantly different regarding the motivation dimensions of segmentation.

Cluster I is the "*consumers of necessity*" segment. This cluster consists of 45 participants, which probably eats fast food out of necessity, since all MFS <3.50, this could be due to working hours, lack of time to prepare home-made meal, or because their children's decision to do so.

Cluster II is the "*fast food lover*" segment. This cluster consists of 84 participants, which are the fast food lovers, since all MFS >3.50, specifically they tend to completely agree that fast food is "convenient and value for money food," while they agree that "fast food for all" consumers, and tend to agree that fast food is of "good food quality."

Lastly, Cluster III is the "*rational customer*" segment. This cluster consists of 66 participants, which are the rational customers, since they do not believe that fast food is of good quality food but do agree and consider fast food as "convenient and value for money food," as well as that "fast food for all" consumers.

23.6 Discussion–Conclusions

This research study has shown some interesting results regarding the habits and preferences of fast food customers. Statistical analysis indicated that the most important element for consuming fast food is that it is perceived as a quick and easy food solution, the saturation feeling that it provides with tasty food at low cost, as well its food variety. Factor analysis for data reduction provided with three factors. The first factor, *good quality* of food includes five items quality of cooking, hygiene, safe to eat, quality of raw materials, and the brand name prestige. The second factor is *food for all* and involves social class, financial class, and age, and the third factor is *convenient and value for money food.* These factors are partially in line with the previous researches. Ma et al. (2016), found in their study that the expectancy (such as fast food is quick, easily accessible, tastes good, and offers a lot of choices) and value constructs were positively related to fast food consumption. According to Dunn et al. (2011), fast food consumption is influenced by specific referent groups, as well as by a general demand for meals that are tasty, satisfying, and convenient. On the other hand, Rydell et al. (2008) in their research found that the most frequently reported reasons for eating at fast food restaurants were: fast food is quick (92%), easy to access (80%), and has good taste (69%). Khan et al. (2013) found that service quality and brand are the key factors for satisfaction in fast food industry. Even more, and as regards the Greek population Kremmyda et al. (2008) and Papadaki et al. (2007) found that Greek university students that live away from home increase fast food consumption sue to accessibility and convenience.

Regarding the results of cluster analysis all segments give as higher final cluster center the dimension "*convenient and value for money food*" is for all segments the highest in rating, which comes partially in the same vein with the study of Ottar Olsen et al. (2009) who segmented fast food/convenience customers based on their benefit and found three consumer groups. These groups are the "convenient", the "ambivalent", and the "dissatisfied" consumer. As to the "*fast food lover*" segment of this study, it has the highest rating of the "*convenient and value for money food*" dimension, which partially is in line with Oni and Matiza's (2014) who found that factors of value for money, convenience, and accessibility were influencing significantly their choice of fast food outlet. Lastly, as to the frequency of visiting fast food restaurants, most of the participants of this study visit them at least once a week, being partially in line with the previous research such as Jiao et al. (2015), who found that most of their participants eat less than two times a week at a fast food or quick service restaurant.

In conclusion, this study suggests that fast food remains an important choice for people to eat. People's choice is influenced by factors such as the quality of the food, the way of cooking, and the prestige of the chain name. Though, 17.4% of the initial sample is not into fast food consumption as they believe that this kind of food is unhealthy, not good for children to get used to and not safe.

This research has as its limitations the small sample size, the focus into one area as well as the ages of participants. Even though with these limitations, it does provide with information of fast food consumption during the economic crisis in Greece.

References

Alsabieh, M., Alqahtani, M., Altamimi, A., Albasha, A., Alsulaiman, A., Alkhamshi, A., et al. (2019). Fast food consumption and its associations with heart rate, blood pressure, cognitive function and quality of life. Pilot study. *Heliyon, 5*(5), e01566.

Bassett, M. T., Dumanovsky, T., Huang, C., Silver, L. D., Young, C., Nonas, C., et al. (2008). Purchasing behavior and calorie information at fast food chains in New York City, 2007. *American Journal of Public Health, 98*(8), 1457–1459.

Berry J. (2011). *Thermopolium*, BBC from: http://www.bbc.co.uk/history/ancient/romans/pompeii_art_gallery_03.shtml. Accessed 18-12-2018.

Biyiri, E. W., Dassanayake, D. M. C., & Dahanayake, S. N. S. (2018). Why Sri Lankans eat at international fast food outlets? Motivations and demographics. In *Proceedings of the 2nd International Research Symposium* (p. 329), Uva Wellassa University, Badulla, Sri Lanka, February 1–2.

Botonaki, A., & Mattas, K. (2010). Revealing the values behind convenience food consumption. *Appetite, 55*(3), 629–638.

Bowman, S. A., Gortmaker, S. L., Ebbeling, C. B., Pereira, M. A., & Ludwig, D. S. (2004). Effects of fast food consumption on energy intake and diet quality among children in a national household survey. *Pediatrics, 113*(1), 112–118.

Bowman, S. A., & Vinyard, B. T. (2004). Fast food consumers vs non-fast food consumers: A comparison of their energy intakes, diet quality, and overweight status. *Journal of American College of Nutrition, 23*(2), 163–168.

Daley, J. (2019). *Recently uncovered thermopolium reminds us that romans loved fast food as much as we do*. SMITHSONIAN.COM, April 3, 2019. Available at website: https://www.smithsonianmag.com/smart-news/romans-loved-fast-food-much-we-do-180971845/. Accessed April 1, 2019.

Dunn, K. I., Mohr, P., Wildon, C. J., & Witterta, G. A. (2011). Determinants of fast food consumption. An application of the theory of planned behaviour. *Appetite, 57*, 349–357.

Ebadi, L., Rakhshanderou, S., & Ghaffari, M. (2018). Determinants of fast food consumption among students of Tehran: Application of planned behavior theory. *International Journal of Pediatrics, 6*(10), 8307–8316.

Farajian, P., Risvas, G., Karasouli, K., Pounis, G. D., Kastorini, C. M., Panagiotakos, D. B., et al. (2011). Very high childhood obesity prevalence and low adherence rates to the Mediterranean diet in Greek children: The GRECO study. *Atherosclerosis, 217*, 525–530.

Ghoochani, O. M., Torabi, R., Hojjati, M., Ghanian, M., & Kitterlin, M. (2018). Factors influencing Iranian consumers' attitudes toward fast food consumption. *British Food Journal, 120*(2), 409–423.

Giannarou, L. (2013). *Cheese pie and souvlaki evolve into a food of crisis*. Available at website: http://www.kathimerini.gr/494639/article/epikairothta/ellada/tyropita-kai-soyvlaki-e3elissontai-se-faghto-ths-krishs.

Goyal, A., & Singh, N. P. (2007). Consumer perception about fast food in India: An exploratory study. *British Food Journal, 109*(2), 182–195.

Grammatikopoulou, M. G., Theodoridis, X., & Chourdakis, M. (2019). International aspects: Abdominal obesity in Greece. In R. Watson (Ed.), *Nutrition in the prevention and treatment of abdominal obesity* (pp. 301–316). Cambridge: Academic Press.
Harnack, L., & French, S. (2003). Fattening up on fast food. *Journal of the American Dietetic Association, 103*(10), 1296–1297.
ICAP Hellas. (2002). *Sector study: Fast food restaurant chains*. Athens, Greece: ICAP Management Consultants, ICAP.
ICAP Hellas. (2008). *Sector study: Fast food restaurant chains*. Athens, Greece: ICAP Management Consultants, ICAP.
ICAP Hellas. (2012). *Sector study: Fast food restaurant chains*. Athens, Greece: ICAP Management Consultants, ICAP.
ICAP Hellas. (2015). *Sector study: Fast food restaurant chains*. Athens, Greece: ICAP Management Consultants, ICAP.
ICAP (2018). *Fast–food restaurant chains*. ICAP Group, Greece (In Greek).
Jiao, J., Moudon, A. V., Kim, S. Y., Hurvitz, P. M., & Drewnowski, A. (2015). Health implications of adults' eating at and living near fast food or quick service restaurants. *Nutrition and Diabetes, 5,* 171.
Kara, A., Kaynak, E., & Kucukemiroglu, O. (1995). Marketing strategies for fast food restaurants: A customer view. *International Journal of Contemporary Hospitality Management, 7*(4), 16–22.
Khan, S., Hussain S. M., & Yaqoob, F. (2013). *Determinants of customer satisfaction in fast food industry*. Available at website: facultyjournal.com: http://www.facultyjournal.com. Accessed April 2019.
Kremmyda, L. S., Papadaki, A., Hondros, G., Kapsokefalou, M., & Scott, J. A. (2008). Differentiating between the effect of rapid dietary acculturation and the effect of living away from home for the first time, on the diets of Greek students studying in Glasgow. *Appetite, 50*(2–3), 455–463.
Lob-Corzilius, T. (2007). Overweight and obesity in childhood—A special challenge for public health. *International Journal of Hygiene and Environmental Health, 210,* 585–589.
Ma, R., Castellanos, D. C., & Bachman, J. (2016). Identifying factors associated with fast food consumption among adolescents in Beijing China using a theory-based approach. *Public Health, 136,* 87–93.
Mamalis, S. (2004). *Consumers attitudes towards fast food restaurants in Greece: An investigation of store image, satisfaction and loyalty* (Doctoral dissertation). Newcastle University. https://theses.ncl.ac.uk/jspui/handle/10443/646.
Mamalis, S. (2009). Critical success factors of the food service industry. *Journal of International Food & Agribusiness Marketing, 21*(2–3), 191–206.
Mamalis, S., Ness, M. R., & Bourlakis, M. A. (2005). Tangible and intangible store image attributes in consumer decision making: The case of fast food restaurants. *WSAES Transactions of Information Science and Applications, 2*(10), 705–1714.
Mamalis, S., Ness, M. R., & Bourlakis, M. A. (2006). Standardization versus customisation. The role of culture. In 98th Seminar, June 29–July 2, 2006, Chania, Crete, Greece (No. 10056). European Association of Agricultural Economists.
Matalas, A. L., & Yannakoulia, M. (2000). Greek street food vending: An old habit turned new. In A. P. Simopoulos & R. V. Bhat (Eds.), *Street foods, world review of nutrition and dietetics (1-24)*. Basel, Switzerland: Karger.
Moreland, K., Wing, S., Diez-Roux, A., & Poole, C. (2002). Neighbor-hood characteristics associated with the location of food stores and foodservice places. *American Journal of Preventative Medicine, 22,* 23–29.
Niemeier, H. M., Raynor, H. A., Lloyd-Richardson, E. E., Rogers, M. L., & Wing, R. R. (2006). Fast food consumption and breakfast skipping: Predictors of weight gain from adolescence to adulthood in a nationally representative sample. *Journal of Adolescent Health, 39*(6), 842–849.
Oni, O. A., & Matiza, T. (2014). Factors influencing consumer choice of fast food outlet: The case of an American fast food franchise brand operating in a predominantly rural community. *Mediterranean Journal of Social Sciences, 5*(20), 802–808.

Ottar Olsen, S., Prebensen, N., & Larsen, T. A. (2009). Including ambivalence as a basis for benefit segmentation: A study of convenience food in Norway. *European Journal of Marketing, 43*(5/6), 762–783.

Papadaki, A., Hondros, G., Scott, J. A., & Kapsokefalou, M. (2007). Eating habits of university students living at, or away from home in Greece. *Appetite, 49*(1), 169–176.

Paeratakul, S., Ferdinand, D. P., Champagne, C. M., Ryan, D. H., & Bray, G. A. (2003). Fast food consumption among US adults and children: Dietary and nutrient intake profile. *Journal of the American Dietetic Association, 103*(10), 1332–1338.

Park, C. (2004). Efficient or enjoyable? Consumer values of eating-out and fast food restaurant consumption in Korea. *International Journal of Hospitality Management, 23*(1), 87–94.

Recordati, G. B. P. (2015). *The food industry: History, evolution and current trend.* https://tesi.luiss.it/15698/1/177941.pdf. Accessed on 20/12/2018.

Rydell, S. A., Harnack, L. J., Oakes, J. M., Story, M., Jeffery, R. W., & French, S. A. (2008). Why eat at fast-food restaurants: Reported reasons among frequent consumers. *Journal of the American Dietetic Association, 108*(12), 2066–2070.

Schroder, M. J. A., & McEachern, M. G. (2005). Fast food and ethical consumer value: A focus on McDonald's and KFC. *British Food Journal, 107,* 212–224.

Tambalis, K. D., Panagiotakos, D. B., Psarra, G., & Sidossis, L. S. (2018). Association between fast food consumption and lifestyle characteristics in Greek children and adolescents; results from the EYZHN (National Action for Children's Health) programme. *Public Health Nutrition, 21*(18), 3386–3394.

Technomic Foodservice Segment Time Series: Limited Service Restaurants (1975–2005). (2004). Chicago, Ill: Technomic Inc. In Austin, S. B., Melly, S. J., Sanchez, B. N., Patel, A., Buka, S., & Gortmaker, S. L. (2005). Clustering of fast food restaurants around schools: A novel application of spatial statistics to the study of food environments. *American Journal of Public Health, 95*(9), 1575–1581.

Thornton, L. E., Bentley, R. J., & Kavanagh, A. M. (2009). Fast food purchasing and access to fast food restaurants: A multilevel analysis of VicLANES. *International Journal of Behavioral Nutrition and Physical Activity, 6*(1), 28. https://doi.org/10.1186/1479-5868-6-28.

Tong, C., & Wong, A. (2016). The effects of corporate social responsibility of fast food restaurants on corporate reputation. *Journal of Marketing and HR, 3,* 126–144.

Tsakiri, T. (2016). *The crisis needs its souvlaki—saturation from grill-cafes.* TO VIMA, 11/5/2016. Available at website: https://www.tovima.gr/2016/05/11/finance/i-krisi-thelei-to-soyblaki-tis-koresmos-apo-psitopwleia-kafeteries/1/. Accessed April 10, 2019.

Wibowo, S. W., & Tielung, M. (2016). Analytical Hierarchy Process (AHP) approach on consumer preference in franchise fast food restaurant selection in Manado City (Study At: Mcdonald's, Kfc, and A&W). *Journal EMBA: Journal Riset Ekonomi, Manajemen, Bisnis dan Akuntansi, 4*(2).

Chapter 24
Prediction Ability of Selected Bankruptcy Models in the Period of Structural Changes

Tomáš Pražák

Abstract Determining the financial stability of a business is a fundamental starting point for deciding on the evaluation of business strategies. A financially sound business is able to generate added value regularly during its business. Conversely, businesses in financial distress can negatively affect the country's economic development. The aim of this paper was to evaluate the predictive ability of selected bankruptcy models in the period of structural changes between 2004 and 2016 in the Visegrad countries. Bankruptcy prediction models such as Altman's bankruptcy model, Index IN05, and Taffler's bankruptcy model were used to meet the objective of the paper. Furthermore, econometric-statistical methods. The predictive capability results show that the Altman's model achieved the highest average abilities, which proved more than 70% of businesses to rank the company financially weak. On the other hand, the sensitivity analysis showed that the IN05 index was the most stable model. Taffler's model has proved to be the least suitable for practical use on businesses in the Visegrad countries.

Keywords Financial distress · Bankruptcy models · Visegrad countries · GDP

JEL Codes G33 · G38

24.1 Introduction

The importance of evaluating the company's financial performance has been steadily increasing in recent years. Because of growing globalization, deepening integration, and the impact of economic structural changes at the beginning of the new millennium, companies have faced the transformation of their business according to the current trends, merging into larger business units, selling their business, or threatening financial distress or bankruptcy.

T. Pražák (✉)
Department of Finance and Accounting, School of Business Administration in Karviná, Silesian University in Opava, Univerzitní náměstí 1934/3, 733 40 Karviná, Czechia
e-mail: prazak@opf.slu.cz

N. Tsounis and A. Vlachvei (eds.), *Advances in Cross-Section Data Methods in Applied Economic Research*, Springer Proceedings in Business and Economics,
https://doi.org/10.1007/978-3-030-38253-7_24

The financial performance and financial soundness of an enterprise is determined by the ability of the enterprise to generate added value, return on invested capital, or return on input. Maximum activity is necessary for the resulting effect of the creation of value added, which is one of the basic prerequisites for effective appreciation of funds. The financial health of a business is determined by the current state of corporate finance, where a financially sound business has an effective amount of capital available to cover its assets, is able to meet its financial obligations and has the ability to turn individual assets into cash as needed. Such an enterprise is attractive to investors, which in turn results in their interest in investing and capital appreciation through the development of new activities or strengthening the capital market position.

A financially sound business does not show signs of a financial threat to its continuing business activity, and it can be assumed that based on its financial performance assessment, there will be no insolvency or overindebtedness in the foreseeable future. Conversely, the financial distress of an enterprise occurs when a business has serious payment difficulties that cannot be resolved other than by a radical change in its activities or structure.

Bankruptcy models (Altman's bankruptcy model—Alt, Taffler's bankruptcy model—Taf, or IN05) are used as early warning systems for potential financial distress, capturing events typical of future corporate decline. Predictive bankruptcy or creditworthy models can be used to model whether an enterprise will meet its obligations on time and to a sufficient extent. The models are based on real company data that has already gone bankrupt. Using formulas and financial ratios, it is predicted whether the company is going to bankrupt or prosper. The bankruptcy forecast can be found several years before the actual bankruptcy.

The aim of the paper is to evaluate to what extent the financial situation of the company, especially the risk of financial distress and bankruptcy, is influenced by the structural changes defined by GDP growth. The analysis of mutual relations will be carried out at the national level for the Visegrad Group countries: Czech Republic (CZE), Hungary (HUN), Poland (POL), Slovakia (SVK). The Visegrad Group was founded on February 15, 1991, in Visegrad, Hungary. The main task of V4 at the time of its creation was the mutual support of all three (now four) postcommunist countries in their efforts to integrate into Euro-Atlantic structures. Despite the common features of individual countries, the transformation process of their economies has taken place differently, and different outcomes of corporate financial performance can be expected.

24.2 Literature Review

The basic models for predicting financial distress and bankruptcy on the basis of financial indicators are Beaver (1966) and Altman (1968). Predictive models are based on the hypothesis that the financial difficulties of an enterprise can be identified by using ratios of financial ratios before they actually occur. William Beaver has developed a one-parameter model for predicting financial distress, whose predictability is growing with a longer forecast horizon. In his analyses, he observed deviations within cash flow, net profit, debt, and turnover indicators. In contrast, Edward Altman developed a multidimensional discriminatory analysis that showed that in most cases, bankruptcy companies could be properly classified at one- to two-year prediction horizons. For its analysis, it first selected 22 indicators divided into liquidity, profitability, debt, solvency, and asset management. Altman's prediction model is the basic method of evaluating the financial health of a company, and its modifications are used by banks and industrial companies.

Taffler's bankruptcy model (Taffler 1983) was also created on these foundations. The first step in compiling this model was to calculate more than 80 selected ratios of all industrial firms between 1968 and 1976 and 46 randomly selected solvent industrial firms. The ratios and coefficients of the Taffler's model indicate four key dimensions of the company's financial profile: profitability, working capital position, financial risk, and liquidity. The predictive ability of Taffler's model has been confirmed over the years by Agarwal and Taffler.

The specifics of the Czech financial statements and the economic situation in the Czech Republic according to Neumaier and Neumaier (2005) reflect the IN credibility index. Like the previous bankruptcy models, this index also includes an analysis of the ratios of activity, profitability, debt, and liquidity. Based on these analyses, four variants of the index were gradually created. The IN95 index is a bankruptcy model created from the lender's perspective, and the market value of the company is not represented among its indicators, unlike the Altman model. This adjustment is appropriate for low liquid capital market conditions. In contrast, the IN99 index is a creditworthiness model constructed from the perspective of the owner. This index was created using a discriminatory analysis, based on which the weights of the IN95 indicators were revised. These two models were subsequently followed by the so-called complex analysis IN01, which combined the previous two models. Subsequently, a modified complex index IN05 was created in 2005 to evaluate the financial situation of the company using one number. According to Neumaier and Neumaier (2005), the IN05 index is similarly successful in predicting possible bankruptcy, such as Altman's bankruptcy analysis, in identifying the threat of bankruptcy.

On the example of the Czech Republic, Basovníková et al. (2018) practical use of Altman's bankruptcy model. They draw attention to the fact that although the Altman's model is suitable for the use of predictions of possible financial distress, they also recommend monitoring other financial indicators, especially return on equity. The comparison of individual models and their ability to identify a company in financial distress was dealt with by Machek (2007). In his article, he analyzed Fast Kralick's test, Taffler's bankruptcy model, IN99 and IN05, and Altman's bankruptcy *Z*-scores for Czech companies from 2007 to 2010. Based on the results of individual models predicting the financial distress of the company, he found that models for practical use of financial distress prediction are Altman's *Z*-scores and IN 99 and IN05 indices. On the other hand, the Kralick's test is the least suitable. Although

Taffler's model was able to draw attention to companies in financial distress, its predictive ability was low compared to other bankruptcy models.

Similarly, Gavurová et al. (2017a) or Gavurová et al. (2017b). On the basis of the previous research in Slovakia, they established a portfolio of four models (Altman's model, Ohlson's model, and IN01 and IN05), which were validated on a sample of 700 Slovak companies. The accuracy of the financial prediction was assessed at three levels. In their articles, they followed the overall accuracy, accuracy of bankruptcy prediction, and inaccuracy in bankruptcy forecasts. The prediction of financial distress in Poland was the goal of Gruszczynski (2014). Based on the results of the individual models, they concluded that the sudden increase in the ratio of short-term liabilities to total assets should be continuously monitored and thoroughly investigated. Both studies also confirmed the high predictive capability of bankruptcy models in the short-term. Dorgai et al. (2016) monitored the ability to predict financial indicators in Hungary.

24.3 Data and Methodology

Permanent solvency is one of the basic conditions for a successful business existence. The ability of a firm to pay means the ability to dispose of the funds required to settle its obligations at the required amount and time. Therefore, in the context of vulnerable solvency, this part of the paper is focused on the development of insolvency of companies in the Czech Republic, Hungary, Poland, and Slovakia for the period of 2010–2016 (Table 24.1). Most corporate insolvency petitions end with a declaration of bankruptcy, or the insolvency petition is dismissed due to a lack of business assets.

However, the financial situation of companies is not only influenced by the decisions of the company management significantly, but also influenced by the macroeconomic environment in which the company is located. The company's financial performance is directly linked to the business cycle. In general, the fact that, at the time of expansion, businesses are expanding their production capacities and falling unemployment, increasing consumer spending and business investment. Conversely, in the event of a recession, both consumers and businesses cut their spending and postpone investments. It is also generally accepted that, at a time of economic expansion and an improving macroeconomic environment, the number of businesses affected

Table 24.1 Development of corporate insolvencies

	2010	2011	2012	2013	2014	2015	2016
CZE	5559	6753	8398	6021	3563	3004	2438
HUN	17,487	30,757	50,224	46,397	60,637	46,967	41,007
POL	665	762	908	926	864	770	616
SVK	830	870	866	880	831	715	692

Source Creditreform (2016)

by financial distress is decreasing and the financial performance of businesses is improving.

The actual growth in real GDP per capita in the Visegrad countries is shown in Fig. 24.1. It can be seen that the global economic crisis of 2008 and 2009 and the subsequent debt crisis of the euro area countries affected the economic development of all countries. However, the only country in the region has not fallen into a deep recession.

In the initial phase of the research, a database of enterprise data from the Visegrad Group countries was created. To this end, the Orbis or Amadeus business data databases were used, and Eurostat, OECD, or central bank databases were available to obtain macroeconomic data. The reference period was between 2004 and 2016, depending on data availability. In the second phase, the bankruptcy models were processed using the MS-Excel tool, which brought the financial results of the company in the given year. The last step was to calculate correlation relationship using the econometric models in econometric software EViews. According to the available results from the Orbis and Amadeus databases, a total amount of 11,014 companies were processed that had available financial data for the period 2004–2016. The number of companies is shown in Table 24.2.

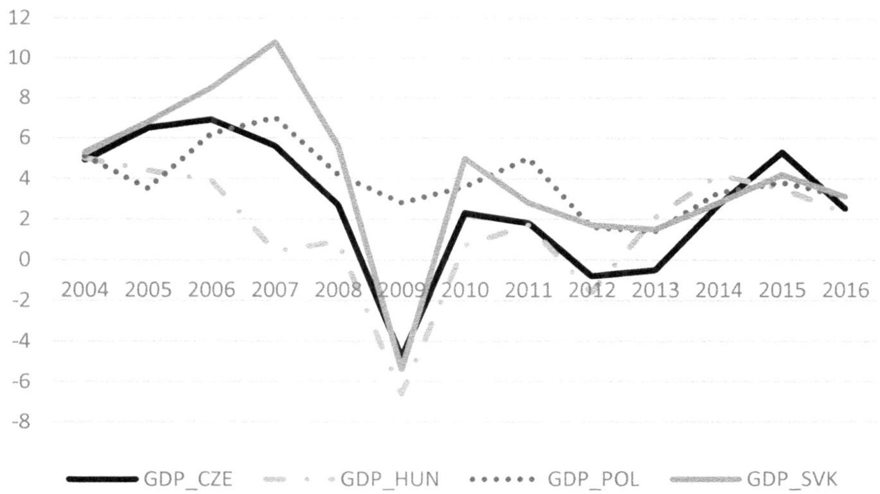

Fig. 24.1 Development of GDP growth. *Source* Eurostat database (2019)

Table 24.2 Number of available companies

Country	CZE	HUN	POL	SVK
Number of companies	4104	1638	4130	1142

Source Orbis and Amadeus database (2019)

Bankruptcy, or predictive, models are early warning systems as they indicate a potential threat to financial health, depending on the behavior of the selected indicators. These models were derived from the actual data for companies that had gone bankrupt or prospered in the past. It is based on the assumption that there have been some anomalies in the company for several years before the bankruptcy, in which the symptoms of future problems are present and which are characteristic of vulnerable companies. They are suitable not only for the current but also for the future decision-making, allowing management to separate and correctly interpret indicators of potential future problems and identify and adjust them in time before serious problems or even bankruptcy occurs. The applications and comparisons of the most frequently used bankruptcy models on the Visegrad Four (V4) were dealt with by Csikosova et al. (2019). On the data of industrial enterprises V4 models IN 95, IN 99, IN01, IN05, original Altman's model Z score and modified models Z' score were applied. In their study, they highlight the factors that should be taken into account when applying bankruptcy models in V4 countries that need to combine available predictive bankruptcy models to assess the financial performance of businesses, as their design is influenced by the country of origin and the time when the model was or construct the resulting index values among themselves and focus in particular on their evolution.

Altman's model

The practical use of Altman's bankruptcy model in the Visegrad Group countries was confirmed by Basovníková et al. (2018), Machek (2007), Gavurová et al. (2017a, b), or Dorgai et al. (2016). Altman's bankruptcy model (Altman Z-score) refers to a model for valuing a business crisis using multiple discriminatory analysis. Altman (2006) firstly selected 22 indicators and divided into liquidity, profitability, indebtedness, solvency, and asset management and tested them on two groups of companies, where one of the groups was bankrupt. Out of the 22 indicators, the five most important indicators were chosen to best predict bankruptcy. This model was derived from real data for companies that have gone bankrupt or prospered in the past. It is based on the assumption that there have been some anomalies in the company several years before the bankruptcy, in which there are indications of the future problems that are characteristic of vulnerable companies.

Altman's bankruptcy model for private firms (Z' score):

$$Z' = 0.717X_1 + 0.847X_2 + 3.107X_3 + 0.42X_4 + 0.998X_5 \tag{24.1}$$

X_1 (current assets − current liabilities)/total assets
X_2 retained earnings/total assets
X_3 earnings before interest and taxes/total assets
X_4 book value of equity/total equity
X_5 sales/total assets

The resulting qualification of the company will be done according to the following:

$Z > 2.9$ enterprise is in a good situation

$1.2 < Z < 2.9$ gray zone of unresolved results
$Z < 1.2$ for bankruptcy is very likely

The first indicator (X_1) expresses the ratio of net working capital to total assets. Net working capital is defined as the difference between current assets and current liabilities. The resulting value of the indicator is the proportion of the company's net liquid assets relative to the total capitalization of the enterprise.

The second indicator (X_2) represents the proportion of retained earnings to total assets. Retained earnings are characterized as a portion of profit that is not used to pay dividends or earn funds and are very often used as an internal source of business finance. The resulting values of the indicator show the leverage effect of the company, where companies with a higher value of retained earnings to total assets have a greater opportunity to use their own financing sources to acquire assets.

The highest weighted indicator in X_3 captures the earnings before interest and taxes (EBIT) share of total assets. The resulting values capture the productivity of corporate assets, regardless of the tax rate.

The fourth ratio (X_4) compares the carrying amount of equity with the carrying amount of total liabilities. Its resulting values show how much equity can fall before it exceeds the total liabilities, indicating the company's financial risk.

The last observed indicator (X_5) shows the relationship between sales and total assets. The resulting values show the company's ability to generate revenue from its assets. The overall score of the Z Score can predict the possible decline with a year ahead with a probability of 94% and a two-year advance with a probability of 72%.

Index IN05

Index IN05 is a comprehensive index for evaluating the financial health of a company through a single number. However, in addition to assessing whether a company is going to go bankrupt or not in the near future, the IN05 index also deals with whether it creates value for its owners. Similar to the Altman index, the IN05 index consists of several subcomponents—coefficients that address specific areas of corporate financial management. According to Kubíčková and Jindřichovská (2015), IN05 is considered by Czech economists to be the most accurate and suitable for use in monitoring Czech businesses and similar economies.

The index of IN05 is:

$$\text{IN05} = 0.13A + 0.04B + 3.97C + 0.21D + 0.09E \tag{24.2}$$

A total assets/foreign capital
B EBIT/interest expenses
C EBIT/total assets
D sales/total assets
E current assets/current liabilities

The resulting qualification of the company will be done according to the following:

IN05 > 1.6 The company creates added value

0.9 < IN01 < 1.6 Gray zone of unresolved results
IN05 < 0.9 Enterprise does not create added value

The resulting value of the X_1 indicator captures the ratio of the company's assets financed by foreign capital, thus informing the company of its debt burden. Conversely, X_2 expresses how high the interest rate is provided by creditors in proportion to how much an enterprise is able to earn. The results of indicators X_3 and X_4 show the ratio of assets that can be covered either by profit or by revenue. Indicator X_5 informs the enterprise of the ratio of current assets financed by short-term foreign funds.

Taffler Bankruptcy Model

Responding to the original Altman's bankruptcy model was the creation of the Taffler's index (Taffler 1983). British economists Taffler and Tisshaw analyzed the financial performance of British businesses on more than 80 ratios, of which they selected four key and assigned specific weights. The Taffler's index is known in two variants—in the original and modified versions.

$$\text{TZ} = 0.53R_1 + 0.13R_2 + 0.18R_3 + 0.16R_4 \tag{24.3}$$

R_1 EBIT/Current Liabilities
R_2 current assets/foreign capital
R_3 short-term liabilities/total assets
R_4 total sales/total assets.

The boundaries of the resulting Taffler's bankruptcy model are as follows:

TZ > 0.3—low probability of financial distress
0.2 < TZ < 0.3—gray zone of companies with potential threat of financial distress
TZ < 0.2—high probability of the upcoming financial distress of the company.

The highest weight in the model is the indicator (X_1) of the EBIT to short-term liabilities of the company. Short-term payables represent payables due within one year, and together with own funds are used to finance the company's normal operations. The main short-term liabilities are short-term bank loans, supplier loans, or payables to employees. The resulting values show the company's ability to cover these short-term liabilities through profit generated before interest and taxation.

The second monitored ratio (X_2) is the ratio of current assets to foreign capital. The resulting value of the indicator represents for the company an overview of the extent to which its short-term assets are financed by foreign sources (short-term and long-term).

The third ratio (X_3) is aimed at monitoring the ratio of short-term liabilities to total assets of the business. The result of the indicator for the company represents the coverage of total assets through short-term liabilities.

In a modified form, the X_4 indicator shows the share of sales in total assets. Individual weights of indicators remain unchanged. The modified option is already considering the existence of a gray zone category in which there are businesses that could not be categorized as low or high probability bankruptcy. As shown in Table 24.5, the cut-off points in this variant are 0.2 and 0.3.

Correlation Analysis

Liou and Smith (2007) conclude that the number of bankruptcies is increasing during the economic recession, while the number of bankruptcies is decreasing. To confirm this hypothesis, Liou and Smith (2007) used correlation analysis.

Correlation represents the correlation of change of two variables, which takes values in the range $<-1; 1>$. Negative correlation values indicate the mutual inverse relationship of two variables. If the quantities develop in the same direction, the correlation coefficient is positive. If the correlation coefficient is zero, the time series are not correlated. The basic element of the correlation analysis is a correlation matrix, where it is possible to observe the statistical significance of the relationship of two variables based on *t*-statistics and probability (Dougherty 2011).

To calculate the Pearson correlation coefficient, it is necessary to know the difference between the value of *X* (macroeconomic variable) and its average value, the difference of *Y* (financial performance of the company measured by bankruptcy models) from its average value, the number of observations *n,* and the standard deviation *S* of both variables. This relationship (Brooks 2002) shows as follows:

$$r_{xy} = \frac{\sum (x_i - \bar{x})(y_i - \bar{y})}{(n-1)s_x s_y}. \tag{24.4}$$

Chow Test for Structural Breaks

Finally, the econometric model Chow test is used to determine the effect of structural changes on the final assessment of bankruptcy models and the interaction of GDP growth. In econometrics, it is most commonly used in time series analysis to test for the presence of a structural break at a period, which can be assumed to be known a priori. The null hypothesis of the Chow test asserts that there is an assumption that the model is independent and identically distributed from normal distribution with unknown variance. The test statistics follows the *F* distribution with k and $N_1 + N_2 - 2k$ degrees of freedom. According to Dougherty (2011), the final equation is shown as follows:

$$F_{\text{Chow}} = \frac{(S_c - (S_1 + S_2))/k}{(S_1 + S_2)/(N_1 + N_2 - 2k)}. \tag{24.5}$$

24.4 Results and Discussion

In the first step, predictive bankruptcy models were applied for the monitored number of enterprises. The resulting values of each model for each state were subsequently divided into bands characterizing their financial health. The numbers of companies in potential financial distress zone are shown in Table 24.3. The results confirm that the largest number of companies in financial distress was in crisis years 2009 and 2012. Table 24.1 shows the average number of companies falling into individual bands in percent. The resulting numbers are different for individual bankruptcy models.

Table 24.3 Number of companies in financial distress zone in %

Model	Alt_CZE	IN05_CZE	Taf_CZE	Alt_HUN	IN05_HUN	Taf_HUN
2004	10.58	21.76	4.84	17.16	32.23	6.35
2005	10.58	22.28	4.98	16.79	33.82	5.62
2006	9.31	21.03	4.67	14.16	31.93	4.15
2007	7.85	17.50	3.18	14.77	34.43	4.58
2008	8.92	23.35	4.42	15.38	36.81	4.70
2009	12.06	28.56	7.12	19.35	38.83	5.25
2010	9.67	24.47	4.25	18.01	38.22	5.56
2011	8.63	22.98	3.45	16.42	38.34	4.33
2012	8.89	25.10	4.11	18.01	42.55	4.40
2013	9.50	25.03	4.08	16.61	37.36	4.58
2014	8.55	19.62	3.09	17.16	33.64	4.03
2015	9.16	18.82	3.43	16.61	31.50	4.82
2016	9.43	20.03	3.60	17.95	31.87	5.62
Model	**Alt_POL**	**IN05_POL**	**Taf_POL**	**Alt_SVK**	**IN05_SVK**	**Taf_SVK**
2004	8.09	19.13	5.52	12.78	38.62	6.22
2005	7.41	19.18	5.59	13.49	39.23	5.60
2006	7.31	17.22	5.30	14.97	39.93	6.74
2007	6.83	14.94	4.33	15.32	37.04	5.78
2008	7.72	19.15	4.87	14.19	42.29	5.25
2009	8.38	19.44	5.52	22.77	50.26	13.22
2010	8.11	18.84	4.60	18.91	43.96	8.32
2011	8.55	20.73	4.75	17.78	42.47	6.57
2012	9.13	23.05	5.57	19.18	47.64	7.44
2013	9.61	21.79	5.59	19.35	46.94	7.53
2014	9.95	19.61	5.52	18.30	43.70	5.60
2015	9.47	19.49	5.21	19.26	43.35	6.65
2016	9.88	21.72	6.20	18.04	41.86	5.25

Source Author's calculations

Table 24.4 Average number of companies in each category in %

Model	Category	CZE	HUN	POL	SVK
Altman	Financial distress zone	9.47	16.80	8.50	17.26
	Gray zone	46.17	57.11	40.82	49.33
	Financial healthy zone	44.32	26.09	50.68	33.41
IN05	Financial distress zone	22.35	35.50	19.56	42.87
	Gray zone	32.74	39.49	26.74	27.08
	Financial healthy zone	44.92	24.96	53.70	30.06
Taffler	Financial distress zone	4.25	4.92	5.27	6.94
	Gray zone	3.67	6.45	4.70	7.58
	Financial healthy zone	92.09	88.63	90.02	85.48

Source Author's calculations

The differences are most evident in the case of the Altman's model and the IN05 model, where there are very different numbers of companies in financial distress and the gray zone. The numbers of financially sound businesses are almost identical in the models. Taffler's model signals only a very noticeable number of businesses in financial distress or in the gray zone. The largest number of enterprises classified as financially distressed or threatened with immediate financial distress in the monitored period was Hungary and Slovakia. At least Poland and the Czech Republic.

Table 24.4 shows the average number of companies categorized per reporting period. The results show that the Altman's bankruptcy model and the IN05 index ranked a similar number of companies as financially sound businesses. The biggest difference was the inclusion of companies in the group of companies at risk of financial distress and included in the gray zone. The IN05 index puts more businesses into the financial distress, as the Altman model, which rather puts them in the gray zone. Taffler's model appears to be the least stringent model for ranking businesses by their financial performance. In all cases, more than 85% of businesses ranked without financial problems.

These bankruptcy models have a predictive ability to estimate the financial performance of businesses for years to come. Based on this, basic statistical methods were applied to determine the predictive ability of selected models in the period under review for the Visegrad Four. First, the number of companies that were put into financial distress for two years was calculated. Subsequently, the average values and standard deviations of the business's predictive ability were calculated. This sensitivity analysis is further illustrated by the coefficient of variation, which monitors the proportion of standard deviation and the average number of companies in distress zone. Despite the fact that Altman's model can predict the largest number of businesses in financial distress for the upcoming years, the IN05 index was the most stable in the year under review. The results in Table 24.5 were influenced by the aforementioned structural changes, especially in 2009 and 2012. It was in these years that the financial performance of companies was the lowest. However, index

Table 24.5 Sensitivity analyses of bankruptcy models

		CZE	HUN	POL	SVK
Altman	Mean	72.16	76.51	74.65	75.75
	Std. dev.	7.49	7.80	5.04	7.57
	Coef. of variation	0.10	0.10	0.07	0.10
IN05	Mean	66.33	74.48	63.66	70.51
	Std. dev.	4.46	2.91	4.98	6.29
	Coef. of variation	0.07	0.04	0.08	0.09
Taffler	Mean	60.62	58.21	66.52	60.87
	Std. dev.	9.50	6.36	8.36	8.57
	Coef. of variation	0.16	0.11	0.13	0.14

Source Author's calculations

IN05 was able to incorporate the possible effects into its current rating. The least stable prediction model would be Taffler's bankruptcy model.

The correlation between the development of the economy and the number of companies at risk of financial distress is evident from the previous results, with the number of businesses with financial problems increasing in the crisis years of 2008–2009 and later also in 2011–2012. This relationship was subsequently quantified using Pearson correlation analysis. Table 24.6 shows statistically significant correlation relations between the selected variables and at the same time confirms the hypothesis that both indicators are strongly correlated. The zero hypothesis for statistical significance was based on t-stat. reject in 9 out of 12 cases where statistically significant relationships can be discussed. The strongest correlation coefficient was achieved in the IN05 index. Conversely, the weakest relationship was confirmed in Taffler's model.

Based on the results of the Chow test in Table 24.7 to determine the effect of structural changes on the resulting values of individual bankruptcy tests and correlations, it was found that the global financial crisis in 2009 had a statistically significant effect on the resulting values in all countries under review. By contrast, the structural

Table 24.6 Correlation analyses

Model	GDP_CZE	GDP_HUN	GDP_POL	GDP_SVK
Altman	−0.3797 (−1.3611)	−0.4923*** (−1.8758)	−0.7025* (−3.2737)	−0.7890* (−4.2595)
IN05	−0.7975* (−4.3848)	−0.7003* (−3.2536)	−0.8440* (−5.2196)	−0.8946* (−6.6390)
Taffler	−0.4500 (−0.1671)	0.0678 (0.2253)	−0.5850** (−2.3925)	−0.7380* (−3.6271)

Source Author's calculations

*, **, *** statistical significance at the level of 1%, 5% and 10%. *T*-statistics in round brackets

Table 24.7 Chow test

Chow breakpoint	F-statistics	Wald statistics
CZE-2009	5.6462**	18.5849*
CZE-2012	4.5623***	16.2148*
HUN-2009	4.9863**	17.4333*
HUN-2012	3.9872***	11.4863**
POL-2009	5.1368**	18.0112*
POL-2012	2.8716	10.5493***
SVK-2009	4.8527**	16.5879*
SVK-2012	3.3254	10.9687***

Source Author's calculations
*, **, *** statistical significance at the level of 1%, 5% and 10%

change in 2012 affected the resulting values in the Czech Republic and Hungary, which, thanks to the setting of their fiscal policy, faced a longer-term crisis.

24.5 Conclusion

Keeping solvency is an important part of financial management and is a measure of the company's sound financial performance for both creditors, banks, suppliers, shareholders, and other financial investors. If the company does not have enough money to pay its debts, it will not be able to meet its immediate obligations, it may become insolvent or insolvent. Conversely, a financially sound business can generate added value not only for its owners, but also for managers or employees. Therefore, monitoring financial performance is still a topical issue.

Bankruptcy models are used in practice to identify the potential threat of financial distress. The object of the financial performance monitoring in this article was selected bankruptcy models, namely Altman's bankruptcy model, Index IN05 and Taffler's bankruptcy model. Already on the basis of the literature review, it can be expected that individual models will show varying results. However, it is important to see how much the results will be different, as each of these models was designed for a different tip of economies. While the Altman's model was originally for American companies, the Taffler model was based on a sample of British companies, and the Index IN05 was based on the example of companies from the Czech Republic.

The aim of this article was to evaluate the predictive ability of selected bankruptcy models in the period of structural changes in companies operating in the Visegrad Four countries. The monitored period was 2004–2016. To fulfill the objective of the thesis, the bankruptcy models and applied econometric-statistical methods were used. A correlation analysis was used to assess the impact of structural changes on business ratings.

The resulting values of individual models show that the number of companies at risk of financial distress increased in the period of structural change. The largest number of enterprises in financial distress assigned the index IN05 and vice versa the least Tafflerův model. A similar number of enterprises were rated by the Altman's model and the IN05 index for corporate financial health. The predictive capability results show that the Altman's model achieved the highest average abilities, which proved more than 70% of businesses to rank the company financially weak. On the other hand, the sensitivity analysis showed that the IN05 index was the most stable model. Taffler's model has proved to be the least suitable for practical use on businesses in the Visegrad countries. The financial assessment of the company is not only influenced by the decisions of the managers, but also by the macroeconomic environment. The correlation analysis only confirms the theory that structural changes have a strong negative impact on the company's financial assessment. For further research, it will be important to include an analysis of the impact of other macroeconomic indicators, such as unemployment, interest rates or exchange rates.

References

Altman, E. (1968). Financial ratios, discriminant analysis and the prediction of corporate bankruptcy. *Journal of Finance, 23*(4), 589–609.

Altman, E. (2006). *Corporate financial distress and bankruptcy* (3rd ed.). New Jersey: Wiley.

Basovníková, M., Konečný, M., Dubový, R., & Masařová, A. (2018). The use of the altman model in evaluation of economic performance of a corporation in the crisis period in the building sector in the Czech Republic. *Acta Universitatis Agriculturae et Silviculturae Mendelianae Brunensis, 66*, 409–421.

Beaver, W. (1966). Financial ratios as predictors of failure. *Journal of Accounting Research, 4*(1), 71–111.

Brooks, C. (2002). *Introductory econometrics for finance*. Cambridge: Cambridge University.

Csikosova, A., Janoskova, M., & Culkova, K. (2019). Limitation of financial health prediction in companies from post-communist countries. *Journal of Risk and Financial Management, 12*(15).

Dorgai, K., Fenyves, V., & Sutó, D. (2016). Analysis of commercial enterprises solvency by means of different bankruptcy models. *Gradus, 3*(1), 341–349.

Dougherty, C. (2011). *Introduction to econometrics* (4th ed.). New York: Oxford University Press.

Gavurová, B., Janke, F., & Packová, M. (2017a). Analysis of impact of using the trend variables on bankruptcy prediction models performance. *Journal of Economics, 65*(4), 370–383.

Gavurová, B., Packová, M., Misanková, M., & Smrčka, L. (2017b). Predictive potential and risks of selected bankruptcy prediction models in the slovak business environment. *Journal of Business Economics and Management, 18*, 1156–1173.

Gruszczynski, M. (2014). Financial distress of companies in Poland. *International Advances in Economic Research, 10*(4), 249–256.

Kubíčková, D., & Jindřichovská, I. (2015). *Finanční analýza a hodnocení výkonnosti firmy.* Praha: C. H. Beck.

Liou, D., & Smith, M. (2007). Macroeconomic variables and financial distress. *Journal of Accounting Business and Management, 14*, 17–31.

Machek, O. (2014). Long-term predictivity ability of bankruptcy models in the Czech Republic: Evidence from 2007–2012. *Central European Business Review, 3*, 14–17.

Neumaierová, I., & Neumaier, I. (2005). Index 05. In *Evropské finanční systémy: Sborník příspěvků z mezinárodní vědecké conference* (pp 143–146). Brno: Masarykova univerzita v Brně.

Taffler, R. (1983). The assessment of company solvency and performance using a statistical model. *Accounting and Business Research*, *15*(52), 295–308.

Chapter 25
The Stability of Money Demand in the Long Run: An Empirical Study from Italy

Chaido Dritsaki

Abstract The stability of money demand is a crucial issue for the effectiveness of monetary policy in each country and is being threatened when important changes are taking place in its monetary policy. Applying ARDL technique and error correction model (ECM) developed by Pesaran et al. (2001), this paper aims to examine the factors that influence money demand in Italy for the period 1960–2017. The results of ARDL technique and ECM show that there is both a long-run and short-run relationship among variables used. Real income, long-run interest rate, and inflation comply with the expectations of monetary theory. Finally, the results of CUSUM and CUSUMSQ stability tests and unit circle confirm the long-run relationship among variables and also that the stability condition is satisfied when money demand for Italy is estimated with M_1 variable for the examined period.

Keywords Money demand stability · ARDL model · Vector error correction model · Stability of the coefficients · Monetary aggregates · Italy

JEL Classification E41 · E52 · C22

25.1 Introduction

The idea that the amount of money in an economy can be accurately measured and analyzed and that changes in this quantity may be related to changes in interest rates, production, and prices has occupied researchers for a long time. Since Keynes's work in 1936, demand for money has been extensively studied by many economists. After WWII, Milton Friedman in 1956, as well as other researchers, led to a common vocabulary with different definitions of money, covering many countries for long periods of time. However, nowadays many of the issues concerning the determinants and dynamics of the demand for money remain unclear. In particular, given the importance of quantification of demand and money supply for policy purposes,

---

C. Dritsaki (✉)
Department of Accounting and Finance, University of Western Macedonia, Kozani, Greece
e-mail: cdritsaki@uowm.gr

N. Tsounis and A. Vlachvei (eds.), *Advances in Cross-Section Data Methods in Applied Economic Research*, Springer Proceedings in Business and Economics,
https://doi.org/10.1007/978-3-030-38253-7_25

economists have focused their attention on specific features of monetary aggregates that appear to vary between countries and time. Such a feature is the stability of money demand. Indeed, due to the volatility of interest rates, exchange rate, inflation and production, demand for money may be very unstable. Therefore, the degree of volatility in demand for money will depend not only on the fluctuations in the components of money demand but also on the degree of correlation between these components. Therefore, the dynamics of money demand varies from country to country, as the short- and long-term dynamics of these components may vary considerably from country to country and from time to time. This is particularly true when shocks change the composition and structure of the financial market.

The function of money demand is one of the macroeconomic relationships that has been more looked into by researchers. This great interest comes from the fact that money demand stability plays an important role in the conduct and adoption of monetary policy for each country. Therefore, the central banks of all countries should apply monetary models and policies based on the estimated relationships between money demand and its determinants.

Few economists would disagree with this view, especially after centralized targets for monetary policy control and implementation were adopted by the central banks. However, despite analytical and empirical efforts, there is no general consensus on the stability (or volatility) of the money demand function. This shows some doubts about one of the fundamental assumptions of monetary targeting, namely the existence of a stable and predictable relationship between money supply and total nominal income (Andersen 1985).

All central banks underline the importance of analyzing money development and the fixed function of money demand for monetary policy purposes. Deutsche Bundesbank, for example, has followed a clear monetary targeting strategy since 1975 and the analysis of monetary aggregates is one of the two pillars of the European Central Bank (ECB) monetary policy strategy. The bank's investigation into the existence and stability of money demand is due, inter alia, to the following two observations:

- The increase of money is related to inflation. Therefore, monetary policy makers use development money as an indicator of future risks to price stability (see McCandless and Weber 1995).
- The procedure of transmitting monetary policy continues being a "black box." If we are able to identify a stable function of money demand, an important element of the monetary transmission mechanism is revealed, which can help to learn more about the transmission of monetary policy (see Mishkin 1995).

The paper is organized as follows. Section 25.2 highlights the main historical events in monetary regimes and policies that potentially could have affected the demand for money in Italy. Section 25.3 presents the main results in the literature related to our analysis. Section 25.4 describes the economic theory. Section 25.5 describes the methodologies employed, Sect. 25.6 reports the main results obtained, and Sect. 25.7 concludes.

25.2 Money Demand in Italy in a Historical Perspective

The first fundamental law on monetary and financial integration was introduced in Italy in 1862, with the creation of a single currency, the Italian lira, which replaced the old coins after national unification. In the period 1861–1870, in the Kingdom of Italy, there were five banks: the Banca Nazionale degli Stati Sardi, the Banca Nazionale Toscana, Banca Toscana di Credito, Banco di Napoli, and Banco di Sicilia. Banca Romana then joined the other five, so the issue of banknotes by many banks was of particular theoretical interest, and this Italian experience was in fact regarded as an example of a competitive money-issuing system (see Gianfreda and Janson 2001).

Before WWI, the convertibility of paper money into gold was maintained in the following periods: 1861–1866, 1882–1885, and 1902–1914. At other times, the government exercised its control with policies that set limits on the issue of paper money and minimum reserves ratios. In addition, the government controlled the banks' official discount rate. This system, however, did not avoid the situation when the banknote issue limits were exceeded due to the fact that the banks were also commercial banks (Muscatelli and Spinelli 2000).

In 1979, Italy kept the exchange rate mechanism (ERM) of the European Monetary System (EMS). The independence of monetary policy from the tax authority, the need for which was initially set by the Governor of the Bank of Italy, Paulo Buffy, in 1975, was achieved in 1981 by the Bank of Italy's "divorce" from the Ministry of Finance. It was suggested that the Bank of Italy was no longer obliged to be the residual buyer in government bond auctions (Favero and Spinelli 1999).

The exchange rate mechanism was abandoned in 1992 due to unsustainable speculative attacks on the Italian Lira. Italy's exit from the ERM required a change in monetary policy to avoid a spiral between exchange rate devaluation and inflation. In the same year, another step was taken toward the independence of the Central Bank, as the treasury was no longer allowed to borrow from the Bank of Italy.

In addition, the power to amend the discount rate, which was previously formally held by the Ministry of Finance in 1992, was officially entrusted to the Italian bank by imposing sanctions to allow for legal independence. Overall, the 1980s and the 1990s marked a change in the monetary regime. Not only did the correlation between public deficits and money generation disappear, but the regulatory framework also underwent significant changes. In November 1996, the Italian currency re-entered the ERM through the introduction of a wider exchange rate band in August 1993. The Lira was the official currency until the end of 2001, as the euro began in 2002 and the ECB became the issuing body and the reference monetary policy institution for all members of the Eurozone (Gaiotti and Secchi 2012).

25.3 Literature Review

25.3.1 Empirical Studies in Italy

This section includes the literature review on the empirical studies on the Italian economy to model stability of money demand.

In his work, Thornton (1998) presents estimates of a stable long-term function of money demand in Italy for the period 1861–1980. The results from Johansen's approach regarding the integration of variables have shown that there is a long-term integrated relationship, both in terms of the demand function and the supply of money function. In both functions, the elasticity of income and interest rates are in line with the size and the sign of monetary theory.

Muscatelli and Spinelli (2000) examine the stability of money demand in Italy for a fairly long period, covering the period of 1861–1996. In particular, they look at how the evolution of the financial system in Italy and policy shifts (changes) have affected the behavior of long-term demand for money, while presenting the structural changes in the stability of money. A second noteworthy conclusion of their work is that there is a two-way causal relationship between money demand, income, interest rate, and the price index.

Caruso (2006) in his work examines the impact of fluctuations in the Milan Stock Exchange on the long-term demand for money in Italy. The empirical results of this work show that stock market fluctuations help to explain temporary movements in liquidity preference. In conclusion, Caruso concludes that though there is a positive correlation between the stock market index that includes dividends and real money balances, the estimated long-term relationship is unstable.

Capasso and Napolitano (2012) investigated the stability of money demand by applying the most recent econometric control procedures in Italy, one of the largest EMU countries, before and after the EMU. Among others, the objective of their work was to ascertain the effect of a change in the currency regime on the monetary aggregates and provide a valid empirical model that would serve as a viable tool for policy performance.

Daniele et al. (2017), following the application of recent econometric technique ARDL, examine the stability of money demand in Italy for the period 1861–2011. The results of their work have shown that instability cannot be ruled out when a function of money demand is assessed irrespective of the use of M_1 or M_2. Then, it is observed that the reason for possible instability in money demand resides in the omission of relevant variables, as it is shown that a fully stable demand for narrow money (M_1) can be obtained from an augmented money demand function involving real exchange rates and its volatility as additional explanatory variables.

25.4 The Economic Theory

The money demand function is of great importance in an IS-LM (Investment/Saving equilibrium-Liquidity preference/Money supply equilibrium) model developed by John Hicks as an attempt to connect Neoclassical and Keynesian theory. The IS/LM model presents the relationship between interest rates and productive output not only in market of goods and services but also in money market. The IS curve represents real economy meaning the production of goods and services. The reduction of interest rates increases output; thus, IS curve is declining. LM curve is increasing and represents the effect of financial sector. A well-known macroeconomic relationship of money demand is the following:

$$\frac{M}{P} = f(Y, \mathrm{OC}) \tag{25.1}$$

where

M represents nominal value of money,
P is price level,
Y is the income, and
OC is the vector of opportunity cost of money holding.

In empirical studies, for the nominal value of money, M_1, M_2, and M_3 are mainly used as variables. For price level, the consumer price index—(CPI) or the GDP deflator is used. For the opportunity cost, the choice of variables differs. Mainly, the nominal short- and long-term interest rates are used. In other studies, inflation rate represents the opportunity cost of money holding instead of holding assets. Moreover, for countries exposed to high inflation, exchange rate equilibrium can be regarded as an alternative variable of opportunity cost.

The long-run relationship of money demand can be formulated as follows:

$$m_t - p_t = \alpha_0 + \beta_1 g_t + \beta_2 R_t + \beta_3 \pi_t + \varepsilon_t \tag{25.2}$$

where

m_t is the logarithm of the nominal M_1 level.
p_t is the logarithm of the CPI.
g_t is the logarithm of real GDP.
R_t is long-term interest rate.
π_t is the annual inflation rate.

Parameters β_1, β_2, and β_3 of the above equation denote income elasticity, semi-elasticity in relation to interest rate, and semi-elasticity in relation to inflation rate, respectively. According to economic theory, real GDP has a positive effect on nominal M_1. On the other hand, variables representing opportunity cost meaning nominal interest rate and inflation rate should have negative effect on nominal M_1. Moreover, it should be noted that income elasticity is important for the determination of monetary expansion which is consistent with the long-run price stability level. Also, the semi-elasticity of interest rate helps to compute the welfare cost of long-term inflation (see Mark and Sul 2003).

25.5 Methodology

25.5.1 *Unit Root Tests*

The first step is to test for integration order for model's variables. For this purpose, we use three basic unit root tests: Dickey–Fuller (1979, 1981) test, Phillips–Peron (1988) test, and Kwiatkowski, Phillips, Schmidt, Shin (1992).

Dickey and Fuller (1979, 1981) have constructed an asymmetric distribution for unit root test, while with Augmented Dickey Fuller test (ADF) they have constructed a parametric test correcting autocorrelation of high order, assuming that the series follows an autoregressive procedure k order AR(k).

Phillips–Perron (1988) suggested a non-parametric test and examined autocorrelation and heteroscedasticity on errors modifying statistical tests. Phillips–Perron test is suitable in any form of autocorrelation as well as assuming that the series follows an ARMA procedure (p, q) unknown order.

Kwiatkowski, Phillips, Schmidt, Shin—KPSS (1992)—test is employed with Lagrange multiplier where the null hypothesis denotes that random walk has zero variance.

25.5.2 *ARDL Model Specification*

Autoregressive distributed lag bounds co-integration method was developed by Pesaran et al. (2001) for investigating the long-run relationship between variables in a VAR model.

The ARDL $(p, q_1, q_2, \ldots, q_k)$ model specification is given as follows: (Pesaran et al. 2001)

$$\alpha(L, p)y_t = \mu + \sum_{i=1}^{k} \beta_i(L, p)x_{1t} + \lambda' w_t + \varepsilon_t \quad \forall t = 1, \ldots, n \tag{25.3}$$

where

$$\alpha(L, p) = 1 - \alpha_1 L - \alpha_2 L^2 - \cdots - \alpha_p L^p$$
$$\beta_i(L, q_i) = \beta_{i0} + \beta_{i1} L + \beta_{i2} L^2 + \cdots + \beta_{iq_i} L^{q_i} \quad \forall i = 1, 2, \ldots, k$$

y_t dependent variable.
μ constant term.

L lag operator.
$w_t = s \times 1$ vector of deterministic variables such as intercept term, time trends, or exogenous variables with fixed lags.

Long-run elasticities of Eq. (25.3) can be calculated as follows:

$$\varphi_i = \frac{\hat{\beta}_i(1, \hat{q})}{\alpha(1, \hat{p})} = \frac{\hat{\beta}_{i0} + \hat{\beta}_{i1} + \cdots + \hat{\beta}_{i\hat{q}}}{1 - \hat{\alpha}_1 - \hat{\alpha}_2 - \cdots - \hat{\alpha}_p} \quad \forall i = 1, 2, \ldots, k \tag{25.4}$$

where

$\hat{p}$ and $\hat{q}_i$, $i = 1, 2, \ldots, k$ are the estimated values of p and q_i.

Long-run coefficients of Eq. (25.3) can be calculated as follows:

$$\varpi = \frac{\hat{\lambda}(\hat{p}, \hat{q}_1, \hat{q}_2, \ldots, \hat{q}_k)}{1 - \hat{\alpha}_1 - \hat{\alpha}_2 - \cdots - \hat{\alpha}_p} \tag{25.5}$$

where

$\hat{\lambda}(\hat{p}, \hat{q}_1, \hat{q}_2, \ldots, \hat{q}_k)$ denotes the OLS estimates of λ in the Eq. (25.3).

To test for the existence of long-run relationship among variables with ARDL method, we use as endogenous each variable of the model and exogenous the same variables as follows:

$$\begin{aligned} \Delta(m-p)_t = {} & \beta_0 + \gamma_T T + \delta_{(m-p)}(m-p)_{t-1} + \delta_g g_{t-1} + \delta_{R_1} R_{1t-1} + \delta_\pi \pi_{t-1} \\ & + \sum_{i=1}^{p} \alpha_{1i} \Delta(m-p)_{t-i} + \sum_{i=0}^{q_1} \alpha_{2i} \Delta g_{t-i} + \sum_{i=0}^{q_2} \alpha_{3i} \Delta R_{1t-i} \\ & + \sum_{i=0}^{q_3} \alpha_{4i} \Delta \pi_{t-i} + \varepsilon_{1t} \end{aligned} \tag{25.6}$$

$$\begin{aligned} \Delta g_t = {} & \beta_0 + \gamma_T T + \delta_g g_{t-1} + \delta_{(m-p)}(m-p)_{t-1} + \delta_{R_1} R_{1t-1} + \delta_\pi \pi_{t-1} \\ & + \sum_{i=1}^{p} \alpha_{1i} \Delta g_{t-i} + \sum_{i=0}^{q_1} \alpha_{2i} \Delta(m-p)_{t-i} + \sum_{i=0}^{q_2} \alpha_{3i} \Delta R_{1t-i} \\ & + \sum_{i=0}^{q_3} \alpha_{4i} \Delta \pi_{t-i} + \varepsilon_{2t} \end{aligned} \tag{25.7}$$

$$\begin{aligned} \Delta R_{1t} = {} & \beta_0 + \gamma_T T + \delta_{R_1} R_{1t-1} + \delta_g g_{t-1} + \delta_{(m-p)}(m-p)_{t-1} + \delta_\pi \pi_{t-1} \\ & + \sum_{i=1}^{p} \alpha_{1i} \Delta R_{1t-i} + \sum_{i=0}^{q_1} \alpha_{2i} \Delta g_{t-i} + \sum_{i=0}^{q_2} \alpha_{3i} \Delta(m-p)_{t-i} \\ & + \sum_{i=0}^{q_3} \alpha_{4i} \Delta \pi_{t-i} + \varepsilon_{3t} \end{aligned} \tag{25.8}$$

$$\Delta\pi_t = \beta_0 + \gamma_T T + \delta_{(m-p)}(m-p)_{t-1} + \delta_g g_{t-1} + \delta_{R_1} R_{1t-1} + \delta_\pi \pi_{t-1} + \sum_{i=1}^{p} \alpha_{1i}\Delta\pi_{t-i} + \sum_{i=0}^{q_1} \alpha_{2i}\Delta g_{t-i} + \sum_{i=0}^{q_2} \alpha_{3i}\Delta R_{1t-i} + \sum_{i=0}^{q_3} \alpha_{4i}\Delta(m-p)_{t-i} + \varepsilon_{4t} \tag{25.9}$$

where

Δ denotes the first differences,
β_0 is the constant (drift),
γ_T is trend coefficient
$\delta_{(m-p)}$, δ_g, δ_{R_1}, and δ_π, are the long-run coefficients and
ε_{1t}, ε_{2t}, ε_{3t}, and ε_{4t} are white noise errors (disturbance terms).

Before estimating Eqs. (25.6), (25.7), (25.8), and (25.9) we should select the optimal lag length. The wrong choice of lag length can lead to biased results on equations' estimation. Moreover, the suitable lag length for each variable of ARDL model is important because we try to avoid non-normality, autocorrelation, and heteroscedasticity of errors terms in an ARDL model. For optimal lag length, we use the Akaike Information Criterion (AIC), Schwarz Bayesian Criterion (SBC), or Hannan–Quinn Criterion (HQC).

Afterwards, the existence of long-run relationship between variables of ARDL model is tested using F statistic, an asymptotic distribution, and we compare it with critical bounds stated in the paper of Pesaran et al. (2001) to ascertain if there exists a co-integrated relationship or not.

The null hypothesis of no co-integration among variables on Eqs. (25.6), (25.7), (25.8), and (25.9) is:

H_0: $\delta_{(m-p)} = \delta_g = \delta_{R_1} = \delta_\pi = 0$ (there is no co-integration—long-run relationship).
H_1: $\delta_{(m-p)} \neq \delta_g \neq \delta_{R_1} \neq \delta_\pi \neq 0$ (there is co-integration—long-run relationship).

Many scientists are interested mainly in long-run relationship between variables. Thus, the concept of co-integration and error correction model (ECM) was developed connecting both the short- and long-run relationship among variables. The error correction model can be formed as follows:

$$\Delta(m-p)_t = \beta_0 + \gamma_T T + \sum_{i=1}^{p} \alpha_{1i}\Delta(m-p)_{t-i} + \sum_{i=0}^{q_1} \alpha_{2i}\Delta g_{t-i} + \sum_{i=0}^{q_2} \alpha_{3i}\Delta R_{1t-i} + \sum_{i=0}^{q_3} \alpha_{4i}\Delta\pi_{t-i} + \lambda_1 \mathrm{ECM}_{t-1} + e_{1t} \tag{25.10}$$

$$\Delta g_t = \beta_0 + \gamma_T T + \sum_{i=1}^{p} \alpha_{1i} \Delta g_{t-i} + \sum_{i=0}^{q_1} \alpha_{2i} \Delta (m-p)_{t-i} + \sum_{i=0}^{q_2} \alpha_{3i} \Delta R_{1t-i} + \sum_{i=0}^{q_3} \alpha_{4i} \Delta \pi_{t-i} + \lambda_2 \mathrm{ECM}_{t-1} + e_{2t} \quad (25.11)$$

$$\Delta R_{1t} = \beta_0 + \gamma_T T + \sum_{i=1}^{p} \alpha_{1i} \Delta R_{1t-i} + \sum_{i=0}^{q_1} \alpha_{2i} \Delta g_{t-i} + \sum_{i=0}^{q_2} \alpha_{3i} \Delta (m-p)_{t-i} + \sum_{i=0}^{q_3} \alpha_{4i} \Delta \pi_{t-i} + \varepsilon_{3t} + \lambda_3 \mathrm{ECM}_{t-1} + e_{3t} \quad (25.12)$$

$$\Delta \pi_t = \beta_0 + \gamma_T T + \sum_{i=1}^{p} \alpha_{1i} \Delta \pi_{t-i} + \sum_{i=0}^{q_1} \alpha_{2i} \Delta g_{t-i} + \sum_{i=0}^{q_2} \alpha_{3i} \Delta R_{1t-i} + \sum_{i=0}^{q_3} \alpha_{4i} \Delta (m-p)_{t-i} + \lambda_4 \mathrm{ECM}_{t-1} + e_{4t} \quad (25.13)$$

The ECM test derives from co-integration models and represents the estimated equilibrium errors. The λ coefficient of ECM is called short-run adjustment coefficient and presents the speed adjustment from equilibrium point or the correction of instability in every period. The sign of λ coefficient must be negative, and its value should be between 0 and 1. Finally, it should be noted that ARDL and ECM models are estimated with least squares method (LS).

25.5.3 Stability and Diagnostic Test

To assure that our estimated model is correctly specified and can be used for forecasting, we should conduct not only the diagnostic test but also the coefficients' stability test. Diagnostic tests examine the model for functional form, non-normality serial correlation, and heteroscedasticity. The stability test is conducted by employing the cumulative sum of recursive residuals (CUSUM) and the cumulative sum of squares of recursive residuals (CUSUMSQ) suggested by Brown et al. (1975). Furthermore, as a final step for the analysis of stability on estimated ARDL model, we test all the inverse roots in relation to the unit circle.

25.6 Empirical Results

Our empirical analysis for money demand of Italy is based on Eq. (25.2). As a proxy for money demand, we use M_1 which contains the monetary circulation. For the estimation and stability of money demand, we use as explanatory variables the gross domestic product, consumer price index, long-run interest rate, and inflation rate as well as ARDL technique. The choice of this technique was made, because it can be applied in small samples and circumvent the problems arising from the stationarity of series. Moreover, this choice is based on the fact that co-integration and error correction model can be applied jointly to determine money demand in Italy in the long-run period and in the short run period.

25.6.1 Data

Time series of the above model is annual covering the period from 1960–2017. Data were derived from World Bank. All variables, except for long-run interest rate and annual rate of inflation, were converted to natural logarithms.

25.6.2 Unit Root Tests

Before continuing to ARDL bounds test, we examine the stationarity of all variables to determine their order of integration. Pesaran et al. (2001) mention that for the integration of time series in an ARDL procedure, time series can be integrated null order $I(0)$ or first order $I(1)$. To determine the integration order of time series in this paper, we use the Dickey–Fuller (1979, 1981), Phillips–Peron (1988), and Kwiatkowski, Phillips, Schmidt, Shin—KPSS (1992) test. The results of the unit root test are presented in Table 25.1.

The results in Table 25.1 show that some variables are integrated null order $I(0)$ and others are integrated order one $I(1)$. Furthermore, because of the small sample, the most proper procedure for co-integration of the series is that of ARDL—autoregressive distributed lags (ARDL) suggested by Pesaran et al. (2001).

25.6.3 Bounds Tests for Co-integration

It was referred that before estimating Eqs. (25.6), (25.7), (25.8), and (25.9), we should choose the optimal lag length. In Fig. 25.1, the lag length of variables is presented using the Akaike criteria (AIC criteria).

Then, in Table 25.2 the results of F statistic are given for the existence of long-run relationship among variables on ARDL model as well as the diagnostic tests for each equation.

According to Narayan (2005), the existing critical values reported in Pesaran et al. (2001) cannot be used for small sample sizes because they are based on large sample sizes. Narayan (2005) provides a set of critical values for sample sizes ranging from

Table 25.1 Unit root tests

Variable	ADF		P-P		KPSS	
Levels						
	C	C, T	C	C, T	C	C, T
m	0.513(0)	−1.988(0)	0.534[6]	−1.970[3]	0.882[6]	0.191[6]**
$m-p$	−1.675(1)	−0.198(0)	−1.788[4]	−0.433[3]	0.526[6]**	0.222[6]
g	−7.448(0)*	−1.459(0)	−7.104[1]*	−1.571[5]	0.865[6]	0.237[6]
R	−1.632(1)	−2.040(1)	−0.830[0]	−1.558[2]	0.297[6]	0.199[6]**
π	−1.491(0)	−2.091(0)	−1.667[3]	−2.169[2]	0.353[6]**	0.153[5]**
First differences						
	C	C, T	C	C, T	C	C, T
Δm	−7.034(0)*	−7.060(0)*	−7.028[5]*	−7.050[6]*	0.202[5]*	0.064[6]*
$\Delta(m-p)$	−5.279(0)*	−5.801(0)*	−5.256[1]*	−5.801[0]*	0.511[4]**	0.123[3]**
Δg	−4.512(0)*	−6.901(0)*	−4.533[4]*	−7.017[6]*	0.926[5]	0.073[6]*
ΔR	−4.786(0)*	−5.216(1)*	−4.538[8]*	−4.480[10]*	0.265[1]*	0.068[3]*
$\Delta\pi$	−6.397(0)*	−6.420(0)*	−6.360[2]*	−6.433[1]*	0.149[2]*	0.072[1]*

1. *, **, and *** show significant at 1%, 5%, and 10% levels, respectively
2. The numbers within parentheses followed by ADF statistics represent the lag length of the dependent variable used to obtain white noise residuals
3. The lag lengths for ADF equation were selected using Schwarz Information Criterion (SIC)
4. Mackinnon (1996) critical value for rejection of hypothesis of unit root applied
5. The numbers within brackets followed by PP statistics represent the bandwidth selected based on Newey and West (1994) method using Bartlett Kernel
6. C Constant, T Trend, Δ First Differences, m logarithm of the nominal M_1 level, p the logarithm of the CPI, g logarithm of real GDP, R long-term interest rate, π annual inflation rate

54 observations. They are 2.01–3.10 at 90%, 2.45–3.63 at 95%, and 3.42–4.84 at 99%.

The results of Table 25.2 show that there are four co-integrating vectors. Thus, we can say that there is a long-run relationship among examined variables of the model.

25.6.4 *Estimated Long-Run and Short-Run Coefficients Using the ARDL Approach*

After the confirmation of long-run relationship among variables and the optimal number of time lags, the next step is to determine the short- and long-run elasticity of co-integrating vectors. The results of equations on long- and short-run dynamic appear in Tables 25.3 and 25.4.

The results in Table 25.3 show that real GDP has a positive long-run effect on nominal M_1. On the other hand, variables representing the opportunity cost, namely

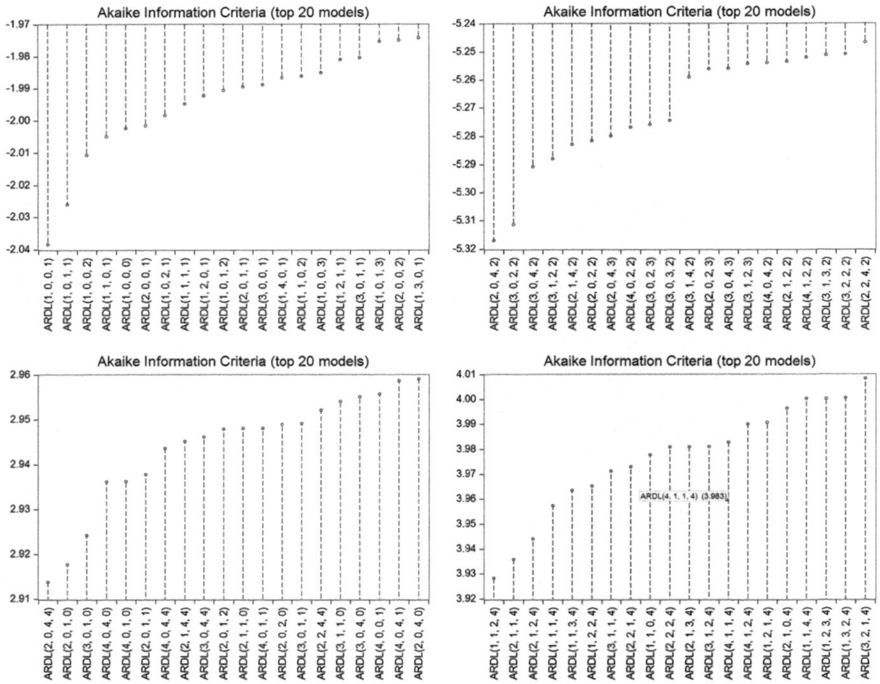

Fig. 25.1 Optimal lag length in Eqs. (25.6), (25.7), (25.8), and (25.9), respectively

Table 25.2 ARDL bounds testing co-integration approach analysis

Bounds testing to co-integration			Diagnostic tests			
Estimated models	Optimal lag length	F-statistics	Jarque-Bera	LM (1)	ARCH (1)	RESET
$F_{m-p}(m-p/g, R_1, \pi)$	(1, 0, 0, 1)	8.258*	0.572	0.025	6.972*	0.527
$F_g(g/m-p, R_1, \pi)$	(2, 0, 4, 2)	5.894*	2.783	0.438	1.239	9.945*
$F_{R1}(R_1/m-p, g, \pi)$	(2, 0, 4, 4)	4.606**	0.157	1.076	0.673	0.836
$F_\pi(\pi/m-p, g, R_1)$	(1, 1, 2, 4)	5.193*	6.665**	0.734	1.144	0.002

*, **, and *** represent significance at 1, 5, and 10% levels, respectively. Appropriate lag length of the variables is selected following AIC

Table 25.3 ARDL long-run results

	Coefficients	S. error	t-statistic
Dependent variable: $m - p$			
g	0.139	0.030	4.500*
R_1	−0.097	0.108	−0.898
π	−0.211	0.189	−1.115
Dependent variable: g			
$m - p$	11.543	1.371	8.416*
R_1	0.944	0.510	1.849**
π	0.283	0.590	0.479
Dependent variable: R_1			
$m - p$	−2.796	1.146	−2.439*
g	0.297	0.093	3.169*
π	0.754	0.130	5.783*
Dependent variable: π			
$m - p$	−6.262	5.551	−1.128
g	0.736	0.608	0.232
R_1	−0.702	0.971	−0.722

*, **, and *** represent significance at 1, 5, and 10% levels, respectively

nominal interest rate and inflation rate, have a negative impact on nominal M_1. The results of this paper agree with economic theory which is referring on long-run relationship of money demand. Due to the fact that real GDP is also statistical significant in 1% level of significance, we can conclude that an increase of GDP by 1% will increase money demand by 0.14% approximately.

The short-run results in Table 25.4 denote that the short-run coefficient on error correction term is negative in all equations and statistical significant in 1% level of significance. This implies that there is a long-run relationship among variables for Italy. Also, this result denotes that short-run variations from the long-run equilibrium are corrected by 4% each year on first equation.

In addition, the results of first equation show a positive relationship between GDP, the long-run interest rate and money demand and negative relationship between money demand and inflation. Because only inflation rate is statistical significant in 1% level of significance, we can claim that an increase on inflation by 1% will reduce money demand in Italy by 0.02% approximately in the short run.

Finally, all diagnostic tests (Table 25.2) satisfy all the assumptions of the linear regression model with autocorrelation and heteroscedasticity being absent, while residuals are normally distributed.

Table 25.4 ARDL short-run results

	Coefficients	S. error	t-statistic
Dependent variable: $\Delta(m - p)$			
Δg	0.076	0.362	0.210
ΔR_1	0.006	0.009	0.661
$\Delta \pi$	−0.018	0.006	−3.089*
ECM_{t-1}	−0.037	0.007	−5.011*
Dependent variable: Δg			
$\Delta g(-1)$	0.239	0.140	1.702***
$\Delta(m - p)$	0.006	0.028	0.231
ΔR_1	0.001	0.002	0.820
$\Delta R_1(-1)$	−0.010	0.002	−4.653*
$\Delta R_1(-2)$	0.002	0.002	0.881
$\Delta R_1(-3)$	−0.003	0.002	−1.825**
$\Delta \pi$	0.002	0.001	1.640***
ECM_{t-1}	−0.001	0.0004	−4.126*
Dependent variable: ΔR_1			
$\Delta R_1(-1)$	0.379	0.116	0.002
$\Delta(m - p)$	0.331	1.443	0.229
Δg	12.612	7.594	1.660***
$\Delta g(-1)$	2.475	6.797	0.364
$\Delta g(-2)$	−3.503	7.003	−0.500
$\Delta g(-3)$	9.396	6.192	1.517
$\Delta \pi$	0.247	0.069	3.564*
ECM_{t-1}	−0.242	0.056	−4.312*
Dependent variable: $\Delta \pi$			
$\Delta(m - p)$	−8.921	2.387	−3.736*
Δg	15.251	11.213	1.360
$\Delta g(-1)$	21.863	11.411	1.915**
ΔR_1	0.779	0.173	4.494*
$\Delta R_1(-1)$	−0.069	0.232	−0.299
$\Delta R_1(-2)$	−0.040	0.214	−0.189
$\Delta R_1(-3)$	0.541	0.175	3.086*
ECM_{t-1}	−0.173	0.036	−4.800*

*, **, and *** represent significance at 1, 5, and 10% levels, respectively

25.6.5 Stability Test

The stability of long-run coefficients is tested from short-run dynamic of the model. On error correction models presented in Table 25.4, the cumulative sum of recursive residuals (CUSUM) and the CUSUM of square (CUSUMSQ) are applied to evaluate parameters' stability. In Fig. 25.2, the results on CUSUM and CUSUMSQ on first equation are presented.

From Fig. 25.2, we can see that the plots of statistics on CUSUM and CUSUMSQ are within the critical bounds at 5% level of significance, denoting that the regression model is stable.

In Fig. 25.3, the results on stability test of the estimated money demand function are presented, checking for all inverse roots of the model.

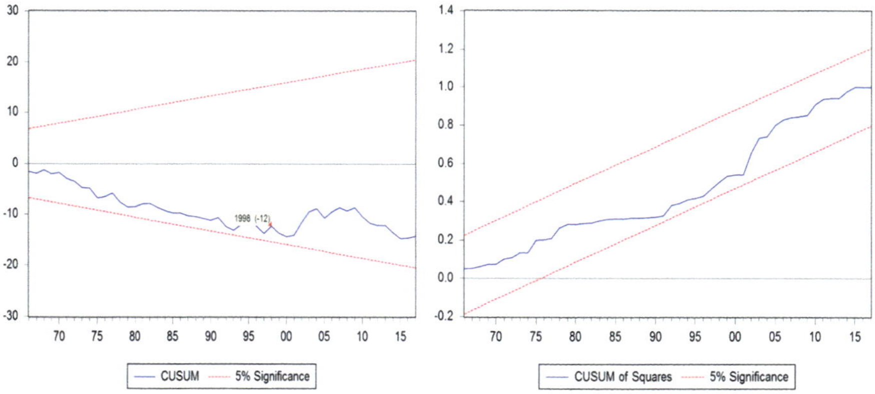

Fig. 25.2 Plot of CUSUM and CUSUMSQ for the coefficient stability of ECM model

Fig. 25.3 Inverse roots for equations presented in Table 25.4

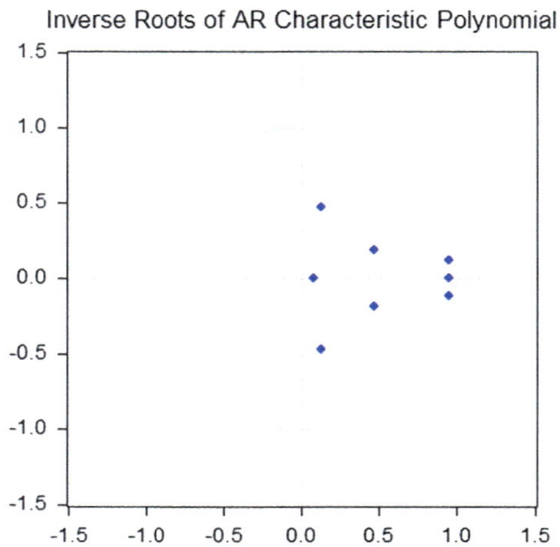

The results in Fig. 25.3 show that all inverse roots of the model are inside the unit circle.

So, the results both in Figs. 25.2 and 25.3 show that the stability condition is satisfied as the plots of CUSUM and CUSUMSQ are within the critical bounds and also that all inverse roots are all strictly inside the unit circle.

25.7 Conclusions and Policy Implications

Friedman and Schwartz on their paper «*A Monetary History of the United States, 1867–1960*» in 1963 argued that money demand is a function of income and interest rate. Later, due to variations on financial markets, money demand was unstable. Specifically, money demand seemed to be non-sensitive in interest rates, and there was an exogenous volatility. Various researchers attributed this volatility on financial markets as well as technological innovations.

The present paper examines the stability of money demand for Italy for the period 1960–2017. For this purpose, we use the currently developed econometric co-integrating technique ARDL and the error correction model ECM for long-run and short-run equilibrium relationship on time series of the model. The results of ARDL technique and ECM show that there is a long-run and short-run relationship among variables used with the real income, long-run interest rate, and inflation to be in accordance with the expectations of monetary theory. Finally, the results of stability tests CUSUM and CUSUMSQ and unit circle confirm the long-run relationship among variables showing that the stability condition is satisfied when money demand in Italy is estimated with M_1 variable for the examined period.

To sum up, we can state that in the examined period real GDP has a positive long-run effect on nominal M_1 for Italy, while variables representing the opportunity costs, namely nominal interest rate and inflation rate, show a negative effect on nominal M_1. The results agree with economic theory which is referring to long-run relationship of money demand. Also, the results on short-run period show a positive relationship among GDP, interest rate, and money demand and a negative one between money demand and inflation.

Appendix

Data Sources (World Bank).
Data (ITALY).
Price index: Consumer Price Index—CPI (Base 2010 = 100) is the price level.
Money level: M_1 is the nominal money variable.
Income: Gross domestic product—GDP (constant 2010 US$).
Long-term interest rate: Average government bond yield (interest rate on government bonds %).

Short-term interest rate: Average deposit rate (interest rate %).
Annual inflation rate: Inflation consumer prices (annual %).

References

Andersen, S. P. (1985). The stability of money demand functions: An alternative approach. *BIS Economic Papers, 14*, 1–72.

Brown, R. L., Durbin, J., & Evans, J. M. (1975). Techniques for testing the constancy of regression relationship over time. *Journal of the Royal Statistical Society: Series B, 37*, 149–192.

Capasso, S., & Napolitano, O. (2012). Testing for the stability of money demand in Italy: Has the euro influenced the monetary transmission mechanism? *Applied Economics, 44*(24), 3121–3133.

Caruso, M. (2006). Stock market fluctuations and money demand in Italy, 1913–2003. *Economic Notes, 35*(1), 1–47.

Daniele, V., Foresti, P., & Napolitano, O. (2017). The stability of money demand in the long-run: Italy 1861–2011. *Cliometrica, 11*(2), 217–244.

Dickey, D. A., & Fuller, W. A. (1979). Distributions of the estimators for autoregressive time series with a unit root. *Journal of American Statistical Association, 74*(366), 427–431.

Dickey, D. A., & Fuller, W. A. (1981). Likelihood ratio statistics for autoregressive time series with a unit root. *Econometrica, 49*(4), 1057–1072.

Favero, C., & Spinelli, F. (1999). Deficits, money growth and inflation in Italy: 1875–1994. *Economic Notes, 28*(1), 43–71.

Friedman, M. (1956). In M. Friedman (Ed.), *The quantity theory of money: A restatement in studies in the quantity theory of money* (pp. 3–21). Chicago: University of Chicago Press.

Friedman, M., & Schwartz, A. J. (1963). *A monetary history of the United States, 1867–1960*. Princeton: Princeton University Press for NBER.

Gaiotti, E., & Secchi, A. (2012). *Monetary policy and fiscal dominance in Italy from the early 1970s to the adoption of the euro: A review*. Questioni di Economia e Finanza (Occasional Papers). Rome: Bank of Italy.

Gianfreda, G., & Janson, N. (2001). Le banche di emissione in Italia tra il 1861 e il 1893: un caso di concorrenza? *Rivista di Politica Economica, 91*(1), 15–74.

Keynes, J. M. (1936). *The general theory of employment, interest and money*. First Published Macmillan Cambridge University Press, for Royal Economic Society in 1936.

Kwiatkowski, D., Phillips, P. C. B., Schmidt, P., & Shin, Y. (1992). Testing the null hypothesis of stationarity against the alternative of a unit root. *Journal of Econometrics, 54*, 159–178.

MacKinnon, J. G. (1996). Numerical distribution functions for unit root and cointegration tests. *Journal of Applied Econometrics, 11*(6), 601–618.

Mark, N., & Sul, D. (2003). Cointegration vector estimation by panel DOLS and long run money demand. *Oxford Bulletin of Economics and Statistics, 65*(5), 655–680.

McCandless, G. T., & Weber, W. (1995). Some monetary facts. *Quarterly Review, 19*(3), 2–11.

Mishkin, F. S. (1995). Symposium on the monetary transmission mechanism. *Journal of Economic Perspectives, 9*(4), 3–10.

Muscatelli, V. A., & Spinelli, F. (2000). The long-run stability of the demand for money: Italy 1861–1996. *Journal of Monetary Economics, 45*, 717–739.

Narayan, P. (2005). The saving and investment nexus for China: Evidence from cointegration tests. *Applied Economics, 37*(17), 1979–1990.

Newey, W. K., & West, K. D. (1994). Automatic lag selection in covariance matrix estimation. *Review of Economic Studies, 61*(4), 631–654.

Pesaran, M. H., Shin, Y., & Smith, R. J. (2001). Bounds testing approaches to the analysis of long run relationships. *Journal of Applied Econometrics, 16*, 289–326.

Phillips, P. C. B., & Perron, P. (1988). Testing for a unit root in time series regression. *Biometrika, 75,* 335–346.

Thornton, J. (1998). The long-run demand for currency and broad money in Italy, 1861–1980. *Applied Economics Letters, 5,* 157–159.

Chapter 26
Can Time-Driven Activity-Based Costing Applied in Show Caves

Nikolaos Kartalis, Ioannis Velentzas and Georgia Broni

Abstract This article aims at studying and implementing the latest and most modern version of activity-based costing, known as time-driven activity-based costing (TD-ABC). Product and service costing is a process of major importance for enterprises to be able to form their pricing policy, but also to control the cost of the produced products or services provided, both partly and totally. Pricing types vary and are determined by different criteria for each case, taking into account the mode of operation and the strategy followed by each business. This costing method was applied to a service provider, in particular show cave organization, providing extremely useful conclusions to the show cave management regarding its operation, being a reliable tool for assessing both its existing and future operations plans.

Keywords Cost management systems · Activity-based costing · Time-driven activity-based costing

JEL Codes M41 · M11

26.1 Introduction

Cost was and still is a permanent "headache" in the world of entrepreneurship. The consecutive effort to reduce cost as much as possible has always been one of the most important fields of study from the managers. During the last decades and specifically after the industrial revolution, there was a rapid development of companies, which it had created the solid ground for more wealth and income increase, but at the same time the use of new resources for production led to the substantial increase of expenditures. When this came to sight, decisions had to be made and methods had to be established in order to trace and reduce cost.

N. Kartalis (✉) · I. Velentzas · G. Broni
University of Western Macedonia, 50100, Kila Kozanis, Greece
e-mail: kartalisdn@gmail.com

N. Tsounis and A. Vlachvei (eds.), *Advances in Cross-Section Data Methods in Applied Economic Research*, Springer Proceedings in Business and Economics,
https://doi.org/10.1007/978-3-030-38253-7_26

Activity-based cost (ABC) systems present a method in which cost is assigned in products or other cost objects based on how much these products or cost objects use the resources of production. Activity, on the other hand, is a procedure which the company uses to produce something. The more the activities, the more the cost. So, the essence of this method lies in the assumption that activities are the reason that cost is been created. In order for a system like that to be implemented has to be done in various stages of implementation. The privileges of ABC are reflected from the complicated procedure of its implementation. All costs information that must be collected from the various parts of the company, sometimes creates problems in the application of the model. On the other hand, this utilities and the emphasis in detail is what gives these systems the liability of their results.

Time-driven activity-based costing was developed with the thought to overcome the difficulties of the ABC implementation. This model presents a different and more practical method for cost tracing in products or other cost objects. The system is based on measuring the time of the activities which they represent the springboard of cost allocation. The important issue with this method is that it can trace the practical capacity so there can be found that in what percentage the company's resources are used correctly, and if so which activities which does not add value and only create cost are traced. Despite all the positive characteristics and the details of these methods (ABC and TD-ABC), most companies still remain loyal to the usage of traditional costing systems.

26.2 Literature Review

Cost is the cash amount that is been sacrificed for goods and services that are expected to bring future or current incomes to the company.[1] Managers pursuit to reduce cost in order to increase the company's efficiency. Some of the most known traditional costing systems are: *The absorption costing*; in this method, it makes no difference if the cost is variable or not. *Variable cost costing*; in this system, the elements of the product cost change with the production stage. *Job-order costing*; this system is applied in companies where, in different periods, we have large production of different kind of products.[2] *Process costing*; the fundamental characteristic of this method is that we have production of large quantities of products that are similar to each other and not specific orders.

According to Cooper and Kaplan (1998), activity-based cost systems can provide great help in a more accurate study of the production process compared to traditional cost systems and that is the reason they provide detailed information regarding cost.

Carolfi (1996) stated that ABC systems provide detailed information about the activities that add value to the product as well as to those which do not. With this information, the company can reduce cost by planning products and processes which

[1] Mowen et al. (2014).

[2] Garrison and Noreen (2002).

consume less activity resources, emphasizing at the same time on eradicating the activities which do not add value to the product. Furthermore, Borthick (1995) makes clear that activities such as measuring, control and displacement increase the length of the production process, and with the current cost systems, there can be a reduce on the production circle aiming in minimizing the delay.

According to Agliati (2002), the basic characteristic of cost systems in a multinational company can be explained by four factors: The structure of production cost of the product, the methodology that is been used for cost tracing, and the allocation methods which support the comparisons between service cost and support cost.

Roztocki and Weistroffer (2005) propose a new frame of work for the evaluation of information by implementing analyzed data based on ABC and fuzzy systems. These systems rely on the thought that they will be useful for companies under development economies, where the economic environment is unstable and exists a lack of historical accounting data.

Anand (2004) presented a practical application of ABC. Issues regarding the implementation of ABC were taken into consideration. These issues had to do with the level of success regarding the stage of implementation of the ABC and the factors which affects it. From the 53 companies that were examined, 23 used ABC systems for the billing the operational feedback of their products. Companies that implemented these systems had a significant advantage in tracing the most accurate information about cost compared to companies that had not implemented ABC systems.

Kaplan and Anderson (2007) presented time-driven activity-based costing. This method demands fewer procedures than the common ABC and yields more accurate information about cost per product unit.

According to Bruggeman and Everaert (2007), TD-ABC isolates different characteristics of each activity by using time equations according to which the time consumed by one activity is an operation of different utilities. According to the equation, time and cost of an activity equal the cost of the object based on its characteristics. The method is been comprised of six stages:

1. Identify of used recourses and activities.
2. Define cost of the resources.
3. Calculation of the practical capacity of every source.
4. Calculate unit cost per time.
5. Calculate the necessary time units of each activity.
6. Calculate cost of every transaction.

Terungwa (2012) studied the practical application of TD-ABC in small service companies and analyzed the profitability of various customers. The purpose of the study was to make clear if the implementation of TD-ABC in small companies can enhance efficiency by causing more profit. For making this study happen, a restaurant was randomly selected and a questionnaire and interview were used for gaining data.

The result showed that using TD-ABC compared to the existed methods already, TD-ABC provides more data and information regarding cost and that managers of small companies can use time equations to calculate the necessary time of the activities so they can improve the costing procedure while increasing profitability.

In an article Monroy et al. (2012), there was a comparison between three methods: ABC, TD-ABC and lean accounting. The comparison was made based on what information each method provides and impact do these informations have. The conclusion was that in lean accounting, decisions are made based on the value stream while in ABC are made in the stage that every product is produced and in the TD-ABC decisions are made based on the status of the product and the stage of the implementation.

Ilhan et al. (2009) studied the profitability of different groups of customers in a four-star hotel in Turkey by implementing TD-ABC. The conclusion was that profitability varied in different groups and a determinant part of this had the implementation of TD-ABC compared to the traditional cost system that had applied already.

26.3 Theory Implication for ABC and TD-ABC

(a) ABC

The effect ABC had, since it was first presented in the 80s, led to substantial changes in regard to the already existed traditional cost systems. According to the traditional cost systems, a large cost pool was used and based on that the cost allocation took place. During the production process, the calculation of direct labor cost was the most common choice for overhead cost allocation, since it was a big part of production cost. There was this thought that a big correlation between direct labors' works, total production units and overhead costs existed.

When companies started to create more products and services, an abundance of production appeared. That inevitably caused a rise to overhead cost because now companies had to invest in production planning, hiring specially qualified mechanics and product designers.[3]

ABC managed to correct mistakes in overhead cost allocation, by interpreting an activity as a cost driver. According to this method, any procedure that consumes overhead resources constitutes an activity in the production process. The bottom of the ABC system lies on the idea that a product creates cost by causing activities which on their turn create cost. This leads us to the conclusion that since the cost is been caused by an activity, a complex in design product will make up a larger part of cost allocation. Next, it will assign the activity cost on products, orders and clients based on the quantity of every consumption of each operational activity.

[3]Garrison and Noreen (2002).

The implementation of an ABC system takes place in these stages[4]:

First Stage ABC.

i. Activities identification, cost pool of activities and quantity of activities.

In this stage, the activities that will make up the backbone of the system are identified. The resources and the activities are shared out in five categories[5]:

- Resources that were obtained and activities which carried out for specific product units or service.
- Resources that were obtained and activities that carried out so a group of similar products was able to be created.
- Resources that were obtained and activities which carried out for the production and sale of one specific product or service.
- Resources that were obtained and activities which carried out for the service of specific customers.
- Resources that were obtained and activities that carried out so they can provide the general capacity and warehouse for the production of goods and services.

ii. Assign overhead cost to activities cost pools.

In the ABC systems, the process of assigning overhead cost derives from the company's general ledger. The methods for this procedure are three: direct, driven and allocated. The precision of the results is better during the direct and driven methods. Also, the cost pool activity provides more information that helps for specific decision to be made.[6]

Second Stage ABC.

i. Calculation of activities indexes.

The activities indexes represent the total cost of each activity, toward the total activity that the company requires so to be able to produce its current product and then to supply it to the customers.

ii. Assign overhead cost to cost objects.

Here, the activity indexes assign with overhead cost the products and services. Each product or service is been assigned depending on how much quantity of the activity has consumed multiplied by its activity index.

---

[4]Hilton (2008), Garrison and Noreen (2002).

[5]Hilton et al. (2008).

[6]Noreen (1991).

(b) TD-ABC

TD-ABC was designed as a simple version of its predecessor ABC. The thought was to simplify the complexity of gathering data. For every resources group, two variables are calculated: Cost per time unit of supply resources and how many times the units of the products consume the available resources.[7]

The implementation process of the TD-ABC comprised of six steps[8]:

1. Identify several resources groups that carry out the activities.
2. Calculate the cost of each group.
3. Calculate the practical capacity of each resources group.
4. Calculate the unit cost of each group by dividing the total cost of resources group with the practical capacity.
5. Define the time needed for each activity with different time drivers.
6. Multiply unit cost with the time needed, for the tracing of the cost in the cost objects.

Companies usually separate cost in direct and indirect, but if we separate cost in three categories by adding overhead cost, then their relationship with cost objects is more suitable. Direct cost can be measured immediately through company's ERP 186 system by gathering continuous information about cost object; in indirect cost where the resource's consumption is not traceable by the first sight, the activity-based cost systems take part as tools for that matter. Overhead cost that is not caused by cost objects such as clients or orders but remains crucial source of information for the company can be calculated by TD-ABC.

Indirect cost is measured and allocated in cost pools. The cost of these used resources is actually the indirect cost compared with the cost object such as clients and orders. The cost objects typically are clients and products, so the starting points for an ABC model are those. TD-ABC is a simple solution specified in relation with the allocation of resource pools. The characteristics of this sector are that cost is not measured. The basic source here is the employees who produce services supported by the systems they use (computers etc.). The resources cost that they have available is calculated to reach resource pool.

(c) Time Drivers

Time drivers are used for the calculation of the usage of resources that is been done by the cost objects. The epitome of TD-ABC lies in the fact that the measuring of resources consumption happens based on time. The capacity of a resource pool can be measured in minutes, hours or even years, with the total of those representing the capacity of the resource pool. There is a difference between paid capacity and practical capacity. For the practical capacity to be calculated the time considered for employees holiday absence, disease and matters of this nature are not included in the resources pool but are taken under consideration by assuming a practical capacity

[7] Kaplan and Anderson (2004).

[8] Kaplan and Anderson (2004).

of 80%.[9] In this model, only the transaction drivers are been considered which are mostly time indexes and they are determined in advance.

Time driver can have three types as variables[10]:

1. Continuous variables: The weight of a pallet or a distance in km.
2. Isolated variables: The number of orders.
3. Index variables: The type of customer (old or new), the type of order (regular or express).

(d) Activities

There are three types of activities:

1. The case where the resource pool is only one activity and one driver.
2. The case where a number of subactivities exist.
3. The complex situation in which the subactivities cannot be identified immediately but they have to be "designed" by a specific method studying the use of resources by the resource pool.

This model reveals us that a process usually comprised of several subactivities but not all steps of each reaction in a procedure are applied. In every process, any likely subactivity has to be traced and explained. Also, there is a fixed time for every activity and subactivity in which this time has to be assumed or even better measured.

(e) Mathematical Formula

The mathematical formula of this system depends on the characteristics of every activity of the company as we mentioned[11]:

$$\text{Cost of event } E \text{ of activity } A = t_{A,E} * C_i$$

C_i cost per time unit
$t_{A,E}$ time consumed by event E of activity A.

Then with the use of time equations, the time that event E of activity A consumes shows us the function of their several characteristics. In the end, the equation has this form[12]:

$$t_{A,E} = \beta_0 + \beta_1 * X_1 + \beta_2 * X_2 + \beta_3 * X_3 + \cdots + \beta_\rho * X_\rho$$

$t_{A,E}$ time needed for the event E of activity A
β_0 fixed time for activity A

[9]Kaplan and Cooper (1998).
[10]Bruggeman et al. (2005).
[11]Bruggemann et al. (2005).
[12]Bruggemann et al. (2005).

β_1 time consumption of a time unit of driver X_i
X_i the time drivers
P the number of time driver that defines the time needed for activity A.

ABC and TD-ABC Comparison

Comparing the two methods, we cannot clearly say which one is better because that depends from the circumstances of each company, the regulations of the country that the company carries out its activity, the kind of company and of course the competitive environment. Regarding the cost tracing, we can say that the basic difference between the two lays on the element of unused capacity which TD-ABC is capable of measuring it while ABC cannot. The time drivers of TD-ABC play a significant part while the cost drivers of ABC are not adequate. Also, ABC requires more time for any kind of upgrade of its system in any new circumstances that may appear, while TD-ABC can simply integrate any change by adding new driver in the time equations.

26.4 Research Method and Findings

The department of the show cave company costing 42,000 € per quarter. The show cave company has seven employees performing the major work. For simplicity, we assume that all costs are committed for the period. They will not vary based on actual work performed. During the most recent period, the show cave company performed three types of activities.

(1) Guiding 40,000 visitors
(2) Performed 500 documents.

We already know that the cost of the department totals 42,000 € which includes all the cost needed to compensate the managers, information technology, etc.

To calculate the practical capacity of the department assume that the seven employees work 480 (8 h * 60 min per hour) minutes per day. This of course is practically impossible because we have launch breaks or maybe some kind of malfunction that can reduce this capacity time. Since there is no inside regulation about breaks, we will assume that the practical capacity is 80% of the paid capacity. Thus, our practical capacity is 480 min * 80% = 384 min per day or 11.520 min per month per employee. Thus, 11,520 min per month * 7 employees = 80,640 per month * 4 (months) = 322,560 min (quarterly).

The formula and calculations for the capacity cost rate are:

$$\begin{aligned}\text{Capacity cost rate} &= \text{Cost of capacity supplied/Practical capacity of resources supplied} \\ &= 42,000\ \text{€}/322,560 = 0.13\ \text{€ per min.}\end{aligned}$$

Now, we calculate the cost driver for the two activities

Activity	Unit time	Cost driver rate 0.13/min
Guiding	60	7.8
Handle paperwork	10	1.3

Then we apply these cost drivers to the two different activities performed in the department.

Activity	Unit time	Quantity	Total minutes	Total costs
Guiding	60	10,000	60,000	7800 €
Handle paperwork	10	1000	10,000	1300 €
Used capacity			70,000	9100 €
Unused capacity (78%)			252,560	32,900 €
Total			322,560	42,000 €

The above analysis reveals that only 22% of the practical capacity (42,000/322,560) of the resources supplied during the period was used for productive work; hence, the 78% of the total expenses of 42,000 € are assigned to customers during the period.

26.5 Conclusion

Between ABC and TD-ABC, there is a difference regarding the simplification of gathering data. Despite the fact that ABC uses very detailed methods on tracing cost, it is difficult and requires a lot of time for its implementation. TDABC came to make this fact easier so it can be a considerable choice by managers.

In this article, we wished to show if truly the TD-ABC application is easy. The basic components of implementation which are the activities were easily tracked down personal observation as well as interviews with the high staff. In organized companies, information such of these can be collected easier by the company's ERP system. Based on our theory, we were able to time measure the activities and form our time equations so further calculate the cost. With our calculations, we were able to reveal the practical capacity, and we can conclude from the results that the practical capacity is at minimum rate compared to the capacity needed for the activities to be carried out. This means that the employees' yields work more than three times their practical capacity which means in the current exist a serious lack of employees.

Regarding cost, in one hand we have less employment cost but one the other hand this lead to customers unsatisfaction and company's loss of the performance.

References

Agliati, M. (2002). *Costing strategies in multinational companies*. DIR Research Division Working Paper.

Borthick, A. F., & Roth H. P. (1995). *Accounting for time: Reengineering business processes to improve responsiveness*. In S. M. Young (Eds.), *Readings in management accounting*. Prentice Hall: Englewood Cliffs, NJ.

Bruggeman, W., & Everaert, P. (2007). Time driven activity-based costing: Exploring the underlying model. *Journal of Cost Management, 21*(2).

Bruggeman, W., Everaert, P., Anderson, S. R., & Levant, Y. (2005). *Modeling logistics costs using time-driven ABC: A case in distribution company*. Belgium: Faculty of Economics, University of Ghent.

Carolfi, I. A. (1996). ABM can improve quality and control costs. *Cost & Management*.

Dalci, I., Tanis, V., & Kosan, L. (2009). Customer profitability analysis with time-driven activity based costing: A case study in a hotel. *International Journal of Contemporary Hospitality Management, 22*(5).

Fladkjaer, H., & Jensen, E. (2011). *The ABC Paradox: Is time-driven ABC relevant for small & medium sized enterprises?* Department of Business & Management, Aalborg University.

Garrison, R. H., & Noreen, E. W. (2002). Managerial accounting (10th Ed.). New York: McGraw-Hill.

Hilton, R. W. (2008). *Managerial accounting: Creating value in a dynamic business environment* (7th Ed.). New York: McGraw-Hill.

Hilton, R.W., Maher, M. W., & Selto, F. H. (2008). *Costo management: Strategies for business decisions* (4th Ed.). New York: McGraw-Hill.

Kaplan, R. S., & Anderson, S. R. (2004). *Time driven activity base costing*. Cambridge, MA: Harvard Business Review.

Kaplan, R. S., & Anderson, S. R. (2007). The innovation of time driven activity based costing. *Cost Management*.

Kaplan, R. S., & Cooper, R. (1998). *Cost & effect: Using integrated cost systems to drive profitability & performance*. Cambridge, MA: Harvard Business School Press.

Manoj, A. (2004). A review of research in the theory & practice of cost management. *South Asian Journal of Management, 11*(1).

Monroy, C. R., Nasiri, A., & Pelaez, M. A. (2012). Activity based costing, time-driven activity based costing & lean accounting: Differences among three accounting systems approach to manufacturing. In *6th International Conference on Industrial Engineering & Industrial Management*, July.

Mowen, M., Hansen, D. R., & Heitger, D. L. (2014). *Cornerstones of managerial accounting* (5th Ed.). South-Western Cengage Learning.

Noreen, E. (1991). Condition under which activity based cost systems provide relevant costs. *Journal of Management Accounting*.

Roztocki, N., & Weistroffer, H. R. (2005). Evaluating information technology investments: A fuzzy activity-based costing approach. *Journal of Information Science & Technology, 2*(4).

Terugwa, A. (2012). Practicability of time-driven activity based costing on profitability of restaurants in Makundi Metropolis of Benue state, Nigeria. *Journal of Contemporary Management*.

Chapter 27
Managerial Decisions in Relation to the Management of Corporate Profitability Performance in the Manufacturing Industry in the Czech Republic

Markéta Šeligová and Zhang Yi

Abstract The aim of the chapter is to evaluate elements of managerial decision making on the profitability of corporate performances in the Czech Republic. In order to achieve the aim, we investigate the relationship between profitability of corporate performance (measured through gross operating profit) and the elements that are the subject of managerial decision making in the production process and which can impact on the profitability of corporate performance. This is mainly the cash conversion cycle (including accounts receivables, accounts payables and inventory), financial assets and financial debt. The correlation analysis, the Granger causality test and the generalized method of moments (GMM) will be used in the assessment of the elements of managerial decision making on the profitability of corporate performances in the Czech Republic. The data sample will include data for the period 2007–2017. The analysis will include companies operating according to the CZ-NACE classification in the manufacturing industry in the Czech Republic. In this research, we used a sample of 3645 manufacturing companies. Using the correlation analysis, the Granger causality test and the GMM showed a statistically significant relationship between the elements of the managerial decision making (such as cash conversion cycle, financial assets, and financial debt) and the gross operating profit in manufacturing companies in the Czech Republic.

Keywords Cash conversion cycle · Gross operating profit · Financial assets · Financial debt

JEL Code M41

M. Šeligová (✉)
Department of Finance and Accounting, School of Business Administration, Silesian University, Univerzitní nám. 1934/3, 733 40 Karviná, Czech Republic
e-mail: seligova@opf.slu.cz

Z. Yi
School of Accounting, Shanxi University of Finance and Economics, 108 Jinyang Road, Taiyuan 030006, Shanxi, China
e-mail: zzyyfree@126.com

N. Tsounis and A. Vlachvei (eds.), *Advances in Cross-Section Data Methods in Applied Economic Research*, Springer Proceedings in Business and Economics,
https://doi.org/10.1007/978-3-030-38253-7_27

27.1 Introduction

Non-financial corporations or the business sector as such are the backbone of the entire Czech economy. In order for businesses to develop their investment activities, they need to have a significant amount of liquidity. If the company does not have the necessary funds, it can also use foreign sources of financing in addition to its own funding to develop its investment activities. The enormous development of theoretical and empirical literature on corporate finance in recent years has brought a plethora of views on how capital structure, corporate liquidity and working capital are important to the value of a business, the profit of a business and its investment decisions.

In connection with financial and corporate characteristics, it is necessary to distinguish what type of business is involved. Whether they are enterprises that can be distinguished by size (small, medium-sized, large, very large), by industry (e.g., manufacturing, construction or services), by ownership (e.g., private, state, cooperative, church, foundation), according to focus and management (profit and non-profit enterprises) and the like.

SMEs are an integral part of the national economy, where they are an important driver of employment. In relation to large enterprises, many studies have pointed to the strong interdependence of medium-sized and large enterprises, where the deterioration in the competitiveness of large enterprises and their potential investment will be reflected in the economic situation of medium-sized enterprises acting as suppliers of individual goods and services. In relation to foreign sources of financing, these enterprises are considered by financial institutions to be a risk group of debtors due to their weak financial strength.

No less important is the division of enterprises by industry. Manufacturing contributes most to the production of capital goods and significantly affects the level of the economy as a whole. It is an important segment of the economy, which is an important vehicle for the development of technology, knowledge and jobs. Different types of liquidity, working capital and different investment opportunities, diversified use of individual sources of funding and their consequent impact on business performance will be characteristic of each type of business.

All manufacturing firms need to understand the association between these two variables to arrive at optimal financial decisions. Though theories exist on the topic, empirical methods are inadequately focused in arriving at conclusions. Use of statistical methods in understanding the relationship is systematic and scientific, which may provide better insight for decision making. Working capital management is most crucial aspect of economic performance of a firm. Effective working capital decisions contribute to the profitability and attainment of overall objectives of an organization on one hand and provide liquidity to the firm on the other. For several reasons, capital budgeting decisions are influenced by operating managers to larger extent and the day-to-day management of liquidity, short-term obligations, uninterrupted operations calls for effective working capital decisions that forms the domain of finance function.

Based on the above, the aim of the chapter is to evaluate elements of managerial decision making on the profitability of corporate performances in the Czech Republic. In order to achieve the aim, the following research question will be identified and evaluated:

- What is the impact of managerial decision making on the profitability of corporate performances in manufacturing industry in the Czech Republic?

The first part of the chapter is focused on literature review. The next section contains the methodology and overview of the data used. The third part of the chapter is devoted to the results and discussion.

27.2 Literature Review

Many authors have concluded in their studies that the elements of managerial decision making and capital structuring are two areas that have an impact on business performance. Some authors have examined the relationship between business profitability and working capital management (inventories, receivables, payables). According to Deloof (2003), working capital management has a significant impact on business performance.

According to Howorth and Westhead (2003), some research has shown that money management firms are larger firms dealing with lower cash sales and cash problems. While smaller businesses focused more on inventory management, less profitable businesses focused on managing their loans. It can be seen from the above that there is a strong relationship between the money transfer cycle in the company and its profitability. The three different components of the cash conversion cycle (liabilities, receivables and inventories) can be managed in a variety of ways to maximize business performance profitability or to increase company growth.

Balasundaram (2010) examined the effect of working capital management on the profitability of manufacturing companies over the period 2003–2007 using correlation analysis and regression analysis. Results of the CCC and return on assets are negatively correlated. It means that the growth of a cash conversion cycle reduces the profitability of companies measured by return on assets (ROA). Furthermore, the growth of inventory conversion period (ICP) was found to increase return on asset companies. Further, the CCC variable is negative at a value of −0.0503 and p value is 0.006. This implies that the increase in the day's cash conversion cycle by 1 day is associated with a decline in ROA by 5.03%. The results suggest that managers can increase the profitability of manufacturing firms by reducing the number of day's inventories and accounts receivable. Working capital management plays a significant role in improved profitability of firms. Firms can achieve optimal management of working capital by making the trade-off between profitability and liquidity.

Chary et al. (2011) argue that theoretically working capital decision affects both liquidity and profitability. Excess of investment in working capital may result in low profitability, and lower investment may result in poor liquidity. Management need to trade off between liquidity and profitability to maximize shareholders wealth. For this reason, in their study, they investigated the companies operating in the pharmaceutical industry for the period from 2003 to 2008 through correlation analysis, regression analysis and Chi-square test. Furthermore, they also showed that the growth of stocks in the company will reduce the profitability of enterprises.

Golas et al. (2013) examined the relationship between working capital and profitability of companies in Poland for the years 2005–2009. The effectiveness of working capital management were evaluated using a cycles of inventories, receivables, liabilities and cash conversion cycle and in relation to rates of return earned on assets. Studies have shown that in industries where these cycles are the shortest achieved the highest rate of return. The beneficial effect of shortening the cycle of working capital on profitability was also verified by using regression analysis.

Lazaridis and Tryfonidis (2006) investigate the relationship of corporate profitability and working capital management from 2001 to 2004. The authors tried to establish using correlation analysis and regression analysis a relationship that is significant between profitability, the cash conversion cycle and its components. The results of research showed that there is statistical significance between profitability, measured through gross operating profit and the cash conversion cycle. Authors found a negative relationship between profitability (measured through gross operating profit) and the cash conversion cycle which was used as a measure of working capital management efficacy. Authors also found that lower gross operating profit is associated with an increase in the number days of accounts payables. The above could lead to the conclusion that less profitable firms wait longer to pay their bills taking advantage of credit period granted by their suppliers. The negative relationship between accounts receivables and firms' profitability suggests that less profitable firms will pursue a decrease of their accounts receivables in an attempt to reduce their cash gap in the cash conversion cycle. Likewise, the negative relationship between number of days in inventory and corporate profitability suggests that a sudden drop in sales accompanied with a mismanagement of inventory will lead to tying up capital at the expense of profitable operations. The authors believe that for this reason managers can create profits for their companies by handling correctly the cash conversion cycle and keeping each different component (accounts receivables, accounts payables, inventory) to an optimum level.

Singh and Pandey (2008) investigate the impact between working capital management and corporate profit using correlation analysis and regression analysis for the period 1990–2007. The ratio has a statistically significant impact on corporate profitability.

Padachi (2006) claims that working capital management will contribute positively to creating a company's value. In his study, he examined the impact of working capital management on corporate performance across industries over the period 1998–2003 using a panel regression analysis. Key variables used in the analysis are inventories days, accounts receivables days, accounts payable days and cash conversion cycle. The regression results show that high investment in inventories and receivables is associated with lower profitability.

27.3 Data and Methodology

Correlation analysis, Granger causality test and panel regression analysis using generalized method of moments (GMM) will be used to determine the impact of managerial decision making on the profitability of corporate performances in manufacturing industry in the Czech Republic. Data to meet the goal of the chapter were drawn from the worldwide Orbis database. This database includes data from the annual reports of individual businesses worldwide. From this database, on annual frequency data were selected for annual reports of manufacturing companies in the Czech Republic from 2007 to 2017. Sample of companies includes 3645 companies in manufacturing industry in the Czech Republic. We used econometrics software EViews 10 to evaluate the relationship between elements of managerial decision making and profitability of corporate performances in the Czech Republic.

Correlation analysis, Granger causality test and panel regression analysis using generalized method of moments will be used to determine the impact of managerial decision making on the profitability of corporate performances in manufacturing industry in the Czech Republic. According to Cohen (2014), the correlation analysis is a suitable method for the initial identification (estimation) of the functional relationship between explained variable and explanatory variable. The correlation relationship can be expressed using the Pearson correlation coefficient, which may take the following form: The Pearson´s correlation coefficient can be expressed using Eq. (27.1):

$$P = \frac{\sum (x_i - \bar{x})(y_i - \bar{y})}{(n-1)s_x s_y} = \frac{\sum (x_i - \bar{x})(y_i - \bar{y})}{\sqrt{\sum (x_i - \bar{x})^2 \sum (y_i - \bar{y})^2}} \tag{27.1}$$

where X represents the mean value matrix of profitability of corporate performances, Y is the mean of the matrix of the values of the individual variables related to the managerial decision making (explanatory variables), and n is the number of observations. Pearson's correlation coefficient values range from -1 to 1. Values close to 1 suggest a positive dependence between the dependent variable and the independent variable; the values approaching -1 have a completely opposite negative relationship. Values approaching 0 show the mutual independence of the variables, where it is not possible to determine unequivocally the dependence between the analyzed variables (there is no linear dependence confirmed here, but it can be a nonlinear dependence between the analyzed variables). The variables are uncorrelated in this case. The statistical significance of the correlation coefficient, which can be tested at 1, 5 and 10% significance, plays an important role in determining the relationship between variables.

Using the correlation analysis and the correlation coefficient, the relationship between the variables can be determined. However, it is impossible to determine how strong the dependence between these variables is, and how is a causal relationship or link between them that examines the relationship between the cause and its consequences within the variables analyzed by us. By contrast, using the Granger causality test, it is only possible to determine which variable may affect another variable.

In the case of Granger's causality, the aim is to reject the zero hypothesis that there is no causal relationship between the variables studied. Engle and Grange (1987), in their study, quantify Granger causality by Eqs. (27.2) and (27.3), where Y_t and X_t represent corporate liquidity and debt funding sources structure, ε_t error or residual component, β_0 and φ_0 constants of causal equations, $\beta_{1t}, \beta_{2t}, \varphi_{1t}$ and φ_{2t} intersections with axes X and Y.

$$\Delta Y_t = \beta_0 + \sum_{i=1}^{\sigma} \beta_{1i} \Delta Y_{t-i} + \sum_{i=1}^{\gamma} \beta_{2i} \Delta X_{t-1} + \varepsilon_{1t} \quad (27.2)$$

$$\Delta X_t = \varphi_0 + \sum_{i=1}^{\gamma} \varphi_{1i} \Delta X_{t-i} + \sum_{i=1}^{\gamma} \varphi_{2i} \Delta Y_{t-1} + \varepsilon_{2t} \quad (27.3)$$

However, it is impossible to determine how strong the dependence between these variables is, and how is a causal relationship or link between them that examines the relationship between the cause and its consequences within the variables analyzed by us. For this reason, a generalized method of moments (GMM) will be used to determine the causal relationship between the variables and to determine the dependence of the endogenous variable on the exogenous variables.

According to Prucha (2014), the problem of panel data is mainly when individual panel data are part of a shorter time series and are unsuitable for the use of least squares in terms of panel regression. According to him, the generalized method of moments (GMM) is a suitable method for examining the functional relationships between variables that are organized into such panel data. On the other hand, the disadvantage is the fact that it is not possible to test the given data within the basic assumptions of the smallest square method, i.e., heteroskedasticity, autocorrelation, normality and multi-collinearity and stationarity.

In order to ensure sufficient reporting ability, all variables will be tested for their statistical significance (for significance levels of 1, 5, and 10%). In addition, the robustness of the model will be verified using Sargan/Hansen *J*-test, which determines to what extent the method is capable of delivering the same results even under load by slight parameter changes. The model is robust in this regard if the results of the Sargan/Hansen test are greater than 0.05.

I will draw from the De Haas and Lelyveld (2010) to construct the model. The relationship between liquidity of companies and structure of debt funding sources will be estimated using the following equations in general form (27.4):

$$L_{it} = \alpha_1 + \beta_1 * \Delta L_{it-1} + \beta_2 * X_{1it} + \beta_3 * X_{2it} + \cdots + \beta_n * X_{nit} + \varepsilon_{it} \quad (27.4)$$

The dependent variable L_{it} is profitability of corporate performance in manufacturing industry in the Czech Republic at time t, L_{it-1} is delayed dependent variable, X_{nit} are elements that are the subject of managerial decision making (cash conversion

Table 27.1. Description of used variables

Variables	Calculation	Expected relationship
Gross operating profit (GOP)	(Sales − cost of goods sold)/(Total assets − financial assets)	Dependent variable
Cash conversion cycle (CCC)	(Number of days inventory + number of days receivables − number of days payables)	−
Fixed financial assets ratio (FA)	Fixed financial assets/Total assets	+
Financial debt ratio (Debt)	(Short-term loans + long-term loans)/Total assets	−

Source Own processing

cycle, financial assets and financial debt), and β_0 and ε_t are model constant and the residual component in the model.

Table 27.1 is a description of the variables used. Dependent variable is presented using gross operating profit. The elements that are the subject of managerial decision making are presented using a cash conversion cycle, financial assets and financial debt. Dependent variable used to evaluate elements of managerial decision making on the profitability of corporate performances in the Czech Republic is represented by gross operating profit. This indicator is an indicator that shows the company's operating performance. Gross operating income is what the company covers its production costs with its sales.

The cash conversion cycle (CCC) is used as a measure of profitability. Cash conversion cycle can be calculated using the following formula:

$$\begin{aligned} \text{CCC} = {} & \text{number of invetory} + \text{number of receivables} \\ & - \text{number of payables} \end{aligned} \tag{27.5}$$

$$\text{Number of inventory} = \frac{\text{Inventory}}{\text{Cost of Goods Sold}} \times 365 \tag{27.6}$$

$$\text{Number of receivables} = \frac{\text{Receivables}}{\text{Sales}} \times 365 \tag{27.7}$$

$$\text{Number of payables} = \frac{\text{Payables}}{\text{Cost of Goods Sold}} \times 365 \tag{27.8}$$

This indicator shows how many days you need to sell inventory and then how many days you need to collect debts and how many days the company needs to pay on average payables. To put it simply, cash conversion cycle means the time needed to convert short-term assets into cash and pay short-term liabilities. In a cash flow management context, the more the longer the cash conversion cycle is, the more resources are needed to finance short-term assets, and as a rule, funding is more expensive and vice versa.

- **A positive cash conversion cycle** (conversion cycle > maturity of payables) expresses the time period in which the firm has to finance operating activities from sources other than personal liabilities (working capital, other short-term liabilities).
- **A balanced cash conversion cycle** (conversion cycle = maturity of payables) occurs when the maturity of liabilities is equal to the conversion cycle.
- **A negative cash conversion cycle** (conversion cycle < maturity of payables) expresses the condition when the maturity of liabilities is shorter than the conversion cycle. A negative cash conversion cycle often arises when a company finances negative working capital or problematic short-term assets, e.g. trade payables.

For this reason, a negative relationship between the elements of managerial decision making and the profitability of corporate performances in the Czech Republic is expected. Shares and participation to other firm are considered as fixed financial assets. This variable is used since for many companies financial assets comprise a significant part of their total assets. This variable will be used in order to obtain an indication how the relationship and participation of one company to others affects its profitability. For this reason, a positive relationship between the elements of managerial decision making and profitability of corporate performances in the Czech Republic is expected.

Another variable used in order to evaluate elements of managerial decision making on the profitability of corporate performances in the Czech Republic includes financial debt. This is used in order to establish relation between the external financing of the company and its total assets. Higher debt represents a higher level of risk of companies. On the other hand, higher debt may mean and larger volume of funding sources because of the cost of external funding. However, it is very important that the company monitors its debt. A high debt ratio can reduce a company's profit, which can easily get into solvency problems. For this reason, a negative relationship between the elements of managerial decision making and the profitability of corporate performances in the Czech Republic is expected.

Table 27.2 describes the descriptive statistics of the used variables. The total of observations is 29,017. On average 23.16% of total assets are financial assets. Overall the average cash conversion cycle ranged at 3.76 days (median 4.08 days).

27.4 Results and Discussion

This part focuses on the results of correlation analysis, Granger causality test and generalized method of moments and their comments. Then, we can evaluate the relationship between elements of managerial decision making and the profitability of corporate performances in the Czech Republic using correlation analysis. Table 27.3 presents results of the correlation analysis using the Pearson's correlation coefficient.

Table 27.3 presents correlative relationship between profitability of corporate performances (dependent variable) and elements of managerial decision making (independent variables). The correlation coefficient is correlation coefficient is 0.2618.

Table 27.2. Descriptive statistics

	GOP	CCC	FA	Debt
Mean	−2.202545	3.768091	0.231637	−0.946271
Median	−2.157276	4.083277	1.730335	−0.751315
Maximum	5.551249	9.410038	0.000951	1.608725
Minimum	−9.827848	−30.09301	9.731370	−13.81551
St. Dev.	1.238858	1.782751	1.012294	0.866664
Skewness	−0.223756	−6.511555	0.588318	−3.062628
Kurtosis	4.964915	64.53226	3.426484	37.93164
Jarque-Bera	4910.110	4,782,751.	1893.793	1,520,658
Probability	0.000000	0.000000	0.000000	0.000000
Sum	−63,911.26	109,338.7	53,148.61	−27,457.96
Sum Sq. Dev.	44,532.86	92,218.65	29,733.85	21,794.11
Observations	29,017	29,017	29,017	29,017

Source Authors' calculations

Table 27.3. Correlation analysis results between profitability of corporate performances and elements of managerial decision making

Variables	CCC	FA	Debt
GOP	−0.2618	0.0020	−0.0316
Probability	(0.0000)	(0.0000)	(0.0000)

Source Authors' calculations

This means that if the cash conversion cycle increases, gross operating profit will also decrease. In addition, a neutral correlation coefficient (0.0020) between financial assets and gross operating profit was demonstrated. Growth in financial assets is likely to be accompanied by growth in gross operating profit. Also, the correlation coefficient is neutral (correlation coefficient is −0.0316) among financial debt and gross operating profit. Increasing financial debt and further debt levels are likely to reduce gross operating profit. All results were demonstrated at a 1% level of statistical significance.

Using the correlation analysis and the correlation coefficient, the relationship between the variables can be determined. However, it is impossible to determine how strong the dependence between these variables is, and how is a causal relationship or link between them that examines the relationship between the cause and its consequences within the variables analyzed by us. By contrast, using the Granger causality test, it is only possible to determine which variable may affect another variable.

Table 27.4 includes the results of the Granger causality test. Within the relationship between cash conversion cycle and gross operating profit, the hypothesis that a cash conversion cycle does not cause a cause can be rejected. This means that there is a causal relationship between cash conversion cycle and gross operating profit. In other words, the cash conversion cycle influences gross operating profit to some extent. The

Table 27.4. Granger causality test results between profitability of corporate performances and elements of managerial decision making

Null hypothesis	Obs.	*F*-statistic	Probability
CCC ≠ GOP	23,287	128.979	8E−30
GOP ≠ CCC		39.3289	4E−10
FA ≠ GOP	24,846	666.718	4E−145
GOP ≠ FA		258.010	9E−58
Debt ≠ GOP	25,029	40.5072	2E−10
GOP ≠ Debt		275.795	1E−61

Source Authors' calculations

number of days that a company converts its inventories and receivables into cash will affect its gross operating profit. The company may experience solvency problems when it is unable to collect funds from the customer for the products sold. On the other hand, gross operating profit has also been shown to affect the cash conversion cycle. The results showed that there is a causal relationship between financial assets and gross operating profit. In this context, the affirmative relationship between variables was confirmed, when financial assets may influence the gross operating profit. An important independent variable is financial debt. Granger causality test has shown a mutually beneficial bond where financial debt will affect gross operating profit and vice versa. All results were found at a level of statistical significance of 1%.

Using a correlation analysis, the link between variables was not confirmed unambiguously. For this reason, the generalized method of moments (GMM) will be used to determine the resulting relationship between structure of debt funding sources and liquidity of medium-sized companies in the Czech Republic.

In line with Table 27.5, statistically significant relationship between elements of managerial decision making and profitability of corporate performances in manufacturing industry in the Czech Republic was demonstrated in one model. The Sargan/Hansen test shows that the robustness of the model has been demonstrated in the above model. All results were tested and confirmed at a statistical significance of 1% (probability is 0.0000).

From Table 27.4 we can see, statistically significant independent variables are gross operating profit of previous period (regression coefficient +0.1475) and cash conversion cycle (regression coefficient −0.1038).

Table 27.5. GMM results between profitability of corporate performances and elements of managerial decision making

Variables	Delayed variable	CCC	FA	Debt	*J*-statistic
GOP	0.1475	−0.1038	0.3010	−0.0625	32.2569
Probability	(0.0000)	(0.0000)	(0.0000)	(0.0000)	

Source Authors' calculations

Using GMM, it was found that the gross operating profit of the previous period has a positive effect on the gross operating profit of the current period. If the gross operating profit of the previous period increases by one unit, the gross operating profit of the current period is likely to increase by 0.1475 units.

Furthermore, it was found that the cash conversion cycle has a significant negative impact on the gross operating profit. If there is an increase in the unit's cash conversion cycle in the company, it will cause a gross operating profit decrease of 0.1038 units.

The relationship between financial assets and gross operating profit has confirmed a positive relationship. For the company, this means that if it increases the financial assets in corporate governance, this is likely to be accompanied by growth in gross operating profit. Using GMM, it has been shown that if a financial assets increase occurs in a unit, the company will record a gain of 0.3010 units.

On the other hand, if we look at the relationship between gross operating profit and financial debt, a negative effect of financial debt on gross operating profit has been demonstrated. For the company, this means that if one financial unit increases financial debt, gross operating profit is reduced by 0.0625 units. If the company uses short-term loans and long-term loans to a greater extent, gross operating profit is likely to decline mainly due to interest payments on loans. Increasing indebtedness can jeopardize the company's solvency and its functioning.

27.5 Conclusion

The aim of this paper was to evaluate elements of managerial decision making on the profitability of corporate performances in the Czech Republic. In order to achieve the aim, we investigate the relationship between profitability of corporate performance (measured through gross operating profit) and the elements that are the subject of managerial decision making in the production process and which can impact on the profitability of corporate performance. This is mainly the cash conversion cycle (including accounts receivables, accounts payables and inventory), financial assets and financial debt.

The correlation analysis, the Granger causality test and the generalized method of moments (GMM) were used in the assessment of the elements of managerial decision making on the profitability of corporate performances in the Czech Republic. The data sample will include data from 2007 to 2017. The analysis included companies operating according to the CZ-NACE classification in the manufacturing industry in the Czech Republic. In this research, we used a sample of 3645 manufacturing companies.

Using the correlation analysis, the Granger causality test and the GMM showed a statistically significant relationship between the elements of the managerial decision making (such as cash conversion cycle, financial assets and financial debt) and the gross operating profit in manufacturing companies in the Czech Republic.

Using the GMM, the positive effect of financial assets on gross operating profit was demonstrated. On the other hand, a negative impact of the cash conversion cycle and financial debt on gross operating profit was demonstrated in the GMM. All resulting relationships were tested at a statistical significance level of 1%. The resulting relationships were confirmed using the Sargan/Hansen test (*J*-statistic), which demonstrates the robustness of the model.

Acknowledgements This paper ensued thanks to the support of the grant IGS/18/2019 "Managerial decisions in relation to the management of corporate profitability performance in the Czech Republic."

References

Balasundaram, N. (2010). Working capital management and its impact on profitability: A study of selected listed manufacturing companies in Sri Lanka.

Chary, S. T., Kastury, R., & Kumar, K. S. (2011). Relationship between working capital and profitability—A statistical approach. *International Journal of Research in Finance and Marketing, 1*(7). ISSN 2231-5985.

Cohen, P., West, S. G., & Aiken, L. S. (2014). *Applied multiple regression/correlation analysis for the behavioral sciences* (2nd Ed.). Psychology Press. ISBN 0-89859-268-2.

De Haas, R., Lelyveld, I. (2010). Internal capital markets and lending by multinational bank subsidiaries. *Journal of Financial Intermediation, 19*(1), 1–25.

Deloof, M. (2003). Does working capital management affect profitability of belgian firms? *Journal of Business Finance & Accounting, 30*(3), 585.

Engle, R. F., & Granger, W. C. (1987). Co-integration and error correction: Representation, estimation, and testing. *Econometrica, 55*, 251–276. ISSN 1468-0262.

Gołaś, Z., Bieniasz, A., & Czerwińska-kayzer, D. (2013). The relationship between working capital and profitability in food industry firms in Poland. *Journal of Central European Agriculture, 14*(1), 52–63. ISSN 1332-9049.

Howorth, C., & Westhead, P. (2003). The focus of working capital management in UK small firms. *Management Accounting Research, 14*, 97–111.

Lazaridis, M., & Tryfonidis, D. (2006). Relationship between working capital management and profitability of listed companies in the Athens Stock Exchange. *Journal of Financial Management and Analysis, 19*(1). ISSN 0970-4205.

Padachi, K. (2006). Trends in working capital management and its impact on firms' performance: An analysis of mauritian small manufacturing firms. *International Review of Business Research Papers, 2*(2), 45–58. ISSN 1832-9543.

Prucha, I. R. (2014). Instrumental variables/method of moments estimation. In M. M. Fisher & P. Nijkamp (Eds.), *Handbook of regional science*. Heidelberg: Springer. ISBN 978-3-642-23430-9.

Singh, P., & Pandey, S. (2008). Impact of working capital management in the profitability of Hindalco Industries Limited. *Journal of Financial Economics, 0*(4), 62–72. ISSN 0304-405X.

Chapter 28
Corruption in the Greek Public Sector: An Empirical Research

Electra Pitoska, Ziaka Vaia and Liana Anastasia

Abstract The phenomenon of corruption and the investigation of methods, institutions, and mechanisms for the control of public officials in carrying out their statutory duties and fight of cases of corruption in the relationship between state—citizen, through any socioeconomic and historical frame. It was and remains a key issue for analysis and discussion, especially in modern democratic societies. The aim of this research is initially through a short bibliographical review to present the definition of corruption, especially corruption in the public sector, the types of corruption, the causes which create this phenomenon and of course the consequences on society and the economy and also to analyze the main mechanisms for combating this phenomenon. On the issue of corruption, an empirical research was carried out. The survey was based on questionnaires in order to record the opinions and estimates of participants on issues such as the degree of corruption perception. After the statistical analysis and the findings presentation, some conclusions show that despite the legislation and measures that have been implemented, Greece is still at the top of the world rankings and is among the most corrupt countries. Also, the existing control mechanisms are not effective and there is a lack of ethics and rules mainly in public administration.

Keywords Corruption · Anticorruption public sector · Greece

JEL Codes D73

E. Pitoska (✉) · Z. Vaia · L. Anastasia
Department of Accounting and Finance, School of Management and Economics, Western Macedonia University of Applied Sciences, Kozani, Greece
e-mail: ilpitoska@yahoo.gr

Z. Vaia
e-mail: ziakabai@yahoo.gr

L. Anastasia
e-mail: anastasia_liana@hotmail.com

N. Tsounis and A. Vlachvei (eds.), *Advances in Cross-Section Data Methods in Applied Economic Research*, Springer Proceedings in Business and Economics,
https://doi.org/10.1007/978-3-030-38253-7_28

28.1 Introduction

Corruption can be characterized as a social illness that derives from social injustice and is plaguing many developing countries today. It has a multifaceted meaning, as there are societies and economic and political systems embracing bribery in the broad sense and corruption in the strict legal sense (Holmes 2006). A well-known definition of corruption is that of the World Bank, which considers corruption to be a misuse of public property for personal gain (Pedersen et al. 2008). The European Commission Report (2014), in accordance with international legal instruments, states that corruption in the broad sense is considered to be "any abuse of power for private gain. "Corruption is a global phenomenon and it has become a multi-billion dollar industry; it has been shown that it is maintained at these terrible levels by developed countries that try to contain developing countries, keeping citizens below the poverty line, while levying a significant "tax" on business development" (Pedersen et al. 2008).

Corruption has been defined as "Cancer" (Wolfensohn 1998), "Enemy" (Gruner 1999) "illness" (Corell 2003) or "scourge" (Transparency International 2005).

In addition, corruption is thought to distort standards of value and to erode compliance (Hamir 1999), resulting in greater public investment, with a lower quality of infrastructure (Schloss 1998; Tanzi and Davoodi 1998).

Corruption is also considered to hamper political and economic progress (Klitgaard 1994), promote the illegal export of resources and presents distrust (Caiden 2001). The tracking/measurement of the phenomenon is done through Indicators such as: "Corruption Perception (CPI)" Index, "Global Corruption Barometer (GCB)" Index, "BPI" Index.

28.2 Forms and Causes of Corruption

Corruption forms vary and include bribery, collusion, embezzlement, extortion, abuse and nepotism (http://www.transparency.org). Corruption is traced in the political and economic sectors.

An important issue is the reason why people are being guilty of corruption. As neoclassical economic theory presents in competitive markets, the main reason is the individual interest. Therefore, if the individual benefit is higher than the cost then corruption is manifested (Chaniotis Theodoros 2005). Also, the more personal the relations between state and citizens through the services are, the higher is the degree of corruption (Treisman 2000). Moreover, the way in which the administrative structure of a state is organized is a basic reason for corruption. Practising state procedures and controls by a few specific individuals results in their monopoly power with increased levels of corruption (Tanzi and Davoodi 1998). One more reason is the ambiguity of tax laws and the ongoing negotiation of the citizens with the bodies of the respective services resulting in increased corruption (Vavoura and Manola 2006).

Furthermore, trade unions and civil organizations play a significant role in distributing resources, as well as religion, which affects governance and corruption (Treisman 2000). One additional cause is the acceptance or not of the corruption phenomenon. The role of education and the educational level are important elements in the adoption of human corruption (Saks 2004).

According to Treisman (2000), the existence of political stability works positively in the fight against corruption. This contributes to the establishment of rules, control mechanisms and structures for the defense of the general interest (Treisman 2000). In the absence of controls or their replacement by informal institutions such as the customer system, the deterrent risk of capture and punishment (Turgul and Anwar 2000) is reduced. The favorable conditions of corruption are also created by intense state intervention, while reduced investment freedom. Private activity is hampered by intense bureaucracy as it becomes more expensive due to illegal wages (Shleifer 2001). On the contrary, according to Barro (1979), the lack of state interventionism leads to inconsiderable limits of the general interest, resulting in the birth of corruption.

The role of the legal system is important and directly dependent on the political status of a country. The interdependence of the two systems often means favor to those in power. Thus, the system becomes clientele and corruption is strengthened and established. When the institutions operate impartially and independently, there is increased control and rigor, thus resulting in a reduction in corruption. Strict penalties are inhibiting the intent of corruption (Reppas 2010).

28.3 Consequences of the Corruption Phenomenon

Tax evasion and avoidance are among the worst antisocial behaviors and, as a complex and structural phenomenon, contribute to reducing the efficiency of the economy and widening social inequalities, as it distorts the distribution and redistribution of economic resources in the short and long term (Pasadis 2013).

The impact and cost of corruption in the public sector are multiple and incalculable. Corruption affects and distorts moral values and principles, undermines democracy and institutions, affects the national economy, and prevents growth. It has an impact on the political and social level, and it is the main cause of the situation in the Public Administration, the operation of Justice and the degradation of the environment. Corruption in the public sector is passed on by the government to citizens by reducing incomes, limiting resources and investing with the consequent impact on economic growth (Reppas 2010). The corrupt social and political environment where corruption evolves adversely affects the economy's course through bribery to cut taxes, fees, and debts. The consequence of all this is the additional tax burden for the state to raise funds that have been deprived of tax evasion (Vavoura and Manola 2006). This additional burden contributes to increased income inequality and poverty since the cost of unpaid taxes is passed on to other groups of taxpayers.

For foreign investment, corruption is a developmental problem since it presents increased transaction costs, cost in money, time, and business risk. It has been observed that in countries with a high corruption index only few foreign investments are made. This has the effect of reducing the growth prospects of a country (Lambropoulou 2016). Because of these conditions, the bureaucracy impedes the lack of attractiveness in domestic investment (Dimitrakos 2008), coupled with the possible bribery and the volatile tax environment.

Of course, corruption is likely to be a lever for the economy. In spite of the negative effects of corruption, studies (Leff 1964) also describe its positive characteristics, such as public servants' pay can positively influence their incitement and performance in the workplace, citizens are helped to resolve their affairs, so it is a means of promoting trade and hindering bureaucracy, and in the case of auctions, offering the best in the sense of the lowest offer is a contribution to reducing government spending.

28.4 Corruption in Greece

Corruption in Greece is a major and time-consuming problem that results in both the deterioration of the reliability of public services and the service they provide to society and, on the other hand, the burden on the national economy. In an effort to tackle its problem, public policy must be shaped to intervene in both prevention and tackling corruption, with various coherent actions, namely to prevent and deter corruption, to identify its origins and eliminates them, to impose sanctions, but also to strengthen internal control mechanisms. The phenomenon of corruption also appears in the private sector but mainly in the public sector. The planning of the anti-corruption strategy of public administration in Greece must be geared to the national anti-corruption strategy. "There is a significant gap between the Member States in the area of anti-corruption measures. For other states, effective prevention has helped to consolidate the reputation that these countries are "clean", while in other countries there was no active action to promote preventative measures" (Lazos 2005).

Greece has begun to implement a more correct approach to fighting corruption. However, as the GRECO Group of States against corruption stresses, its legislation is still "too complicated". This is exacerbated by a low level of law enforcement, and risk assessment does not seem to be a common practice in defining future targeted actions.

28.5 Empirical Investigation

28.5.1 The Research Methodology

After the literature review, a field survey was organized in order to investigate the phenomenon of corruption in general and in the public sector in particular, in June 2018. The employees of the Decentralized Administration of Epirus—Western Macedonia (spatial competence of Western Macedonia) and in particular the employees of the services of the prefectures of Kozani, Florina, Kastoria, and Grevena were selected This choice of the research field was made on the one hand because it was considered to be an average representative state of state employees, on the other, because the region in question has a full range of competencies, specializations and services. It is also noted that research was also organized for educational reasons, except for academic requirements.

For the purposes of the survey, a properly structured questionnaire was prepared, with three (3) question sets and eighteen (18) in total questions. The questionnaire was compiled after searching for questionnaires from other surveys and was basically based on the World Barometer and International Transparency questionnaires.

The first section of the questionnaire includes five (5) questions concerning the demographic data of the sample, and in particular gender, age, level of education, place of residence and social class to which they belong.

The second section contains twelve (12) questions referring to the perception of corruption in the public sector, the assessment of the degree of corruption in the public sector in relation to the private sector, the importance of personal relations in the transactions with the public, the percentage of citizens who have been bribed. In addition to the above, in the same section there are questions reporting corruption incidents and more specifically if citizens are willing to report a corruption incident and to which body, and in different circumstances, why they would not complain.

Furthermore, questions are included about the forms of corruption, citizens' assessment of the corrupt body, the causes of the corruption phenomenon, but the effectiveness of state actions and control mechanisms.

The third and final section of the questionnaire includes a single question about assessing the effectiveness of proposals to reduce the corruption phenomenon.

The questionnaire was distributed electronically to the employees of the Decentralized Administration of Epirus of Western Macedonia (spatial competence of Western Macedonia), i.e. the prefectures of Kozani, Florina, Kastoria, and Grevena, which have a total of 275 and were given sufficient time to answer/participate. The survey was completed in September and a total of ninety-four (194) active officials attended.

The questionnaire used was anonymous because the purpose of the survey is to capture the views, perceptions, and attitudes of individuals about corruption, so anonymity was considered necessary to give honest answers without the fear of revealing their personal details.

Moreover, it has been decided that the questions should be brief and understandable so that individuals can easily complete them. At the same time, efforts have been made to avoid unnecessary and unintelligible questions, so as to require as little time as possible.

28.5.2 The Findings of the Survey

After the statistical processing of the replies, the following are observed:

With regard to demographic data, all respondents are divided into two sexes as follows: 55.2% women and 44.8% men. Another important parameter is the sample age, where the 45–55 age group participates by 38.7%, followed by ages 35–45 (33%) and then a uniform distribution between the ages 25–35 years (12%), & 55+ (9.8%), while the lowest representation comes from the age group 18–25 (6.7%). Regarding the level of education of the participants in the survey, the majority are graduates with 45.4% graduates, followed by holders of postgraduate/doctoral degree with 23.3%, followed by secondary education graduates with a percentage of 24.2% and finally the compulsory education staff of 5.2%. Greater representation was made by the employees of the prefecture of Kozani with an overwhelming majority (50%), followed by the employees of the prefecture of Grevena (18%), and the employees of the prefectures of Kastoria and Florina with 17.5% and 14.4% respectively. Most of the respondents classify themselves in the middle class (61.9%), while 27.3% in the working class and a small 10.8% in the upper social class.

As far as the perception of corruption in the public sector is concerned, participants with an overwhelming percentage (46.4%) believe that corruption in the public sector is a very important problem. A smaller percentage (35.1%) believes that it is a major problem, while (15.5%) of respondents believe that corruption is not a big problem, with the impression that none of the respondents think corruption is at all problem (Fig. 28.1).

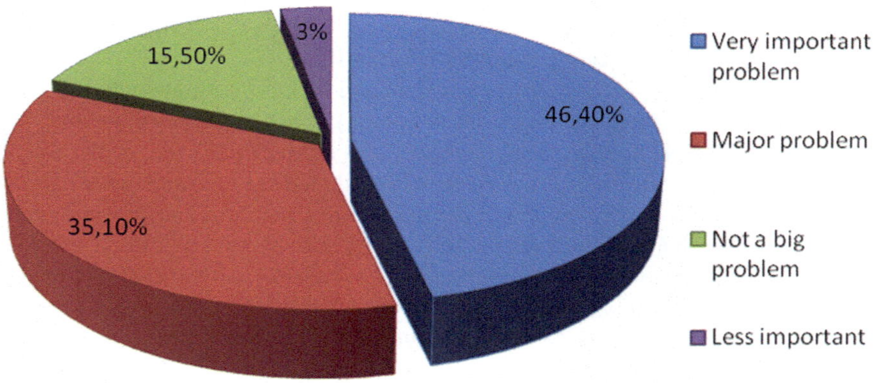

Fig. 28.1. Corruption perceptions in the public sector

Participants' views differ on the question of whether the public sector in Greece is more corrupt than the private sector since 31.9% believe that the public sector is just as corrupt as the private sector. Fewer (15.5%) believe that the public sector is far more corrupt than the private sector. In contrast, 9.8% consider the private sector more corrupt.

The importance of personal contacts—transactions in the public sector in order to make any request for the majority (31.9%) is considered very important. In a smaller percentage (27.3%) they are considered very important, for some (21.7%) they are quite important. A small percentage (12.4%) believes that personal contacts are a bit significant and an even smaller (6.7%) that it is not at all important in transactions with the public sector to make any request.

In assessing the extent of corruption in Greece, media with political parties and parliament occupy the top positions since, according to respondents, the most corrupt institutions are in the country, followed by tax offices and town planning in the fourth and fifth place respectively while in the next positions the army is ranked among NGOs and DEKOs and in the last positions the judiciary, the police, and the army, while the civil servants are ranked last.

Out of ten participants, an extraordinarily high percentage (65%) said they were never asked to bribe while 28% said they had been asked to bribes and have shown that 40.2% is a "courtesy gift", 26.8% because "it is the only way to serve and speed up a process, reflecting the problem of bureaucracy in corruption." Finally, a very small percentage (6.2%) replied that they would bribe to achieve a better price (Fig. 28.2).

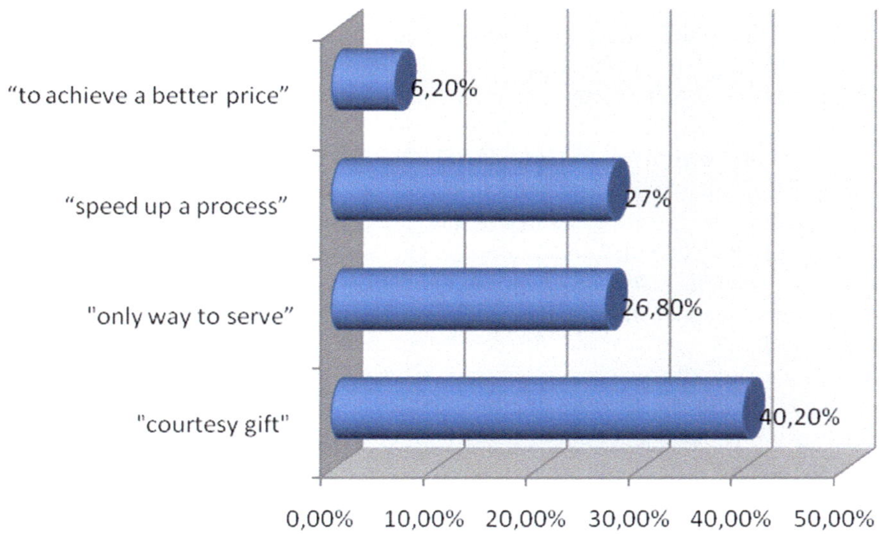

Fig. 28.2. Causes-reasons for bribery

With regard to the assessment of respondents about what actions are corruption, most of the participants estimate at about equal rates that the consideration for a policeman or the consideration for an urban planning officer or a taxi exchange is far too corrupt, while fewer corrupt actions, the provision of a doctor's consideration, as well as the use of personal contacts or relationships for the recruitment of a relative in the public or private sector, and finally the minority of questions Managing considers as very corrupt energy use personal contacts or relationships to shift family member in the military.

Due to the public corruption, the lack of appropriate control mechanisms seems to be the dominant workers' attitude; as equally important is slowing the administration of justice and non-attribution of responsibility and then uncontrolled power and lack of individual ethics. On the other hand, least important are the lack of transparency, the lack of clear regulations, the great bureaucracy and the vague legislative framework, and the inadequate level of salary.

Concerning the intention to report corruption, participants with an extremely high percentage (62.4%) said they were willing to report corruption, reflecting their intense willingness to participate actively in combating this phenomenon, while a significantly lower percentage (22, 7%) responded negatively and a percentage (14.9%) replied I do not know/do not answer.

As far as the anti-corruption agencies are concerned, the Ombudsman is the first in the preferences of the participants with 43.4%, while the second in line with 37.9% is the directly involved service and then it follows a uniform distribution of answers of the participants (about 27%) that they would file a corruption incident with the Prosecutor on a special telephone line and only a small percentage (13.1%) replied that they would file corruption charges at the media.

In an impressively large percentage (62.3%), the participants would not file a corruption complaint because they believe that it would have no effect, thus capturing the general notion that there are no credible/appropriate control mechanisms. A much smaller percentage (24.5%) said they were afraid of the consequences of such a complaint and then a percentage (21.7%) did not know who they could report a corruption incident while a percentage (11.3%) replied I do not know/reply.

Regarding the effectiveness of the state's actions, about half of the participants (44.3%) estimate that they are a little efficient and, in a smaller percentage (29.9%), their assessment is moderate. Even less (18.6%) consider that they are not effective at all, while a very small percentage (6.2%) considers that the state's actions are very effective. It is impressive that the percentage (1%) that the state's anti-corruption actions are very effective is negligible/very small (Fig. 28.3).

Regarding the effectiveness of proposals to reduce corruption in the public sector, most of the respondents believe that, in order to tackle corruption, laws must be applied quickly for all and without exceptions, Several respondents also consider organizing anti-corruption awareness campaigns to make citizens more active and severe punishment being effective ways of tackling corruption while fewer believe that improving democratic institutions, simplifying procedures, e-government, and upgrading services are less effective ways of tackling corruption. Few people believe that appropriate staff selection policies and know-how exchange can limit corruption.

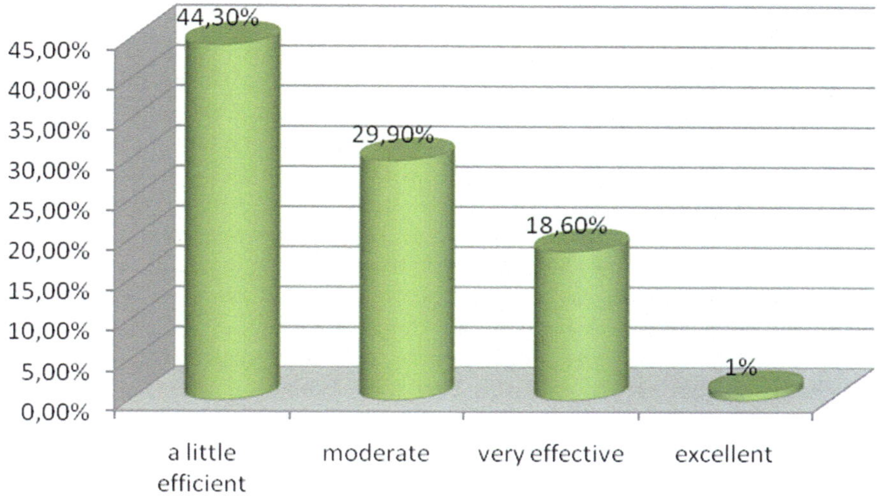

Fig. 28.3. Estimation of the effectiveness of state actions

28.6 Summary—Conclusions

After the literature review and empirical investigation, the following conclusions are drawn:

- In recent years, Greece has made significant progress in addressing the corruption phenomenon since according to the International Transparency Report in 2015 it was ranked 58th in 2015 compared to the 69th in 2014 and the 80th and 96th 2013 and 2012 respectively. Legislative and institutional initiatives such as the creation of the DYNAMICS program, torturing and criminalizing corruption offenses such as active and passive bribery and bribery of a judge contributed to the improvement.
- An important innovation was the introduction of the Public Prosecutor's Office and Prosecutor's Office against Corruption, the establishment of an independent authority to prevent money laundering, the establishment of the economic police, and the creation of the General Secretariat against Corruption.
- Despite all the legislation and measures that have been implemented, Greece is still at the top of the world rankings and is among the most corrupt countries. In 2018, it fell from the 67th place to the 59th place in 2017 out of 180 countries in the latest ranking based on the CPI Corruption Perception Index. Last year, Greece scored a total of 48 points, and this year it scored only 45.
- The phenomenon of corruption is very intense in Greece since both international surveys and participants in empirical research highlight the problem of corruption as a dominant issue that hinders the development of democratic institutions and processes, considering that it is a very serious problem. This leads to the preservation of .the mentality that if you do not own 'means', you won't carry out a task in the Greek public. This is reflected in our research since a large percentage

responded that personal contacts—transactions in the public sector are necessary to carry out any request.

- The control mechanisms are not effective and this is reflected in the empirical investigation by the participants' assessment that the lack of appropriate control mechanisms is one of the most important factors in the creation of corruption.
- There is no clear legislative framework for the powers of each control mechanism, which leads to the overlapping of responsibilities between different agencies. There is, therefore, no specialized body that only evaluates and manages the allegations of corruption, which prevents the citizen from reporting incidents of corruption. The overwhelming majority of respondents consider the complaint of a corruption incident to be ineffective in eliminating the phenomenon.
- The labyrinth of the legislative framework and the overlapping of competences by many of the control mechanisms mentioned above contribute to the fairness of justice and, as it is very clearly reflected in the empirical investigation, is considered a deterrent to tackling corruption.
- There is a clear lack of ethics and rules of conduct (mainly) in the public administration since most of the assessment is that non-attribution of responsibilities combined with the uncontrolled power of some state officials and the lack of individual ethics are among the most important factors in creating the phenomenon of corruption in public administration.
- Updating through various actions to tackle corruption and its negative consequences has resulted in public wake-up and mobilization by requiring public officials accused of corruption charges to be accountable to justice. They are also willing to help themselves in the fight against corruption since the overwhelming majority of citizens are willing to report a corruption incident.
- Finally, the urgent desire of citizens to fight the ill-fated phenomenon of corruption that has taken enormous proportions in the world is primarily equality, that is to apply laws quickly for all and without exceptions, and secondarily direct responsibility, the improvement of democratic institutions, the simplification of procedures and other actions that help to overcome it.

References

Barro, R. J. (1979, October). On the determination of the public debt. *The Journal of Political Economy, 87*(5, Part 1), 940–971.

Caiden, G. E. (2001). Corruption and governance. In G. E. Caiden, O. P. Dwivedi, & J. Jabbra (Eds.) *Where corruption lives* (pp. 15–38) Bloom Weld, CT: Kumarian Press.

Chaniotis Theodoros. (2005). Economic theory, money and intense corruption. Available at: http://www.kathimerini.gr/218762/article/oikonomia/ellhnikh-oikonomia/oikonomikh-8ewria-xrhma-kai-entonh-diaf8ora. Access August 28, 2016.

Corell, H. (2003). *The high-level political conference for the purpose of signing the United Nations convention against corruption*. Merida, Mexico: United Nations.

Dimitrakos, D. (2013). *"The Pandemic of Corruption" 2008*. International Transparency of Greece National Research on Transparency in Greece 2013.

EU Anti-Corruption Report Anti-Corruption Strategies. (2014). Available at: http://ec.europa.eu/dgs/home-affairs/e-library/documents/policies/organized-crime-and-human-trafficking/corruption/docs/acr_2014_en.pdf. Access September 18, 2016.

Gruner, J. (1999). Is it the professional duty of the accountant to expose corruption? *Accountancy Ireland, 31*(3), 16.

Gurgur, T., & Shah, A. (2000). *Localization and corruption: Panacea or Pandora's box*. World Bank.

Hamir, M. A. (1999). *Keynote address corruption democracy and good governance in Africa: Essays on accountability and ethical behavior* (pp. 1–8).

Holmes, L. (2006). *Rotten state corruption post-communism and neoliberalism*. Durham, London: Duke University Press.

International Transparency-Hellas Available at: http://old.transparency.gr/Content.aspx?page=4. Access September 28, 2016.

Klitgaard, R. (1994). A framework for a country programme against corruption. In *Accountability and transparency in international development: The launching of transparency international* (pp. 55–73).

Lambropoulou, M. (2016). *Economic analysis of corruption*. Administrative Information. Available at: http://docplayer.gr/11838655-I-oikonomiki-analysi-tis-iafthoras-sto-imosio-tomea.html. Access September 18, 2016.

Lazos, G. (2005). *Corruption and anti-corruption Athens*.

Leff, N. (1964). *Economic development through bureaucratic corruption*. American Behavioral Scientist.

Pasadis, S. (2013). *An empirical approach to the role of economics and corruption in Greece* (pp. 38–39). Diploma thesis.

Pedersen, H., & Johannsen, L. (2008). *Corruption: Commonality causes and consciences comparing 15 ex-communist countries*. Paper prepared for the 13th NISPAcee.

Reppas, P. (2010. May). Corruption: The causes and consequences lecture notes in the course "Economic Development" of the Department of Economic and Regional Development of the Panteion University.

Saks, L. R. (2004). *Corruption in America*. United States: Harvard University and NBER.

Schloss, M. (1998). Comparing corruption for development: The role of government business and civil society. In Transparency International and the International Bank for Reconstruction and Development (Ed.) *New perspectives on combating corruption* (pp. 1–11) Washington: Transparency International.

Shleifer, A. (2001). *Legal origins* National Nureau of economic research.

Tanzi, V., & Davoodi, H. (1998). Roads to nowhere: How corruption in public investment hurts growth. In *New perspectives on combating corruption* (pp. 33–42).

Treisman, D. (2000). The causes of corruption: A cross-national study. *Journal of Public Economics, 76*, 399–457. https://www.amherst.edu/media/view/.../Treisman2000.pdf.

Vavouras, I., & Manola, G. (2006). *Introduction to macroeconomic concepts* (p. 298). Athens: Papazisis Athens. Chapter 27.

Wolfensohn, J. (1998). Corruption impedes development-and hurts the poor. *International Journal of Government Auditing, 25*(4), 1–2.

Chapter 29
Household Income as a Predictor of Body Mass Index Among Adults in Poland: A Multilevel Analysis

Anna Sączewska-Piotrowska and Damian Piotrowski

Abstract The relationship between body mass index (BMI) and different predictors is very important aspect from the point of view of the whole society because the costs of preventing and fighting the overweight and obesity are borne by everyone. This study investigates the relationship important from the point of view of economists, i.e., between BMI and income household. This relationship was examined against other relationships. Linear multilevel models were fitted, with 18,534 adult Polish individuals nested in 9786 households and 66 subregions (Nomenclature of Territorial Units for Statistics 3—NUTS 3). We used data from the Social Diagnosis project (individual and household level) and from Statistics Poland (subregion level). We found that BMI was significantly associated with individual and household characteristics. Individuals in households from higher income categories (middle- and high-income) had higher values of BMI compared to low-income households. Two variables from subregion level (green areas and length of bicycle tracks) were related statistically insignificant with BMI. Just less than 0.5% of the unexplained variance was located on the subregion level. The study highlighted the importance of the household environment (household characteristics explain 14–18% of variance) which confirms that treating individuals as a part of households in which attitudes and behavior are shaped is a correct approach.

Keywords Body mass · Household income · Poland

JEL Codes I18 · I31 · I38

A. Sączewska-Piotrowska (✉)
University of Economics in Katowice, 1 Maja 50, 40-287 Katowice, Poland
e-mail: anna.saczewska-piotrowska@ue.katowice.pl

D. Piotrowski
Medical University of Silesia, Al. Legionów 49, 41-902 Bytom, Poland
e-mail: dpiotrowski@sum.edu.pl

N. Tsounis and A. Vlachvei (eds.), *Advances in Cross-Section Data Methods in Applied Economic Research*, Springer Proceedings in Business and Economics,
https://doi.org/10.1007/978-3-030-38253-7_29

29.1 Introduction

A rapid increase in the prevalence of overweight and obesity is a global problem. In 2014, over 600 million adults were classified as obese (according to body mass index (BMI)) and more than 1.9 billion adults were overweight (World Health Organization 2016). The prevalence of overweight and obesity in Poland increased significantly between 1975 and 2016. In the mid-1970s of the twentieth century, 40.2 and 10.7% of the adults ($\geq$18 years old) were overweight and obese, respectively. Overweight and obesity estimates from 2016 show that 58.3% of the adults in Poland were overweight and 23.1% were obese (World Health Organization 2019). World Health Organization model predicts that in 2030 28% of men and 18% of women will have BMI $\geq$ 30 (World Health Organization 2013), i.e., will obese. The more overweight and obese people, the more diseases in society, for example, type 2 diabetes, cardiovascular disease, osteoarthritis, and various cancers (World Health Organization 2000; Mokdad et al. 2003). The more sick people in society, the higher cost of health care. Therefore, determination of factors related to increased BMI values is very important from the point of view of individual and also from the point of view of the whole society. Many researchers from different fields have studied the correlation between various indicators and BMI (Drewnowski and Spencer 2004; Clarke et al. 2009; Dupuy et al. 2011; Devaux and Sassi 2013; Costa-Font et al. 2014; Kim 2016). One of the considered predictors may be a household income. Numerous studies conducted in developed countries (Ball and Crawford 2005; Villar and Quintana-Domeque 2009) demonstrated a negative association between income and BMI. The situation in Poland may be different. After economic transformation in Poland in 1989, the society is more affluent (Sączewska-Piotrowska 2018). These positive changes in Polish economy have occurred relatively recently and therefore the relationship between income and BMI can be different than in the countries considered as developed for a longer period of time. This situation is reflected in the results of the conducted research. Single-level analysis results show no statistically significant correlation between low income and the prevalence of obesity (Mazur et al. 2008); some of them show a statistically significant correlation between socioeconomic status and overweight prevalence (Kowalkowska et al. 2014). The results of research in Poland are not as unambiguous as in the case of research on developed countries.

Previous studies of the determinants of BMI in Poland mostly focused on individual-level characteristics. But individuals are nested in households or families, and the households or families are nested in cities, regions, communities, etc. BMI may be associated with factors not only from the individual level, but characteristics from the other levels can be also significant.

The aim of the study was to evaluate the relationship between income household and BMI in Poland. For this purpose, the multilevel models were estimated. Individual-, household-, and subregion-level characteristics in Poland were included in the models, which allowed to look broadly at the BMI predictors with special attention to household income.

29.2 Methods

29.2.1 Data Source

The study was conducted based on data from the Social Diagnosis project (Council for Social Monitoring 2016) and from the Statistics Poland (2019a). The Social Diagnosis project is a panel study conducted in Poland. Each subsequent wave involves all available households from the previous wave and households from a new representative sample. Eight waves have been conducted from 2000 to 2015. Data from the 2015 wave were used in the study. The sample was 18,534 adults, 9786 households, and 66 subregions (Nomenclature of Territorial Units for Statistics 3—NUTS 3). The division into 66 subregions was valid until 31 December 2014; since 1 January 2015, there have been 73 subregions in Poland. The Social Diagnosis database contains information about belonging to 66 subregions. The Social Diagnosis base provided data about individual and household-level variables, while on the Web site of the Statistics Poland the data from subregion level are available.

29.2.2 Outcome Variable

BMI was used as the outcome variable. The data from Social Diagnosis project provided complete BMI data. BMI was calculated as weight (kg) divided by the square of height (m^2).

29.2.3 Individual-Level Variables

The Social Diagnosis collected data about many individual variables which may be linked to BMI. Sex, education, age, and information about physical activity were included in models. Sex was modeled as a dummy variable with females as the reference category. Four categories of education were included: lower secondary or below, basic vocational, secondary, and tertiary. Age was also divided into four categories: 34 and less, 35–44, 45–59, and 60 and above. The question, if the respondent practices any sport or physical activity, was used to measure physical activity. Simply division for yes (lack of physical activity) and no (physically active) was used.

29.2.4 Household-Level Variables

The most important variable (from the point of our purpose) is household income. We decided to divide the income into three categories (low, middle, and high) taking into account the poverty and affluence lines: 60 and 200% of the median income. We have focused on lines in relative terms as a percent of the median. This approach is used by Eurostat to calculate at-risk-of-poverty rate (European Commission 2010) and by many authors to calculate the range of affluence or range of richness (Brzeziński 2010; Franzini et al. 2016; Törmälehto 2017). There was calculated equivalized income in order to take account of the differences in a household's size and its composition. There was used the modified OECD (Organisation for Economic Co-operation and Development) equivalence scale. This scale (Hagenaars et al. 1994) assigns 1 to the first adult of the household, 0.5 to each subsequent adult aged 14 or more, and 0.3 to children (each person under 14).

The other household-level variables were included: place of resident and household size. The first variable was dichotomized (urban and rural areas), and the second was categorized into five categories: 1, 2, 3, 4, 5, and more members.

29.2.5 Subregion-Level Variables

Two variables from subregion level were included in the analysis: green areas (ha/1000 ha) and length of bicycle tracks (km/10,000 km^2). The data about these factors (for 2015) were provided by Statistics Poland. According to the Statistics Poland green areas are defined as 'areas including technical infrastructure and buildings functionally associated with them, covered with vegetation, located in the village of dense buildings or cities, used for the aesthetic, recreational, therapeutic or shielding purposes, in particular parks, lawns, promenades, boulevards, botanical and zoological gardens, children's playgrounds, historic gardens and cemeteries, as well as street greenery and the greenery located near squares, historic fortifications, buildings, landfill sites, airports, railway and industrial buildings' (Statistics Poland 2019b). Bicycle track is defined by the Statistics Poland as 'road or its part intended for bicycle traffic, determined the appropriate road signs; a bicycle track is separated from other roads or road the same way by design or by using road traffic safety equipment' (Statistics Poland 2019c). Green area and length of bicycle tracks are presented in Fig. 29.1.

It is clear that the subregions composed of big cities (Kraków, Łódź, Poznań, Szczecin, Warszawa, Wrocław) or which include big cities (Katowicki subregion, Trójmiejski subregion) are in a better situation in terms of green areas and length of bicycle tracks.

29.2.6 Statistical Analysis

First, descriptive statistics were used to characterize the relationship between BMI and individual-level variables. After testing the normality (Kolmogorov–Smirnov test), group differences were tested via analysis of variance.

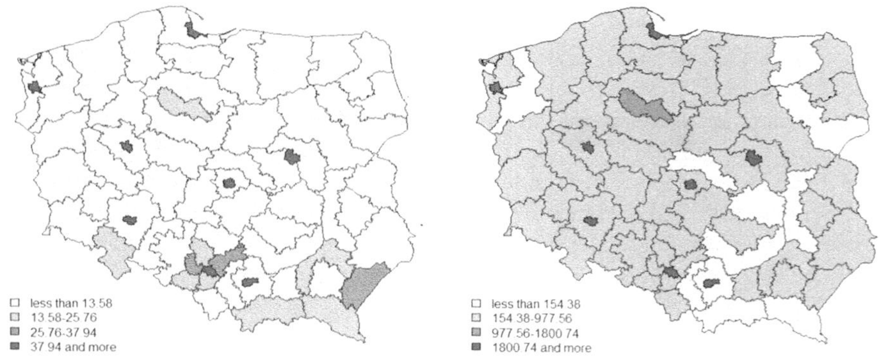

(a) green areas **(b)** length of bicycle tracks

Fig. 29.1 Subregions in Poland—boundaries, green areas, and length of bicycle tracks © EuroGeographics for the administrative boundaries

In the next step, three-level models were estimated, with continuous outcome variable BMI for individuals (level 1) nested within households (level 2) and subregions (level 3). Four models were constructed in increasing order of complexity. Model 1 (the null model) incorporated only household-specific and subregion-specific random effects to model between-household and between-subregion variation in BMI:

$$\mathrm{BMI}_{ijk} = \eta_{000} + h_{00k} + u_{0jk} + r_{ijk},$$

where BMI_{ijk} is BMI score of individual i from household j in subregion k, η_{000} is a intercept, h_{00k} is a random effect from the level 3 (subregion), u_{0jk} is a random effect from the level 2 (household), and r_{ijk} is a random effect from the level 1 (individual). Model 1 can be written in multilevel notation:

$$\text{Level 1}: Y_{ijk} = \beta_{0jk} + r_{ijk}$$

$$\text{Level 2}: \beta_{0jk} = \gamma_{00k} + u_{0jk}.$$

$$\text{Level 3}: \gamma_{00k} = \eta_{000} + h_{00k}$$

The second model included individual-level predictors (Model 2), then household-level predictors were added (Model 3), and subregion-level variables were additionally included (Model 4). Finally, Model 4 was specified as:

$$\begin{aligned}\mathrm{BMI}_{ijk} = {} & \eta_{000} + \eta_{001}(\text{paths\_ log})_k + \eta_{002}(\text{areas\_ log})_k + \gamma_{010}(\text{middle})_{jk} \\ & + \gamma_{020}(\text{high})_{jk} + \gamma_{030}(\text{urban areas})_{jk} + \gamma_{040}(2)_{jk} + \gamma_{050}(3)_{jk} + \gamma_{060}(4)_{jk} \\ & + \gamma_{070}(5\text{ and more})_{jk} + \beta_{100}(\text{male}) + \beta_{200}(\text{basic vocational})\end{aligned}$$

$$+ \beta_{300}(\text{secondary}) + \beta_{400}(\text{tertiary}) + \beta_{500}(35 - 44) + \beta_{600}(45 - 59)$$
$$+ \beta_{700}(60 \text{ and above}) + \beta_{800}(\text{lack of physical activity}) + h_{00k} + u_{0jk} + r_{ijk}.$$

To understand how variance in the dependent variable decomposes across levels the intraclass correlation coefficient (ICC) was calculated. In three-level models, ICC is defined as the proportion of variance that occurs at each level (Kim 2009). A chi-squared test was used to compare the estimated models and to choose the best-fitted model.

The descriptive analysis (percentages, mean, and standard deviation), normality test (Kolmogorov–Smirnov test), and the differences between groups (ANOVA test) were performed using Statistica (TIBCO Software Inc. 2017). The model parameters were estimated using restricted maximum likelihood (REML). The models were fitted in R program (R Core Team 2018) with lme4 package (Bates et al. 2015).

29.3 Results

Table 29.1 shows the characteristics of the study sample. The majority of the sample (56.01%) was female. The largest share had people from age category 60 and above (35.33%), with secondary education (33.27%), and not practicing any sport (65.98%). Most of the surveyed households (30.26%) had two people. Just over half (57.31%) of the households was from urban areas. Three-quarters of the households were from the middle-income category.

BMI was significantly associated with all considered individual-level variables (sex, age, education, and lack of physical activity). BMI was higher among men, among people from higher age categories, from lower education categories and among physically inactive people. The results of the comparison of BMI between groups are presented in Table 29.2.

The results of the multilevel analysis are shown in Table 29.3. The fit of estimated models is shown in Table 29.4.

Based on ICC values from the Model 1, it can be stated that 13.94% of the total variation in BMI was explained by differences in the household level, 0.43% in the subregion level, whereas 85.62% is explained by individual predictors. The intercept in Model 1 refers to the mean BMI of all adults (26.43 kg/m^2).

With the inclusion of individual predictors, adults' mean BMI was 23.18 kg/m^2; i.e., this is the mean BMI controlling for individual variables. Males had higher (1.19 kg/m^2) BMI than females, high educated people had lower (0.39 kg/m^2) BMI than people with a low level of education, young people had lower (2.09 kg/m^2 compared to 35–44, 3.27 kg/m^2 compared to 45–59, 3.88 kg/m^2 compared to 60 and more) BMI than people from higher age categories, and physically inactive people had higher (0.26 kg/m^2) BMI than active people. Model 2 shows that 81.99% of the variance in BMI was at the individual level, with 17.67 and 0.34% associated

Table 29.1 Sample characteristics

	Characteristics	Percent of sample
Individual characteristics ($n = 18{,}534$)	*Sex*	
	Male	43.99
	Female	56.01
	Age	
	34 and less	22.02
	35–44	15.62
	45–59	27.02
	60 and above	35.33
	Education	
	Lower secondary or below	19.95
	Basic vocational	28.42
	Secondary	33.27
	Tertiary	18.36
	Lack of physical activity	
	Yes	65.98
	No	34.02
Household characteristics ($n = 9786$)	*Number of members*	
	1	21.67
	2	30.26
	3	17.84
	4	16.27
	5 and more	13.96
	Place of resident	
	Urban areas	57.31
	Rural areas	42.69
	Household income	
	Low	15.14
	Middle	75.59
	High	9.26

with household and subregion levels, respectively. Model 2 fits better than Model 1 (reduction in deviance: $\chi^2 = 2{,}754.380$; $p < 0.001$).

In Model 3, the addition of the household-level variables showed that mean BMI is now 22.67 kg/m^2. Adults from middle- and high-income households had higher (0.54 kg/m^2 and 0.58 kg/m^2, respectively) BMI than adults from low-income households. Additionally, people from urban areas had lower (0.31 kg/m^2) BMI than people from rural areas, and people from four-person households had higher (0.35 kg/m^2)

Table 29.2 Comparison of BMI between groups—individual level

Variables	Values	Mean	SD	*P*-value[a]
Sex	Male	27.00	4.04	$p < 0.001$
	Female	25.90	4.84	
Age	34 and less	23.76	3.91	$p < 0.001$
	35–44	25.87	4.27	
	45–59	27.10	4.32	
	60 and above	27.70	4.45	
Education	Lower secondary or below	26.94	4.90	$p < 0.001$
	Basic vocational	27.06	4.36	
	Secondary	26.04	4.42	
	Tertiary	25.37	4.34	
Lack of physical activity	Yes	26.82	4.60	$p < 0.001$
	No	25.53	4.29	

[a]Group differences tested via analysis of variance

BMI than people from one-person households. The fit of Model 3 was better than that of the previous models (reduction in deviance: $\chi^2 = 56.378$; $p < 0.001$).

Model 4, after full adjustment for contextual variables, showed no significant association of BMI with green areas and length of bicycle tracks. The fit of Model 4 was worse than that of the Model 3 (there was no reduction in deviance).

29.4 Discussion

Our data indicate that the majority of variance in BMI can be explained by individual-level characteristics. Household characteristics explain 14–18% of the variance. Sub-region characteristics explain only less than 0.5% of the variance. Our finding is consistent with previous studies. For example, a study by Sund et al. (2010) conducted in an adult Norwegian population shows that about 83% of the variation in BMI was at the individual level and 13–15% at the family level. Only about 1% and less than 1% of the variance was explained by ward- and municipality-level[1] characteristics, respectively.

Based on results of two-level regression analyses, Robert and Reither (2004) reported that in the USA some of the total variability in BMI among women and men (about 6% and 11%, respectively) was due to variations between communities, although most of the variability was due to variation between individuals. Hoehner et al. (2011) conducted a cross-sectional analysis in Texas. They examined the association between neighborhood walkability BMI, and they found that only a small

[1]The municipalities are equivalent to NUTS5 (Structural Business Statistics Methodology 2005).

Table 29.3 Results of the multilevel linear regression—the predictors of BMI in the sample

Predictors	Model 1			Model 2			Model 3			Model 4		
	Estimates	CI	*p*	Estimates	CI	*p*	Estimates	CI	*p*	Estimates	CI	*p*
Individual characteristics												
(Intercept)	26.43	26.33–26.53	**<0.001**	23.18	22.96–23.41	**<0.001**	22.67	22.33–23.02	**<0.001**	22.67	21.97–23.37	**<0.001**
Sex												
Male				1.19	1.07–1.30	**<0.001**	1.17	1.05–1.29	**<0.001**	1.17	1.05–1.29	**<0.001**
Female				–			–			–		
Education												
Lower secondary or below				–			–			–		
Basic vocational				0.12	−0.07–0.30	0.215	0.10	−0.08–0.29	0.274	0.11	−0.08–0.29	0.263
Secondary				−0.11	−0.29–0.07	0.222	−0.11	−0.30–0.08	0.244	−0.11	−0.29–0.08	0.257
Tertiary				−0.39	−0.61 to −0.17	**<0.001**	−0.39	−0.61 to −0.16	**0.001**	−0.38	−0.61 to −0.15	**0.001**
Age												
34 and less				–			–			–		
35–44				2.09	1.89–2.30	**<0.001**	2.10	1.89–2.30	**<0.001**	2.09	1.89–2.30	**<0.001**
45–59				3.27	3.09–3.45	**<0.001**	3.31	3.13–3.49	**<0.001**	3.31	3.13–3.49	**<0.001**
60 and more				3.88	3.70–4.06	**<0.001**	3.99	3.79–4.19	**<0.001**	3.99	3.79–4.19	**<0.001**
Lack of physical activity												
Yes				0.26	0.12–0.40	**<0.001**	0.26	0.12–0.40	**<0.001**	0.26	0.12–0.40	**<0.001**
No				–			–			–		
Household characteristics												
Income												

(continued)

Table 29.3 (continued)

Predictors	Model 1			Model 2			Model 3			Model 4		
	Estimates	CI	*p*	Estimates	CI	*p*	Estimates	CI	*p*	Estimates	CI	*p*
Low							–			–		
Middle							0.54	0.34–0.74	**<0.001**	0.54	0.34–0.74	**<0.001**
High							0.58	0.29–0.87	**<0.001**	0.58	0.30–0.87	**<0.001**
Place of resident												
Urban areas							−0.31	−0.46 to − 0.16	**<0.001**	−0.29	−0.45 to − 0.14	**<0.001**
Rural areas							–			–		
Household size												
1							–			–		
2							0.10	−0.13–0.33	0.415	0.09	−0.14–0.32	0.435
3							0.13	−0.12–0.39	0.308	0.13	−0.13–0.39	0.318
4							0.35	0.08–0.62	**0.011**	0.34	0.07–0.61	**0.012**
5 and more							0.25	−0.02–0.52	0.075	0.24	−0.03–0.51	0.082
Subregion characteristics												
Tracks_log										0.02	−0.11–0.16	0.730
Areas_log										−0.07	−0.19–0.06	0.288
Random effects												
σ^2	17.63			14.66			14.64			14.64		
τ_{00}	$2.87_{\text{HOUSEHOLD}}$			$3.16_{\text{HOUSEHOLD}}$			$3.12_{\text{HOUSEHOLD}}$			$3.12_{\text{HOUSEHOLD}}$		
	$0.09_{\text{SUBREGION}}$			$0.06_{\text{SUBREGION}}$			$0.06_{\text{SUBREGION}}$			$0.06_{\text{SUBREGION}}$		
ICC (%)	$13.94_{\text{HOUSEHOLD}}$			$17.67_{\text{HOUSEHOLD}}$			$17.82_{\text{HOUSEHOLD}}$			$17.82_{\text{HOUSEHOLD}}$		
	$0.43_{\text{SUBREGION}}$			$0.34_{\text{SUBREGION}}$			$0.34_{\text{SUBREGION}}$			$0.34_{\text{SUBREGION}}$		
Observations	18,534			18,534			18,534			18,534		

Table 29.4 Fit of models

Model	Df	AIC	BIC	logLik	Deviance	Chisq	Chi Df	Pr(>Chisq)
Model 1	4	108,397	108,428	−54,194	108,389			
Model 2	12	105,659	105,752	−52,817	105,635	2,754.380	8	<2.2e−16***
Model 3	19	105,616	105,765	−52,789	105,578	56.378	7	7.945e−10***
Model 4	21	105,618	105,783	−52,788	105,576	1.815	2	0.4035

Significant codes 0 '***' 0.001 '**' 0.01 '*' 0.05 '.' 0.1 '·' 1

amount of the variance in BMI was explained by the neighborhood of residence in the intercept-only model for women and men (ICC = 0.05 and 0.04, respectively).

Multilevel analysis was also conducted in Australia. King et al. (2006) showed that area-level social disadvantage explains 2.1% of the variance for men and 3.5% of the variance for women (model after adjustment for age and survey type). Feng and Wilson (2015) found that neighborhood-level factors accounted for 4.9% of the overall variation in BMI, whereas 20.1% was attributable to household-level factors. They conducted their analysis based on Australian National Health Survey (2011–2012).

Ross et al. (2007) investigated the influence of neighborhood and metropolitan area characteristics on BMI in urban Canada in 2001. In the null model, the amount of variation in BMI among men that was attributable to neighborhoods and metropolitan areas was 4.39% and 1.35%, respectively, and among the women—4.44% and 1.42%, respectively.

A different approach was presented by Mowafi et al. (2011). The authors examined the association between area-level education and BMI among adults in Cairo (Egypt). They found that 1.6–2.6% of the variance was attributable to level 2 (neighborhood education level).

Vaezghasemi et al. (2016) presented the results of two- and three-level multilevel analysis from four waves of Indonesian Family Life Surveys. Based on the last wave from 2007, they found that variation in BMI attributable to districts was 1.5% and attributable to households 15%.

The definitely higher influence of regional characteristics (level of provinces) showed a study conducted by Raftopoulou (2017). Based on Spanish National Health Survey (2011–2012), the author showed that 10.45% of the total BMI variance is determined at the regional level (she analyzed two-level structure—personal and regional level).

BMI and household income is the most important association from the point of view of our purpose. Previous analyses suggest that there is a significant relationship between BMI and household income. Our finding concerning the direction of between

BMI and income is not in agreement with the majority of previous studies. Ross et al. (2007) conducted research in urban Canada for men and women separately. They found that higher BMI is seen in lower income categories among the women. The relation of BMI among the men was characterized by a gradient of lower BMI across decreasing income categories. King et al. (2006) also showed differences between men and women. In Canada belonging to the lowest income category (household income $20,799 or less) compared to the highest category ($78,000 or more) was associated with higher BMI among the women. There was no significant relationship between income group among the men. The study conducted by Feng and Wilson (2015) showed that BMI was lower among participants with high disposable incomes (average household gross income expressed in quintiles). Hernández-Yumar et al. (2018) basing on Spanish National Health Survey (2011–2012) showed that members of low-income households (lowest to 1st tertile) compared to members of high-income households (>2nd tertile) were characterized by higher BMI.

The relationship between BMI and family income was examined by Sund et al. (2010). This study showed no significant association with family income in Norway, but the income was treated as a continuous variable (in our study, income was a categorical variable). Raftopoulou (2017) findings suggest that individuals in Spain with higher net income (also treated as a continuous variable) tend to exhibit lower levels of BMI.

Our finding showing higher BMI in higher income groups can be explained by different nutritional habits in Poland and in other countries (the USA and Western Europe). According to research conducted by Uramowska-Zyto and Kozłowska-Wojciechowska (2003), nutritional habits in low-income rural areas were better than in the high-income capital city of Warsaw.

The authors are aware of one limitation in this study. Data regarding individuals' weight and height (and therefore BMI value) come from subjects' statement. The data would have been more reliable, if they had come from actual measurements performed on surveyed group. This mentioned bias was taken into consideration while choosing data.

29.5 Conclusion

Individuals in households from higher income categories (middle and high income) had a higher BMI than individuals from low-income households. Poland is a developed country, but the changes in the economy took place relatively recently and possibly therefore household income and BMI are connected in a different way than in the USA and Western Europe. The alarming fact is that high-income groups are the reference groups for different groups in society. Therefore, in the future, an increase in BMI prevalence in lower-income groups can be expected.

References

Ball, K., & Crawford, D. (2005). Socioeconomic status and weight change in adults: A review. *Social Science and Medicine, 60*(9), 1987–2010.

Bates, D., Maechler, M., Bolker, B., & Walker, S. (2015). Fitting linear mixed-effects models using lme4. *Journal of Statistical Software, 67*(1), 1–48. https://doi.org/10.18637/jss.v067.i01.

Brzeziński, M. (2010). Income affluence in Poland. *Social Indicators Research, 99*(2), 285–299.

Clarke, P., O'Malley, P. M., Johnston, L. D., & Schulenberg, J. E. (2009). Social disparities in BMI trajectories across adulthood by gender, race/ethnicity and lifetime socio-economic position: 1986–2004. *International Journal of Epidemiology, 38*(2), 499–509.

Costa-Font, J., Hernández-Quevedo, C., & Jiménez-Rubio, D. (2014). Income inequalities in unhealthy life styles in England and Spain. *Economics & Human Biology, 13,* 66–75.

Council for Social Monitoring. (2016). Integrated database. http://www.diagnoza.com. Accessed September 11, 2016.

Devaux, M., & Sassi, F. (2013). Social inequalities in obesity and overweight in 11 OECD countries. *European Journal of Public Health, 23*(3), 464–469.

Drewnowski, A., & Spencer, S. (2004). Poverty and obesity: The role of energy density and energy costs. *The American Journal of Clinical Nutrition, 79*(1), 6–16.

Dupuy, M., Godeau, E., Vignes, C., & Ahluwalia, N. (2011). Socio-demographic and lifestyle factors associated with overweight in a representative sample of 11–15 year olds in France: Results from the WHO-collaborative health behaviour in school-aged children (HBSC) cross-sectional study. *BMC Public Health, 11,* 1–11.

European Commission. (2010). Algorithms to compute social inclusion indicators based on EU-SILC and adopted under the open method of coordination. Doc. LC-ILC/39/09/EN-rev.1. http://www.dst.dk/ext/747139308/0/. Accessed February 20, 2019.

Feng, X., & Wilson, A. (2015). Do neighbourhood socioeconomic circumstances not matter for weight status among Australian men? Multilevel evidence from a household survey of 14691 adults. *British Medical Journal Open, 5,* 1–9.

Franzini, M., Granaglia, E. &, Raitano, M. (2016). Extreme inequalities in contemporary capitalism. Should we be concerned about the rich? Springer, Switzerland.

Hagenaars, A. J. M., de Vos, K., & Zaidi, M. K. (1994). *Poverty statistics in the late 1980s: Research based on micro-data.* Luxembourg: Office for Official Publications of the European Communities.

Hernández-Yumar, A., Wemrell, M., Abásolo Alessón, I., González López-Valcárcel, B., Leckie, G., & Merlo, J. (2018). Socioeconomic differences in body mass index in Spain: An intersectional multilevel analysis of individual heterogeneity and discrimatory accuracy. *PLoS ONE, 13*(12), 1–23.

Hoehner, C. M., Handy, S. L., Yan, Y., Blair, S. N., & Berrigan, D. (2011). Association between neighborhood walkability, cardiorespiratory fitness and body-mass index. *Social Science and Medicine, 73*(12), 1707–1716.

Kim, J. S. (2009). Multilevel analysis: An overview and some contemporary issues. In R. E. Millsapm & A. Maydeu-Olivares (Eds.), *The SAGE handbook of quantitative methods in psychology* (pp. 337–361). Los Angeles, London: SAGE.

Kim, Y. (2016). The long-run effect of education on obesity in the US. *Economics & Human Biology, 21,* 100–109.

King, T., Kavanagh, A. M., Jolley, D., Turrell, G., & Crawford, D. (2006). Weight and place: A multilevel cross-sectional survey of area-level social disadvantage and overweight/obesity in Australia. *International Journal of Obesity, 30,* 281–287.

Kowalkowska, J., Wadolowska, L., Wuenstel, J. W., Słowińska, M. A., & Niedźwiedzka, E. (2014). Socioeconomic status and overweight prevalence in Polish adolescents: The impact of single factors and a complex index of socioeconomic status in respect to age and sex. *Iranian Journal of Public Health, 43*(7), 913–925.

Mazur, A., Klimek, K., Telega, G., Hejda, G., Wdowiak, L., & Małecka-Tendera, E. (2008). Risk factors for obesity development in school children from south-eastern Poland. *Annals of Agricultural and Environmental Medicine, 15*(1), 281–285.

Mokdad, A. H., Ford, E. S., Bowman, B. A., Dietz, W. H., Vinicor, F., Bales, V. S., et al. (2003). Prevalence of obesity, diabetes, and obesity-related health risk factors, 2001. *JAMA, 289*(1), 76–79.

Mowafi, M., Khadr, Z., Subramanian, S. V., Bennett, G., Hill, A., & Kawachi, I. (2011). Are neighborhood education levels associated with BMI among adults in Cairo, Egypt? *Social Science and Medicine, 72*(8), 1274–1283.

R Core Team. (2018). *R: A language and environment for statistical computing*. R Foundation for Statistical Computing, Vienna, Austria. https://www.R-project.org/. Accessed December 27, 2018.

Raftopoulou, A. (2017). Geographic determinants of individual obesity risk in Spain: A multilevel approach. *Economics and Human Biology, 24,* 185–193.

Robert, S. A., Reither, E. N. (2004). A multilevel analysis of race, community disadvantage, and body mass index among adults in the US. *Social Science & Medicine, 59*(12), 2421–2434.

Ross, N. A., Tremblay, S., Khan, S., Crouse, D., Tremblay, M., & Berthelot, J. M. (2007). Body mass index in urban Canada: Neighborhood and metropolitan area effects. *American Journal of Public Health, 97*(3), 500–508.

Sączewska-Piotrowska, A. (2018). Zamożność dochodowa gospodarstw domowych. Determinanty, dynamika, zróżnicowanie przestrzenne [Income affluence of households. Determinants, dynamics, spatial differentiation]. Wydawnictwo Uniwersytetu Ekonomicznego w Katowicach, Katowice.

Statistics Poland. (2019a). https://bdl.stat.gov.pl/BDL/start. Accessed February 27, 2019.

Statistics Poland. (2019b). https://stat.gov.pl/en/metainformations/glossary/terms-used-in-official-statistics/3198,term.html. Accessed February 27, 2019.

Statistics Poland. (2019c). https://stat.gov.pl/en/metainformations/glossary/terms-used-in-official-statistics/3704,term.html. Accessed February 27, 2019.

Structural Business Statistics Methodology. Statistisk sentralbyrå—SSB (Statistics Norway). (2005). https://ec.europa.eu/eurostat/ramon/nat_methods/SBS/SBS_Meth_NO.pdf. Accessed January 04, 2019.

Sund, E. R., Jones, A., & Midthjell, K. (2010). Individual, family, and area predictors of BMI and BMI change in an adult Norwegian population: Findings from the HUNT study. *Social Science and Medicine, 70*(8), 1194–1202.

TIBCO Software Inc. (2017). Statistica (data analysis software system), version 13. http://statistica.io. Accessed October 02, 2018.

Törmälehto, V. M. (2017). *High income and affluence: Evidence from the European Union statistics on income and living conditions (EU-SILC)*. Statistical Working Papers, Brussels: European Union.

Uramowska-Zyto, B., & Kozłowska-Wojciechowska, M. (2003). Zachowania żywieniowe rodzin ubogich [Nutrition behavior of poor families]. *Roczniki PZH, 54,* 221–229.

Vaezghasemi, M., Ng, N., Eriksson, M., & Subramanian, S. V. (2016). Households, the omitted level in contextual analysis: Disentangling the relative influence of households and districts on the variation of BMI about two decades in Indonesia. *International Journal for Equity in Health, 15,* 1–11.

Villar, J. G., & Quintana-Domeque, C. (2009). Income and body mass index in Europe. *Economics and Human Biology, 7,* 73–83.

World Health Organization. (2000). *Obesity: Preventing and managing the global epidemic*. Report of a WHO consultation. Technical Report Series 894. Geneva: WHO.

World Health Organization. (2013). *Nutrition, physical activity and obesity*. Poland. http://www.euro.who.int/__data/assets/pdf_file/0020/243317/Poland-WHO-Country-Profile.pdf?ua=1. Accessed March 29, 2019.
World Health Organization. (2016). *Obesity and overweight fact sheet*. http://www.who.int/mediacentre/factsheets/fs311/en/. Accessed March 21, 2019.
World Health Organization. (2019). *Global health observatory data repository*, Geneva. http://apps.who.int/gho/data/node.home. Accessed March 29, 2019.

Chapter 30
Inflation as Reflecting Macroeconomic Gaps: An Analysis for Emerging Economies

Ricardo Ramalhete Moreira

Abstract This article is tested for the hypothesis regarding the causality relationships between a macroeconomic gap, especially the investment–domestic savings' gap, and the inflation rate. For empirical purposes, Dumitrescu and Hurlin (Econ Modell 29:1450–1460, 2012) method for Granger causality in panel data was applied to the annual series from 1995 to 2014, covering a group of 50 emerging and developing countries. The empirical findings indicated a corroboration of the tested hypothesis, according to which an increase in the macroeconomic gap is accompanied by a rise in inflation rates.

Keywords Inflation · Macroeconomic gaps · Causality · Emerging economies

JEL Codes E31 · E21 · E22

30.1 Introduction

The inflation rate can be regarded as an adjustment mechanism facing macroeconomic disequilibria. In a mainstream view, the investment–domestic savings' gap determines the behavior of the inflation (Clark et al. 1994; Clark and Laxton 1995; MacDonald 1997; Laxton and Pesenti 2003). For instance, if the investment rate is higher than the domestic savings rate, there will be an excessive domestic demand over the GDP, thereby stimulating higher inflation rates (Clarida et al. 1999). In other words, the output level stays above the potential output, which is accompanied by an increase in the inflation rate, resembling the theoretical results of the New Keynesian Phillips curve.

We can then formalize the conventional hypothesis as follows:

R. R. Moreira (✉)
Professor of Economics, Federal University of Espírito Santo, Vitória, Brazil
e-mail: ricardo.moreira@ufes.br

N. Tsounis and A. Vlachvei (eds.), *Advances in Cross-Section Data Methods in Applied Economic Research*, Springer Proceedings in Business and Economics,
https://doi.org/10.1007/978-3-030-38253-7_30

$$p_t = \alpha + \sum_{j=1}^{n} \beta_j \, p_{t-j} + \sum_{i,j=1}^{n} \chi_{ij} \, x_{it-j} + \delta_t \qquad (30.1)$$

where p_t represents the inflation rate as a dependent variable, while x_{it-j} represents the possible i-explanatory variables or causes—especially the investment–domestic savings' gap for our study—fixed in j possible time lags. In turn, χ_{ij} are the associated coefficients, while δ_t stands for a stochastic residual. Moreover, we also take into account the potential inertia of the dependent variable so that its past values can influence its current ones. Thus, $\sum_{j=1}^{n} \beta_j \, p_{t-j}$ stands for such a potential inertia component.

Based on the conventional perspective, although investment–domestic savings' gaps are assumed to explain inflation rate behavior, one could raise the question about which forces determine such gaps at an initial moment. At the limit, all the variables that can affect investment and domestic savings decisions are potential candidates, including even the inflation. In this case, we allow for a type of circularity (endogeneity) commonly disregarded in works dealing with the issue. Past values of the investment–domestic savings' gap are also an explanatory variable at the current level that we should take into account, as expressed in Eq. (30.1).

The remainder of the paper is structured as follows. The second section shows the dataset and the methodological strategy for empirical purposes. Finally, the third section analyzes the findings, which are followed by concluding remarks and the references.

30.2 Dataset and Methodological Strategy

The annual time series were all collected from the International Monetary Fund *(IMF) World Economic Outlook Database* for a group of 50 emerging and developing countries from 1995 to 2014 ($T = 20$), thus encompassing 1000 observations. The variables are gap = gap between investment and domestic savings rates, both measured as a ratio to GDP; p = accumulated annual inflation rate. Although it would be better if we used quarterly or even monthly data, as it would expressively increase our number of observations, these IMF time series are available only on an annual basis. Table 30.1 shows the group of 50 countries used in this work, while Table 30.2 highlights some descriptive statistics, and Figs. 30.1, 30.2, and present the graphical behavior of the two series for each country.

Before performing the causality analysis for the panel data, it is important to assess the integration order of the time series to avoid spurious estimates. For robustness reasons, we applied four unit root tests for panel data, i.e., the tests of Levin et al. (2002), Im et al. (2003) and ADF-Fisher, which is decomposed into two methods, the Fisher Chi-square and the Choi Z. Table 30.3 presents the results of these tests.

Based on the results, gap and p are $I(0)$. Figures 30.1 and 30.2 also confirm these findings. In this case, we did not perform the co-integration analysis proposed for

Table 30.1 50 emerging and developing countries

1. Armenia	11. Croatia	21. Haiti	31. Malawi	41. Nigeria
2. Azerbaijan	12. Djibouti	22. Hungary	32. Malaysia	42. Pakistan
3. The Bahamas	13. Dominica	23. India	33. Mauritania	43. Panama
4. Bahrain	14. Dominic. Rep.	24. Jamaica	34. Mexico	44. Peru
5. Brazil	15. Ecuador	25. Kazakhstan	35. Moldova	45. Philippines
6. Cameroon	16. Egypt	26. Kenya	36. Morocco	46. Poland
7. Chile	17. El Salvador	27. Kuwait	37. Mozambiq.	47. Romania
8. China	18. Ethiopia	28. Kyrgyz Rep.	38. Namibia	48. Russia
9. Rep. of Congo	19. Ghana	29. Lesotho	39. Nepal	49. Rwanda
10. Costa Rica	20. Guatemala	30. Libya	40. Nicaragua	50. Saudi Arab.

Source Prepared by the author

Table 30.2 Descriptive statistics for our 50 emerging and developing countries

	gap (% of GDP)	p(%)
Mean	2.39	9.03
Median	2.78	5.40
Maximum	48.04	411.76
Minimum	−51.10	−9.86
St. Dev.	10.65	19.30

Source Prepared by the author

panel data in Pedroni (1999), Kao (1999), and Maddala and Wu (1999). Instead, we used gap and p in level values. Dumitrescu and Hurlin (2012) test for Granger causality in panel data is based on Wald statistics of mean non-causality over the cross-sectional units. The test recognizes the heterogeneity of the causality relationships among the cross-sectional units as well as the heterogeneity of the model used to test the Granger causality (Tugcu 2014).

Initially, we adopted such a specific empirical method for two main reasons, an economic reason and a statistical one. Regarding the former, causality tests are suitable when an economic relationship is sensitive to theoretical controversies concerning the associated causality. The relation between the investment–domestic savings' gap and inflation rate is exposed, as mentioned above, to different visions, especially with regard to the causality path. Thus, Dumitrescu and Hurlin (2012) test in panel data has a strong appeal for our research.

On the other hand, when it comes to the statistical reason, the main advantage of this heterogeneous panel data causality test in relation to existing frameworks, such as in Holtz-Eakin et al. (1988), is that it does not impose homogeneous coefficients on the lagged variables across countries. In other words, Dumitrescu and Hurlin (2012) test allows for estimating Granger causality for each country individually and, in

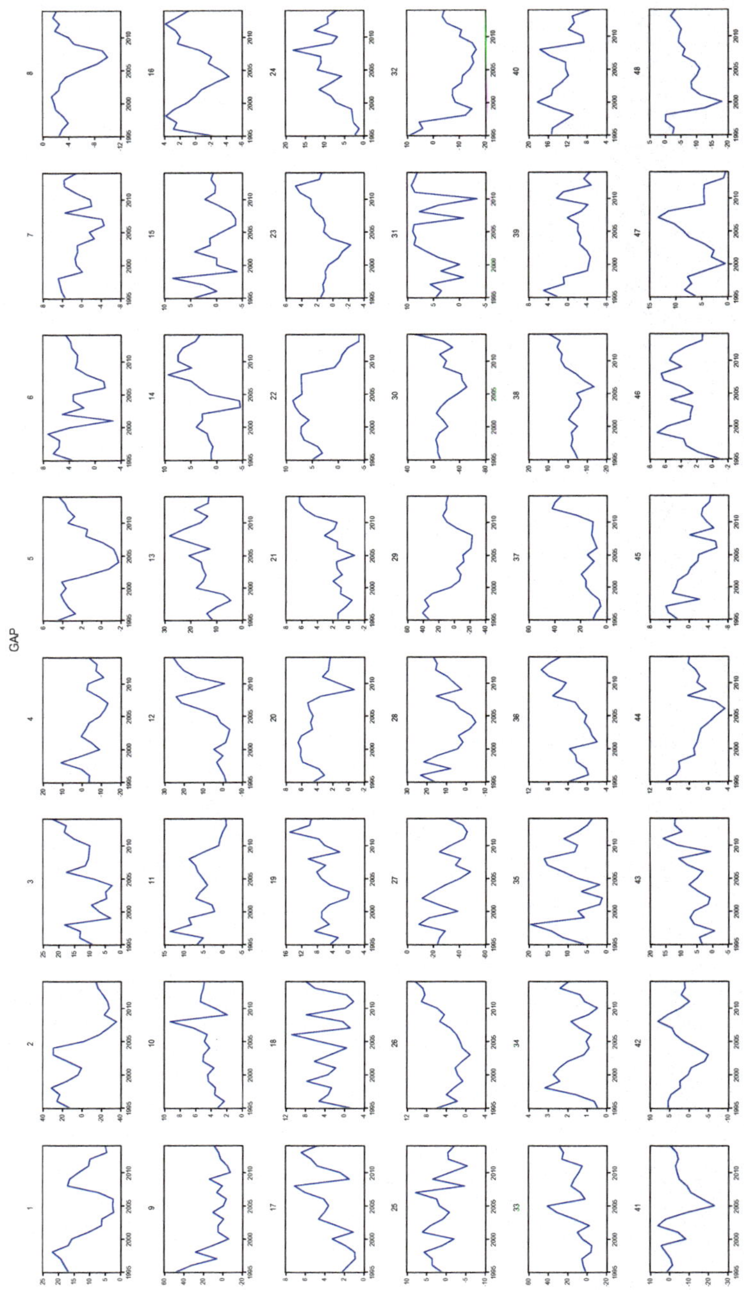

Fig. 30.1 Investment–domestic savings' gap in the panel data. *Source* Prepared by the author

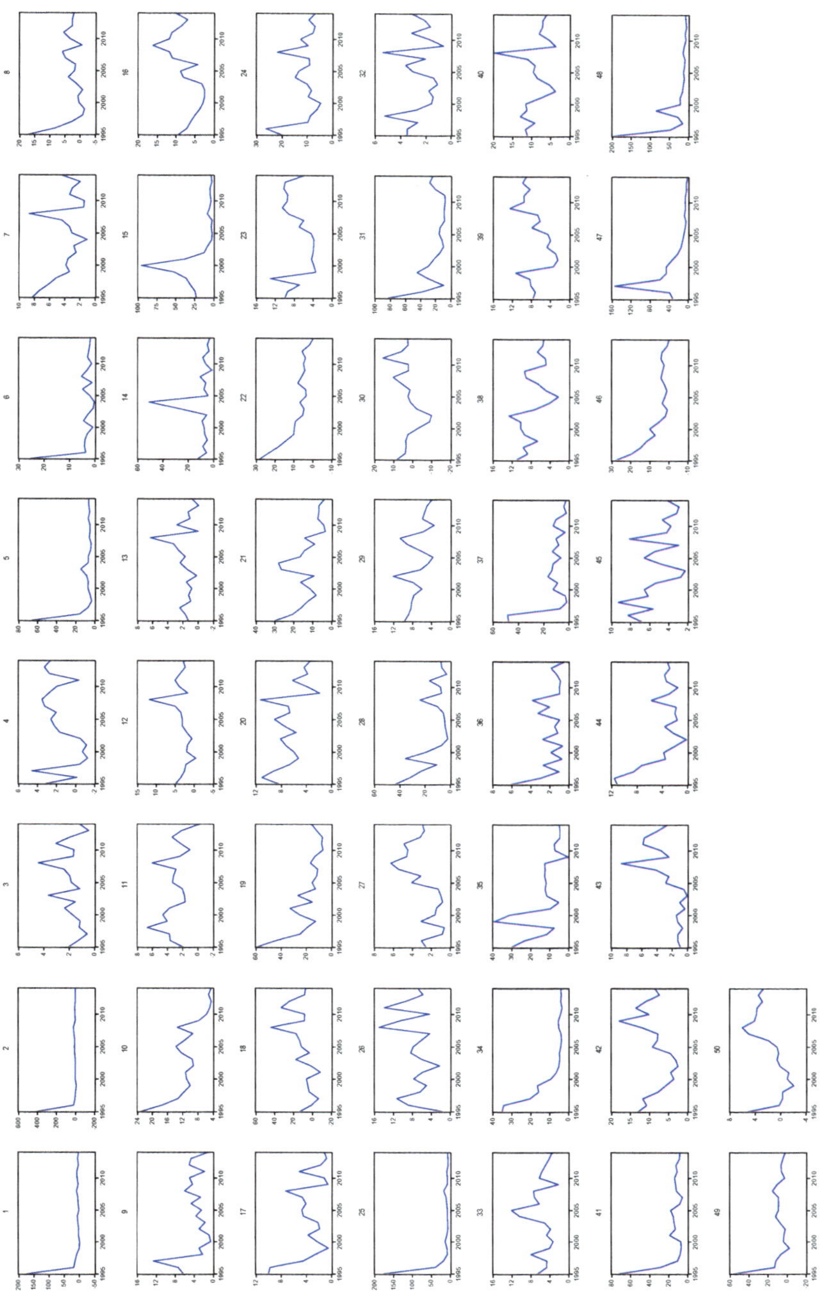

Fig. 30.2 Annual inflation in the panel data. *Source* Prepared by the author

Table 30.3 Unit root tests for the panel data (prob.)

	gap	*p*
Levin, Lin and Chu	0.0000	0.0000
Im, Pesaran and Shin	0.0000	0.0000
ADF—Fisher Chi-square	0.0000	0.0000
ADF—Choi *Z*-stat	0.0000	0.0000

Note Lags in each test were defined by the Schwarz criterion
Source Prepared by the author

the second stage, averaging the individual Wald statistics to measure a standardized causality statistic. Furthermore, the test has very good small sample properties, even with cross-sectional dependence (Herzer 2016). Therefore, this relatively new Granger causality test for panel data is preferable, as our sample is not so large, particularly with regard to time (1995–2014) and also due to common cross-sectional dependence among the data. Finally, we performed the test for 1, 2, and 3 lags to allow it the potential to capture more delayed effects between the variables.

30.3 Causality Findings and Some Correlation Measures

In Table 30.4, we can observe the results from the Granger causality test for panel data proposed by Dumitrescu and Hurlin (2012). We tested for the relation between *p* and gap.

The test rejects the null hypothesis of non-Granger causality from the gap to *p* in all three specifications. Thus we can assume that, based on our panel data, changes in the gap between investment and domestic savings rates are followed by changes in the accumulated annual inflation rate 1, 2, and 3 years forward. The inverse causality relation was not corroborated. The null hypothesis of non-Granger causality from *p* to gap was accepted in all the three specifications. In short, for the 50 emerging and developing countries, we confirmed the conventional hypothesis according to which

Table 30.4 Dumitrescu–Hurlin's Granger causality for panel data

Lags	Null hypothesis	*W*-stat.	*Z*-bar-stat.	Prob.
1	*p* does not homogeneously cause gap	1.39433	0.98404	0.3251
	gap does not homogeneously cause *p*	1.99107	3.31916	0.0009
2	*p* does not homogeneously cause gap	2.71298	0.86958	0.3845
	gap does not homogeneously cause *p*	3.48889	2.80093	0.0051
3	*p* does not homogeneously cause gap	3.9878	0.40559	0.6850
	gap does not homogeneously cause *p*	5.1543	2.39519	0.0166

Source Prepared by the author

Table 30.5 Measures of correlation between gap and *p*

	Ordinary correlation	Spearman rank-order	Kendall's tau
Coef.	0.063	0.139	0.095
Stat.*	1.998	4.419	47,221.000
Prob.	0.046	0.000	0.000

**t*-stat for ordinary and Spearman's correlations, and scores for Kendall's tau

economic policies aiming to stabilize inflation dynamics should control monetary and fiscal instruments correlated to investment and domestic savings rates over time.

We tested ordinary, Spearman's, and Kendall's correlation measures for gap and *p* (Table 30.5). We found that there exists a positive correlation.[1] It means that when gap increases there exists a rise of the inflation rate 1, 2 and 3 years forward in our Panel Data.

30.4 Concluding Remarks

The macroeconomic relations between the investment–domestic savings' gap and inflation rate were assessed through the conventional perspective (Clark et al. 1994; Clark and Laxton 1995; MacDonald 1997; Laxton and Pesenti 2003), that is, the former causing the latter over time.

Based on panel data composed of 50 emerging and developing countries, from 1995 to 2014, we found empirical results supporting such a vision. In other words, that inflation dynamics can be explained by factors affecting differences between investment and domestic savings rates. When investment rises (or domestic savings decline) *ceteris paribus,* there exists a rise in inflation rates over a term of 3 years. However, when inflation rates change *ceteris paribus*, we did not find gap changes as a response. Hence, monetary and fiscal countercyclical policies that aim to stabilize consumer prices can be efficient if their instruments are effective in controlling investments and domestic savings over time.

In short, our empirical article has highlighted the robustness of the conventional perspective, particularly applied to the relation from investment–domestic savings' gap to inflation rates over our panel data, based on the Dumitrescu–Hurlin Granger causality approach.

[1]Although all the estimated coefficients have small values, it is important to regard them as a preliminary step. Indeed, our main goal in the present work was to assess causality relations between the studied variables. More robust measures of correlation require multiple regression analysis in panel data, thereby taking into account control variables affecting the behavior of the dependent time series across countries.

References

Clarida, R., Galí, J., & Gertler, M. (1999). The science of monetary policy: A new Keynesian perspective. *Journal of Economic Literature, 37,* 1661–1707.

Clark, P. B., & Laxton, D. (1995). "Exchange rate effects of fiscal consolidation" annex to *World Economic Outlook* IMF October.

Clark, P. B., Bartolini, L., Bayoumi, T., & Symansky, S. (1994). *Exchange rates and economic fundamentals: A framework for analysis*. Occasional Paper No. 115. Washington, DC: IMF.

Dumitrescu, E. I., & Hurlin, C. (2012). Testing for Granger non-causality in heterogeneous panels. *Economic Modelling, 29,* 1450–1460.

Herzer, D. (2016). Unions and income inequality: A heterogeneous panel co-integration and causality analysis. *Labour, 30,* 318–346.

Holtz-Eakin, D., Newey, W., & Rosen, H. S. (1988). Estimating vector autoregressions with panel data. *Econometrica, 56,* 1371–1396.

Im, K., Pesaran, H., & Shin, Y. (2003). Testing for unit roots in heterogeneous panels. *Journal of Econometrics, 115,* 53–74.

Kao, C. D. (1999). Spurious regression and residual-based tests for cointegration in panel data. *Journal of Econometrics, 90,* 1–44.

Laxton, D., & Pesenti, P. (2003). Monetary rules for small, open, emerging economies. *Journal of Monetary Economics, 50,* 1109–1146.

Levin, A., Lin, C., & Chu, C. J. (2002). Unit root tests in panel data: Asymptotic and finite-sample properties. *Journal of Econometrics, 108,* 1–24.

MacDonald, R. (1997). *What determines real exchange rates? The long and short for it.* IMF Working Paper No. 21.

Maddala, G. S., & Wu, S. (1999). A comparative study of unit root tests with panel data and a new simple test. *Oxford Bulletin of Economics and Statistics, 61,* 631–652.

Pedroni, P. (1999). Critical values for cointegration tests in heterogeneous panels with multiple regressors. *Oxford Bulletin of Economics and Statistics, 61,* 653–670.

Tugcu, C. T. (2014). Tourism and economic growth nexus revisited: A panel causality analysis for the case of the Mediterranean Region. *Tourism Management, 42,* 207–2012.

Chapter 31
Digital Currencies: Its Features and Macroeconomic Implications

Osama Samih Shaban

Abstract Central banks are producing traditional paper currencies within controls and under a corresponding inventory of metals or a basket of currencies, but digital currencies are not subject to any controls of any kind which may create a fertile environment of economic instability. The purpose of this paper is to explore the macroeconomics implications of digital currencies, in addition to examine the extent to which digital currencies are currently used as a form of money, and also to determine whether digital currencies pose a material risk to monetary or financial stability. In order to achieve the objectives of this paper, the study examined the digital currencies currently in use, and it analyzed its performance, and expectations, and finally, the study provides its point of view about possible risk associated with digital currencies in use and its effect to our economy.

Keywords Digital currencies · Macroeconomic policy · Inflation rate · Financial stability

JEL Codes E44 · E42

31.1 Introduction

Digital currency is a type of currency available only in digital form, and has no physical presence. It has characteristics similar to physical currencies, but allows for instant transactions and unlimited transfer of ownership. Examples include virtual currencies, blind currencies, or even "digital compulsory cash" issued by the central bank (Wikipedia 2019).

Digital currencies or electronic currencies are also defined as virtual currencies that are traded through the Internet, perhaps the most famous is Bitcoins. It has become famous because of the four advantages of conversion speed, low cost, privacy

O. S. Shaban (✉)
Accounting Department, Faculty of Business, Al-Zaytoonah University of Jordan, 130, Amman 11733, Jordan
e-mail: drosama@zuj.edu.jo

N. Tsounis and A. Vlachvei (eds.), *Advances in Cross-Section Data Methods in Applied Economic Research*, Springer Proceedings in Business and Economics,
https://doi.org/10.1007/978-3-030-38253-7_31

protection and its decentralization. This means that any intangible currency that an individual can not feel is an electronic currency. This means that the credit cards and the money that is transferred and received through electronic banks are considered an electronic currency system, but eventually, when it is touched and felt it is again considered cash currency (FinancierWorldwide.com 2019).

Digital currencies are considered crypto currency, and the name is derived from two sections, the first is crypto, and the second is the currency, and the abbreviation is cryptography. In other words, digital currencies are digital assets designed to act as a medium for exchange of money or anything of value in a transaction. They rely on cryptography to secure these processes, to control the addition and deletion of units, and finally to document and validate these processes (Houben and Snyers 2018).

Digital currencies have captured the thoughts of many people, and it have raised the concern, fear, and panic of many people also, but the most important that everyone agrees that digital currencies technological revolution will change the form of funds in this world, and it is expected to affect the world's largest and most important financial institutions and their mode of operation.

Many e-currencies are now traded at the Forex market, and its value is increasing in hysterical way as a result of the supply and demand. For example, in December 2017, the Bitcoin's price exceeded $17,000 per unit, and since the number of Bitcoins is limited (21 million Units) only, which increased the competition of the currency circulated among investors. Central banks are producing traditional paper currencies within controls and under a corresponding inventory of metals or a basket of currencies, but digital currencies are not subject to any controls of any kind which may create a fertile environment of economic instability (Forbes.com 2019).

The purpose of this paper is to explore the macroeconomics implications of digital currencies, in addition to examine the extent to which digital currencies are currently used as a form of money, and also to determine whether digital currencies pose a material risk to monetary or financial stability.

The problem of the study arises out of that central banks are producing traditional paper currencies within controls and under a corresponding inventory of metals or a basket of currencies, but digital currencies are not subject to any controls of any kind which may create a fertile environment of economic instability, which eventually may impose possible risk to our economy, so the main question can be asked, what are the consequences and material risk that digital currencies can pose to monetary or financial stability?

The structure of this paper starts with the introduction, then, the second part discusses the literature review of the digital currencies and its features, limitations, and expectations, and finally, the study provides its point of view about possible risk associated with digital currencies in use and its effect to our economy.

31.2 Literature Review and Theoretical Framework

Digital currencies are decentralized currencies, meaning that no government or institution can control the production of more units, and they are controlled by a technology called block chain. The block chain was defined in the book Block-chain Revolution by the writer Tapscott and Tapscott (2016) argued that block chain is considered as a platform that can help us create the digital relationships that will reshape the world of business and transforms the old order of human affairs for the better. In the sense that every economic or financial transaction occurs on the system is recorded and encrypted in a block, and linked to other blocks to form a series of blocks. The digital currency system or the Betquin system is a decentralized system for sending and receiving money characterized by many features, such as super speed, where the transfer of what you want in less than a few seconds, unlike the traditional banks that take days. The second feature is low cost, as the cost of money transfers is almost free or negligible. The third one is the protection and transparency, as every economic or financial operation is saved in a mass and distributed to millions of computers around the world, making the process of penetration is impossible in practice, and the financial process takes place in front of the world, making attempts to manipulate them impossible. Finally, decentralized, which means it is non-affiliated to any central bank. The way digital currencies work makes them very unique in comparison to conventional systems in financial transactions whether online or in real fact (Hern 2019).

The most famous digital currencies emerged in the year 2009 is the Bitcoin encoded by Satoshi Nakamoto, Bitcoin is the most popular digital currency in the world now, and it has the highest market value. In 2011, Charlie Lee, a former Google engineer, invented a coin named LTC, which appeared as an alternative to the Bitcoin, but could not reach the level of Bitcoin. In the year 2013, appeared the most popular digital currency named Ripple. Ripple ranked third in the world of digital currencies in terms of liquidity, the currency of the ripple differs from the currency of the Bitcoin, the Bitcoin seeks to replace the traditional banking system, but the former one seeks to support it (FinancierWorldwide.com 2019).

In January 2014, Evan Duffield created Dash, a digital currency that is considered one of the top ten cryptocurrencies in the world in terms of market capitalization. Dash has been among the top-tier cryptocoins almost since its launch in 2014. Also in April 2014, the Monero digital currency was created. Monero (XMR) is an open-source cryptocurrency focuses on fungibility, privacy, and decentralization. Monero uses an obfuscated public ledger, meaning anybody can broadcast or send transactions, but no outside observer can tell the source, amount, or destination. In the same year, the Chinese government launched its digital currency, the NEO, in order to strengthen its economy. In the year 2015, the Russian programmer Vitalik Buterin invented the second and best digital currency ever, the Ethereum coin, the Ethereum is a virtual or digital currency working under decentralized platform which is extremely important and dangerous at the same time. Ethrium threatens the function of governments, since it allows the creation of intelligent contracts in a way that simulates conventional contracts, ensures that all clauses of the contract are met and ensures that none of the terms of the contract is violated, namely the role of power in real life (arincen.com 2019). Table 31.1 shows the top 30 Cryptocurrencies by Market Capitalization.

A key attraction of digital currencies are their low transactions fees. But these fees may need to rise as usage grows and may eventually be higher than those charged by incumbent payment systems. Also most digital currencies incorporate a pre-determined path toward a fixed eventual supply. In addition to making it extremely unlikely to achieve widespread usage in the long run. A fixed money supply may also harm the macroeconomy, it could contribute to deflation in the prices of goods and services, and in wages. Also, it could lead to the inability of the money supply to vary in response to demand would likely cause greater volatility in prices and real activity.

From the perspective of economic theory, whether a digital currency maybe considered to be money depends on the extent to which acts as:

- A store of value
- A medium of exchange
- A unit of account.

Meeting these definitions does not necessarily imply that an asset will be regarded as money for legal and regulatory purposes. At present, digital currencies are used by relatively few people, data suggest that digital currencies are primarily viewed as stores of value, and not typically used as media of exchange. Also, there is little evidence of digital currencies being used as units of account (Ali et al. 2014). Since digital currencies have become popular in recent years, some analysts and experts have begun to study the effects of these new assets on the future of societies. Experts are divided between supporters of the emerging industry and oppose it, like the famous economist Nouriel Roubini who finds that digital coins are worthless. Also, he stated that block chain is "no better than an Excel spreadsheet." He also pointed out block chain as "the most overhyped technology ever," while noting that Bitcoin and other cryptocurrencies are the mother of all bubbles (cointelegraph.com 2019).

At the conference on the promotion of foreign investment in the UAE's financial markets, experts and analysts have identified five risk factors for investors in the encrypted digital currency markets, which have lost more than 60% of their value since the beginning of the year. They also stressed that there will a great risk on the national currency, as it will work on replacing the national currency with the digital currencies, and eventually, it will drain the state's wealth and resources. There is also a direct negative impact on real-regulated investments, as well as lower purchases of gold and precious metals, and negative impact in the real estate, stocks, and trade sectors (arabi21.com 2019).

Table 31.1 Top 30 cryptocurrencies by market capitalization

No.	Name	Market capitalization ($)	Price ($)	Volume (24 h) ($)	Change (24 h) (%)
1	Bitcoin	94,182,635,792	5,333.24	13,583,223,761	0.90
2	Ethereum	18,139,984,206	171.51	5,679,120,370	1.59
3	XRP	13,618,269,274	0.324470	971,528,910	1.13
4	Bitcoin Cash	5,193,306,795	292.71	1,148,623,934	2.38
5	EOS	4,936,756,135	5.24	1,738,249,659	1.50
6	Litecoin	4,738,782,753	77.11	2,553,381,780	1.38
7	Binance Coin	3,448,585,971	24.43	235,532,647	3.31
8	Tether	2,611,123,330	1.01	11,118,750,057	−0.17
9	Stellar	2,191,679,885	0.113185	229,677,965	1.73
10	Cardano	1,961,835,310	0.075667	76,993,139	4.19
11	TRON	1,680,508,198	0.025202	338,728,823	1.75
12	Monero	1,156,670,306	68.31	103,067,517	0.61
13	Dash	1,069,520,551	122.04	258,923,623	1.10
14	Bitcoin SV	1,021,575,350	57.59	114,408,266	2.53
15	Tezos	878,100,104	1.33	4,223,561	1.26
16	IOTA	862,029,355	0.310135	10,489,863	1.94
17	NEO	703,556,975	10.82	240,662,620	3.80
18	Ethereum Classic	651,483,327	5.93	362,613,154	1.41
19	Maker	611,252,998	611.25	1,239,281	0.68
20	Ontology	606,353,558	1.23	75,014,776	0.50
21	NEM	577,344,677	0.064149	23,933,749	1.78
22	Basic Attenti…	526,048,377	0.420858	104,198,057	−7.49
23	Zcash	431,234,363	67.67	180,002,688	−0.05
24	Crypto.com Chain	421,711,407	0.081694	591,100	−2.32
25	VeChain	384,038,155	0.006925	17,494,037	2.72
26	Dogecoin	332,551,927	0.002790	35,620,263	1.67
27	Bitcoin Gold	298,901,365	17.07	15,909,143	2.67
28	Waves	261,674,676	2.62	19,485,221	1.56
29	OmiseGO	258,950,073	1.85	73,370,918	0.79
30	Augur	251,598,126	22.87	13,546,730	12.63

Source coinmarketcap.com

31.3 Methodology

The methodology adopted in this paper has covered the top ten digital currencies which represented the study sample. The study community is formed of more than 100 digital currencies formally circulated in the market. The study conducted the performance analysis among the study sample depending on the information provided by the website named CoinDesk. The data collected are covering one full year started by April,28, 2018, and ended by the date of performing this research paper on April, 29, 2019. The data were collected on a daily basis and for a period of 365 days. According to performance analysis conducted on the top ten digital currencies, Tables (31.2, 31.3, 31.4, 31.5, 31.6, 31.7, 31.8, 31.9, 31.10 and 31.11), Figs. (31.1, 31.2, 31.3, 31.4, 31.5, 31.6, 31.7, 31.8, 31.9, and 31.10) illustrate the individual performance of these currencies. Finally, all digital currencies were grouped in a single performance analysis, and it is illustrated in Table 31.12 and Fig. 31.11.

Bitcoin is the leading digital currency, its performance during the 2018 is the worst. The difference of closing prices between the beginning and end of year shows a loss of $4292.568, representing down performance of 45.5% in 2018.

Ethereum is the second leading digital currency, its performance during the 2018 is the worst performance of all. The difference of closing prices between the beginning

Table 31.2 One-year performance analysis of Bitcoin

No.	Name	Closing prices from 29/4/2018	Closing prices up to 28/4/2019
1	Bitcoin	9444.1425	5151.5745

Source www.coindesk.com

Table 31.3 One-year performance analysis of Ethereum

No.	Name	Closing prices from 29/4/2018	Closing prices up to 28/4/2019
2	Ethereum	693.961	153.910

Source www.coindesk.com

Table 31.4 One-year performance analysis of Litecoin

No.	Name	Closing prices from 29/4/2018	Closing prices up to 28/4/2019
3	Litecoin	117.4751	71.94302

Source www.coindesk.com

Table 31.5 One-year performance analysis of XRP

No.	Name	Closing prices from 29/4/2018	Closing prices up to 28/4/2019
4	XRP	0.6097	0.3055

Source www.coindesk.com

Table 31.6 One-year performance analysis of Bitcoin Cash

No.	Name	Closing prices from 29/4/2018	Closing prices up to 28/4/2019
5	Bitcoin Cash	988.5081	270.0236

Source www.coindesk.com

Table 31.7 One-year performance analysis of Stellar

No.	Name	Closing prices from 29/4/2018	Closing prices up to 28/4/2019
6	Stellar	0.2906	0.0997

Source www.coindesk.com

Table 31.8 One-year performance analysis of Cardano

No.	Name	Closing Prices from 29/4/2018	Closing Prices up to 28/4/2019
7	Cardano	0.2189	0.0689

Source www.coindesk.com

Table 31.9 One-year Performance analysis of Tron

No.	Name	Closing Prices from 29/4/2018	Closing Prices up to 28/4/2019
8	Tron	0.0603	0.0240

Source www.coindesk.com

and end of year shows a loss of 540.051, representing down performance of 78% in 2018.

Litecoin is the third leading digital currency, and its performance during the 2018 was also nightmare. The difference of closing prices between the beginning and end of year shows a loss of 45.53208, representing down performance of 38.7% in 2018.

XRP is ranked in the fourth position among the leading digital currency, its performance during the 2018 represents crisis for investors. The difference of closing

Table 31.10 One-year performance analysis of Monero

No.	Name	Closing prices from 29/4/2018	Closing prices up to 28/4/2019
9	Monero	155.8641	64.5718

Source www.coindesk.com

Table 31.11 One-year performance analysis of dash

No.	Name	Closing prices from 29/4/2018	Closing prices up to 28/4/2019
10	Dash	305.4615	113.4173

Source www.coindesk.com

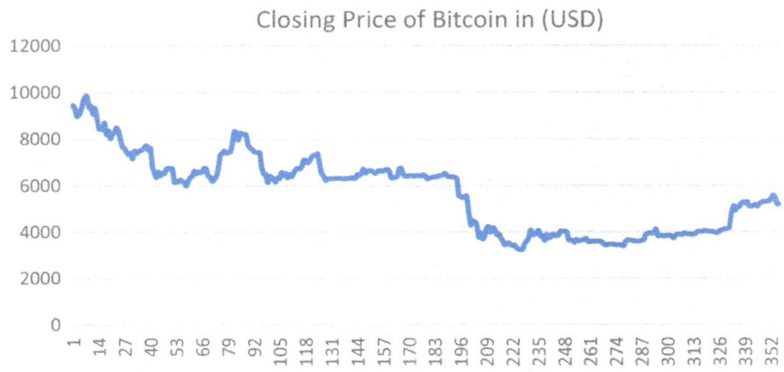

Fig. 31.1 Closing price of Bitcoin in (USD)

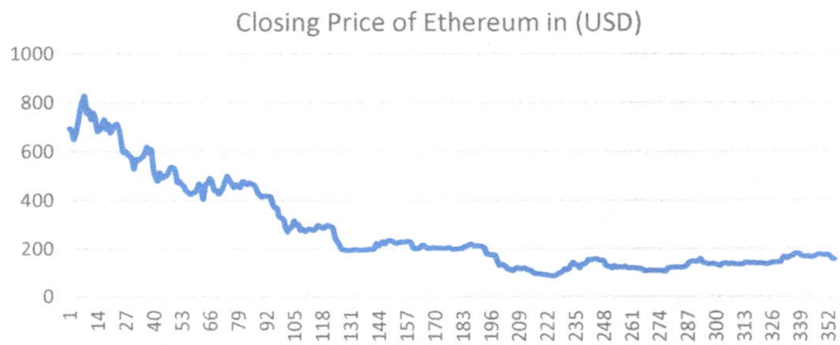

Fig. 31.2 Closing price of Ethereum in (USD)

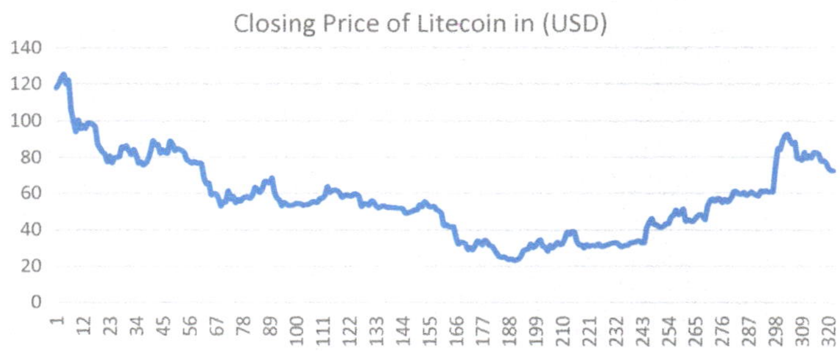

Fig. 31.3 Closing price of Litecoin in (USD)

prices between the beginning and end of year shows a loss of 0.3042, representing down performance of 50% in 2018.

Bitcoin Cash is ranked in the fifth position among the leading digital currency, its performance during the 2018 is also one of the worst performance of all. The difference of closing prices between the beginning and end of year shows a loss of 718.4845, representing down performance of 72% in 2018.

Fig. 31.4 Closing price of XRP in (USD)

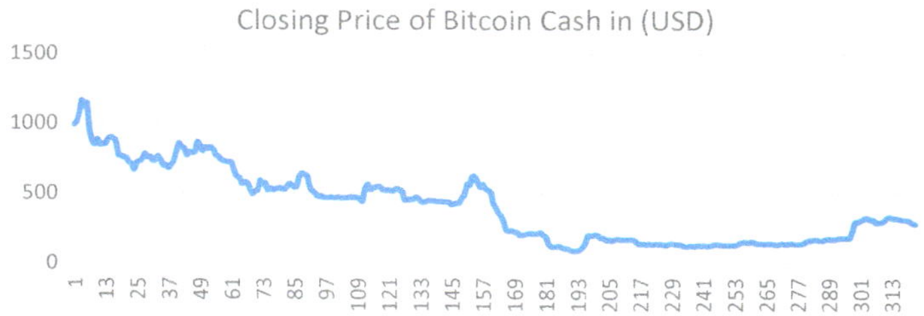

Fig. 31.5 Closing price of Bitcoin Cash in (USD)

Fig. 31.6 Closing price of Stellar in (USD)

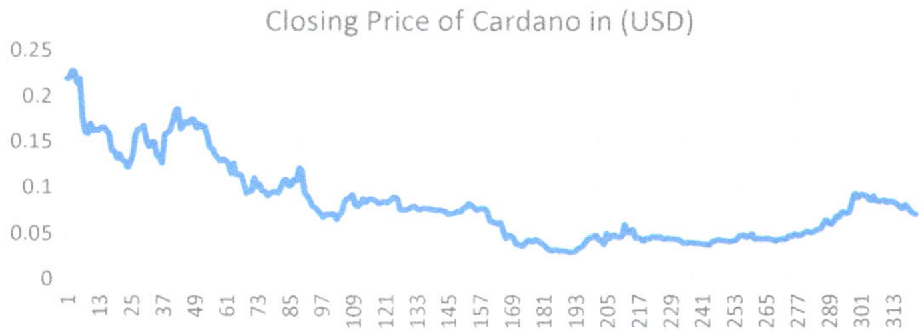

Fig. 31.7 Closing price of Cardano in (USD)

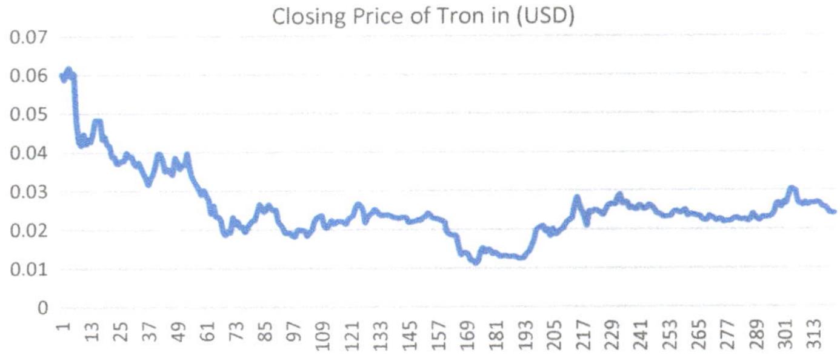

Fig. 31.8 Closing price of Tron in (USD)

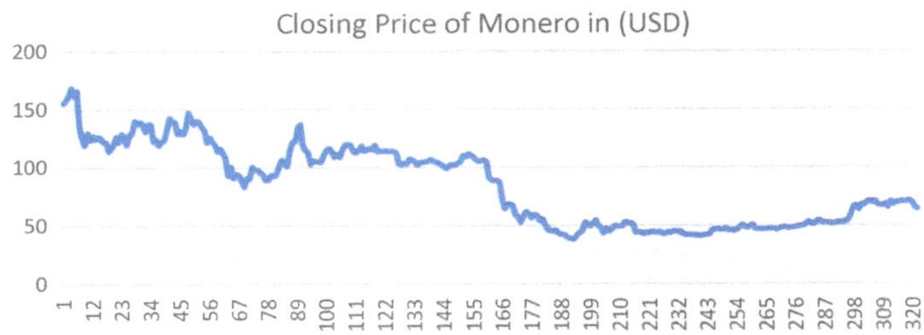

Fig. 31.9 Closing price of Monero in (USD)

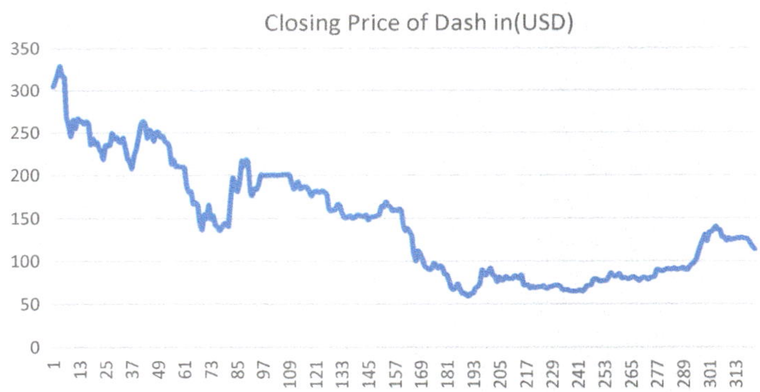

Fig. 31.10 Closing price of Dash in (USD)

Stellar is ranked in the sixth position among the leading digital currency, its performance during the 2018 is also devastating investors. The difference of closing prices between the beginning and end of year shows a loss of 0.1909, representing down performance of 65.7% in 2018.

Cardano is ranked in the seventh position among the leading digital currency, its performance during the 2018 is also devastating investors. The difference of closing

Table 31.12 One-year performance analysis of top ten digital currencies

No.	Name	Closing prices from 29/4/2018	Closing prices up to 28/4/2019	Difference
1	Bitcoin	9444.1425	5151.5745	−4292.568
2	Ethereum	693.961	153.910	−540.051
3	Litecoin	117.4751	71.94302	−45.53208
4	XRP	0.6097	0.3055	−0.3042
5	Bitcoin Cash	988.5081	270.0236	−718.4845
6	Stellar	0.2906	0.0997	−0.1909
7	Cardano	0.2189	0.0689	−0.15
8	Tron	0.0603	0.0240	−0.0363
9	Monero	155.8641	64.5718	−91.2923
10	Dash	305.4615	113.4173	−192.0442

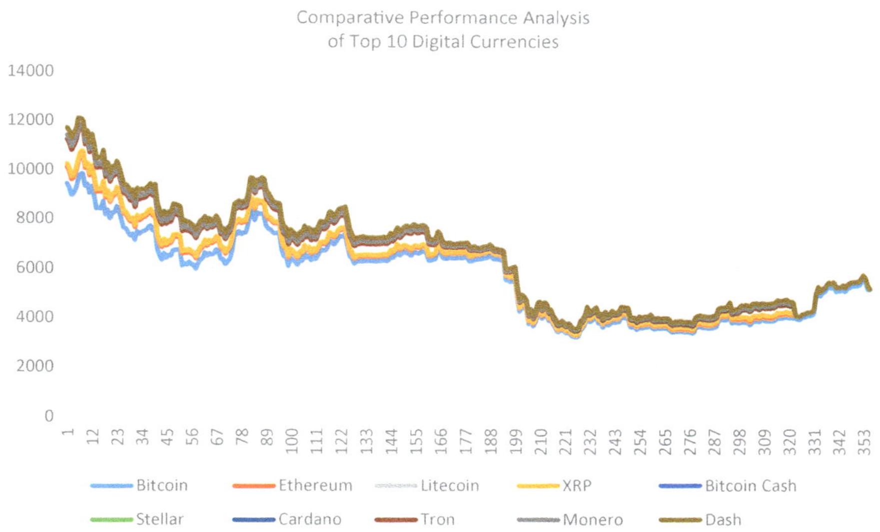

Fig. 31.11 Comparative performance analysis of top ten digital currencies

prices between the beginning and end of year shows a loss of 0.15, representing down performance of 68.8% in 2018.

Tron is ranked in the eighth position among the leading digital currency, its performance during the 2018 is nightmare. The difference of closing prices between the beginning and end of year shows a loss of 0.0363, representing down performance of 60.2% in 2018.

Monero is ranked in the ninth position among the leading digital currency, its performance during the 2018 is horrible. The difference of closing prices between the beginning and end of year shows a loss of 91.2923, representing down performance of 58.6% in 2018.

Dash is ranked in the tenth position among the leading digital currency, its performance during the 2018 is also horrible. The difference of closing prices between the beginning and end of year shows a loss of 192.0442, representing down performance of 62.9% in 2018.

Chart Comparative Performance Analysis of top ten Digital Currencies.

31.4 Results and Recommendations

- It is noticed from above Tables (31.2, 31.3, 31.4, 31.5, 31.6, 31.7, 31.8, 31.9, 31.10, 31.11 and 31.12), and Figs. (31.1, 31.2, 31.3, 31.4, 31.5, 31.6, 31.7, 31.8, 31.9, 31.10, and 31.11), that the top digital currencies are all having declining performance during the one-year period started from 29/4/2018, and ending by 28/4/2019. Evidence supporting our conclusion is witnessed by the news reported telling that, after the market value of the digital currencies reached high score levels of $800 billion, it lost more than half a trillion dollars from its market value in a month of trading.
- Digital currencies are not subject to any control of any official bodies such as central banks, but money is issued and transactions are controlled collectively through the Internet, without authority or guardianship that protects the rights of customers.
- The limited supply of high demand for digital currencies has made them volatile. Evidence of such conclusion is reported by Steven Strongin, head of global investment research in Goldman Sachs said "the market value of digital currencies is vulnerable to further decline, and the correlation between them is worrying about the value of the resulting assets." Also, The famous economist Nouriel Roubini sees that digital currencies are worthless.
- On the other hand, there is few economist who's in favor of digital currencies, Naderoub Shadyev, a specialist in the field of technology, block chain and digital currencies, which was interviewed by "Forbes" newspaper said "that digital currencies can be of great value to the global economy and societies. This is because of the great importance role that money plays in the development of societies, which can be applied to the digital currencies such as Bitcoin. Money acts as a store of value, a medium of exchange, and a unit of account. With the development of the Internet and the spread of the new digital economy, an effort is being made to move from physical assets as a store of value to digital assets that play the same role.
- Digital currencies cause gaps in the bank's financial statements and its transactions, leading to the inability to track economic activities, and thus, the power and ability to control the course of transactions will be in the hands of people rather than governments, and ultimately, if widely adopted, can politicize money. Therefore, experts, financial institutions, and institutions called for an end to the illegal actions

resulting from the use of digital currencies and thus greater control should be imposed to eliminate fraud.

- Finally, digital currencies do not currently pose a material risk to monetary or financial stability, but further control and regulations should be imposed to its transactions and operations.

References

Ali, R., Barrdear, J., Clews, R., & Southgate, J. (2014). *The economics of digital currencies.* Quarterly Bulletin, Q3. Bank of England.

arabi21.com. (2019). Five risks associated with digital currencies. Accessed April 22, 2019. Available at http://www.arabi21.com.

arincen.com. (2019). Crypto-currency. Accessed April 22, 2019. Available at http://www.arincen.com.

Coindesk.com. (2019). Bitcoin performance during 2018. Accessed April 22, 2019. Available at http://www.coindesk.com.

cointelegraph.com. (2019). Crypto critic of blockchain. Accessed April 22, 2019. Available at http://www.cointelegraph.com.

FinancierWorldwide.com. (2019). The rise of digital currency. Accessed April 22, 2019. Available at http://www.FinancierWorldwide.com.

Forbes.com. (2019). Supply and demand in currency markets. Accessed April 28, 2019. Available at http://www.forbes.com.

Hern, A. (2019). Bitcoin and cryptocurrencies—What digital money really mean for our future. Accessed April 22, 2019. Available at http://www.theguardian.com.

Houben, R., & Snyers, A. (2018). *Cryptocurrencies and bolckchain: Legal context and implications for financial crime, money laundering and tax evasion.* Policy Department for Economic, Scientific and Quality of Life Policies, European Parliament. Accessed April 25, 2019. Available at: http://www.europarl.europa.eu/supporting-analyses.

Tapscott, D., & Tapscott, A. (2016). *Blockchain revolution: How the technology behind Bitcoin is changing money, business, and the world.* Brilliance Audio; Unabridged edition.

Wikipedia. (2019). Digital currency. Accessed April 22, 2019. Available at http://www.https://www.wikipedia.org.

Chapter 32
Technology Progress, Trade Openness, and Income Inequality: A Cross-Country Empirical Study

Yih-Luan Chyi and Yi-Hsuan Su

Abstract Since the 1990s, many countries encountering trade liberalization and rapid technological progress have experienced rising within-country income inequality. This paper investigates relationships between trade openness and income inequality in both cross-country and country-specific framework. Using a panel of 61 countries over a period from 1975 to 2005, this study estimates a threshold regression model to identify an inverted-U relationship between openness and inequality with threshold effects of technological progress. On the one hand, income inequality among individuals in countries with less advanced technologies might be getting worse when their trade becomes more opened. On the other hand, for countries with a higher degree of technology advancement, trade openness tends to improve their income inequality.

Keywords Trade openness · Technological progress · Income inequality

JEL Classifications F14 · F62 · O30

32.1 Introduction

According to the World Bank dataset of global Gini coefficients, the within-country income inequality varies significantly across high-income and low-income countries as demonstrated in Fig. 32.1. In particular, there have been rising trends of income inequality in selected OECD countries for the past three decades.[1] What

[1]See Martin and Förster (p. 12, 2013).

Y.-L. Chyi (✉)
Department of Economics, National Tsing Hua University, 30013 Hsin-Chu, Taiwan
e-mail: ylchyi@mx.nthu.edu.tw

Y.-H. Su
National Applied Research Laboratories, Science & Technology Policy Research and Information Center, 10636 Taipei, Taiwan
e-mail: altonsu@gmail.com

N. Tsounis and A. Vlachvei (eds.), *Advances in Cross-Section Data Methods in Applied Economic Research*, Springer Proceedings in Business and Economics,
https://doi.org/10.1007/978-3-030-38253-7_32

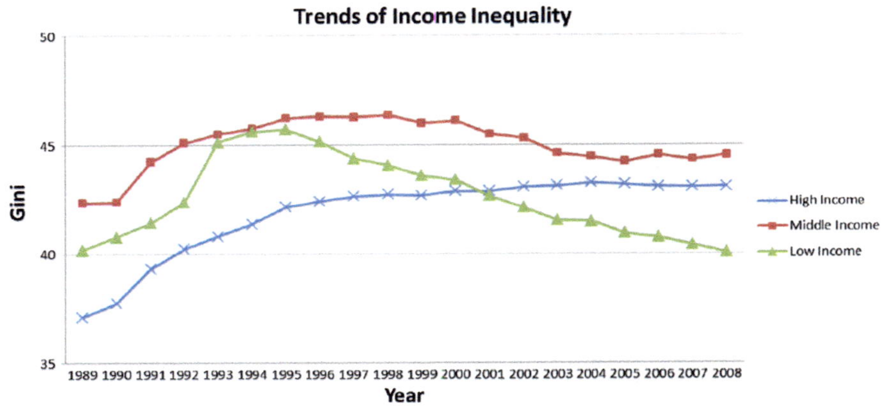

Fig. 32.1 Income inequality for countries with different income levels

are likely reasons for the increasing within-country inequality and the variation of cross-country inequality during the past 30 years? Widely accepted explanations for the prominent evidence in income inequality still remain unsettled. Moreover, it is especially important to know the underlying relationships between income inequality and its contributing factors, considering the wave of globalization is most likely irreversible.

Along with the deepening international integration, does the worldwide income distribution become more unequal? Many researchers have suggested that trade liberalization, as a factor, could interact with income inequality both theoretically and empirically. However, their empirical relationships are rather inconclusive. Using aggregate income data and its own estimates of domestic income distribution to construct worldwide data of individual income, Sala-i-Martin (2002) finds that global income inequality has declined during the 1980s and 1990s. In addition, most of the global income differentials can be explained by cross-country inequality, instead of the within-country inequality. Similar to the studies of Calderón and Chong (2001) and Dollar and Kraay (2004), Sala-i-Martin's findings support a hypothesis that the trade liberalization is helpful in improving income inequality. On the other hand, combining individual country's household survey data into one global dataset, Milanovic (2002) finds that global income inequality has risen noticeably from 1988 to 1993 because of the increasing cross-country inequality, not the within-country inequality. Later on, Lundberg and Squire (2003), Easterly (2005), and Milanovic and Squire (2005) confirm that trade liberalization is relevant in explaining the rising income inequality.

Some recent studies challenge previously emphasized importance of trade liberalization in explaining income inequality. For instance, Jaumotte et al. (2013) suggest that technological progress relative to trade openness has a greater influence on income inequality. Firms' active participation in innovation and adoption of new technology could facilitate spread of the state-of-the-art ideas and thus encourage productivity growth. However, impacts of technological progress on income distribution may be different across countries with various degrees of technology advancement. The puzzling distributional effects may be related to the possibility that technological progress could be skill-biased rather than neutral. In general, Acemoglu (2001) suggests that technological progress is either skill-biased or unskilled-biased.

There are many studies on the effects of openness or technological change on income inequality; however, the link between them still remains inconclusive. Recently, theoretical and empirical studies suggest that the nonlinear effects of trade openness have important implications (Helpman et al. 2010, 2014). To shed some light on the distributional effects of openness for countries with different levels of technology, we use a panel threshold regression model introduced by Hansen (1999) to estimate nonlinear relations between variables of interests over time. Using a panel of 61 countries over a 31-year period from 1975 to 2005, our main findings indicate that it is crucial to account for technological changes when investigating the distributional effects of openness. The empirical results show that openness is important in explaining income inequality, but its effects depend on the level of technological progress. The threshold effects of technology and an inverted-U relationship are identified when examining the impacts of trade on income inequality. On the one hand, countries with a relatively low degree of technological advancement tend to go through deteriorating income inequality when they become more open. On the other hand, when countries have developed into relatively advanced ones in technology, their trade openness could become helpful in improving income inequality.

The rest of the paper is organized as follows. In the next section, relevant literature is reviewed. In Sect. 32.3, the empirical methodology and the data are presented. Section 32.4 shows our empirical results with discussions. Section 32.5 provides a conclusion.

32.2 Literature Review

32.2.1 Openness to Trade

The traditional Heckscher-Ohlin (HO) model implies that when an economy becomes more opened, in developed countries, inequality rises, while in developing countries, inequality declines.[2] However, the empirical results provided by Hanson and Harrison (1999) and Goldberg and Pavcnik (2007) both show that inequality increases in developing countries.

The model developed by Helpman et al. (2010) (thereafter the HIR model) provides essential and inspiring insights. Departing from Melitz (2003) model, the HIR

[2]Based on the HO model, the Stolper–Samuelson theorem predicts that after trade is opened, wages of skilled workers in developed countries should increase relative to the wages of unskilled workers; conversely, the wages of unskilled workers in developing countries should also increase.

model introduces a number of alternative elements, including standard Diamond–Mortensen–Pissarides search and matching frictions; bargaining between workers and employers; ex post match-specific heterogeneity in a worker's ability; and firms' screening activities. They incorporate these features into their theoretical analysis in order to investigate the link between wage inequality and trade openness. The HIR model indicates that sectoral wage inequality is highly associated with the heterogeneity of firm productivity. In addition, inconsistent with the predictions of the Stopler–Samuelson theorem that wage inequality rises in developed countries and declines in developing ones, the HIR model shows that once the economy takes part in the international market, wage inequality will rise in all kinds of countries; and that the relationship between wage inequality and the degree of exposure to trade is at first increasing and later decreasing. In specific, the impact of trade openness on inequality will depend on the initial level of trade openness.

Lundberg and Squire (2003) investigate the empirical relationship between openness and income inequality using an unbalanced panel dataset of 125 countries over the period from 1960 to 1998. They find a negative correlation between trade openness and income growth among the poorest 40% of the population, but a strong and positive correlation among the remaining groups. This result implies that when countries become more open, their income distributions may be more uneven.

32.2.2 Technological Progress

Regarding the relationship between technological change and income inequality, some studies address the issue from a theoretical perspective. Vindigni (2002) develops a theoretical model with endogenous human capital and technological progress to show dynamic general equilibrium relations among technological change, human capital accumulation, and income inequality. Vindigni's main findings indicate that the skill premium becomes higher and thus income distribution could be less equal due to skill-biased technological progress in imperfect credit markets. Besides, the HIR model suggests that more dispersed firm productivity may be a potential source of rising wage inequality. Since the distribution of firm productivity could be driven mainly by innovations and technological progress, technological changes may play an essential role in explaining wage inequality.

Furthermore, Acemoglu (1998) endogenizes the direction of technological change into models originally developed by Romer (1990), Aghion and Howitt (1992) and Grossman and Helpman (1991). Technology improvements in skill-complementary and labor-complementary machines have different implications in the sense that the labor-complementary machines replace old skills and favor non-skilled labor, while the skill-complementary machines replace non-skilled labor and favor skilled labor. According to Acemoglu (1998), the influence of an increase in the supply of skills on skill premium depends on two competing forces, i.e., the conventional substitution effect and the directed technology effect. The substitution effect can simply be demonstrated as a movement along a downward sloping demand curve of skilled labors, while the directed technology effect may be illustrated as a shift of the skilled-labor demand curve. Initially, no effort is devoted in changing direction of technology, and hence, the demand for skilled labor remains stable in response to a rising supply of skilled labor. As a result, the substitution effect dominates, the skill premium decreases and thus wage inequality declines. Later on, more supply of skilled workers leads to a larger market for skill-complementary technologies. In addition, higher profits from invention may motivate inventors to dedicate more effort in creating skill-complementary technologies. Thus, the demand for skilled labor rises in response to a rising supply of skilled labor. In this case, the directed technology effect dominates. The rising premium can attract more individuals to invest in education and skills, and again encourages the skilled-biased technological progress. According to Acemoglu (2001), technological change of USA during the late eighteenth and early nineteenth centuries is unskilled-biased, while new machines and technologies adopted since the post-war period tend to be skilled-complementary. Hence, Acemoglu's model implies a likely path of wage inequality to decline at first and then rise significantly over time, which is consistent with the experience of USA over the past century.

32.2.3 Technology and Trade

Among the limited theoretical literature on trade openness, technological change and income inequality, Dinopoulos and Segerstrom (1999) propose a new dynamic general equilibrium model with international trade to analyze income distributional effects of R&D-related technological change and trade liberalization. The arrival of innovations is endogenously determined by firms' R&D investment, and technological change is driven by the process of creative destruction noted by Schumpeter (1942). Their model provides a critical channel through which trade liberalization can affect the relative wages of skilled workers. Assuming that R&D is the skilled-labor intensity activity, trade openness may positively affect profitability of innovation and thus boost R&D investment. Subsequently, there will be higher relative wages of skilled workers and deteriorating wage inequality. Their study suggests that more liberalized trade not only stimulates skill upgrading and technological progress but also provides explanations for the wage inequality in both countries.

Acemoglu (1998) also discusses the distributional effects of directed technological change in an open economy. Technologies traded with less developed countries (LDCs) should be relatively unskilled-biased and lead to a decrease in income inequality. However, in some cases, such as with a lack of international property rights protection system, trade simply raises the relative prices of the skill-intensive goods, promotes skill-complementary technologies, and thereby increases income inequality.

In sum, existing studies provide inconsistent results regarding the relationships among trade openness, technological changes, and income inequality. This paper attempts to investigate empirically the following hypotheses.

Hypothesis 1 The relationship between trade openness and income inequality is nonlinear and displays an inverted-U pattern.

Hypothesis 2 The relationship between technology and income inequality is positive since the directed technology effect could dominate the substitution effect.

The first hypothesis is based on the implications of the HIR model, suggesting that with different degree of trade participation, income inequality will rise at first and later decline. The second hypothesis is inferred from Acemoglu (1998). However, our sample periods start from 1975 and may only cover the time during which most of the new technologies are skilled-biased instead of the skill-replacing ones. In this case, the directed technology effects are likely to dominate and a positive relationship between technology and income inequality may be expected. This paper will identify potential relationships between income inequality and technology along the process of international integration. It is interesting to discover if the relationships manifest themselves as a Kuznets inverted-U curve[3] or a Great U-Turn[4]?

32.3 Empirical Methodology

32.3.1 The Panel Threshold Regression Model

While conventional panel regressions are used in many existing empirical studies, this paper employs the panel threshold regression model introduced by Hansen (1999). When the value of threshold variable is identified, the threshold regression model allows us to pinpoint the turning point objectively. This method is useful not only in identifying the nonlinear relationship between technological progress and income inequality but also in detecting their relationship over time.

The observations used in the panel threshold regression model should come from a balanced panel $\{y_{it}, q_{it}, x_{it}, 1 \le i \le n, 1 \le t \le T\}$. The subscript i denotes the individual, and the subscript t denotes time. Also, y_{it} is a scalar of the dependent variable, q_{it} is a scalar representing the threshold variable, and x_{it} is a k vector of independent variables. The panel threshold regression model takes the form shown as

$$y_{it} = \mu_i + \beta_1' x_{it} I(q_{it} \le \gamma) + \beta_2' x_{it} I(q_{it} > \gamma) + \varepsilon_{it} \tag{32.1}$$

where I (·) is an indicator function. Equation (32.1) can be expressed as

[3]Kuznets (1953) used data of industrial countries in the nineteenth and twentieth centuries to show the result of inverted U-shaped relationship between growth and income inequality. In the initial stage of industrial development, income inequality rises. With further development, income inequality tends to narrow down.

[4]Harrison and Bluestone (1988) described the situation of upswing in family income inequality starting around 1969 in USA by using the term of "The Great U-Turn."

$$y_{it} = \begin{cases} \mu_i + \beta_1' x_{it} + \varepsilon_{it}, \ q_{it} \le \gamma \\ \mu_i + \beta_2' x_{it} + \varepsilon_{it}, \ q_{it} > \gamma \end{cases} \tag{32.2}$$

The threshold variable may be an element of x_{it} and its value q_{it} being smaller or larger than the threshold γ splits the sample into two groups. This model allows the regression parameters, denoted as β_1 and β_2, to differ depending on the value of q_{it}. It is required for the elements of x_{it} not to be time invariant for the identification of β_1 and β_2. The threshold variable q_{it} is assumed not to be time invariant.

To determine whether the threshold effect is statistically significant, the hypothesis of no threshold effect in (1) can be represented by the linear constraint as

$$H_0 : \beta_1 = \beta_2.$$

Under the null hypothesis, H_0, the threshold γ is not identified, so traditional tests have nonstandard distributions. Hansen (1996) suggests a bootstrap procedure to simulate the asymptotic distribution of the likelihood ratio test and demonstrates that p-values constructed from the bootstrap simulation are asymptotically valid. The null hypothesis of no threshold effect is rejected if the p-value is smaller than the critical value. According to Hansen (1999), the bootstrap size does not have an accelerated rate of convergence relative to conventional asymptotic approximations since the asymptotic distribution is non-pivotal. In some situations, there may exist multiple thresholds. If two thresholds can be detected, the double threshold regression model takes the form as:

$$y_{it} = \mu_i + \beta_1' x_{it} I(q_{it} \le \gamma_1) + \beta_2' x_{it} I(\gamma_1 < q_{it} \le \gamma_2) + \beta_3' x_{it} I(\gamma_2 < q_{it}) + \varepsilon_{it}. \tag{32.3}$$

32.3.2 *Data and Variables*

a. Dependent variable: Gini index

The major problem for the data of the Gini index previously available is that they are collected from various sources and lack comparability across countries. In this study, we adopt the Gini index from the Standardized World Income Inequality Database (SWIID) constructed by Solt (2009). Solt has made great effort in overcoming the issue of data comparability and availability. SWIID maximizes the comparability of income inequality data for 153 countries and for as many years as possible from 1960 to the present.[5] Gini indices of both gross and net income inequality data are provided by SWIID. The gross income inequality data, denoted as gini_market, represents the

---

[5]SWIID uses the data collected by the Luxembourg Income Study to standardize data from many sources including United Nations University's World Income Inequality Database, the OECD Income Distribution Database, the Socio-Economic Database for Latin America and the Caribbean

Gini index of inequality in household pre-tax and pre-transfer income. And the net income inequality data, denoted as gini_net, represents the Gini index of inequality in household income after taxes and transfers, namely disposable income. To avoid the disturbances from government policies and to clearly capture the impacts of trade openness and technological changes on income inequality, this study uses the data of gross income inequality as the dependent variable in our empirical analysis.

b. Independent and control variables

As for independent variables, trade openness is measured by the ratio of trade to GDP, where trade is the sum of the exports and imports of goods and services. Besides trade openness, our analysis takes into account financial openness, represented by FDI. We first sum up the net inflow and outflow of FDI, then calculate the ratio of FDI to GDP to proxy for financial openness. To measure technological changes, this study uses proxies as ratios of high-technology products to manufactured exports, and high-technology products defined as those with high R&D intensity, such as in aerospace, computers, pharmaceuticals, scientific instruments, and electrical machinery. Since access to education may affect income inequality (Willen et al. 2004), our analysis also considers a human capital variable, the average years of education completed among people over age 15, from the Barro-Lee Educational Attainment Dataset constructed by Barro and Lee (2013). The variables concerning educational attainment in Barro-Lee's database are provided every five years, and therefore, we take the mean of two available data for those gap years. Lastly, this study controls for variables regarding country-specific characteristics, such as population, unemployment, and the Internet user. Including Internet users as a control variable has three reasons. First, in constructing the composite index of globalization, the variable of Internet users is often viewed as an important component in the channel of information flows, for example, the GlobalIndex proposed by Raab et al. (2007) and the KOF index constructed by Dreher (2006). Second, the development of the personal computer and the Internet is widely cited to be a good proxy for technological diffusion, as mentioned by Hall (2010). Last but not least, since the prevalence of the Internet relies on the installation of fixed-line phones or cables, and fixed-line phones and cables are highly related to the telecommunication infrastructure (see Hyytinen and Toivanen 2011).

The data of all independent and control variables are collected from the World Bank's World Development Indicators database, except the educational data are collected from the Barro-Lee Educational Attainment Dataset.[6] A list of summary of the definitions and the data sources of all dependent and independent variables is shown in Table 32.1. Summary statistics of those variables are provided in Table 32.2. A report of the pair-wise correlation matrix of all variables is demonstrated in Table 32.3. Table 32.4 shows a list of countries used in our analysis.

---

generated by CEDLAS and the World Bank, Eurostat; the World Bank's PovcalNet, the UN Economic Commission for Latin America and the Caribbean, the World Top Incomes Database, national statistical offices around the world, and many other.

[6]The latest updated version of Barro-Lee Educational Attainment Dataset is available on this website: http://www.barrolee.com/.

Table 32.1 List of variables

Variables	Notation	Definition	Data sources
Gini_market	GINI	Gini index of inequality in household pre-tax and pre-transfer income	The Standardized World Income Inequality Database (SWIID)
Trade	Trade	The sum of exports and imports of goods and services (% of GDP)	World Bank's World Development Indicators database (WDI)
Technology	hiTech	High-technology exports (% of manufactured exports)	
FDI	FDI	The net inflow and outflow of FDI (% of GDP)	
Population	Popu	Total population of a country	
Unemployment	Unem	Unemployment rate (% of total labor force)	
Internet users	Inter	Internet users (per 100 people)	
Average schooling	Avg_sch	Average years of total schooling, age 15+, total	Barro-Lee Educational Attainment Dataset

Table 32.2 Summary statistics

Variable	Mean	Median	Std. Dev.	Min.	Max.
Gini_market	44.38346	43.7448	9.232669	18.38571	79.35268
Trade	66.65456	55.1601	58.69855	0	444.1004
Technology	6.749891	0	12.13123	0	74.99461
FDI	2.304619	0.87797	5.460417	−28.62426	101.4665
Population	7.68e+07	21,000,000	1.92e+08	826,000	1.33e+09
Unemployment	5.044316	4.8	5.275026	0	27.2
Internet users	5.296943	0	14.10616	0	84.83
Average schooling	6.988024	7.165	3.007583	0	13

Table 32.3 Pair-wise correlation matrix of all variables

Correlation	Gini	FDI	Trade	hiTech	Popu	Unem	Avg_sch	Inter
Gini	1.0000							
FDI	0.0017	1.0000						
Trade	0.0050	0.4619	1.0000					
hiTech	0.0214	0.3582	0.3624	1.0000				
Popu	0.0162	−0.0532	−0.2148	0.0291	1.0000			
Unem	0.0197	0.1115	0.0637	0.0882	−0.1228	1.0000		
Avg_sch	−0.3854	0.2029	0.1169	0.3843	−0.1323	0.1682	1.0000	
Inter	−0.0366	0.3464	0.1852	0.4485	−0.0499	0.0697	0.3873	1.0000

Table 32.4 Countries used in analysis

Income level	Name of countries	Number of countries
High income	Australia, Canada, Denmark, Finland, France, Germany, Greece, Hong Kong, Ireland, Italy, Japan, South Korea, Netherlands, New Zealand, Norway, Poland, Portugal, Puerto Rico, Singapore, Spain, Sweden, Switzerland, Trinidad and Tobago, UK, USA, Uruguay	26
Upper middle	Argentina, Brazil, Bulgaria, China, Colombia, Costa Rica, Hungary, Iran, Jordan, Malaysia, Mauritius, Mexico, Panama, Peru, South Africa, Thailand, Tunisia, Turkey, Venezuela.	19
Lower middle	Egypt, El Salvador, India, Indonesia, Morocco, Nigeria, Pakistan, Philippines, Sri Lanka, Ukraine, Zambia	11
Low income	Bangladesh, Kenya, Malawi, Sierra Leone, Tanzania	5
Total number of countries		61

Notes The income level of countries is following the World Bank classifications

32.4 Empirical Results

In this study, we use a panel of 61 countries over a 31-year period from 1975 to 2005 to perform our empirical analysis in three steps. First, we try to verify Hypothesis 1 proposed from the HIR model to examine whether there exists a nonlinear relationship between trade openness and income inequality. In this phase, we take trade as the threshold variable and test if it has threshold effects in affecting income inequality. Second, we validate Hypothesis 2 by testing whether technological progress influences income inequality in a nonlinear pattern. In this step, the technological progress is used as the threshold variable. Finally, we take a further step to examine whether technology contributes threshold effects in the relationship between trade and income inequality, and whether trade plays an important role in identifying a nonlinear relationship between technological progress and income inequality. We illustrate the empirical results in Table 32.5.

We first examine whether the role of trade has the threshold effect in shaping income inequality and reveal that all tests for single, double, and triple thresholds are statistically insignificant, along with their bootstrap *p*-values of 0.702, 0.840, and 0.766, respectively. Thus, Hypothesis 1 is rejected, and it is inconsistent with the predictions of the HIR model as well as the empirical findings in Brazil's case. Yet, the positive and statistically significant coefficient of trade in the first regime, 0.034, indicates that income inequality tends to rise when a country is open to trade. This finding is consistent with some empirical studies suggesting an increase in wage inequality following trade openness (Goldberg and Pavcnik 2007; Menezes-Filho et al. 2008). The potential reason for the inconsistency of our empirical finding with

Table 32.5 Empirical results of threshold regression

	Analysis (I)	Analysis (II)	Analysis (III)
Test for single threshold			
F_1	19.32	86.55	36.16
p-value	0.76	0.02**	0.28
Threshold	75.00	27.49	2.43
Test for double threshold			
F_2	14.06	26.56	63.90
p-value	0.83	0.28	0.04**
Thresholds	37.66; 75.00	1.59; 27.49	2.43; 27.49
Test for triple threshold			
F_3	12.51	21.09	8.05
p-value	0.73	0.32	0.81
Thresholds	37.66; 75.00; 217.57	1.59; 9.35; 27.49	0.14; 4.37; 27.49
Coefficient of regressors			
FDI_{it-1}	0.0928 (1.78)*	0.0329 (0.66)	−0.0103 (−0.20)
hiTech_{it-1}	–	–	0.0453 (2.09)**
$\text{Popu}_{it-1}/10^7$	0.2888 (6.08)***	0.2643 (5.68)***	0.3027 (6.48)***
Unem_{it-1}	0.0286 (0.94)	0.0155 (0.52)	−0.0079 (−0.26)
Avg_ sch_{it-1}	−0.8436 (−4.49)***	−1.2669 (−6.52)***	−1.2486 (−6.38)***
Inter_{it-1}	0.1046 (8.31)***	0.0775 (6.08)***	0.0802 (6.39)***
$\text{Trade}_{it-1}I(\text{Trade}_{it-1} \leq 75)$	0.0340 (3.31)***	–	–
$\text{Trade}_{it-1}I(75 < \text{Trade}_{it-1})$	−0.0008 (−0.11)	–	–
$\text{hiTech}_{it-1}I(\text{hiTech}_{it-1} \leq 27.49)$	–	0.2309 (9.15)***	–
$\text{hiTech}_{it-1}I(27.49 < \text{hiTech}_{it-1})$	–	0.0022 (0.14)	–
$\text{Trade}_{it-1}I(\text{hiTech}_{it-1} \leq 2.43)$	–	–	−0.0110 (−1.56)
$\text{Trade}_{it-1}I(2.43 < \text{hiTech}_{it-1} \leq 29.15)$	–	–	0.0281 (3.66)***
$\text{Trade}_{it-1}I(29.15 < \text{hiTech}_{it-1})$	–	–	−0.0173 (−1.97)**

Notes 1. F_1, F_2, and F_3 are LR test statistics for threshold effect
2. 500 bootstrap replications were used for each of the three bootstrap tests
3. t-statistics are in parentheses next to the coefficient estimate of regressors
*significant at 10%;**significant at 5%;***significant at 1%

theoretical predictions from the HIR model may be partly due to our neglecting a critical factor such as technological progress, stressed by Acemoglu.

We proceed to verify the linkage between technological changes and income inequality. The test for a single threshold value is statistically significant with a bootstrap p-value 0.02, representing that technological progress has the threshold effect on income inequality. As a result, the econometric specification in analysis (II) takes the form of a single threshold regression model shown as:

$$\begin{aligned}\mathrm{GINI}_{it} &= \mu_i + \theta_1\mathrm{FDI}_{it-1} + \theta_2\mathrm{Popu}_{it-1} + \theta_3\mathrm{Unem}_{it-1} + \theta_4\mathrm{Avg\_sch}_{it-1} \\ &\quad + \theta_5\mathrm{Inter}_{it-1} + \beta_1\mathrm{hiTech}_{it-1}I(\mathrm{hiTech}_{it-1} \leq \gamma_1) \\ &\quad + \beta_2\mathrm{hiTech}_{it-1}I(\gamma_1 < \mathrm{hiTech}_{it-1}) + e_{it}\end{aligned} \tag{32.4}$$

where Trade_{it-1} denotes trade openness; FDI_{it-1} denotes financial openness; hiTech_{it-1} denotes the level of technological development; Popu_{it-1} denotes the nation's total population; Unem_{it-1} denotes the unemployment rate; $\mathrm{Avg\_sch}_{it-1}$ denotes the average years of schooling; and Inter_{it-1} denotes the Internet users per 100 people.

The point estimates of the single threshold, γ_1, is 27.49, suggesting that the pattern between technological change and income inequality depends on the level of technological development. The results of the threshold regression show that in the first regime, the link between technological progress and income inequality is highly significant and positive with a coefficient of 0.231, implying that a country with a relatively low level of technology will experience rising income inequality in the process of technological development. After the level of technology grows above a certain threshold value, a smaller coefficient of 0.002 than that in first regime suggests that the upward trend of income inequality tends to ease, though it is not supported by any statistical significance level.

The empirical results do not reject Hypothesis 2. Since our sample peroid is likely to cover only the era in which most of the new technologies are skilled-biased, in this case, the directed technology effects may dominate the substitution effects. In addition, our sample countries include 26 high and 19 upper-middle income ones out of 61 countries. Most countries are capable of exploring the new IT technologies. Therefore, it is expected to find negative distributional effect of technological development.

Finally, based on theoretical and empirical work of Dinopoulos and Segerstrom (1999), Acemoglu (1998), and Jaumotte et al. (2013), we extend to incorporate the role of trade and technology simultaneously into the threshold regression function and detect their threshold effect. We find that when technology is taken as the threshold variable, a nonlinear relationship between trade and income inequality can be identified. In the test for the threshold of technological development, we find the test for a double threshold F2 is significant with a bootstrap p-value of 0.04, indicating there exists double thresholds for technological development in the process that trade openness affects income inequality. In this situation, the econometric specification in analysis (III) takes the form of a double threshold regression model shown as:

$$\begin{aligned}\text{GINI}_{it} = {} & \mu_i + \theta_1 \text{FDI}_{it-1} + \theta_2 \text{hiTech}_{it-1} + \theta_3 \text{Popu}_{it-1} \\ & + \theta_4 \text{Unem}_{it-1} + \theta_5 \text{Avg\_ sch}_{it-1} + \theta_6 \text{Inter}_{it-1} \\ & + \beta_1 \text{Trade}_{it-1} I(\text{hiTech}_{it-1} \leq \gamma_1) \\ & + \beta_2 \text{Trade}_{it-1} I(\gamma_1 < \text{hiTech}_{it-1} \leq \gamma_2) \\ & + \beta_3 \text{Trade}_{it-1} I(\gamma_2 < \text{hiTech}_{it-1}) + e_{it} \end{aligned} \tag{32.5}$$

The point estimates of the two thresholds, γ_1 and γ_2, are 2.43 and 27.49, dividing all the countries into three classifications, and the relationship between trade and income inequality displays different trends in three stages.

In the first regime, when the ratio of high-technology products to manufactured exports is below 2.43%, trade openness has no statistically significant relationship with income inequality. Nevertheless, the coefficient of trade openness is significantly positive in the second regime and becomes significantly negative in the third regime. This finding indicates that when the level of technological progress of a country is relatively low, more exposure to international trade will increase income inequality; once the level of technological progress rises above a threshold value, income inequality could improve along with rising trade liberalization.

Our empirical findings have important implications. First, after taking the role of technology into consideration, Hypothesis 1 is no longer rejected. The nonlinear relationship between trade and income inequality becomes highly significant, and our results imply that technological progress plays a critical role in explaining their linkage. More importantly, the nonlinear relationship exhibits an inverted-U pattern, which is consistent with the prediction of the HIR model. Second, besides confirming the importance of technology in addressing the issue of income inequality, our empirical findings to some extent support Acemoglu's arguments about the impacts of trade on income inequality when the direction of technology is taken into account. Generally speaking, in the process of international integration, developing countries tend to attract trading of unskilled-biased technologies due to their larger supply of unskilled labor. Consequently, some of the developing countries may experience an improving income inequality. Acemoglu (2001) emphasizes that conventional calculations underestimate the impact of trade on income inequality because they ignore the change in the direction of technological change induced by trade. And such a reverse relationship between trade and income inequality when incorporating the role of technology is confirmed by our empirical findings. When in the third regime, the level of technology in a country is relatively high, we expect that the conventional substitution effect may dominate again as a result of the sufficiently large supply in skills and depress income inequality.

32.5 Conclusions

The issue of income inequality has caught researchers' attentions for centuries; however, it is difficult to discern the distributional effects of some critical causes. Motivated by the theoretical framework of the HIR model and Acemoglu's model with directed technological change, this study examines the effects of trade openness and technological progress on income inequality. Based on related literature, we investigate and test two hypotheses. Hypothesis 1 refers to the nonlinear and an inverted-U relationship between trade openness and income inequality. Hypothesis 2 refers to the complicated relationship between technological progress and income inequality. With a panel of 61 countries with the time span of 31 years from 1975 to 2005, we use the econometric method of panel threshold regression model to perform our empirical analysis in three steps. In analysis (I), when the investigation simply focuses on the effect of trade openness on income inequality, it fails to detect nonlinearity between trade openness and income inequality and thus rejects Hypothesis 1 in the first stage of our empirical analysis. In analysis (II), we proceed to examine the effect of technological progress on income inequality. The results show that there is a single threshold about the level of technology. Below a threshold value, where the ratio of high-technology products to manufactured exports amounts to 27.49%, the development of technology leads to an increase in income inequality. When the level of technological progress is above the threshold, the ongoing rising trend of income inequality is flatter despite statistical insignificance. The results in analysis (II) are consistent with the implications of Acemoglu's model and support Hypothesis 2, since our sample may only cover the later period with more skill-complementary technologies. Therefore, the development of technology tends to worsen income inequality. In the final stage, we jointly consider the trade openness and technological progress in our empirical specification. As a result, we find that after incorporating technological progress into investigation, a nonlinear and inverted-U relationship between trade openness and income inequality in different stages of technological development can be identified. Moreover, our empirical results confirm Acemoglu's arguments that taking into account the direction of technological progress will change a negative relationship between trade openness and income inequality into a positive one. In sum, to illuminate the issue of income inequality, this study identifies the threshold effects of technological changes on income inequality in the era of globalization. Moreover, the observed phenomenon of increasing income inequality could be just an interim phenomenon instead of representing the outcome of a final stage of international integration.

References

Acemoglu, D. (1998). Why do new technologies complement skills? Directed technological change and wage inequality. *The Quarterly Journal of Economics, 113*(4), 1055–1089.

Acemoglu, D., (2001). *Directed technological change*. NBER Working Paper No. 8287.

Aghion, P., & Howitt, P. (1992). A Model of growth through creative destruction. *Econometrica, 60*(2), 323–351.

Barro, R., & Lee, J.-W. (2013). A new data set of educational attainment in the world, 1950–2010. *Journal of Development Economics, 104,* 184–198.

Calderón, C., & Chong, A. (2001). External sector and income inequality in interdependent economies using a dynamic panel data approach. *Economics Letters, 71*(2), 225–231.

Dinopoulos, E., & Segerstrom, P. (1999). A Schumpeterian model of protection and relative wages. *American Economic Review, 89*(3), 450–472.

Dollar, D., & Kraay, A. (2004). Trade, growth, and poverty. *Economic Journal, 114*(493), F22–F49.

Dreher, A. (2006). Does globalization affect growth? Evidence from a new index of globalization. *Applied Economics, 38*(10), 1091–1110.

Easterly, W. (2005). Globalization, prosperity, and poverty. In A. Harrison (Ed.), *Globalization and poverty*, University of Chicago Press for NBER. forthcoming.

Goldberg, P., & Pavcnik, N. (2007). Distributional effects of globalization in developing countries. *Journal of Economic Literature, 45,* 39–82.

Grossman, G., & Helpman, E. (1991). Quality ladders in the theory of growth. *Review of Economic Studies, 58,* 43–61.

Hall, J. D. (2010). The diffusion of technology, education and income inequality: Evidence from developed and developing countries. In *The 2009 Dynamics, Economic Growth, and International Trade (DEGIT) Conference Paper*. Philadelphia: Drexel University.

Hansen, B. E. (1996). Inference when a nuisance parameter is not identified under the null hypothesis. *Econometrica, 64,* 413–430.

Hansen, B. E. (1999). Threshold effects in non-dynamic panels: Estimation, testing, and inference. *Journal of Econometrics, 93,* 345–368.

Hanson, G. H., & Harrison, A. (1999). Trade liberalization and wage inequality in Mexico. *Industrial and Labor Relations Review, 52*(2), 271–288.

Harrison, B., & Bluestone, B. (1988). *The great U-turn: Corporate restructuring and the polarizing of America*. New York, NY: Basic Books.

Helpman, E., Itskhoki, O., Muendler, M., & Redding, S. (2014). *Trade and inequality: From theory to estimation*. NBER Working Paper No. 17991.

Helpman, E., Itskhoki, O., & Redding, S. (2010). Inequality and unemployment in a global economy. *Econometrica, 78*(4), 1239–1283.

Hyytinen, A., & Toivanen, O. (2011). Income inequality and technology diffusion: Evidence from developing countries. *The Scandinavian Journal of Economic, 113*(2), 364–387.

Jaumotte, F., Lall, S., & Papageorgiou, C. (2013). Rising income inequality: Technology, or trade and financial globalization? *IMF Economic Review, 61*(2), 271–309.

Kuznets, S. (1953). *Shares of upper income groups in income and savings*. New York, NY: National Bureau of Economic Research.

Lundberg, M., & Squire, L. (2003). The simultaneous evolution of growth and inequality. *The Economic Journal, 113*(487), 326–344.

Martin, J. P., & Förster, M. (2013). Inequality in OECD countries: The facts and policies to curb it. See http://insights.unimelb.edu.au/vol15/pdf/Martin.pdf.

Melitz, M. J. (2003). The impact of trade on intra-industry reallocations and aggregate industry productivity. *Econometrica, 71,* 1695–1725.

Menezes-Filho, N. A., Muendler, M.-A., & Ramey, G. (2008). The structure of worker compensation in Brazil, with a comparison to France and the United States. *Review of Economics and Statistics, 90,* 324–346.

Milanovic, B. (2002). True world income distribution, 1988 and 1993: First calculation based on household surveys alone. *Economic Journal, 112*(476), 51–92.

Milanovic, B., & Squire, L. (2005). *Does tariff liberalization increase wage inequality? Some empirical evidence*. World Bank Policy Research Working Paper, No. 3571. Washington, DC: World Bank.

Raab, M., Ruland, M., Schönberger, B., Blossfeld, H.-P., & Hofäcker, D. (2007). GlobalIndex-A multidimensional approach to globalization measurement. *TransEurope Project*, http://www.transeurope-project.org.

Romer, P. (1990). Endogenous technological change. *Journal of Political Economy, 98*(5), Part 2: The Problem of Development: A Conference of the Institute for the Study of Free Enterprise Systems, S71-S102.

Sala-i-Martin, X. (2002). *The disturbing "rise" of global income inequality*. NBER Working Paper 8904, http://www.nber.org/papers/w8904. http://www.columbia.edu/~xs23/papers/GlobalIncomeInequality.htm.

Schumpeter, J. A. (1942). *Capitalism, socialism, and democracy*. New York, NY: Harper and Row.

Solt, F. (2009). Standardizing the World Income Inequality Database. *Social Science Quarterly, 90*(2), 231–242. SWIID Version 4.0, September 2013.

Vindigni, A. (2002). *Income distribution and skilled biased technological change*. Working Paper No. 464, Industrial Relations Section, Princeton, University.

Willen, P., Hendel, I., & Shapiro, J. (2004). *Educational opportunity and income inequality*. NBER Working Paper No. 10879.

World Development Indicators. (2014). The World Bank-World Databank. http://databank.worldbank.org/data/home.aspx.

Chapter 33
Implementation of Local Volatility in Piterbarg's Framework

Alexis Levendis and Pierre Venter

Abstract The stock market crash of 1987 proved to be a major turning point in financial markets as the Black–Scholes model assumption of constant volatility was violated. A new phenomena known as the "volatility smile" were observed post the crisis, and this has been one focus area of quantitative finance researchers over the past couple of decades. Almost 20 years after the crash now known as "Black Monday", the 2007 global financial crisis occurred which showed that numerous other factors need to be considered when pricing derivatives. Collateral, for instance, is considered by Piterbarg. In this paper, we present a local volatility model used to price arithmetic Asian call options in the Piterbarg framework.

Keywords Interpolation · Local Volatility · Monte Carlo · Collateral

33.1 Introduction

The Black and Scholes (1973) model introduced the fundamental building blocks for option pricing as we know it today. The model makes two important assumptions, (1) the volatility is constant throughout the tenor of the option and (2) the interest rate is constant and risk-free. The first assumption of constant volatility proved to be flawed after the stock market crash of 1987, also known as "Black Monday". The reason for this is that the demand for out-the-money put options increased post the crash since investors started using these instruments as insurance to protect their assets. The second assumption of a risk-free interest rate broke down after the 2007 global financial crisis when large banks such as Lehman Brothers defaulted.

Many researchers have tried to address the shortcomings in the Black and Scholes (1973) model. Dupire (1994) shows that there is a deterministic function for volatility of the spot price and time $\sigma_{BS_{LV}}(S_t, t)$ which can be obtained from quoted European

A. Levendis (✉) · P. Venter
College of Business and Economics, University of Johannesburg,
Johannesburg, South Africa
e-mail: alexilevendis@gmail.com

N. Tsounis and A. Vlachvei (eds.), *Advances in Cross-Section Data Methods in Applied Economic Research*, Springer Proceedings in Business and Economics,
https://doi.org/10.1007/978-3-030-38253-7_33

call option prices. Piterbarg (2010) developed a framework post the credit crisis which relaxes the assumption of a risk-free interest rate and includes the intricacies of the repo and collateralisation markets. His framework uses three different interest rates including r_F (the unsecured funding rate paid on funds used to finance the derivative), r_C (the collateral rate paid on collateral received) and r_R^S (the rate gained in a repurchase agreement into which an underlying asset S is entered into). The relationship between the three interest rates is given by $r_C \leq r_R^S \leq r_F$. Recently, von Boetticher (2017) extended the work done by Dupire (1994) where he derived formulas for the local volatility $\sigma_{P_{LV}}(S_t, t)$ in the Piterbarg (2010) framework.

In this paper, we will consider S&P 500 call option data with a variety of strike prices and maturities as at 4 October 2018. First, we will calculate implied volatilities using the closed-form solutions for European call options derived by von Boetticher (2017). Next, we show how to interpolate these implied volatilities using natural cubic splines (Press et al. 1993) in the strike direction and linear interpolation in the time to maturity direction using the total implied variance (Kahalé 2004). The interpolation will lead to a smooth implied volatility surface which is not necessarily arbitrage-free, but we present a necessary condition which must be satisfied and show how to calculate it. The remainder of this paper is structured as follows: Sect. 33.4 shows how implied volatilities can be transformed into local volatilities by making use of the formula derived by von Boetticher (2017), Sect. 33.5 presents the implementation of our local volatility model and the impact of collateral on European and arithmetic Asian call option prices in the Piterbarg framework.

33.2 Piterbarg Implied Volatility

Given the market quoted price of a European call option, the implied volatility is defined as the volatility that must be used as input into an option pricing model in order to return the quoted price. It is important to note here that the implied volatility is dependent on the choice of option pricing model.

The closed-form solution of a European call option to the Black and Scholes (1973) partial differential equation

$$\frac{\partial V}{\partial t} + r S_t \frac{\partial V}{\partial S_t} + \frac{1}{2}\sigma_{BS}^2 S_t^2 \frac{\partial^2 V}{\partial S_t^2} = r V, \tag{33.1}$$

is given by

$$V(S_t, t) = S_t N(d_1) - K e^{-r(T-t)} N(d_2), \tag{33.2}$$

where V is the value of the derivative, r is the risk-free interest rate, K is the strike price, σ_{BS} the volatility of the underlying in the Black and Scholes (1973) framework, T is the maturity date, $N(.)$ is the cumulative standard normal distribution and S_t the stock price at time t. d_1 and d_2 are defined as follows:

$$d_1 = \frac{\ln(\frac{S_t}{K}) + (r + \frac{\sigma_{BS}^2}{2})(T - t)}{\sigma_{BS}\sqrt{T - t}},$$
$$d_2 = d_1 - \sigma_{BS}\sqrt{T - t}.$$

The closed-form solution (33.2) can be used to retrieve the implied volatility by treating σ_{BS} as the only unknown in the equation.

Piterbarg (2010) extends the Black and Scholes (1973) model to take collateral agreements into account and derives the following partial differential equation:

$$\frac{\partial V}{\partial t} + r_R^S S_t \frac{\partial V}{\partial S_t} + \frac{1}{2}\sigma_P^2 S_t^2 \frac{\partial^2 V}{\partial S_t^2} = r_F V - (r_F - r_C)C, \tag{33.3}$$

where C is the amount of collateral posted in the trade and σ_P is the volatility of the underlying in the Piterbarg (2010) framework.

The closed-form solution to this equation was derived by von Boetticher (2017) where he considered three different types of collateral payments including a fully collateralised (FC) trade, zero collateral (ZC) as well as partial collateral (PC). The respective solutions for a European call option are

$$V_{\text{FC}}(S_t, t) = e^{-\int_t^T r_C(u)du}(S_t e^{\int_t^T r_R^S(u)du} N(d_1) - KN(d_2)), \tag{33.4}$$
$$V_{\text{ZC}}(S_t, t) = e^{-\int_t^T r_F(u)du}(S_t e^{\int_t^T r_R^S(u)du} N(d_1) - KN(d_2)), \tag{33.5}$$
$$V_{\text{PC}}(S_t, t) = e^{-\int_t^T r_F(u)du}(S_t e^{\int_t^T r_R^S(u)du} N(d_1) - KN(d_2)) \times(1 + \int_t^T \theta(r_F(s) - r_C(s))ds), \tag{33.6}$$

where $\theta \in [0, 1]$ and d_1 and d_2 are defined as follows:

$$d_1 = \frac{\ln(\frac{S_t}{K}) + \int_t^T r_R^S(u)du + \frac{1}{2}\sigma_P^2(T - t)}{\sigma_P\sqrt{T - t}},$$
$$d_2 = d_1 - \sigma_P\sqrt{T - t}.$$

Note the integrals of the interest rates in the solutions. This is because they are determined from the respective repo/funding/collateral curves and not a unique, constant risk-free rate. Equations (33.4)–(33.6) can be used to calculate the implied volatility of an option once the type of collateral agreement is known. The closed-form solution of a European call option in the Black and Scholes (1973) framework differs from the solution in the Piterbarg (2010) framework which will lead to different implied volatilities.

European call option prices are only quoted for a limited set of strikes and maturities in the market. We are required to fill the gaps if the implied volatility surface is going to be of any use going forward. The next section will focus on techniques on how to interpolate these values in the strike direction and time to maturity direction which will lead to a smooth surface.

33.3 Simple Interpolation of Implied Volatility

Given a function $f(x)$ defined on $[a, b]$ and a set of nodes

$$a = x_0 < x_1 < x_2 < \cdots < x_n = b,$$

a cubic spline interpolant, G, for f satisfies the following conditions:

- G is a cubic polynomial, G_j on $[x_j, x_{j+1}]$ for $j = 0, 1, \ldots, n-1$,
- $G(x_j) = f(x_j)$ for $j = 0, 1, \ldots, n$,
- $G_{j+1}(x_{j+1}) = G_j(x_{j+1})$ for $j = 0, 1, \ldots, n-2$,
- $G'_{j+1}(x_{j+1}) = G'_j(x_{j+1})$ for $j = 0, 1, \ldots, n-2$,
- $G''_{j+1}(x_{j+1}) = G''_j(x_{j+1})$ for $j = 0, 1, \ldots, n-2$,
- $G''(x_0) = G''(x_n) = 0$.

Given a set of $n + 1$ data values $\{(x_0, f(x_0), (x_1, f(x_1)), \ldots, (x_n, f(x_n))\}$, we will create n cubic polynomials of the form

$$G_j(x) = a_j + b_j(x - x_j) + c_j(x - x_j)^2 + d_j(x - x_j)^3, \tag{33.7}$$

for $j = 0, 1, \ldots, n-1$.

The objective is to find the coefficients a_j, b_j, c_j and d_j (a total of $4n$ unknowns) subject to the conditions listed above.

Solving a_j for $j = 0, 1, \ldots, n-1$ is simple since the known values of the function f can be substituted

$$G_j(x_j) = a_j = f(x_j). \tag{33.8}$$

Now, n equations remain with $3n$ unknowns. Calculating the first derivative of G yields n more equations

$$G'_j(x) = b_j + 2c_j(x - x_j) + 3d_j(x - x_j)^2, \tag{33.9}$$

for $j = 0, 1, \ldots, n-1$. This leads to $2n$ equations and $3n$ unknowns.

The continuity of the second derivative at the nodal points produces n more equations

$$G''_j(x) = 2c_j + 6d_j(x - x_j), \tag{33.10}$$

for $j = 0, 1, \ldots, n-1$. We now have $3n$ equations and $3n$ unknowns, and hence, we can proceed to solve the remaining coefficients.

Let $h_j = x_{j+1} - x_j$. Then, from (33.8) to (33.10), we have

$$\begin{aligned} G'(x_j) &= b_j, \\ G'(x_{j+1}) &= b_{j+1} = b_j + 2c_j h_j + 3d_j h_j^2, \\ G''(x_j) &= 2c_j, \\ G''(x_{j+1}) &= 2c_{j+1} = 2c_j + 6d_j h_j. \end{aligned}$$

For $j = 0, 1, \ldots, n-1$ we have the following set of equations:

$$\begin{aligned} a_{j+1} &= a_j + b_j h_j + c_j h_j^2 + d_j h_j^3, \\ b_{j+1} &= b_j + 2c_j h_j + 3d_j h_j^2, \\ c_{j+1} &= c_j + 3d_j h_j. \end{aligned}$$

We can calculate d_j by a simple transformation

$$d_j = \frac{c_{j+1} - c_j}{3h_j}.$$

Using the natural boundary conditions $G''(x_0) = G_0''(x_0) = 2c_0 = 0$ and $G''(x_n) = G_{n-1}''(x_n) = 2c_n = 0$ and also the fact that the quantities a_j, d_j and h_j are known, we can form a set of $n+1$ equations with $A\mathbf{c} = \mathbf{y}$ where

$$A = \begin{bmatrix} 1 & 0 & 0 & 0 & \ldots & 0 \\ h_0 & 2(h_0 + h_1) & h_1 & 0 & \ldots & 0 \\ \vdots & \vdots & \vdots & \vdots & & \vdots \\ 0 & 0 & 0 & h_{n-2} & 2(h_{n-2} + h_{n-1}) & h_{n-1} \\ 0 & 0 & 0 & 0 & 0 & 1 \end{bmatrix}$$

$$\mathbf{c} = \begin{bmatrix} c_0 \\ c_1 \\ c_2 \\ \vdots \\ c_{n-1} \\ c_n \end{bmatrix}$$

$$\mathbf{y} = \begin{bmatrix} 0 \\ \frac{3}{h_1}(a_2 - a_1) - \frac{3}{h_0}(a_1 - a_0) \\ \frac{3}{h_2}(a_3 - a_2) - \frac{3}{h_1}(a_2 - a_1) \\ \vdots \\ \frac{3}{h_{n-1}}(a_n - a_{n-1}) - \frac{3}{h_{n-2}}(a_{n-1} - a_{n-2}) \\ 0 \end{bmatrix}$$

The implied volatility surface is defined as

$$\sigma_{\text{imp}} : (K, \tau) \rightarrow \sigma_{\text{imp}}(K, \tau),$$

where τ is the time to maturity.

Given a limited number of market implied volatilities at different strikes (K) and expiry times (τ), we will apply the natural cubic spline algorithm (Press et al. 1993) shown above to interpolate implied volatilities in the strike (K) direction for each given time to expiry (τ). Note that great care must be taken when selecting the options to include in the cubic spline algorithm. This is because of the so-called "butterfly spread arbitrage". The existence of the butterfly spread requires that $\frac{\partial^2 \sigma_{\text{imp}}}{\partial K^2} \geq 0$. The proof of the convexity in K condition can be found in Roper (2010).

Once the gaps are filled in the strike (K) direction, all that remains is to interpolate the implied volatilities in the time to maturity (τ) direction. Define the total implied variance as in Kahalé (2004)

$$w(K, \tau) = \sigma^2_{\text{imp}}(K, \tau)\tau.$$

For $\tau_2 > \tau_1$, we require that $w(K, \tau_2) > w(K, \tau_1)$ else calendar arbitrage will exist. Proof of the monotonicity in (τ) can be found in Roper (2010). Interpolation in the total implied variance direction is a simple algorithm:

- Assume $0 < \tau_1 < \tau_2 < \tau_3 < \cdots < \tau_{n-1} < \tau_n$ are the known times to expiry obtained from market data.
- For each interpolated and given strike (K), calculate the gradient $m = \frac{\sigma_{\text{imp}}(K, \tau_j) - \sigma_{\text{imp}}(K, \tau_{j-1})}{\tau_j - \tau_{j-1}}$ for $j = 2, 3, \ldots, n$.
- Fill the gaps with the formula $w(K, \tau) = m \times (\tau - \tau_j) + w(K, \tau_j)$ for $j = 1, 2, \ldots, n-1$.
- Transform the total implied variance back to implied volatility $\sigma_{\text{imp}}(K, \tau) = \sqrt{\frac{1}{\tau} \times w(K, \tau)}$.

Once an implied volatility surface has been constructed, the next step is to calculate local volatilities from this surface. The following section will focus on local volatility in the Piterbarg (2010) framework.

33.4 Piterbarg Local Volatility

In the Black and Scholes (1973) framework, the stock price evolution is described by the stochastic differential equation

$$dS_t = rS_t dt + \sigma_{BS} S_t dW_t, \tag{33.11}$$

where r is the unique risk-free interest rate, the rate which is relaxed by Piterbarg (2010).

By now, it should be clear that the assumption of constant volatility is unrealistic. Dupire (1994) extended the Black and Scholes (1973) equation by investigating a risk-neutral process of the form

$$dS_t = rS_t dt + \sigma_{BS_{LV}}(S_t, t) S_t dW_t, \tag{33.12}$$

where the instantaneous volatility $\sigma_{BS_{LV}}$ is a deterministic function of the spot and time. His work led to the Dupire equation which allows us to calculate local volatility $\sigma_{BS_{LV}}$ as a function of Black and Scholes (1973) implied volatility σ_{BS},

$$\sigma^2_{BS_{LV}}(K, \tau) = \frac{\sigma^2_{BS} + 2\tau\sigma_{BS}\frac{\partial\sigma_{BS}}{\partial\tau} + 2rK\tau\sigma_{BS}\frac{\partial\sigma_{BS}}{\partial K}}{(1 + Kd_1\sqrt{\tau}\frac{\partial\sigma_{BS}}{\partial K})^2 + K^2\tau\sigma_{BS}(\frac{\partial^2\sigma_{BS}}{\partial K^2} - d_1\sqrt{\tau}(\frac{\partial\sigma_{BS}}{\partial K})^2)}, \tag{33.13}$$

where

$$d_1 = \frac{\ln(\frac{S_t}{K}) + (r + \frac{\sigma^2_{BS}}{2})\tau}{\sigma_{BS}\sqrt{\tau}}.$$

By first constructing an implied volatility surface from known option prices at different strikes and maturity dates, it is possible to construct a local volatility surface using Eq. (33.13). Derman and Kani (1994) used a binomial tree to deduce $\sigma_{BS_{LV}}(S_t, t)$ numerically from the volatility smile. They showed that the volatility of liquid index options can be used to construct an entire implied tree which will correctly value standard calls and puts that define the volatility smile. The fact that the local volatility surface can reproduce the volatility smile for European call and put options makes the model very attractive.

In the Piterbarg (2010) framework, the stock drifts at the repurchase rate r^S_R

$$dS_t = r^S_R S_t dt + \sigma_{P_{LV}}(S_t, t) S_t dW_t. \tag{33.14}$$

The reason for this is that if we enter into a repurchase agreement today, we sell the underlying S and agree to buy it back at a premium r^S_R.

The extension of the Dupire (1994) equation to the Piterbarg (2010) framework was derived by von Boetticher (2017). The local volatility function $\sigma_{P_{LV}}$ in terms of Piterbarg (2010) implied volatility σ_P is given by

$$\begin{aligned} \sigma^2_{P_{LV}}(K, \tau) &= \frac{\sigma^2_P + 2\sigma_P\tau(\frac{\partial\sigma_P}{\partial\tau} + r^S_R K\frac{\partial\sigma_P}{\partial K})}{(1 + Kd_1\sqrt{\tau}\frac{\partial\sigma_P}{\partial K})^2 + K^2\tau\sigma_P(\frac{\partial^2\sigma_P}{\partial K^2} - d_1\sqrt{\tau}(\frac{\partial\sigma_P}{\partial K})^2)}, \\ d_1 &= \frac{\ln(\frac{S_t}{K}) + \int_t^T r^S_R(s)ds + \frac{1}{2}\sigma^2_P\tau)}{\sigma_P\sqrt{\tau}}. \end{aligned} \tag{33.15}$$

In the next section, we will present our numerical results based on S&P 500 call option data. We will make use of Eq. (33.15) to construct the local volatility surface which will then be used to price European and arithmetic Asian call options.

33.5 Numerical Results

33.5.1 Data

S&P 500 call option data as at 4 October 2018 was obtained from https://www.barchart.com/stocks/quotes/$SPX/options. European call option prices with strikes ranging from $2855 to $2950 in intervals of $5 and expiries 1 day, 8 days, 13 days and 18 days were included in the investigation. The surface below shows a visualisation of the data.

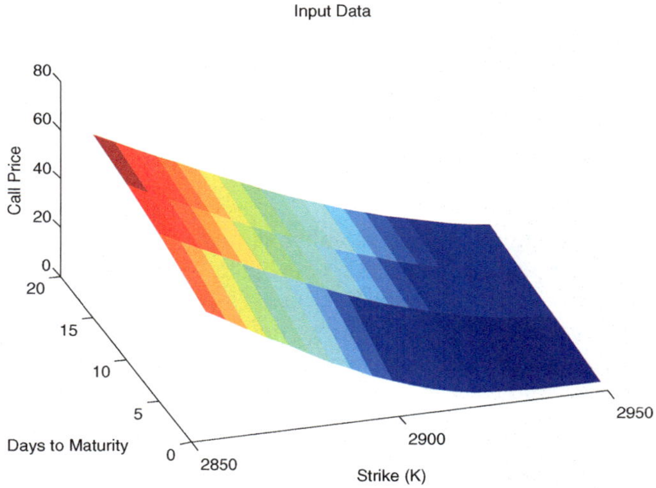

33.5.2 Calculating Implied Volatility and Interpolation

Using our dataset in Sect. 33.5.1, we will consider the scenarios where zero collateral and full collateral are posted in the trade. Recall from Sect. 33.2 that von Boetticher (2017) derived the closed-form solution to European call options in the Piterbarg (2010) framework. The closed-form solutions are given by

$$V_{\text{ZC}}(S_t, t) = e^{-\int_t^T r_F(u)du}(S_t e^{\int_t^T r_R^S(u)du} N(d_1) - KN(d_2)), \tag{33.16}$$

$$V_{\text{FC}}(S_t, t) = e^{-\int_t^T r_C(u)du}(S_t e^{\int_t^T r_R^S(u)du} N(d_1) - KN(d_2)), \tag{33.17}$$

where

$$d_1 = \frac{\ln(\frac{S_t}{K}) + \int_t^T r_R^S(u)du + \frac{1}{2}\sigma_P^2(T-t)}{\sigma_P\sqrt{T-t}},$$
$$d_2 = d_1 - \sigma_P\sqrt{T-t}.$$

We will assume that $r_F = 6\%$, $r_R^S = 5\%$, $r_C = 4\%$ and that we are working with 252 trading days in a year. The closed-form solutions then simplify to

$$V_{\text{ZC}}(S_t, t) = e^{-r_F(T-t)}(S_t e^{r_R^S(T-t)} N(d_1) - KN(d_2)), \tag{33.18}$$
$$V_{\text{FC}}(S_t, t) = e^{-r_C(T-t)}(S_t e^{r_R^S(T-t)} N(d_1) - KN(d_2)), \tag{33.19}$$

where

$$d_1 = \frac{\ln(\frac{S_t}{K}) + r_R^S(T-t) + \frac{1}{2}\sigma_P^2(T-t)}{\sigma_P\sqrt{T-t}},$$
$$d_2 = d_1 - \sigma_P\sqrt{T-t}.$$

We are now equipped to apply Eqs. (33.18) and (33.19) to our data and calculate the implied volatilities σ_P. A simple way to do this is to use the *Goal Seek* functionality in Microsoft Excel. The graphs below show the calculated implied volatilities for each time to expiry.

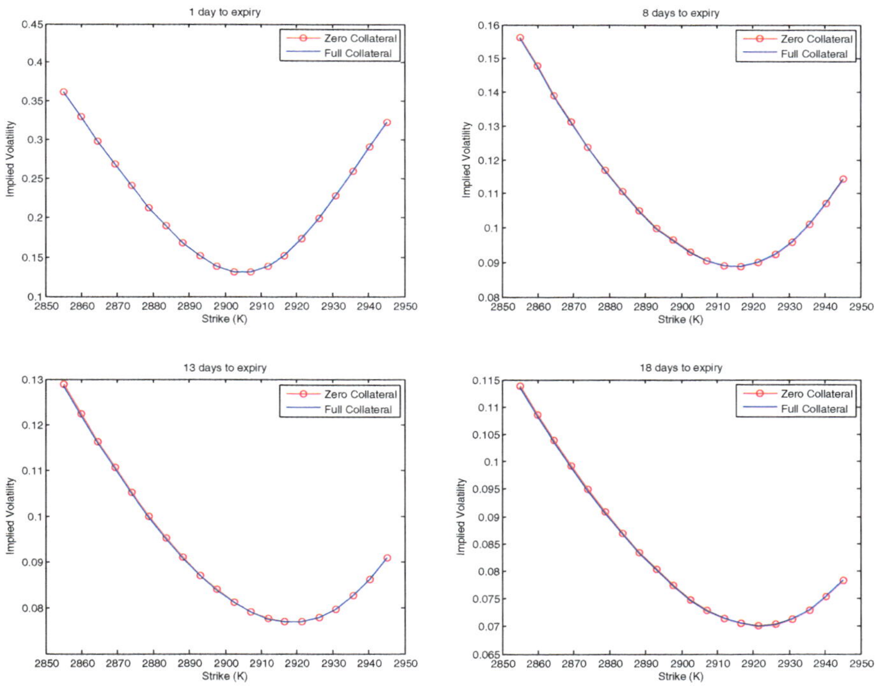

The graphs show that implied volatilities for zero collateral trades versus full collateral trades do not differ much for short times to expiration, but a closer investigation reveals that the implied volatilities for zero collateral trades are slightly higher compared to full collateral trades. To illustrate the concept, an enlarged graph for the 18-day European call options is shown below.

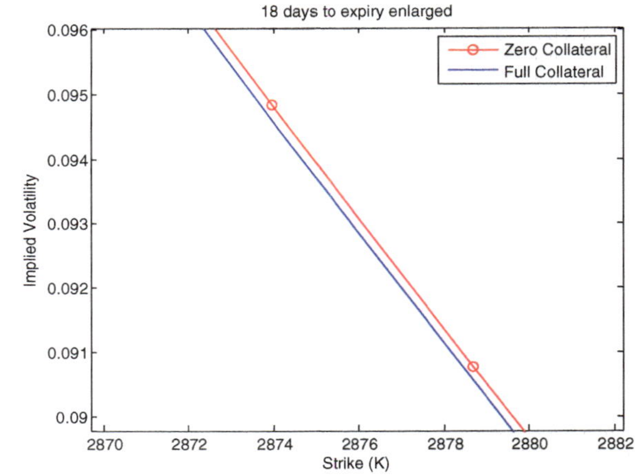

The difference should become more apparent for options with longer expiry dates because the effect of discounting will be greater than in the short term.

The next step is to decide which options to include in our cubic spline interpolation algorithm. This step is critical since our algorithm is not necessarily free from arbitrage. From the data, we have call options at strike intervals of \$5, i.e. $h = 5$. The local volatility formula requires that $\frac{\partial^2 \sigma_P}{\partial K^2} \geq 0$. Therefore, we need to do a sense check upfront to investigate whether the second derivative with respect to K is positive across strikes. We can calculate the second derivative by using the central finite difference formula

$$\frac{\partial^2 \sigma_P}{\partial K^2}(K, \tau) \approx \frac{\sigma_P(K+h, \tau) - 2\sigma_P(K, \tau) + \sigma_P(K-h, \tau)}{h^2}. \tag{33.20}$$

We will use the call options starting from strike \$2855 to \$2945 with $h = 10$ as input into the cubic spline algorithm to avoid arbitrage.

We want to interpolate the implied volatilities in such a way that it is easy to read the values of the surface when we apply our Monte Carlo simulation. We choose $\Delta K = 1$ and $\Delta \tau = \frac{1}{252}$ and proceed to interpolate the implied volatilities using cubic splines in the strike (K) direction and linear interpolation in the time to maturity (τ) direction as explained in Sect. 33.3. Our interpolation leads to a 3-D surface which is used as input into the local volatility formula. Below, we show the implied volatility surfaces for the zero collateral scenario and full collateral scenario.

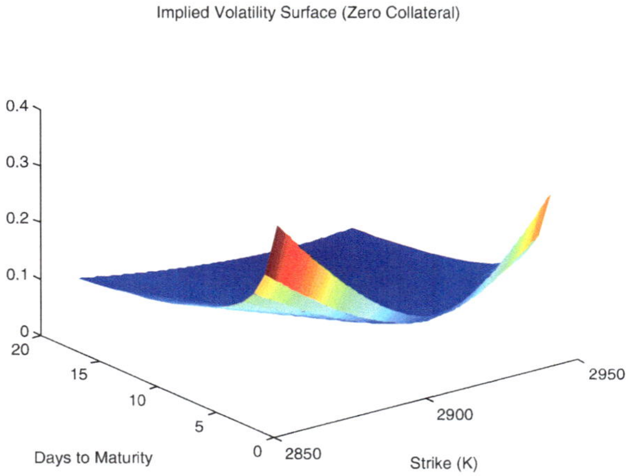

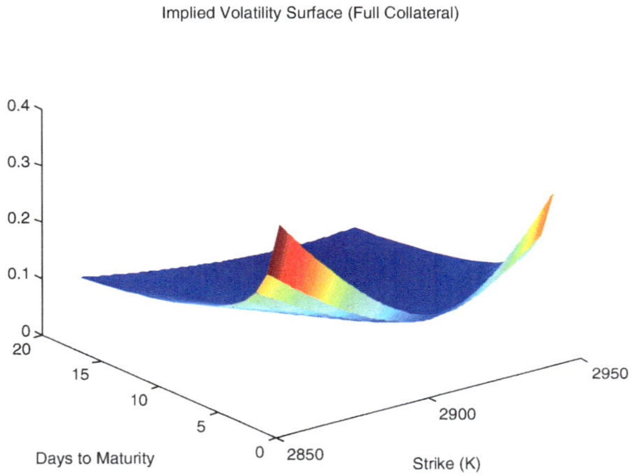

33.5.3 Calculating Local Volatility

The implied volatility surface can be transformed into a local volatility surface by making use of the formula derived by von Boetticher (2017)

$$\sigma^2_{P_{LV}}(K,\tau) = \frac{\sigma_P^2 + 2\sigma_P\tau\left(\frac{\partial\sigma_P}{\partial\tau} + r_R^S K\frac{\partial\sigma_P}{\partial K}\right)}{\left(1 + Kd_1\sqrt{\tau}\frac{\partial\sigma_P}{\partial K}\right)^2 + K^2\tau\sigma_P\left(\frac{\partial^2\sigma_P}{\partial K^2} - d_1\sqrt{\tau}\left(\frac{\partial\sigma_P}{\partial K}\right)^2\right)}, \tag{33.21}$$

where a constant r_R^S leads to d_1 taking the form

$$d_1 = \frac{\ln\left(\frac{S_t}{K}\right) + r_R^S\tau + \frac{1}{2}\sigma_P^2\tau}{\sigma_P\sqrt{\tau}}.$$

Our local volatility surfaces for the zero collateral and full collateral scenarios are shown below.

Local Volatility Surface (Zero Collateral)

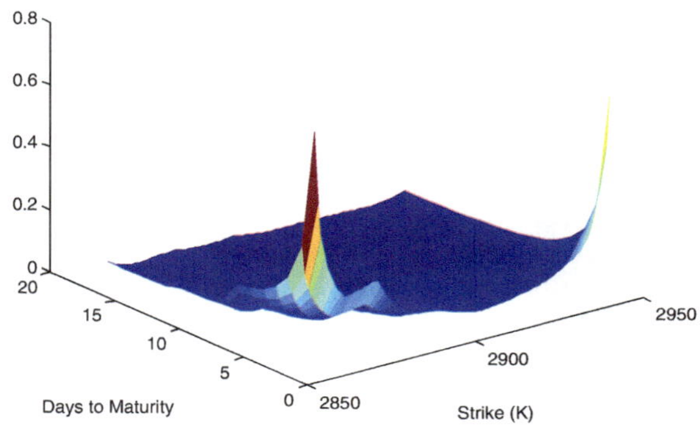

Local Volatility Surface (Full Collateral)

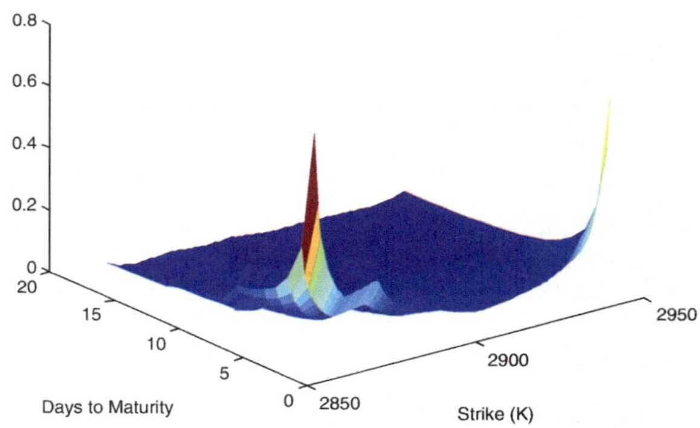

The rule of thumb is that the local volatility surface should increase twice as fast as the implied volatility surface. Our local volatilities are in line with this rule.

Recall that the stock drifts at r_R^S in the Piterbarg (2010) framework. In other words, the stock price process is described by the stochastic differential equation

$$dS_t = r_R^S S_t dt + \sigma_{P_{LV}}(S_t, t) S_t dW_t. \tag{33.22}$$

If we choose the time steps in our Monte Carlo simulation to be exactly the same as the time spacing in our local volatility surface, then it will be simple to observe the local volatilities directly from the surface. Therefore, we will choose $\Delta t = \frac{1}{252}$. Finally, we put all our work into action by pricing European and arithmetic Asian call options.

33.5.4 Pricing in Action

Before we can apply our local volatility model, we need to determine the accuracy of our local volatility surface calibration. This can be done by pricing the European call options in Sect. 33.5.1 with a Monte Carlo simulation using our local volatility surface. If our results are close to the actual market prices, then we know we have done a good job in calibrating the surface, and we can proceed to use the local volatilities to price more complex options. The graphs below show the accuracy of our Monte Carlo simulation when compared to the actual prices of the 13-day and 18-day European call options. We simulated 5000 price paths in our investigation.

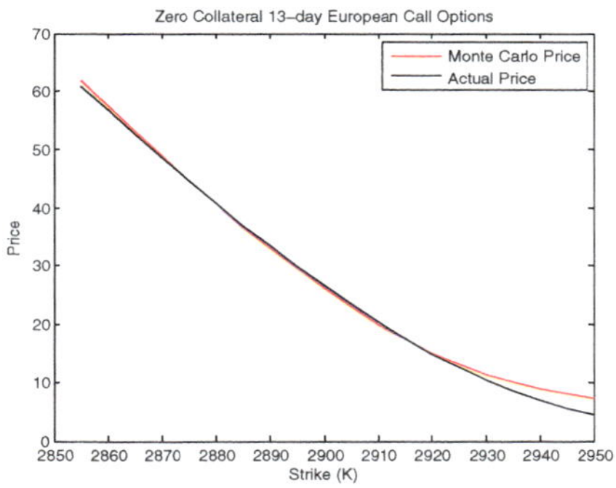

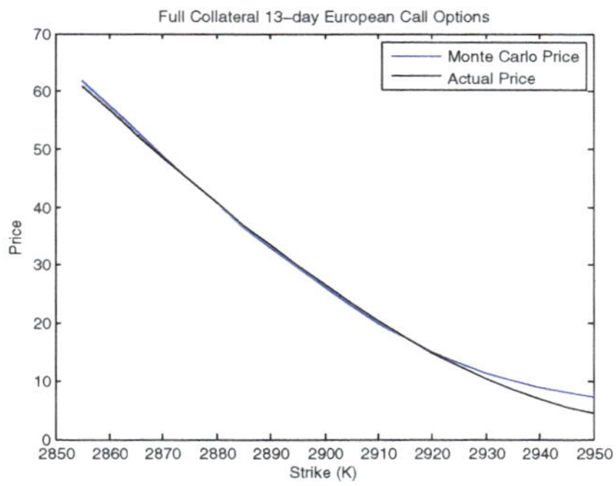

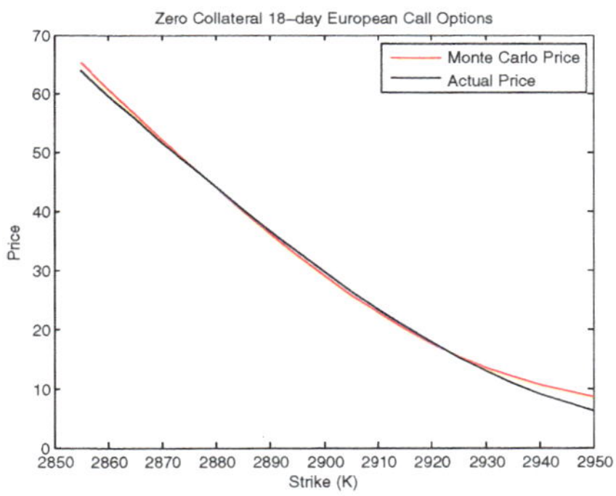

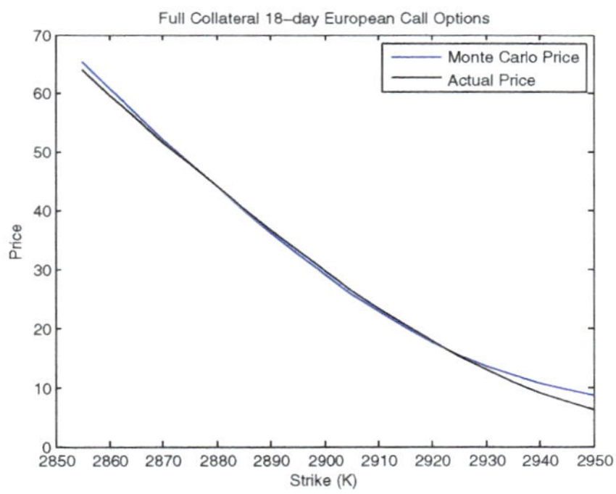

The graphs indicate that our local volatilities have been calibrated well since the results obtained from the Monte Carlo simulation are close to the actual market prices. We proceed to use our zero collateral and full collateral local volatility surfaces to price more complex options.

An Asian option is a contract where the payoff of the option is determined by the average underlying price over some pre-set period of time. In this paper, we will consider Asian call options that can only be exercised at the date of expiry and that an arithmetic average applies. In mathematical terms, the average A of the underlying over the interval $[0, T]$ is given by

$$A(0, T) = \frac{1}{T} \int_0^T S(t)dt. \tag{33.23}$$

There is no closed-form solution for the price of an arithmetic Asian call option. Therefore, numerical methods (Monte Carlo or partial differential equations) are applied.

In order for us to assess the impact of collateral on the price of European and Asian calls, we look at options that expire in 180 days. Since 180 days to maturity falls outside the domain of our local volatility surface, we need a way of extrapolating volatilities. We do this by simply taking $\sigma_{P_{LV}}(S_{t_{\max}}, t_{\max})$ for volatilities outside the surface domain. The graph below shows the prices of 180-day European and Asian calls for zero and full collateral scenarios.

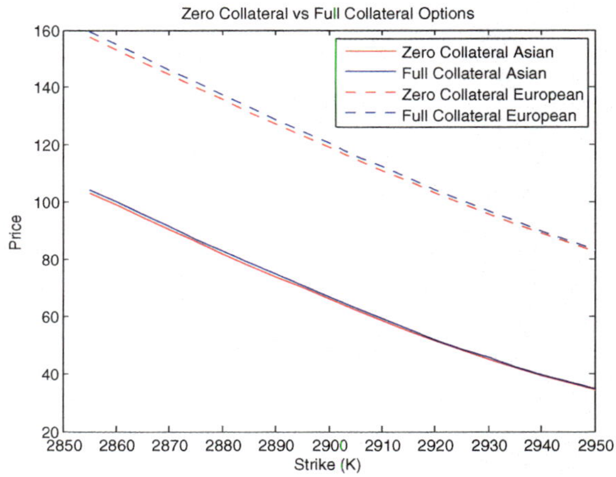

The first thing to mention is that an arithmetic Asian call option is cheaper compared to a European call option. This is because an arithmetic Asian call option is based on the average stock price over some pre-set period which means that there is less volatility. Less volatility implies a lower price.

Next, we draw our attention to the impact of collateral on the option prices. For European and Asian call options, a fully collateralised trade is more expensive than an uncollateralised trade. When the trade is fully collateralised, we discount off the collateral curve. If no collateral is posted, we discount using the funding curve. An important assumption in the Piterbarg (2010) framework is that $r_C \leq r_R^S \leq r_F$. In the event of the issuer defaulting, the holder of the option will still receive the value of the derivative if full collateral is posted making the option more expensive when compared to a zero collateral trade. The graph shows that the further in-the-money the option, the greater the price difference between fully collateralised and zero collateral trades. The further out-the-money the option, the smaller the difference in price. This should make intuitive sense because the holder of an option will lose out substantially if the issuer defaults with the option being far in-the-money. If the option is far out-the-money, it is more likely that the option will not be exercised and end worthless by the time of expiry for both zero collateral and full collateral scenarios.

33.6 Conclusion

In this paper, we have attempted to give the reader a practical approach on how to implement local volatility in the Piterbarg (2010) framework by using a simple interpolation algorithm and running a Monte Carlo simulation. We have shown that the presence of collateral leads to lower implied volatilities when compared to zero collateral trades, which in turn also leads to lower local volatilities. An interesting finding from our research is that full collateral options that are far in-the-money display a greater difference in price when compared to zero collateral options. This price difference becomes less evident for out-the-money options. The reasoning behind this is credit risk. The further in-the-money an option holder, the more collateral he would expect to account for the probability of the issuer defaulting and being unable to meet payment obligations.

Derivative pricing has come a long way since the early days of Black and Scholes (1973). As markets become even more complex, the need for development in the field of quantitative finance will become increasingly more important. Areas for future research may include the application of local volatility to FX options and the application of the SABR model to interest rate derivatives in the Piterbarg (2010) framework.

References

Black, F., & Scholes, M. (1973). The pricing of options and corporate liabilities. *Journal of Political Economy*, *81*(3), 637–654.
Derman, E., & Kani, I. (1994). Riding on a smile. *Risk*, *7*(2), 32–39.
Dupire, B. (1994). Pricing with a smile. *Risk*, *7*(1), 18–20.
Kahalé, N. (2004). An arbitrage-free interpolation of volatilities. *Risk*, *17*(5), 102–106.
Piterbarg, V. (2010). Funding beyond discounting: Collateral agreements and derivatives pricing. *Risk Magazine*, *23*(2), 97–102.
Press, W., Flannery, B., Teukolsky, S., & Vetterling, W. (1993). *Numerical recipes in C: The art of scientific computing*. Cambridge: Cambridge University Press.
Roper, M. (2010). Arbitrage free implied volatility surfaces. *Risk*, *7*(1), 18–20.
von Boetticher, S. T. (2017). The Piterbarg Framework For Option Pricing. Ph.D. diss.

Chapter 34
Trends in the Italian Movie Sector: Evidence from Box Office Performances

Anna Maria Bagnasco

Abstract The paper provides an empirical analysis of box office performances for a sample of top 10 and top 50 grossing movies from 2014 to 2018. We use data of box office revenues to calculate the distribution of total box office revenues on the movies considered in the sample. Descriptive evidence documents a concentration of revenues on a small number of movies. Moreover, we try to understand whether the variables *domestic box office revenues* and *number of copies distributed of a movie* have a relation to the total box office revenues.

Keywords Movie economics · Box office performance · Domestic market share

JEL Codes L83

34.1 Introduction

In the last two years, film activity shows a relevant decrease: All the benchmarks compared to the previous year display a negative trend (Table 34.1).

In two years, there was a loss in absolute terms of 19.3 million viewers (−18.4%, 2018 vs. 2016).

According to the latest edition of the Yearbook of Entertainment Activity (SIAE 2018) the débâcle of the cinema in the last two years was because there were no films that were able to draw people to the theaters. In 2016, the movie "Quo Vado" attracted almost 10 million spectators, while the most watched film in 2017, "Beauty and the Beast," had 3.4 million, and, in 2018, "Bohemian Rhapsody," almost 3 million. The top three grossing movies in 2017 and in 2018 did not reach the admissions of the top 1 grossing movie in 2016 (see Table 34.2).

The success of Zalone's film shows that the demand for cinema in the theater exists and people are willing to pay to consume films: but how many features lead the box

A. M. Bagnasco (✉)
IULM, Milan, Italy
e-mail: annamaria.bagnasco@iulm.it

N. Tsounis and A. Vlachvei (eds.), *Advances in Cross-Section Data Methods in Applied Economic Research*, Springer Proceedings in Business and Economics,
https://doi.org/10.1007/978-3-030-38253-7_34

Table 34.1 Italian movie market

	2018	2017	2016
Admissions	85,903,642	92,264,159	105,293,454
Box office (€)	555,445,373	584,554,941	661,295,946
USA (%)	60.0	66.4	55.7
ITA + COP (%)	23.0	17.7	29.1
Others (%)	17.5	16.0	15.2

Source Anica-Cinetel (2019)

Table 34.2 Admissions 2016–2018

	Movie	Admissions
2016	Quo Vado?	9,964,606
2017	La Bella E La Bestia	8,537,323
	Cattivissimo Me 3	
	50 Sfumature Di Nero	
2018	Bohemian Rapsody	7,688,198
	Avengers: Infinity War	
	50 Sfumature Di Rosso (Fifty Shades Freed)	

Source ANICA (2017, 2018, 2019)

office revenues? The first question we investigate is the distribution of revenues among the movies on the screens.

34.2 Where Is the Focus of the Box Office?

With the aim of understanding the behavior of the Italian movie market, we use the data set on Top-50 motion pictures, consisting of the top 50 revenue-earning motion pictures each year. We considered a time frame of six years, from 2013 to 2018, and the success criterion we used in this analysis is the volume of gross sales at the box office in the considered years. We concentrated the analysis both on top 10 and top 50 films that showed top ranks in each year on the considered gross sales lists. The results are summarized in Fig. 34.1.

As Fig. 34.1 suggests, a small number of films collected the largest amount of the total revenues.

In each considered year, the top 10 grossing movies, around 2% of the total movies, collected a percentage of between 20 and 30% of the total revenues: The correlation between top 10 grossing movies and total revenues is 0.79 ($p = 0.064$), a high value, although not statistically significant due to the small sample size.

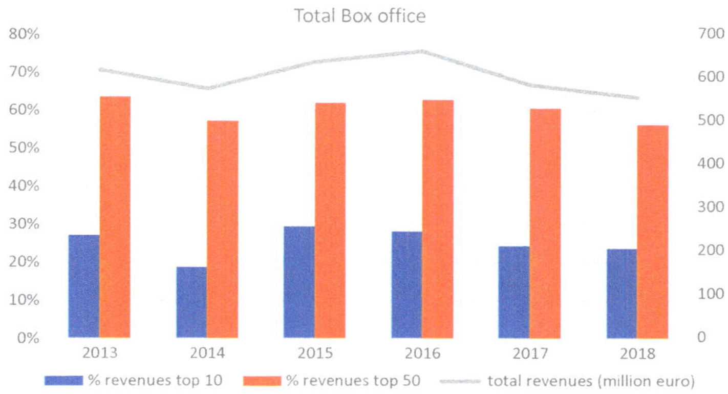

Fig. 34.1 % of revenues for top 10 and top 50 grossing movies

A similar result emerges with respect to data on the top 50 grossing movies. A percentage of around 10% of the total movies accounted for a percentage of between 56 and 63% of the total revenues: The correlation between top 50 grossing movies and total revenues is 0.86 ($p = 0.028$).

We used the same methodology with respect to top 10 and top 50 grossing domestic films and total revenues: Our aim was to understand whether the same relation holds when limiting the analysis on domestic products. In Fig. 34.2a, b, we represent the percentage of revenues for domestic grossing movies in the top 10 and in top 50 respectively. In the third figure, all the data are represented with respect to total revenues.

The empirical analysis shows no statistically significant correlation with total revenues: $r = 0.70$ ($p = 0.121$) and $r = 0.27$ ($p = 0.601$) for the Italian top 10 and top 50, respectively.

The core business of the theatrical system is closely dependent on the nature and type of the supply: The impact of mainstream films is more than ever preponderant. This is one of the most evident aspects of the recent evolution of the market. A big impact on the 2016 figures was due to the performance made by Checco Zalone: His film "Quo Vado" reached an audience of almost 10 million and registered a box office revenue of €65,365,655 million.

Considering the strong impact of the Zalone successes in the year, we have tried to understand whether a good performance at the domestic box office is able to lead the total box office.

Fig. 34.2 % of revenues for domestic grossing movies in top 10 and in top 50 and total revenues

34.3 Domestic Box Office Versus Total Box Office: Which Relationship?

We analyzed the relationship between the domestic box office revenues and the total ones. The hypothesis we want to test is whether a good performance at the domestic box office leads to a good performance in the total box office.

We use data on total revenues and percentage of revenues for domestic features from 2000 to 2018.

In the next figure, we show the linear regression analysis performed on these variables, assuming percentage of box office as explicative (independent) variable and total box office as dependent variable (ITA % of box office: mean = 24.9, SD = 4.9 total box office: mean = 582.8, SD = 70.3) (Fig. 34.3).

It can be seen that the coefficient of determination $R^2 = 0.43$ does not confirm a strong relationship between the variables.

This result is particularly interesting for at least two reasons: *in primis*, total box office can increase when the domestic share decreases (and vice versa); moreover, the same correlation between 1968 and 1998 gave as result $R^2 = 0.95$ (Celata 2008).

The first observation brings us to consider that in the Italian movie sector, there is no coherence among different actors along the supply chain: film makers release a large number of films every year, but moviegoers often prefer the ones from other nationalities, in particular the USA, over domestic films in the theaters.

Are foreign movies better than domestic ones? The second aspect deserves a deeper investigation:

today's context is defined by the multiplication of windows and an evolution beyond standardized modes of access that can serve any kind of content. This dramatically changes the traditional movie supply chain.

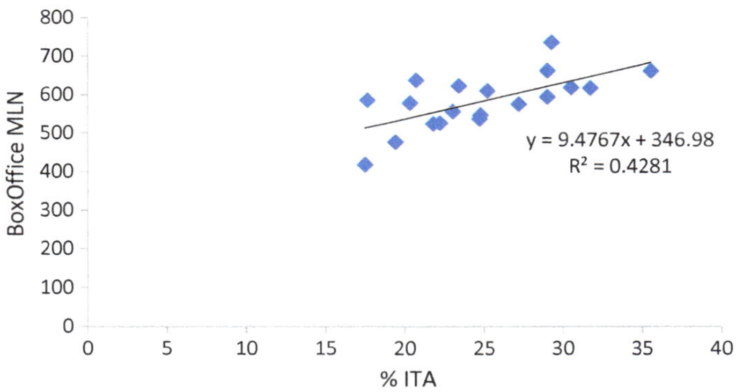

Fig. 34.3 Regression between the % of revenues generated by Italian films and total box office, 2000–2018

34.4 Looking for Italian Features

With the aim of understanding some of the trends in the Italian movie market, we used data from Italian features: The sample includes all the 210 Italian pictures that were run during 2018.

In the first step, we analyzed the revenues distribution over the 210 features. The results are impressive and are summarized in Fig. 34.4, using the Lorenz curve.

Within the graphic, it also emerges that 81% of the grossing movies in our sample accounted for 9.3% of the total box office revenue, while the top 10% of grossing movies in our sample accounted for 70% of the total box office revenue. The Gini index is 0.842.

In the second step of our analysis, we tried to understand whether it was possible, on the basis of available data, to identify a possible indicator of the box office.

We analyzed the relationship between the revenues of grossing movies and the number of copies distributed for each film. Descriptive statistics for the variables are reported in Table 34.3 and the graphic in Fig. 34.5.

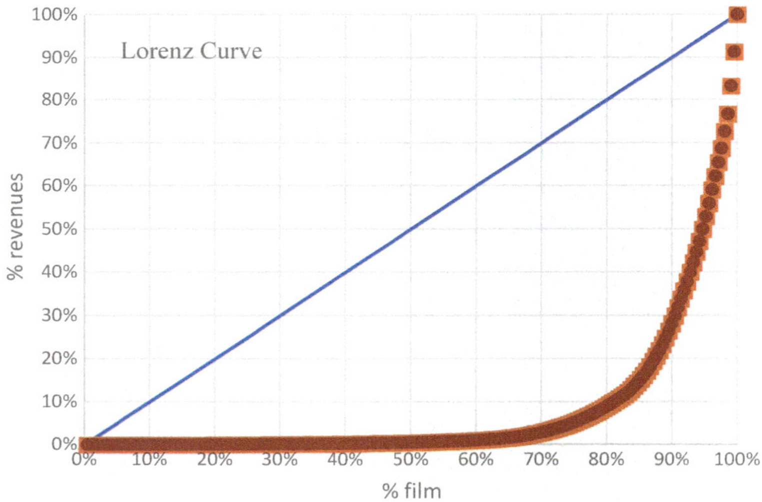

Fig. 34.4 Lorenz curve: the revenue's distribution over Italian films

Table 34.3 Descriptive statistics

Variable	Mean	Standard deviation	Minimum	Maximum
Total revenue (€)	501,500	1,254,963	96	9179,618
Number of copies	104.3	152.6	1	691

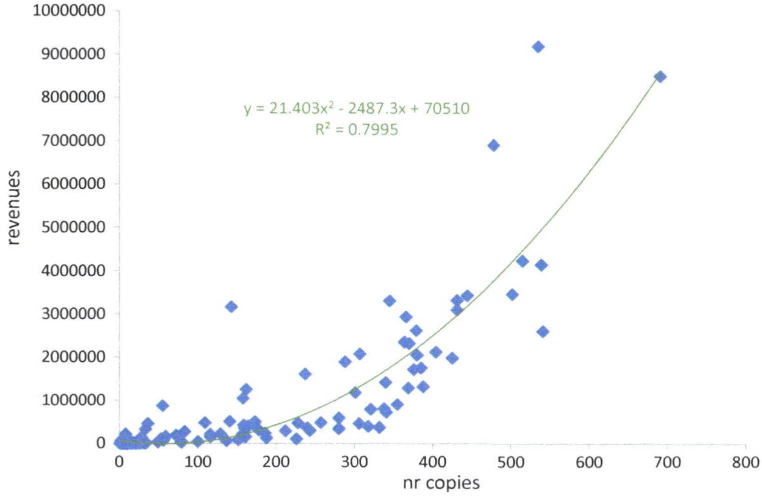

Fig. 34.5 Regression between revenues and number of copies

The relationship is well approximated by the second-degree curve in the graphic above (Fig. 34.5). It can be seen that the coefficient of determination $R^2 = 0.80$ confirms a strong relationship between the variables.

We can infer that the number of copies is a good predictor for the success of a movie.

The distributor chooses a release pattern, the number and location of theaters in which the film will "exhibit" for audience. Distributors also choose a date for when to release their film for exhibition, looking for high demand periods and seeking to avoid playing against films that are strong substitutes.

The number of theaters and their locations for the initial release are based on the distributor's a priori estimate of demand. The size of initial release determines the number of copies that are needed for distribution for each of the theaters: The higher the number of copies, the more promotion investment there is by the distributors. Surely, it could be difficult for a film with a small number of copies on the national screens to be seen, known, and appreciated. In our sample, only 32 films have had a distribution of more than 100 copies, while 102 films had had a distribution of less than 20 copies, and 49 films (25.3% of the sample) were available in one or two copies.

So, why do filmmakers produce film? Not for moviegoers: People often cannot know their films exist.

The number of viewers who are able to see the film is limited by the availability of theaters booked in the release.

34.5 Conclusion

The empirical analysis shows that in the Italian movie market, the trend for a whole season depends on a very limited number of titles: less than 10% of films accounted for more than 50% of total revenues.

There is no doubt that cinema-going is an activity that does not allow for long-term planning: To confirm the volatility of the film industry and its market, the figures and historical series of admissions in theater show that the audience response is not a known fact and does not guarantee incomes of stable positions. Precisely for this reason, it is necessary to create real *events* to communicate to the public through targeted and common marketing actions in order to maximize their impact at local or national level in a long-term perspective and as part of an organic strategy. Also the huge success of "Quo Vado" has become an event, partly thanks to distribution which almost ended up in a monopoly (more than half of Italian screens showed the movie) and to aggressive marketing: This phenomenon brought back the old idea of going to the cinema as a collective ritual, something that has been missing for a long time in Italy. Even without expecting to reach Zalone's success, our results suggest that more intensive promotion and a broader distribution could be a good strategy to implement for domestic production.

We certainly must not fall into the error of thinking that the huge success of "Quo Vado" can cure the historical problems of our sector.

To increase the number of people regularly going to the cinema, it is necessary to strengthen the supply in the summer and keep diversifying our product.

In this paper, we have analyzed some trends in the Italian movie sector: the results could be a starting point to investigate more deeply the problems and potentialities of the sector.

References

Anica (2017), I dati del mercato cinematografico anno 2016, http://www.anica.it/allegati/dati%20cinema%202016_cinetel.pdf.

Anica (2018), Il cinema in sala nel 2017: Il box office. http://www.anica.it/allegati/dati_cinema_2017.pdf.

Anica (2019), Il cinema in sala nel 2018: I dati del box office. http://www.anica.it/allegati/Dati/Box%20office%202018%20italia_tabella.pdf.

Anica, Cinetel (2019) I dati del mercato cinematografico nel 2018. https://www.cinetel.it/pages/studi_e_ricerche.php.

Celata, G. (2008). *Dispensa di economia del cinema, Economia dell'informazione e della comunicazione*. Roma: Università La Sapienza. http://opentsrl.net/activities/cinema/2008.5.11-DispenseEconomiadelCinema.pdf.

SIAE. (2018). *Yearbook of the entertainment activity 2017*, Roma. https://www.siae.it/sites/default/files/16_32_2017_Yearbook_of_Entertainment_Activity.pdf.

Chapter 35
Feedback of Macroeconomic Indicators to Shocks in Second-Tier Stock Market Development and Innovation Within Kaleckian Framework: Hong Kong Case Study

Trang Nguyen, Taha Chaiechi, Lynne Eagle and David Low

Abstract Despite the importance of second-tier stock markets in supporting SMEs (Small and Medium Enterprise) development and innovation, the dynamic impacts of second-tier stock markets development and innovation on macroeconomic indicators remain under-explored. This study aims to bridge the gap both theoretically and empirically. Accordingly, the theoretical model of Kaleckian–Post-Keynesian macroeconomics is extended and an empirical model is specified and estimated for the case of Hong Kong. A Structural Vector Error Correction (SVEC) estimation technique and impulse response function are adopted for empirical analysis. The results determine that Hong Kong's macroeconomic indicators exhibit small but positive feedback to shocks in the second-tier market development and innovation in the short run. Specifically, various channels of growth including private investment, domestic savings, and productivity growth are found to be responsive to shocks in the second-tier market development indicators. Meanwhile, shocks to innovation indicators effectively induce responses of the following growth channels: private investment, domestic savings, productivity growth, and employment.

Keywords Second-tier stock market · Innovation · Kaleckian–Post-Keynesian economics · Structural VEC (SVEC) model · Impulse response function

JEL Classifications E62 · G32

T. Nguyen (✉) · T. Chaiechi · L. Eagle · D. Low
Discipline of Economics, College of Business, Law and Governance, James Cook University, Cairns, Australia
e-mail: thiminhtrang.nguyen2@my.jcu.edu.au

N. Tsounis and A. Vlachvei (eds.), *Advances in Cross-Section Data Methods in Applied Economic Research*, Springer Proceedings in Business and Economics,
https://doi.org/10.1007/978-3-030-38253-7_35

35.1 Introduction

Recent years have witnessed increasing attention on the pivotal role of second-tier stock markets in financing landscape for Small and Medium Enterprises (SMEs). World Federation of Exchanges (2015) acknowledged second-tier stock markets as an important alternative source of funding for SMEs. Second-tier stock markets, by offering a platform for long-term equity financing on a continuous basis, have effectively fulfilled a significant 5.8% of global SMEs' credit gap that is estimated at USD 3.2 trillion by the International Finance Corporation—IFC (2013). Undoubtedly, a shortage of credit is one of the major obstacles in realizing SMEs' potentials.

Having a second-tier stock market in place benefits not only for such growing aspirant enterprises but also for investors. On one hand, being listed on this platform provides SMEs a credible identity and prevents them from being over-leveraged at different stages of growth. On the other hand, this fundraising platform can be seen as a vehicle for early-stage investors (i.e. angel investors and venture capitalists) to exit their investments, which then encourages them to make further investments in start-ups. As pointed out by Sestanovic (2016), equity-financed SMEs tend to be more stable and resilient during the financial crises than debt-financed SMEs.

Additionally, second-tier stock markets appear to increasingly become a critical source of finance for SMEs that may have limited access to traditional sources of finance for innovation. This is due to the fact that the companies listed on second-tier stock markets mainly operate in innovative sectors such as information technology, media, telecommunications, biotechnology, environmental protection, and renewable energy. Accordingly, the development of second-tier stock market can be considered as a cardinal stimulus for innovation, which consequently arouses output demand and boosts economic growth.

Despite the significance of second-tier stock markets in supporting SMEs' development and innovation, there is a paucity of research on the dynamic impacts of second-tier stock markets on macroeconomic indicators. Moreover, a great deal of studies on innovation-growth nexus fails to examine this relationship within an integrated macroeconomic framework. Therefore, in the absence of such attempts, the objective of this study is to explore the dynamic responses of macroeconomy to shocks in indicators of second-tier stock market development and innovation within an extended Kaleckian–Post-Keynesian framework.

Among the growing number of the second-tier stock markets across the world (51 markets as of 2016), the Growth Enterprise Market (GEM) in Hong Kong, emerges as one of the world's most successful examples of a stock market for SMEs (Peterhoff et al. 2014), making it attractive for researchers. Accordingly, the empirical analysis of the Hong Kong case study provides insights into the potential contributions of the GEM development and innovation to the economic growth process in Hong Kong (Table 35.1).

Table 35.1 Hong Kong's Growth Enterprise Market (GEM) and innovation indicators

Second-tier stock market	GEM	Innovation indicators	
Established by	HKEX	No. of patent applications	14,092
Market opened	1999	Percentage of labour force	0.4%
No. of listed firms	260	No. of trademark applications	36,181
Market capitalization[a]	40.1	Percentage of labour force	0.9%
Percentage of GDP (%)	12.6%	High-technology exports[a]	0.4
Trading value[a]	19.0	Percentage of GDP (%)	0.1%
Percentage of GDP (%)	6.0%		

Notes HKEX is Hong Kong Stock Exchange; GEM is Growth Enterprise Market; [a]in US$ billion

35.2 Literature Review

Greenwood and Jovanovic (1990) are among the first to promote the role of stock markets as being to mobilize savings, distribute resources, and foster long-term economic growth. Pagano (1993) suggested the three key channels through which stock market development contributes to growth: (i) the increasing proportion of savings that are transmitted to investments; (ii) the changing savings rate which affects investments; and (iii) the efficiency of capital allocation. Furthermore, stock markets can facilitate growth through various channels such as liquidity provision, information dissemination, corporate governance control, and risk distribution. Stock markets provide liquidity that helps investors enhance the allocation of funds and reduce the risk of losing all of their investment funds in projects that do not pay off for a long time (Bencivenga et al. 1996). Stock markets can reduce the cost of acquiring information by generating and disseminating corporate information to the public. Reducing the information asymmetry problem thus assists investors in the decision-making process and improves resource allocation (Levine 2005). Stock markets are capable of controlling elements of corporate governance by tying managers' compensation to the performance of the company's shares in the market. Consequently, stock markets help align the interest of principles (investors) and agents (managers), thereby improving investors' confidence and fostering efficient resource allocation (Jensen and Murphy 1990). Moreover, stock markets also provide a mechanism allowing a transfer of risk from parties who undertake investments to parties who finance the investments, thus risk distribution can increase the savings rate and allocate resources efficiently (Levine 2005).

Schumpeter (1912) acknowledged innovation as one of the major stimuli to economic growth because institutions, entrepreneurs, and technology changes are the cores of growth and can be influenced by government policy. According to Solow (1956), technological advances typically increase the productivity of capital and thus induce further investments. As such, the resulting capital formation should be regarded as a facilitator of growth. Romer (1986, 1990) asserted that industrial innovation is the key determinant of economic growth due to its direct impact on the production process and product release procedure. Kirchhoff (1994) and Wennekers and Thurik (1999) further postulated that innovation helps promote productivity and growth through motivating new business establishment, which further boosts employment and outputs. Additionally, Grossman and Helpman (1994) laid stress on the important role of innovation in the endogenous growth model, specifically, the important role of technology improvements in pursuing a rapid and sustainable economic growth in the face of depletable natural resources.

In spite of an extensive body of empirical literature on stock market-growth nexus (for examples, see Boubakari and Jin 2010; Ali and Aamir 2014; Azam et al. 2016), there is a paucity of research focusing on second-tier stock markets. Also, a great deal of researches fails to examine the dynamic interaction between stock markets and economic growth within an integrated macroeconomic model. In addition, the empirical studies on the innovation-growth nexus are voluminous (for examples, see Hasan and Tucci 2010; Agénor and Neanidis 2015; Pradhan et al. 2016), however, this nexus has yet been tested within an integrated system of macroeconomic functions. Therefore, in the absence of such attempts, this study aims to explore the dynamic impacts of second-tier stock market development and innovation on different sources of economic growth.

35.3 Extended Kaleckian Macroeconomic Model

As previously mentioned, a Kaleckian–Post-Keynesian macroeconomic model was employed and extended to explore the dynamic impacts of the second-tier stock market development and innovation on macroeconomic indicators. The model, which was initially proposed by Marglin and Bhaduri (1990) and later complemented by Stockhammer and Onaran (2003), captures both profit-led and wage-led growth regimes. The goods market was augmented by a demand-driven labour market, the Marxian reserve army effect,[1] and technological progress. Accordingly, the goods market consists of behavioural functions for private investment, domestic savings, and net export, which are then supplemented by the functions of distribution, labour productivity, and employment. Following Chaiechi (2012), this study further extended the model by incorporating second-tier stock market development and innovation into the functions of private investment, domestic savings, productivity, and employment. The extended model is presented below.

$$\text{Accumulation } g_t^i \equiv \frac{I_t}{K_t} = \alpha_0 + \alpha_1 z_{t-1} + \alpha_2 \pi_{t-1} - \alpha_3 r_t + \alpha_4 \text{gx}_{t-1} + \alpha_5 \text{smd}_t + \alpha_6 \text{inn}_t \tag{35.1}$$

$$\text{Savings } g_t^s \equiv \frac{S_t}{K_t} = \beta_1 z_t + \beta_2 \pi_t + \beta_3 \text{smd}_t + \beta_4 \text{inn}_t \tag{35.2}$$

[1]Marxian reserve army effect refers to a situation that higher unemployment diminishes the bargaining power of workers and therefore stimulates higher profits.

$$\text{Income distribution } \pi_t = \gamma_0 + \gamma_1 z_t + \gamma_2 u_t + \gamma_3 \text{gx}_t \tag{35.3}$$

$$\text{Productivity growth } \text{gx}_t = \tau_0 + \tau_1 g_t^i + \tau_2 z_t + \tau_3 \text{smd}_t + \tau_4 \text{inn}_t \tag{35.4}$$

$$\text{Net export } \text{nx}_t = -\delta_1 z_t + \delta_2 \pi_t \tag{35.5}$$

$$\text{Unemployment } u_t = \lambda_0 - \lambda_1 g_t^i - \lambda_2 \Delta z_t - \lambda_3 \pi_t + \lambda_4 u_{t-1} + \lambda_5 \text{gx}_t - \lambda_6 \text{inn}_t \tag{35.6}$$

$$\text{Market equilibrium } g_t^i = g_t^{\text{stotal}} = g_t^s - \text{nx}_t \tag{35.7}$$

where g_t^i is the growth of capital accumulation, I_t is private investment, K_t is physical capital stock, g_t^s is domestic savings, z_t is capacity utilization, π_t is profit share or income distribution, nx_t is net export, u_t is unemployment rate, gx_t is productivity growth, r_t is interest rate, smd_t is SME stock market development indicator, and inn_t is innovation indicator.

Equation (35.1) demonstrates the growth of investment, which is a function of expected rate of profit (driven by profit share and capacity utilization), interest rate (Hein 2004; Kalecki 1968), technology advance (reflected in productivity growth) (Kalecki 1968). Duménil and Lévy (1989) asserted that stock markets, which are among the common types of financial intermediary, can accommodate the capital requirement for investment and production. Aghion and Howitt (1998) placed emphasis on the important role of technological innovation in providing new opportunities for investment in physical and human capital. Thus, theoretically, it is essential to include second-tier stock market development and innovation in the equation of capital accumulation.

Equation (35.2) represents a plain Cambridge savings function, which is subject to income distribution behaviour of workers and capitalists (Lavoie 1992; Marglin 1984), such that capitalists have a higher marginal propensity to save than workers. The development of stock markets increases the proportion of savings that are transformed into productive investments and thus may change the interest rate on savings (Pagano 1993). Stock markets provide a mechanism for risk distribution which can increase the saving interest rate and allocate resources efficiently (Levine 2005). Aghion et al. (2016) posited that the growth stemming from innovation allows domestic sectors to easily adopt the current frontier technology. For those countries which are distant from the frontier, a corporation with foreign experts is required. As such, domestic savings are vital for innovation and thus growth since it enables the local firms to have equity stakes in the corporation, which in turn mitigates the agency problem. Therefore, the indicators of second-tier stock market development and innovation were entered into the equation of domestic savings.

Equation (35.3) defines the supply-side of the model. Capacity utilization rate can change the unit labour cost, which is the basis for price establishment. Unemployment rate signifies the Marxian reserve army effect, which refers to a situation that higher unemployment diminishes the bargaining power of workers and therefore stimulates higher profits. Productivity growth can have distributional effects in the short run since distributional issues are mainly due to the division of productivity gains rather than the output itself.

Equation (35.4) presents the growth of labour productivity, which is a function of capital accumulation (as a result of technological advancements) and capacity utilization (which is measured by the existing machinery and equipment that are put into service). King and Levine (1993) postulated that stock market development promotes productivity growth through the process of directing capital into productive investments and diversifying investment risks, thereby leading to long-term economic stimulation. Technological innovation is essential for the development of new leading-edge goods and services, which in turn induces consumption and growth. Process innovation leads to additional productivity growth throughout different stages of the company's development (Huergo and Jaumandreu 2004). Accordingly, the inclusion of second-tier stock market development and innovation in a productivity growth equation is desirable.

Equation (35.5) exhibits a net export function. Domestic demand for imports gives rise to the negative impact of capacity utilization on net export. Profit share is considered as an indicator of international competitiveness because it is driven by the unit labour cost (Blecker 2002; Bowles and Boyer 1995).

Equation (35.6) shows the function of labour market. Employment depends on effective demand for output (Kalecki 1968), thus, for a given productive capacity, employment depends on capacity utilization. If demand for labour mainly depends on wages, then profit share, which is a proxy for wages, can capture the effect of real wage per labour after accounting for labour productivity. If a technological advance does not align with an increase in the effective demand for output, then it will engender unemployment. Technological innovation may instigate job destruction in the short term, however, the impact in the long term is likely to be positive as the compensation mechanism leads to a higher demand for labour. Since the key macroeconomic variables are considered in a system of integrated equations, the long-run impact of innovation is reflected in the employment function.

Equation (35.7) describes the goods market equilibrium in the long run. Capital stock is established at a certain equilibrium level where investment will be equal to savings for a normal rate of capital utilization.

35.4 Data and Variables Characteristics

The data of macroeconomic indicators, second-tier stock market development and innovation in Hong Kong were retrieved from various issues of the National Statistics Departments, International Financial Statistics (IFS-IMF), World Bank Database (WDI), and Bloomberg Database for the period of 2009:M7–2016:M12. Variables used in this study are defined in Table 35.2 as follows:

Table 35.2 Variable definitions

Variable	Notation	Definition
Macroeconomic indicator (MED)	INV	*Investment* is measured by the growth of physical capital stock Investment = [Physical Capital Stock + (1—Capital Depreciation Rate) × Gross fixed capital formation]/Physical Capital Stock
	SAV	*Savings* is normalised by physical capital stock
	AW	*Income Distribution* or *Profit Share* is measured following Dutt (1995) approach. Income Distribution = [1—(Wage Rate × Labour Force/Nominal GDP)] × Capacity Utilisation I Capacity Utilisation = Nominal GDP/Physical Capital Stock
	GX	*Productivity Growth* is the growth rate of (Nominal GDP/Labour Force)
	NX	*Net Export* is the difference between export and import normalised by nominal GDP
	UN	*Unemployment Rate*
Growth Enterprise Market indicator (GEM)	GCAP	*Growth Enterprise Market (GEM) capitalisation* is normalised by nominal GDP
	GTRA	*Growth Enterprise Market (GEM) traded value* is normalised by nominal GDP
	GTUR	*Growth Enterprise Market (GEM) turnover ratio* is measured by dividing stock market traded value by stock market capitalization
Innovation Indicator (INN)	PTA	*Patent applications* of residents and non-residents per thousand labours
	TMA	*Trademark applications* of residents and non-residents per thousand labours
	HTE	*High-technology export* is normalized by nominal GDP

Notes All variables have been adjusted for seasonality and in the case of variables for which only quarterly or annually data are available, monthly data were generated using interpolation techniques

Table 35.3 reports the descriptive statistics of all variables, showing that most of the variables are non-normal distributed due to positive/negative skewness, large values of kurtosis, and highly significant Jarque–Bera statistics.

Table 35.3 Descriptive statistics

Variables	INV	SAV	AW	GX	NXY	UN	GCAP	GTRA	GTUR	PTA	TMA	HTE
Mean	0.14	0.27	0.42	0.04	−0.23	0.04	0.85	0.06	0.06	0.28	0.77	0.003
Median	0.14	0.26	0.41	0.04	−0.23	0.03	0.84	0.05	0.06	0.28	0.79	0.003
Maximum	0.16	0.35	0.48	0.10	−0.13	0.06	1.78	0.25	0.16	0.33	0.87	0.005
Minimum	0.12	0.23	0.38	−0.05	−0.34	0.03	0.38	0.01	0.02	0.26	0.56	0.001
Std. Dev.	0.01	0.03	0.03	0.03	0.05	0.01	0.32	0.04	0.03	0.02	0.08	0.001
Skewness	−0.58	0.92	0.57	−0.76	0.001	1.96	0.65	2.54	1.14	0.29	−0.80	0.53
Kurtosis	3.19	3.46	1.97	5.25	2.39	5.98	2.92	11.00	3.86	2.05	2.88	1.99
Jarque-Bera	5.18***	13.43*	8.84**	27.64*	1.40	91.02*	6.34**	336.87*	22.40*	4.69***	9.57*	8.14**

Notes *, **, *** indicate that the test statistic is significant at 1%, 5%, and 10%, respectively

35.5 Preliminary Analysis

Before examining the feedback of Hong Kong's macroeconomic indicators to shocks in the Growth Enterprise Market (GEM) development and innovation, preliminary analysis of stationarity, lag order selection, cointegration, and block exogeneity issue are indispensable. The tests were performed and the results were presented in the following sub-sections.

35.5.1 Stationarity

To test for stationarity of all variables, Augmented Dickey–Fuller (ADF) and Phillips and Perron (PP) unit root tests were performed for both level 0 [I(0)] and level 1 [I(1)]. The results, as reported in Table 35.4, confirm that all variables are integrated at first difference, implying stationarity at the first order of integration. Thus, all I(1) variables should be used in subsequent analysis.

35.5.2 Lag Length Selection

Lag length selection is necessary not only for the estimates of autoregressive coefficients to be consistent and reliable but also for the inferences of impulse response analysis to be accurate. The lag order is selected based on the following information criteria: LR (sequentially modified likelihood ratio), FPE (Final Prediction Error), AIC (Akaike Information Criterion), SC (Schwarz Information Criterion), and HQ (Hannan–Quinn Information Criterion). As shown in Table 35.5, LR, FPE, and AIC criteria consistently selected lag 4 while HQ criterion suggested lag 2. Therefore, the VAR/VEC model with lag 4 should be set up for further analysis.

35.5.3 Cointegration

As all variables are integrated at first difference, cointegration relationship may exist between the variables. To test for this relationship, a VAR-based cointegration rank test was performed following the method of Johansen (1991, 1995). The results are displayed in Table 35.6 where the trace test statistic and the maximum eigenvalue test statistic were used to detect the number of cointegrating equations at 5% level of significance. As can be seen, the maximum eigenvalue statistics identified fewer cointegrating equations than the trace statistics (4 vs. 5 equations). This is probably due to the low power of the test when the cointegration relation is rather close to the unit circle or the non-stationary bound (Johansen and Juselius 1990). The minimum amount of reported cointegrating equations was used for subsequent analysis.

Table 35.4 Stationary tests

Variables—I(0)	INV	SAV	AW	GX	NXY	UN	GCAP	GTRA	GTUR	PTA	TMA	HTE
ADF—C	−2.0	−1.7	−1.7	−2.2	−2.2	−3.5**	−0.9	−2.8***	−2.4	−1.1	−1.9	−1.0
ADF—C&T	−2.0	−1.0	−1.1	−1.8	−2.1	−2.5	−1.6	−2.8	−2.5	−1.1	1.0	−2.2
PP—C	−2.6	−1.1	−1.6	−5.0*	−5.8*	−4.1*	−1.0	−3.2**	−2.6***	−1.0	−2.6	−0.8
PP—C&T	−2.6	−1.5	−1.0	−4.9*	−5.6*	−3.2***	−1.7	−3.2	−2.8	−1.0	1.0	−2.2
Variables—I(1)	INV	SAV	AW	GX	NXY	UN	SCAP	STRA	STUR	PTA	TMA	HTE
ADF—C	−3.9*	−3.6*	−4.5*	−3.9*	−12.5*	−6.2*	−7.3*	−7.6*	−7.4*	−5.7*	−5.5**	−4.1*
ADF—C&T	−3.9**	−3.9**	−4.7*	−3.6**	−12.5*	−7.2*	−7.3*	−7.6*	−7.4*	−5.8*	−5.6*	−5.6*
PP—C	−4.3*	−14.9*	−4.4*	−5.1*	−21.4*	−11.3*	−15.3*	−7.6*	−10.5*	−5.9*	−3.2**	−5.7*
PP—C&T	−4.3*	−18.7*	−4.6*	−5.0*	−21.4*	−8.1*	−15.6*	−7.5*	−10.4*	−6.0*	−5.6*	−5.7*

Notes *, **, *** indicate the test statistic is significant at 1%, 5%, and 10%, respectively; C represents constant; C&T represents constant and trend

Table 35.5 Lag length selection

Lag	Log likelihood	LR	FPE	AIC	SC	HQ
0	1867.87	NA	3.80e−27	−43.81	−43.64[a]	−43.74
1	1935.06	123.31	1.83e−27	−44.54	−43.34	−44.06[a]
2	1969.90	59.01	1.90e−27	−44.52	−42.27	−43.61
3	2033.21	98.32	1.03e−27	−45.16	−41.88	−43.84
4	2081.83	68.64[a]	8.15e−28[a]	−45.45[a]	−41.14	−43.72

Notes [a]indicates lag order selected by the criterion

Accordingly, there were at least four long-run equilibrium relationships among the variables. The results, expectedly, also confirmed our theoretical model specification based on the Kaleckian–Post-Keynesian macroeconomic framework as discussed previously in Sect. 35.3.

35.5.4 Block Exogeneity Wald Test

The exogeneity issue really matters the application of SVAR/SVEC model because without appropriate validation of exogeneity of the variables, the model would become too restrictive and that may mislead the dynamic relationships between the variables in the system (Huh 2005). The Block exogeneity Wald test was, therefore, performed to examine whether including the indicators of GEM market development and innovation into the model encounters the exogeneity issue. The result shows that only the variable of patent applications (PTA) is purely exogenous to the model, indicating that it does not explain economic development. On the other hand, market capitalization, traded value, and turnover ratio of the GEM (GCAP, GTRA, and GTUR, respectively), trademark applications (TMA), and high-technology exports (HTE) can be treated as endogenous variables, suggesting their contributions to Hong Kong's economic development. These endogenous variables can then be included in the model and imposed a shock to examine the impulse response function (Table 35.7).

35.6 VEC Residuals and Stability Condition

Based on the outcomes of preliminary analysis, a VEC model was established for a set of identified endogenous variables representing macroeconomic development, the GEM market development, and innovation in Hong Kong. To ensure all inferences and further estimations from the VEC models are consistent and reliable, testing for any sign of misspecification of the models is desirable. As shown in Table 35.8, the model residuals contain zero autocorrelation (up to lag 12) and are normally

Table 35.6 Johansen cointegration rank test

No. of CE(s) at most	0	1	2	3	4	5	6	7	8	9	10
Trace statistic	417.5*	330.6*	256.2*	192.1*	133.3*	95.6	61.4	34.5	19.9	5.7	0.2
Max-Eigen statistic	87.0*	74.3*	64.1*	58.7*	37.7	34.3	26.8	14.7	14.2	5.5	0.2

Notes *, ** indicate that the test statistic is significant at 1% and 5%, respectively; CE(s) is cointegrating equation(s)

Table 35.7 Block exogeneity Wald test

Variables	INV	SAV	AW	GX	NXY	UN	GCAP	GTRA	GTUR	PTA	TMA	HTE
Chi-sq (df = 4)	68.3**	75.3*	61.2**	70.3*	60.9**	106.4*	106.5*	87.3*	86.0*	48.5	65.7**	60.0***

Notes *, **, *** indicate that Chi-squared statistic is significant at 1%, 5%, and 10%, respectively; df is the degree of freedom

Table 35.8 VEC residuals diagnostics

VEC residual serial correlation LM tests		
Lag	Rao F-stat	P-value
2	0.866	0.790
4	0.879	0.764
6	0.976	0.553
8	0.861	0.798
10	0.880	0.763
12	1.176	0.180
VEC residual normality tests		
Joint test:	Jarque-Bera	P-value
	28.522	0.159
VEC residual white heteroscedasticity tests		
Joint test:	Chi-sq	P-value
	4920.86	0.352

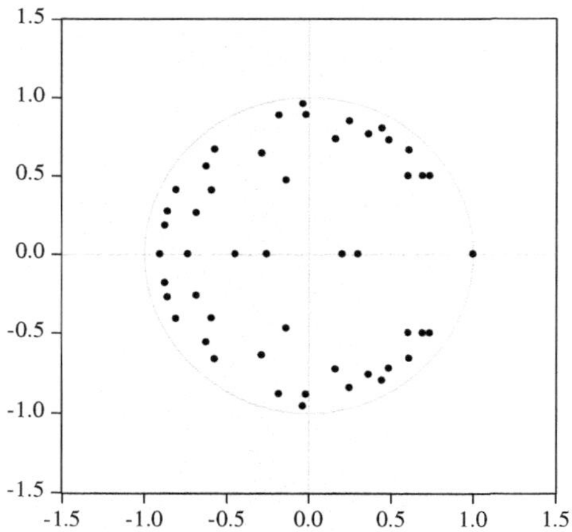

Fig. 35.1 VEC stability condition

distributed and homoscedastic with the regressors. Given the absence of serial correlation, non-normality, and heteroscedasticity in the residuals, the model is thus well-specified. Moreover, the stability condition of the model was also tested using the inverse roots of autoregressive (AR) characteristic polynomial. As depicted in Fig. 35.1, all inverse AR roots of the model lie in or on the unit circle, indicating that the stability condition was not violated.

35.7 Structural VEC Identification and Estimation

To investigate the feedback of Hong Kong economy to shocks in the indicators of the GEM market development and innovation, a structural VEC (SVEC) model was employed with short-run restrictions[2] on structural innovations of the estimated system. Short-run restrictions were determined using a lower triangular Cholesky factorization approach. As such, all elements above the diagonal are restricted to be zero and the Cholesky order of lower diagonal elements are identified following a recursive structure Wold-causal chain. Following the Kaleckian theory of growth and distribution, private investment is thus supposed to be the growth engine and generates effective circles of growth in domestic savings, income distribution, productivity, net export, and employment. Therefore, in the Cholesky ordering, private investment is placed first and employment is placed last.

Since the focus is to examine the dynamic impacts of the GEM market development and innovation on macroeconomic indicators in Hong Kong, the variables of the GEM market development and innovation were entered into the Cholesky ordering. The GEM market development is placed before innovation due to the fact that the GEM helps SMEs raise equity capital to implement R&D activities to enhance their technologies or intellectual properties. The identified Cholesky ordering can be presented in the following vector.

$$\begin{aligned} Y_t &= (\text{INV}_t, \text{SAV}_t, \text{AW}_t, \text{GX}_t, \text{NX}_t, \text{UN}_t, \text{GEM}_t, \text{INN}_t) \\ &= (\text{MED}_t, \text{GEM}_t, \text{INN}_t) \end{aligned} \tag{35.8}$$

where $\text{MED}_t = (\text{INV}_t, \text{SAV}_t, \text{AW}_t, \text{GX}_t, \text{NX}_t, \text{UN}_t)$. This vector can now be written in SVEC representation, which allows structural shocks to be imposed in the estimated system, as below:

$$\Delta Y_t = \Pi Y_{t-1} + \Gamma_1 \Delta Y_{t-1} + \cdots + \Gamma_{p-1} \Delta Y_{t-p+1} + B\varepsilon_t \tag{35.9}$$

where $\Pi = \alpha\beta^{\top}$ is cointegration matrix in which α is the loading matrix and β is the matrix of the coefficients of the long-run relationships; the dimension of α and β is Kxr where K is the number of endogenous variables and r is the cointegration rank or the number of cointegrating relationships between the variables; $\Gamma_i = -(I - A_1 - \cdots A_i)$ where I is integration order and A_i are $K \times K$ coefficient matrices for $i = 1, \ldots, p$; $u_t = B\varepsilon_t$ and $\varepsilon_t \sim N(0, I_K)$ is the underlying structural shocks; B is short-run matrix which required at least $r(r-1)/2$ number of restrictions to be imposed.

Given the identified endogenous variables representing the GEM market development and innovation (as noted in Sect. 35.5.4), the structure of the SVEC matrix for subsequent analysis appears as follows:

[2]Long-run restrictions were not imposed to avoid the problems of finite time series data (Faust and Leeper 1997), near-observational equivalence of shocks with permanent effects and shocks with persistent effects (Erceg et al. 2005), and weak-instrumental problem (Gospodinov 2010).

$$\Delta Y_t = (\text{MED}_t, \text{GCAP}_t, \text{GTRA}_t, \text{GTUR}_t, \text{TMA}_t, \text{HTE}_t) \quad (35.10)$$

To identify shock, a number of short-run restrictions (i.e., $K(K-1)/2$) were imposed on the contemporaneous matrix B. Table 35.9 reports the estimation results, which appear to align with the Kaleckian model of growth and distribution. Accordingly, investment fosters productivity growth and effectively promote the mobilization of domestic savings. The positive influence of investment on income distribution suggests that a higher level of investment is associated with a higher rate of profit share, implying a profit-led system of capital accumulation. Savings have an impact on income distribution through the marginal propensity to save. Productivity grows together with the level of savings since the improvement in productivity requires capital investment, which can be financed by savings. Income distribution positively affects productivity growth through the rate of capacity utilization, such that unit labour cost changes pro-cyclically with capacity utilization rate, which in turn is a measure of labour productivity. The last five rows of the matrix indicate the contemporaneous effects of macroeconomic indicators on the GEM market development and innovation.

35.8 Structural VEC Impulse Response Analysis

Having the SVEC model estimated in the previous section, impulse response analysis was conducted to examine the dynamic response of Hong Kong's macroeconomic indicators to shocks in the GEM market development and innovation. It is noted that only endogenous variables are imposed shocks, accordingly, they are market capitalization (GCAP), traded value (GTRA), turnover ratio (GTUR), trademark applications (TMA), and high-technology exports (HTE). The responses of investment, savings, productivity growth, and unemployment are on the focus since the indicators of the GEM market development and innovation have been incorporated in these equations according to the Kaleckian's theory, as discussed in Sect. 35.3.

Figures 35.2 and 35.3 present the impulse response function for 30 months ahead with Cholesky one standard deviation shocks imposed on the SVEC system. The response is considered to be statistically significant at 5% if the zero baselines do not fall within the bootstrapped 95% confidence bands. The speed of adjustment following a structural shock is measured by the number of months before the response lines intersect with the zero baselines.

As can be seen, investment and savings are responsive to shocks in the GEM market capitalization and trademark applications in the first 3–4 months. The feedback of productivity growth to shocks in the GEM market turnover and trademark applications are immediately positive up to 4 months ahead before die out afterward. However, productivity growth shows some delays (around 4 months) in response to shocks in the GEM market traded value and high-technology export. These responses

Table 35.9 SVEC matrix estimation

Variable	INV	SAV	AW	GX	NX	UN	GCAP	GTRA	GTUR	TMA	HTE
INV	0.0019	0	0	0	0	0	0	0	0	0	0
SAV	0.0015	0.0052	0	0	0	0	0	0	0	0	0
AW	0.0010	0.0006	0.0024	0	0	0	0	0	0	0	0
GX	0.0026	0.0014	0.0023	0.0053	0	0	0	0	0	0	0
NX	0.0097	−0.0041	0.0117	0.0055	0.0188	0	0	0	0	0	0
UN	0.0000	−0.0001	0.0000	0.0000	0.0002	0.0004	0	0	0	0	0
GCAP	0.0102	0.0161	0.0091	−0.0037	0.0076	0.0078	0.0525	0	0	0	0
GTRA	0.0047	0.0041	0.0038	0.0002	0.0021	0.0002	0.0113	0.0094	0	0	0
GTUR	0.0023	0.0047	−0.0016	0.0000	0.0018	−0.0004	0.0058	0.0098	0.0030	0	0
TMA	0.0000	0.0005	−0.0006	0.0004	0.0012	0.0004	0.0003	0.0014	0.0005	0.0015	0
HTE	0.00002	0.0000	0.00003	0.0000	0.0000	−0.00002	0.00002	0.0000	0.00002	0.0000	0.0001

Notes Grey highlights indicate the parameter is statistically significant either at 1%, 5%, or 10%

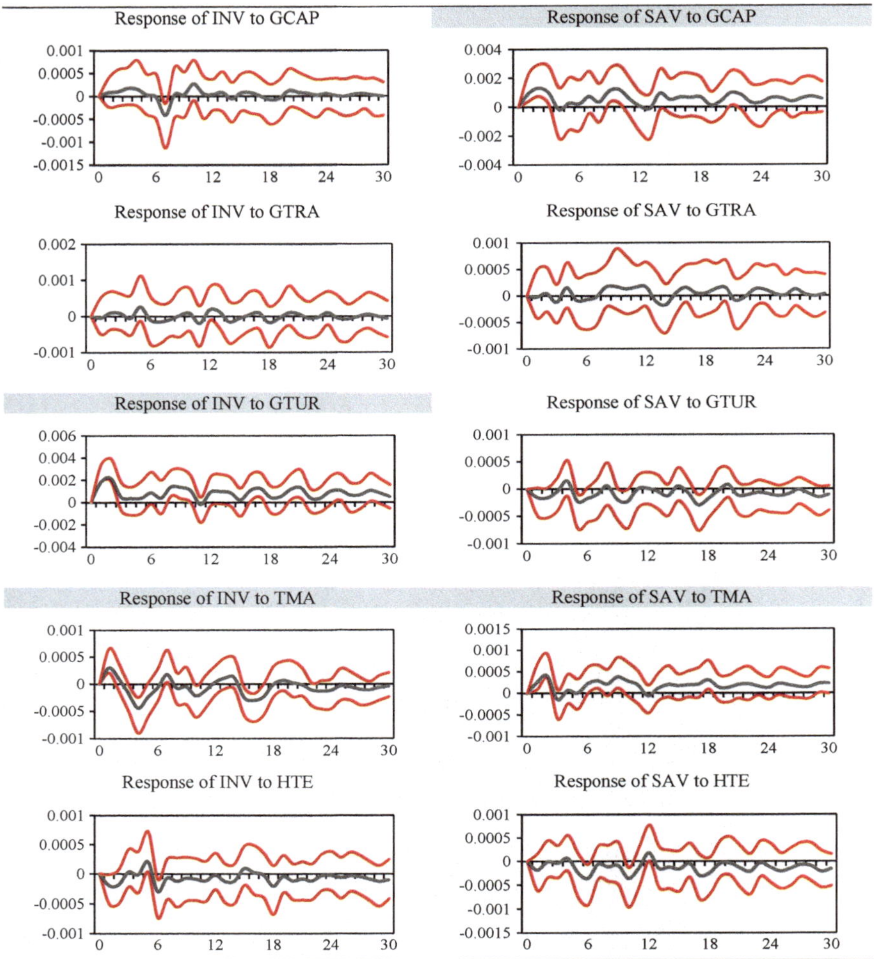

Fig. 35.2 Responses of investment and savings to orthogonal shocks to the GEM and innovation. *Notes* Grey highlights indicate the impulse response functions are significant at 5%

last for just 1–3 months before become insignificant. Shock in trademark applications, at the same time, causes an instant decrease in unemployment, which then bounces back but quickly drops down again.

Overall, shocks in various indicators of the GEM market development and innovation trigger small but positive feedback in different channels of economic growth in Hong Kong. The positive feedback appears to be statistically significant in the short run only. The GEM market development affects the growth process through the following channels: private investment, domestic savings, and productivity growth,

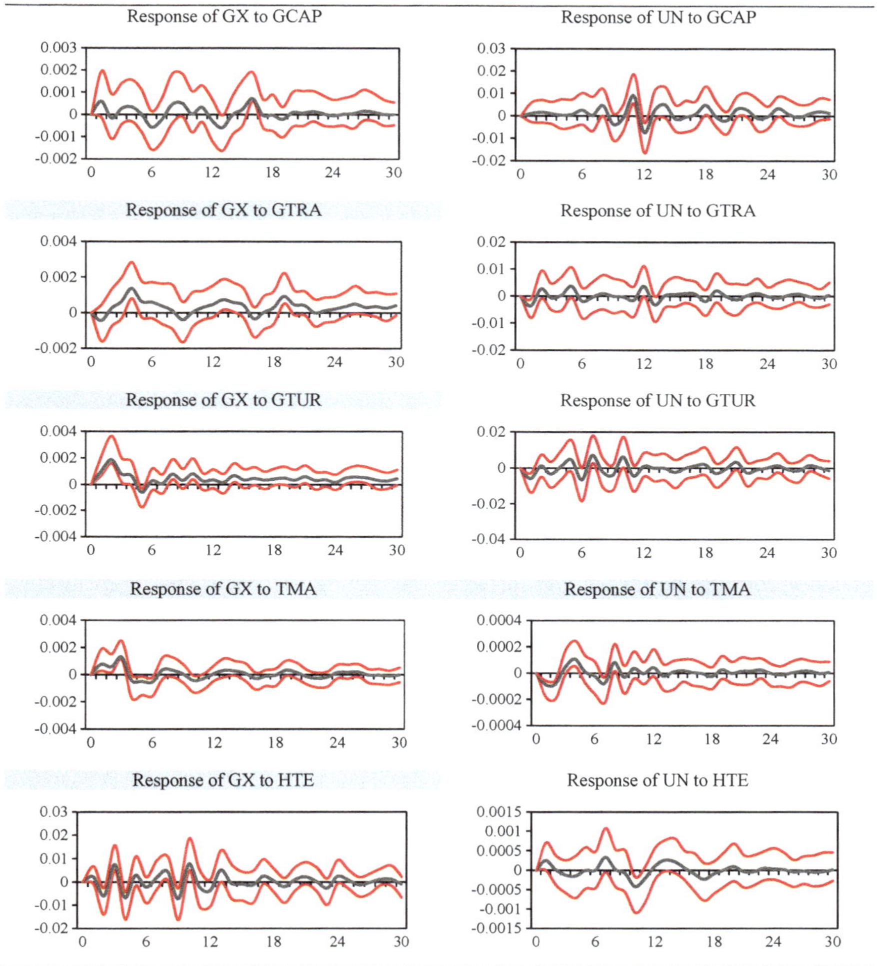

Fig. 35.3 Responses of productivity and unemployment to orthogonal shocks to the GEM and innovation. *Notes* Grey highlights indicate the impulse response functions are significant at 5%

while innovation influences growth through these channels and employment channels. The current small contribution of the GEM and innovation to economic development in Hong Kong is probably due to the fact that the GEM is still at early stage of development and high-technology export just accounts for a very small portion of GDP (see Table 35.1).

35.9 Conclusion

This study examined the feedback of Hong Kong economy to shocks imposed on the indicators of the Growth Enterprise Market (GEM) development and innovation. Accordingly, the Kaleckian–Post-Keynesian model of growth and distribution in an open economy was extended by integrating the indicators of the GEM market development and innovation into the functions of private investment, domestic savings, productivity growth, and employment. For empirical analysis, a structural VEC (SVEC) model and the corresponding impulse response function (IRF) with short-run restrictions were adopted based upon the results of cointegration and block exogeneity tests.

The results show evidence of positive feedback of Hong Kong macroeconomic indicators to shocks in the GEM market development and innovation in the short run. Specifically, various channels of growth including private investment, domestic savings, and productivity growth are found to be responsive to shocks in the GEM market development indicators. Meanwhile, shocks to innovation indicators effectively induce responses of the following growth channels: private investment, domestic savings, productivity growth, and employment. As such, the implication of our findings is that incorporating the second-tier stock market development and innovation into the Kaleckian model of growth and distribution can improve the model specification and further extend the Kaleckians' theoretical framework. Moreover, our findings are also relevant to policymakers in the sense that any policies that foster the development of the GEM and innovation could potentially induce an overall crowding-in effect on private investment, and growth in domestic savings, productivity, and employment in Hong Kong.

References

Agénor, P.-R., & Neanidis, K. (2015). Innovation, public capital, and growth. *Journal of Macroeconomics, 44*(3), 252–275.

Aghion, P., Comin, D., Howitt, P., & Tecu, I. (2016). When does domestic savings matter for economic growth? *IMF Economic Review, 64*(3), 381–407.

Aghion, P., & Howitt, P. (1998). *Endogenous growth theory*. Cambridge, MA: Mit Press.

Ali, M., & Aamir, N. (2014). Stock market development and economic growth: Evidence from India, Pakistan, China, Malaysia and Singapore. *International Journal of Economics, Finance and Management Sciences, 2*(3), 220–226. https://doi.org/10.11648/j.ijefm.20140203.13.

Azam, M., Haseeb, M., Samsi, A. B., & Raji, J. O. (2016). Stock market development and economic growth: Evidence from Asia-4 countries. *International Journal of Economics and Financial Issues, 6*(3), 1200–1208.

Bencivenga, V. R., Smith, B. D., & Starr, R. M. (1996). Equity markets, transactions costs, and capital accumulation: An illustration. *The World Bank Economic Review, 10*(2), 241–265.

Blecker, R. (2002). Distribution, demand and growth in neo-Kaleckian macro-models. In Setterfiled (Ed.), *The economics of demand-led growth*. Cheltenham, UK: Edward Elgar.

Boubakari, A., & Jin, D. (2010). The role of stock market development in economic growth: Evidence from some Euronext countries. *International Journal of Financial Research, 1*(1), 14–20.
Bowles, S., & Boyer, R. (1995). Wages, aggregate demand, and employment in an open economy: An empirical investigation. In G. Epstein, H. Gintis (Eds.), *Macroeconomic policy after the conservative era. Studies in investment, saving and finance*. Cambridge: University Press.
Chaiechi, T. (2012). Financial development shocks and contemporaneous feedback effect on key macroeconomic indicators: A post Keynesian time series analysis. *Economic Modelling, 29*(2), 487–501.
Duménil, G., & Lévy, D. (1989). The real and financial determinants of stability: The law of the tendency toward increasing instability. In: W. Semmler (Ed.), *Financial dynamics and business cycles: New perspectives*. Armonk, New York: M.E. Sharpe.
Dutt, A. (1995). Internal finance and monopoly power in capitalist economies: A reformulation of Steindl's growth model. *Metroeconomica, 46*(1), 16–34.
Erceg, C., Gust, C., & Guerrieri, L. (2005). Can long-run restrictions identify technology shocks? *Journal of the European Economic Association, 3*(6), 1237–1278.
Faust, J., & Leeper, E. (1997). When do long-run identifying restrictions give reliable results? *Journal of Business & Economic Statistics, 15*(3), 345–353.
Gospodinov, N. (2010). Inference in nearly nonstationary SVAR models with long-run identifying restrictions. *Journal of Business & Economic Statistics, 28*(1), 1–12.
Greenwood, J., & Jovanovic, B. (1990). Financial development, growth, and the distribution of income. *The Journal of Political Economy, 98*(5), 1076–1107.
Grossman, G., & Helpman, E. (1994). Endogenous innovation in the theory of growth. *Journal of Economic Perspectives, 8*(1), 23–44.
Hasan, I., & Tucci, C. (2010). The innovation–economic growth nexus: Global evidence. *Research Policy, 39*(10), 1264–1276.
Hein, E. (2004). Money, credit and the interest rate in Marx's economic. On the similarities of Marx's monetary analysis to Post-Keynesian economics. *International Papers in Political Economy, 11*(2), 1–47.
Huergo, E., & Jaumandreu, J. (2004). Firms' age, process innovation and productivity growth. *International Journal of Industrial Organization, 22*(4), 541–559.
Huh, H. -S. (2005). A simple test of exogeneity for recursively structured VAR models. *Applied Economics, 37*(20), 2307–2313.
International Finance Corporation—IFC. (2013). *Closing the credit gap for formal and informal micro, small, and medium enterprises*. Retrieved from Washington D.C. http://www.ifc.org/wps/wcm/connect/4d6e6400416896c09494b79e78015671/Closing+the+Credit+Gap+Report-FinalLatest.pdf?MOD=AJPERES.
Jensen, M., & Murphy, K. (1990). Performance pay and top-management incentives. *Journal of Political Economy, 98*(2), 225–264.
Johansen, S. (1991). Estimation and hypothesis testing of cointegration vectors in Gaussian vector autoregressive models. *Econometrica: Journal of the Econometric Society, 59*(6), 1551–1580.
Johansen, S. (1995). *Likelihood-based inference in cointegrated vector autoregressive models*. Oxford University Press.
Johansen, S., & Juselius, K. (1990). Maximum likelihood estimation and inference on cointegration—With applications to the demand for money. *Oxford Bulletin of Economics and Statistics, 52*(2), 169–210.
Kalecki, M. (1968). Trend and business cycles reconsidered. *The Economic Journal, 78*(310), 263–276.
King, R., & Levine, R. (1993). Finance, entrepreneurship and growth. *Journal of Monetary Economics, 32*(3), 513–542.
Kirchhoff, B. (1994). *Entrepreneurship and dynamic capitalism: The economics of business firm formation and growth*. Westport: Praeger.

Lavoie, M. (1992). *Foundations of post-Keynesian economic analysis: Aldershot*. UK: Edward Elgar.
Levine, R. (2005). Finance and growth: Theory and evidence. *Handbook of Economic Growth, 1*, 865–934.
Marglin, S. (1984). *Growth, distribution, and prices*. Cambridge, MA: Harvard University Press.
Marglin, S., & Bhaduri, A. (1990). Profit squeeze and Keynesian theory. In S. A. Marglin & J. B. Schor (Eds.), *The golden age of capitalism. Reinterpreting the postwar experience*. Oxford: Clarendon Press.
Pagano, M. (1993). Financial markets and growth: An overview. *European Economic Review, 37*(2–3), 613–622.
Peterhoff, D., Romeo, J., & Calvey, P. (2014). *Towards better capital market solutions for SME financing*. Retrieved from http://www.oliverwyman.com/content/dam/oliver-wyman/global/en/files/insights/financial-services/2014/July/FINAL3_BetterCapitalMarketMechanismsSMEs.pdf.
Pradhan, R., Arvin, M., Hall, J., & Nair, M. (2016). Innovation, financial development and economic growth in Eurozone countries. *Applied Economics Letters, 23*(16), 1141–1144.
Romer, P. (1986). Increasing returns and long-run growth. *Journal of Political Economy, 94*(5), 1002–1037.
Romer, P. (1990). Endogenous technological change. *Journal of Political economy, 98*(5, Part 2), 71–102.
Schumpeter, J. A. (1912). *The theory of economic development*. Cambridge: Harvard University Press.
Sestanovic, A. (2016). SME stock exchanges—Should they have a greater role? *Journal of Finance and Law, 4*(1), 59–74.
Solow, R. (1956). A contribution to the theory of economic growth. *The Quarterly Journal of Economics, 70*(1), 65–94.
Stockhammer, E., & Onaran, Ö. (2003). The effect of distribution on accumulation, capacity utilization and employment: Testing the wage-led hypothesis for Turkey. In R. Holt, S. Pressman (Eds.), *Empirical work in Post Keynesian Economics*. Routledge.
Wennekers, S., & Thurik, R. (1999). Linking entrepreneurship and economic growth. *Small Business Economics, 13*(1), 27–56.
World Federation of Exchanges. (2015). *WFE Report on SME Exchanges (with inputs from the World Bank Group's Finance and Markets Global Practice)*. Retrieved from https://www.world-exchanges.org/home/index.php/research/wfe-research#sr.

Chapter 36
Market Tightness on the CEE Emerging Stock Exchanges in the Context of the Non-trading Problem

Joanna Olbrys

Abstract According to literature, the following three dimensions of market liquidity as special liquidity characteristics are usually distinguished: (1) market depth, (2) market tightness, and (3) market resiliency. The purpose of this study is to explore market tightness as one of dimensions of market liquidity on seven small Central and Eastern European (CEE) emerging stock markets in the Czech Republic, Hungary, Slovakia, Slovenia, Lithuania, Estonia, and Latvia, in the context of serious problems with stock illiquidity. The number of companies that reveal a substantial non-trading problem is large. In the study, daily percentage relative spread is employed as a proxy of market tightness on the investigated stock exchanges. The research sample covers the period from January 2, 2012 to December 30, 2016. Furthermore, to verify the stability of the obtained results, tests based on the time rolling-window approach are provided. In general, the average daily market tightness is quantitatively similar to the investigated markets, taken separately. However, the market tightness significantly differs among stocks and the results are not homogenous in sub-periods. Moreover, the influence of the non-trading effect on daily value of a stock tightness on the CEE stock exchanges is crucial.

Keywords Dimensions of market liquidity · Market tightness · Percentage relative spread · Daily data · Non-trading problem · CEE stock exchanges

JEL Codes G12 · G15 · G17

36.1 Introduction

Dimensions concept discovers liquidity through several measures that capture distinctive liquidity aspects. However, there is no unanimity in determining dimensions of market liquidity among the researchers. For example, Kyle (1985) distinguished the following three dimensions of market liquidity as special liquidity characteristics:

J. Olbrys (✉)
Bialystok University of Technology, Wiejska 45A, Bialystok 15-351, Poland
e-mail: j.olbrys@pb.edu.pl

N. Tsounis and A. Vlachvei (eds.), *Advances in Cross-Section Data Methods in Applied Economic Research*, Springer Proceedings in Business and Economics,
https://doi.org/10.1007/978-3-030-38253-7_36

(1) market depth, (2) market tightness, and (3) market resiliency. Wong and Fung (2002) emphasized that another concept is immediacy, but it incorporates elements of all three dimensions, and it does not have to be considered as a separate dimension. Bernstein (1987) pointed out the following three dimensions: (1) market depth, (2) market breadth, and (3) market resiliency. Ranaldo (2001) mentioned four aspects: (1) market depth, (2) market tightness, (3) market resiliency, and (4) trading time. In general, market depth is defined as the ability to buy or sell a certain amount of an asset without influence on the quoted price. This dimension of market liquidity has been explored more extensively than other dimensions. Moreover, there has been quite extensive research on spread which may be treated as a proxy of market tightness. Tightness is described as the cost of turning around a position over a short period of time. The least empirical investigation has been conducted on market resiliency because this dimension of liquidity is especially difficult to estimate (Olbrys and Mursztyn 2019).

The aim of this study is to explore market tightness as one of the dimensions of market liquidity on seven small Central and Eastern European (CEE) emerging stock markets in the Czech Republic, Hungary, Slovakia, Slovenia, Lithuania, Estonia, and Latvia.

The Polish stock exchange is not included in the research because it is large compared to the other CEE stock exchanges. However, all three dimensions of market liquidity have been previously assessed on the Polish stock market. Olbrys and Mursztyn (2017) have investigated market depth and market tightness for intraday data from the Warsaw Stock Exchange (WSE). Olbryś (2017) has conducted the research on interaction between market depth and market tightness on the WSE. Olbrys and Mursztyn (2019) have introduced a new methodology for stock resiliency measurement based on Discrete Fourier Transform, which has been utilized in empirical experiments on the WSE. However, to the best of the author's knowledge, the findings regarding comparative analyses of daily market tightness on seven small CEE stock exchanges in Czechia, Hungary, Slovakia, Slovenia, Lithuania, Estonia, and Latvia are novel.

The remainder of the study is organized as follows. Section 36.2 specifies a methodological background concerning measurement of market tightness. Section 36.3 describes the data. In Sect. 36.4, we present and discuss the empirical results for daily data from seven small CEE stock exchanges. The last section encompasses the conducted research with a brief summary.

Nomenclature	
PSE	Prague Stock Exchange (Czechia)
BSE	Budapest Stock Exchange (Hungary)
BSSE	Bratislava Stock Exchange (Slovakia)
LJSE	Ljubljana Stock Exchange (Slovenia)
NASDAQ Vilnius	Stock Exchange in Vilnius (Lithuania)

(continued)

(continued)

Nomenclature	
NASDAQ Tallinn	Stock Exchange in Tallinn (Estonia)
NASDAQ Riga	Stock Exchange in Riga (Latvia)
Czechia	New official short name of the Czech Republic (since July 1, 2016)
CEE	Central and Eastern European countries
%RS	Percentage relative spread

36.2 Market Tightness as One of Market Liquidity Dimensions

According to the literature, various versions of the bid/ask spread are recognized as proper measures for market tightness because they approximate the cost of execution of a trade. However, the relative spread is the most frequently used. This measure is sometimes referred to as inside bid/ask spread (e.g. Levin and Wright 1999; Acker et al. 2002), proportional quoted spread bid/ask (e.g. Chordia et al. 2000; Foran et al. 2015), or percentage quoted spread bid/ask (e.g. Korajczyk and Sadka 2008; Fong et al. 2017).

In this research, daily percentage relative spread RS_t is employed as a proxy of market tightness. Considering that the bid/ask prices are not public information on the CEE stock exchanges, the best bid price is approximated by the highest price at time t, while the best ask price is approximated by the lowest price at time t. Then daily percentage relative spread value is given by Eq. (36.1):

$$RS_t = \frac{200 \cdot \left(P_t^H - P_t^L\right)}{P_t^H + P_t^L}, \tag{36.1}$$

where P_t^H, P_t^L are the highest and lowest prices at time t, respectively (Olbryś 2017; Olbrys and Mursztyn 2017). Percentage relative spread is in fact a measure of illiquidity. A high value of percentage relative spread denotes high market tightness and low liquidity. Conversely, a small value of percentage relative spread denotes low market tightness and high liquidity. The RS_t value at time t is equal to zero when $P_t^H = P_t^L$. Percentage relative spread is the measure most extensively used, as it is quite easy to estimate and it makes tightness of different equities comparable to each other. In this study, daily values of percentage relative spread are calculated based on the highest and lowest prices for a stock on each trading day.

36.3 Data Description and Problems with Asset Illiquidity

In this research, daily data for seven small CEE stock markets are used. Data is coming from Bloomberg under the license agreement between Bloomberg and Bialystok University of Technology (the grant No. 2016/21/B/HS4/02004). The data set contains the opening, high, low, and closing prices, as well as volume for a security over each trading day, in the period from January 2, 2012 to December 30, 2016 (five years). Specifically, the database holds 1252 (for the PSE), 1240 (for the BSE), 1244 (for the BSSE), 1245 (for the LJSE), 1245 (for the NASDAQ Vilnius), 1251 (for the NASDAQ Tallinn), and 1242 (for the NASDAQ Riga) trading days, respectively. The Warsaw Stock Exchange (WSE) is not included in the research because it is large compared to the other CEE stock exchanges. For comparison, at the end of 2016, the total number of listed stocks was equal to 881 (WSE), 23 (PSE), 41 (BSE), 71 (BSSE), 37 (LJSE), 34 (NASDAQ Vilnius), 17 (NASDAQ Tallinn), and 32 (NASDAQ Riga) (Olbryś 2018).

It is a commonly known fact that a large number of the CEE stock markets listed companies reveal a substantial non-trading problem. We refer to non-trading as a lack of transactions over a particular period when a stock exchange is open for trading. The lack of transactions means that daily volume (in items) is equal to zero, e.g., (Nowak and Olbryś 2016; Olbryś 2018). Therefore, to mitigate this problem, we excluded the stocks that exhibited extraordinarily many non-traded days during the whole sample period. Specifically, because the analyzed CEE stock markets were extremely illiquid, the basic condition concerning the maximum number of non-traded days for these markets was equal to 373, which constituted about 30% of all trading days. The number of zeros in daily volume was tremendously high for the BSSE-traded companies. The total number of stocks on the BSSE was equal to 71, while only 3 out of them met basic conditions. Finally, 10 (Prague), 18 (Budapest), 3 (Bratislava), 9 (Ljubljana), 15 (Vilnius), 12 (Tallinn), and 7 (Riga) companies were contained in the data set. Table 36.1 presents information about the companies after the reduction due to a stock illiquidity, in alphabetical order according to the company's name (74 firms in total for all exchanges).

36.4 Comparative Study of Daily Market Tightness on the CEE Stock Exchanges

In the first step, daily market tightness is estimated by using percentage relative spread (1) for each stock that is contained in the database (see Table 36.1). Furthermore, to verify the stability of the empirical results, the time rolling-window approach is employed. The whole sample period covers five years, therefore robustness tests based on the 2-year rolling-window are provided. Three 2-year time windows are utilized: (1) Window 1 (January 2012–December 2014), (2) Window 2 (January 2013–December 2015), and (3) Window 3 (January 2014–December 2016). Finally,

Table 36.1 Companies contained in the database (January 2012–December 2016)

	Stock exchange	Index	Market Cap. EUR Billion, December 2016	The number of companies	Companies
1	Prague Stock Exchange	PX	22.19	10	CETV, CEZ, FOREG, KOMB, PEGAS, RBAG, TABAK, TELEC, UNIPE, VIG.
2	Budapest Stock Exchange	BUX	21.27	18	ANY, APPENINN, PANNONIA, ELMU, EMASZ, ESTMEDIA, FHB, GSPARK, MTELEKOM, MOL, NUTEX, OPIMUS, OTP, PANNERGY, PLOTINUS, RABA, RICHT, ZWACK
3	Bratislava Stock Exchange	SAX	5.28	3	SLN1, TMR, VUB
4	Ljubljana Stock Exchange	SBI-TOP	5.00	9	GRVG, IEKG, KRKG, LKPG, MELR, PETG, POSR, TLSG, ZVTG
5	NASDAQ Vilnius	OMXV	3.50	15	AVG1L, APG1L, GRG1L, KNF1L, LNR1L, LNA1L, LGD1L, PTR1L, PZV1L, RSU1L, SAB1L, TEO1L, VLP1L, VBL1L, ZMP1L
6	NASDAQ Tallinn	OMXT	2.29	12	ARC1T, MRK1T, TVEAT, BLT1T, EEG1T, HAE1T, NCN1T, OEG1T, PRF1T, SFG1T, TAL1T, TKM1T
7	NASDAQ Riga	OMXR	0.80	7	GRD1R, BAL1R, GZE1R, LSC1R, OLF1R, SAF1R, VSS1R

the average value of daily market tightness is estimated for each stock, within the whole sample period and each time window. Summarized empirical results of average daily tightness during four investigated periods are presented in Tables 36.2, 36.3, 36.4, 36.5, 36.6, 36.7, and 36.8. Standard deviations are given in brackets. The numbers of zeros in daily volume and in the %RS daily values concern the whole sample period.

Several results in Tables 36.2, 36.3, 36.4, 36.5, 36.6, 36.7, and 36.8 are worth special notice. The influence of the non-trading effect on a stock tightness is crucial. The numbers of zeros in daily volume and in the %RS daily values are tremendously high for many companies from all exchanges, except for the PSE (Table 36.2). In general, the PSE-traded companies are the most liquid as a group. The mean value of daily market tightness varies between 0.56% (Table 36.4) and 2.46% (Table 36.3), and is quantitatively similar to the investigated markets, taken separately. However, the market tightness significantly differs among stocks. One can observe that the low value of daily market tightness might be confusing in the case of extremely illiquid companies. Although usually a small value of daily percentage relative spread denotes high liquidity, the small average daily value of tightness for such firms does not mean high liquidity or the low daily cost of an execution of a trade. For example, the average daily tightness on the BSSE (Table 36.4) is especially low in all investigated periods, while the BSSE-traded companies are extremely illiquid.

The next goal of this study is to assess whether the mean results of market tightness during the whole sample period and time-windows significantly differ compared to each other. To address this issue, we utilize the Z-statistic for independent large sample means:

$$Z = \frac{\acute{x}_1 - \acute{x}_2}{\sqrt{\frac{s_1^2}{n_1} + \frac{s_2^2}{n_2}}}, \tag{36.2}$$

where $\acute{x}_1$ and $\acute{x}_2$ are sample means, s_1^2 and s_2^2 are sample variances, and n_1, n_2 denote sample size, respectively. The following two-tailed hypothesis is tested:

$$\begin{matrix} H_0 : \mu_1 = \mu_2 \\ H_1 : \mu_1 \neq \mu_2 \end{matrix}, \tag{36.3}$$

where μ_1 and μ_2 are the expected values of tightness for each stock during the compared periods, and the null hypothesis states that two expected values are equal. Table 36.9 contains the summarized findings of the tests for all companies. Calculations of the Z-statistic values (2) are based on the sample empirical results presented in Tables 36.2, 36.3, 36.4, 36.5, 36.6, 36.7, and 36.8. The null hypothesis is rejected when $|Z| > 1.96$ (the critical value of Z statistic at 5% significance level is equal to 1.96).

The summarized results of the significance test for the difference between two means presented in Table 36.9 are not homogenous during the investigated periods. These findings indicate that the hypothesis H_0 is outweighed by the hypothesis H_1

Table 36.2 Summarized results of average daily values of market tightness on the PSE(in %)

	Company	Number of zeros in daily volume	Number of zeros in %RS daily values	Whole sample (1252 days)	Window 1 (751 days)	Window 2 (749 days)	Window 3 (751 days)
1	CETV	0	2	3.24 (2.98)	3.69 (3.56)	3.25 (3.39)	2.80 (2.38)
2	CEZ	0	1	2.07 (2.18)	2.07 (2.68)	2.08 (2.71)	2.09 (2.65)
3	FOREG	1	9	1.90 (1.43)	1.69 (0.98)	1.86 (1.42)	1.96 (1.63)
4	KOMB	0	0	2.14 (1.11)	2.15 (1.13)	1.93 (0.93)	2.03 (1.02)
5	PEGAS	0	1	1.43 (0.96)	1.18 (0.65)	1.33 (0.93)	1.52 (1.10)
6	RBAG	0	0	2.59 (1.54)	2.70 (1.58)	2.40 (1.38)	2.43 (1.55)
7	TABAK	0	3	1.33 (0.82)	1.25 (0.78)	1.10 (0.59)	1.27 (0.81)
8	TELEC	1	3	2.22 (2.46)	1.78 (1.76)	2.40 (2.85)	2.41 (2.79)
9	UNIPE	0	19	1.72 (1.13)	1.49 (1.04)	1.74 (1.24)	2.02 (1.24)
10	VIG	4	11	1.82 (1.20)	1.63 (0.97)	1.63 (0.92)	1.92 (1.31)
Mean	–	–	–	2.05	1.96	1.97	2.05
Std. Dev.	–	–	–	0.56	0.75	0.61	0.44
Median	–	–	–	1.99	1.73	1.90	2.02
Max	–	–	–	3.24	3.69	3.25	2.80
Min	–	–	–	1.33	1.18	1.10	1.27

Table 36.3 Summarized results of average daily values of market tightness on the BSE (in %)

	Company	Number of zeros in daily volume	Number of zeros in %RS daily values	Whole sample (1240 days)	Window 1 (739 days)	Window 2 (743 days)	Window 3 (749 days)
1	ANY	19	66	1.53 (2.20)	1.78 (1.38)	1.56 (1.12)	1.31 (0.95)
2	APPENINN	1	1	2.79 (1.79)	3.03 (1.97)	3.23 (2.00)	2.66 (1.52)
3	ELMU	294	566	1.46 (16.22)	1.35 (2.75)	1.56 (2.74)	1.57 (2.20)
4	EMASZ	153	379	1.45 (10.95)	1.54 (2.52)	1.68 (2.58)	1.37 (1.82)
5	ESTMEDIA	29	192	7.33 (7.40)	7.54 (5.19)	8.15 (5.38)	7.51 (5.41)
6	FHB	4	12	2.54 (2.17)	2.81 (2.18)	2.60 (2.19)	2.54 (2/48)
7	GSPARK	179	360	1.28 (10.29)	1.29 (1.58)	1.33 (1.48)	1.28 (1.36)
8	MOL	0	0	1.94 (0.93)	2.05 (0.97)	1.91 (0.86)	1.81 (0.86)
9	MTELEKOM	0	0	1.71 (0.92)	1.92 (0.98)	1.78 (0.95)	1.54 (0.86)
10	NUTEX	322	633	3.66 (18.63)	3.75 (5.40)	2.54 (4.76)	2.95 (4.99)
11	OPIMUS	65	355	4.66 (10.98)	3.33 (2.98)	4.15 (4.36)	5.51 (5.37)
12	OTP	1	1	2.31 (1.27)	2.49 (1.34)	2.33 (1.28)	2.15 (1.15)
13	PANNERGY	0	5	2.37 (1.85)	2.58 (2.13)	2.72 (2.12)	2.27 (1.42)

(continued)

Table 36.3 (continued)

	Company	Number of zeros in daily volume	Number of zeros in %RS daily values	Whole sample (1240 days)	Window 1 (739 days)	Window 2 (743 days)	Window 3 (749 days)
14	PANNONIA	2	8	3.03 (2.14)	3.39 (2.40)	3.04 (2.02)	2.63 (1.67)
15	PLOTINUS	192	470	0.76 (13.37)	0.68 (1.09)	0.81 (1.15)	0.92 (1.17)
16	RABA	20	65	1.77 (2.24)	2.03 (1.45)	1.77 (1.23)	1.60 (1.18)
17	RICHT	0	0	1.91 (0.95)	1.88 (0.92)	1.99 (0.97)	1.98 (1.02)
18	ZWACK	86	281	0.80 (8.02)	0.87 (1.19)	0.79 (1.06)	0.71 (0.95)
Mean	–	–	–	2.41	2.46	2.44	2.35
Std. Dev.	–	–	–	1.57	1.54	1.66	1.67
Median	–	–	–	1.93	2.04	1.95	1.89
Max	–	–	–	7.33	7.54	8.15	7.51
Min	–	–	–	0.76	0.68	0.79	0.71

Table 36.4 Summarized results of average daily values of market tightness on the BSSE (in %)

	Company	Number of zeros in daily volume	Number of zeros in %RS daily values	Whole sample (1244 days)	Window 1 (746 days)	Window 2 (746 days)	Window 3 (745 days)
1	SLN1	334	910	0.82 (2.13)	0.87 (2.11)	0.79 (2.04)	0.68 (1.93)
2	TMR	316	812	0.20 (0.47)	0.27 (0.50)	0.22 (0.48)	0.13 (0.43)
3	VUB	294	805	1.02 (2.28)	1.12 (2.38)	0.97 (2.32)	0.89 (2.24)
Mean	–	–	–	0.68	0.75	0.66	0.56
Std. Dev.	–	–	–	0.43	0.44	0.39	0.39
Median	–	–	–	0.82	0.87	0.79	0.68
Max	–	–	–	1.02	1.12	0.97	0.89
Min	–	–	–	0.20	0.27	0.22	0.13

Table 36.5 Summarized results of average daily values of market tightness on the LJSE (in %)

	Company	Number of zeros in daily volume	Number of zeros in %RS daily values	Whole sample (1245 days)	Window 1 (742 days)	Window 2 (748 days)	Window 3 (752 days)
1	GRVG	16	74	2.71 (1.98)	2.53 (1.91)	2.48 (1.74)	2.87 (1.94)
2	IEKG	201	530	3.51 (6.32)	4.09 (7.43)	3.23 (4.56)	3.32 (4.32)
3	KRKG	0	1	1.50 (0.99)	1.68 (1.00)	1.54 (0.98)	1.34 (0.96)
4	LKPG	18	94	2.26 (2.00)	2.70 (2.31)	2.46 (2.04)	2.08 (1.56)
5	MELR	171	455	1.41 (2.07)	2.08 (2.27)	1.73 (2.34)	0.94 (1.84)
6	PETG	1	17	1.60 (1.17)	1.75 (1.30)	1.55 (1.14)	1.49 (0.98)
7	POSR	173	399	1.28 (1.58)	1.27 (1.80)	1.46 (1.68)	1.48 (1.44)
8	TLSG	8	48	1.77 (1.31)	1.86 (1.34)	1.96 (1.37)	1.71 (1.25)
9	ZVTG	3	49	1.85 (1.35)	1.99 (1.54)	1.83 (1.26)	1.70 (1.03)
Mean	–	–	–	1.99	2.22	2.03	1.88
Std. Dev.	–	–	–	0.72	0.82	0.59	0.76
Median	–	–	–	1.77	1.99	1.83	1.70
Max	–	–	–	3.51	4.09	3.23	3.32
Min	–	–	–	1.28	1.27	1.46	0.94

Table 36.6 Summarized results of average daily values of market tightness on the NASDAQ Vilnius (in %)

	Company	Number of zeros in daily volume	Number of zeros in %RS daily values	Whole sample (1245 days)	Window 1 (746 days)	Window 2 (746 days)	Window 3 (748 days)
1	AVG1L	185	414	1.63 (2.14)	1.93 (2.08)	1.62 (2.18)	1.20 (2.10)
2	APG1L	21	166	0.94 (0.80)	1.18 (0.87)	0.89 (0.77)	0.71 (0.68)
3	GRG1L	32	288	0.92 (1.02)	0.89 (1.03)	0.97 (1.05)	0.97 (1.05)
4	KNF1L	74	289	1.07 (1.23)	0.84 (1,02)	0.96 (1.03)	1.26 (1.35)
5	LNR1L	286	643	0.84 (1.50)	0.94 (1.61)	0.96 (1.63)	0.97 (1.65)
6	LNA1L	136	352	0.77 (1.06)	0.97 (0.97)	0.77 (0.84)	0.61 (1.08)
7	LGD1L	315	656	0.82 (1.50)	0.98 (1.63)	0.75 (1.34)	0.70 (1.29)
8	PTR1L	80	269	1.42 (1.41)	1.67 (1.41)	1.54 (1.42)	1.24 (1.37)
9	PZV1L	366	769	0.61 (1.12)	0.71 (1.20)	0.71 (1.21)	0.58 (1.14)
10	RSU1L	334	748	0.60 (0.99)	0.70 (1.01)	0.65 (0.95)	0.51 (0.94)
11	SAB1L	7	115	1.30 (1.16)	1.31 (1.17)	1.25 (1.12)	1.31 (1.09)
12	TEO1L	10	86	0.73 (0.64)	0.68 (0.65)	0.76 (0.64)	0.76 (0.66)
13	VLP1L	71	443	0.87 (1.07)	0.97 (1.07)	0.86 (1.07)	0.90 (1.20)
14	VBL1L	292	731	0.59 (1.04)	0.78 (1.19)	0.66 (1.09)	0.44 (0.92)
15	ZMP1L	301	613	0.73 (1.43)	0.76 (1.22)	0.64 (1.04)	0.68 (1.53)
Mean	–	–	–	0.92	1.02	0.93	0.86
Std. Dev.	–	–	–	0.31	0.37	0.31	0.29
Median	–	–	–	0.84	0.94	0.86	0.76
Max	–	–	–	1.63	1.93	1.62	1.31
Min	–	–	–	0.59	0.68	0.64	0.44

Table 36.7 Summarized results of average daily values of market tightness on the NASDAQ Tallinn (in %)

	Company	Number of zeros in daily volume	Number of zeros in %RS daily values	Whole sample (1251 days)	Window 1 (749 days)	Window 2 (747 days)	Window 3 (750 days)
1	ARC1T	228	532	2.15 (3,25)	2.80 (3.76)	2.06 (3.33)	1.42 (2.11)
2	MRK1T	60	261	1.13 (1.26)	1.18 (1.42)	1.06 (1.14)	0.95 (0.92)
3	TVEAT	2	101	1.00 (0.76)	1.04 (0.82)	1.01 (0.74)	0.96 (0.66)
4	BLT1T	68	244	2.22 (2.22)	2.46 (2.37)	2.02 (1.93)	1.97 (2.05)
5	EEG1T	226	640	1.09 (1.61)	1.15 (1.74)	1.12 (1.69)	1.07 (1.69)
6	HAE1T	120	432	0.91 (1.13)	0.94 (1.26)	0.88 (1.03)	0.82 (0.96)
7	NCN1T	148	584	0.99 (1.38)	1.11 (1.48)	0.94 (1.29)	0.86 (1.21)
8	OEG1T	0	39	1.19 (0.81)	1.36 (0.90)	1.14 (0.78)	1.00 (0.68)
9	PRF1T	143	527	1.05 (1.45)	1.19 (1.57)	0.94 (1.36)	0.84 (1.26)
10	SFG1T	11	108	1.60 (1.35)	1.63 (1.38)	1.60 (1.43)	1.65 (1.47)
11	TAL1T	0	5	1.28 (0.84)	1.28 (0.88)	1.32 (0.87)	1.29 (0.81)
12	TKM1T	6	74	0.97 (0.81)	1.00 (0.87)	0.85 (0.67)	0.90 (0.68)
Mean	–	–	–	1.30	1.43	1.25	1.14
Std. Dev.	–	–	–	0.45	0.59	0.43	0.37
Median	–	–	–	1.11	1.19	1.09	0.98
Max	–	–	–	2.22	2.80	2.06	1.97
Min	–	–	–	0.91	0.94	0.85	0.82

Table 36.8 Summarized results of average daily values of market tightness on the NASDAQ Riga (in %)

	Company	Number of zeros in daily volume	Number of zeros in %RS daily values	Whole sample (1242 days)	Window 1 (743 days)	Window 2 (740 days)	Window 3 (745 days)
1	GRD1R	77	257	1.34 (1.53)	1.37 (1.51)	1.39 (1.57)	1.38 (1.59)
2	BAL1R	175	541	1.45 (2.95)	1.46 (3.01)	1.48 (3.07)	1.55 (3.14)
3	GZE1R	87	351	0.97 (1.28)	0.99 (1.08)	0.82 (0.97)	0.91 (1.42)
4	LSC1R	223	472	1.79 (2.52)	1.97 (2.65)	1.82 (2.45)	1.53 (2.27)
5	OLF1R	79	217	1.09 (1.13)	1.25 (1.21)	1.16 (1.18)	1.01 (1.17)
6	SAF1R	284	580	1.16 (1.84)	1.29 (2.05)	1.19 (1.90)	0.95 (1.62)
7	VSS1R	295	616	1.10 (1.81)	1.16 (2.01)	1.22 (1.86)	1.11 (1.65)
Mean	–	–	–	1.27	1.36	1.30	1.21
Std. Dev.	–	–	–	0.28	0.31	0.31	0.27
Median	–	–	–	1.16	1.29	1.22	1.11
Max	–	–	–	1.79	1.97	1.82	1.55
Min	–	–	–	0.97	0.99	0.82	0.91

Table 36.9 Summarized results of the significance test for the difference between two means of daily tightness values for the CEE-traded companies

		WS/W1	WS/W2	WS/W3	W1/W2	W1/W3	W2/W3	Sum
PSE (10 firms)	H_0	3	5	5	2	2	5	22
	H_1	7	5	5	8	8	5	38
BSE (18 firms)	H_0	8	14	11	6	4	7	50
	H_1	10	4	7	12	14	11	58
BSSE (3 firms)	H_0	2	3	2	3	1	2	13
	H_1	1	0	1	0	2	1	5
LJSE (9 firms)	H_0	3	4	3	2	0	3	15
	H_1	6	5	6	7	9	6	39
NASDAQ Vilnius (15 firms)	H_0	6	14	8	6	5	7	46
	H_1	9	1	7	9	10	8	44
NASDAQ Tallinn (12 firms)	H_0	8	10	5	6	3	9	41
	H_1	4	2	7	6	9	3	31
NASDAQ Riga (7 firms)	H_0	6	6	5	6	4	4	33
	H_1	1	1	2	1	3	3	11

Notation: WS—whole sample; W1—Window 1; W2—Window 2; W3—Window 3 in most cases for the PSE, BSE, and LJSE exchanges. The opposite observation concerns the BSSE, NASDAQ Vilnius, NASDAQ Tallinn, and NASDAQ Riga. This is mainly the consequence of the non-trading effect which might induce serious biases in various statistical measures due to extraordinarily many zeros that are present in the %RS time series.

36.5 Conclusion

The main aim of this paper was to assess daily market tightness as one of market liquidity dimensions on seven small Central and Eastern European (CEE) emerging stock markets in the Czech Republic, Hungary, Slovakia, Slovenia, Lithuania, Estonia, and Latvia, in the context of serious problems with stock illiquidity. Daily percentage relative spread was employed as a proxy of market tightness. The research sample covered the period from January 2, 2012 to December 30, 2016. To verify the stability of the empirical results, the 2-year time rolling-window approach was employed. In general, the mean results of daily market tightness during the whole sample and time-window sub-samples are quantitatively similar to the investigated markets, considered separately. The average daily tightness varies between 0.56 and 2.46%. However, the findings substantially differ between stocks. Moreover, summarized results of the significance test for the difference between two means of daily tightness values indicate that the empirical findings are not homogenous during the investigated periods. The evidence is that the cost of turning around a position over a day is diverse and this evidence is rather in accordance with the investor's intuition. Furthermore, it is worthwhile to note that the low value of daily market tightness might be confusing in the case of extremely illiquid companies. While usually a small value of daily percentage relative spread denotes high liquidity, the small average daily value of tightness for such firms does not mean high liquidity or the low cost of an execution of a trade. To sum up, the influence of the non-trading problem on daily value of a stock tightness on small emerging CEE stock exchanges is crucial.

Acknowledgements This study was supported by the grant "Comparative research on commonality in liquidity on the Central and Eastern European stock markets" from the National Science Centre in Poland, No. 2016/21/B/HS4/02004.

References

Acker, D., Stalker, M., & Tonks, I. (2002). Daily closing inside spreads and trading volumes around earnings announcements. *Journal of Business Finance & Accounting, 29*(9/10), 1149–1179.

Bernstein, P. L. (1987). Liquidity, stock markets, and market makers. *Financial Management, 16*(2), 54–62.

Chordia, T., Roll, R., & Subrahmanyam, A. (2000). Commonality in liquidity. *Journal of Financial Economics, 56*, 3–28.

Fong, K. Y. L., Holden, C. W., & Trzcinka, C. (2017). What are the best liquidity proxies for global research? *Review of Finance, 2,* 1355–1401.
Foran, J., Hutchinson, M. C., & O'Sullivan, N. (2015). Liquidity commonality and pricing in UK. *Research in International Business and Finance, 34,* 281–293.
Korajczyk, R., & Sadka, R. (2008). Pricing the commonality across alternative measures of liquidity. *Journal of Financial Economics, 87*(1), 45–72.
Kyle, A. S. (1985). Continuous auctions and insider trading. *Econometrica, 53*(6), 1315–1336.
Levin, E. J., & Wright, R. E. (1999). Explaining the intra-day variation in the bid-ask spread in competitive dealership markets—A research note. *Journal of Financial Markets, 2*(2), 179–191.
Nowak, S., & Olbryś, J. (2016). Direct evidence of non-trading on the Warsaw Stock Exchange. *Research Papers of Wroclaw University of Economics, 428,* 184–194.
Olbryś, J. (2017). Interaction between market depth and market tightness on the Warsaw Stock Exchange: A preliminary study. In: K. Jajuga, L. Orlowski, K. Staehr (Eds.), *Contemporary trends and challenges in finance. Springer Proceedings in Business and Economics* (pp. 103–111). Cham: Springer.
Olbryś, J. (2018). The non-trading problem in assessing commonality in liquidity on emerging stock markets. *Dynamic Econometric Models, 18,* 67–79.
Olbrys, J., & Mursztyn, M. (2017). Dimensions of market liquidity: The case of the Polish stock market. In: N. Tsounis, A. Vlachvei (Eds.) *Advances in applied economic research. Springer Proceedings in Business and Economics* (pp. 151–166). Cham: Springer.
Olbrys, J., & Mursztyn, M. (2019). Measuring stock market resiliency with Discrete Fourier Transform for high frequency data. *Physica A: Statistical Mechanics and Its Applications, 513,* 248–256.
Ranaldo, A. (2001). Intraday market liquidity on the Swiss Stock Exchange. *Swiss Society for Financial Market Research, 15*(3), 309–327.
Wong, J., & Fung, L. (2002). Liquidity of the Hong Kong stock market since the Asian financial crisis. *Proceedings of the Third Joint Central Bank Research* Conference (pp. 180–211). Basel, Switzerland: Bank for International Settlements.

Chapter 37
Impact of Corporate Governance on CSR in Slovak Insurance Companies

Janka Grofčíková, Katarína Izáková and Dagmar Škvareninová

Abstract Corporate governance creates important signals that the company sends to its surroundings. It affects the performance of the company and consequently the satisfaction of owners and employees, the trust of creditors, clients, and all other interest groups. There are several ways to gain their trust and satisfaction. One of them is to present information on financial support for activities that are called corporate social responsibility (CSR). The application of the CSR in practice is all the more important in companies providing insurance services, which are often referred to in the literature as trust-based products. There is only little attention paid to the research of corporate governance in relation to corporate social responsibility in insurance companies. Therefore, in our contribution, we examine the impact of selected determinants of corporate governance on corporate social responsibility information disclosure in insurance companies based in Slovakia. We use the basic methods of regression and correlation analysis to quantify this relationship. The selection of explanatory determinants of CG is carried out in accordance with the assumption of shareholders' and stakeholders' theories of management. The goal is to find out which set of variables will better explain the impact of corporate governance on CSR reporting. The results of the analysis showed that the model based on stakeholder's theory assumptions explains the changes in reporting CSR information better.

Keywords Corporate governance · Corporate social responsibility · Insurance companies

JEL Codes M14 · G22

J. Grofčíková (✉) · K. Izáková · D. Škvareninová
Department of Finance and Accounting, Faculty of Economics, Matej Bel University, Tajovského 10, Banská Bystrica, Slovakia
e-mail: janka.grofcikova@umb.sk

K. Izáková
e-mail: katarina.izakova@umb.sk

D. Škvareninová
e-mail: dagmar.skvareninova@umb.sk

N. Tsounis and A. Vlachvei (eds.), *Advances in Cross-Section Data Methods in Applied Economic Research*, Springer Proceedings in Business and Economics,
https://doi.org/10.1007/978-3-030-38253-7_37

37.1 Introduction

The importance of the insurance industry for the entire economy is undeniable, since it results from its ability to mitigate unfavorable financial situation of individuals and businesses that arises as a result of undesirable events. The main role of the insurance industry lies in the process of raising funds professionally and efficiently in order to cover risk. Therefore, trust of clients in insurance is a crucial aspect. As a matter of course, insurance companies are expected to set the right standards for corporate governance (CG) and corporate social responsibility (CSR) to be able to build this trust and keep their clients loyal. It is recommended to treat CG and CSR as two sides of the same coin, as it motivates companies to do their business with respect to the benefit of the whole society.

Specificities of corporate governance have been studied by some authors. Apparently, with regard to systemic importance, their studies mainly focus on corporate governance in the banking sector. Among them, Adams (2012), Beltratti and Stulz (2012) examined corporate governance and management of banks in the period before and after the financial crisis. Although the banking and insurance sectors are closely interconnected, the aspects of corporate governance in insurance have yet to be investigated to a sufficient range. These issues are, however, partly examined in the work of Ricci (2014). His work is devoted to seeking comprehensive and systematic insight into academic studies which are focused on analyzing recent legislation and interventions in the field of management and corporate governance in insurance.

In our paper, we will try to interconnect these basic concerns. We will examine selected key determinants of corporate governance and management of companies operating in the insurance sector in terms of two basic approaches to company management. Consequently, we will assess their impact on corporate social responsibility. Therefore, the aim of our study is to examine the impact of selected corporate governance and financial performance determinants on corporate social responsibility reporting in insurance companies in Slovakia.

37.2 Literature Review

Recently, the importance of management and corporate governance of companies have been investigated by several authors, e.g., Cadbury (1992), Shleifer and Vishny (1997), Millstein (1998), and others. However, they mainly focus on enterprises operating in the non-financial sphere. One of these, Adrian Cadbury is supposedly a person who initiated the Code of Corporate Governance, since in 1992 he drafted the first code including the principles of corporate governance. The concept of corporate governance indicates the system by which companies are managed and controlled. With regard to this concept, the role of shareholders is to appoint the Director and auditors as well as to establish supervision to ensure that appropriate control structures are implemented (Cadbury 2002). Musa et al. (2014) further completes this argument since he assumes that the application of corporate governance principles, alongside the impact on innovation potential, also has an impact on business performance.

Furthermore, Zahroh and Hamidah (2016) study the relationship between corporate governance and performance. They are examined in relation to the size of the Board of Directors and their independence, as well as to the independence of the audit committee, the quality of audit, and the level of implementation of corporate governance. Besides these, other papers examine the internationalization of corporate governance (Grofčíková 2016, 2017), the influence of selected corporate governance determinants on corporate performance which is mostly measured through return on assets (ROA) and return on equities (ROE) in a representative sample of monitored enterprises from, Japan (Mizuno 2010), Slovakia (Grofcíková and Izáková 2018) or the UK (Akbar et al. 2016).

Relationships between company governance, its size, financial reporting risk, and performance are reviewed also by Halim et al. (2017). On the one hand, findings of their research highlight the significant role of the risk management committee, the auditors' trustworthiness, and the independence of the audit committee. On the other hand, the importance of the suitable size of the Board of Directors, the frequency of its meetings, and its corporate performance are also discussed. Bartkowiak and Borkowski (2014) emphasize the importance of the financial review which is an inevitable part of an efficient corporate governance system.

Procházka (2017) pays attention to the ROA that is understood as a variable, depended on the factors that characterize the monitored subjects, including the factors characterizing their ownership.

Ferreira and Matos (2008) found that institutional investors prefer investment into large, well-managed companies with effective corporate governance, since they are prerequisites for better business performance, higher valuation, and overall revenue stability. The study of the relationship between ownership and performance of enterprises in Central European countries was further supplemented by the authors Machek and Kubíček (2018). They have proved the fact that there is an inverted U-shaped relationship between ownership and financial performance.

Institutions also deal with corporate governance issues. One of them is the Organization for Reconstruction and Development (OECD). In 1999, this organization developed the first set of corporate governance principles, which was subsequently revised and supplemented in 2004 and 2015. The current valid version was developed in cooperation with the OECD Corporate Governance Committee and the states of G20. This document consists of 6 separate chapters.

In the Slovak Republic, compliance with the principles of corporate governance that relate to insurance companies is also regulated by Act no. 39/2015 Collection of laws on insurance. Section 7 paragraph (2) letter (m) of this Act states that "demonstration of the ability to comply with the control system and corporate governance pursuant to Sections 23 to 30" is one of the conditions for granting the authorization for insurance activities. In accordance with this law, insurance companies are obliged to implement and apply an effective management and corporate governance system that ensures reliable and prudent management of the business. Under Section 23, insurance companies are obliged, for example, to take appropriate measures to prevent conflict of interest with the aim of independent risk management, introduce, and apply rules and procedures in the form of a written conception to risk management, also to internal control, internal audit, submission of information for supervisory purposes, disclosure and reporting, handling of complaints, and others. In Slovakia, the insurance companies have been complying with this obligation as early as 2016, and together with the annual report, they also submit a report on solvency and financial conditions. However, we have found that the statutory key functions, which include (1) the function of risk management, (2) the compliance function, (3) the internal audit function, and (4) the actuary function are respected, but at different qualitative levels. The European frame Solvency II is an effective instrument for supervising insurance sector. It was implemented in Slovak legislation by the Act on Insurance No. 39/2015 Collection of laws with effect from January 1, 2016. Through supporting of responsible governance and risk management, Solvency II enhances protection of insured entities. Harmonized notification and reporting of information provides key information to supervisors and enables to response to adverse developments in a sufficient time period.

37.2.1 Approaches to Basic Models of Corporate Governance and Management

The responsibility of corporate governance bodies helps build the trust, transparency, and accountability environment which is needed to support long-term investments, financial stability, and corporate integrity, and thereby foster stronger growth and a more inclusive society.

Corporate governance deals with issues of property rights, contractual relationships, proprietary control mechanisms, and organizational forms of businesses, decides on, and manages integration processes (takeovers, mergers, acquisitions) as well as relationships with stakeholders. There are several approaches to management and corporate governance which are related to company theories.

Agency theory examines relationships between shareholders and top management of an enterprise. Jensen and Meckling (1976) provide an explanation of the relationships between these two groups. Shareholders, who provide investment capital and take financial risk, appoint team of experts and management specialists (agents) who make decisions on their behalf and protect their interests. To eliminate the risk that agents will prefer their own interests, shareholders must provide appropriate control mechanisms, in the form of internal and external audits. The positive impact of control mechanisms on business operation is confirmed also by Dey (2008). He states that companies with an effective audit committee are less likely to experience problems. Several other studies, based on agency theory, reflect how different motivations of directors and agents affect the financial performance of companies. Possible negative consequences of agency theory are mitigated by reasonable suggestions for incentives for managers (Gjesdal 1982). Concentration of ownership in the hands of one or a small number of owners may, according to Shleifer and Vishny (1986), reduce the company's loss of value by inefficient diversification of the company's business. Agency theory assumes that the interests of business shareholders and managers are different. In case the interests of these two groups are the same, then the stewardship theory better reflects management processes.

Both of these theories have gradually broadened the view of the role of stakeholders in enterprises, which resulted in the basis for the stakeholder theory. The key focus of this theory is to improve the balance between the interests of the various stakeholders' groups in such a way that each group achieves a degree of satisfaction (Abrams 1951). Interest groups include mostly suppliers, customers, employees, investors, creditors, state and local authorities, civic activities and movements, the media, or the local community. In our paper, we focus on the four basic and frequently mentioned interest groups, including shareholders, managers, creditors, and employees. With regard to this theory, the role of corporate governance is to adequately protect and satisfy the interests of all interest groups. Näsi (1995) states that in the long term the company must do to satisfy every interest group. The satisfaction is related to what these groups give to the company, and what they receive from the company. Accordingly, an enterprise is no longer seen as a means of capitalizing the shareholders' investments, but as an entity that capitalizes the investments of all interest groups. Over the last decade, stakeholder concerns have been complemented with corporate social responsibility (CSR).

37.2.2 Corporate Social Responsibility

Hučka et al. (2007) treat corporate social responsibility as a separate field that exists alongside the company's management, but in any case, they is a close link between these two fields. According to corporate social responsibility includes economic, legal, ethical and philanthropic (charitable) responsibilities that society expects from the enterprise. Through the level of social responsibility, the company demonstrates its sensitive approach to society problems and at the same time it indicates the quality of cooperation with stakeholders. Carroll and Shabana (2010) analyze how business entities benefit from the policies of social corporate responsibility. Wolska (2013) highlights the importance of compliance with CSR conditions as well as benefits which result from a non-particularist and non-individualist approach to social responsibility.

The focus of corporate social responsibility is to build relationships in order to involve all stakeholders in business activities and projects. In addition to this, this concept also includes human resources, formal and legal conditions, and the protection of the environment on a voluntary basis. The aspects of corporate social responsibility are basically defined in seven major areas: (1) corporate governance,

(2) employee behavior, (3) human rights, (4) integrity in customer relationships, (5) the environment, (6) business integrity, and (7) social obligations. Friedman (1970) tried to prove the fact that the prior social obligation of business is to maximize benefits, but only with compliance to the laws and fundamental moral principles.

Another important area of CSR includes projects targeting local communities. In this area, the attention is paid to cooperation with social institutions and non-governmental organizations, promotion of educational and cultural activities, project development and internship activities as well as various forms of education and initiatives that focus on cooperation with educational institutions and research centers.

With regard to this, Nordic countries are a positive example. In these countries, corporate social responsibility is highly developed and is mostly based on the idea of sustainable development, the concept of the economy serving society, the perception of environmental awareness at the individual and corporate levels, the state policy that support the idea of CSR, building the infrastructure to raise awareness of CSR, honesty and competence of government officials, and effectively functioning non-governmental organizations.

37.2.3 Characteristics of Insurance Market in Slovakia

Information about the effectiveness of the insurance market, its scope, performance, and concentration is assessed through insurance market indicators, such as number of employees, number of insurance contracts, and others. The main indicators include the amount of premiums written through which the concentration of the insurance market in the economy or the region is assessed.

In 2001, Slovenská poisťovňa, a. s. was assessed to be the best insurer in the insurance market in the Slovak Republic (in 2003 Slovenská poisťovňa, a. s. was acquired by Allianz, Allianz hereinafter). Its share in the insurance market, calculated on the basis of the amount of written premiums on total premiums written, was 46.6% that year and it gradually decreased to 33.4% (in 2006) and to 25% (in 2017).

With regard to importance, Kooperativa poisťovňa, a. s. Vienna Insurance Group (Kooperativa hereinafter) has the second position in the Slovak insurance market. Kooperativa together with the Komunálna poisťovňa, a. s. and Poisťovňa Slovenská sporiteľňa, a. s. (PSLSP hereinafter) belong to the Vienna Insurance Group. Through the ownership of these three insurance companies, Austrian investment capital is greater than German capital.

Through a merger of Kooperativa and PSLSP on April 1, 2018, Kooperativa acquired 7% of the share of PSLSP in its portfolio and became the most important insurance company in the Slovak market. Consequently, Allianz moved down to the second position.

Table 37.1 Five largest insurance companies in SR according to the share (in %) of total premium written in sector

2017 (16 insurance companies)		2012 (18 insurance companies)		2007 (24 insurance companies)	
Insurance company	Share	Insurance company	Share	Insurance company	Share
Allianz	24.65	Allianz	27.58	Allianz	32.53
Kooperativa	19.15	Kooperativa	23.22	Kooperativa	21.93
Generali	9.19	Generali	8.57	Česká poisťovňa-Slovensko	6.56
Komunálna poisťovňa	7.99	Komunálna poisťovňa	7.83	Amslico poisťovňa	6.38
Poisťovňa SLSP	6.31	Amslico poisťovňa	5.89	NN životná poisťovňa	4.64
Total PW in sector (mil. €)	*2167.4*	*Total PW in sector (mil. €)*	*2114.3*	*Total PW in sector (mil. €)*	*1915.0*

PW Premium written

Changes in concentration of the insurance market and position of the five important insurance companies in Slovakia in 2007, 2012 and 2017 are presented in Table 37.1. We also indicate the total number of insurance companies in the Slovak insurance market in these years. In 2007, the five largest insurers had 72.05% share of premiums written, and in 2017, 67.29%.

Other quantitative indicators of the insurance market include the number of insurance employees, and indication of the level of occupation and human resource. Ferreira and Matos (2008) and Musa et al. (2017) recommend gender diversity alongside with the diverse skills of senior representatives of corporate bodies. For this reason, one of the determinants we will observe is the gender, as measured by the ratio of women in the Board of Directors. Apparently, these senior positions are mostly held by men. In the annual The Global Gender Gap Report published by WEF it is stated that Scandinavian countries have a high ratio of women in social processes, which ensures an equal status for female and male. In 2018, Slovakia was ranked in the 83rd position out of 149 countries assessed. Comparatively, Slovenia held the 11th position. According to the European Parliament, companies listed on the stock exchange market in the EU should undergo transparent recruitment procedures that would allow at least 40% of females to become non-executive members in Boards of Directors or Supervisory Boards by the year 2020 (In 2013, the ratio of women in the positions of non-executive members in the Boards of the largest EU companies was only 17.6%).

37.3 Methodology

This paper presents the results of research that focuses on the impact of selected corporate governance determinants on corporate social responsibility reporting in insurance companies based in the Slovak Republic. For this purpose, we make use of a multiple linear regression model. Relationships between corporate social responsibility, corporate financial performance, and corporate governance have been characterized in the previous part of the paper. As seen in the text above, authors examine these relationships mostly in the companies which operate in the non-financial sphere. However, not enough attention is paid to entities operating in the financial sector, i.e., insurance companies.

With regard to these facts, our research is mainly focused on this specific group of business entities. In accordance with the records of the National Bank of Slovakia, there were 16 insurance companies headquartered in the Slovak Republic and 22 branches of foreign insurance companies operating in the Slovak Republic as of December 31, 2017. In compliance with the valid legislation, branches of foreign insurance companies are not obliged to establish management bodies, which are in the joint-stock companies represented by the Board of Directors and the Supervisory Board. Our research sample consists of 16 insurance companies based in the Slovak Republic. The research in these companies is, besides other aspects, focused also on the size and structure of the Board of Directors, which is one of the key determinants of corporate governance and management. Taking a statistical point of view into consideration, these entities form a basic set.

The information that is processed in our research is obtained from the annual reports of individual insurance companies for the year 2017, which are publicly available either on the Web sites of these insurance companies or in the Register of Financial Statements. Initially, we intended to process data for more than one calendar year to investigate changes over the particular time period. However, we have encountered the problem of year-to-year comparability of the information presented in the annual reports of individual insurers and found discrepancies between individual insurance companies. The structures and the content of annual insurance reports were not comparable; therefore, the data could not be obtained in a continuous chronological order. In some years, the information was reported, hence in the years that followed, the structure and content of the information reports were changed, or the information relevant to the research was not reported at all. Owing to the insufficient amount of information required for processing, we have faced a problem to examine several selected parameters of management and corporate governance of companies over a longer period of time. This is the reason why our research is focused on the following parameters as they are fully comparable in the research sample. Therefore, the information concerning parameters on corporate social responsibility reporting and the information on selected corporate governance determinants concern no more than the year 2017.

37.3.1 Researched Variables

37.3.1.1 Corporate Social Responsibility Disclosure

The dependent variable in our research is represented by corporate social responsibility disclosure that has been surveyed in insurance companies in the Slovak Republic. We examined 26 reported social responsibility parameters in total. These are divided into 8 groups, namely education (5 parameters), health (3), sports (5), humanitarian aid (5), employees (4), the environment (1), science and research (2), and culture (1 parameter). Insurance companies mostly reported their support in the fields of education, sports, and humanitarian aid. These were followed by staff support, support to health as well as science and research. Support to environment and culture were reported only in a small number of insurance companies. The volume of funds which were invested by insurance companies into particular areas cannot be compared, since this information was published irregularly.

In order to formulate the regression model, we have calculated the corporate social responsibility disclosure index for each insurance company as the ratio of the reported CSR information to the total number of monitored information, expressed as:

$$\text{CSRD Index}_i = \frac{\sum_{d=1}^{26} \text{CSR}_{d_i}}{\sum \text{CSR}_d}, \quad (37.1)$$

where i = the insurance company, CSR_{di} = the monitored corporate social responsibility parameter in the insurance company "i," the binary coding was used in this case (code 1 denotes the case when the parameter was reported, code 0 denotes the case when the insurance company did not report the parameter), $\sum \text{CSR}_d$ = the grand total of the monitored parameters, which is 26.

The average CSRD index was 23.9%. Taking the 26 monitored parameters into consideration, this means an average of 6.21 parameters in a particular insurance company.

37.3.1.2 Independent Variables

With regard to the stated objectives of this paper, we have selected independent variables. For a list of independent variables and their measurement methods, see Table 37.2.

The most frequently studied determinant of corporate governance is the size of the Board of Directors and its structure. These determinants are related to the independent variables which are in the table indicated from x_1 to x_5. In the set of independent variables, the shareholders' status is represented by the variables from x_6 to x_8. The group of employees is represented by the variables x_9 and x_{10}. The variable x_{11} is

Table 37.2 Independent variables and their measurement

Description	Symbol	Measurement
X_1: Board members	BM	Total number of members with chairman in the Board of Directors
X_2: Woman in Board	WB	Ratio of women in the Board of Directors
X_3: Education of Board members	EB	Ratio of the Board of Directors members with university degree
X_4: Independence of BM	IB	Ratio of independent members in the Board of Directors
X_5: Foreign Board members	FB	Ratio of members with residence outside the SR in the Board of D
X_6: 5 largest shareholders	LSH	Sum of percentage of 5 largest shareholders
X_7: Number of institutional investors	NII	Number of institutional investor
X_8: Institutional investors	PII	Sum of percentage of institutional investor on the share capital
X_9: Employees	EMP	Total number of employees
X_{10}: Managers	MAN	Percentage of managers on total number of employees
X_{11}: Total indebtedness	TI	Total indebtedness (total liabilities/asset)
X_{12}: Premium written	PW	Premium written in EUR
X_{13}: Return on equity	ROE	Return on equity (net profit/equity)

used to examine the impact of the "creditors" group on corporate social responsibility reporting. Premium written and ROE perform the role of control variables.

37.3.2 Regression Model Construction

Through a multiple linear regression analysis, we will investigate the relationships between the selected independent and dependent variables. In order to assess multicollinearity of explanatory variables that enter into the regression model, a variable inflation factor (VIF) is used. The reference value of VIF is 10. Variables with VIF < 10 can be evaluated as weakly, insignificantly linear dependent. The independence of random errors has been tested in accordance with the Durbin–Watson test. Statistical tests were performed with the use of SPSS program. If required, this might be complemented with a test of statistical relevance of the autocorrelation coefficient of the first degree.

The regression model, which will be the result of our research, can be formulated as follows:

$$y = \beta_0 + \beta_1 x_1 + \beta_2 x_2 + \cdots + \beta_n x_n + \varepsilon, \quad (37.2)$$

Table 37.3 Regression models variables according to corporate governance approach

Corporate governance model	Model symbol	Independent variables (symbols from Table 37.2)
Shareholders' model	$CSRD_{SH}$	BM, WB, IB, EB, FB, LSH, NII, PW, ROE
Stakeholders' model	$CSRD_{ST}$	BM, WB, IB, EB, FB, LSH, PII, PW, MAN, EMP, TI

where y = an explained, dependent variable, β = a regression coefficient, x = a selected independent, explanatory variable, ε = a random error, and n = a number of explanatory variables.

We will formulate 2 regression models. The available independent variables that refer to the basics of two corporate governance models will be included in these models. These two models of corporate governance have been also defined by Škare and Hasić (2015). These two models refer to (1) an shareholders' governance model; this model assumes that only the interests of the shareholders should be taken into account, as they are considered to be the owners of their shares as well as co-owners of the company, and (2) stakeholders' governance model, according to which the interests of all stakeholders should be taken into account within the process of the company management; this model at the same time assumes that the shareholders are not the only entities that may undergo the risks in the company. For our research, we take the following into consideration: shareholders, employees (executive staff), management (managing staff), and creditors.

Consequently, with the use of an analysis ANOVA, we will compare the relevance and validity of these models with respect to the economic environment in which these insurance companies operate. The list of variables included in the individual models is shown in Table 37.3. Through the T test, the statistical relevance of the variables included in the final model will be evaluated.

37.4 Empirical Results and Discussion

37.4.1 Descriptive and Correlation Analysis

Table 37.4 shows the descriptive characteristics of all the variables which are included in regression models.

Table 37.5 shows the results of the correlation analysis of individual independent variables with the dependent variable. At the level of significance $\alpha = 0.1$, we will verify the hypothesis related to the existence of dependence between the selected independent variable and the dependent variable (H_0: $\rho = 0$, H_1: $\rho \neq 0$). The statistical software SPSS has been used in this case.

We can say that at the selected level of significance there is a statistically significant dependence between LSH * CSRDI, between NII * CSRDI, between EMP * CSRDI,

Table 37.4 Descriptive statistics of variables

Variables	Min	Max	Mean	Std. dev.	Variables	Min	Max	Mean	Std. dev.
CSRDI	0.0385	0.6154	0.2390	0.1754	NII	1.0000	2.0000	1.4286	0.5136
BM	2.0000	7.0000	4.0714	1.2688	PII	0.0000	1.0000	0.9282	0.2672
FB	0.0000	1.0000	0.2633	0.3248	EMP	36	1516	428	449
WB	0.0000	0.7500	0.2597	0.2016	MAN	0.0146	0.2489	0.1284	0.0713
EB	0.5000	1.0000	0.9071	0.1685	TI	0.5420	0.9300	0.8021	0.1069
IB	0.0000	1.0000	0.5677	0.3907	PW	8,294,000	566,668,000	149,277,571	169,969,379
LSH	0.9958	1.0000	0.9996	0.0011	ROE	−0.1790	0.2370	0.1022	0.1077

Table 37.5 Correlation analysis of variables

Variables	Pearson's *R* (Sig.)	Partial correlation (Sig.)		Variables	Pearson's *R* (Sig.)	Partial correlation (Sig.)	
		$CSRDI_{SH}$	$CSRDI_{ST}$			$CSRDI_{SH}$	$CSRDI_{ST}$
BM * CSRDI	0.33 (0.25)	−0.09 (0.86)	0.99** (0.02)	PII * CSRDI	−0.12 (0.69)	x	−0.91* (0.09)
FB * CSRDI	−0.27 (0.35)	0.42 (0.40)	−0.98** (0.02)	EMP * CSRDI	0.60** (0.02)	x	−0.92* (0.07)
WB * CSRDI	−0.16 (0.59)	0.56 (0.25)	−0.98** (0.02)	MAN * CSRDI	−0.50* (0.06)	x	−0.99** (0.01)
EB * CSRDI	−0.19 (0.51)	0.67 (0.14)	−0.89 (0.10)	TI * CSRDI	0.26 (0.36)	x	0.86 (0.13)
IB * CSRDI	0.06 (0.84)	−0.26 (0.61)	0.67 (0.33)	PW * CSRDI	0.59** (0.03)	0.41 (0.42)	0.35 (0.65)
LSH * CSRDI	−0.57** (0.03)	−0.66 (0.15)	−0.90* (0.09)	ROE * CSRDI	0.40 (0.15)	−0.12 (0.83)	x
NII * CSRDI	−0.54** (0.04)	−0.75* (0.08)	x				

*Correlation is significant at the 0.1 level (2-tailed). **Correlation is significant at the 0.05 level (2-tailed). ***Correlation is significant at the 0.1 level (2-tailed)

MAN * CSRDI, PW * CSRDI. These dependencies might be interpreted as moderate. Through partial correlation, we measure the direction and intensity of the relationship of the selected independent variable to the dependent variable that is disposed of the impact of the other variables. In all cases, we can see a shift in the value of the correlation coefficient.

37.4.2 Regression Analysis

In this part of the paper, we will formulate two linear regression models. The variables listed in Table 37.3 will be included in these models in accordance with the theories related to two basic models for corporate governance. For this purpose, we will use the SPSS statistical software and the enter and backward methods.

Shareholders' Governance Model (Model $CSRDI_{SH}$)

In this part of the paper, we will formulate a model based on the theories related to shareholders' governance. The general regression function, which explains the impact of the selected variables on corporate social responsibility reporting, is indicated in a pattern 3.

$$\begin{aligned} CSRDI_{SH} = {} & \beta_0 + \beta_1 BM + \beta_2 WB + \beta_3 IB + \beta_4 EB + \beta_5 FB \\ & + \beta_6 LSH + \beta_7 NII + \beta_8 PW + \beta_9 ROE + \varepsilon. \end{aligned} \quad (37.3)$$

A specific pattern of the model will depend on the results of the regression analysis summarized in Table 37.6. Through SPSS, we have formulated 8 potential models.

The results of the ANOVA test show the results of the F statistics for H_0: none of the explanatory variables is related to the variable explained, H_1: H_0 has not been proved. At the level of significance $\alpha = 0.1$, models 1 and 2 seem statistically insignificant. On the other hand, models 3 to 8 proved to be statistically significant. The insignificance of models 1 and 2 may be due to the low number of companies surveyed. However, the data of the basic set which include the information from all insurance companies based in the Slovak Republic have been processed, and this is the reason why we cannot edit the scope of the file.

The significance of models 1 and 2 may also be affected by the choice of explanatory variables and their possible multicollinearity. The results of the correlation analysis are included in Sect. 37.4.1. The multicollinearity of the variables has been tested through the variance inflation factor (VIF). Its values do not exceed the reference value 10 in any of the models as well as for any variable. The highest VIF at 5.987 has been detected for the LSH variable in model 1; the lowest VIF with the value of 1.001 has been detected for both variables included in model 8.

Through Durbin–Watson test (DW), we have evaluated the independence of the residues ε_i. Their values are indicated for each suggested model in Table 37.6. This test we complemented with a test of coefficient of autocorrelation. Consequently, a zero hypothesis on the residual independence (H_0: the residues ε_i are independent, H_1: the residues ε_i are interdependent) has been formulated. Based on the comparison of the autocorrelation coefficients with the critical value of the cyclic coefficient of autocorrelation for $\alpha = 0.05$ and $n = 16$, we can accept a zero hypothesis on the independence of the residues.

Taking the results of these tests, as well as our attempt to include the most independent variables that has been monitored in the model into account, we will formulate the following regression function that is also based on the assumptions of the shareholders' governance model:

$$\mathrm{CSRDI_{SH}} = \beta_0 + \beta_1\mathrm{WB} + \beta_2\mathrm{IB} + \beta_3\mathrm{EB} + \beta_4\mathrm{FB} + \beta_5\mathrm{LSH} + \beta_6\mathrm{NII} + \beta_7\mathrm{PW} + \varepsilon. \tag{37.4}$$

This model corresponds to model 3 in Table 37.6, which can be considered significant by the ANOVA test. Table 37.7 lists the values of individual regression coefficients, t statistics, p-values, and VIFs.

We will formulate the following regression model to explain the impact of FB, WB, EB, IB, LSH, NII, and PW on the CSRD index:

$$\begin{aligned}\mathrm{CSRDI_{SH}} = {} & 138.013 + 0.535\mathrm{WB} - 0.054\mathrm{IB} + 0.851\mathrm{EB} + 0.203\mathrm{FB} \\ & - 138.403\mathrm{LSH} - 0.290\mathrm{NII} + 3.769\mathrm{E} - 10\mathrm{PW} + \varepsilon. \end{aligned} \tag{37.5}$$

The variables "constant," EB, SLH, and NII are considered important at the level of significance $\alpha = 0.1$. In this model, there is a strong correlation ($R = 90.4\%$)

Table 37.6 Regression analysis—CSRDI shareholders governance model

Variables	Model number	1	2	3	4	5	6	7	8
	Entered	BM, WB, IB, EB, FB, LSH, NII, PW, ROE							
	Removed		BM	ROE	IB	FB	WB	LSH	EB
Model summary	*R*	0.905	0.905	0.904	0.897	0.877	0.851	0.816	0.785
	R square	0.820	0.818	0.817	0.805	0.769	0.724	0.666	0.616
	Adj. *R* square	0.414	0.528	0.604	0.638	0.625	0.601	0.566	0.546
	Std. err. of the est.	0.134	0.120	0.110	0.105	0.107	0.117	0.115	0.118
	Durbin–Watson	2.799	2.787	2.729	2.698	3.134	2.913	2.633	2.186
ANOVA	*F* value	2.021	2.816	3.827	4.815	5.341	5.905	6.658	8.824
	Sig.	0.260	0.135	0.061*	0.029**	0.019**	0.013**	0.009***	0.005***

*Correlation is significant at the 0.1 level (2-tailed). **Correlation is significant at the 0.05 level (2-tailed). ***Correlation is significant at the 0.01 level (2-tailed)

Table 37.7 Multiple regression for $CSRDI_{SH}$

Var.	Unstd. coeff.	Std. error	*t*-value	Sig.	VIF	Var.	Unstd. coeff.	Std. error	*t*-value	Sig.	VIF
Constant	138.013	62.956	2.192	0.071*		IB	−0.054	0.085	−0.629	0.552	1.181
FB	0.203	0.175	1.157	0.291	3.447	LSH	−138.403	63.226	−2.189	0.071*	5.431
WB	0.535	0.314	1.702	0.140	4.273	NII	−0.290	0.092	−3.153	0.020**	2.384
EB	0.851	0.375	2.273	0.063*	4.247	PW	3.769E−10	2.588E−10	1.456	0.196	2.063

*Correlation is significant at the 0.1 level (2-tailed). **Correlation is significant at the 0.05 level (2-tailed). ***Correlation is significant at the 0.01 level (2-tailed)

between the output variable CSRD index and the independent variables. Through this model, we can explain 81.7% variability of the reporting index of the information on social responsibility of the insurance companies. Adjusted *R* square is of the value of 60.4%, which we also consider to be sufficient and relevant.

Stakeholders' Governance Model (Model $\mathbf{CSRDI_{ST}}$)

In this part of the paper, we will formulate a regression model based on stakeholders' governance theory. The pattern of regression function with all the explanatory variables that are monitored is indicated in pattern 6.

$$\mathrm{CSRDI_{ST}} = \beta_0 + \beta_1\mathrm{BM} + \beta_2\mathrm{WB} + \beta_3\mathrm{IB} + \beta_4\mathrm{EB} + \beta_5\mathrm{FB} + \beta_6\mathrm{LSH} + \beta_7\mathrm{PII} + \beta_8\mathrm{PW} + \beta_9\mathrm{MAN} + \beta_{10}\mathrm{EMP} + \beta_{11}\mathrm{TI} + \varepsilon. \quad (37.6)$$

We will reassess the relevance of the individual independent variables by relevant statistical tests, the results of which are shown in Table 37.8.

Two models for this analysis have been designed by the linear regression tool in SPSS program. Both models confirm the existence of a strong correlation between dependent and independent variables (99.5%). These models can account for up to 99.1% (99.0%) of CSRD index variability. In both proposed models presented in Table 37.8, the standard error in estimation is significantly lower (4.25 and 3.70%) compared to the $\mathrm{CSRDI_{SH}}$ model. The results of the ANOVA test show that both proposals can be considered statistically significant at the level of significance $\alpha = 0.05$. Durbin–Watson's statistics was supplemented by a statistical significance of the 1st degree autocorrelation coefficient for non-standardized and studentized residues. We have accepted a zero hypothesis on the independence of the residues at the level of significance $\alpha = 0.05$.

Multicollinearity of the variables has been evaluated through VIF. In the first proposed model, we detected a high VIF for three variables (EB, PW, and EMP). For this reason, we prefer the second designed model, which excludes the premium written variable. The results of the regression analysis of this modified model are shown in Table 37.9.

We will formulate the following regression model to explain the impact of BM, FB, WB, EB, IB, LSH, PII, EMP, MAN, and TI on the CSRD index:

$$\mathrm{CSRDI_{ST}} = 88.169 + 0.159\mathrm{BM} - 0.881\mathrm{WB} + 0.102\mathrm{IB} - 0.858\mathrm{EB} - 0.471\mathrm{FB} - 86.805\mathrm{LSH} - 0.202\mathrm{PII} - 3.849\mathrm{MAN} - 7.477\mathrm{E} - 4\mathrm{EMP} + 0.337\mathrm{TI} + \varepsilon. \quad (37.7)$$

All variables can be considered as significant at the level of significance $\alpha = 0.1$. In this model, there is a strong correlation ($R = 99.5\%$) between the output variable CSRD index and independent variables. With this model, we can explain the 99% variability of the reporting index of the CSR information. Adjusted *R* square is of the value of 95.5%, which we consider to be an excellent result.

Table 37.8 Regression analysis—CSRDI stakeholders governance model

Model	Variables		Model summary					ANOVA	
	Entered	Removed (Backward)	R	R square	Adj. R square	Std. err. of the est.	Durbin–Watson	F value	Sig.
1	BM, WB, IB, EB, FB, LSH, PII, PW, MAN, EMP, TI		0.995	0.991	0.941	0.0425	2.562	19.933	0.049**
2		PW	0.995	0.990	0.955	0.0370	2.166	28.898	0.009***

*Correlation is significant at the 0.1 level (2-tailed). **Correlation is significant at the 0.05 level (2-tailed). ***Correlation is significant at the 0.01 level (2-tailed)

Table 37.9 Multiple regression for $CSRDI_{ST}$

Var.	Unstd. coeff.	Std. error	*t*-value	Sig.	VIF	Var.	Unstd. coeff.	Std. error	*t*-value	Sig.	VIF
Constant	88.169	23.022	3.829	0.031**		LSH	−86.805	23.076	−3.762	0.033**	6.441
BM	0.159	0.021	7.669	0.005***	6.552	PII	−0.202	5.033E−2	−4.021	0.028**	1.716
FB	−0.471	0.052	−9.009	0.003***	2.739	EMP	−7.477E−4	9.496E−5	−7.874	0.004***	17.291
WB	−0.881	0.109	−8.081	0.004***	4.582	MAN	−3.849	0.336	−11.468	0.001***	5.439
EB	−0.858	0.126	−6.820	0.006***	4.264	TI	0.337	0.111	3.039	0.056*	1.332
IB	0.102	0.035	2.921	0.061*	1.755						

*Correlation is significant at the 0.1 level (2-tailed). **Correlation is significant at the 0.05 level (2-tailed). ***Correlation is significant at the 0.01 level (2-tailed)

The regression coefficients of the variables related to LSH, NII, and PII are negative. These parameters represent a shareholders' group, whose main interest focuses on a growth of the assets of an insurance company. Therefore, we can assume that an increase in the ownership of the majority shareholders results in an increases in the pressure to redistribute dividend profits, which is to the detriment of providing part of the profit to finance social policies and higher social responsibility.

Negative coefficients have also been detected in the case of the variables related to EMPs and MAN, whose main interest is to negotiate an advantageous wage policy and various labor benefits that are cost-effective in terms of accounting as they reduce the company's disposable income. Therefore, a company can invest less to develop its social responsibility.

We have quantified the positive correlation coefficient for the variable related to total indebtedness (TI). This might be explained by an ability of a company to use drawn or retained foreign resources to fund corporate social responsibility.

The results related to the structure of the Board of Directors are with opposite correlations in the formulated models, which could have been caused by the exclusion of a number of members of the Board of Directors from the $CSRDI_{SH}$ model.

However, we can see that the $CSRDI_{ST}$ (pattern 7) has a better reporting ability in comparison with the $CSRDI_{SH}$ model (pattern 5), since it contains a higher number of explanatory variables and also more statistically significant variables. In our opinion, it more precisely explains the dependent variable. Moreover, this model is better suited to the economic environment in which the monitored insurance companies operate, i.e., the environment with a malfunctioning capital market and a strong position of banks, financial intermediaries, and established labor law legislation.

37.5 Conclusion

Our paper examined the impact of selected corporate governance determinants on corporate social responsibility information reporting in insurance companies based in Slovakia. Basic methods of regression and correlation analyses were used in order to quantify the results of our research. Finally, based on the regression analysis, we quantified a dependent variable through selected explanatory variables. The regression formulas were formulated from a set of variables and in compliance with corporate governance, agency, and stakeholders' theories. Eventually, the results of the analysis proved that the model based on the stakeholders' theory better reflects changes in reporting on corporate social responsibility. We assume that our research is beneficial since yet no similar research on these specific issues in the insurance industry has been carried out.

Acknowledgements This paper has been supported by the Scientific Grant Agency of Slovak Republik under project VEGA No. 1/0749/18 "Research on the application of corporate governance principles in companies in Slovakia." The authors would like to express their gratitude to the Scientific Grant Agency of The Ministry of Education, Science, Research, and Sport of the Slovak Republic for financial support of this research and publication.

References

Abrams, F. W. (1951). Management's responsibilities in complex world. *Harvard Business Review, 29,* 54–64.

Act No. 39/2015 on insurance.

Adams, R. B. (2012). Governance and the financial crisis. *International Review of Finance, 12*(1), 7–38. https://doi.org/10.1111/j.1468-2443.2011.01147.x.

Akbar, S., Poletti-Hughes, J., El-Faitouri, R., Zulfiqar, S., & Shah, A. (2016). More on the relationship between corporate governance and firm performance in the UK: Evidence from the application of generalized method of moments estimation. *Research in International Business and Finance, 38,* 417–429.

Bartkowiak, P., & Borkowski, M. (2014). Financial review as an element of corporate governance in the Polish legal regulations. *Journal of International Studies, 7*(2), 70–82. https://doi.org/10.14254/2071-8330.2014/7-2/6.

Beltratti, A., & Stulz, R. M. (2012). The credit crisis around the globe: Why did some banks perform better? *Journal of Financial Economics, 105*(1), 1–17. https://doi.org/10.1016/j.jfineco.2011.12.005.

Cadbury, A. (1992). *Report of the committee on the financial aspects of corporate governance*. London: Gee & Co. Ltd.

Cadbury, A. (2002). *Corporate governance and chairmanship: A personal view* (p. 280). Oxford: OUP. https://doi.org/10.1093/acprof:oso/9780199252008.001.0001.

Carroll, A. B., & Shabana, K. M. (2010). The business case for corporate social responsibility: A review of concepts, research and practice. *International Journal of Management Reviews, 12*(1), 85–105. https://doi.org/10.1111/j.1468-2370.2009.00275.x.

Dey, A. (2008). Corporate governance and agency conflicts. *Journal of Accounting Reseach, 46*(5), 1143–1181. https://doi.org/10.1111/j.1475-679X.2008.00301.x.

Ferreira, M. A., & Matos, P. (2008). The colors of investors' money: The role of institutional investors around the world. *Journal of Financial Economics, 88*(3), 499–533. https://doi.org/10.1016/j.jfineco.2007.07.003.

Friedman, M. (1970). The social responsibility of business is to increase its profits. *The New York Times Magazine*, September 13, 1970. http://umich.edu/~thecore/doc/Friedman.pdf. Accessed February 22, 2019.

G20/OECD Principles of Corporate Governance. http://www.oecd.org/corporate/principles-corporate-governance.htm. Accessed February 22, 2019.

Gjesdal, F. (1982). Information and incentives: The agency information problem. *The Review of Economic Studies, 49*(3), 373–390. https://doi.org/10.2307/2297362.

Grofčíková, J. (2016). Globalization and its impact on the corporate financial management and control. In Globalization and its socio-economic consequences. *16th International Scientific Conference. Proceedings Part II*, Žilina, pp. 547–555.

Grofčíková, J. (2017). Impact of globalization on the financial management processes. In Globalization and its socio-economic consequences. *17th International Scientific Conference*, Žilina, pp. 589–596.

Grofčíková, J., & Izáková, K. (2018). Corporate governance and firm performance in Slovakia. In: Globalization and its socio-economic consequences. *18th International Scientific Conference*, Rajecké Teplice, pp. 532–539.

Halim, E. H., Mustika, G., Sari, R. N., Anugerah, R., & Mohd-Sanusi, Z. (2017). Corporate governance practices and financial performance: The mediating effect of risk management committee at manufacturing firms. *Journal of International Studies, 10*(4), 272–289. https://doi.org/10.14254/2071-8330.2017/10-4/21.

Hučka, M., Malý, M., & Okruhlica, F. (2007). *Správa společností*. Praha: Kernberg Publishing.

Jensen, M. C., & Meckling, W. H. (1976). Theory of the firm: Managerial behavior, agency costs and ownership structure. *Journal of Financial Economics, 3*(4), 305–360. https://doi.org/10.1016/0304-405X(76)90026-X.

Machek, O., & Kubíček, A. (2018). The relationship between ownership concentration and performance in Czech Republic. *Journal of International Studies, 11*(1), 177–186. https://doi.org/10.14254/2071-8330.2018/11-1/13.

Millstein, I. M. (1998). *Corporate governance: Improving competitiveness and access to capital in global markets: A report to the OECD*. https://doi.org/10.1787/9789264162709-en.

Mizuno, M. (2010). Institutional investors, corporate governance and firm performance in Japan. *Pacific Economic Review, 15*(5), 653–665.

Musa, H., Debnárová, L., Musová, Z., & Krištofík, P. (2017). Gender equality and corporate governance in Slovakia. *Ekonomika a management, 20*(1), 98–100. https://doi.org/10.15240/tul/001/2017-1-007.

Musa, H., Musová, Z., & Debnárová, L. (2014). Responsibility in the corporate governance framework and financial decision making process. *Procedia Economics and Finance, 23*(2015), 1023–1029. https://doi.org/10.1016/S2212-5671(15)00371-8.

Näsi, J. (Ed.). (1995). *Understanding stakeholder thinking*. ISBN-10: 9519601368.

Procházka, D. (2017). The impact of ownership and other corporate characteristics on performance of V4 companies. *Journal of International Studies, 10*(2), 204–218. https://doi.org/10.14254/2071-8330.2017/10-2/15.

Ricci, O. (2014). *Corporate governance in the European insurance industry*. Basingstroke: Palgrave Macmillan. https://doi.org/10.1787/9789264162709-en.

Shleifer, A., & Vishny, R. W. (1986). Large shareholders and corporate control. *Journal of Political Economy, 94*(3/1), 461–488.

Shleifer, A., & Vishny, R. W. (1997). A survey of corporate governance. *Journal of Finance, 52*(2).

Škare, M., & Hasić, T. (2015). Corporate governance, firm performance and economic growth—Theoretical analysis. *Journal of Business Economics and Management, 17*(1), 35–51.

Wolska, G. (2013). Corporate social responsibility in Poland—Theory and practice. *Journal of International Studies, 6*(2), 45–53. https://doi.org/10.14254/2071-8330.2013/6-2/4.

Zahroh, N., & Hamidah. (2016). The role of corporate governance in firm performance. *SHS Web of Conferences, 34*(13003). https://doi.org/10.1051/shsconf/20173413003.

Chapter 38
Heston Nandi Option Pricing Model Applied to the CIVETS Indices

Niel Oberholzer and Pierre J. Venter

Abstract The purpose of this study is to make use of the Heston Nandi model to approximate option price surfaces for the CIVETS (Colombia, Indonesia, Vietnam, Egypt and South Africa) countries' equity indices. Daily data from 2010 to 2018 was used. The statistical properties of the return series show signs of leptokurtosis and volatility clustering, which is consistent with the stylised facts of financial returns. The approximated call option price surface is consistent with what is found in the market. The approximated option prices for Egypt and Turkey are slightly higher due to greater historical volatility, and a higher risk-free rate.

Keywords GARCH · Heston nandi · CIVETS · Volatility surface

38.1 Introduction

The CIVETS countries consist of Colombia, Indonesia, Vietnam, Egypt, Turkey and South Africa. These countries are all emerging market economies that are characterised by a diverse and dynamic economic activities, an young growing population and a fairly stable and developing finical system. As investors are seeking higher and better returns, countries like the CIVETS are attracting more investment capital away from more traditional investments. The increase of capital investment flow leads to an increase in the demand for more sophisticated derivative instrument. These instruments enable the investor to hedge and reduce financial risk exposure that may result from uncertainty and an increase in volatility.

The increase in the use of derivatives instruments resulted in renewed focus on the correctness of option pricing models. Since, the defining of the Black and Scholes

N. Oberholzer · P. J. Venter (✉)
Department of Finance and Investment Management, University of Johannesburg, Auckland Park, Johannesburg 2006, South Africa
e-mail: pventer@uj.ac.za

N. Oberholzer
e-mail: nielo@uj.ac.za

N. Tsounis and A. Vlachvei (eds.), *Advances in Cross-Section Data Methods in Applied Economic Research*, Springer Proceedings in Business and Economics,
https://doi.org/10.1007/978-3-030-38253-7_38

(BS) option pricing model which is based on the assumption that the underlying asset price follows and Geometric Brownian motion (GBM) with a log-normal and constant volatility many studies has shown that BS model results in systematic biases. Amongst these biases is the under-pricing of out-the-money options, options on financial assets with low volatility (Gultekin et al. 1982), the U-shaped implied volatility curve, and "volatility smile", in relationship to exercise price (Rubinstein 1985).

Since the defining of the BS researchers has developed option valuation or pricing models that incorporated stochastic volatility (Heston 1993). This resulted in two types of volatility models. The continuous-time stochastic volatility models and the discrete time generalised auto-regressive conditional heteroskedasticity (GARCH) models. However, it must be noted that a related class of volatility models is the implied binomial tree or deterministic volatility models of Derman and Kani (1994), Dupire (1994) and Rubinstein (1994).

The UN model provides major improvement on the BS, Dumas et al. (1998) which uses a separate implied volatility for each option fitted the volatility smile. A further benefit of the HN model application is that the HN model captures the correlation of volatility with returns and the path dependence in volatility. The GARCH model as stated by HM only requires a finite number of parameters need to be estimated regardless of the length of the time series. This leads to a more simplified value estimation process.

In this research paper, the focus will be on the applying of the Heston Nandi (HN) option pricing model to the CIVETS. The application of the HN option pricing model will provide a better insight into the determining of the implied volatility. The HN model, a stochastic volatility model, which assumes that the volatility of the underlying asset is not of a constant nature nor is it deterministic but it follows a random process. Therefore, implying that progression of the volatility is determined by an exogenous process. Unlike the BS where volatility is treaded as an constant. The remainder of the research paper will be as follows. Section 38.2 will provide a short literature review, Sect. 38.3 will outline the methodology, the empirical results will be reported in Sect. 38.4 and finally, the concluding remarks are discussed in Sect. 38.5.

38.2 Literature Review

Even though options are an derivative of an asset, the underlying issue to option valuation and pricing is whether the option price are consistent with time series properties of the underlying asset and its price (Bates 1997). In option pricing, three characteristics of consistency or the lack thereof have been observed in relationship to second moments, any changes in second moments and higher-order moments. The first characteristics of consistency relate to the levels of conditional volatility underlying the specific asset used. Thus, implying testing for arbitrage between the option price and the underlying assets time series. However, it is not easy to identify which moments are inconsistent in the obtaining of arbitrage profits (Bates 1997).

The second characteristics of consistency concern relate to the persistence of the mean-reverting volatility process as evident from the ARCH/GARCH model volatility processes. This concern centres around the term structure of volatility as inferred from the different option maturities and the consistencies in relationship with predictable changes in volatility. In other words, does the term structure of implicit volatility predict or detriment changes in the implicit or does the actual volatility predict or detriment changes in the implicit volatility. The last concern in regards to option pricing centres around the higher moments, i.e. skewness and kurtosis of the underlying conditional distribution. This concern relates to the explaining of the "volatility smile". In other words, the providing of evidence of leptokurtosis implicit in the option price.

The BS model by Black and Scholes is a seminal work in regards to option pricing theory. Despite subsequent enhancements to option pricing theory, the BS still remains one of the most used pricing models. One of the big benefits of the BS is that it relates the spot return distribution of spot returns to the cross-sectional properties of the option price (Heston 1993). However, despite its ongoing successful use and implementation, the BS model still presents certain concerns (Rubinstein 1985). One of the big critiques against the BS is that it makes a strong assumption in regards to equity returns and the normality of the distribution. Under the BS, it is assumed that equity returns are normally distributed with a constant variance. This assumption at best is not correct as the BS does not depend on the mean spot return.

In order to resolve the critique regarding the theoretical assumption of time-varying volatility, Scott (1997), Hull and White (1987) and Wiggins (1987) generalised the BS to allow for stochastic volatility. Further enhancements to the theoretical assumption in the BS was made by Melino and Turnbull (1990), Eisenberg and Jarrow (1994) and Stein and Stein (1991). However, these enhancements were based on the BS that did not deliver a close-form solution in regards to the calculation of volatility. Heston and Nandi (2000) offered a further solution to this problem in their stochastic process model. In this model, it is assumed that the volatility of an asset is not constant, nor even deterministic; however, it follows a random (GARCH) process.

A stochastic volatility model, as defined by HN, are very useful as they explain in a self-consistent way why options with different strikes and different expirations have differed BS implied volatility, i.e. volatility smiles (Gatheral 2003). In many instances, the distribution of equity returns reflects volatility clustering, high peaks and fat tails relative to normal distributions. The volatility clustering, high peaks and fat tails are reflective of the different characteristics of distributions and there different variables. This reflects the importance of applying a model that treads model variance as a random variable (Gatheral 2003).

The empirical performance of the HN model in traded markets was studied by Fiorentini et al. (2002). The authors used a time series approach based on an indirect inference in the estimation of the model parameters. The results obtained in this study indicate that the HN model over-priced calls that were out-of-the-money and under-priced in-the-money class. The authors to state that the daily volatility risk premium reflected volatile behaviour. However, the authors to concluded that the impact of the daily volatility risk premium has a negligible impact on the pricing performance of Heston's model.

As with the study by Fiorentini et al. (2002), Moyaert and Petitjean (2011) considered the performance of the NH model versus the BS and (Bates 1997) for daily option prices, puts and calls, on the Eurostoxx500 equity Index. According the authors, the (Bates 1997) model outperformed the short-term out-of-the options, while the HN performed better. The HN model also provided the best hedging performance, best average in regards to volatility. In closing, the authors highlight that in terms of hedging error, the HN outperformed the option contracts that mature in-the-money.

In a study by Singh and Dixit (2016), the author compares the effectiveness of the HN option pricing model to the Indian Index option market. The study compares the HN and BS models based on the moneyness, volatility of the underlying and time-to-expiration of the options. The results obtained indicated that the HN model outperforms the BS model when using an liquidity-weighted performance metrics. The authors continue by stating that the HN model outperformed the BS model for both put- and call options. Singh and Dixit (2016) concluded by stating that the HN also outperformed the BS on an statistical evaluation.

Labuschagne et al. (2017) made use of three univariate GARCH models to determine the best-fitting model for the CIVETS countries. In addition, the authors generated volatility skews using the GARCH models in Duan (1995) framework. The results showed that the GJR-GARCH model was the most reliable for Colombia and Egypt. The EGARCH model was the best fit for Indonesia, Turkey and SA. The results delivered no clear best-fitting model for Vietnam. The model generated volatility skews that were consistent with what is obtained in the market.

In a recent study, Labuschagne et al. (2014) made use of the HN model to determine the effect of the global financial crisis on implied volatility of the ASEAN nations. The results showed that the implied volatility skews were consistent with the market. Furthermore, implied volatility was higher during the crisis period, which is consistent with expectations.

38.3 Methodology

In this paper, option price surfaces are approximated using the approach by Heston and Nandi (2000). The model makes two important assumptions. The asset return process under the physical measure is given by,

$$R_t = \ln\left(\frac{S_t}{S_{t-1}}\right) = r + \lambda\sigma_t^2 + \sigma_t z_t.$$

where, S_t is the asset price at time t, r is the continuously compounded risk-free rate, and z_t is a normal disturbance. In this study, the central bank rate of each country is used as aproxy for the risk-free rate, this is consistent with Labuschagne et al. (2017). The conditional variance is formulated as follows,

$$\sigma_t^2 = \omega + \alpha z_t + \beta \sigma_t^2.$$

The parameters λ, ω, α, and β are estimated using maximum likelihood.

The fair price of an equity option is the expectation of the discounted pay-off under the risk-neutral measure (Hull 2012). Under the risk-neutral measure, z_t is replaced by z_t^*, which is a standard normal variable. Given the estimated parameters and the risk-free rate, the price at time t of a call option is given by,

$$C_t = \exp\{-r(T-t)\}\,\tilde{\mathbb{E}}\left[\max\left(S_T - K, 0\right)\right].$$

where T is the time to maturity, S_T is the underlying asset price at maturity, K is the strike price and $\tilde{\mathbb{E}}[\cdot]$ denotes the expectation under the risk-neutral measure.

38.4 Empirical Results

In this section, the empirical results are discussed. This section is divided into two subsections. One which covers the statistical properties of the return series considered in this study. The seconds subsection focuses on the Heston Nandi GARCH coefficients and approximated option prices.

38.4.1 Data Analysis

The data used in this study was obtained from the Thomson Reuters Datastream databank. Daily data from January 2010 until August 2018 was used. The following equity indices were obtained (Table 38.1).

In this subsection, the statistical properties of the CIVETS equity indices will be investigated. The line graphs of the different index levels are plotted in Fig. 38.1.

Table 38.1 Equity indices

Country	Equity index
Colombia	IGBC
Indonesia	IDX composite
Vietnam	HOCHIMINH
Egypt	HERMES
Turkey	BIST national 100
SA	FTSE/JSE top 40

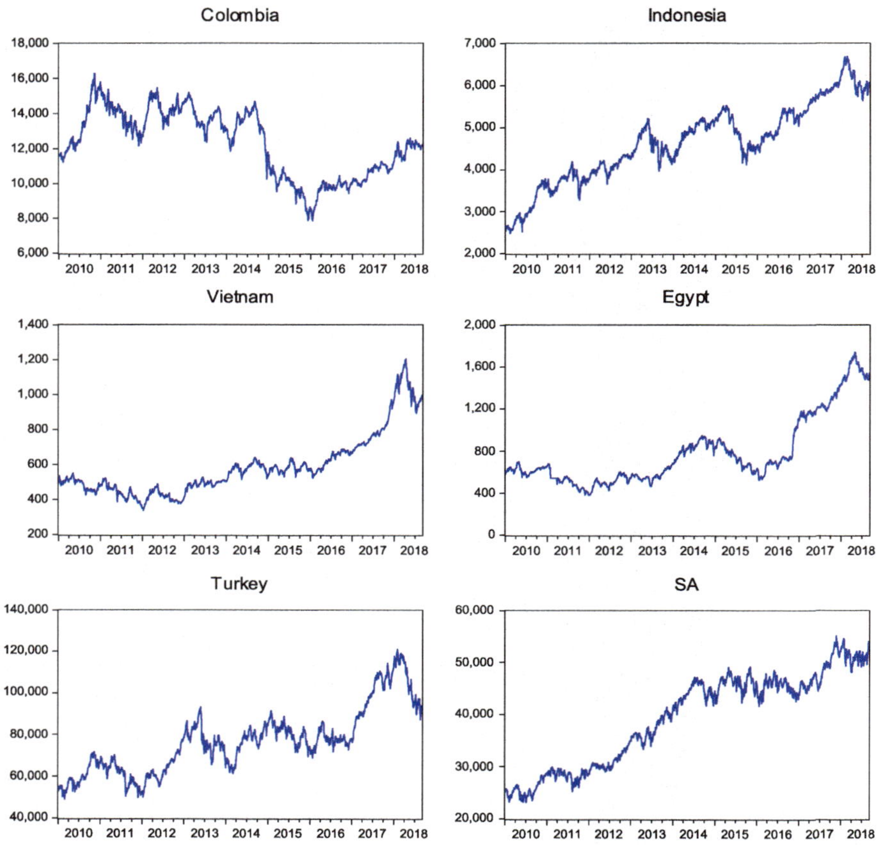

Fig. 38.1 Line graphs: equity indices

The Colombia equity index seems to be downward trending. All the other variables seem to be upward trending. The logarithmic returns are illustrated below. The logarithmic returns are denoted by R_i for each country i (Fig. 38.2).

The mean of the return series considered is close to zero. Furthermore, there seem to be signs of volatility clustering. This will be formally tested in the next section. The histograms of the return series considered are plotted in Fig. 38.3.

The histograms indicate signs of leptokurtosis when compared to the normal distribution. A constant mean close to zero, leptokurtosis and signs of volatility clustering are consistent with the stylised facts of financial returns as explained by Danielsson (2011).

The descriptive statistics in Table 38.2 confirm expectations of leptokurtosis (the kurtosis is greater than three in each case). The Jarque–Bera test statistic indicates that the return series are not normally distributed. Moreover, the measure of dispersion (standard deviation) shows that Egypt is the most volatile.

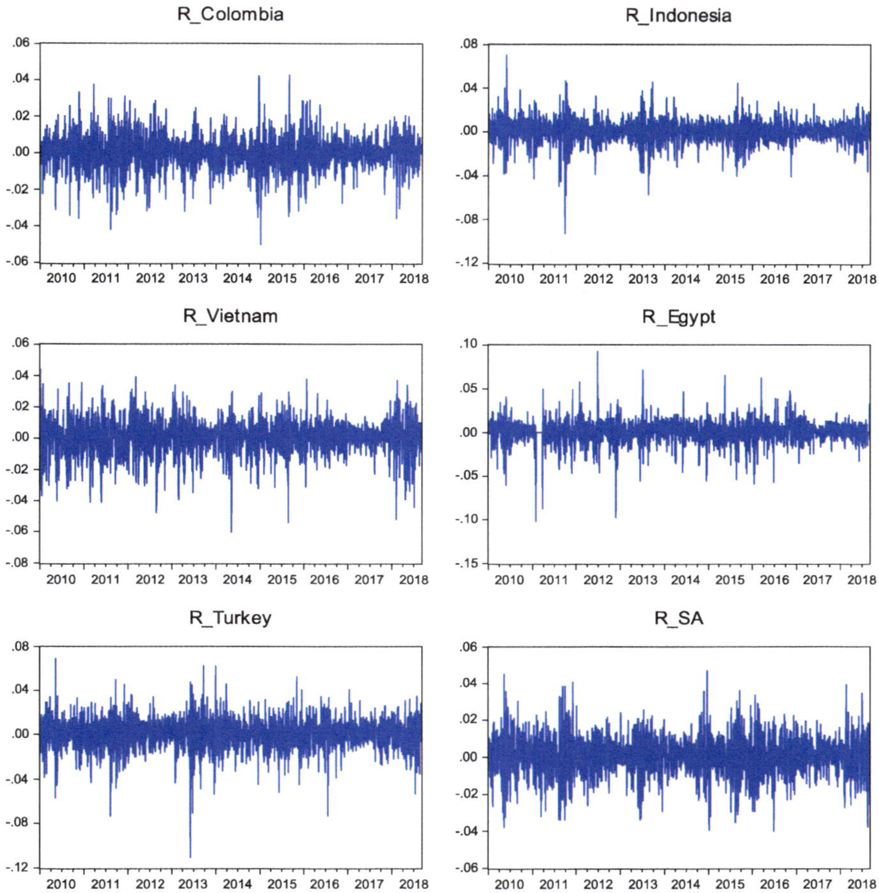

Fig. 38.2 Line graphs: logarithmic returns

38.4.2 Heston Nandi GARCH Analysis

In order to estimate the Heston Nandi GARCH parameters, it is necessary to confirm that ARCH effects (or volatility clustering) are present in the return series. The ARCH LM test below indicated that ARCH effects are present for all the return series considered in this study (Table 38.3).

The Heston Nandi GARCH estimated parameters of the different return series considered are reported in Table 38.4.

The parameters reported above were used to construct a call option price surface for the CIVETS countries' equity indices. The following parameters were assumed: the underlying asset price $S_0 = 100$, the strike prices $K = 80, 81, \ldots, 120$, and number of days until maturity $T = 30, 40, \ldots, 360$ (Fig. 38.4).

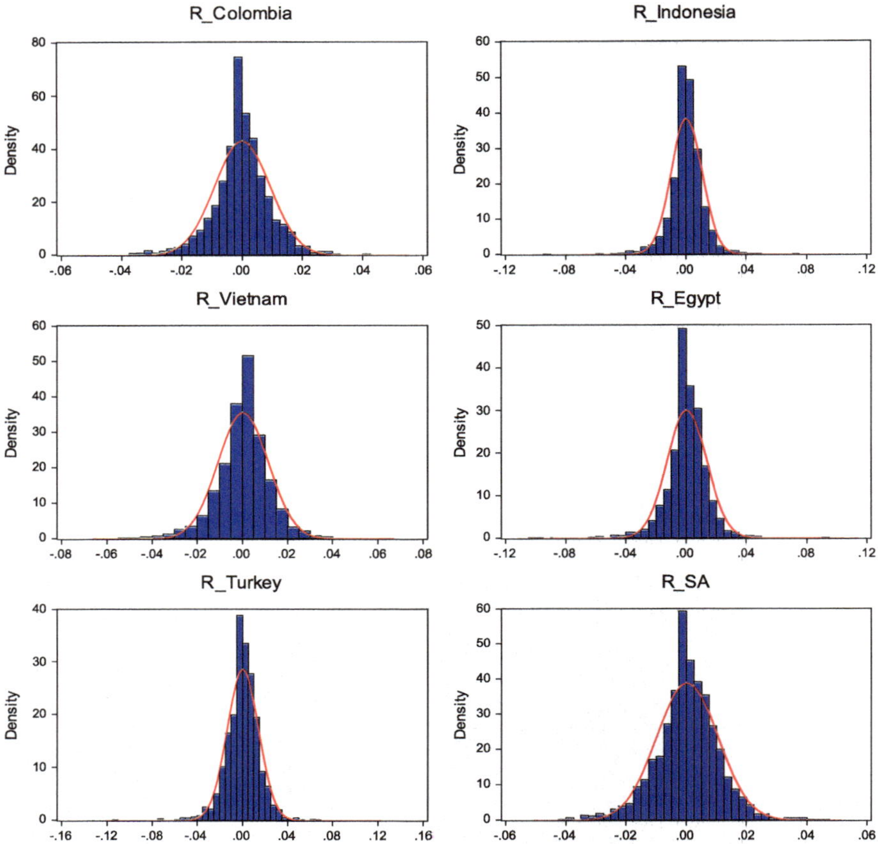

Fig. 38.3 Histograms: logarithmic returns

Table 38.2 Descriptive statistics

	$R_{Colombia}$	$R_{Indonesia}$	$R_{Vietnam}$	R_{Egypt}	R_{Turkey}	R_{SA}
Mean	0	0.0004	0.0003	0.0004	0.0002	0.0003
Median	0	0.0004	0.0003	1.00E−04	0.0003	0.0002
Maximum	0.0427	0.0701	0.044	0.0923	0.069	0.0468
Minimum	−0.0501	−0.093	−0.0605	−0.1023	−0.1106	−0.0405
Std. Dev.	0.0092	0.0104	0.0112	0.0133	0.014	0.0103
Skewness	−0.2388	−0.5961	−0.4781	−0.6296	−0.5402	−0.1381
Kurtosis	5.4822	9.7499	5.2773	10.2642	7.0355	4.5857
Jarque–Bera	601.6997	4424.129	574.4575	5118.287	1643.437	243.9566
Observations	2260	2260	2260	2260	2260	2260

Table 38.3 ARCH LM test

	F-Statistic	Obs*R-squared
Colombia	80.8072	78.0832
Indonesia	42.7553	41.9976
Vietnam	115.6082	110.0725
Egypt	44.7469	43.9159
Turkey	38.1655	37.5642
SA	28.6646	28.3302

Table 38.4 Heston-Nandi GARCH parameters

	λ	ω	α	β
Colombia	−1.813	1.76E−26	7.64E−06	0.9058
Indonesia	1.152	4.06E−32	8.65E−06	0.913
Vietnam	−0.6849	2.32E−22	1.04E−05	0.9132
Egypt	−3.93	1.65E−05	2.26E−05	0.7734
Turkey	−5.793	2.1E−13	1.33E−05	0.9307
SA	0.1937	2.91E−24	5.73E−06	0.943

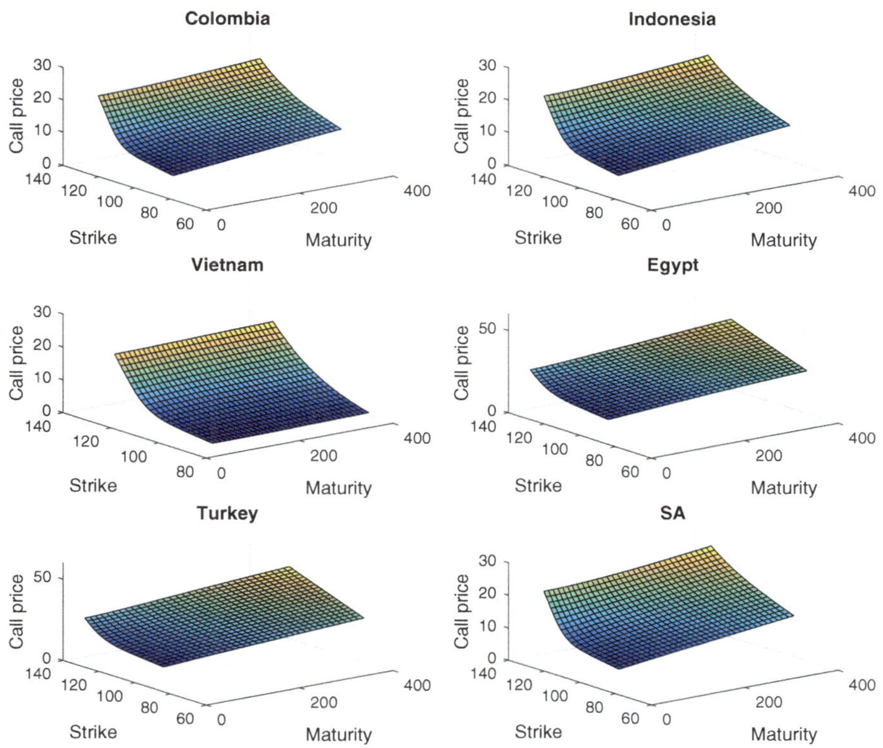

Fig. 38.4 Call option price surfaces

The call option prices are consistent with expectations and what is usually obtained from the market. The approximated prices for Egypt and Turkey are higher. This is due to the greater volatility (as shown in Table 38.2), and the higher risk-free rate. The results obtained are consistent with the results of Labuschagne et al. (2017). The put option price surfaces can be easily obtained using put-call parity (Hull 2012).

38.5 Conclusion

The purpose of this study was to make use of the Heston Nandi model to approximate option price surfaces for the CIVETS countries' equity indices. Daily data from 2010 to 2018 was used. The initial data analysis shows that the statistical properties of the return series show signs of leptokurtosis and volatility clustering, this is consistent with the stylised facts of financial returns. Furthermore, the approximated call option price surface is consistent with what is found in the market. The approximated option prices for Egypt and Turkey are slightly higher due to greater historical volatility, and a higher risk-free rate. Areas for future research might include comparing the Heston Nandi model to other volatility models (Dupire 1994; Heston 1993) and extending the approach followed in this paper to the pricing of exotic derivatives.

References

Bates, D. S. (1997). The skewness premium: Option pricing under asymmetric processes. *Advances in Futures and Options Research*, *9*, 51–82.

Danielsson, J. (2011). *Financial risk forecasting: The theory and practice of forecasting market risk with implementation in R and Matlab* (Vol. 588). Wiley: Wiley.

Derman, E., & Kani, I. (1994). Riding on a smile. *Risk*, *7*(2), 32–39.

Duan, J. C. (1995). The GARCH option pricing model. *Mathematical Finance*, *5*(1), 13–32.

Dumas, B., Fleming, J., & Whaley, R. E. (1998). Implied volatility functions: Empirical tests. *The Journal of Finance*, *53*(6), 2059–2106.

Dupire, B. (1994). Pricing with a smile. *Risk*, *7*(1), 18–20.

Eisenberg, L., & Jarrow, R. (1994). Option pricing with random volatilities in complete markets. *Review of Quantitative Finance and Accounting*, *4*(1), 5–17.

Fiorentini, G., Leon, A., & Rubio, G. (2002). Estimation and empirical performance of Heston's stochastic volatility model: The case of a thinly traded market. *Journal of Empirical Finance*, *9*(2), 225–255.

Gatheral, J. (2003). Modeling the implied volatility surface. Global Derivatives and Risk Management, Barcelona.

Gultekin, N. B., Rogalski, R. J., & Tinic, S. M. (1982). Option pricing model estimates: Some empirical results. *Financial Management*, pp. 58–69.

Heston, S. L. (1993). A closed-form solution for options with stochastic volatility with applications to bond and currency options. *The Review of Financial Studies*, *6*(2), 327–343.

Heston, S. L., & Nandi, S. (2000). A closed-form GARCH option valuation model. *The Review of Financial Studies*, *13*(3), 585–625.

Hull, J. C. (2012). *Options, futures, and other derivatives*. London: Pearson Education.

Hull, J., & White, A. (1987). The pricing of options on assets with stochastic volatilities. *The Journal of Finance*, *42*(2), 281–300.

Labuschagne, C. C., Oberholzer, N., & Venter, P. J. (2017). Univariate GARCH model generated volatility Skews for the CIVETS stock indices. In *Advances in Applied Economic Research* (pp. 333–347). Cham: Springer.

Melino, A., & Turnbull, S. M. (1990). Pricing foreign currency options with stochastic volatility. *Journal of Econometrics*, *45*(1–2), 239–265.

Moyaert, T., & Petitjean, M. (2011). The performance of popular stochastic volatility option pricing models during the subprime crisis. *Applied Financial Economics*, *21*(14), 1059–1068.

Rubinstein, M. (1985). Nonparametric tests of alternative option pricing models using all reported trades and quotes on the 30 most active CBOE option classes from August 23, 1976 through August 31, 1978. *The Journal of Finance*, *40*(2), 455–480.

Rubinstein, M. (1994). Implied binomial trees. *The Journal of Finance*, *49*(3), 771–818.

Scott, L. O. (1997). Pricing stock options in a jump diffusion model with stochastic volatility and interest rates: Applications of Fourier inversion methods. *Mathematical Finance*, *7*(4), 413–426.

Singh, S., & Dixit, A. (2016). Performance of the Heston's stochastic volatility model: A study in Indian index options market. *Theoretical Economics Letters*, *6*(02), 151.

Stein, E. M., & Stein, J. C. (1991). Stock price distributions with stochastic volatility: An analytic approach. *The Review of Financial Studies*, *4*(4), 727–752.

Wiggins, J. B. (1987). Option values under stochastic volatility: Theory and empirical estimates. *Journal of Financial Economics*, *19*(2), 351–372.

Chapter 39
The Impact of TV Advertising on Brand Credibility

Eva Kicova, Viera Bartosova and Jozsef Popp

Abstract Due to Nielsen cross-channel report, there is overall growing media consumption. Driving, that is, a growth in digital consumption. There is assumption that consumers replace TV screens to spend more time on social media. Another marketer's assumption said that while TV is a great place to run big international marketing campaigns, digital video and display ads can be targeted to reach specific local markets, making them more efficient for small and midsize business budgets. This paper deals with these myths, we have collected, facts and real data to refute these hypotheses. The main purpose is to investigate the relationship between brand credibility and brand presence in TV commercials. What is more, paper describes advertising effectiveness measurements to assess brand credibility. Case study shows results before and after TV advertising on brand credibility of the chosen company. A meta-analysis was performed on three months observation. The findings indicated a positive linear relationship between brand presence in TV and brand credibility. As a conclusion, paper offers suggestion for cross-media strategy.

Keywords Brand · Brand building · Brand awareness · Credibility

JEL codes M31 · M37

E. Kicova (✉) · V. Bartosova
Faculty of Operation and Economics of Transport and Communications, Department of Economics, University of Zilina, Univerzitna 1, 010 26 Zilina, Slovak Republic
e-mail: eva.kicova@fpedas.uniza.sk

V. Bartosova
e-mail: viera.bartosova@fpedas.uniza.sk

J. Popp
Faculty of Economics and Business, Department of Agricultural Economics, University of Debrecen, Institute of Sectoral Economics and Methodology, Böszörményi út 138, Debrecen 4032, Hungary
e-mail: popp.jozsef@econ.unideb.hu

N. Tsounis and A. Vlachvei (eds.), *Advances in Cross-Section Data Methods in Applied Economic Research*, Springer Proceedings in Business and Economics,
https://doi.org/10.1007/978-3-030-38253-7_39

39.1 Introduction

Companies are aware that the ability to communicate effectively and efficiently with their customers on target markets is critical to their success. The main goal of marketing communication is to inform, persuade and remind customers about products or services of that company, or brand offers (Teixeira et al. 2012). Nowadays, marketers have many channels to choose from and to communicate and advertise. The Internet has become the most discussed topic. Many researchers and practitioners assumed that classic TV ads are no longer important, because people watch TV less. Therefore, we see some questions, television and the Internet—are they competitive media or complementary? Or will the Internet be a new TV? There is a big discussion between key media players and marketers. However, broadcasting does not move from television to Internet, it still remains in the same numbers, and the Internet is just another channel. This can be called mainly as distribution extension. Global figures underline the power of TV advertising (ATO 2017).

What is more, in 2017, on the occasion of World Television Day, TV broadcasters and trade bodies from around the world have joined together for the first time to release global figures demonstrating TV's resilience and strength as an advertising medium. They formed Global TV Group as a new databank. Major media players are exchanging unfiltered transparent, reliable data and fresh insights for TV (Global TV Group 2018).

39.2 Myths About TV Advertising

To prove the power of TV ads, there are seven myths face with real facts and charts.

1. **People watch TV less**

As can be seen, total TV time consumption is rising from year to year. We can assume that people are mostly working in creative sector, so they need to relax by watching and not thinking. TV reaches approximately 70% of a country's population a day, 90% in a week and nearly everyone in a month (ATO 2017). It is the unique combination of this reach together with the huge volume of time spent on watching TV that makes it such a powerful form of advertising. Following figure shows that TV has the greatest portion of media consumptions as well (Figs. 39.1 and 39.2).

Time	**3:17 h**	**3:40 h**	**3:45 h**
Year	**2008**	**2013**	**2018**

Fig. 39.1 TV time consumption

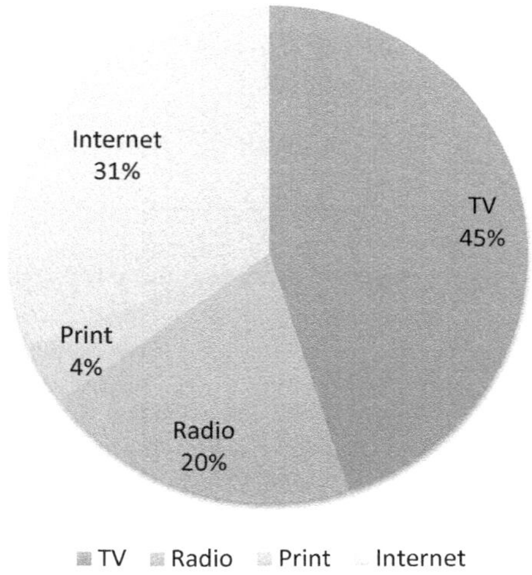

Fig. 39.2 Media consumption on a regular day

2. **People watch mostly video on laptops or PC**

Real numbers:

- 94% of households have TV screens,
- And more than 30% households have two or more TV screens that are in regular use,
- 99% of TV programme is still watching on TV screens.

TV, in all its forms, is the world's favourite video. On average, based on the available data, TV accounts for 90% of the average viewer's video time. For the younger millennial audience, who are the most enthusiastic experimenters with all forms of video, it is also the largest proportion of their video time at around 73% of the total.

3. **Millennials do not watch TV, they spend more time on social media**

So-called millennial's TV viewing increases as they get older and have children.

- 4–14 years old children watching 1:43 h/day,
- 15–24 years old teenagers watching 1.06 h/day,
- 25–34 years old young people watching 2:31 h/day,
- For example, in Italy, 16–24 s watch 2h 13 a day; 25–34 s watch 2h 38 and 25–34 year olds with children watch 3h 23 (Nelsen 2018).

4. **Media multitasking, while watching TV is a big trend**

According to online survey, we realized in the end of 2018, about 50% of those who reported multitasking (38%) said they always or often used the Internet while watching TV. Over a fifth of that group watched another video online while watching TV, ***with a third of that group saying that they research products seen in commercials***.

- According to new numbers from, 56% of heavy multitaskers are in the age 18–34,
- while watching TV surveyed respondents using 28% smartphone, 15% laptops, 6% PC, 5% tablets.

5. **Watch the news on TV in the Internet age is an anachronism**

   - 36% people daily watching news on TV, 20% people weekly searching for news on TV,
   - 26% people daily searching for news on the Internet, 14% searching for several times a week,
   - on the other hand, we have also multitaskers here, half-surveyed respondents reported reading online news content while watching TV (ATO 2017).

6. **In west countries, TV was replaced by Netflix, YouTube and other Social media**

In Fig. 39.3, we can see that despite the new comers as SVOD services, such as Netflix or big trend of the online video platforms, mainly YouTube, TV consumption has remained steadfast around the globe.

7. **TV advertising revenue is decreasing, TV does not have a good ROI**

According to research from Nelsen (2018) displayed in Fig. 39.4, TV is the best for generating revenue and even for profit. TV is the most effective form of advertising, generating 71% profit, with a short-term profit rate of 62% over all other form of advertising (radio, print, online video, out-of-home advertising, etc.).

In conclusion, we can assume that the television market is changing. However, the TV market is changing very slowly and in a completely different way than the sceptics had anticipated. It changes in different directions, but numbers still show that this is the most effective way of advertising.

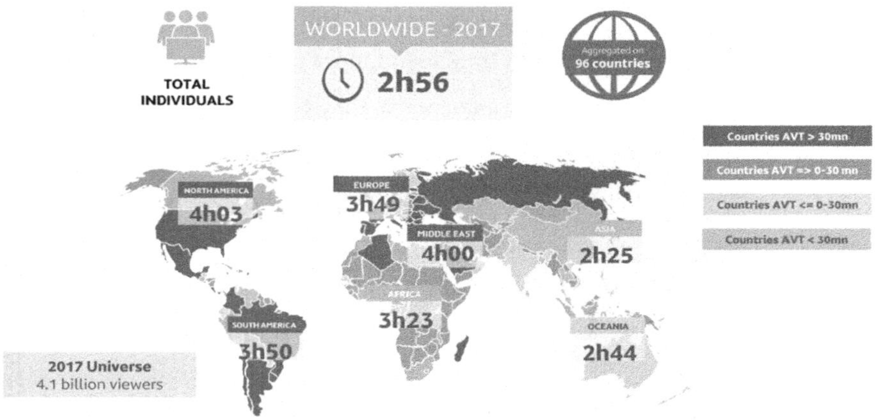

Fig. 39.3 Globe TV consumption in average

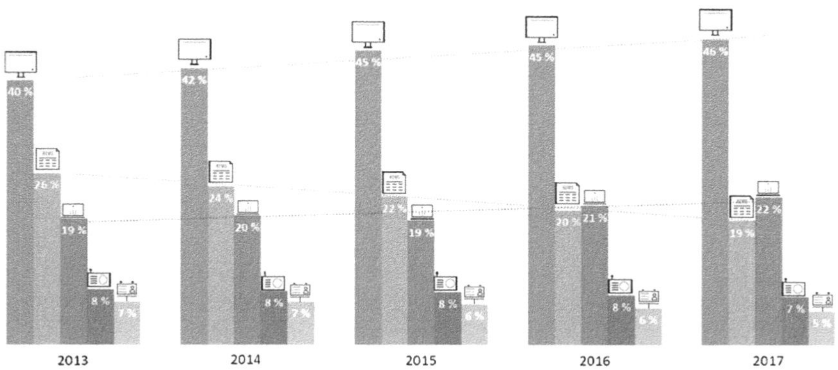

Fig. 39.4 Revenue coming from TV, print, Internet (digital), radio and OOH advertising

39.3 TV Advertising and Effectiveness Measures

Marketers use advertising for long-term brand building, it is a paid form of controlled, non-personal and outward communication (Keller 2007). It promotes ideas, goods and services of an identifiable source aimed at a specific target market in order to inform, remind or persuade consumers to act (Percy and Elliott 2005). There is always advertising in the centre of marketing communication plan that should support brand equity, brand awareness and of course in long-term distance, brand credibility (Krizanova et al. 2015). The aim of marketers is to create strong association with brand, in other words the advertising message strategy is an indication of what the marketer and advertiser wish to accomplish through the advertisement. Level of consumer involvement or interaction is more than required for advertising to be effective (Stefanikova et al. 2015).

Zaichkowsky (1986) first explained how involvement is built on the foundation of personal relevance. He proposed three levels of involvement, namely personal factors (such as personality, needs, values and interests), the object or stimuli factors (the source and content of communication) and situational factors (such as the occasion, temporal perspectives and physical surroundings). These antecedents of involvement determine the level of involvement the consumer has with the relevant product, brand and advertising message (Valaskova et al. 2018). Advertising, therefore, works mainly by communicating a persuasive informational message to build strong brands (Gajanova et al. 2019). High attention levels have been linked with improved recall (Fox 2018) and are, therefore, normally regarded as being important for successful communication (Percy and Elliott 2005), particularly in the case of ***television advertising***. Moreover, it is necessary to distinguish between advertisement recall and brand recall. Sometimes, consumers remember the advertisement but not the brand. This is mostly a risk with highly creative advertisements and unfamiliar brands (Rubinson 2009). On the other hand, brand recall occurs when consumers can remember the brand name in an advertisement, which can be ascribed to message elements that encourage usefulness, such as differentiation, positioning and features (Aaker 2003; Keller 2007).

There are numerous measures of advertising effectiveness in current literature. Advertising effectiveness is stated as the encoding of brand information in memory. This is measured by recognition and recall (Kliestik et al. 2018). The message response involvement theory denotes that varying amounts of motivation, opportunity and ability that directly affect the attention given to brand processing (Stefko et al. 2014).

One of the most well-known advertising models, the elaboration ***likelihood model*** (ELM), purports that active or attentive processing produces attitude changes that are more predictive of behaviour than inattentive processing. Specific factors are also indicated to which the changes in marketing and emphasis on the marketing communication element can be attributed.

All advertising messages require an instrument or medium to reach the target audience. Peleckis et al. (2018) argue that the term media is typically applied to advertising (i.e. television, magazines, radio, Internet, etc.), although the concept of media is relevant to all marketing communication tools. Television is often chosen by advertisers because of its ability to utilize audio and visual effects in the advertising message. This allows for increased creativity and impact with which the advertising message can be presented (Krizanova 2013). Furthermore, despite changes in the television industry, such as the ability for viewers to control their viewing of television commercials, research empirically argues that the effectiveness of television advertising remains significant (Svabova et al. 2018).

39.3.1 Television Advertising Effectiveness

When measuring the effectiveness of television advertising, one should keep in mind that processing of and responses to television advertising do not always occur immediately after exposure to the advertisement intervention. This is referred to as the *sleeper effect*. Many persuasive messages, therefore, do not have an initial effect, but changes in behaviour take place after a period. In general terms, this is any delayed effect that arises as a result of some intervention (Svabova et al. 2018). Results from a study show that attitudes formed on the basis of repeated advertisement exposure are more accessible from memory and are held with more confidence than attitudes based on a single advertisement exposure (Gajanova et al. 2019). In addition, marketers believe that a television advertisement is only effective when the consumers who see the advertisement know which brand is being advertised. When measuring brand recognition, respondents are required to recognize a stimulus, which might be a word, object or image, as something they have previously seen (Keller 2007). Krizanova et al. (2015) suggests that a strong brand presence helps to reinforce the link between the message and the brand.

Romaniuk (2009) suggests that the longer a brand is shown in an advertisement, the more likely respondents will be able to store that information in their memory. Results from another study support this notion and explain that attention and encoding variability contribute independently to brand name memory, suggesting that brand presence assists in reinforcing the brand name in memory (Kliestik et al. 2018). Additionally, marketers conclude that the decision to zap (fast-forward) through an advertisement depends on how the brand is presented within the advertisement (Kliestik et al. 2018). The ability of an advertisement to concentrate consumers' visual attention reduces avoidance significantly, and the likelihood that consumers will zap through an advertisement can be decreased with a 'pulsing strategy' in which brand images are shown more frequently for a shorter period of time within the advertisement instead of longer at the beginning or end.

39.3.2 Trust and Impact of TV Advertising

In this part, we will show other facts and numbers that confirm the relationship between brand awareness, brand credibility and presence on TV advertising.

TV is the most trusted form of advertising and remains most likely to make consumers laugh, move them to tears or trigger emotions. TV is by far the most trusted form of advertising in Canada. 36% of adults named TV the most trustworthy advertising compared to 10% for Internet advertising. In the UK, 58% stated television is where they are most likely to find advertising that makes them feel emotional in comparison to 9% for social media and 6% for newspapers.

Effectiveness: Advertisers invest in TV advertising because it works. Studies around the world demonstrate TV's many effects—and the positive impact it has on other media.

For example:

- In Australia, on average, TV campaign achieves sales revenues (ROI) of $ 1.70 per $ 1 invested.
- In Belgium, TV generates almost three times the brand recall of YouTube (42% vs. 15%).
- In the USA, disruptor brands such as Airbnb and Fitbit saw an immediate significant lift in website visits once their first TV campaign launched (figures from 13 brands feature a lift, ranging from 11% to 1 075%).
- In France, the traffic of an advertiser's website during a TV campaign increases by 44%.
- In the UK, adding TV to a campaign generates a 40% increase in effectiveness.
- German research has shown that, when added to a radio, outdoor or magazine campaign, TV boosts the ROI by +222%, +123% and +112%, respectively.

39.4 Case Study of No Name Brand in Three Months

Goal: Gain new customers and increase brand awareness branding, brand did not have TV advertisement before.
Process: TV advertising for three months and as additional channel use YouTube videos.
Starting point: Brand credibility 13.7%.

Brands, they have share of voice bigger than theirs share of market they tend to grow in time.

Therefore, it is important to invest into strong campaigns with emotional message. This linear relationship can be seen in Fig. 39.5.

Results: Brand increased by 93%, from 13.7% to 26.50% (start comparison and end of campaign). Our no name brand has been on same the level with market leaders what is connected to brand credibility. Estimated impact on sales of tens of millions of euros. All these figures were measured by brand lift method, online survey that we made. The campaign was started 25 April 2018 and finished 20 July 2018.

Suggestion: How to plan the most effective cross-media campaign.

- Planning a brand campaign in combination of online + TV
- Synergy of both media during their daily consumption = stronger intervention for smaller budgets
- TV generates a surface airstrike and an overall audience
- Online
  - The digital generation interferes with their native TV (non TV viewers)
  - Remarketing + segmented targeting to trigger an online action (purchase)
  - Key point: total TV and online interventions are more effective than catching up with TV more intervention by increasing GRP intervention (we increase the frequency of heavy TV users; we do not speak only to online users) (Fig. 39.6).

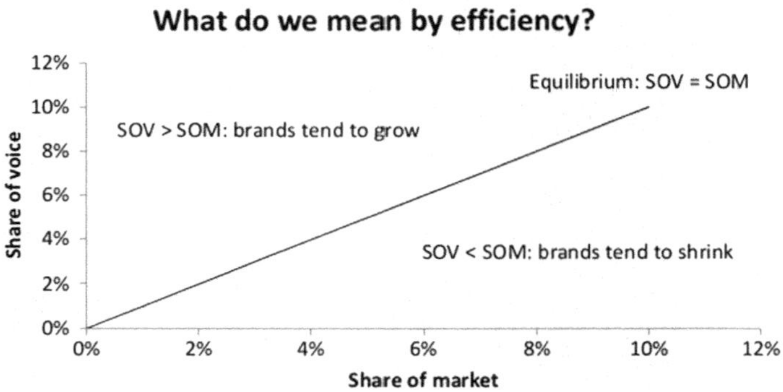

Fig. 39.5 Relation between SOV and SOM

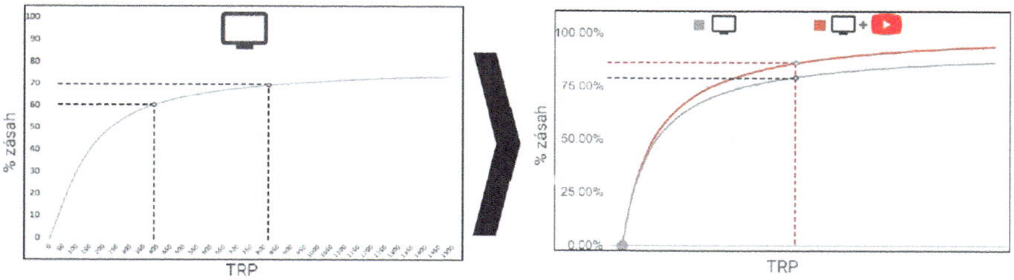

Fig. 39.6 Planning effective TV intervention

With the same budget, it is possible to achieve an intervention that would be purely on TV only ***two times more*** expensive and unreachable online.

Acknowledgements This paper is an outcome of the science project APVV-15-0505: Integrated model of management support for building and managing the brand value in the specific conditions of the Slovak Republic.

References

Aaker, D. A. (2003). Brand building—budování značky (p. 312). Brno: Computer Press.

ATO–Nielsen Admosphere. (2017). *Lifestyle survey*.

Fox, M. A. (2018). Drive-in theatres, technology, and cultural change. *Economics, Management, and Financial Markets, 13*(2), 24–39.

Gajanova, L., Nadanyiova, M., & Moravcikova, D. (2019). The use of demographic and psychographic segmentation to creating marketing strategy of brand loyalty open access indicator image. *Scientific Annals of Economics and Business, 66*(1), 65–84.

Keller, K. L. (2007). *Strategic brand management*. Praha: Grada Publishing.

Kliestik, T., Kovacova, M., Podhorska, I., & Kliestikova, J. (2018). Searching for key sources of goodwill creation as new global managerial challenge. *Polish Journal of Management Studies, 17*(1), 144–154.

Krizanova, A., Majerová, J., Kliestik, T., & Majercak, P. (2013). Theoretical aspects of brand building in seafood industry. *NAŠE MORE, 60*(5–6), 105–112.

Krizanova, A., et al. (2015). Building a Brand in the Context of Sustainable Development. In *Proceedings of International Conference on Management Engineering and Management Innovation* (pp. 79–84). Changsha: PRC.

Macdonald, E. K., & Sharp, B. M. (2000). Brand awareness effects on consumer decision making for a common, repeat purchase product: A replication. *Journal of Business Research, 48*(1), 5–15.

Nelsen NNTV Program Report. *All broadcast and cable*. 1/01/2018–11/18/2018. Live + 7.

Peleckis, K., Peleckiene, V., & Peleckis, K. (2018). The search for balance and equilibrium of negotiating powers under distorted market competition. *Ekonomicko-manazerske spektrum, 12*(2), 67–82.

Percy, L., & Elliott, R. (2005). *Strategic advertising management*. New York: Oxford University Press.

Rodrigues, P., & Martines, F. V. (2016). Perceptual and behavioural dimensions: measuring brand equity consumer based. *Journal of Fashion Marketing and Management, 20*(4), 507–519.

Romaniuk, J. (2009). The efficacy of brand-execution tactics in TV advertising, brand placements, and internet advertising. *Journal of Advertising Research, 49*(2), 143–150. https://doi.org/10.2501/S0021849909090187.

Rubinson, J. (2009). Empirical evidence of TV advertising effectiveness. *Journal of Advertising Research, 49*(2), 20–226. https://doi.org/10.2501/S0021849909090321.

Stefko, R., Bacik, R., & Fedorko, R. (2014). Facebook content analysis of banks operating on Slovak market. *Polish Journal of Management Studies, 10*(1), 145–152.

Stefanikova, L., Rypakova, M., & Moravcikova, K. (2015). The impact of competitive intelligence on sustainable growth of the enterprises. In: *Conference: 4th World Conference on Business, Economics and Management. Book Series: Procedia Economics and Finance Vol. 26* (pp. 209–214). Ephesus, Turkey: WCBEM.

Svabova, L., Kramarova, K., & Durica, M. (2018). Prediction model of firm's financial distress. *Ekonomicko-manazerske spektrum, 12*(1), 16–29.

Teixeira, T., Wedel, M., & Pieters, R. (2012). To zap or not to zap: How to insert the brand in TV commercials to minimize avoidance. *New Strategy, 4*(1), 14–22.

Valaskova, K., Kliestikova, J., & Krizanova, A. (2018). Consumer perception of private label products: An Empirical research. *Journal of Competitiveness, 10*(3), 149–163.

Zaichkowsky, J. L. (1986). Conceptualising involvement. *Journal of Advertising, 15*(2), 4–14. https://doi.org/10.1080/00913367.1986.10672999.

Chapter 40
Large Shareholders and Profitability of Telecommunication Firms in Eastern Europe and the Black Sea Region

Ioannis Antoniadis, Theodoros Parganas and Kontstantinos Spinthiropoulos

Abstract This paper examines the relationship between the performance of the firm and ownership structure in the telecommunication companies of Eastern Europe and the Black Sea region. More specifically we focus on the ownership percentage the large shareholder of the company owns and its effect on profitability measures of performance (ROA and ROE) of the firms. A balanced panel is used for 14 telecommunication companies from 11 countries of the region is used for the period 2012–2015. Our results indicate the existence of a non-linear relationship between large shareholder ownership and performance, suggesting the existence of agency problems.

Keywords Corporate governance · Ownership · Performance · Large shareholders · Agency problem · Telecommunications

JEL classification L22 · L96

I. Antoniadis (✉)
Department of Regional Development and Cross Border Studies, University of Western Macedonia, Kozani, Greece
e-mail: iantoniadis@uowm.gr

T. Parganas
Hellenic Telecommunications Organization, Kozani, Greece
e-mail: t.parganas@gmail.com

K. Spinthiropoulos
Department of Administrative Science and Technology, University of Western Macedonia, Kozani, Greece
e-mail: spinthiropoulos@gmail.com

N. Tsounis and A. Vlachvei (eds.), *Advances in Cross-Section Data Methods in Applied Economic Research*, Springer Proceedings in Business and Economics,
https://doi.org/10.1007/978-3-030-38253-7_40

40.1 Introduction

Ownership structure and its importance for corporate governance and performance are well recognized by relevant literature (Shleifer and Vishny 1997; Demsetz and Villalonga 2001; Davies et al. 2005; Kostyuk et al. 2018). Along with the separation of ownership and control, can create potential conflicts of interests between shareholders, managers, and stakeholders, a situation is known as the principal-agent problem (Fama and Jensen 1983) and has been the basis for the agency theory (Fama 1980).

The existence of large shareholders has been suggested as a remedy for the issue. Large shareholders have stronger incentives and power to directly and actively monitor managers, in the case of separation of ownership and control (Agrawal and Knoeber 1996; La Porta et al. 1999; Welch 2003). Concentrated ownership could also give rise however to another type of agency problem (Antoniadis et al. 2008), between large shareholders, minority shareholders and other stakeholders, as the former may take advantage of their dominant position and power in the firm, expropriating the latter for their personal benefit (Shleifer and Vishny 1986; La Porta et al. 1999; Andres 2008; Hamadi 2010).

The telecommunications industry has been a case for the role of large shareholders in their management and governance (Zambarloukou 2010; Cai and Tylecote 2008). During the last 20 years, technology breakthroughs and innovations in have elevated the importance of the sector for the development of the national and regional economies (Goddard and Gillespie 2017). Globalization and the free flow of capital across countries and regions have affected significantly not only the operation, growth, and profitability of the companies. The increasing growth for technology products and services related to telecommunications, liberalization of the markets, in national and global level, have fuelled the growth of the sector with the creation of new companies, and led to a wave of mergers and acquisitions in the sector, leading to significant changes in the ownership structure of the firms in the industry (Baller et al. 2016; Bradshaw 2017; Mark and Specht 2019).

Considering the importance of the sector for the economic development of a country and the effect it has on promoting innovation it is important to examine the effect ownership structure and most specifically large shareholders have on the profitability of telecommunications firms. We examine 14 firms in the industry from 11 countries of Eastern Europe and the Black Sea Region for 4 years (2012–2015), in order to identify the nature of agency problems associated with the existence of large shareholders in their corporate ownership structure. Using panel data, we found that there is a non-linear relationship between the percentage of ownership held by the large shareholder and profitability ratios, indicating the existence of agency problem as profitability decreases as the percentage of larger shareholder rises, but only until a certain level.

The rest of this paper is structured as follows. Section 40.2 briefly presents the financial status of the sector in the examined geographic area. Section 40.3 reviews the relevant literature on the importance of corporate governance and the relationship between ownership structure, performance, and the agency problem. Section 40.4 discusses the methodology and variables used in our analysis, along with the characteristics of the sample, followed by the presentation of the empirical results of the performed econometric analysis, in Sect. 40.5. Finally, Sect. 40.6 concludes the paper offers a brief discussion on the presented results and suggestions for further study.

40.2 The Telecommunications Sector

Recent data concerning global informatics and telecommunications for 2016–2017 showed that there is a growing trend in the fundamentals of the industry. The overall value of the market is steadily rising by 1.2% in 2016 and 1.7% in 2017, reaching 1.788 and 1.818 trillion euros, respectively (SEPE 2016).

According to further data provided by SEPE (2016), the development and growth of the telecommunication sector in the South-East Europe region showed mixed trends. Russian and Polish market has displayed signs of dynamic growth, whereas in most countries of the region the prospects of development for the sector were weak or stable. The value of the market fell by 1.1% in 2016 reaching 49 billion euros in 2016 and has shown anemic signs of recovery in 2017 by 0.5%, reaching 49.2 billion euros.

The profitability of the 14 telecommunications firms in the region measured by the return of assets and return on equity can be seen in Graph 40.1a. There is an obvious decrease in the profitability of the firms measured by ROA and ROE. The mean value of the total assets is found to have an increasing trend for the years 2014 and 2015 (Graph 40.1b). Considering the decrease in the profitability of the firms during these years, and the increase in the mean value of total assets during these years we can assume that the companies in the region have been investing heavily in new technologies like 4G that had a toll in their profitability indices.

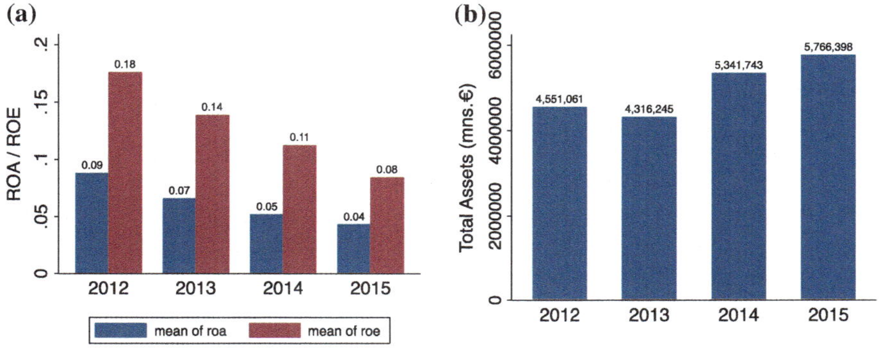

Graph 40.1 **a** Profitability of telecommunications firms (2012–2015), **b** total assets (2012–2015)

However, at the same time, there was a change in the ownership structure of the firms, which led to an increase in the ownership concentration of the firms. The mean value of the percentage that the larger shareholder owns has risen from 61.33% in 2012 to 66.02% in 2015. Therefore, we could speculate that there is some evidence in the expropriation of minority shareholders as larger shareholders have increased their power, directing funds in investments, hindering short term profitability.

40.3 Literature Review

Corporate governance has progressed from being a way of ensuring providers of capital to get a return on their investment (Shleifer and Vishny 1997), to a complex nexus of mechanisms that aim in dealing and reducing conflicts of interests between the firm, shareholders, and stakeholders (Goergen and Renneboog 2006). Ownership structure and corporate governance have been an important topic that has been researched by a number of studies (Arouri et al. 2011; Isik and Soykan 2013; Koystuk et al. 2018).

Ownership from large shareholders is identified as an important mechanism for reducing conflicts between the various stakeholders of the company, hence, controlling agency costs. That is also important in today's corporate environment, where increased competition, and technological breakthroughs renders necessary the study of the factors affecting profitability and efficiency of firms, especially for the telecommunications and technology firms. Ownership structure and the existence of large shareholders is also important for this relationship since the need for diversification of business activities and investments in new technologies, proposed by managers may be blocked by large shareholders in favour of financial performance (Thomsen and Perdersen 2000).

In that regard, numerous studies have examined the relationship of ownership structure and firm performance, shedding light on the various aspects of the issue. One of the pioneering researches of the field is the one of Morck et al. (1988), who introduced the concept of the non-linear relationship between ownership and performance examining managerial ownership with a piece-wise regression. Their results showed that performance rises until a certain level of ownership but beyond that, managerial entrenchment will result in decreased performance. Demsetz and Vilallonga (2001) have also found that there is a non-linear relationship between financial performance and ownership structure, using 2SLS regression, as performance rises along with ownership concentration, but when large shareholders power exceeds a certain level expropriation effect sets in, that impacts negatively the performance of the firm. Their results also considered industry effects and other financial variables. In another research on the relationship of ownership structure and firm performance Thomsen and Pedersen (2000), have examined ownership structure in the largest European countries, highlighting the role of concentrate ownership, shareholder identity, and its effect on financial performance, again in a nonlinear fashion, as higher levels of ownership diminished the positive effect of increased monitoring.

A research conducted by Scholten (2014), concerning 80 Dutch listed companies, documented this non-linear relationship, between profitability measured by ROA and ownership concentration. For shareholders' percentages larger than 48% profitability was found to be affected in a negative way. Similar results were provided by Zeitun and Tian (2007) as far as ROE is concerned, especially in the cases where the larger shareholder was the State (SOE). Kapopoulos and Lazaretou (2007) examined 175 Greek listed firms, following the methodology of Demsetz and Villalonga (2001) and found that a more concentrated ownership structure and less diffused ownership is positively related to firm profitability.

Arouri et al. (2011) also demonstrated the negative effect that concentrated ownership has on the financial performance of banks in the GCC countries. In a similar study performed by Isik and Soykan (2013), 164 industrial firms listed on the Istanbul Stock Exchange (BIST) were examined during 2003–2010. Their results also indicate the importance of large shareholders on the performance of the examined firms, both in terms of profitability (ROA), and firm value (Tobin's Q). Desoky and Mousa (2013) also found that concentrated ownership has a significant effect on the performance of the Egyptian firms, in terms of profitability measured by ROE. Ownership concentration was found to have a concave relationship with the performance for firms in Central and Eastern Europe that operate in less developed institutional systems (Balsmeier and Czarnitzki 2017).

We should also note that the inclusion of financial variables, like the size of the firm, liquidity, leverage, etc., is also very important in order to control for the different characteristics of the examined firms, (Vlachvei and Notta 2008; Notta et al. 2010; Desoky and Mousa 2013). Eljelly (2004) for example surveying listed Sri Lankan industrial firms found that liquidity has a significant effect on the profitability of the firms. Comparable results are provided by Saleem and Rehman (2011) for the oil companies in Pakistan where liquidity was found to have a significant relation with ROA but insignificant for ROE. Leverage has also been found to have a negative effect on profitability (Notta et al. 2010), while Isik and Soykan (2013) found that size of the firm had a positive and significant effect on profitability but negative to the value of the firm measured by Tobin's Q.

In conclusion, after a short review of the literature, we can assume that there is a non-linear relationship between ownership structure and the larger shareholders' percentage in the firm and the two main measures of profitability namely ROA and ROE, which is also affected by a number of control variables like liquidity and leverage. In the following section, the proposed model to estimate this relationship is presented along with the data and methodology that was used.

40.4 Data and Methodology

In the present research, we have examined a sample of 14 companies that operate in the telecommunications sector from 11 countries of the Eastern Europe and the Black Sea Region, for a 4 year period of time (2012–2015). Financial and ownership data were collected by the annual reports of the companies.

The variables we are going to examine as dependents variables measuring the profitability of the firms are, return on assets (ROA), and return on equity (ROE). The independent variables are the larger shareholders' percentage of shares (OWN), the logarithm of the total assets of each firm (SIZE), the debt to equity ratio (LEVERAGE) and the liquidity (LIQUIDITY) ratio. The 3 latter variables are used as control variables for the financial characteristics of the firms. Also in order to capture the non-linear relationship described by the literature, we use the squared ownership percentage (OWNSQ), using a different approach compared to Isik and Soykan (2013), and extending the work of Aruri et al. (2011) who used a linear model.

Table 40.1 presents the descriptive statistics of the used variables for the pooled sample. It is important to note the high levels of ownership concentration observed in our sample, as the mean value for the larger ownership (OWN) of our sample is 62.92% As far as the profitability of the firms is concerned the mean value of ROA and ROE for the pooled sample is 0.0622 (6.22%) and 0.1279 (12.79%), respectively.

In order to assess the relationship between profitability and the percentage the larger shareholder holds, a performance regression (40.1) is estimated:

$$\text{Profitability}_{it} = \alpha_0 + \beta(\text{ownership})_{it} + \gamma\,(\text{control variables})_{it} + u_{it}, \quad (40.1)$$

where i stands for the firm and $t = 2012–2015$ and u_{it} represents the disturbance term, and *Profitability*$_{it}$ is ROA, and ROE. Therefore, the estimated regressions will be the following:

$$\begin{aligned}\text{ROA}_{it} &= a + b\_1 \cdot \text{OWN} + b\_2 \cdot \text{OWN}^2 + b\_3 \cdot \text{SIZE} + b\_4 \cdot \text{LEVERAGE} \\ &\quad + b\_5 \cdot \text{LIQUIDITY} + u_{it} \\ \text{ROE}_{it} &= a + b\_1 \cdot \text{OWN} + b\_2 \cdot \text{OWN}^2 + b\_3 \cdot \text{SIZE} + b\_4 \cdot \text{LEVERAGE} \\ &\quad + b\_5 \cdot \text{LIQUIDITY} + u_{it}\end{aligned}$$

In the following section, the empirical results of the panel data regression are presented and discussed.

Table 40.1 Descriptive statistics

	Mean	Std. Dev.	Min	Max
ROA	0.06227	0.05447	−0.11668	0.19563
ROE	0.12795	0.14546	−0.36176	0.52150
OWN	0.62923	0.20926	0.40000	1.00000
OWNSQ	0.43895	0.310781	0.16000	1.00000
SIZE	13.42779	2.48415	8.91731	17.13423
LEVERAGE	1.20285	0.99095	0.11000	4.16000
LIQUIDITY	0.61263	0.68488	0.00934	2.86034

40.5 Empirical Results

Table 40.2 demonstrates Pearson's Correlation matrix. Our results show that there is not a significant multicollinearity problem except for the case of the square of ownership (OWNSQ) and (OWN) that seems to be highly correlated and this relation is statistically significant.

In Table 40.3 the results of the regression are presented using the fixed effects model. We must note that in both regressions both Breuch and Pagan multiplier test and Hausman test rejected random effects in favor of fixed effects. More specifically the value of the Hausman test was $X^2 = 18.25$ ($p = 0.0026$) for ROA model and $X^2 = 18.97$ ($p = 0.0019$) for the ROE model, suggesting the use of fixed-effects model. The R^2 values are also satisfactory and according to relevant literature.

From the results of the ROA regression, we verify the existence of a non-linear relationship between larger shareholder ownership performance and profitability measured as ROA, in a 0.1 level of statistical significance. However, it is interesting to note that this relationship is opposite to the one expected by literature (Demsetz and Villalonga 2001; Scholten 2014) as profitability seems to decrease as the shareholder's percentage rises, until a certain point and then rises as the values of the coefficients for OWN and OWNSQ are −2.370 and 1.602, respectively. As far as the other control variables are concerned, leverage has a negative and statistically significant effect on profitability as expected (Notta et al. 2010; Isik and Soykan 2013), while the size of the firm and liquidity are not statistically significant.

This relationship is also present and stronger in the case of the ROE regression, as the estimated coefficients are statistically significant at a 0.01 level of significance.

Table 40.2 Correlation matrices

Panel A: dependent variable ROA						
	ROA	OWN	OWNSQ	SIZE	LEVERAGE	LIQUIDITY
ROA	1.0000					
OWN	−0.4029	1.0000				
OWNSQ	−0.4114	0.9970	1.0000			
SIZE	0.1446	0.2120	0.1805	1.0000		
LEVERAGE	−0.1731	0.0964	0.1131	−0.0219	1.0000	
LIQUIDITY	0.3210	0.1685	0.1783	0.1058	−0.4315	1.0000
Panel B: dependent variable ROE						
ROE	1.0000					
OWN	−0.4050	1.0000				
OWNSQ	−0.4081	0.9970	1.0000			
SIZE	0.1136	0.2120	0.1805	1.0000		
LEVERAGE	0.2222	0.0964	0.1131	−0.0219	1.0000	
LIQUIDITY	−0.0037	0.1685	0.1783	0.1058	−0.4315	1.0000

Table 40.3 Panel Data results

	(1)	(2)
	ROA	ROE
OWN	−2.370*	−8.677***
	(1.252)	(3.042)
OWNSQ	1.602*	5.817***
	(0.832)	(2.022)
SIZE	−0.00908	0.0303
	(0.0327)	(0.0794)
LEVERAGE	−0.0384***	−0.0747**
	(0.0135)	(0.0329)
LIQUIDITY	0.0209	0.0167
	(0.0155)	(0.0377)
Constant	1.006*	2.708*
	(0.584)	(1.419)
Observations	56	56
R-squared	0.328	0.297
F(5,37)	3.61	3.13
Number of firms	14	14

Standard errors in parentheses, *** $p < 0.01$, ** $p < 0.05$, * $p < 0.1$

Again the identified relationship is opposite to the one proposed by the literature (Morck et al. 1988) as the function is convex and the values of the coefficients for OWN and OWNSQ are −8.677 and 5.817 respectively. The effect of control variables on ROE is similar to the ones identified in the ROA case.

These findings are interesting since they contradict the private benefits hypothesis (Isik and Soykan 2013). However, we should take under consideration the characteristics of the examined sample, and more specifically the ownership structure of the firms in question. The mean values of the percentage the larger shareholder own in the firms is very big (62.92%) and bigger than relevant studies (i.e. Isik and Soykan (2013) reported a mean value of 48.57%).

Therefore, it is possible that the private benefits derived by expropriating minority shareholders, diminish as the stake owned by the larger shareholder rises. Large shareholders with lower levels of ownership, but sufficient control, may lead companies to invest more funds in new technologies, at the expense of current profitability, compared to companies where the large shareholders hold a bigger stake in the company. Since the mean value of the total assets employed by the firms has risen significantly during 2013–2015, indicating investments or mergers and acquisition activities this can be a plausible explanation. Additionally, we should also consider the identity of the shareholders since it is an important factor that affects both the agency problem and the decisions for investments (Thomsen and Pedersen 2000). The existence of state-owned enterprises or firms where the main shareholder is another foreign firm have a significant effect on the priorities set by management, concerning the trade-off between current profitability and investments (Zeitun and Tian 2007; Cai and Tylecote 2008), and that difference is reflected in our econometric results.

40.6 Conclusions

The aim of this paper was to investigate the relationship between large shareholders and the profitability of firms. In order to do that we have examined a sample of 14 telecommunications firms of Eastern Europe and the Black Sea Region for a 4-year period of time (2012–2015), using financial and ownership data.

Our results indicated the high levels of ownership concentration in the firms of the sector in this region, along with a decline in the profitability, and an increase in investments depicted in the rise of the value of total assets. Although our findings are statistically significant documenting the relationship between profitability and large shareholders and their value as a mechanism of corporate governance, contradicts relevant literature. More studies examine lower levels of ownership concentration while our study examined a sample with firms where large shareholders own significant percentages of shares. It is possible to argue that although profitability falls as ownership rises due to minority shareholders' expropriation, at a higher level of ownership concentration private benefits stemming from that behaviour diminish, and large shareholders focus on profitability as a priority.

Our research, however, comes with some limitations. The size of the sample is very small, limiting the inclusion of more variables that would help us understand the examined relationship in greater depth. More research should be conducted expanding the time period examined and the examined region to include more firms in the sector. Also, other sectors can be examined to shed more light on the relationship of ownership and performance of the firm, adding more variables concerning the characteristics of the shareholders and their engagement in the decision-making process and the governance of the firm.

References

Agrawal, A., & Knoeber, C. R. (1996). Firm performance and mechanisms to control agency problems between managers and shareholders. *Journal of Financial and Quantitative Analysis, 31,* 377–397.

Andres, C. (2008). Large shareholders and firm performance: An empirical examination of founding-family ownership. *Journal of Corporate Finance, 14*(4), 431–445.

Antoniadis, I., Lazarides, T., Sarrianidis, N., & Goupa, H. (2008). The impact of agency problem in firm value and the greek stock exchange market financial crisis. In *International Conference on Applied Economics–ICOAE,* (p. 27).

Arouri, H., Hossain, M., & Muttakin, M. B. (2011). Ownership structure, corporate governance and bank performance: Evidence from GCC countries. *Corporate Ownership and Control, 8*(4D), 365–372.

Baller, S., Dutta, S., & Lanvin, B. (2016). *Global Information Technology Report 2016*. Geneva: Ouranos.

Balsmeier, B., & Czarnitzki, D. (2017). Ownership concentration, institutional development and firm performance in Central and Eastern Europe. *Managerial and Decision Economics, 38*(2), 178–192.

Bradshaw, M. J. (2017). Foreign direct investment and economic transformation in Central and Eastern Europe. In *Foreign Direct Investment and Regional Development in East Central Europe and the Former Soviet Union* (pp. 41–58). Routledge.

Cai, J., & Tylecote, A. (2008). Corporate governance and technological dynamism of Chinese firms in mobile telecommunications: A quantitative study. *Research Policy, 37*(10), 1790–1811.

Davies, J. R., Hiller, D., & McColgan, P. (2005). Ownership structure, managerial behavior, and corporate value. *Journal of Corporate Finance, 11*, 645–660.

Demsetz, H., & Villalonga, B. (2001). Ownership structure and corporate performance. *Journal of Corporate Finance, 7*(3), 209–233.

Desoky, A. M., & Mousa, G. A. (2013). An empirical investigation of the influence of ownership concentration and identity on firm performance of Egyptian listed companies. *Journal of Accounting in Emerging Economies, 3*(2), 164–188.

Eljelly, A. M. (2004). Liquidity-profitability tradeoff: An empirical investigation in an emerging market. *International Journal of Commerce and Management, 14*(2), 48–61.

Fama, E. F. (1980). Agency problems and the theory of the firm. *Journal of Political Economy, 88*, 288–307.

Fama, E. F., & Jensen, M. C. (1983). Separation of ownership and control. *Journal of Law and Economics, 26*(2), 301–325.

Goddard, J. B., & Gillespie, A. E. (2017). Advanced telecommunications and regional economic development. In *Managing the city* (pp. 84–109). Routledge.

Goergen, M., & Renneboog, L. (2006). Corporate governance and shareholder value. *Commercial management of projects: Defining the discipline,* (pp. 100–131).

Hamadi, M. (2010). Ownership concentration, family control, and performance of firms. *European Management Review, 7*(2), 116–131.

Isik, O., & Soykan, M. E. (2013). Large shareholders and firm performance: evidence from Turkey. *European Scientific Journal, ESJ, 9*(25).

Kapopoulos, P., & Lazaretou, S. (2007). Corporate ownership structure and firm performance: Evidence from Greek firms. *Corporate Governance: An International Review, 15*(2), 144–158. https://doi.org/10.1111/j.1467-8683.2007.00551.x.

Kostyuk, A., Mozghovyi, Y., & Govorun, D. (2018). Corporate governance, ownership and control: A review of recent scholarly research. *Corporate Board: Role, Duties and Composition, 14*(1), 50–56.

La Porta, R., Lopez-de-Silanes, F., & Shleifer, A. (1999). Corporate ownership around the world. *Journal of Finance, 54*(2), 471–517.

Mark, A., & Specht, W. (2019). Assessment of the telecommunications sector from the capital market perspective. In *Future Telco*, (pp. 25–34). Springer, Cham.

Morck, R., Shleifer, A., & Vishny, R. (1988). Management ownership and market valuation: an empirical analysis. *Journal of Financial Economics, 20*(1), 293–315.

Notta, O., Vlachvei, A., & Samathrakis, V. (2010). Competitiveness—the case of Greek food manufacturing firms. *International Journal of Arts and Sciences, 3*(7), 211–225.

Saleem, Q., & Rehman, R. U. (2011). Impacts of liquidity ratios on profitability. *Interdisciplinary Journal of research in business, 1*(7), 95–98.

SEPE (2016). *ICT Market Report 2016/2017 Update.* (*in Greek*). Available at http://www.sepe.gr/files/1/EITO/12thReport/e-Book/files/assets/common/downloads/publication.pdf. Accessed on 27 July 2017.

Shleifer, A., & Vishny, R. W. (1986). Large shareholders and corporate control. *Journal of Political Economy, 94*(3), 461–488.

Shleifer, A., & Vishny, R. W. (1997). A survey of corporate governance. *The Journal of Finance, 52*(2), 737–783.

Scholten, M. H. M. (2014). *Ownership structure and firm performance: Evidence from the Netherlands* (Bachelor's thesis). University of Twente.

Thomsen, S., & Pedersen, T. (2000). Ownership structure and economic performance in the largest European companies. *Strategic Management Journal, 21*(6), 689–705.

Welch, E. (2003). The relation between ownership structure and performance in listed Australian companies. *Australian Journal of Management, 28*(3), 287–305.

Vlachvei, A., & Notta, O. (2008). Firm growth, size, and age in Greek firms. In *Proceedings of International Conference on Applied Economics*, (pp. 915–21).

Zambarloukou, S. (2010). Ownership, corporate governance and industrial relations in the banking and telecommunications sectors: the case of Greece. *Industrial Relations Journal, 41*(3), 233–248.

Zeitun, R., & Gang Tian, G. (2007). Does ownership affect a firm's performance and default risk in Jordan? *Corporate Governance: The International Journal of Business in Society, 7*(1), 66–82.

Chapter 41
Use of Differential Equations in Firms Behavior in an Oligopoly Market

Th. Monovasilis, Z. Kalogiratou, N. Tsounis, G. Bertsatos and S. Moustakli

Abstract Computational biology models of the Volterra–Lotka family, known as competing species models, are used for modeling an oligopoly market. More specifically, a duopoly market is considered. Equilibrium of the two companies is derived under different assumptions about sectoral demand and cost functions. More specifically, at first, linear demand functions are considered, and then two cases of isoelastic demand function are used.

Keywords Differential equations · Oligopoly

JEL Codes C62 · C63

41.1 Introduction

Computational biology models of the Volterra–Lotka family Murray (2002), known as competing species models, are used for modeling an oligopoly market Varian (2003). These models are described by systems of the first-order ordinary differential equations (ODEs) of the form

---

Th. Monovasilis · N. Tsounis · G. Bertsatos · S. Moustakli
Department of Economics, University of Western Macedonia, Kastoria, Greece
e-mail: monoba@kastoria.teiwm.gr

N. Tsounis
e-mail: tsounis@kastoria.teiwm.gr

Z. Kalogiratou (✉) · G. Bertsatos · S. Moustakli
Department of Informatics, University of Western Macedonia, Kastoria, Greece
e-mail: kalogira@kastoria.teiwm.gr

N. Tsounis and A. Vlachvei (eds.), *Advances in Cross-Section Data Methods in Applied Economic Research*, Springer Proceedings in Business and Economics,
https://doi.org/10.1007/978-3-030-38253-7_41

$$
\begin{aligned}
y_1' &= f_1 (y_1, y_2, \ldots, y_n) \\
y_2' &= f_2 (y_1, y_2, \ldots, y_n) \\
\vdots \quad & \quad \vdots \\
y_n' &= f_n (y_1, y_2, \ldots, y_n)
\end{aligned}
\tag{41.1}
$$

where

$$t \in [t_0, T], \quad y_1(t_0) = y_{10}, y_1(t_0) = y_{20}, \ldots, y_n(t_0) = y_{n0}.$$

Means that the rate of change y_i' depends on the other companies $y_1, y_2, \ldots, y_n$. The above is an autonomous problem where t does not appear explicitly.

In this work, we construct a system of ODEs from demand and cost functions. In Sect. 41.2, linear demand and cost functions are considered. In Sects. 41.3 and 41.4, two cases of isoelastic demand function are considered under the assumption of linearity of the cost functions.

41.2 Linear Demand Function

Consider the case of n companies, the demand function

$$P = \alpha - \beta Q$$

where $Q = q_1 + q_2 + \cdots + q_n$ and q_i is the quantity produced by the i company. Consider also linear cost functions

$$C_i(q) = \gamma_i + \delta_i q$$

for the i company. Then, the profit function of the i company is

$$
\begin{aligned}
\Pi_i(q_1, q_2, \ldots, q_n) &= P q_i - C_i(q_i) \\
&= (\alpha - \beta(q_1, q_2, \ldots, q_n))\, q_i - (\gamma_i + \delta_i q_i)
\end{aligned}
$$

The marginal profit is

$$
\begin{aligned}
\frac{\partial \Pi_i}{\partial q_i}(q_1, q_2, \ldots, q_n) &= \frac{\partial}{\partial q_i}(\alpha - \beta(q_1 + q_2 + \cdots + q_n))\, q_i - \frac{\partial}{\partial q_i}(\gamma_i + \delta_i q_i) \\
&= -\beta q_i + \alpha - \beta(q_1 + q_2 + \cdots + q_n) - \delta_i \\
&= \alpha - \delta_i - \beta(q_1 + q_2 + \cdots + q_n + q_i)
\end{aligned}
$$

the proportional rate of change is analog to the marginal profit therefore

$$\frac{q_i'}{q_i} = c_i \frac{\partial \Pi_i}{\partial q_i}(q_1, q_2, \ldots, q_n)$$

$$\frac{q_i'}{q_i} = c_i \left(\alpha - \delta_i - \beta(q_1 + q_2 + \cdots + q_n + q_i)\right)$$

$$q_i' = c_i \left(\alpha - \delta_i - \beta(q_1 + q_2 + \cdots + q_n + q_i)\right) q_i \tag{41.2}$$

Consider the case of two companies

$$\begin{aligned} q_1' &= c_1 \left(\alpha - \delta_1 - \beta(2q_1 + q_2)\right) q_1 \\ q_2' &= c_2 \left(\alpha - \delta_2 - \beta(q_1 + 2q_2)\right) q_2 \end{aligned} \tag{41.3}$$

When $q_1' = 0$ and $q_2' = 0$

$$\begin{aligned} c_1 \left(\alpha - \delta_1 - \beta(2q_1 + q_2)\right) q_1 &= 0 \\ c_2 \left(\alpha - \delta_2 - \beta(q_1 + 2q_2)\right) q_2 &= 0 \end{aligned}$$

There are four equilibrium points

EP1

$$q_1 = q_2 = 0$$

EP2

$$q_1 = 0, \quad \text{and} \quad q_2 = \frac{\alpha - \delta_2}{2\beta}$$

EP3

$$q_1 = \frac{\alpha - \delta_1}{2\beta}, \quad \text{and} \quad q_2 = 0$$

EP4

$$q_1 = \frac{\alpha - 2\delta_1 + \delta_2}{3\beta}, \quad q_2 = \frac{\alpha + \delta_1 - 2\delta_2}{3\beta} \quad \text{and} \quad Q = q_1 + q_2 = \frac{2\alpha - \delta_1 - \delta_2}{3\beta}$$

If the two companies have the same cost function $C(q) = \gamma + \delta q$, then

$$q_1 = q_2 = \frac{\alpha - \delta}{3\beta}$$

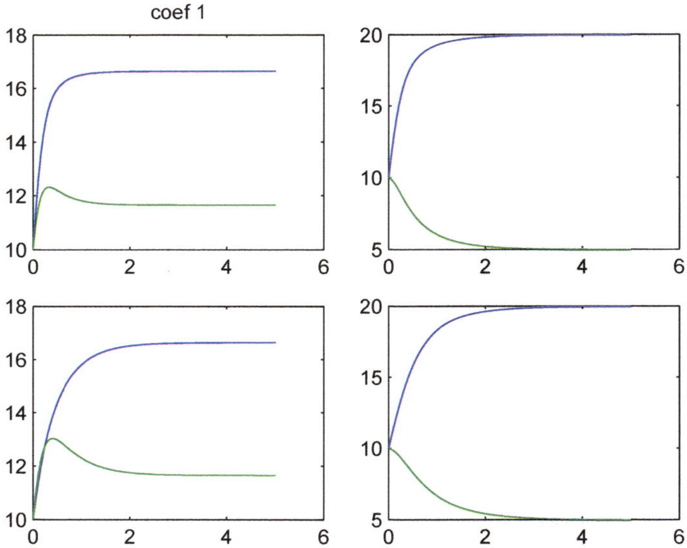

Fig. 41.1 Equal starting values

We have solved system (41.3) for several parameter sets. The system (41.3) is solved numerically, and the classical fourth-order Runge–Kutta method has been employed Butcher (2008). In Fig. 41.1, the quantity curves of the two companies with equal starting values $q_1(0) = q_2(0) = 10$, coefficients for the demand function $\alpha = 10$, $\beta = 0.2$ and the coefficients set are given below

nw $c_1 = 1, c_2 = 1, \delta_1 = 1, \delta_2 = 2,$
ne $c_1 = 1, c_2 = 1, \delta_1 = 1, \delta_2 = 4,$
sw $c_1 = 0.5, c_2 = 1, \delta_1 = 1, \delta_2 = 2,$
se $c_1 = 0.5, c_2 = 1, \delta_1 = 1, \delta_2 = 4.$

In Fig. 41.2, we have used different starting values $q_1(0) = 10$, $q_2(0) = 20$, coefficients for the demand function $\alpha = 10$, $\beta = 0.2$, the same cost function with $\delta_1 = \delta_2 = 1$ and

nw, sw $c_1 = 0.5, c_2 = 1,$
ne, se $c_1 = 0.2, c_2 = 1.$

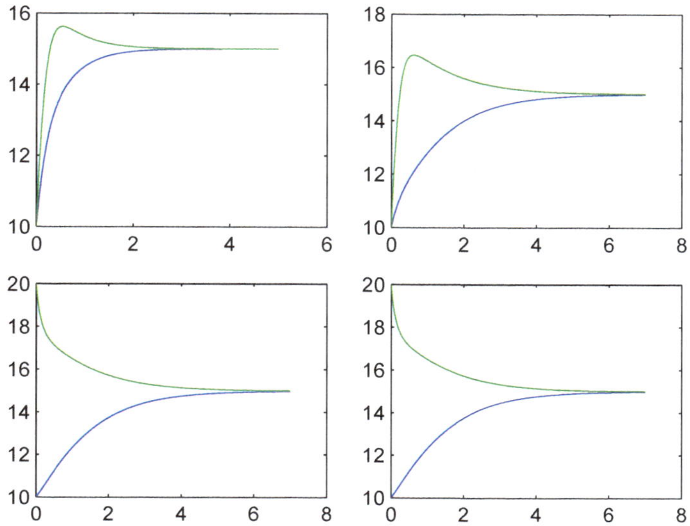

Fig. 41.2 Different starting values

41.3 Isoelastic Demand Function I

Let us consider the demand function

$$P = \frac{\alpha}{Q} \qquad \text{or} \quad P = \frac{\alpha}{q_1 + q_2 + \cdots + q_n}$$

Then, the profit function of the i company is

$$\begin{aligned} \Pi_i(q_1, q_2, \ldots, q_n) &= Pq_i - C_i(q_i) \\ &= \frac{\alpha q_i}{q_1 + q_2 + \cdots + q_n} - (\gamma_i + \delta_i q_i) \end{aligned}$$

The marginal profit is

$$\begin{aligned} \frac{\partial \Pi_i}{\partial q_i}(q_1, q_2, \ldots, q_n) &= \frac{\partial}{\partial q_i} \frac{\alpha q_i}{q_1 + q_2 + \cdots + q_n} - \frac{\partial}{\partial q_i}(\gamma_i + \delta_i q_i) \\ &= \alpha \frac{(q_1 + q_2 + \cdots + q_n) - q_i}{(q_1 + q_2 + \cdots + q_n)^2} - \delta_i \end{aligned}$$

the proportional rate of change is analog to the marginal profit therefore

$$\frac{q_i'}{q_i} = c_i \frac{\partial \Pi_i}{q_i}(q_1, q_2, \ldots, q_n)$$

$$\frac{q_i'}{q_i} = c_i \left(\alpha \frac{(q_1 + q_2 + \cdots + q_n) - q_i}{(q_1 + q_2 + \cdots + q_n)^2} - \delta_i \right)$$

$$q_i' = c_i \left(\alpha \frac{(q_1 + q_2 + \cdots + q_n) - q_i}{(q_1 + q_2 + \cdots + q_n)^2} - \delta_i \right) q_i$$

Consider the case of two companies

$$q_1' = c_1 \left(\alpha \frac{q_2}{(q_1 + q_2)^2} - \delta_1 \right) q_1$$
$$q_2' = c_2 \left(\alpha \frac{q_1}{(q_1 + q_2)^2} - \delta_2 \right) q_2$$

There is one equilibrium point

$$q_1 = \frac{\alpha d_2}{(d_1 + d_2)^2}, \quad \text{and} \quad q_2 = \frac{\alpha d_1}{(d_1 + d_2)^2}$$

41.4 Isoelastic Demand Function II

Let us consider the demand function

$$P = \frac{\alpha}{\sqrt{Q}} \quad \text{or} \quad P = \frac{\alpha}{\sqrt{q_1 + q_2 + \cdots + q_n}}$$

Then, the profit function of the i company is

$$\begin{aligned} \Pi_i(q_1, q_2, \ldots, q_n) &= P q_i - C_i(q_i) \\ &= \frac{\alpha}{\sqrt{q_1 + q_2 + \cdots + q_n}} q_i - (\gamma_i + \delta_i q_i) \end{aligned}$$

The marginal profit is

$$\begin{aligned} \frac{\partial \Pi_i}{\partial q_i}(q_1, q_2, \ldots, q_n) &= \frac{\partial}{\partial q_i} \left(\frac{\alpha q_i}{\sqrt{q_1 + q_2 + \cdots + q_n}} \right) - \frac{\partial}{\partial q_i} (\gamma_i + \delta_i q_i) \\ &= \frac{\alpha \left(2(q_1 + q_2 + \cdots + q_n) - q_i \right)}{2 \left(q_1 + q_2 + \cdots + q_n \right)^{3/2}} - \delta_i \end{aligned}$$

the proportional rate of change is analog to the marginal profit therefore

$$\frac{q_i'}{q_i} = c_i \left(\frac{\alpha \left(2(q_1 + q_2 + \cdots + q_n) - q_i \right)}{2 \left(q_1 + q_2 + \cdots + q_n \right)^{3/2}} - \delta_i \right)$$

$$q_i' = c_i \left(\frac{\alpha \left(2(q_1 + q_2 + \cdots + q_n) - q_i\right)}{2\left(q_1 + q_2 + \cdots + q_n\right)^{3/2}} - \delta_i \right) q_i$$

Consider the case of two companies

$$q_1' = c_1 \left(\alpha \frac{q_1 + 2q_2}{2(q_1 + q_2)^{3/2}} - \delta_1 \right) q_1$$

$$q_2' = c_2 \left(\alpha \frac{2q_1 + q_2}{2(q_1 + q_2)^{3/2}} - \delta_2 \right) q_2$$

There are three equilibrium points

EP1

$$q_1 = 0, \quad \text{and} \quad q_2 = \frac{\alpha^2}{4\delta_2^2}$$

EP2

$$q_1 = \frac{\alpha^2}{4\delta_1^2}, \quad \text{and} \quad q_2 = 0$$

EP3

$$q_1 = \frac{9\alpha^2(2\delta_2 - \delta_1)}{4(\delta_1 + \delta_2)^3}, \quad \text{and} \quad q_2 = \frac{9\alpha^2(2\delta_1 - \delta_2)}{4(\delta_1 + \delta_2)^3}$$

41.5 Conclusions

Computational biology models of the Volterra–Lotka family, known as competing species models, are used for modeling an oligopoly market. More specifically, a duopoly market is considered. Equilibrium of the two companies is derived under different assumptions about sectoral demand and cost functions. More specifically, at first, linear demand functions are considered, and then two cases of isoelastic demand function are used.

Acknowledgements This work has been funded by Project No. 80318, University of Western Macedonia.

References

Butcher, J. C. (2008). *Numerical methods for ordinary differential equations*. Wiley.
Murray, J. D. (2002). *Mathematical biology*. New York: Springer.
Varian, H. (2003). *Microeconomic analysis*. New York: Norton.

Chapter 42
Competitiveness Index of EU Food and Beverage Manufacturing Industries

Ourania Notta and Aspasia Vlachvei

Abstract The objective of this study is the analysis of the current state of the EU food and beverage industry's competitiveness. The present study aims to derive a composite indicator (Industrial Competitiveness Index, ICI) for food and beverage competitiveness using data for 28 EU countries for the period 2008–2016 and to present and discuss the results for each of 10 food and beverage subsectors for each of 28 EU countries. Also, the analysis focuses on the comparison of the relevant results for the two periods 2008–2016 and 2003–2007 (from our earlier research) in order to draw conclusions about the effects of both enlargement of EU on the competitiveness index of food and beverage industry and the effects of economic crisis on competitiveness. Our results suggest that despite the substantial decrease of the indices, the "old" EU countries are the competitive leaders in the food and beverage industry.

Keywords Competitiveness · Food and beverages

JEL code L66

42.1 Introduction

The last forty years there is a growing academic and political debate over better ways to conceptualize and measure competitiveness. Although there are several attempts to define the concept of competitiveness either on a nation/country, industry, or firm level, (EU Commission 2003; OECD 1996; IMD 2004; Martin et al. 1991; Buckley

O. Notta (✉)
Department of Agriculture (Agricultural Economics Program), International Hellenic University, P.O. Box 141, 57400 Thessaloniki, Greece
e-mail: ournotta@farm.teithe.gr

A. Vlachvei
Department of Economics, University of Western Macedonia, Kastoria Campus, Fourka Area, 52100 Kastoria, Greece
e-mail: vlahvei@kastoria.teiwm.gr

N. Tsounis and A. Vlachvei (eds.), *Advances in Cross-Section Data Methods in Applied Economic Research*, Springer Proceedings in Business and Economics,
https://doi.org/10.1007/978-3-030-38253-7_42

et al. 1988; Krugman 1994), there are still troubles with understanding its meaning, its measurement, and its determinants. According to Porter and Rivkin (2012), the wide misunderstanding of the concept of competitiveness has dangerous consequences for political discourse as well as policy and corporate choices that are all also evident today.

Since competitiveness seems to be a multivariable determined concept, the most appropriate way to estimate the level of competitiveness is by using multidimensional or composite indicators (indices) of competitiveness. On the other hand, composite indicators could be associated with several arguments like which are the most appropriate variables to be used (individual indicators), which are the weights representing their relative importance, and which will be the aggregation method (Notta and Vlachvei, 2018; Vlachvei and Notta 2017; Vlachvei et al. 2017; Siudek and Zawojska 2014).

Following Fisher and Schornberg (2007), we developed an Industrial Competitiveness Index as a composite measure for relative and multidimensional economic performance of EU F&D manufacturing industries, covering differences in levels and development of profitability, productivity, and growth for 2003–07 (Notta and Vlachvei 2018). The main advantage of this approach is the aggregation of the different dimensions of the competitiveness concept into one final index score, on which an overall assessment can be based. In this way, industry ranking tables for EU and individual country can be obtained (Notta and Vlachvei 2018). Meanwhile, the political and economic situation in EU changed. The enlargement of EU led to the entry of 11 new members, which make up 40% of the 28 countries currently. Also, the global debt crisis in 2008–09 following the collapse of the US subprime mortgage market led to the 2008 economic recession with a severe impact across the global economy including EU economy.

The main objective of this work is the analysis of the current state of the EU food and beverage industry's competitiveness. The aim of this paper is to derive a composite indicator (Industrial Competitiveness Index, ICI) for food and beverage competitiveness using data for 28 EU countries for the period 2008–2016 and to present and discuss the results for each of 10 food and beverage subsectors for each of 28 EU countries. Also, the analysis will focus on the comparison of the relevant results for the two periods 2008–2016 and 2003–2007 (from our earlier research) in order to draw conclusions about the effects of both enlargement of EU on the competitiveness index of food and beverage industry and the effects of economic crisis on competitiveness. This study contributes to the literature on the discussion of the indices of competitiveness and the progress of competitiveness of EU food and beverage manufacturing industries.

The structure is as follows: After this Introduction section, competitiveness is discussed theoretically. In the third section, the methodology, a composite indicator for sector competitiveness is derived using data for 28 EU countries and the results are presented, along with the main conclusions.

42.2 Literature Review

Microeconomic concepts and indicators of competitiveness have a solid theoretical base because they focus on the essential characteristics of producers in competition for market share and profits or ability to export (Siggel 2006). This ability can be measured by the size or increase of market share (e.g., Mandeng 1991), by export performance (e.g., Balassa 1965), by price ratios (e.g., Durand and Giorno 1987), cost competitiveness (e.g., Turner and Golub 1997; Siggel and Cockburn 1995), or by more complex and multidimensional indicators (e.g., Porter 1990; Buckley et al. 1992; Oral 1993; Siggel 2006). Multidimensional indicators are the most popular in the business economics literature. A review by Waheeduzzaman and Ryans (1996) also pointed out that the competitiveness concept involves different disciplines, such as comparative advantage and/or the price competitiveness perspective, the strategy and management perspective, and the historical and sociocultural perspectives. Competitiveness can also be treated as a dependent, independent, or intermediary variable, depending on the perspectives from which we approach the issue. This variety of levels and approaches actually reflects the wide applications of this concept.

Whatever the levels of focus are, competitiveness is ultimately concerned with the long-term performance of the subject related to its competitors, which is the result of being competitive. Nevertheless, competitiveness is also concerned with what factors lead to being competitive, as well as how it can be achieved. For example, in Oral's (1986) model of the competitiveness of industrial firms, competitiveness is a function of the firm's industry mastery, its cost superiority, and the political–economic environment around it, implying a need for both external and internal considerations of competitiveness. Feurer and Chaharbaghi (1994) viewed competitiveness as an interaction between the level of customer and shareholder values through matching and improving the organization's capabilities, offerings and potential, as well as the organization's ability to act and react through its financial strength. Corbett and Wassenhove (1993) also suggested that a firm's competitiveness has price, place, and product dimensions. Therefore, competitiveness should be considered a multidimensional concept.

Among the micro-economic indicators measuring more than one dimension, the perhaps best known one is the concept of Porter (1990), while Buckley et al. (1992) and Oral (1993) are also interesting attempts to capture more than one dimension of the concept. Porter (1990) developed the "Diamond Model" in which he identified four interrelated factors necessary for sustaining competitiveness: these are firm strategy, structure and rivalry, demand conditions, related supporting industries and factor conditions (key factors that are created, e.g., skilled labor, capital, and infrastructure). The government acts as facilitator in this model encouraging firms to become competitive and creating the environment that enables firms to increase productivity and become more competitive by improving the infrastructure and investing in specialized education and engineering. In fact, it is a multitude of factors that influence the competitiveness of producers, but Porter models them by classifying them under these four facets of a diamond. These facets can be viewed as dimensions along which competitiveness can be measured. Porter's concept has attracted very wide interest in the business and political communities, perhaps because of its comprehensive nature. Buckley et al. (1988) suggested the application of a threefold measure of competitiveness, including competitive performance, competitive potential, and management process. Their model emphasizes the interrelationship of these three kinds of measures. The concepts proposed by Porter (1990) and Buckley et al. (1992) include both static and dynamic aspects. The latter integrates three characteristics of firms or industries, their competitive performance, competitive potential, and their process of management. It is multidimensional and dynamic in that it focuses on the potential of firms to adjust to exogenous changes and to achieve comparative advantage in the future. The indicators of cost and price competitiveness, as well as various composite indicators based on potential (e.g., Porter 1990; Buckley et al. 1992; and Oral 1993), are ex-ante in the sense that they demonstrate a capacity to compete. Ex-post indicators have the advantage that they prove de facto the point of successful competition, but rarely reveal the sources of competitiveness. Ex-ante indicators, on the other hand, tend to show the main sources of the advantage, although the advantage may not yet be realized. Ex-post competitiveness measures the outcome of the competition, while ex-ante measurement reflects the potential competitiveness.

Ajitabh and Momaya (2004) approach includes two strategic levels: (a) assets and performance (an enterprise's competitiveness depends on the combination of tangible and intangible assets, e.g., human resources, material inputs, industry infrastructure, technology, reputation, trademarks), and (b)processes within organization, which together provide competitive advantage and can be termed as sources of competitiveness.

All the research shows that when using the term competitiveness, we need to consider not only the resulting performance or the potential or asset to generate this performance, but also the process for doing so. Nevertheless, in order to apply a multidimensional framework, it is necessary to consider the constructs for competitiveness that are more appropriate and more readily operationalized for it.

Mann et al. (2002) propose the concept of competitiveness as having four characteristics. First, competitiveness is long-term oriented; second; competitiveness is controllable, relating to the various resources and capabilities of a firm rather than simply the favorable external conditions leading to superior performance competitiveness. Competitiveness is also a relative concept, concerned with how competitive a firm is when compared to the rest of the industry. The last characteristic is concerned with its dynamic nature, which involves the dynamic transformation of competitive potentials through the competitive process into outcomes, corresponding to the framework suggested by Buckley et al. (1988).

42.2.1 Competitiveness' Index Composition

Also studies attempted to create a complex measure of competitiveness. Lipovatz et al. (2000) consider labor productivity, vertical integration, technological innovation, and firm size to be critical factors for industrial competitiveness and apply multivariate analysis to assess these factors in the Greek food and beverage industries. They find that productivity evolution correlates primarily with organizational and structural changes and, to a lesser extent, with growth rate and technological innovations. A reduction in raw material consumption per unit product has a positive impact on labor productivity.

Another study, by Fischer and Schornberg (2007), evaluates the competitiveness of the food and drink manufacturing sector in 13 EU countries by calculating profitability, productivity and output growth, and aggregating them into a single competitiveness index per country and product following the United Nations "Human Development Index method," that is to say attributing scores depending on the maximum and minimum values among countries. According Fischer and Schornberg (2007) profitability certainly is a key variable for assessing sector competitiveness (EU Commission 2005) and value added as a percentage of turnover is a kind of profit margin that one often has to rely. Market shares are usually defined as the proportion (percentage) of the total available market (or segment) output or sales that is produced or sold by a company or an industry (Werden 2002; Notta and Vlachvei 2018).

Wijnands et al. (2008) measured the competitiveness of eight subsectors, benchmarked them with four leading world economies, assessed the effect of differences in legal requirements, and predicted future developments using scenario analysis. International economics indicators supplemented with data on legal issues from a survey conducted by leading experts were used to measure competitiveness. They calculated five indicators: (a) annual growth in a sector's share of real value added compared with growth in the total industry, (b) annual growth in terms of the Balassa Index, (c) Growth in the export share on the world market, (d) annual growth in labor productivity of the sector, and (e) annual growth in real value added of the sector. Then, they standardize them so that all have the same mean (0) and the same variance (1), and use the (unweighted) mean value of these standardized scores to compute an overall measure of competitiveness.

Laureti and Viviani (2011) aggregated different dimensions in order to obtain a synthetic measure of firm competitiveness (FC). The synthetic measure of firm competitiveness is obtained using a data envelopment analysis (DEA) approach as a weighted average of three financial measures: return on sales (ROS), return on assets (ROA), and return on equity (ROE). The obtained FC indicator ranges from zero to one for each firm, with higher values indicating a better relative competitiveness. Then a Tobit model is considered to measure the influence of different factors on the measured competitiveness, like productivity. They found that productivity has a substantial effect on firm competitiveness in both "Machinery and mechanical equipment" and "Textile and clothing sectors" and it is stronger in 2002 than in 2005.

It is interesting to note that weights can have a significant effect on the overall composite index and the rankings. Different weights may be assigned to indicators to reflect their economic significance, statistical adequacy, cyclical conformity, speed of available of data, etc. A number of weighting techniques are available of which some are derived from statistical models, such as factor analysis, data envelopment analysis, and unobserved components models or from participatory methods like budget allocation, analytic hierarchy processes, and conjoint analysis. Bowen and Moesen (2011) focus to the issue of aggregation, that is, how to select the weights to be applied to the primitive subindicators (variables) used to form a composite index. They test how the ranking of countries based on the World Economic Forum's (WEF') Global Competitiveness Index (GCI) is changed when the underlying primitive data dimensions of this composite index are aggregated using weights that are endogenously determined for each country, instead of aggregated using the WEF's fixed set of weights applied to all countries. They claim that their approach determines endogenously the "best" weights a given observational unit (e.g., country) on the basis of its revealed performance on each primitive subdimension underlying a composite index. The ranking of countries based on the values of a composite competitiveness index that uses the proposed endogenous weight method is then compared to the ranking based on the WEF's competitiveness index for the year 2006. The rankings are then compared and assessed to determine if the observed difference in the rankings are statistically significant. A comparison of the ranking of countries on the basis of the value of each index reveals that countries do undergo a change in their competitiveness rank when endogenous weights are used.

42.3 Methodology-Competitive Index Measurement, Results, and Discussion

Buckley et al. (1988) suggested the application of a threefold measure of competitiveness, including competitive performance, competitive potential, and management process. Their model emphasizes the interrelationship of these three kinds of measures. It is multidimensional and dynamic in that it focuses on the potential of firms to adjust to exogenous changes and to achieve comparative advantage in the future. Following Buckley et al. (1988), Fischer and Schornberg (2007) overall, simultaneously consider competitive performance (effectiveness as the status of competitiveness), competitive potential (efficiency reveals something about the ability to be competitive in the future), and competitive process (growth as dynamic aspect of competitiveness; Buckley et al. 1988, p 183). So they define competitiveness as a function of profitability, efficiency/productivity, and growth COMPS = f (PROS, EFFS, GROS). That is, they calculate a composite measure for relative and multidimensional economic performance as measured by profitability, productivity, and output growth.

They use the aggregation method for the calculation of an index by taking averages of the different variables. This is the simplest and widely used approach and covers their interest in tracking changes in competitiveness levels (and not only ranks) over time, industries, and countries.

Following Fischer and Schornberg (2007), we build a single composite index, (Industrial Competitiveness Index, ICI), on the methodology used for the calculation of the United Nations' Human Development Index (see United Nations Development Programme, UNDP 2002). We transform all measures into individual indices that are combined into three component indices (one each for profitability, productivity and growth). Then, we use overall maximum $M_k^{\max}$ and minimum $M_k^{\min}$ values rather than the extrema of every particular year and every industry in the calculation process. Thus, the lowest value recorded across industries/units (j) in our period of investigation (years t) will have a zero score for a particular measure k while the highest overall value will receive the score of 100. Hence, the individual index subindicators scores I_{ki} are calculated as follows:

$$I_{ki} = \frac{M_k^{tj} - M_k^{\min}}{M_k^{\max} - M_k^{\min}} \times 100$$

where I_{ki} is the ith subindicator of the kth unit, $j = 1,\ldots..k,\ldots K$ is used to index units and $i = 1,\ldots, M$ to index subindicators. These component indices are then aggregated into the Industrial Competitiveness Index (ICI) by taking their averages which implies equal weighting. Equal weighting reflects a judgment that the different component indices have equal importance within the evaluation process. ICI is the composite indicator of the kth unit on which a final ranking of the analyzed industries and countries is based.

42.3.1 Data

Europe's food and drink industry is a major contributor to Europe's economy, ahead of other manufacturing sectors. That means: 4.57 million people employed throughout the EU, a turnover of €1.1 trillion and €230 billion in value added, which make it the largest manufacturing industry in the EU for 2015. Food and drinks ranked first in the share of total manufacturing value added in 2015, contributing 12.1% to the total manufacturing. In terms of turnover, the food and beverage sector in 2015 covering 15.2% of the total turnover of the manufacturing sector. In half of the EU's 28 Member States, the food and drink industry is the biggest employer within manufacturing. At the same time, the EU is the largest exporter of food and drink products in the world. In 2017, extra-EU exports reached €110 billion, with a trade surplus of €35 billion (FoodDrinkEurope 2018). The data for the empirical analysis were taken from Eurostat databases (Eurostat 2019) covering structural business statistics. In the annual detailed enterprise statistics, manufacturing sectors are classified according to the statistical classification of economic activities in the European Community. For the 28 EU food and beverage processing sector and its subsectors, profitability as gross operating surplus over turnover (GOS in €m/TURN, in €m), productivity as gross value added per employee (GVA/employee, in €m), and growth of production value (PROD, in €m) were available. Output growth is measured as the ratio of subsector's annual production value of year t over production value of year $t - 1$. The period of investigation was 2008–2016. We used 2008 data for the calculation of growth variable. All data were thoroughly checked for outliers, given the significance of the overall maxima and minima in the index calculation. In order to buffer the inherent year-to-year volatility in our data, we calculated a eight-year average (arithmetic means), for 2008–2016. All data were thoroughly checked for outliers, given the significance of the overall maxima and minima in the index calculation. Due to the calculation of eight-year averages, the impact of missing data was minimized.

42.3.2 Results

In Table 42.1, the first column lists overall ICI scores (calculated as unweighted means of the industry ICI scores of all countries) for the food and beverage industries of 28 EU countries for period 2008–16. According the results reporting in the first

Table 42.1 Industrial Competitiveness Index scores for food and beverages subsectors in EU-28 for 2008–2016 and 2003–2007

Industry category	ICI (2008–16)	ICI (2003–07)
C110 Manufacture of beverages	27.90	36.17
C108 Manufacture of other food products	25.83	31.13[a]
C107 Manufacture of bakery & farinaceous products	24.18	–
C106 Manufacture of grain mill products, starches & starch products	23.94	30.27
C103 Processing and preserving of fruit and vegetables	23.77	28.54
C109 Manufacture of prepared animal feeds	23.16	27.37
C104 Manufacture of vegetable & animal oils and fats	23.00	29.83
C102 Processing and preserving of fish, crustaceans & molluscs	2232	25.60
C101 Processing and preserving of meat & production of meat products	21.99	23.85
C105 Manufacture of dairy products	21.54	26.32

Note Industries are ranked by ICI 2008–16
[a]Manufacture of Confectionery & other food products
Source Authors' calculations from Eurostat data

table, the beverage industry with ICI score 27.90, following by the manufacture of miscellaneous food products (ICI score 25.83), the manufacture of bakery and farinaceous products (ICI score 24.18) and the manufacture of grain mill products, starches, and starch products (ICI score 23.94) are the most competitive industrial activities among the 28 EU countries during the period 2008–16. The processing and preserving of fruit and vegetables (23.77), the manufacture of prepared animal feed (23.16) and the manufacture of vegetable and animal oils and fats (23.00) are in the middle positions of the competitive list. In the last three places as the least competitive industries are the processing and preserving of fish, crustaceans, and molluscs (22.32), the processing and preserving of meat and production of meat products (21.99) and the manufacture of dairy products (21.54).

The second column of Table 42.1, presents the overall ICI scores for the food and beverage industries of 17 EU countries for period 2003–2007 from our previous research results (Notta and Vlachvei 2018). By comparing the results between the two periods, some interesting findings arise. First, there is a substantial decrease of the index in all industries. Second, despite the substantial decrease of the index, the most competitive industries in the present period were also the most competitive during 2003–2007. Finally, the ranking of the ten subindustries remains almost the same with slight discrepancies mainly due to the lack of data for some industries from some countries (e.g., there are no data for the large Denmark's dairy industry).

Table 42.2 reports countries' Industrial Competitiveness Index Scores for food and beverages sectors in EU-28 for 2008–2016. The results show that Ireland (30.85) ranked first by a wide margin from UK (27.39), the second country in the ranking. The third most competitive EU food processing country is Austria (26.52) following by Netherlands (26.36) and Belgium (25.75). The first ten places in the ranking are complemented by Norway, Greece, Finland, Italy, and Spain, in this order. Cyprus and Luxembourg hold the last places with 19.23 and 13.04 ICI score, respectively.

In Table 42.3, we compare the countries' Industrial Competitiveness Index scores for food and beverages sectors in EU between the two periods 2008–2016 and 2003–07. Comparing the results for the current period 2008–2016 with previous period 2003–07, it is interesting that despite the substantial decrease of the indices, the four first countries (Ireland, UK, Austria, and Netherlands) were also the most competitive in the same order during 2003–2007. Belgium food and drink industry raises 3 places in the ranking (from the 8th to 5th rank) while Greece fell into the ranking (from 5th to 7th) mainly due to economic crisis. Norway held the 6th position while Finland and Italy went up in the rankings ((from the 12th to 8th rank and 11th to 9th, respectively). Spain held the 10th position, while the "new" countries Poland, Bulgaria, and Slovenia are the new entries in the list of the first 17 countries. Altogether, seven countries have maintained their ranking in the ranking of the food and drink industries' competitiveness in Europe, five countries have been ranked higher, two countries (Greece and Germany) have fallen, and three "new" countries are new entrants to the list of the first 17 countries.

Table 42.2 Countries' Industrial Competitiveness Index scores for food and beverages sectors in EU-28 for 2008–2016

Country	ICI (2008–16)
Ireland	30.85
United Kingdom	27.39
Austria	26.52
Netherlands	26.36
Belgium	25.74
Norway	25.71
Greece	25.65
Finland	25.44
Italy	25.01
Spain	24.82
Sweden	24.66
Poland	24.30
France	24.10
Bulgaria	23.77
Germany	23.54
Czechia	23.34
Slovenia	23.21
Lithuania	23.18
Romania	23.00
Denmark[a]	22.97
Portugal	22.93
Hungary	22.91
Croatia	22.84
Slovakia	21.93
Latvia	21.73
Estonia	21.19
Cyprus	19.27
Luxembourg	13.04

Note [a]Not available data for dairy industry

Table 42.4 presents the ICI scores for the individual EU country for each food and beverage industries. In total of 28 countries, the beverage manufacturing sector is the most competitive sector in half of them (14 countries) (Austria, Belgium, Czechia, France, Croatia, Italy, Lithuania, Greece, Luxemburg, Netherlands, Portugal, Romania, Spain, Sweden), the second most competitive industry in 8 countries (Germany, Denmark, Estonia, Finland, Poland, Slovenia, Slovakia, and Ireland), and the third most competitive industry in 2 countries (Bulgaria and Hungary). By comparing the

Table 42.3 Countries' Industrial Competitiveness Index scores for food and beverages sectors in EU for 2008–2016 and 2003–07

COUNTRY	ICI (2008–16)	Rank	Country	ICI (2003–2007)
Ireland	30.85	1◀1	Ireland	36.32
United Kingdom	27.39	2◀2	United Kingdom	33.34
Austria	26.52	3◀3	Austria	31.74
Netherlands	26.36	4◀4	Netherlands	31.09
Belgium	25.74	5▲8	Greece	31.05
Norway	25.71	6◀6	Norway	30.01
Greece	25.65	7▼5	Luxemburg	29.79
Finland	25.44	8▲12	Belgium	28.81
Italy	25.01	9▲11	Denmark[a]	28.73
Spain	24.82	10◀10	Spain	28.18
Sweden	24.66	11▲14	Italy	27.68
Poland	24.30	NEW ENTRY	Finland	27.05
France	24.10	13▲15	Germany	26.99
Bulgaria	23.77	NEW ENTRY	Sweden	26.16
Germany	23.54	15▼13	France	25.77
Czechia	23.34	16◀16	Czech Republic	24.50
Slovenia	23.21	NEW ENTRY	Portugal	23.71

Note [a]Not available data for dairy industry

results between the two periods, in 9 from 10 countries (Belgium, Czechia, France, Greece, Luxemburg, Netherlands, Portugal, Spain, and Sweden) beverage industry remains the most competitive sector. The 10th country was Finland whose beverage industry has fallen in second place. The beverage sector comprises both alcoholic and non-alcoholic beverages. The sector is rooted in the economy and enjoys a strong connection with the industries throughout its value chain. This goes from the agricultural sector with raw ingredients; to the packaging and raw materials industries; through to the transport and distribution sectors and finally to the supermarkets, shops, bars and restaurants were the products are sold. The sector contributes revenue, jobs, and investment. In addition, the beverage industry delivers employment and provides an important source of tax revenue for many governments.

Finally, manufacture of grain mill products, starches, and starch products represents the first position concerning competitiveness sector for six countries (Cyprus, Denmark, Estonia, Finland, Hungary, and UK), the second position for two countries (Bulgaria, Lithuania), and the third position for six countries (Austria, Belgium, Germany, Netherlands, Norway, and Sweden).

Table 42.4 Industrial Competitiveness Index scores per country and per industry for 2008–2016

Country	C101	C102	C103	C104	C105	C106	C107	C108	C109	C110
Austria	23.09	28.02*[b]	26.77	25.16	23.68	27.92[c]	25.82	25.34	26.96	32.40[a]
Belgium	23.18	24.42	26.93[b]	24.85	23.69	26.58[c]	26.18	25.96	23.48	32.13[a]
Bulgaria	21.24	25.76[a]	24.31	23.76	21.84	25.48[b]	23.65	23.72	22.70	25.19[c]
Cyprus	21.86	–	25.39[b]	–	23.49	25.79[a]	23.58	25.32[c]	22.76	24.55
Czechia	20.27	24.26[c]	22.90	22.17	21.41	21.64	22.54	24.06	24.49[b]	29.69[a]
Germany	21.91	21.85	23.69	22.30	22.75	24.42[c]	24.20	24.26	25.03[a]	24.95[b]
Denmark	22.96	22.74	24.95	28.14[c]	–	29.05[a]	24.08	25.46	23.27	29.02[b]
Estonia	22.30	20.83	24.12[c]	21.83	22.60	27.27[a]	22.93	23.64	–	26.40[b]
Greece	23.72	25.50	25.18	26.67[c]	23.80	24.87	26.67[b]	26.17	24.58	29.36[a]
Spain	23.35	23.22	25.30[c]	23.66	24.70	24.89	24.70	25.91[b]	23.60	28.91[a]
Finland	22.78	23.31	24.58	27.92[c]	23.16	28.97[a]	23.70	27.01	24.03	28.94[b]
France	21.14	22.08	23.33	24.87[b]	23.17	24.61	24.25	24.73[c]	23.62	29.15[a]
Croatia	21.99	24.52[b]	22.35	22.37	22.02	18.94	23.19	23.30[c]	22.48	27.23[a]
Hungary	20.70	17.35	23.76	24.94[b]	21.51	27.50[a]	23.01	23.13	23.30	23.93[c]
Ireland	22.69	25.45	25.74	33.82*[c]	24.05	25.83	25.69	62.16*	24.94	38.07*[b]
Italy	22.14	23.80	23.83	24.94	24.19	25.61	26.00[c]	27.12[b]	24.12	28.40[a]
Lithuania	20.21	22.28	24.19	21.87	22.05	25.17[b]	21.77	23.80	24.44[c]	26.00[a]
Luxembourg	20.86[c]	–	–	–	–	–	25.98[b]	–	–	31.42[a]
Latvia	22.35	22.40	23.68[c]	13.73	22.12	19.55	23.13	23.68[b]	23.99[a]	22.60
Netherlands	22.93	23.80	26.07	24.13	24.66	26.64[c]	25.86	29.43[b]	25.47	34.61[a]
Norway	24.04*	25.06	26.38	22.71	27.03*	27.02[c]	23.51	28.36[a]	26.92	26.11

(continued)

Table 42.4 (continued)

Country	C101	C102	C103	C104	C105	C106	C107	C108	C109	C110
Poland	21.17	23.17	24.68	23.31	22.26	23.65	25.26	28.09[a]	24.43	26.95[b]
Portugal	21.10	21.85	24.35[b]	22.29	22.77	22.13	22.69	23.84[c]	22.12	26.17[a]
Romania	20.96	23.17	23.73[c]	24.03[b]	22.10	21.54	21.89	23.21	22.55	26.86[a]
Sweden	22.03	22.29	23.30	26.77[b]	23.32	26.00[c]	23.16	25.26	23.08	31.42[a]
Slovenia	20.99	23.02	24.63[c]	20.73	23.09	21.47	22.76	26.88[a]	22.21	26.35[b]
Slovakia	20.00	17.87	21.52	21.09	20.88	25.83	23.80	23.54[c]	20.00	24.79[b]
UK	23.68	24.65	29.83*[c]	30.34	26.79	31.16*	27.10*	29.81	30.82*[b]	19.72

Note *First position concerning competitiveness country for the sector
[a]First position concerning competitiveness sector for the country
[b]Second position concerning competitiveness sector for the country
[c]Third position concerning competitiveness sector for the country
Source Authors' calculations from Eurostat data

42.4 Conclusions

Our results show that the beverage manufacturing, the manufacture of miscellaneous food products, the manufacture of bakery and farinaceous products and the manufacture of grain mill products, starches, and starch products are the most competitive industrial activities in 2008–16. Comparing these results with previous period (2003–2007), it is interesting that despite the substantial decrease of the index, all these industries were also the most competitive during 2003–2007 period. Also the ranking of the ten subindustries remains almost the same.

The results also show that Ireland ranked first by a wide margin from UK the second country in the ranking following by Austria and Netherlands in the period 2008–2016. Comparing these results with the previous period, it is interesting that despite the substantial decrease of the indices, these four first countries were also the most competitive in the same order during 2003–2007. Altogether, seven "old" countries have maintained their ranking in the ranking of the food and drink industries' competitiveness in Europe, five "old" countries have been ranked higher, only two "old" countries (Greece and Germany) have fallen, and only three "new" countries are new entrants to the list of the first 17 countries confirming that the "old" EU countries are the competitive leaders in the food and beverage industry.

Finally, despite the enlargement of EU and the effect of economic crisis during the examined period, the results are consistent with our results (Notta and Vlachvei 2018), for the previous period 2003-2007 supporting the credibility of this index.

References

Ajitabh, A., & Momaya, K. (2004). Competitiveness of firms: review of theory, frameworks and models. *Singapore Management Review, 26*(1), 45–61.

Balassa, B. (1965). *Trade liberalization and 'revealed' comparative advantage, manchester school*, No. 33, May.

Bowen, H. P., & Moesen, W. (2011). Composite competitiveness indicators with endogenous versus predetermined weights an application to the world economic forum's global competitiveness index. *Competitiveness Review: An International Business Journal, 21*(2), 129–151.

Buckley, P., Pass, C., & Prescott, K. (1988). Measures of international competitiveness: Critical survey. *Journal of Marketing Management, 4,* 175–200.

Buckley P. J., Pass C. L., & Prescott K. (1992). The Meaning of Competitiveness. In *Servicing international markets: Competitive strategy of firms*. Cambridge: Blackwell Publishers.

Corbet, C., & Wassenhove, L. (1993). Trade offs? What trade offs? competence and competitiveness in manufacturing strategy? *California Management Review, 35*(4), 107–122.

Durand, M., & Giorno, C. (1987). Indicators of international competitiveness: conceptual aspects and evaluation. *OECD Economic Studies, 9*(Autumn), 147–182.

Eurostat. (2019). *Annual detailed enterprise statistics for industry*. Retrieved 27 May 19 from https://ec.europa.eu/eurostat/data/database.

EU Commission. (2003). *European competitiveness report*. http://europa.eu.int/comm/enterprise/enterprise_policy/competitiveness/doc/comprep_2003_en.pdf. Accessed 5 Dec 2004.

EU Commission. (2005). *EU sectoral competitiveness indicators*. http://europa.eu.int/comm./enterprise/enterprise_policy/competitiveness/doc/eu_sectoral_competitiveness_indicators.pdf. Accessed 24 May 2005.
Fischer, C., & Schornberg, S. (2007). Assessing the competitiveness situation of EU food and drink manufacturing industries: An index–based approach. *Agribusiness, 23*(4), 473–495.
Feurer, R., & Chaharbaghi, K. (1994). Defining competitiveness: A holistic approach. *Management Decision, 32*(2), 49–58.
FoodDrinkEurope. (2018). *Data and trends of the EU food and drink industry 2018*. https://www.fooddrinkeurope.eu/publication/data-trends-of-the-european-food-and-drink-industry-2018/. 11 Oct 2018.
International Institute for Management Development (IMD). (2004). *World competitiveness yearbook*. http://www.imd.ch/wcy.
IMD. (2004). *World competitiveness yearbook 2003*. Lausanne, Switzerland: IMD.
Krugman, P. (1994). Competitiveness: A dangerous obsession. *Foreign Affairs, 73,* 28–44.
Laureti, T., & Viviani, A. (2011). Competitiveness and productivity: A case study of Italian firms. *Applied Economics, 43*(20), 2615–2625. https://doi.org/10.1080/00036840903357439.
Lipovatz, D., Mandaraka, M., & Mourelatos, A. (2000). Multivariate analysis for the assessment of factors affecting industrial competitiveness: The case of Greek food and beverage industries. *Applied Stochastic Models in Business and Industry, 16,* 85–98.
Mann, T. W. Y., Lau, T., & Chan, K. F. (2002). The competitiveness of small and medium enterprises: A conceptualization with focus on entrepreneurial competencies. *Journal of Business Venturing, 17,* 123–142.
Mandeng, O. J. (1991). International competitiveness and specialization. *CEPAL Review, 45*(December), 39–52.
Martin, L., Westgren, R., & van Duren, E. (1991). Agribusiness competitiveness across national boundaries. *American Journal of Agricultural Economics, 73,* 1456–1464.
Notta, O., & Vlachvei, A. (2018). Competitiveness index. In Tsounis & Vlachvei (Eds.), *Advances in panel data analysis in applied economic research* (pp. 693–705). Springer.
Oral, M. (1986). An industrial competitiveness model. *IIE transactions, 18*(2), 148–157.
Oral, M. (1993). A methodology for competitiveness analysis and strategy formulation in glass industry. *European Journal of Operational Research, 68*(1), 9–22.
Organisation for Economic Co-operation and Development. (1996). *Globalisation and competitiveness: Relevant indicators* (STI Working Papers 5). http://www.oecd.org/LongAbstract/0,2546,en_2649_33703_1885987_1_1_1_1,00 + html. Accessed 10 Oct 2004.
Porter, M. (1990). *The competitive advantage of nations*. New York: Free Press.
Porter, Michael E., & Rivkin, Jan W. (2012). Choosing the United States. *Harvard Business Review, 90*(3), 80–91.
Siggel, E., & Cockburn, J. (1995). *International competitiveness and its sources: A method of development policy analysis*. Concordia University Department of Economics (Discussion Paper 9517).
Siggel, E. (2006). International competitiveness and comparative advantage: A survey and a proposal for measurement. *Journal of Industry, Competition and Trade, 6*(2), 137–159.
Siudek, T., & Zawojska, A. (2014). Competitiveness in the economic concepts, theories and empirical research. *Acta Scientiarum Polonorum. Oeconomia, 13*(1).
Turner, A., & Golub, S. (1997). Towards a system of unit labor cost-based competitiveness indicators for advanced, developing and transition countries. In *Staff Studies for the world economic outlook, IMF.*
United Nations Development Programme. (2002). *Deepening democracy in a fragmented world* (Human Development Report). Retrieved 15 Oct 2004 from http://hdr.undp.org/reports/view_reports.cfm?type_1.
Vlachvei, A., Notta, O., Karantininis, K., & Tsounis, N. (2017). *Factors affecting firm competitiveness and performance in the modern business world* (pp. 1–358). IGI Global.

Vlachvei, A., & Notta, O. (2017). Firm competitiveness: theories, evidence, and measurement. In *Factors affecting firm competitiveness and performance in the modern business world* (pp. 1–42). IGI Global.

Wijnands, J. H. M., Bremmers, H., van der Meulen, B. M. J., & Poppe, K. J. (2008). An economic and legal assessment of the EU food industry's competitiveness. *Agribusiness, 24*(4), 417–439.

Waheeduzzaman, A. N. M., John K. R., Jr., et al. (1996). Definition, perspectives and understanding of international competitiveness: A quest for common ground. *Competitiveness Review 6*(2), 7–26.

Werden, G. (2002). Assigning market shares for antitrust anlysis. In D. Slottje (Ed.), *Measuring market power. Contributions to economic analysis series* (Chap. 1, pp. 1–29). Amsterdam (North Holland): Elsevier Science.

Chapter 43
Mathematical Modeling of the Brewery Sector in Greece with the Use of Differential Equations

Z. Kalogiratou, Th. Monovasilis, N. Tsounis, G. Bertsatos and S. Moustakli

Abstract Computational biology models of the Volterra–Lotka family, known as competing species models, are used for modeling an oligopoly market, with application to the brewery sector in Greece. Parameter estimation with nonlinear least squares is performed. The findings show the company with the larger market share is experiencing a strong competition from all the other companies of the sector; the coefficient is negative and its value is −0.59. However, the coefficient for the "rest of the companies" in the sector has a positive sign although its value is small, about 0.07. This indicates that smaller companies of the sector benefited by the increase of sales of the first company maybe because they are targeting consumers with different tastes offering a completely differentiated product.

Keywords Differential equations · Duopoly · Brewery sector

JEL Codes C62 · C63 · D43

43.1 Introduction—The Brewery Sector in Greece

The brewery factory was established in Greece in 1864 under the brand name of FIX. Since then, there has been a lot of mobility in the sector. Many brands and companies were established over the years, and some of them are still active. Large brewers adapted to market conditions and have expanded their production, with only a few commercial brands, highlighting their particular characteristics and their origin.

Z. Kalogiratou (✉) · G. Bertsatos · S. Moustakli
Department of Informatics, University of Western Macedonia, Kastoria, Greece
e-mail: kalogira@kastoria.teiwm.gr

Th. Monovasilis (✉) · N. Tsounis · G. Bertsatos · S. Moustakli
Department of Economics, University of Western Macedonia, Kastoria, Greece
e-mail: monoba@kastoria.teiwm.gr

N. Tsounis
e-mail: tsounis@kastoria.teiwm.gr

N. Tsounis and A. Vlachvei (eds.), *Advances in Cross-Section Data Methods in Applied Economic Research*, Springer Proceedings in Business and Economics,
https://doi.org/10.1007/978-3-030-38253-7_43

Today, there is a small number of brewery manufactures with several (about forty) “small breweries” or “microbreweries” which have been active at the local level.

Domestic beer production involves a limited number of large brewers, which have systematic and organized breweries and have extensive distribution networks. These companies have a long-standing presence in the industry, modern facilities and products with strong brands. The domestic beer market circulates a plethora of brands, some of which are imported by production companies to enrich the variety of their products. These large breweries either creating new products or adding new brands to their products in order to maintain or even strengthen their position on the market. In addition, they are constantly pursuing their differentiation, sometimes renewing the packaging of products.

Microbreweries produce beer in small batches and are limited in distribution. The number of microbrewers has seen a significant increase in recent years and from six in 2009, currently estimated at around 40 companies. The tendency to produce more special and more specialized products has led to the establishment of these breweries. In most of the country’s prefectures, there is a small brewery. Regions such as Santorini, Crete, Serres, Argos, Corfu, Tinos, Euboea, Halkida, Chios, Melissenka have already been small or large breweries, many of which have been created mostly over the last five years.

However, although the number of microbreweries has been considerably increased due to competition from the large companies of the sector, their market share is still small.

The paper proceeds as follows: in Sect. 43.2, the mathematical model for describing an oligopoly market is developed. In Sect. 43.3, the brewery sector is modeled by considering the sector consist of two companies: the largest company and the rest of companies that are considered as one. Section 43.4 concludes.

43.2 Mathematical Modeling

Systems of first order ODEs are considered of the form

$$\mathbf{y}'(\mathbf{t}) = \mathbf{f}(\mathbf{t}, \mathbf{y}), \quad \mathbf{t} \in [\mathbf{t_0}, \mathbf{T}], \quad \mathbf{y}(\mathbf{t_0}) = \mathbf{y_0}.$$

where

$$\begin{aligned} \mathbf{y}(\mathbf{t}) &= (y_1(t), y_2(t), \ldots, y_n(t))' \\ \mathbf{f} &= (f_1, f_2, \ldots, f_n)' \end{aligned}$$

We consider the autonomous problem where t does not appear explicitly

$$\begin{aligned} y_1' &= f_1(y_1, y_2, \dots, y_n) \\ y_2' &= f_2(y_1, y_2, \dots, y_n) \\ \vdots & \quad \vdots \\ y_n' &= f_n(y_1, y_2, \dots, y_n) \end{aligned}$$

Means that the rate of change y_i' depends on the other companies $y_1, y_2, \dots, y_n$.

A simple case is to consider linear right hand side functions f_i

$$\begin{aligned} y_1' &= b_1 + a_{11}y_1 + a_{12}y_2 + \cdots + a_{1n}y_n \\ y_2' &= b_2 + a_{21}y_1 + a_{22}y_2 + \cdots + a_{2n}y_n \\ \vdots & \quad \vdots \\ y_n' &= b_n + a_{n1}y_1 + a_{n2}y_2 + \cdots + a_{nn}y_n \end{aligned}$$

in this case, we can find the analytic solution.

We are rather interested in the proportional rate of change $y_i'(t)/y_i(t)$ in which case we can write

$$\begin{aligned} y_1' &= g_1(y_1, y_2, \dots, y_n)\, y_1 \\ y_2' &= g_2(y_1, y_2, \dots, y_n)\, y_2 \\ \vdots & \quad \vdots \\ y_n' &= g_n(y_1, y_2, \dots, y_n)\, y_n \end{aligned}$$

we now assume that the functions g_i are linear which is the case of linear demand and linear cost functions and we conclude the following model

$$\begin{aligned} y_1' &= (b_1 + a_{11}y_1 + a_{12}y_2 + \cdots + a_{1n}y_n)\, y_1 \\ y_2' &= (b_2 + a_{21}y_1 + a_{22}y_2 + \cdots + a_{2n}y_n)\, y_2 \\ \vdots & \quad \vdots \\ y_n' &= (b_n + a_{n1}y_1 + a_{n2}y_2 + \cdots + a_{nn}y_n)\, y_n \end{aligned}$$

43.3 Modeling the Brewery Sector

The main brewery company in Greece for the last decades has been *Athenian Brewery*; in 2009, it represented the 83.5% of the sector but as new breweries entered the market, its share reduced to 50.5%. Over the years *Olympic Brewery*, a subsidiary of Carlsberg Group born by the merger of *Mythos Brewery* and *Olympic Brewery* become the second company of the sector with share 29, 32 and 33% for the years 2015, 2016 and 2017. There are several other small companies having in descending order 7, 4.5 and 4% (three companies following *Olympic Brewery*) in 2017.

We consider the *Athenian Brewery* and the rest of the sector explained by a system of two differential equations of the form

$$\begin{aligned} y_1' &= (b_1 + a_{11} y_1 + a_{12} y_2)\, y_1 \\ y_2' &= (b_2 + a_{21} y_1 + a_{22} y_2)\, y_2 \end{aligned}$$

we will estimate the parameters b_1 and b_2 and a_{ij} s using data from 2009 to 2017. We denote y_{1j}, y_{2j} the values of the functions $y_1(t)$, $y_2(t)$ at time t_j. This is observed data and they are approximated by $y_1(t)$, $y_2(t)$ using the nonlinear least-squares approximation method. The nonlinear least-squares problem that has to be solved is described below and this can be achieved by using an iterative method.

$$\min \sum_{j=1}^{n} \left(\left(y_1(t_j) - y_{1j}\right)^2 + \left(y_2(t_j) - y_{2j}\right)^2 \right)$$

where $j = 1, 2, \ldots, n$ denote discrete moments of time t.

The approximating functions $y_1(t)$ $y_2(t)$ are not known but can be found as the solutions of a system of two differential equations. This problem is well known in numerical analysis, and it is a problem of parameter estimation in ordinary differential equations. The system of ODEs is solved numerically, using a fourth-order Runge–Kutta method (Butcher 2008) and the nonlinear least-squares function in MATLAB Optimization Toolbox is used for solving the nonlinear least-squares problem. Nonlinear optimization methods are iterative methods, and therefore, an initial estimate of the parameters is required to start the iterative process. Further, it is noted that these kinds of methods may only give local solutions. To obtain the initial estimate of the parameters following the work by Kalogiratou et al. (2012, 2013), the nonlinear problem is transformed into a set of linear least-squares problems, one for each company. Then these linear problems are solved and an initial estimate for the parameters is found to be used are an input into the nonlinear method. From the above system of differential equations for each t_j, we have:

$$\begin{aligned} y_1'(t_1) &= (b_1 + a_{11} y_1(t_1) + a_{12} y_2(t_1))\, y_1(t_1) \\ y_1'(t_2) &= (b_1 + a_{11} y_1(t_2) + a_{12} y_2(t_2))\, y_1(t_2) \\ &\vdots \quad \vdots \\ y_1'(t_n) &= (b_1 + a_{11} y_1(t_n) + a_{12} y_2(t_n))\, y_1(t_n) \end{aligned}$$

and

$$
\begin{aligned}
y_2'(t_1) &= (b_2 + a_{21} y_1(t_1) + a_{22} y_2(t_1))\, y_2(t_1) \\
y_2'(t_2) &= (b_2 + a_{21} y_1(t_2) + a_{22} y_2(t_2))\, y_2(t_2) \\
\vdots \quad &\quad \vdots \\
y_2'(t_n) &= (b_2 + a_{21} y_1(t_n) + a_{22} y_2(t_n))\, y_2(t_n)
\end{aligned}
$$

The derivatives can be approximated using finite differences

$$
y_i(t_j) = \frac{y_i(t_{j+1}) - y_i(t_j)}{t_{j+1} - t_j} = y_i(t_{j+1}) - y_i(t_j)
$$

since we have observations for each year.

We derive two linear least-squares problems to solve

$$
\begin{aligned}
b_1 + a_{11} y_1(t_1) + a_{12} y_2(t_1) &= \frac{y_1(t_2) - y_1(t_1)}{y_1(t_1)} \\
b_1 + a_{11} y_1(t_2) + a_{12} y_2(t_2) &= \frac{y_1(t_3) - y_1(t_2)}{y_1(t_2)} \\
\vdots \quad &\quad \vdots \\
b_1 + a_{11} y_1(t_{n-1}) + a_{12} y_2(t_{n-1}) &= \frac{y_1(t_n) - y_1(t_{n-1})}{y_1(t_{n-1})}
\end{aligned}
$$

and

$$
\begin{aligned}
b_2 + a_{21} y_1(t_1) + a_{22} y_2(t_1) &= \frac{y_2(t_2) - y_2(t_1)}{y_2(t_1)} \\
b_2 + a_{21} y_1(t_2) + a_{22} y_2(t_2) &= \frac{y_2(t_3) - y_2(t_2)}{y_2(t_2)} \\
\vdots \quad &\quad \vdots \\
b_2 + a_{21} y_1(t_{n-1}) + a_{22} y_2(t_{n-1}) &= \frac{y_2(t_n) - y_2(t_{n-1})}{y_2(t_{n-1})}
\end{aligned}
$$

After solving these two linear least-squares problems, we derive coefficients

$$
b_1 = 0.495134426266375, \quad a_{11} = -0.094199934594501, \\
a_{12} = -0.155160361498928
$$

and

$$
b_2 = 1.624351990174309, \quad a_{21} = -0.188578521255324, \\
a_{22} = -0.515409512290269
$$

We use these coefficients as starting (initial) values for the nonlinear least-squares MATLAB function (fminsearch). The resulting coefficients for the nonlinear problem are

$$\begin{aligned} a_{11} &= -0.315337677189593, \quad a_{12} = -0.587922150892131, \\ b_1 &= 1.965121477405442 \\ a_{21} &= 0.069559191154965, \quad a_{22} = -0.077899438933097, \\ b_2 &= 0.025060347534725 \end{aligned}$$

In Figs. 43.1 and 43.2, the observed values and the functions $y_1(t)$ and $y_2(t)$ are shown for the starting coefficients. In Figs. 43.3 and 43.4, the observed values and the

Fig. 43.1 Fitting with the starting coefficients Athenian Brewery

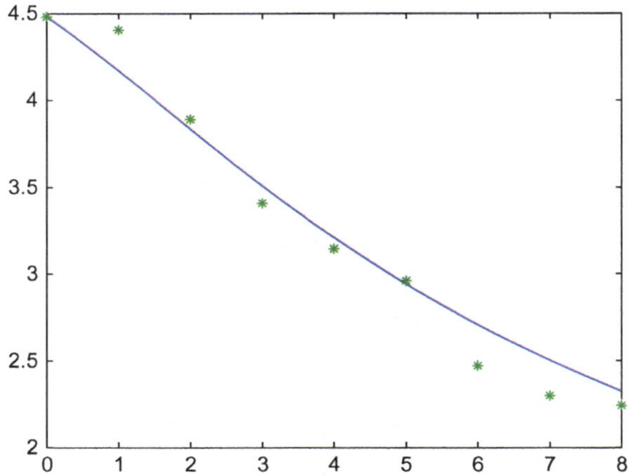

Fig. 43.2 Fitting with the starting coefficients other companies

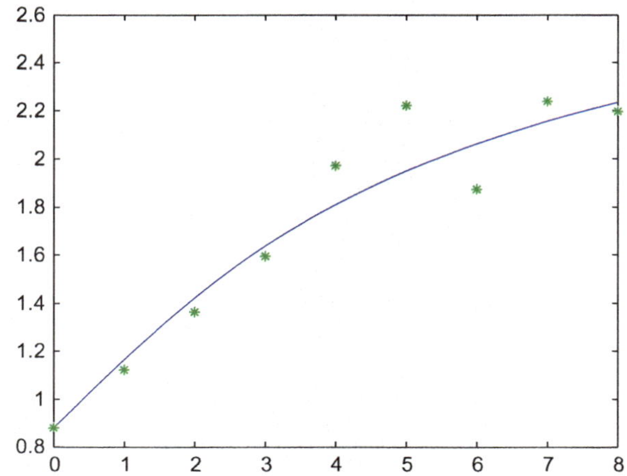

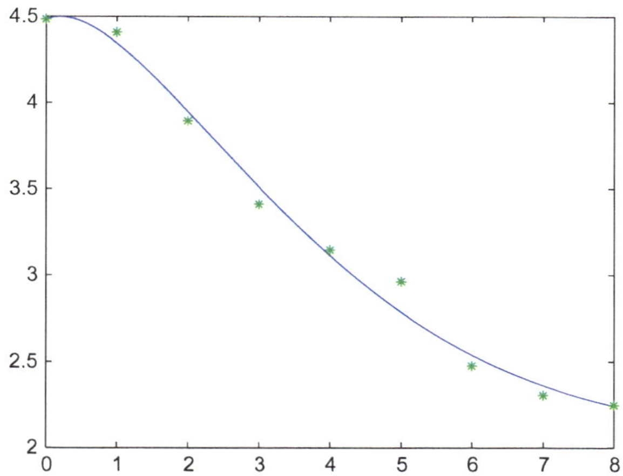

Fig. 43.3 Fitting with the optimal coefficients Athenian Brewery

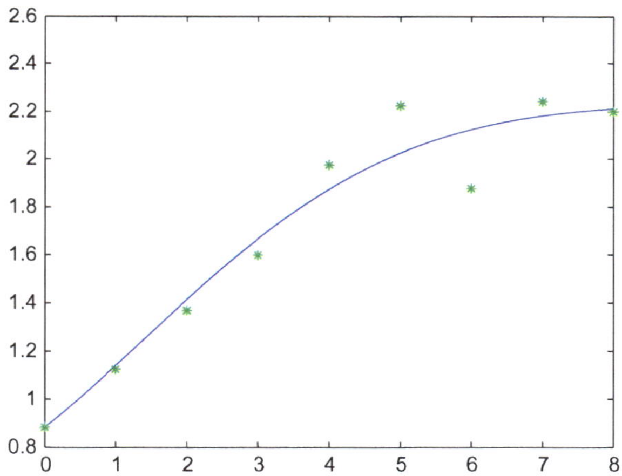

Fig. 43.4 Fitting with the optimal coefficients other companies

functions $y_1(t)$ and $y_2(t)$ are shown for the optimal coefficients found by fminsearch. In Figs. 43.5 and 43.6, the long-term behavior of the sector is presented. In the long run, the system approaches the equilibrium point

$$\lim_{t\to\infty} y_1(t) = 210.53 \quad \text{and} \quad \lim_{t\to\infty} y_2(t) = 221.04$$

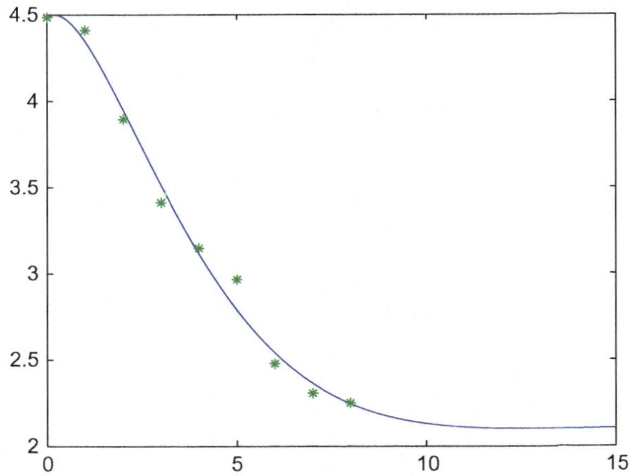

Fig. 43.5 Long-term behavior Athenian Brewery

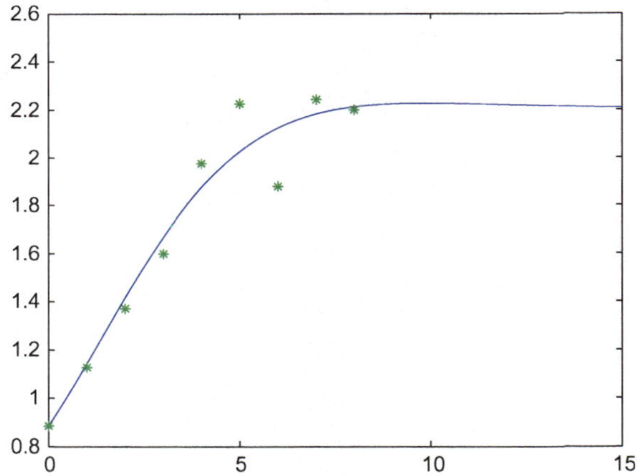

Fig. 43.6 Long-term behavior other companies

43.4 Conclusions

An attempt has been made to model the brewery sector in Greece using ODEs. The sector was considered to consist of two companies, the one that has the largest market share and the second comprising all the other breweries. From the estimated coefficients, it is seen that the company with the larger market share is experiencing a strong competition from all the other companies of the sector; the coefficient is negative and its value is -0.59. However, the coefficient for the "rest of the companies" in the sector has a positive sign although its value is small, about 0.07. This indicates that smaller companies of the sector benefited by the increase of sales of the first company maybe because they are targeting consumers with different tastes offering a completely differentiated product.

Acknowledgements This work has been funded by Project No. 80318, University of Western Macedonia.

References

Butcher, J. C. (2008). *Numerical methods for ordinary differential equations*. Wiley.
Kalogiratou, Z., Monovasilis, Th, & Tsounis, N. (2012). Modeling regional employment. An application in high technology sectors in Greece. *Procedia Economics and Finance*, *1*, 213–218.
Kalogiratou, Z., Monovasilis, Th, Moustakli, S., & Tsounis, N. (2013). Modeling the mobile telecommunications sector in Greece. *Procedia Economics and Finance*, *5*, 385–393.

Chapter 44
New Approach to the Elaboration of Algerian Risks-Industrial Index (IR)

Assia Khenoussi and Hanya Kherchi Medjden

Abstract In this article, we propose to set out some avenues to adapt the Algerian industrial risk index to national data. Firstly, we evaluate the methods used in Algeria to calculate this index while conducting an econometric and statistical study. This study improves that the Algerian index (RI) is explained to more than 96 of various anomalies in these methods who have reached their limits and we will propose a new approach to calculate this index, this last consists in the correction of the weights of all coefficients in the French formula by the method of the weighting of the gross domestic product (GDP), Algerian and French, respectively, as first place to stop our index at its base 1000 in January 2009, and from this date this last one will take half-yearly values readjusted by the values of the other indices that they compose it namely: ICC (construction cost index) of CNAT (national technical assistance center), IPPI (industrial producer price index), IPI (industrial production index) source national statistics office (N.O.S). By validating the transitivity property of our new index, we will establish exclusively a direct application on an insurance portfolio. The results provided by this new approach show an incorrect reclassification of the risks obtained, over the same period, by the two old approaches and the new index, which shows a risk management of insurance contracts problem for the insurer.

Keywords R.I. index · Risk management · Econometric modeling · Composite index

JEL Codes G 22 · G21 · G32.

A. Khenoussi (✉) · H. Kherchi Medjden
ENSSEA Algiers, Kolea University pole, Tipaza, Algeria
e-mail: khenoussi-assia@hotmail.fr

H. Kherchi Medjden
e-mail: hanya.kherchi@gmail.com

N. Tsounis and A. Vlachvei (eds.), *Advances in Cross-Section Data Methods in Applied Economic Research*, Springer Proceedings in Business and Economics,
https://doi.org/10.1007/978-3-030-38253-7_44

44.1 Introduction

The evolution of industrial accidents has taken on a dangerous and tragic turn with more than 19.000 accidents recorded between 1992 and 2009 according to the Office of Risk Analysis and Industrial Pollution (BARPI) (http://www.aria.developpement-durable.gouv.fr/). The increase accident statistics make the action of controlling fire risk a challenge for industrialists, between assuming or transferring the risk, the industrials tend to share these risks with to underwrite a policy's insurance, whose insurers offer negotiated insurances formulas (Pozanna 2015). This agreement is materialized by the subscription of an insurance policy and the determination of a risk premium to be paid "insurance premium."

At the company underwriting the industrial risk fire insurance contract, the risk manager assumes the processing of these insurance contracts in a risk management process where the risks are classified (Morlaye 2006). The introduction of the risk into one of the classes is based on the value of the content of the insured property discounted by a reference index called the "Industrial Risk Index" or the "R.I" index, while respecting the proportional rule of capital, the values of the insured property must be as accurate as possible when subscribing to business risk fire insurance policies to avoid the problem of underinsurance, to this end, the insured capital is subject to indexation in order to protect itself against inflation. Hence, the performance of the management plans for these contracts in the property and casualty insurance company is relatively linked to the relevance of this index, which is the subject of our study.

Risk management is a process used to evaluate risks faced by a firm or an individual and to minimize costs involving these risks. A risk manager uses indicators in order to classify all risks. An index is an indicator expressing the relative variation of the value of a good between two situations, current situation and basic situation. The index of the industrial risks (IR) is an indicator used by insurance markets in order to update amounts appearing in the contract of fire insurance. For the case of Algeria, in order to calculate this index, two methods are used. The first method focuses on the results of the Plenary Assembly of Damage Insurance Companies (A.P.S.A.D), where the second is based on data got from the National Office of Statistics (N.O.S). The econometric analysis of the model applied in Algeria shows that the contribution of the independent variable in the linear model measured by the coefficient of determination (R square) is very high. That is 96% of the variation of the dependent variable (IR Algerian) is explained by the independent variable (IR French).

The aim of this paper is to propose a realistic and operational approach to calculate the Algerian risks industrials index "RI." The estimated model is built on the basis of the correction of all weights, related to the coefficients of the formula of RI by the method of the gross domestic product (GDP), weighting by fixing our new index to the basis of 1000 in the year 2009, in order to anticipate the evolution of this index, explained by the other indices: construction cost index (ICC), industrial production price index (IPPI) and industrial production index (IPI). Finally, after the validation of the circularity property of our new index, we will develop a case study on data corresponding to the portfolio of the non-life insurance branch. A number of outcomes related to reclassifications to obtained wrong risks and various differences on the same period will be the subject of an analysis borrowed from the risk management.

44.2 A Review of the Literature on the RI Index and Its Applications

In order to prevent the economic and monetary phenomenon *inflation*, the insurer uses techniques to discount insured values, and the industrial risks index (RI) presents the better adjustment method used in the insurance market. Statistically, the RI index is a 1000 base index (Lambert-Faivre 1991), whose composite structure reflects the evolution of the main items included in an industrial risk contract like construction, equipment and goods.

In France, according to Lambert-Faivre (1991), the formula of the RI is calculated by (Eq. 44.1)

$$\mathrm{RI} = 45 + 2.26A + 1.71B + 0.8C + 1.42D \tag{44.1}$$

Where, the 45 is a constant value introduced by the Plenary Assembly of Damage Insurance Company in 1975, for the two reasons to stabilize the approved contracts (depreciation deducted) and reflect the cost of the actuarial value.

- **A**: FNB index National Federation of Buildings of the construction cost which was fixed at base 1 in 1941.
- **B**: Labor cost index, for mechanical and electrical industries which was fixed at base 100 in 1997 National Institute of Statistics and Economic Studies (N.I.S.E.S).
- **C**: Index of the industrial sales price for metallurgical products, which was fixed at base 100 in 1990 (N.I.S.E.S).
- **D**: Selling price index of the intermediate goods, which was fixed at a base of 100 in 1990 (N.I.S.E.S).

R.I index is used in different fields mainly:

1. Periodic adaptation of the industrial risk prices.
2. Values updating such as insured values bonus and franchises.
3. Modification of threshold values to upgrade from simple to industrial risk price. In this price upgrade, the threshold is defined as a value of the content (equipment and goods) whether insured or not, in a number of times of RI (100, 350, 600 or 1000) (Fig. 44.1).

According to the study published by the Algerian National Insurance Council N.I.C (2004),[1] the approach of the Algerian industrial insurer has always been based

[1]Source: National Insurance Council; IR index and RS tarif revision, 2004.

Fig. 44.1 Classification of insured risks model

Table 44.1 Methods used by the NIC to calculate the IR Index

Method	Method 1	Method 2
Principle	Use the French RI	Use NOS data and French RI
Method's used	RI(1) = RI Fr * [PC * TC + (1−PC)]	RI(2) = RI Fr * IG /100
	RI Fr: the value of French RI, of the first quarter of the year N−1	IG: general index of prices equal to the average index of the production cost/100 at the first quarter of the year n−1
	TC: the exchange rate the rate of in the first quarter of the year n−1/100	
	PC: the convertible part	
RI declared value	RI = Min [RI(1); RI(2)]	

on the French methodology, where the permanent secretariat of (N.I.C) is in charge of calculating and publishing every six months the RI applicable in the Algerian economy. In the present study, we divided our research into two parts; we evaluated the current Algerian method in the calculation of the RI and then proposed a new method for more accurate determination of the Algerian RI.

44.2.1 Evaluation of the Algerian Method for RI Calculation

The methodology for determining the value of the Algerian industrial risk index is based on two methods available in the study published by the National Insurance Council (N.I.C 2004) the latter methods are summarized in Table 44.1.

44.2.1.1 The First Method

This method is based on the results of the Plenary Assembly of the Insurance Companies Damages (A.P.S.A.D). The value of the index is defined by

$$\mathrm{RI} = \mathrm{RIFr} * [\mathrm{PC} * \mathrm{TC} + (1 - \mathrm{PC})] \quad (44.2)$$

This method is applicable only if the insured has the possibility to give, for one or more unit's sufficient technical information and support, making it possible to recalculate the price of his units; it involves establishing a reconstruction scenario.

This method is mainly based on the samples method which in itself is based on the estimation of the actual cost value using a method widely applied in the engineering companies of one or several units by estimating the cost of equipment, materials, civil engineering works in the assembly and engineering services to build, where the units originated from the active country and taking into consideration the respective parts of materials, works, and services, which may be of local or foreign origin (Lambert-Faivre 1991).

The statistical evaluation of the first and second methods reveals a number of critical points and limitations of these methods. For the sample method, which is not an easy task given the problems related to the evolution of techniques, as well as the problems related to the evolution of prices, there are then anomalies in the formula for calculating the RI index where the multiplication of two values, one in dinars and the other in euros, gives a value in dinars:

Indice RI = RI Fr * [PC * TC + (1 − PC)]

Indice RI in DZD = RI Fr in Euro * [PC(in DZD) * TC + (1−PC)]

44.2.1.2 Second Method

The second method is where the RI index is determined on the data of the Algerian National Statistical Office (NOS) and the French RI index given by the formula (Eq. 44.3)

$$\text{Algerian IR} = \text{French IR} * \text{GI} \tag{44.3}$$

GI: General index of prices equal to the average index of the production cost/100. The value of the reported industrial risk index is the minimum index value calculated by both methods. In order to validate the robustness of these methods used by the National Insurance Council (N.I.C), we proceeded by a simple simulation of the results with real data.

44.2.1.3 Simulation of the Outcomes from both Methods of the (N.I.C) Study Using Real Data

In order to evaluate the second method, which is based in its calculation on the French RI index value and on the cost evolution in Algeria in the various industrial sectors since 1999, we proceed to determine the level of contribution of each variable in the dependent value in the Algerian RI index model, and we proceed to the econometric estimation of Eq. 44.3.

1. **Econometrical study of the RI model**
   The model of the Algerian IR index in the following form:
   Algerian IR Index = French IR * IG
   We will bring the model to a linear form by including the logarithm, and the formula of the index will become:

$$\log \text{RI Algerian} = \log \text{RI French} + \log \text{IG} \tag{44.4}$$

2. **The estimated of the parameters of the model**
   To evaluate the second method, which is based on the French RI and the evolution of costs since 1999 in Algeria, aiming to test the contribution level of each variable in the model of the Algerian RI, we proposed an economic estimation of the logarithmic model according to the following formula:

$$Log \text{ RI Algerian} = log \text{ RI French} + log \text{ IG} \tag{44.5}$$

   The estimated model with the IG variable shows that: the not significant the log variable IG is (P-st 0.85385 >5%) (Table 44.2), we deduce means that the value of the Algerian RI index published by this method is explained by the value of the French RI index at over 96%. Who asserted the hypothesis that the log IG variable is not significant in the Algerian log RI model.
   A second estimation of the model without the variable Log IG 3 With a significant student likelihood of 0.000 < 5%, and R^2 = 0.96% that means that 96% of the variation in the dependent variable (log Algerian RI) is depended by the French RI variable.

Table 44.2 Estimate Of the parameters in the model of RI Algerian index (ONS method's)

Variable	Coefficient	Std. error	t-statistic	Prob
log RI Fr	1.180529	0.0007985	147.8452	0.0000
log IG	0.005491	0.029530	0.18593221	0.8538
R-Squared	0.968193	Mean dependent var		10.02572
Adjusted R-squared	0.0967096	S.D. dependent var		0.167071
S.E of regression	0.030305	Akaike infocriterion		−4.092635
Sum squared resid	0.026634	Schwarz criterion		−4.000120
Log likelihood	65.43584	Hannan–Quinncriter		−4.062477
Durbin–Watson stat	0.685115			

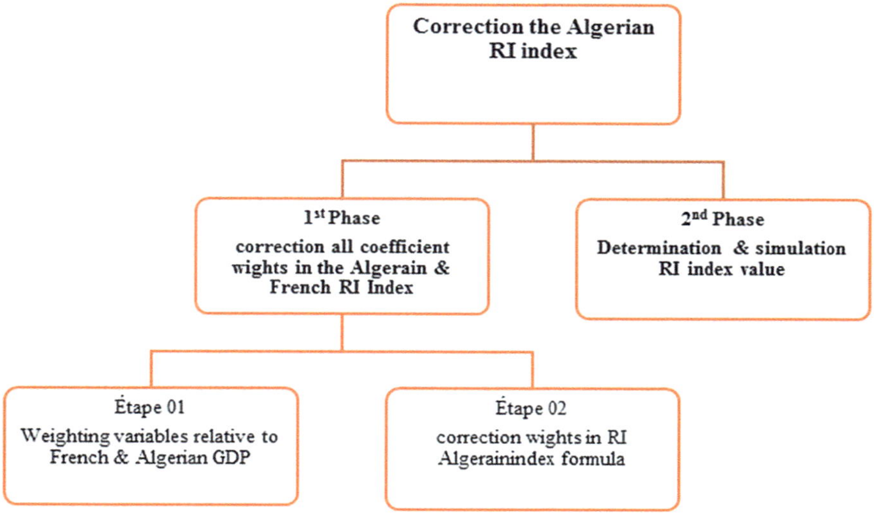

Fig. 44.2 Methodology to correct the Algerian industrial index

44.3 A New Methodology for the Elaboration of the IR Index

44.3.1 Description of the Method

This methodology is based on the weighted distribution of the factors that make up the RI index, by identification, using the contribution of each variable, in the formula of the index in the Algerian and French gross domestic product (GDP) of each of these countries (Table 44.3).

Table 44.3 Restimate Of the parameters in the model of RI Algerian index (ONS method's)

Variable	Coefficient	Std. error	t-statistic	Prob
log RI Fr	1.182009	0.000631	1872.555	0.0000
R-Squared	0.968155	Mean dependent var		10.02572
Adjusted R-squared	0.0968155	S.D. dependent var		1.167071
S.E of regression	0.029814	Akaike infocriterion		−4.15596
Sum squared resid	0.026666	Schwarz criterion		−4.109702
Log likelihood	65.41737	Hannan–Quinncriter		−4.140881
Durbin–Watson stat	0.682988			

44.3.1.1 Basic Hypotheses

For a type of industrial industry:

- 30% goods
- 45% material
- 25% building.

44.3.2 The Development Method

Will take place in two major phases (Fig. 44.2), the first one contains two steps, one for determining the contributions in each variable in the French and Algerian GDP and the other to correct the coefficients of the Algerian formula, and the second phase is where we will determine, and stop the level of the Algerian IR index at its base 1000, we test it and validate it.

1. **Correction of the weights of the coefficients of the Algerian RI index**

a. The weight correction in the Algerian index formula

$$\mathrm{RI} = 45 + 2.26A + 1.71B + 4.02C + 6.56D = 5229 \tag{44.6}$$

The share of industry in GDP in this year is about 14%, the share of each industrial sector in the value added of the sector (Table 44.4) [date base source INSEE (http://www.insee.fr/) and ONS (http://www.ons.dz/)].

- The choice of data from Algerian data[2]: In the absence of the data, as regards the share of the industrial workforce in the mechanical and electrical industry, we will substitute them by share industrial production index (IPI) of the production of the steel, mechanical, metallurgical, electrical and electronic industries (I.S.M.M.E.E), published by the National office of statistics (N.O.S), and we will be interested only in the mechanical and electrical industry.

[2]Elaborate by the authors with data from INSEE and N.O.S (National office of statistics [?] and French national institute for statistical and economic studies http://www.insee.fr/.

Table 44.4 The share of each variable in the Algerian and French GPD

Variable	Algerian GPD (%)	French GPD (%)
Industry	6	14
Industrial labor (mechanical and electric)	0.17	3.78
Metallurgical production	0.93	2.38
Intermediate goods	4.9	7.84
Construction	6.21	6

For the construction cost, we will take the added value of the Public works and Hydraulics Building Sector (BTPH) but without the share of oil services and public works.

b. The weight correction in the Algerian index formula
In 2009, the formula of the RI index stopped at

$$5229 = \text{RI} = 45 + 2.26A + 1.71B + 4.02C + 6.56D \tag{44.7}$$

We stop the value of the Algerian RI index, at its base 1000 on January 1, 2009, we formulate the expression of the Algerian index by identification, with that of the French index in January 2009, with the new coefficients correct we obtain the following formula

$$\text{RI} = 45 + 2.34A + 0.077B + 4.04C + 4.1D \tag{44.8}$$

where:
The constant, which represents the fixed portion 4.5%, is a stabilizing element for contracts most often, underwritten "obsolete deducted," returns to the Algerian experts in pricing the determined.
A: construction cost index based on (CNAT) data, base 100; the base year 1991 [?].
B: production price index (IPI) (source N.O.S) for (ISMMEE), where the sum of mechanical and electrical industries is taken, base 100, base year 1989.
C: price index for metallurgical products (source N.O.S): producer price index (IPPI) for metallurgical products, base 100, base year 1989.
D: index of the price of intermediate goods, which is significantly represents the commodity, we will take the index of the industrial producer price, without those of metallurgy (source N.O.S) base 100; the base year 1989.

2. **Simulation and validation of the new model of the Algerian IR index**

a. Taking the year 2009 as base year, it is from January first, we will readjust the value of this index quarterly, according to the data of the N.O.S and the C.N.A.T (Ministry of Housing), and each year, there will be an adjustment of the coefficients

of the variables according to the rates of their contribution in the construction of the GDP of fact that this last is published annually.
On an Excel spreadsheet, the values of the RI Base 1000 index on January 1, 2009, calculated on the basis of the values, are output from the variables at the beginning of the previous quarter. The new RI index stabilized in value during the period from Q1 2009 to April 1, 2015.

b. Validation of the IR Index Model
The R.I. index is a composite price-indicator that interprets the variations of the other simple index that constitute it in an industrial structure. This index is considered a Laspeyres index, and it is equal to the arithmetic mean of the elementary corresponding indices (prices or quantities) weighted by the initial period values. Moreover, this index is a chained index and has properties that it must check the calculation of chained series. The method used consists in calculating the evolutions from one date to the next and in forcing the transitivity
We have

$$I_{t/t'} = 1000 * \left[\frac{I_{t/t-1}}{1000} * \frac{I_{t/t-2}}{1000} * \cdots * \frac{I_{t'+1/t'}}{1000} \right] \tag{44.9}$$

$$I_{Q_{2-2015}/Q_{1-2009}} = 1000 * 1.003514254 \tag{44.10}$$

We deduce that the RI index is circular (Eq. 44.10); if the weights have changed a lot, since the base period, this index risks losing all concrete meaning.

44.3.3 Application of the IR Index to a Portfolio of Contracts

A panel data of 5606 insurance contracts used in our application provided by an Algerian insurance company, underwritten in one year, classified by their characteristics (region, agency, class, branch, branch, insured, subscription date, effect, expiry, insured capital, contained value, container value, net premium, total premium). A procedure for the treatment of property and casualty insurance risks at company level was made according to the value of the R.I index for this period estimated on 27.261 DZD for the first half and 27.663 DZD for the policies written in the second half on the basis of the (N.C.I) (Fig. 44.3 and Table 44.5).

The policies are classified according to the severity of the risk, determined by separate thresholds that distinguish between simple risks (R.S), the risk with industrial or commercial character (R.I.C) and business risks (R.E).

This threshold is expressed with:

- The value of the content assured is multiplied with value of the RI index (350 or 1000),
- If the indicated threshold is 350, this means that up to a content value of 350 as compared to the RI index, the risk is classified in the RS multi-risk housing

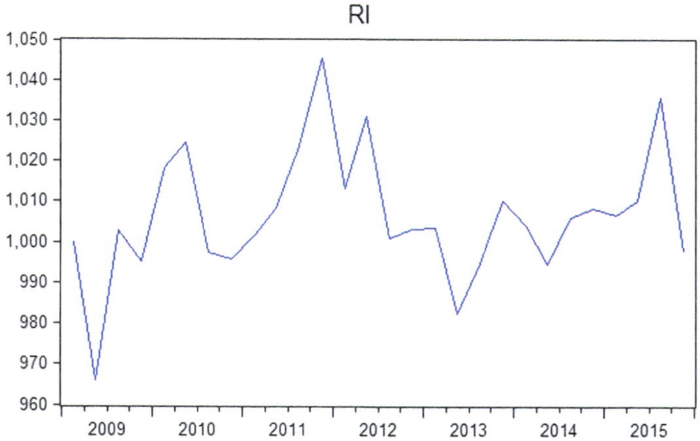

Fig. 44.3 Evolution of the value of the new Algerian index IR base 1000

Table 44.5 Calculates chained series of the index

$Ich_{t+1} = Ich_t + Ich_{t+1/t}$	Ich_t	IR index	Year
1000	1000	1000	2009 Q_1
965,966413	0,965966413	965,966413	2009 Q_2
1002,80909	1,038140747	1002,80909	2009 Q_3
1008,23781	1,00222601	1008,23781	2014 Q_4
1006,46677	0,998243431	1006,46677	2015 Q_1
1010,00375	1,003514254	1010,00375	2015 Q_2

Table 44.6 Amounts of the assured risks in 2012 according to CNA RI index

Period	RE	RIC	RS
Q_1	92 165 374,93	22 872 706,25	3 773 145,93
Q_2	33 345 410,05	23 704 226,63	3 694 131,15
Q_3	24 584 432,06	17 919 212,52	2 643 873,93
Q_4	56 408 523,59	27 046 450,33	3 913 204,59

(MRH), between 350 and 1000 times, the value of the index the risk is covered by the RIC multi-risk professional (MRP) and above 1000 times (Tables 44.6 and 44.7).

Table 44.7 Amounts of the assured risks in 2012 according to the new index

Période	RE	RIC	RS
Q_1	91959248,16	9771894,67	17080084,29
Q_2	33399569,29	8621182,15	18723016,39
Q_3	25571379,36	6098296,18	13477842,97
Q_4	60607622,37	6506462,22	20254093,36

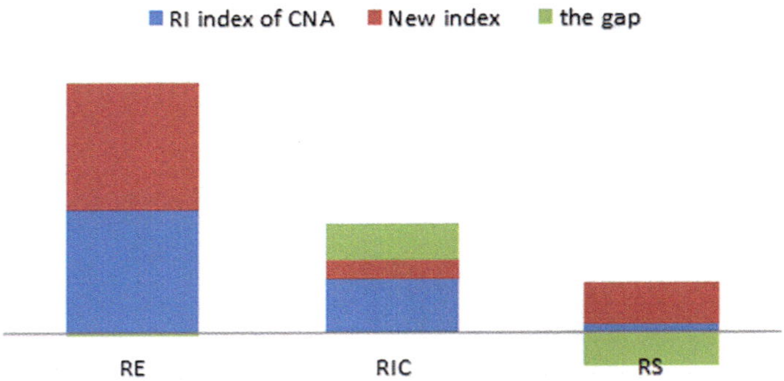

Fig. 44.4 Premium amounts with both indices

44.4 Conclusion

The non-adjustment of the limit values in the tariff of simple risks (with NIC index) and the periodic non-adjustment of the RI index result in the insurers misclassifying certain simple risks into the industrial risks category with premium rates higher than they should have for the policyholders concerned. The management of contracts with the new index is reporting (Fig. 44.4):

- Overestimate for some industrial and commercial contracts (RIC) for an amount of +60 544 760.51 DZD.
- Underestimation of some contracts with an amount of −5 034 078.55 DZD in the business risk class and an amount of −55 510 681.4 DZD for simple risks (SR), this underestimation may lead the company to a critical situation "underinsurance."

This denounces undesired consequences, since this amount is no longer representative of the real values of insurable property in the fire insurance contract, as well as for the industrial risk tariff, which continues to be set without taking into account the evolution of the IR index. The results of this study allowed us to confirm the basic hypotheses set out in the introduction: The methods previously used in Algeria to calculate the RI index have reached their limits. The Algerian IR index follows the evolution of that of France, and it is far from the Algerian reality. However, the elaboration technique to correction Algerian IR based on purely Algerian data, we have been proposed the new present method with success.

Finally, it can be said that our work has highlighted the necessity of using both actuarial techniques and risk management in particular to understand insurance issues.

Acknowledgements We would like to declare that the authors have not receipt funding from an external source. And we like to express our gratitude to Mr. Zerrouki, professor of actuarial science at the ENSSEA in Algiers, with whom we have the chance to discuss and work on the idea of this method.

References

http://www.aria.developpement-durable.gouv.fr.

http://www.insee.fr.

Lambert-Faivre, Y. (1991). Risques & assurances des entreprises. In *Précis Dalloz*, 3rd ed. (p. 162).

Morlaye, F. (2006). Risque management en assurance. *Economica*. Paris.

Pozanna, T. (2015). *Gestion du risque & assurance d'entreprise. Les regards sur la sécurité industrielle*. FONCS.edit.

Study of the Algerian National Insurance Council (N.I.C). (2004). *Indice RI & révision du tarif RS* (p. 10). http://www.cna.dz/Documentation/Travaux-du-CNA/Etudes/Indice-des-risques-industriels.

The national statistical office (N.S.O). Statistical review of economic accounts (pp. 669–670). P02. http://www.ons.dz.

Chapter 45
The Impact of Tourism Demand on Tax Revenues and Bank Loans in Turkey

Mustafa Şit, Ahmet Şit and Haydar Karadağ

Abstract The aim of this study is to investigate the impact of tourism demand on tax revenues and the bank loans granted to the tourism sector in Turkey. The data covers the period 2007Q1–2018Q3. The methods used included the tests of normality, heteroscedasticity, autocorrelation, CUSUM stability, unit root, Johansen cointegration, VECM error correction model and Quantile Regression. As a result, the hypothesis that the increase in tourism demand will increase the tax revenues and use of loans is supported. The findings may serve as a guide for tourism and fiscal policies. The tourism sector should be supported by public policies to obtain higher tax revenues.

Keywords Tourism demand · Tax revenues · Bank loans · Quantile regression test

JEL Classification E62 · C32 · L83

45.1 Introduction

Tourism is one of the main dynamics in terms of country economies. It has many benefits such as contributing to economic development of a country or regional economy, increasing employment, contributing to macro balances by providing foreign exchange inflow to the country and improving the worldwide image of a country. As the number of tourists coming to the country increases, tourism revenues will

---

M. Şit (✉)
Faculty of Tourism and Hotel Management, Harran University, Sanliurfa, Turkey
e-mail: msit@harran.edu.tr

A. Şit
Social Sciences Vocational School, Kilis 7 Aralık University, Kilis, Turkey
e-mail: ahmetsit@kilis.edu.tr

H. Karadağ
Faculty of Economics and Administrative Sciences, Rize Recep Tayyip Erdoğan University, Rize, Turkey

N. Tsounis and A. Vlachvei (eds.), *Advances in Cross-Section Data Methods in Applied Economic Research*, Springer Proceedings in Business and Economics,
https://doi.org/10.1007/978-3-030-38253-7_45

increase. As a result, the revenue of tourism companies and consequently their profitability will increase. The taxes that businesses will have to pay will also increase unless they are tax-exempt.

In a report prepared by the World Travel and Tourism Council (WTTC 2009), it was estimated that the share of tax revenues generated by the direct, indirect and induced effects of tourism demand in total tax revenues would be over 10% by the year 2020 (Kırca and Topal 2017: 98).

Moreover, as the number of tourists increases, tourism businesses resort to capacity building. For capacity extension, they will need more investments; thus, more financial resources. Businesses without capital adequacy will increase their capacity by resorting to foreign resources. Today, bank loans are the most common foreign resource for businesses in the tourism sector. Tourism businesses with the aim of building capacity will prefer to use more bank loans.

The hypothesis that has been tested in this study is that the increase in tourism demand will also increase tax revenues and the bank loans given to the sector in the national economy. In the study, firstly, the literature related to the subject has been presented and the methodology of the research has been explained. Afterwards, the findings of the analysis have been interpreted within the framework of the hypothesis proposed.

45.2 Literature

First, Archer (1982) suggested a positive relationship between tourism demand and tax revenues. Archer explained his theory with the tourism multiplier approach. In many other studies following Archer's study, it was confirmed that the increasing demand in tourism also increased tax revenues (Var and Quayson 1985; Wanhill 1994; Archer and Fletcher 1996; Sinclair 1997). For the economy of Singapore, Khan et al. (1990) investigated the data in 1983. They found that direct and indirect effects of tourism expenditures had an impact on production, income and employment.

In the study conducted on the Malaysian economy, Mazumder et al. (2009) reached similar results. In another study, Palmer and Riera (2003) found that tourism movements in the Balearic Islands caused a significant amount of tax revenue. Yusaku (2002) stated that the increase in tourism demand would create an impact on the income—spending cycle in the economy. In a study conducted on Turkey's economy, Kırca and Topal (2017), examined the long-term relationship between tax revenues and tourism demand with 1998Q1–2016Q4 data. As a result of the research, it was determined that there was a statistically significant and long-term correlation between tax revenues and tourism demand in Turkey. According to the estimator results, the increase in tourism demand positively affects tax revenues.

However, studies on the impact of tourism demand on bank loans are limited. Mowlana and Smith (1990) found that the demand for tourism grew in line with financial services. In his study, Archer (1995) revealed that tourism demand in Bermuda had a positive impact on the finance sector in the country. Cao et al. (2017) stated that tourism and financial loans were correlated and that credit crunch limited the expansion capacity of tourism companies.

In addition, there are also studies focusing on the relationship between tourism demand and financial markets (Chudik and Fratzscher 2011; Galesi and Sgherri 2009). Alzboun (2014) conducted a study on sustainability practices and financial links in the hotel industry in Jordan. He found that high-class and chain hotels had more financial leakage than low-class hotels.

45.3 Data Set and Method

In the study, the number of tourists coming to the country, tax revenues and the bank loans granted to the tourism sector (hotels and restaurants) were taken as the variables of the tourism demand. Tax revenues were retrieved from the official website of the Revenue Administration, bank loans were retrieved from the official website of the Banks Association of Turkey, and the number of tourists as tourism demand was retrieved from the official website of the Association of Turkish Travel Agencies. The data covers the period 2007Q1–2018Q3. Since the 2018Q4 data were not given precisely for each variable, they were not evaluated.

The methods used in the study included the tests of normality, heteroscedasticity, autocorrelation, CUSUM stability, Johansen cointegration, and Quantile Regression. Johansen cointegration test indicates whether there is a cointegrated relationship among variables. In order to perform the Johansen cointegration test, all of the variables must be stationary at the same level (Akpolat and Altıntaş 2013: 120).

The Quantile Regression reveals the effects of the different aspects of the distribution of each variable. It provides different levels of estimation for each of the variables. The relationship between dependent and independent variables can also be estimated by OLS regression method. However, Quantile regression test is different from OLS. The OLS regression estimates the conditional expectation of a response variable taking into account the hierarchical data structure, but cannot characterize the whole conditional distribution of the dependent variable (Baum 2013).

Quantile regression investigates the relationship between dependent and independent variables throughout the distribution. Thus, it portrays how tourism demand affects bank loans and tax revenues at various intervals (Volgushev et al. 2013).

The emergence of different results in different quantiles can be interpreted as the dependent variable reacting differently to the changes in explanatory variables at different points of conditional distribution (Kurtoğlu 2011: 38).

For these reasons, Quantile regression method was used in the study. The two models used in the study are as follows:

$$Q_1\left(\ln \text{Tax}_{i,t}\right) = \alpha_{i+}^{q}\beta_{i,1}^{q} \ln \text{Tourism}_{i,t-1+}\varepsilon \tag{45.1}$$

$$Q_2\left(\ln \text{Loan}_{i,t}\right) = \alpha_{i+}^{q}\beta_{i,2}^{q} \ln \text{Tourism}_{i,t-1+}\varepsilon \tag{45.2}$$

In the equation, Q represents the dependent variables, β; the independent variables and ε; the margin of error. In other words, while tax revenues are the dependent variable in model 1, loans granted to the sector are the dependent variable in model 2.

45.4 Findings

When the variables used in the study; namely tourism demand, tax revenues and bank loans are taken as an amount, they correspond to large figures. Therefore, the data were analyzed by taking their logarithms. Descriptive statistics for the logarithms of the variables used in the study are given in Table 45.1.

In the Jarque–Bera values, H_0 is rejected as the prob values exceed 0.05, so the series is distributed normally. Furthermore, the skewness and kurtosis values ranging from −2.56 to 2.56 show that the series are stationary.

A centered VIF value between 1 and 5 indicates that there is no multiple collinearity among variables. VIF (Variance Separation Factor) refers to how the parameter and variance estimates differ from the actual value as a result of the multiple collinearity. Therefore, the closer the VIF value is to 0, the better it is for analysis. A VIF value greater than 5 indicates that there is multiple collinearity among the variables (Tarı 2011: 161–162).

As seen in Table 45.2, the fact that the VIF values of the variables used in the study are over 10 indicates that there is a multiple collinearity problem among the variables. Since there is multiple collinearity, the analysis could not be continued with this data. The first differences of the series should be taken and continued. When the first differences of the series are taken, the VIF values range from 1 to 5 (VIF = 3.017049). This result indicates that the problem of multiple collinearity among variables is resolved.

According to Table 45.3, there is no autocorrelation problem.

Table 45.1 Descriptive statistics

	LNTOURIST	LNTAX	LNLOAN
Mean	15.74399	18.12895	16.96870
Median	15.71414	18.18399	16.91598
Maximum	16.51441	18.93455	18.37558
Minimum	14.77157	17.34014	15.58384
Std. dev.	0.496695	0.453951	0.822006
Skewness	−0.155410	−0.003967	−0.071292
Kurtosis	1.908549	1.850206	1.754626
Jarque-Bera	2.522089	2.589094	3.077104
Probability	0.283358	0.274022	0.214692

Table 45.2 Multiple collinearity

				First Difference
	Coefficient	Uncentered	Centered	Centered
Variable	Variance	VIF	VIF	VIF
LNTAX	0.707258	49244.70	30.20127	3.017049
LNLOAN	0.215698	13179.79	30.20127	3.017049
C	58.26551	12336.19	NA	NA

Table 45.3 Autocorrelation test

Breusch-Godfrey serial correlation LM test				
Lag length	1	2	3	4
Prob. F (1.42)	0.3011	0.0000	0.0000	0.0000
Prob. chi-square (1)	0.2794	0.0000	0.0000	0.0000

Figure 45.1 shows the analyses of the structural breaks in the series. In both graphs, the blue lines within the orange lines indicate that the series is stationary. There is no structural break in the series.

According to the PP unit root test results which are more reliable than those of ADF, all series are stationary at level (I_0); in other words, they do not include unit root (Table 45.4).

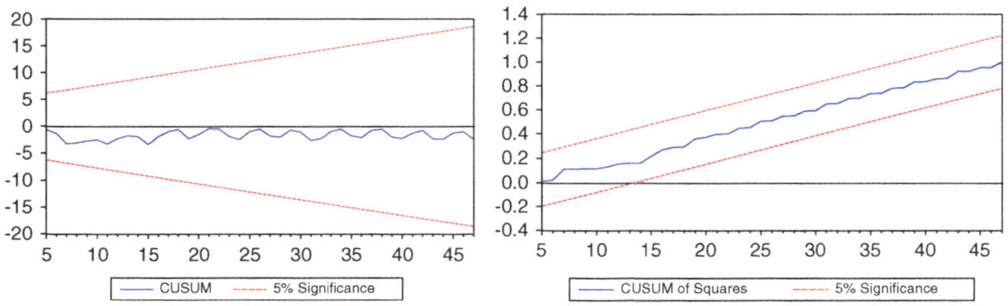

Fig. 45.1 Cusum and cusum square graphs

Table 45.4 Unit root test results

	ADF		Philips Perron		
	T Statistic	Prob	T Statistic	Prob	Stability
LNLOAN	−19.19006	0.0000	−28.08407	0.0000	Series is stable at level
LNTAX	−14.11823	0.0000	−20.65906	0.0000	Series is stable at level
LNTOURIST	−3.390988	0.0669	−12.57774	0.0000	Series is stable at level

Once the unit root test has been performed, the lag length of the series should be determined in order to perform the Johansen cointegration test.

According to Table 45.5, the lag length was determined as 5.

The H_0 hypothesis is rejected since the prob values in both models are below 0.05. There is a cointegration relationship among the series. Subsequently, the error correction model was tested (Table 45.6).

For the error correction model to be valid, the error terms found in the models must be stationary in the series. When the unit-roots of the error terms found for Model 1 and 2 were viewed, it was concluded that the error terms found in both models were stationary in the series. Therefore, error correction model was applied. The error correction model results for Model 1 and 2 are given in Table 45.7.

According to Table 45.7, one-unit deviation in tax revenues compared to the previous year in Model 1 is corrected by 57% in the following period. The one-unit deviation in loans granted to the sector is corrected by 92%.

According to Table 45.8, tourism demand affects tax revenues at a maximum range of 0.10 (about 26%). It has been concluded that the demand for tourism also affects the maximum amount of loans granted to the sector in the range of 0.10 (about 33%).

45.5 Conclusion

As a result of the study, the series were found to have a normal distribution according to Jarque-Bera values. There was also no multiple linear connections between the series according to Centered VIF value. According to CUSUM and CUSUM-squared charts, there was no structural break in the series. As a result of ADF and PP unit root tests, it was found that the series did not have unit roots and that they were stationary. The Johansen cointegration test results revealed that there was a long-term relationship between tourism demand with tax revenues and bank loans in Turkey. According to the VECM error correction model, the deterioration in balance in the previous period is corrected by 0.57 for tax revenues and corrected by 0.57 for loans in the following period.

According to the Quantile Regression analysis results, the fact that the prob value is lower than 0.05 indicates that the model is significant. There is a significant relationship between loans granted to the sector and tax revenues with tourism demand. When the level of being affected is examined, the increase in the demand for tourism has a strong impact on the loans granted to the sector by 33% and tax revenues by 26%. These findings are consistent with the literature. More tourists arriving in the country cause tourism businesses to grow and use more loans. Thus, while the revenues and profits of growing businesses increase, the amount of tax collected from tourism businesses also increases. As a result, the hypothesis that the increase in tourism demand will increase the tax revenues and use of loans is supported. The findings may serve as a guide for tourism and fiscal policies. The tourism sector should be supported by public policies to obtain higher tax revenues.

Table 45.5 Determination of lag length

Lag order selection criteria												
Lag	LogL		LR		FPE		AIC		SC		HQ	
	Model 1	Model 2	Model 1	Model 2	Model 1	Model 2	Model 1	Model 2	Model 1	Model 2	Model 1	Model 2
0	−21.389	−30.114	NA	NA	0.011	0.018	1.231	1.690	1.317	1.776	1.261	1.720
1	6.108	20.607	50.653	93.435	0.003	0.001	−0.005	−0.768	0.252	−0.510	0.086	−0.676
2	43.727	65.966	65.338	78.781	0.000	0.000	−1.775	−2.945	−1.344	−2.514	−1.621	−2.792
3	65.208	78.568	35.049*	20.561	0.000	0.000	−2.695	−3.398	−2.091*	−2.795*	−2.480	−3.183
4	70.013	85.376	7.3336	10.391*	0.000	0.000	−2.737	−3.546	−1.961	−2.770	−2.461	−3.270
5	*76.063*	*92.003*	*8.5963*	*9.416*	*0.000**	*8.910**	*−2.845**	*−3.684**	*−1.897*	*−2.736*	*−2.508**	*−3.347**
6	77.434	94.498	1.8040	3.283	0.000	9.878	−2.707	−3.605	−1.586	−2.484	−2.308	−3.206
7	79.238	97.165	2.1839	3.228	0.000	0.000	−2.591	−3.535	−1.298	−2.242	−2.131	−3.075
8	80.433	98.986	1.3211	2.012	0.000	0.000	−2.443	−3.420	−0.978	−1.955	−1.922	−2.899

* Denote appropriate lag length

Table 45.6 Johansen cointegration test results

Variables	Lag length	Eigenvalue	0.05 Critical value	Prob
Model 1	5	0.250829	15.49471	0.0000
Model 2	5	0.273974	15.49471	0.0110

Table 45.7 Error correction model results

	Coefficient	t-statistic	Prob
Model 1	0.030264	0.738652	0.4642
EC (−1)	−0.570482	−2.971671	0.0049
Model 2	−0.072019	−1.283983	0.2062
EC (−1)	−0.923962	−4.314583	0.0001

Table 45.8 Quantile regression results

	Quantile	0.10	0.20	0.30	0.40	0.5	0.60	0.70	0.80	0.90
Model 1	Prob	0.000*	0.001*	0.009*	0.017*	0.354	0.472	0.768	0.789	0.474
	Coef	0.256	0.219	0.191	0.153	0.048	0.035	0.013	0.010	0.027
	T-Stat	4.699	4.44	3.578	2.473	0.934	0.724	0.295	0.268	0.721
Model 2	Prob	0.000*	0.000*	0.016*	0.123*	0.625	0.557	0.572	0.516	0.89
	Coef	0.328	0.284	0.204	0.102	0.022	0.026	0.022	0.021	0.004
	T-Stat	4.052	3.912	2.503	1.568	0.491	0.59	0.568	0.654	0.139

* Denote appropriate lag length

References

Akpolat, A. G., & Altıntaş, N. (2013). Enerji Tüketimi İle Reel GSYİH Arasındaki Eşbütünleşme Ve Nedensellik İlişkisi: 1961-2010 Dönemi. *Bilgi Ekonomisi ve Yönetimi Dergisi, 8*(2), 115–127.

Alzboun, N. (2014). Assessment of the effect of sustainability practices on financial leakage in the hotel industry in Jordan. *All Dissertations*, 1425.

Archer, B. H. (1982). The value of multipliers and the policy implications. *Tourism Management, 3*(4), 236–241.

Archer, B. (1995). Importance of tourism for the economy of Bermuda. *Annals of Tourism Research, 22*(4), 918–930.

Archer, B., & Fletcher, J. (1996). The economic impact of tourism in the Seychelles. *Annals of Tourism Research, 23*(1), 32–47.

Baum, C. F. (2013). *Quantile regression*. http://fmwww.bc.edu/EC-CS. Accessed March 15, 2019.

Cao, Z., Li, G., & Song, H. (2017) Modelling the interdependence of tourism demand: The global vector autoregressive approach. *Annals of Tourism Research, 67*, 1–13.

Chudik, A., & Fratzscher, M. (2011). Identifying the global transmission of the 2007–2009 financial crisis in a GVAR model. *European Economic Review, 55*(3), 325–339.

Galesi, A., & Sgherri, S. (2009). *Regional financial spillovers across Europe: A global VAR analysis* (IMF Working Papers 09/23). International Monetary Fund.

Khan, H., Seng, C. F., & Cheong, W. K. (1990). Tourism multiplier effects on Singapore. *Annals of Tourism Research, 17*(3), 408–418.

Kırca, M., & Topal, M. H. (2017). Türkiye'de Turizm Talebinin Vergi Gelirleri Üzerindeki Etkisinin Analizi. *Balkan and Near Eastern Journal of Social Sciences, 3*(2).

Kurtoğlu, F. (2011). Quantile Regresyon: Teorisi ve Uygulamaları, Dissertation, University of Cukurova.

Mazumder, M. N. H., Ahmed, E. M., & Al-Amin, A. Q. (2009). Does tourism contribute significantly to the Malaysian economy? Multiplier analysis using IO technique. *International Journal of Business and Management, 4*(7), 146–159.

Mowlana, H., & Smith, G. (1990). Tourism, telecommunications and transnational banking: A framework for policy analysis. *Tourism Management, 11*(4), 315–324.

Palmer, T., & Riera, A. (2003). Tourism and environmental taxes. With special reference to the Balearic ecotax. *Tourism Management, 24*(6), 665–674.

Sinclair, M. T., & Stabler, M. (1997). *The economics of tourism*. London: Routledge.

Tarı, R. (2011). *Ekonometri*. Kocaeli: Umuttepe Yayınları.

Var, T., & Quayson, J. (1985). The multiplier impact of tourism in the Okanagan. *Annals of Tourism Research, 12*(4), 497–514.

Volgushev, S., Birke, M., Dette, H., & Neumeyer, N. (2013). Significance testing in quantile regression. *Electronic Journal of Statistics, 7*, 15–145.

Wanhill, S. (1994). The measurement of tourist income multipliers. *Tourism Management, 15*(4), 281–283.

WTTC. (2009). *Economic impact research*. https://www.wttc.org/. Accessed May 14, 2019.

Yusaku, H. (2002). The expansions of the essays on tourism multiplier model. *The Economic Journal of Takasaki City University of Economics, 45*(1), 15–33.

Chapter 46
VaR and ES Calculation with a Bayesian Dynamic tCopula-GARCH Model

Justyna Mokrzycka

Abstract The aim of the study is to calculate one-day forecasts of the Bayesian value-at-risk (VaR) and expected shortfall (ES) for two kinds of bivariate portfolios and two kinds of datasets. The Bayesian inference for VAR(1)-tCopula-GARCH(1,1), VAR(1)-tBEKK(1,1), and VAR(1)-tDCC(1,1) models and the predictive distribution of ordinary return rates of portfolio are used. The Bayesian VaR and ES fully take into account uncertainty of parameters of model. Moreover, the study also presents the one-day forecasts of VaR with using conditional autoregressive value at risk (CAViaR) with asymmetric slope and ES with employing conditional autoregressive expectiles (CARE) also with asymmetric slope. In order to compare the forecasts of VaR and ES obtained from different models, we use non-Bayesian criteria. The research shows that the calculation of VaR and ES with using tCopula-GARCH model and tBEKK model (or tDCC model for the second dataset) gives similar values of one-day forecasts, taking into account correlation coefficients between predictions from different methods. Moreover the model, which has the highest explanatory power (the highest marginal data density), not in all cases gives the best prediction the VaR and ES considering the non-Bayesian criteria.

Keywords Value-at-risk · Expected shortfall · tCopula-GARCH model · Multivariate GARCH model · Bayesian inference

JEL Classification G11 · G17

46.1 Introduction

The accurate evaluation of risk, especially a portfolio risk, is one of the most interesting areas of research. From practical point of view, this issue is crucial. Both an underestimation of risk and an overestimation of risk may have negative consequences for investors. One of the most commonly used measures of risk is value-at-risk. The VaR measures the least portfolio loss that may occur with established

J. Mokrzycka (✉)
Cracow University of Economics, ul. Rakowicka 27, 31-510 Cracow, Poland

N. Tsounis and A. Vlachvei (eds.), *Advances in Cross-Section Data Methods in Applied Economic Research*, Springer Proceedings in Business and Economics,
https://doi.org/10.1007/978-3-030-38253-7_46

probability α over a certain time horizon, in this research a one-day horizon. This measure has not the property of subadditivity (Artzner et al. 1999); it means that the VaR of the portfolio may exceed the sum of the VaR of each asset in the portfolio. Moreover, the VaR does not specify the potential size of loss, which may happen when loss is greater than the VaR. On the other hand, the VaR is still commonly used by financial institutions and recommended by their regulators, especially in banking sector (see, e.g., Capital Adequacy Directive by the Bank of International Settlement in Basel). Expected shortfall is also risk measure, but it is a subadditive. ES is the conditional expectation of the loss given that the loss is larger than the VaR level.

In this work, the prediction of these two measures of risk for bivariate portfolios is based on using Bayesian bivariate parametric statistical models. We employ Bayesian VAR(1)-tCopula-GARCH(1,1), VAR(1)-tBEKK(1,1), and VAR(1)-tDCC(1,1) models for daily logarithmic rates of return of assets in portfolio. To calculate the one-day forecast of VaR and ES, we use a bivariate predictive distribution of future returns of assets. To employ Bayesian inference makes it possible to take into account uncertainty of parameters of model in the forecasts. In the Bayesian statistical model, the parameters are random variables, which have a priori and a posteriori densities. Moreover to compare the results, we also use other approaches to the prediction these measures; it is based on nonparametric specifications: CAViaR for the VaR and CARE for the ES (Engle and Manganelli 2004).

Over the last decade, quite numerous works about prediction of the VaR or the ES based on parametric statistical models using copulas or multivariate GARCH specification were published (see, e.g., Cherubini et al. 2004; Paralo and Hotta 2006; Huand et al. 2009; Weiss 2013). The results of Bayesian inference for the prediction of these measures with using MSF-SBEKK and SV-GARCH models for large portfolio are presented by Pajor and Osiewalski (2012). To the best of author's knowledge, no results of the prediction the VaR and ES with using predictive distributions and the Bayesian inference in tCopula-GARCH specification have been presented in the relevant literature so far.

In this study, we use the same empirical data as in Mokrzycka (2019) and choose one specification from the Copula-GARCH class of models and from the multivariate GARCH class. Selected models, according to results present by Mokrzycka (2019), have the best explanatory power in its class. In this work, we calculate and assess of the quality of forecasts of the VaR and ES. This is the other issue than comparing the explanatory power of models. The models which are overall leaders of ranking may not be very accurate in some particular aspects—such as tail behavior and risk measurement.

The paper has the following structure. In Sect. 46.2, the concept of portfolio VaR and ES, notation, CAViaR and CARE methods, and non-Bayesian assessment of the forecast are briefly presented. In Sect. 46.3, the Bayesian Copula-GARCH and MGARCH models and Bayesian prediction are shortly discussed. In Sect. 46.4, we present the empirical results of one-day forecasts of the VaR and ES for two kinds of portfolios and two kinds of empirical data. The chapter ends with conclusions.

46.2 Value-at-Risk and Expected Shortfall

Let us consider portfolio consisting of two assets, $S_{t,i}$ denotes the price of asset i at time t, and a_i is the number of units of asset i possessed in given time. The value of the portfolio at time t has the following formula $W_t = a_1 S_{t,1} + a_2 S_{t,2}$, $\left(S_{t,i} > 0, a_i > 0, i = 1, 2, t = 1, \ldots, T\right)$.

The one-period ordinary return rate of the portfolio is $R^*_{t:t+1} = \frac{W_{t+1} - W_t}{W_t}$, $R^*_{t:t+1} = \omega_{t,1} R_{t:t+1,1} + \omega_{t,1} R_{t:t+1,2}$, where $R_{t:t+1,i} = \frac{S_{t+1,i} - S_{t,i}}{S_{t,1}}$, $i = 1, 2$ and $\omega_{t,i} = \frac{a_i S_{t,i}}{W_t}$ denotes the share of asset i in portfolio value at time t. Let Ψ_T is the set of observations on asset prices up to time T. Both notations and definitions in this section is the same as in the paper Pajor and Osiewalski (2012). The one-period ahead value-at-risk for a long trading position with given probability level α, $\mathrm{VaR}^L_{T:T+1}(\alpha)$ is defined by the following formula:

$$P(W_{T+1} \le W_T - \mathrm{VaR}^L_{T:T+1}(\alpha)|\Psi_T) = \alpha, \tag{46.1}$$

which can be written as

$$P\left(R^*_{T:T+1} \le -\frac{\mathrm{VaR}^L_{T:T+1}(\alpha)}{W_T}|\Psi_T\right) = \alpha. \tag{46.2}$$

The one-period ahead value-at-risk for a short trading position with given probability level α, $\mathrm{VaR}^S_{T:T+1}(\alpha)$ is defined

$$P(W_{T+1} \ge W_T + \mathrm{VaR}^S_{T:T+1}(\alpha)|\Psi_T) = \alpha, \tag{46.3}$$

$$P\left(R^*_{T:T+1} \ge \frac{\mathrm{VaR}^S_{T:T+1}(\alpha)}{W_T}|\Psi_T\right) = \alpha. \tag{46.4}$$

The VaR is α-quantile (or $(1-\alpha)$-quantile for a short trading position) of the conditional distribution of one-period ahead return of the portfolio, given Ψ_T.

The one-period ahead expected shortfall for a long trading position with given probability level α, $\mathrm{ES}^L_{T:T+1}(\alpha)$, is defined as

$$\mathrm{ES}^L_{T:T+1}(\alpha) = -E[W_{T+1} - W_T|W_{T+1} \le W_T - \mathrm{VaR}^L_{T:T+1}(\alpha), \Psi_T], \tag{46.5}$$

and respectively for a short trading position:

$$\mathrm{ES}^S_{T:T+1}(\alpha) = -E[W_{T+1} - W_T|W_{T+1} \ge W_T - \mathrm{VaR}^S_{T:T+1}(\alpha), \Psi_T]. \tag{46.6}$$

The ES is the conditional expectation of portfolio profit and loss, given the VaR level is exceeded.

In empirical study based on Bayesian inference (see Sect. 46.3), we assume that we observe daily return rates of assets for $t = 1, \ldots, T$ and we want to predict $R^*_{T:T+1}$, one-day forecasts return of the portfolio kept at time T. In modeling, the logarithmic rates of return are used $y_{i,t+1} = \ln\left(\frac{S_{t+1,i}}{S_{t,i}}\right) = \ln\left(R_{t:t+1,i} + 1\right)$. In order to calculation one-day forecasts of the VaR (Eqs. 46.2 and 46.4), we use the nonlinear function of future logarithmic returns: $R^*_{T:T+1} = -1 + \omega_{T,1}\exp\left(y_{1,T+1}\right) + \omega_{T,2}\exp\left(y_{2,T+1}\right)$. The same approach is used for calculation the one-day forecasts of ES.

Let we denote $D_{t:t+1} = W_{t+1} - W_t$ as daily value changes of portfolio value. Apart from Bayesian inference for the rates of return, we also employ the conditional autoregressive value-at-risk with asymmetric slope (Engle and Manganelli 2004) and conditional autoregressive expectiles also with asymmetric slope (Taylor 2008). Let $q_t(\alpha)$ is the conditional α-quantile of $D_{t-1:t}$, $I_{(-\infty,0)}(\cdot)$ denotes the characteristics function of the interval $(-\infty, 0)$, and then the CAViaR with asymmetric slope is described by the following equation:

$$q_t(\alpha) = \beta_0 + \beta_1 q_{t-1}(\alpha) + \beta_2|D_{t-2:t-1}| + \beta_3|D_{t-2:t-1}|I_{(-\infty,0)}(D_{t-2:t-1}). \quad (46.7)$$

The CARE model has the following structure:

$$\mu_t(\tau) = \gamma_0 + \gamma_1\mu_{t-1}(\tau) + \gamma_2|D_{t-2:t-1}| + \gamma_3|D_{t-2:t-1}|I_{(-\infty,0)}(D_{t-2:t-1}), \quad (46.8)$$

where $\mu_t(\tau)$ means conditional τ expectile, i.e.,

$$\mu_t(\tau) = \underset{\mu}{\arg\min}\, E\left[\left|\tau - I_{(-\infty,0)}(D_{t-1:t} - \mu)\right|(D_{t-1:t} - \mu)^2|\Psi_{t-1}\right]. \quad (46.9)$$

Given τ the best choice of $\boldsymbol{\gamma} = \left[\gamma_0, \gamma_1, \gamma_2, \gamma_3\right]'$ is:

$$\hat{\gamma} = \underset{\gamma}{\arg\min} \sum_{t=1}^{T} \left|\tau - I_{(-\infty,0)}(D_{t-1:t} - \mu_t(\tau))\right|(D_{t-1:t} - \mu)^2. \quad (46.10)$$

We estimate the ES using conditional expectiles (Taylor 2008):

$$\mathrm{ES}^L_{t:t+1}(\alpha) = -\left[1 + \frac{\tau}{(1-2\tau)\alpha}\right]\mu_t(\alpha) + \left[1 + \frac{\tau}{(1-2\tau)\alpha}\right]E(D_{t-1:t}|\Psi_{t-1}). \quad (46.11)$$

We assume $E(D_{t-1:t}|\Psi_{t-1}) = 0$. In order to obtain forecasts of ES for a short trading position, we use Eq. (46.11) to the series $\{D_{t:t+1}\}$ multiplied by minus one.

For backtesting the one-day forecasts of the VaR obtained using methods (Bayesian inference described in Sect. 46.3 and CAViaR methods), we use popular non-Bayesian: the Kupiec test and we calculate the loss functions ("tick" and Lopez) as $L^j = \frac{1}{p}\sum_{t=T}^{T+p-1} l^j_{t:t+1}$, where $\in \{L, S\}$, p is number of forecasts and for

- the "tick" loss

$$l^L_{t:t+1} = \begin{cases} (\alpha-1)\big[D_{t:t+1} + \mathrm{VaR}^L_{t:t+1}(\alpha)\big], & \text{if } D_{t:t+1} < -\mathrm{VaR}^L_{t:t+1}(\alpha), \\ \alpha\big[D_{t:t+1} + \mathrm{VaR}^L_{t:t+1}(\alpha)\big], & \text{if } D_{t:t+1} \geq -\mathrm{VaR}^L_{t:t+1}(\alpha); \end{cases}$$

$$l^S_{t:t+1} = \begin{cases} (\alpha-1)\big[\mathrm{VaR}^S_{t:t+1}(\alpha) - D_{t:t+1}\big], & \text{if } D_{t:t+1} > \mathrm{VaR}^S_{t:t+1}(\alpha), \\ \alpha\big[\mathrm{VaR}^S_{t:t+1}(\alpha) - D_{t:t+1}\big], & \text{if } D_{t:t+1} \leq \mathrm{VaR}^S_{t:t+1}(\alpha); \end{cases}$$

- the Lopez loss

$$l^L_{t:t+1} = \begin{cases} 1 + \big[D_{t:t+1} + \mathrm{VaR}^L_{t:t+1}(\alpha)\big]^2, & \text{if } D_{t:t+1} < -\mathrm{VaR}^L_{t:t+1}(\alpha), \\ 0, & \text{if } D_{t:t+1} \geq -\mathrm{VaR}^L_{t:t+1}(\alpha); \end{cases}$$

$$l^S_{t:t+1} = \begin{cases} 1 + \big[\mathrm{VaR}^S_{t:t+1}(\alpha) - D_{t:t+1}\big]^2, & \text{if } D_{t:t+1} > \mathrm{VaR}^S_{t:t+1}(\alpha), \\ 0, & \text{if } D_{t:t+1} \leq \mathrm{VaR}^S_{t:t+1}(\alpha). \end{cases}$$

For backtesting the one-day forecasts of the ES obtained with using methods (Bayesian inference described in Sect. 46.3 and CARE methods), we compute the mean error (MA), the mean absolute error (MAE), and the mean absolute percentage error (MAPE) (Zhu and Galbraith 2011).

$\mathrm{MA}^j(\alpha) = \mathrm{ES}^{A,j}(\alpha) - \mathrm{AL}^j(\alpha)$, where $j \in \{L, S\}$ and $\mathrm{ES}^{A,j}(\alpha)$ is the average predictive ES:

$$\mathrm{ES}^{A,L}(\alpha) = \frac{1}{J^L} \sum_{t=T}^{T+p-1} I_{(-\infty,0)}\big(D_{t:t+1} + \mathrm{VaR}^L_{t:t+1}(\alpha)\big)\mathrm{ES}^L_{t:t+1}(\alpha),$$

$$J^L = \sum_{t=T}^{T+p-1} I_{(-\infty,0)}\big(D_{t:t+1} + \mathrm{VaR}^L_{t:t+1}(\alpha)\big).$$

$$\mathrm{ES}^{A,S}(\alpha) = \frac{1}{J^S} \sum_{t=T}^{T+p-1} I_{(0,+\infty)}\big(D_{t:t+1} - \mathrm{VaR}^S_{t:t+1}(\alpha)\big)\mathrm{ES}^S_{t:t+1}(\alpha),$$

$$J^S = \sum_{t=T}^{T+p-1} I_{(0,+\infty)}\big(D_{t:t+1} - VaR^S_{t:t+1}(\alpha)\big).$$

$\mathrm{AL}^j(\alpha)$ is the average loss on the portfolio if the loss exceeds $\mathrm{VaR}^j_{t:t+1}(\alpha)$:

$$\mathrm{AL}^L(\alpha) = \frac{1}{J^L} \sum_{t=T}^{T+p-1} I_{(-\infty,0)}\big(D_{t:t+1} + \mathrm{VaR}^L_{t:t+1}(\alpha)\big)|D_{t:t+1}|,$$

$$\mathrm{AL}^S(\alpha) = \frac{1}{J^S}\sum_{t=T}^{T+p-1} I_{(0,+\infty)}\big(D_{t:t+1} - \mathrm{VaR}^S_{t:t+1}(\alpha)\big)|D_{t:t+1}|.$$

$$\mathrm{MAE}^L(\alpha) = \frac{1}{J^L}\sum_{t=T}^{T+p-1} I_{(-\infty,0)}\big(D_{t:t+1} + \mathrm{VaR}^L_{t:t+1}(\alpha)\big)\big|\mathrm{AL}^L(\alpha) - \mathrm{ES}^L_{t:t+1}(\alpha)\big|,$$

$$\mathrm{MAE}^S(\alpha) = \frac{1}{J^S}\sum_{t=T}^{T+p-1} I_{(0,+\infty)}\big(D_{t:t+1} - \mathrm{VaR}^S_{t:t+1}(\alpha)\big)\big|\mathrm{AL}^S(\alpha) - \mathrm{ES}^S_{t:t+1}(\alpha)\big|.$$

$$\mathrm{MAPE}^L(\alpha) = \frac{1}{|\mathrm{AL}^L(\alpha)|J^L}\sum_{t=T}^{T+p-1} I_{(-\infty,0)}\Big(D_{t:t+1} + \mathrm{VaR}^L_{t:t+1}(\alpha)\Big)\Big|\mathrm{AL}^L(\alpha) - \mathrm{ES}^L_{t:t+1}(\alpha)\Big|,$$

$$\mathrm{MAPE}^S(\alpha) = \frac{1}{|\mathrm{AL}^S(\alpha)|J^S}\sum_{t=T}^{T+p-1} I_{(0,+\infty)}\Big(D_{t:t+1} - \mathrm{VaR}^S_{t:t+1}(\alpha)\Big)\Big|\mathrm{AL}^S(\alpha) - \mathrm{ES}^S_{t:t+1}(\alpha)\Big|.$$

If the $\mathrm{MA}^j(\alpha)$ is negative (positive), then the model tends to underestimate (overestimate) risk (Zhu and Galbraith 2011).

46.3 The Bayesian Model and Prediction

Let us consider a bivariate observation on return rates $\boldsymbol{y}_t = [y_{1,t}, y_{2,t}]'$, $t = 1, \ldots, T$, which follows the VAR(1) process:

$$\begin{bmatrix} y_{1,t} \\ y_{2,t} \end{bmatrix} = \begin{bmatrix} \varphi_{1,0} \\ \varphi_{2,0} \end{bmatrix} + \begin{bmatrix} \varphi_{11} & \varphi_{12} \\ \varphi_{21} & \varphi_{22} \end{bmatrix}\begin{bmatrix} y_{1,t-1} \\ y_{2,t-1} \end{bmatrix} + \begin{bmatrix} z_{1,t} \\ z_{2,t} \end{bmatrix}, t = 1, \ldots, T. \tag{46.12}$$

The parameters of (46.12) are collected in $\boldsymbol{\varphi}_0 = [\varphi_{1,0}, \varphi_{2,0}]'$ and $\boldsymbol{\varphi} = \begin{bmatrix} \varphi_{11} & \varphi_{12} \\ \varphi_{21} & \varphi_{22} \end{bmatrix}$. We assume that all eigenvalues of $\boldsymbol{\varphi}$ lie inside the unit circle. The vector $z_t = [z_{1,t}, z_{2,t}]'$ represents a bivariate white noise defined as some conditionally heteroskedastic process.

In this work, the z_t apart from the Copula-GARCH model is also described by the popular tSBEKK(1,1) and tDCC(1,1) structures. For details about this structure, you may see Baba et al. (1989), Engle (2002) or Osiewalski et al. (2006). Stochastic processes $\{z_{i,t}\}$, $i = 1, 2$ follow the GARCH(1,1) structure:

$$\begin{aligned} z_{i,t} &= \varepsilon_{i,t}\sqrt{h_{i,t}}, \\ h_{i,t} &= \alpha_{i,0} + \alpha_{i,1} z^2_{i,t-1} + \beta_{i,1} h_{i,t-1}, \end{aligned} \tag{46.13}$$

where $\alpha_{i,0} > 0$, $\alpha_{i,1} \geq 0$, $\beta_{i,1} \geq 0$, $\alpha_{i,1} + \beta_{i,1} < 1$. For independent and identically distributed random variables $\varepsilon_{i,t}$ we assume symmetric t-Student distribution with zero mean and unit precision. Note that we do not standardize the noise, so that $E\left(\varepsilon_{i,t}^2\right) = \nu_i/(\nu_i - 2)$ if $\nu_i > 2$.

The Copula-GARCH model, proposed by Patton (2006) and Jondeau and Rocklinger (2006), uses a conditional copula and Sklar's theorem (Sklar 1959) to describe dependence between the components of $\boldsymbol{\varepsilon}_t = (\varepsilon_{1,t}, \varepsilon_{2,t})'$. The conditional density function of $\boldsymbol{\varepsilon}_t$ has the following representation:

$$p_{\boldsymbol{\varepsilon}_t}\left(\varepsilon_{1,t}, \varepsilon_{2,t}|\Psi_{t-1}\right) = c_t\left(t_1\left(\varepsilon_{1,t}|\Psi_{t-1}\right), t_2\left(\varepsilon_{2,t}|\Psi_{t-1}\right)|\Psi_{t-1}\right) \\ \times f_{t_1}\left(\varepsilon_{1,t}|\Psi_{t-1}\right) f_{t_2}\left(\varepsilon_{2,t}|\Psi_{t-1}\right),$$

where c_t is the density of conditional t-Student dynamic copula, whereas t_{ν_1} and $f_{t_{\nu_1}}$ are the univariate symmetric t-Student cumulative distribution and density function, respectively, with ν_1 degree of freedom. The parameter ρ of the t-Student copula is varying on time as proposed by Tse and Tsui (2002):

$$\rho_t = (1 - \alpha - \beta)\rho + \alpha\xi_{t-1} + \beta\rho_{t-1}$$

where $\alpha \geq 0, \beta \geq 0, \alpha + \beta < 1$ and $\xi_t = \frac{\sum_{i=0}^{1} \varepsilon_{1,t-i}\varepsilon_{2,t-i}}{\sqrt{\sum_{i=0}^{1} \varepsilon_{1,t-i}^2 \varepsilon_{2,t-i}^2}}$.

Let $\boldsymbol{\theta} \in \Theta \subset R^m$ be a vector of parameters consisting of the elements of $\boldsymbol{\varphi}_0$ and $\boldsymbol{\varphi}$ as well as the parameters of the volatility process. The Bayesian statistical model is uniquely determined by the joint probability (density) function of observations (included the forecasted ones) and parameters:

$$p(\widetilde{\boldsymbol{y}}, \boldsymbol{\theta}) = p(\widetilde{\boldsymbol{y}}|\boldsymbol{\theta})p(\boldsymbol{\theta}), \tag{46.14}$$

where $\widetilde{\boldsymbol{y}} = \left[\boldsymbol{y}_1, \ldots, \boldsymbol{y}_T, \boldsymbol{y}_{T+1}\right] = \left[\boldsymbol{y}, \boldsymbol{y}_{T+1}\right]$ is the matrix of observations ($\boldsymbol{y}_{T+1}$ is forecasted), $p(\widetilde{\boldsymbol{y}}|\boldsymbol{\theta})$ is the sampling density, and $p(\boldsymbol{\theta})$ represents the prior density. Bayesian inference relies on the decomposition of the joint density in Eq. (46.14):

$$p\left(\boldsymbol{y}, \boldsymbol{y}_{T+1}, \boldsymbol{\theta}\right) = p\left(\boldsymbol{y}_{T+1}|\boldsymbol{y}, \boldsymbol{\theta}\right)p(\boldsymbol{y}|\boldsymbol{\theta})p(\boldsymbol{\theta}) = p\left(\boldsymbol{y}_{T+1}|\boldsymbol{y}, \boldsymbol{\theta}\right)p(\boldsymbol{\theta}|\boldsymbol{y})p(\boldsymbol{y}),$$

where $p(\boldsymbol{y})$ is the marginal data density, defined as

$$p(\boldsymbol{y}) = \int_{\Theta} p(\boldsymbol{y}|\boldsymbol{\theta})p(\boldsymbol{\theta})\mathrm{d}\boldsymbol{\theta}.$$

The joint posterior density—predictive density function:

$$p\left(\boldsymbol{\theta}, \boldsymbol{y}_{T+1}|\boldsymbol{y}\right) = p\left(\boldsymbol{y}_{T+1}|\boldsymbol{y}, \boldsymbol{\theta}\right)p(\boldsymbol{\theta}|\boldsymbol{y}),$$

where the $p\big(y_{T+1}|y,\theta\big)$ is the sampling predictive density, and $p(\theta|y) = \frac{p(y,\theta)}{p(y)} = \frac{p(y|\theta)p(\theta)}{p(y)}$ is the posterior density (Osiewalski and Pajor 2010).

In order to prediction of future returns and calculation of the VaR according to Eqs. (46.2) and (46.4), we use the Bayesian predictive distribution:

$$p\big(y_{T+1}|y\big) = \int_{\Theta} p\big(y_{T+1}|y,\theta\big)p(\theta|y)\mathrm{d}\theta.$$

The predictive distribution of the one-day ordinary returns $R^*_{t:t+1}$ is directly obtained from $p\big(y_{T+1}|y\big)$. The foundation of Bayesian VaR and ES assessment can be found in Osiewalski and Pajor (2010), Pajor and Osiewalski (2012).

In order to complete the Bayesian AR(1)-tSBEKK(1,1) model, we use the same prior density as Osiewalski et al. (2006) and for the Bayesian VAR(1)-tDCC(1,1) model the same prior density as Osiewalski and Pipień (2005). The prior density for the VAR(1)-tCopula-GARCH(1,1) specification is similar as for tDCC, for details you may see Mokrzycka (2019).

Due to a rather complicated form of the joint data and parameters' distribution, $p(\tilde{y},\theta)$, to obtain the Bayesian predictive distribution usually requires numerical techniques. To that end, in our paper we resort to the Monte Carlo method with importance sampling (MCIS). The histogram of Bayesian predictive distribution is obtained by 1 million draw from the importance function. The details of this approach can be found in Geweke (1989). In this work, for the importance function we take the one of the multivariate t-Student distribution with 3 degrees of freedom, which remains in accordance with Evans and Swartz (1995) or Osiewalski and Pipień (1999). The other parameters of this distribution (i.e., the mean vector and covariance matrix) were estimated iteratively, based on at least 100,000 initial passes of the algorithm, with monitoring the numerical errors.

46.4 Empirical Study

In our empirical study, we consider $p = 518$ (from September 22, 2015 till September 21, 2017) one-day forecasts $\mathrm{VaR}^j_{t:t+1}(\alpha)$, $\mathrm{ES}^j_{t:t+1}(\alpha)$ of two bivariate portfolios and $\alpha \in \{0.01, 0.05, 0.1\}$, $j \in \{L, S\}$, $t = T, \ldots .T + p - 1$. Portfolio no. 1 consists of one unit of each assets, i.e., $a_1 = 1, a_2 = 1$. Portfolio no. 2 is constructed that the share of each assets in the time T portfolio value is $\frac{1}{2}$, $\big(\omega_{T,1} = \omega_{T,2} = \frac{1}{2}\big)$, $T =$ 21.09.2015. Moreover, we use two kinds of datasets. As the datasets we use the same data as Mokrzycka (2019): the series of logarithmic daily returns of two exchange rates: EUR/PLN and USD/PLN, and the series of logarithmic daily returns of two stock market indices: SP500 and BUX, over the period August 1, 2005, till September 21, 2015. BUX Index prices from September 22, 2015 till September 21, 2017 have been converted into USD. The choice of this empirical data and also the Bayesian tCopula-GARCH and MGARCH models is deliberate. One of the purposes of this work is to compare the assessment of forecasts of the VaR and ES obtained with using Copula-GARCH and MGARCH models (AR(1)-tCopula-GARCH(1,1) and AR(1)-tSBEKK(1,1) models for exchange rates and VAR(1)-tCopula-GARCH(1,1) and VAR(1)-tDCC(1,1) models for stock market indices). According to Mokrzycka (2019), the AR(1)-tSBEKK(1,1) structure has the highest explanatory power for the exchange rates and the VAR(1)-tCopula-GARCH(1,1) structure for the stock market indices. Now, our results point to that the predictions of the VaR and ES with using the model which has the higher explanatory power may have worse assessment in different trading position or probability level α.

For Bayesian estimation of models, the whole dataset available at time $T + k, (k = 0, 50, 150, \ldots, 450)$ is used. The Bayesian models are re-estimated for every 50 new observations. We calculate the predictive distributions of logarithmic returns $r_t = \left(r_{t,1}, r_{t,2}\right)$ and next calculate the predictive distribution of ordinary returns rates of portfolio $R^*_{t:t+1}$ (see Sects. 46.2 and 46.3). Thus, we obtain 518 distributions for one-day forecast horizon for every portfolio and dataset. For example, in Fig. 46.1, we present the first predictive distributions of $R^*_{T:T+1}$, $(T = 21.09.2015)$ for portfolio no. 1 for exchange rates. The $\text{VaR}^L_{T:T+1}(\alpha)$ is α-quantile of the predictive distribution and $\text{ES}^L_{T:T+1}(\alpha)$ is conditional expectation given that the $\text{VaR}^L_{T:T+1}(\alpha)$ is exceeded (see Sect. 46.2).

In Figs. 46.2 and 46.3, we present the 518 one-day forecasts $\text{VaR}^j_{t:t+1}(\alpha)$ and $\text{ES}^j_{t:t+1}(\alpha)$, respectively, where $\alpha \in \{0.01, 0.05, 0.1\}$, $j \in \{L, S\}$, $t = T, \ldots .T + 517$ for portfolio no. 1 for the stock market indices. These forecasts are obtained by using: Bayesian VAR(1)-tCopula-GARCH(1,1), VAR(1)-tDCC(1,1) models, and CAViaR or CARE methods. As we can see the forecasts obtained in Bayesian models are quite similar.

Tables 46.1 and 46.2 display the value of the assessment criteria for forecast the VaR and ES (see Sect. 46.2, the best case is in bold) for the exchange rates portfolios. For the VaR there are: the p-value of the Kupiec test, the "tick" loss and the Lopes loss functions. For the ES: the mean errors (MA), the mean absolute errors (MAE), and the mean absolute percentage errors (MAPE). The criteria are

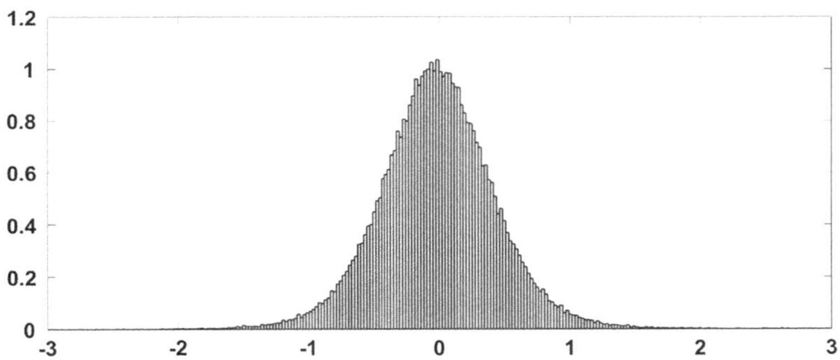

Fig. 46.1 Histogram of the predictive distribution $R^*_{T:T+1}$ (portfolio no. 1) in AR(1)-tCopula-GARCH(1,1) model for exchange rates $(T = 21.09.2015)$

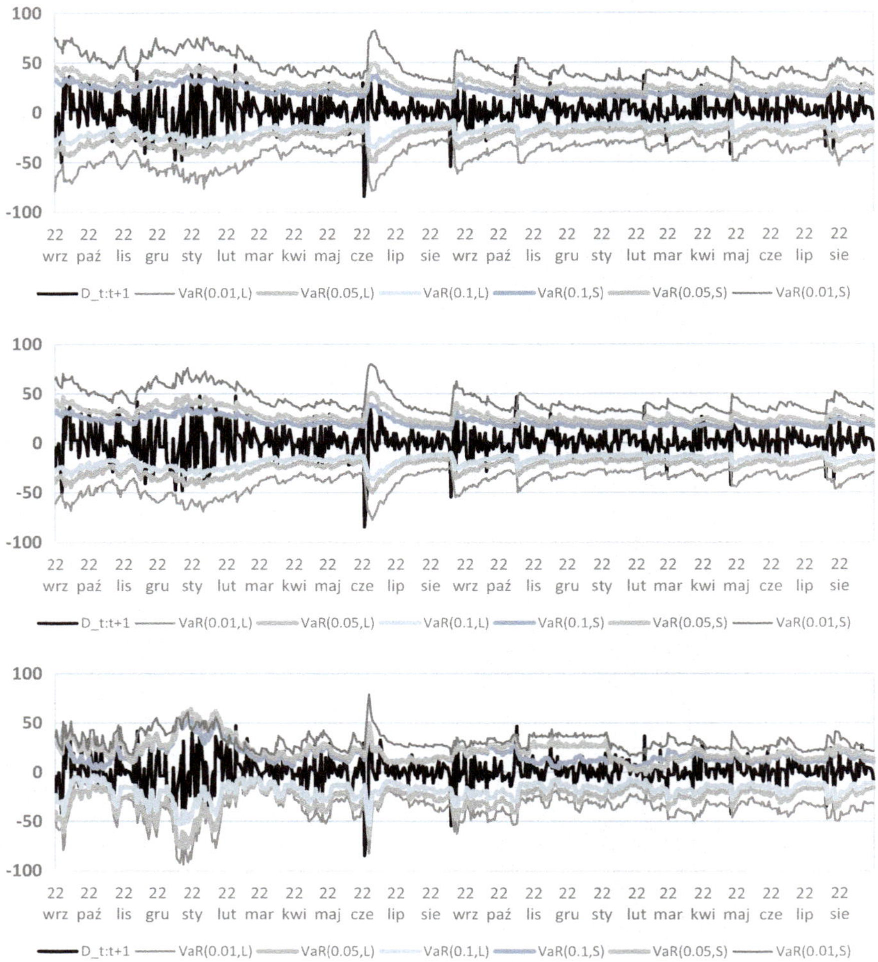

Fig. 46.2 One-day forecasts of VaR (-VaR for long trading position) with using VAR(1)-tCopula-GARCH(1,1) model (at the top), VAR(1)-tDCC(1,1) model (in the middle), and CAViaR model with asymmetric slope (at the bottom) for market indices portfolio no. 1

calculated for different probability level α, long and short trading positions and portfolio no. 1 (Table 46.1), portfolio no. 2 (Table 46.2). We notice that we may not conclude which model is better to prediction, the assessment of quality of one-day forecasts the VaR or ES depends on the particular criterion. The model with the highest explanatory power AR(1)-tBEKK(1,1) (Mokrzycka 2019) is definitely worse than AR(1)-tCopula-GARCH(1,1) for the long trading position, $\alpha = 0.1$ (portfolio no. 1) and the short trading position, $\alpha = 0.05$ (portfolio no. 2). The CAViaR and CARE methods generally have worse assessment than Bayesian Copula-GARCH

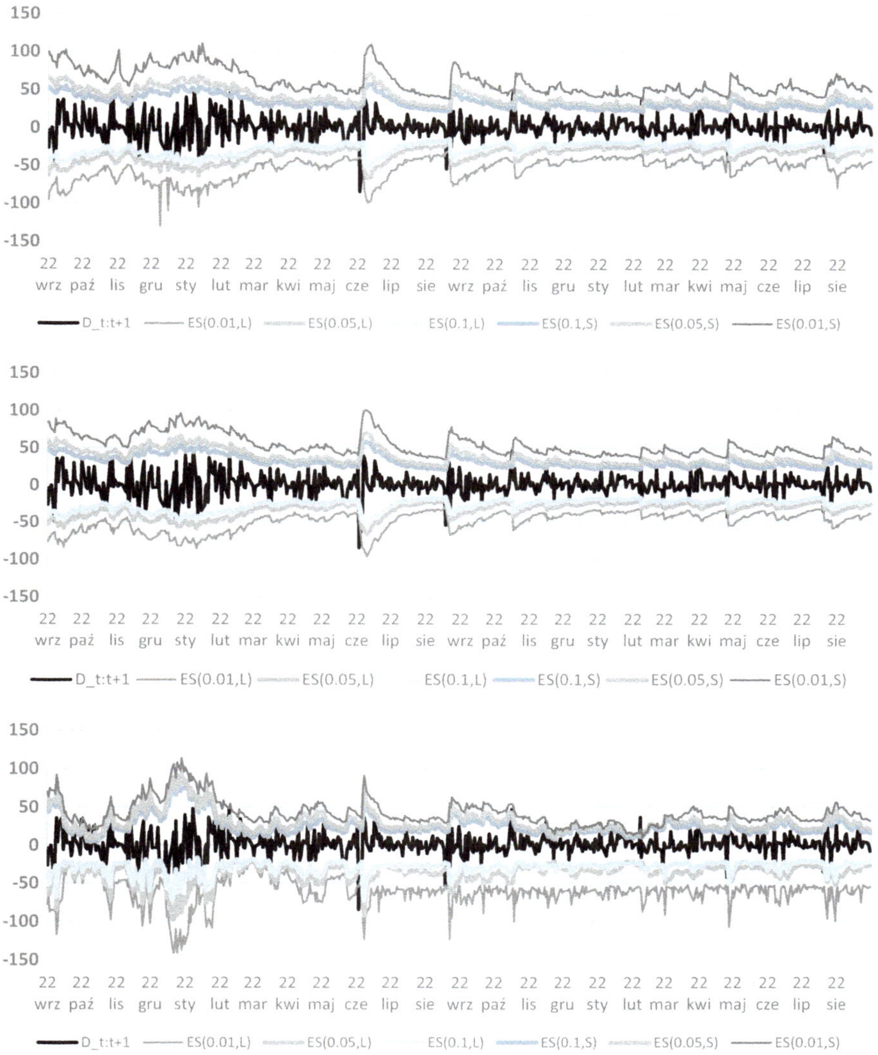

Fig. 46.3 One-day forecasts of ES (-ES for long trading position) with using VAR(1)-tCopula-GARCH(1,1) model (at the top), VAR(1)-tDCC(1,1) model (in the middle), and CARE model with asymmetric slope (at the bottom) for market indices portfolio no. 1

Table 46.1 *p*-Values for the Kupiec test, the "tick" loss and the Lopes loss functions for $\mathrm{VaR}_{t:t+1}^{\{L,S\}}(\alpha)$ and the mean errors (MA), the mean absolute errors (MAE), and the mean absolute percentage errors (MAPE) for $\mathrm{ES}_{t:t+1}^{\{L,S\}}(\alpha)$ for the exchange rates portfolio no. 1

	$\alpha = 0.01$			$\alpha = 0.05$			$\alpha = 0.1$		
	tCopula	tBEKK	CAViaR/CARE	tCopula	tBEKK	CAViaR/CARE	tCopula	tBEKK	CAViaR/CARE
Long trading position									
p-value	0.0239	0.0239	0.4456	0.2161	0.3077	0.0809	0.4758	0.7910	0.0229
"tick"	0.0011	0.0011	0.0010	0.0037	0.0037	0.0040	0.0064	0.0064	0.0068
Lopez	0.0019	0.0019	0.0135	**0.0386**	0.0405	0.0676	**0.0908**	0.0966	0.1313
MA	0.0011	0.0001	0.0568	0.0120	0.0122	**0.0084**	**0.0066**	0.0074	0.0069
MAE	0.0011	0.0001	0.0573	**0.0126**	0.0139	0.0183	**0.0096**	0.0115	0.0230
MAPE	0.0105	0.0013	0.6774	**0.1732**	0.1919	0.2781	**0.1485**	0.1802	0.3966
Short trading position									
p-value	0.4456	0.7239	0.9363	0.6759	0.8256	0.2348	0.7910	0.5736	0.9766
"tick"	0.0016	0.0015	0.0015	0.0048	0.0048	**0.0045**	0.0074	0.0074	**0.0072**
Lopez	0.0136	**0.0117**	0.0097	0.0542	**0.0523**	0.0619	0.0967	**0.0929**	0.1006
MA	−0.0138	−0.0111	**−0.0009**	**−0.0047**	−0.0047	0.0067	−0.0029	−0.0039	**0.0016**
MAE	**0.0182**	0.0240	0.0386	**0.0111**	0.0130	0.0164	**0.0091**	0.0106	0.0157
MAPE	**0.1330**	0.1680	0.2588	**0.1241**	0.1447	0.1983	**0.1255**	0.1451	0.2222

Table 46.2 p-Values for the Kupiec test, the "tick" loss and the Lopes loss functions for $\mathrm{VaR}_{t:t+1}^{\{L,S\}}(\alpha)$ and the mean errors (MA), the mean absolute errors (MAE), and the mean absolute percentage errors (MAPE) for $\mathrm{ES}_{t:t+1}^{\{L,S\}}(\alpha)$ for the exchange rates portfolio no. 2

	$\alpha = 0.01$			$\alpha = 0.05$			$\alpha = 0.1$		
	tCopula	tBEKK	CAViaR/CARE	tCopula	tBEKK	CAViaR/CARE	tCopula	tBEKK	CAViaR/CARE
Long trading position									
p-value	0.0239	0.0239	0.4456	0.5515	0.3077	0.0539	0.4758	0.9065	0.0032
"tick"	0.0011	0.0011	0.0010	0.0038	0.0038	0.0042	0.0066	**0.0065**	0.0070
Lopez	0.0019	0.0019	0.0135	0.0444	**0.0405**	0.0695	**0.0908**	0.0985	0.1410
MA	0.0001	−0.0023	0.0472	0.0143	0.0124	**0.0104**	**0.0066**	0.0075	−0.0002
MAE	0.0001	0.0023	0.0472	0.0151	**0.0143**	0.0161	**0.0099**	0.0114	0.0063
MAPE	0.0006	0.0208	0.5743	0.2025	**0.1933**	0.2208	**0.1511**	0.1762	0.1054
Short trading position									
p-value	0.4456	0.7239	0.4456	0.8256	0.8256	0.1184	0.6793	0.5736	0.5432
"tick"	0.0016	0.0015	0.0015	0.0048	0.0048	**0.0047**	0.0075	0.0075	**0.0073**
Lopez	0.0136	**0.0117**	0.0136	0.0523	0.0523	0.0658	0.0948	**0.0929**	0.1084
MA	**−0.0086**	−0.0113	0.0256	**−0.0037**	−0.0045	0.0178	**−0.0026**	−0.0036	0.0047
MAE	**0.0179**	0.0231	0.0426	**0.0115**	0.0130	0.0243	**0.0100**	0.0112	0.0184
MAPE	**0.1293**	0.1603	0.3129	**0.1252**	0.1425	0.2877	**0.1355**	0.1500	0.2591

and MGARCH specifications. It is worth notice that for long trading position and $\alpha = 0.01$ (portfolio no. 1 and 2) only the CAViaR method is proper considering the Kupiec test (at 0.05 significance level). Taking into account MA, the methods in many cases overestimate risk for the long trading position and underestimate for the short trading position.

Tables 46.3 and 46.4 display the value of the assessment criteria for forecast the VaR and ES (see Sect. 46.2, the best case is in bold) for the stock market indices portfolios. The criteria are calculated for different probability level α, the long and short trading positions and portfolio no. 1 (Table 46.3), portfolio no. 2 (Table 46.4). Similarly as previous we may not conclude which model is better to prediction, the assessment of quality of one-day forecasts of the VaR or ES depends on the particular criterion. The model with the highest explanatory power VAR(1)-tCopula-GARCH(1,1) (Mokrzycka 2019) is definitely worse than VAR(1)-tDCC(1,1) for long trading position, $\alpha = 0.01$ (portfolio no. 1). The CAViaR and CARE methods rarely have better assessment than Bayesian Copula-GARCH and MGARCH specifications. It is worth notice that for a short trading position and $\alpha = 0.05$ (portfolio no. 1) any of using methods is not proper considering the Kupiec test (at 0.05 significance level). Taking into account MA, the methods in many cases underestimate risk for the long trading position and overestimate for the short trading position.

Tables 46.5 and 46.6 display the correlation coefficients values between the forecasts of the VaR and ES for the exchange rates portfolios and the stock market indices portfolios, respectively. The calculation shows that the tCopula-GARCH specification leads to the VaR and ES assessments that are highly correlated with the ones based on MGARCH structures for each portfolio and each dataset. Moreover, if we compare the correlation coefficient between CAViaR (or CARE) and other methods, then the forecast from MGARCH specifications in many cases is highly correlated with the forecast from CAViaR (or CARE).

46.5 Conclusions

In this paper, bivariate Bayesian: AR(1)-tCopula-GARCH(1,1) with dynamic t-Student copula and AR(1)-tSBEKK(1,1) models are employed to model logarithmic daily returns of two exchange rates: EUR/PLN and USD/PLN. Also, the bivariate Bayesian: VAR(1)-tCopula-GARCH(1,1) model with dynamic t-Student copula and VAR(1)-tDCC(1,1) specifications are used to model logarithmic daily returns of two stock market indices: SP500 and BUX.

The main aim of the research was to calculate and assess the quality of one-day forecasts of the Bayesian value-at-risk and expected shortfall for two kind of bivariate portfolio. The predictive distributions of ordinary returns rates of portfolios are used, the VaR is the α-quantile of these distributions and the ES is a conditional expectation given that the VaR is exceeded. Moreover, the study also presents the forecasts of VaR with using conditional autoregressive value-at-risk with asymmetric slope and ES with employing conditional autoregressive expectiles also with asymmetric slope.

Table 46.3 p-Values for the Kupiec test, the "tick" loss and the Lopes loss functions for $\text{VaR}_{t:t+1}^{\{L,S\}}(\alpha)$ and the mean errors (MA), the mean absolute errors (MAE), and the mean absolute percentage errors (MAPE) for $\text{ES}_{t:t+1}^{\{L,S\}}(\alpha)$ for the market indices portfolio no. 1

	$\alpha = 0.01$			$\alpha = 0.05$			$\alpha = 0.1$		
	tCopula	tDCC	CAViaR/CARE	tCopula	tDCC	CAViaR/CARE	tCopula	tDCC	CAViaR/CARE
Long trading position									
p-value	0.9363	0.7239	0.0004	0.6759	0.6983	0.3077	0.6793	0.4758	0.9065
"tick"	0.6467	**0.6092**	0.6187	1.8238	**1.7720**	1.8086	2.9226	**2.8558**	2.9045
Lopez	7.9347	**7.1988**	7.7867	16.3871	15.2948	**12.4363**	26.4423	24.4376	**22.7467**
MA	−14.125	**−10.280**	13.3808	**−0.2350**	−2.0874	1.2190	**−1.2360**	−1.5609	1.7233
MAE	14.1254	**10.2800**	14.8928	8.4585	8.7151	**7.7586**	7.6465	7.5685	**5.9924**
MAPE	0.2771	**0.2178**	0.5575	0.2507	0.2513	**0.2368**	0.2672	0.2623	**0.2242**
Short trading position									
p-value	0.1087	0.1087	0.0592	0.0088	0.0323	0.0049	0.0730	0.1019	0.1113
"tick"	0.4737	0.4570	**0.4203**	1.5689	1.5491	1.5029	**1.5897**	2.5564	2.4974
Lopez	0.1898	**0.0117**	1.0801	2.5764	2.6492	5.0084	**7.1544**	7.3339	10.0898
MA	4.6624	**−1.0670**	7.3888	3.8567	3.1981	4.1347	5.2833	3.7635	**0.3943**
MAE	5.4254	**2.0409**	13.7516	6.7092	7.9576	9.0860	8.6133	7.5026	**7.2623**
MAPE	0.1300	**0.0489**	0.3605	0.1984	0.2307	0.3841	0.2863	**0.2561**	0.3261

Table 46.4 p-Values for the Kupiec test, the "tick" loss and the Lopes loss functions for $\mathrm{VaR}^{\{L,S\}}_{t:t+1}(\alpha)$ and the mean errors (MA), the mean absolute errors (MAE), and the mean absolute percentage errors (MAPE) for $\mathrm{ES}^{\{L,S\}}_{t:t+1}(\alpha)$ for the market indices portfolio no. 2

	$\alpha = 0.01$			$\alpha = 0.05$			$\alpha = 0.1$		
	tCopula	tDCC	CAViaR/CARE	tCopula	tDCC	CAViaR/CARE	tCopula	tDCC	CAViaR/CARE
Long trading position									
p-value	0.7239	0.0254	0.7239	0.9839	0.0539	0.9839	0.8610	0.3011	0.8610
"tick"	**0.7344**	0.7367	0.7461	**2.2432**	2.2493	2.2634	3.6142	**3.6030**	3.6103
Lopez	23.8442	25.1997	**20.2789**	**37.4497**	41.7184	43.2431	**51.3403**	57.7908	54.0434
MA	−13.2273	−4.8049	**4.6797**	−4.4195	−3.3126	**2.9423**	−2.4211	−3.8492	**−0.9330**
MAE	**13.2273**	6.3583	20.1028	5.9589	**4.5326**	11.3555	**4.7158**	5.9005	5.8421
MAPE	**0.2160**	0.1212	0.3098	0.1458	**0.1225**	0.2478	**0.1401**	0.1840	0.1756
Short trading position									
p-value	0.5873	0.7239	0.5873	0.2161	0.4196	0.2161	0.3874	0.4528	0.3874
"tick"	**0.4203**	0.5037	0.5555	1.8288	**1.8224**	1.9556	**3.0122**	3.0290	3.1710
Lopez	1.1682	**0.0117**	2.5394	**7.0490**	9.0328	13.1008	**15.2938**	20.0604	24.9591
MA	**3.1939**	5.8496	68.0621	3.1561	**2.2702**	10.2888	2.7762	**0.9186**	1.7914
MAE	**4.7814**	11.7149	217.1512	7.1418	**5.5676**	41.8562	5.2354	**4.0027**	12.7499
MAPE	**0.0901**	0.2188	1.6019	0.1728	**0.1482**	0.6642	0.1576	**0.1278**	0.3243

Table 46.5 Correlation coefficients between $\text{VaR}_{t:t+1}^{\{L,S\}}(\alpha)$ and $\text{ES}_{t:t+1}^{\{L,S\}}(\alpha)$ from different models for portfolios of the exchange rates

	Portfolio no. 1			Portfolio no. 2		
	$\alpha = 0.01$	$\alpha = 0.05$	$\alpha = 0.1$	$\alpha = 0.01$	$\alpha = 0.05$	$\alpha = 0.1$
Long trading position (VaR)						
Corr(tCopula, tBEKK)	0.9671	0.9650	0.9580	0.9440	0.9672	0.9635
Corr(tCopula, CAViaR)	0.2134	0.6541	0.7515	0.3778	0.0774	−0.0589
Corr(tBEKK, CAViaR)	0.3293	0.7047	0.7930	0.3832	0.0712	−0.0723
Short trading position (VaR)						
Corr(tCopula, tBEKK)	0.9631	0.9597	0.9603	0.9613	0.9655	0.9637
Corr(tCopula, CAViaR)	0.2875	0.6587	0.4307	0.1685	0.1617	0.1604
Corr(tBEKK, CAViaR)	0.3905	0.7460	0.5376	0.3606	0.3161	0.3347
Long trading position (ES)						
Corr(tCopula, tBEKK)	0.9656	0.9671	0.9673	0.9205	0.9246	0.9274
Corr(tCopula, CARE)	0.8051	0.8374	0.8248	0.0816	0.1423	0.0157
Corr(tBEKK, CARE)	0.7983	0.8200	0.8032	0.0751	0.1469	0.0212
Short trading position (ES)						
Corr(tCopula, tBEKK)	0.9440	0.9564	0.9464	0.9212	0.9117	0.8937
Corr(tCopula, CARE)	0.3778	0.5513	0.4889	0.5831	0.5325	0.3405
Corr(tBEKK, CARE)	0.3832	0.5647	0.4958	0.5878	0.5576	0.3461

The results point to that we may not conclude which model is better to prediction, and the assessment of quality of one-day forecasts of the VaR or ES depends on the particular criterion. The CAViaR and CARE methods rarely have better assessments of the VaR and ES than Bayesian tCopula-GARCH and MGARCH specifications. Taking into account portfolios of the stock market indices and the mean errors, the methods, in many cases, underestimate risk for the long trading position and overestimate for the short trading position. For portfolios of exchange rates the opposite is true, the methods, in many cases, overestimate risk for the long trading position and underestimate for the short trading position. The results shows that the tCopula-GARCH specification leads to the VaR and ES assessments that are highly correlated with the ones based on MGARCH structures for each portfolio and each dataset.

Table 46.6 Correlation coefficients between $\text{VaR}_{t:t+1}^{\{L,S\}}(\alpha)$ and $\text{ES}_{t:t+1}^{\{L,S\}}(\alpha)$ from different models for portfolios of the stock market indices

	Portfolio no. 1			Portfolio no. 2		
	$\alpha = 0.01$	$\alpha = 0.05$	$\alpha = 0.1$	$\alpha = 0.01$	$\alpha = 0.05$	$\alpha = 0.1$
Long trading position (VaR)						
Corr(tCopula, tDCC)	0.9456	0.9470	0.9457	0.9085	0.9078	0.9110
Corr(tCopula, CAViaR)	0.2357	0.4603	0.2919	0.4076	0.2494	0.2163
Corr(tDCC, CAViaR)	0.3036	0.5388	0.3883	0.5837	0.3969	0.3594
Short trading position (VaR)						
Corr(tCopula, tDCC)	0.9482	0.9497	0.9439	0.9150	0.9228	0.9245
Corr(tCopula, CAViaR)	0.5528	0.6457	0.6774	0.1808	0.4711	0.3741
Corr(tDCC, CAViaR)	0.6565	0.6846	0.7326	0.3964	0.5527	0.3747
Long trading position (ES)						
Corr(tCopula, tDCC)	0.9238	0.9455	0.9479	0.8929	0.9080	0.9143
Corr(tCopula, CARE)	0.3183	0.4911	0.4907	0.2831	0.2665	0.2263
Corr(tDCC, CARE)	0.3399	0.5185	0.5045	0.3136	0.2829	0.2356
Short trading position (ES)						
Corr(tCopula, tDCC)	0.9433	0.9500	0.9488	0.9024	0.9172	0.9197
Corr(tCopula, CARE)	0.7216	0.6582	0.6567	0.6140	0.6835	0.6121
Corr(tDCC, CARE)	0.7408	0.6806	0.6695	0.6310	0.6329	0.5542

Acknowledgements The author would like to thank Anna Pajor for valuable comments on the manuscript. This work was supported by the funds of Ministry of Science and Higher Education granted to the Faculty of Finance and Law at Cracow University of Economics for research conducted by young researchers and Ph.D. students.

References

Artzner, P., Delbaen, F., Eber, J.-M., & Heath, D. (1999). Coherent measures of risk. *Mathematical Finance, 9,* 203–228.

Baba, Y., Engle, R. F., Kraft, D. F., & Kroner, K. F. (1989). Multivariate simultaneous generalized ARCH, Department of Economics, *Working Paper*, University of California at San Diego.

Cherubini, U., Luciano, E., & Vecchiato, W. (2004). *Copula Methods in Finance*. England: Wiley.

Engle, R. F. (2002). Dynamic Conditional correlation—A simple class of Multivariate GARCH Models. *Journal of Business and Economic Statistics, 20,* 339–350.

Engle, R., & Manganelli, S. (2004). CAViaR: conditional autoregressive value at risk by regression quantiles. *Journal of Business and Economic Statistics, 22,* 367–381.

Evans, M., & Swartz, T. (1995). Methods for approximating integrals in statistics with special emphasis on Bayesian integration problems. *Statistical Science, 10*(3), 254–272.

Geweke, J. (1989). Bayesian inference in econometric models using Monte Carlo integration. *Econometrica, 57,* 1317–1339.

Huang, J. J., Lee, K. J., Liang, H., Lin, & W. F. (2009). Estimation value at risk of portfolio by conditional copula-GARCH method. *Insurance: Mathematics and Economics, 45*, 315–324.
Jondeau, E., & Rockinger, M. (2006). The Copula-GARCH model of conditional dependencies: An international stock market application. *Journal of International Money and Finance, 25,* 827–853.
Mokrzycka, J. (2019). Bivariate Bayesian comparison of bivariate Copula-GARCH and MGARCH models. *Central European Journal of Economic Modelling and Econometrics, 11,* 47–71.
Osiewalski, J., & Pajor, A. (2010). Bayesian value-at-risk for a portfolio: Multi- and univariate approaches using MSF-SBEKK models. *Central European Journal of Economic Modelling and Econometrics, 2,* 253–277.
Osiewalski, J., Pajor, A., & Pipień, M. (2006). Bayesian analysis of main bivariate GARCH and SV models for PLN/USD and PLN/DEM (1996–2001). *Dynamic Econometric Models, 7,* 25–35.
Osiewalski, J., & Pipień, M. (2005). Bayesian analysis of dynamic conditional correlation using bivariate GARCH models. *Acta Universitatis Lodziensis Folia Oeconomica, 192,* 213–227.
Osiewalski, J., & Pipień, M. (1999). Bayesian forecasting of exchange rates using GARCH models with skewed t conditional distributions. In *Marcromodels '98, Proceedings of the 25-th International Conference* (Vol. 2, pp. 195–218). Łódź: Absolwent.
Pajor, A., & Osiewalski J. (2012). Bayesian value-at-risk and expected shortfall for a large portfolio (multi- and univariate approaches). *Acta Physica Polonica A, 121*(2-B), 101–109.
Paralo, H. P., & Hotta, L. K. (2006). Using conditional copula to estimate value at risk. *Journal of Data Science, 4,* 93–115.
Patton, A. J. (2006). Modelling asymmetric exchange rate dependence. *International Economic Review, 47*(2), 527–556.
Sklar, A. (1959). Fonctions de répartition à n dimensions et leurs marges. *Publications de l'Institut de Statistique de L'Université de Paris, 8,* 229–231.
Taylor, J. W. (2008). Estimating value at risk and expected shortfall using expectiles. *Journal of Financial Econometrics, 6,* 231–252.
Tse, Y. K., & Tsui, A. K. C. (2002). A multivariate GARCH model with time-varying correlations. *Journal of Business & Economic Statistic, 20,* 351–362.
Weiss, G. N. F. (2013). Copula-GARCH versus dynamic conditional correlation: an empirical study on VaR and ES forecasting accuracy. *Review of Quantitative Finance and Accounting, 41*(2), 179–202.
Zhu, D., & Galbraith, J. W. (2011). Modeling and forecasting expected shortfall with the generalized asymmetric student-t and asymmetric exponential power distributions. *Journal of Empirical Finance, 18,* 765–778.

Chapter 47
Competitive Differentiation in the Digital Environment and Social Networks

Tatiana Corejova, Maria Rostasova, Alexandra Rovnanova and Marek Valica

Abstract Differentiation of services means the inclusion of new services that represent variations to those services that are already part of a range of services. Differentiation of services exists on the basis of service with a real or perceived, rational or emotional value and occupying a place in the mind of the customer. The extent to which these values are important to the customer determines whether they have differentiated themselves. The contribution deals with the so-called virtual value chains in the digital environment e.g. in the two worlds: in physical and in virtual world of information. The comparison of selected social network based on the value chain is included too. This virtual world provides an opportunity to penetrate into the world of electronic business as a new centre of value formation. In buying electronic services with the use of market place in the form of virtual sphere, there are services in the form of digital information which are provided through information channels. Building a virtual value chain through which a company integrates information that is necessary for ensuring processes in the value chain provide managers with an ability to "see" these information flows in the value chain from the beginning to the end as the basis for differentiation as well as for success on the market.

Keywords Competitive differentiation · Value chain

JEL Codes M14

47.1 Introduction

Each differentiation relies on the attributes of difference, singularity and uniqueness. The formation of these attributes occurs in order to achieve the competitive advantage of the company. Uniqueness moves the company into a leading position among

T. Corejova (✉) · M. Rostasova · A. Rovnanova · M. Valica
University of Zilina, Univerzitna 8215/1, 01026 Zilina, Slovakia
e-mail: tatiana.corejova@uniza.sk

N. Tsounis and A. Vlachvei (eds.), *Advances in Cross-Section Data Methods in Applied Economic Research*, Springer Proceedings in Business and Economics,
https://doi.org/10.1007/978-3-030-38253-7_47

competitors (Pavco 2010). If the aim of the company is to differentiate itself, it should follow all forms of differentiation. Its goal should be to differentiate itself as much as possible from competitors in order to attract new customers. Being different in just one point is not enough, it is necessary to support differentiation in various forms. Companies are forced to develop new product features that will attract customers and will help company to differentiate itself from competitors (Papula 1995). Differentiation of companies in the market, however, affects not only products, but also processes, technologies, people and image.

A more permanent competitive advance can be created with the following forms of differentiation:

- differentiation based on technical development, which is particularly suitable for technologically demanding industries;
- differentiation based on services, where the company's advantage is the ability to provide extensive after-sales services;
- differentiation based on brand attractiveness;
- differentiation based on adaptation towards specific age groups or socio-economic groups.

Such sources of differentiation are diverse and unlimited. According to Samuelson and Barnett (2006), differentiation strategy is looking for a competitive advantage especially in a wide range of customer segments. In addition, product differentiation may create barriers to entry and increase the market power of producers. The consumers usually choose products that bring them the greatest value (Kotler et al. 2007). The key to acquiring and retaining customers is therefore to better understand their needs and buying process than competitors and offer them a higher value. The better the company can present itself as a supplier of higher value for the target markets, the more competitive advantage it will gain, whether it offers lower prices than competitors or a greater benefit by which it justifies its higher prices (Kotler et al. 2007).

Differentiation of services means the inclusion of new services that represent variations to those services that are already part of a range of services (Birnerova 2013). Differentiation of services makes it possible to adapt the service to requirements of an individual customer (Čorejová and Rostášová 1999).

According to Trout and Rivkin (2008), more and more companies have a problem to differentiate. Differentiation of services exists on the basis of service with a value that is real or perceived, rational or emotional and occupying a place in the mind of the customer. The extent to which these values are important to the customer determines whether they have differentiated themselves. Approaches of other authors to differentiation are very similar. They consider differentiation as something different, unique and singular from existing products.

47.2 Theoretical Framework of Competitive Differentiation

Kotler (1998) emphasizes that the offer of the service provider should be markedly different from the offers of competition. Customers expect the provision of service-enriched with its further properties and they look for innovation of the service. The main problem of the service provider who wants to be different is that the innovations in this sector can be quickly copied and imitated. Company can differ from competition mainly by the quality of provided services in all its parameters. Kotler (2007) highlights the fact that positioning must begin by differentiation of the marketing offer of a service company that differs from the competition in the way customers expect.

We can, therefore, say that the customer evaluates the price, value and quality aspects of the product when purchasing the required service. The use of the value chain is one of the ways to achieve a higher added value. The value chain is used to identify the way the product is distinguished by value (Payne 1996).

The company has to constantly seek new ways to synchronize its special abilities with changing opportunities and threats on the market. If the company makes a reckoning of differentiation by developing the quality or reliability of services or other intangible resources, it gains a much more secure position. Such advantages are much more difficult to imitate (Papula 1995).

Porter (1992) defines two basic competitive advantages:

- Low costs—the so-called driving forces of costs decide about their behaviour within individual activities.
- Uniqueness—the basis for this competitive advantage is the choice of appropriate policy, mutual ties with suppliers, distributors, timing and other aspects.

In differentiation, it depends on the ability of the company to offer the customer a unique and exceptional value in terms of quality, utility, characteristics, durability or after-sales services. The company should carefully choose one or more characteristics that customers regard as essential in the given industry and try to satisfy these needs (Porter 1992). Service providers often complain that it is not easy to distinguish their service from a competitor. If customers perceive the offer as relatively equivalent, they stop being interested in supplier and follow the price. Alternatively, to price competition differentially acts the offer, delivery conditions and the image of the supplier. Payne (1996) takes into account as one of the possibilities of differentiation the value chain as a tool for achieving higher added value.

47.3 Value Chain as the Basis of Differentiation

Differentiation results from the so-called value chain of the company and the potential source of uniqueness can be conditioned by any value-creating activity (Payne 1996; Porter 1992; Lesakova 2014). Porter (1992) suggests the use of the value chain as one of the tools to achieve higher added value. The value chain of industry represents a way of thinking about competitive advantage from the point of view of the strategic advantage or disadvantage of each activity that is involved in creating the final offer for the end customer (Sedláčková and Buchta 2006). The value chain of industry shows in detail the value creation system and is composed of all the activities that create value within the industry (Rostasova and Stofkova 2003).

The main reason for using this tool of analysis is that the chain is actually a system that simultaneously presents the way. Differentiation stems from the value chain of a given company. A potential source of uniqueness is virtually any value-creating activity.

47.4 Social Media and Social Networks

Socialization is closely linked to the area where one moves and lives. For the past few years, since the massive arrival of the internet and media, almost everyone lives his/her part of life even digitally. If a person wants to socialize in every environment he/she lives in, it was only a matter of time when different groups started to occur on the internet. As man tends to associate with other people on the basis of certain criteria, of which probably the most common is the sphere of interests, even on the internet the first social groups were based on sharing common interests by a certain group of people the size of which was sufficient for the network to become widespread.

Online internet environment is a dimension of progress that constantly moves the possibilities of marketers and it offers new creative and effective possibilities for promotion. The current trend in online environment is dominated by social networks which represent a part of modern social media. Janouch (2010) writes about social media as online media where "content is created and shared by users. Social media are constantly changing as their content changes, as well as with adding many features. Social media are a place of collective wisdom where the opinions on a particular product are mostly true. This is why social media enjoy greater popularity than traditional media. The social media are characterized by rating, voting on anything, writing comments and commenting on comments and other similar activities. People can easily communicate about anything."

The social media have now become a regular part of integrated marketing communication (Qualman 2012). Kaplan and Haenlein (2009) described social media as "a set of Internet applications built on the ideological and technological foundations of Web 2.0 that enable the creation and exchange of user-generated content."

Social media serve to bring together and develop social contacts. Their advantage is that their content can be created, edited or commented by any registered user. Thus, they provide a great deal of space for creativity and ideas which are then easily spread among the users. They are superior to social networks because they include blogs, wiki sites, chat rooms, Social Bookmarking, and so on. They are used by more than 70% of the internet population and more than 50% of registered Facebook users follow them every day (Kaplan and Henlein 2009).

The term social network was first used in 1954 (Barnes 1954). Nowadays, the concept of social network can be defined as a set of people, some of which are linked by bonds or relationships and this set then forms the overall network of relationships, i.e. social network. Social networks are actually a product that enables communication and sharing of information in a more or less durable way, what differs it from chat or phone. A characteristic feature of social networks is the existence of profiles presented by people. Those should correspond to real people or companies, but this may not always be true.

The messages in the social networks are spread on the principle of monitoring of activities and people's opinions that are interested in individual users and who are classified as their friends (Prikrylová and Jahodová 2010). These friends follow each other, their interests, what are they doing right now or what are they about to do, and so on. Social networks work on the principle of registration and creation of your own profile. This profile can be subsequently followed by either an unlimited number of other registered users or only by users who are tagged as friends by the author of profile (Vaynerchurk 2016).

Nowadays, social networks are no longer just a tool for personal communication, but they also become an important information channel for the corporate sphere. Most of the large and medium-sized companies are currently using them for communication purposes—about 35% of them have already integrated social media into their company's overall communication strategy and an absolute majority of them even perceives them as a great opportunity for business. The most common reason for engaging social network media into business communication is the consolidation of brand reputation, dialogue with customers (customer feedback) or an effort to support the visits of company websites. However, it is interesting that more than half of the companies surveyed allow their employees unlimited access to Internet social networks. Today, social media represent a fast and especially extremely effective communication tool. Its priority mission – within the frame of personal and corporate communication, as well as political marketing - is to inform online, in real-time and space about everything that is happening, with the opportunity to share textual, audio and visual (static and dynamic) communication contents, with the additional possibility of immediate and direct feedback: these are the benefits that are not offered by any other type of communication.

Social media, according to the most recent surveys, are actively used by around 70% of the world's Internet population (more than 2.2 billion), with about 1.5 billion active users on the largest social network Facebook. Each social network is unique, it has its typical visitors, it works on its specific forms of content and offers companies different opportunities for promotion.

Social networks are characterized by a large scope, availability around the world and a high number of users. To identify the competitive differentiation, we focused on crucial global social networks (Facebook, Instagram, YouTube, Google+, LinkedIn and Twitter). SWOT analysis and analysis of value chains were used.

47.5 Comparison of Selected Social Networks Differentiation Based on Value Chain

The number of active social network users compared to the total population was 42% in 2018, which represents approximately 3.2 billion users. The penetration of social networks in individual regions, expressed as a percentage compared to the total population in the world, is different. For example, in the United States, it is up to 70%, in Western Europe 54%, in Southern Europe 54% compared to 6% in Central Africa. The largest number of social network users is in East Asia, while in Central Asia it is the least.

The most widely used social networks are Facebook and YouTube, followed by Messenger, Instagram, Google+, Twitter and finally LinkedIn. Most of the time users (aged 18–34) spend on the social network Facebook, on the contrary, at least it is on Google+. Facebook dominates among social networks (see Table 47.1).

Comparison of *traffic and use of social networks* showed that Facebook is the most used and the most visited social network, with the largest number of users up to about 2.1 billion. Facebook users use the social networking site on average for up to 15 days per month and open and check the news on it up to 8 times a day on average. Regarding active Facebook users, they are especially young people aged 25–34 who make up to 25% of all users of this social network. Up to 73% of social network users visit Facebook, 42% of the total are active contributors and use the Facebook site during the month. However, social network YouTube is better in this aspect. Its site is visited by up to 82% of all social network users, but only 24% of users are active contributors to it. This parameter is different mainly because YouTube social network is primarily used for watching videos, but only a small percentage of users actually use it to the active contribution of their videos.

Table 47.1. Heatmap of comparison of social networks

	Facebook	YouTube	Twitter	LinkedIn	Instagram	Google+
Number of users (mil.)	2.167	1,500	330	260	800	376
Average daily accesses to the network	8	8	5	3	6	2
Average number of days spent per month on the network	15	14.2	7.5	5.8	11	3.2
Those who visited the page during the month	73%	82%	36%	25%	Together with FB	29%
Active using and contributing to network	42%	24%	22%	13%	Together with FB	21%

Resource: Rovňanová (2018)

Regarding the number of YouTube users, it is placed second after Facebook, with a total of about 1.5 billion users. The average number of days spent on this social network by users is about 14.2 days on average. The number of user accesses to this social network per day is the same as for Facebook—8 times, and the most active users are 16–24-year-old, who make up 31% of all users. The social network Instagram is ranked third. The number of users of this social network dedicated to sharing photos is significantly lower than the previous two networks, at around 800 million users. The most active users of Instagram are, like in all other groups, people aged 16–24, who make up 37% of all users. The average number of days spent on this social network by users is approximately 11 days per month. The number of daily network accesses is on average 6 times. The social network Twitter ranked fourth with the number of users up to 330 million.

The average number of days spent on this social network by users is approximately 7.5 days per month. The number of daily network accesses is 5 times a day on average. The most active users of Twitter are people aged 25–34. 36% of social network users visit Twitter at least once a month, but only 22% of users are actively using it and contributing to it. The social network Google+ ranked fifth with about 370 million users. The average number of days spent on this website is only 3.2 days per month. The number of daily network accesses is only 2 times a day on average. Only 29% of social network users visit the Google+ page, 21% of users actively contribute and use this site over the course of the month. The most active users are 25–34 years old, similarly like on Facebook, Twitter and LinkedIn. The social network LinkedIn ranked sixth with about 260 million users. The most active users of LinkedIn are people aged 25–34, due to the fact that it is a professional network focusing mainly on the professional level of users.

The average number of daily network accesses is 3 times a day and the average number of days spent on this network is 5.8 per month. 25% of social network users visit LinkedIn at least once a month, but only 13% of users are actively using it and contributing to it.

Inbound logistics—In principle, inbound logistics of social networks is basically not so different. It refers to the ways the company acquires resources and uses them according to its needs. The range of resources used by social networks includes hardware, several types of technologies and office supplies. Generally, value chain analysis analyses the process of receiving and storing raw materials until they are transferred to the final goods. However, in regard to business models of companies, tangible resources such as hardware and technologies used by the company are only secondary and the primary resources for attracting customers are intangible. Social networks offer their customers unique intangible "products" of informative nature that is content. From this point of view, inbound logistics of content is highly cost-effective because the content is uploaded by users in the forms of texts, pictures and videos without any additional costs for business. Social networks differ only in the form of content that can be uploaded to each social network. Facebook allows its users to upload content in the form of text, picture, video, etc. Users of YouTube can upload video content with short comments; Instagram allows its users to upload only photos and short videos; Google+ is similar to Facebook and allows its users to upload video, text, images; Twitter allows its users to upload a limited amount of text and to attach a link to a short video or image since in this case, it is a microblogging network; with regard to the social network LinkedIn, it is possible to contact our "friends" through news.

Business activities and sales—Facebook is available in more than 90 different languages and the company has offices and data centres in more than 30 countries worldwide. In addition, there are five support offices and more than 35 sales offices worldwide. Operations on Facebook primarily include the transformation of raw content into user-friendly format through profile page, timeline, real-time updates, news feed, notifications, local friends, applications, and so on. Main sources of value of business operations are connected with a consistent improvement of content creation practices. Twitter is available worldwide in 33 different languages and has more than 35 offices all around the world. Twitter has become the largest provider of current news worldwide. Tweets are posted by users in real-time and can be followed by anyone. The main sources of value for users are current news that informs them about the current situation in the world. LinkedIn is available in more than 200 countries worldwide in 24 different languages. LinkedIn has become the best professional network in the world with branches in 23 different countries. It is a professional network that allows users to promote themselves through their CVs. It is possible to find contacts on people around the world who work in the same industry or have the same interests. YouTube is available in more than 30 different languages all around the world. This multilingual support brings a long way to the usefulness of users and increase of web traffic. YouTube is one of the biggest earning factors for its parent company Google, simply because of the number of viewers visiting pages daily and the revenue earned from advertising. YouTube has a simple but excellent design.

Outbound logistics is related to the storage and distribution of finished products to customers. For social networks, outbound logistics is connected with the provision of content to its users through relevant sites and applications. E-commerce is the main source of value addition because there are no additional costs for business related to the outbound logistics aspect of business.

Social networks are based on the 7P marketing concept. Since their establishment, social media companies have been constantly expanding their target segment of customers and use multi-segment type of position focused on several customer segments along with various social media platforms.

Individual social networks do not have a physical department of customer services due to the online nature of their business. Range of customer service platforms includes a phone number for customers, online help communities for all customers and options toolbar within the website designed to help users with technical issues.

Infrastructure of social networks includes a wide range of support systems and functions such as finance, planning, quality control and general management. Due to the nature of business, infrastructure of data centres represents one of the critical success factors.

Individual networks approach human resource management with innovative concepts reflecting digital environment and 4A possibilities. Facebook uses unconventional employee recruitment and selection procedures with a particular emphasis on the suitability of potential candidates on organizational culture of the social media company. Such practices include participation in six-week training camp, using employee recommendations and internal resources for recruitment and a lack of attention for formal education. The number of Twitter employees is currently around 3770. Recruitment of new employees is carried out through various theories, later selection and subsequent training of selected employees. The number of LinkedIn employees is approximately 9200. It is expected that the number of employees will increase in the foreseeable future as it is with other social networks as the number of users increases each day. Recruitment of new employees is carried out through various methods. Google, which owns the Google+ social network, has always tried to employ the most qualified and competent individuals to ensure they excel in research and development of their technologies and systems. In fact, the company often gives challenges and tests which help recipients to sort out the vast amount of CVs they receive. The number of YouTube employees and the extent and complexity of its business increased significantly when Google bought this video server in 2006. The company uses unconventional recruitment and selection procedures. Concerning Google+ and YouTube, it is not possible to determine the exact number of employees as they fall under Google and some employees work at several positions.

Technology development is considered by all social networks as a critical factor of success in the current market. Twitter is trying to be our "digital face to the world", so it strives to be the best in the area of current world affairs. It wants to provide the best and the newest information to all users. LinkedIn is slowly becoming the best professional network in the world which is connected with the fact that the number of new users still increases. As for the social network Google+, it is trying to rival its biggest competitor—Facebook, but it is not successful in this task. The number of users is increasing but compared to Facebook it is only a negligible amount. Social networks Facebook and YouTube are doing the best. Expenses of Facebook for research and development were USD 4.82 billion, USD 2.67 billion, and USD 1.42 billion in 2015, 2014, and 2013. The latest development introduced by the company is "software that provides students with a full view of their academic responsibility for the year in each class and divides them into adjustable lesson modules they can solve at their own pace. "

Procurement activity within the chain of support operations of Facebook is related to ways resources are acquired for business. Facebook has 49 branches around the world and "it has built for huge data centres with two more sites under construction as of September 2016. "Considering the size and scope of Facebook business activities, the company carries out complex procurement activities on the global scale with the aim to use the best resources in order to maintain competitive advantages.

47.6 Discussion and Conclusion

Impetus to the debate on objective issue can currently be the area of value chains which has been complemented by new approaches towards the creation of value chains. It deals with the so-called virtual value chains (Rayport and Sviokla 1995) because the service companies compete in two worlds: in physical world—visible and touchable and in virtual world of information. This virtual world provides an opportunity to penetrate into the world of electronic business as a new centre of value formation. New information market place is considerably different from the physical market. In buying electronic services with the use of market place in the form of virtual sphere, there are services in the form of digital information which are provided through information channels.

Service companies, therefore, need to create the value in physical world but also in virtual world. It is necessary to bear in mind the fact that the processes for the value formation are not equal in both worlds. Understanding of differences and harmony between the processes with added value of physical world and information world will help to see more clearly the strategic problems of service companies in the current period. A proper understanding of the two interacting processes which create the added value for customers brings new conceptual and tactical tasks.

Building a virtual value chain through which a company integrates information that is necessary for ensuring processes in the value chain provide managers with an ability to "see" these information flows in the value chain from the beginning to the end.

It is, therefore, possible to ask whether the model of value chain works with information such as supporting elements of processes creating the value for customers or whether this information is the source of the value itself. In the services sector, we can find a lot of examples when managers often use information about inventory, production, and logistics or they use them to monitor and control these processes but rarely use this information for creating new value for customers.

With the use of an integrated information base, companies can begin to carry out activities that add value more effective and efficient through information and with information. In other words, these information-based activities mirror the steps in the physical value chain. When companies move a whole range of activities with added value from a market place to a virtual space, they will thus create a virtual value chain.

Once companies become experts to manage their value-added activities within a parallel value chain, they are ready to develop these new relationships.

Managers must consciously focus on the principles that govern the creation of values and the use of both value chains, alone and in combination. These two value-added processes are fundamentally different. The physical value chain is composed of a linear sequence of activities with defined input and output points. By contrast, the virtual value chain is nonlinear—there is a matrix of possible inputs and outputs that can be accessed and distributed through a wide range of channels.

Companies create new markets and new relationships with existing markets by applying five generic value-adding steps of information world to each activity of virtual value chain.

Digital property, unlike physical, is not consumed. Companies that create the value of digital assets may be able to renew them through countless transactions, thus changing the competitive dynamics in the industry.

The virtual value chain newly defines economies of scale, allowing small companies to achieve low unit costs for products and services on the market where large companies dominate.

In the virtual space, companies can redefine their economies of scale by outlining a set of digital assets that provide value in many diverse markets. Thanks to digital assets, companies have new relationships with customers and expand their reach. By using the virtual value chain, they can coordinate markets and provide a wider range of high-quality products and services.

Lower transaction costs allow companies to manage and track information that would be too costly to capture and process a few years ago. As companies collect, organize, select, synthesize and distribute information in the virtual space in managing material and final products on the market, they have the ability to "perceive and react" to customer requests easier than to produce and sell products and services.

Managers must evaluate their business meetings, their strengths and weaknesses, opportunities and risks, along with value chains from both worlds, virtual and physical.

Acknowledgements This contribution was undertaken as a part of the research projects 1/0152/18 VEGA Business and business models and platforms in the digital environment and 1/0087/18 VEGA Enhancing competitiveness of the Zilina region by increasing influence of the University of Zilina in the region and in Zilina town.

References

Analýza konkurencie a konkurenčné stratégie. (2008). http://referaty.aktuality.sk/analyza-konkurencie-a-konkurencne-strategie/referat-26639. Accessed 2.

Barnes, J. A. (1954). Class and committees in a Norwegian Island Parish. *Human Relations, 7,* 39–58.

Birnerová, E. (2013). *Marketing služieb*. 2. vyd. EDIS, ISBN 978-80-554-0636-7.

Čorejová, T., & Rostášová, M. (1999). *Diagnostický postup v manažérstve kvality v pošte*. Žilina: EDIS. 94s. ISBN 80-7100-619-X.

Digital Life in 2025. http://www.pewinternet.org/2014/03/11/digital-life-in-2025/. Accessed July 18, 2016.

Digital Marketing 2016. http://www.digitalmarketing-conference.com/world-digital-2016/. Accessed July 18, 2016.

EU Parliament. (2016). *The internal market*. http://www.europarl.europa.eu/atyourservice/sk/displayFtu.html?ftuId=FTU_5.9.4.html. Accessed April 14, 2019.

Janouch, V. (2010). *Internetový marketing*. Computer Press. ISBN 978-80-251-2795-7.

Jednotný digitálny trh pre Európu. http://itas.sk/jednotny-digitalny-trh-pre-europu. Accessed April 14, 2019.

Kaplan, A. M., & Haenlein, M. (2009). *The challenges and opportunities of social media*. Paris: ESCP Europe.

Kotler, P. (1998) *Marketing management: Analýza, plánovaní, využití, kontrola*. Praha: Grada Publishing. 710 s. ISBN 80-7169-600-5.

Kotler, P., Wong, V., Saunders, J., & Armstrong, G. (2007). *Moderní marketing* 4.vyd. Praha: Grada Publishing. ISBN 978-80-247-1545-2.

Lesáková, D., a kol. (2014). *Strategický marketing*. Bratislava: Vydavateľstvo SPRINT, 353 s. ISBN 978-80-89085-92-7.

Papula, J., a kol. (1995). *Strategický manažment*. Bratislava: Ekonóm. 197 s. ISBN 80-225-0680-X.

Pavco. (2010). Konkurenčné stratégie a dosahovanie konkurenčnej výhody: diferenciácia, nákladové vodcovstvo a fokálne stratégie. Diploma work. http://www.cutn.sk/Library/Thesis/2010/Pavco.pdf. Accessed April 14, 2019.

Payne, A. (1996). *Marketing služieb*. Praha: Grada Publishing. 247 s. ISBN 80-7169-276-X.

Porter, M. E. (1992). *Konkurenční výhoda: Jak vytvořit a udržet si nadpruměrný výkon*. Praha: Victoria Publishing, 626 s. ISBN 80-85605-12-0.

Prikrilová, J., & Jahodová, H. (2010). *Moderní marketingová komunikace*. Grada. ISBN 978-80-247-3622-8.

Qualman, E. (2012) Socialnomics: How social media transforms the way we live and do business. Wiley. ISBN 978-11-182-8278-6.

Rayport, J. F., & Sviokla, J. (1995). Exploiting the virtual value chain. *Harvard Business Review*. https://hbr.org/1995/11/exploiting-the-virtual-value-chain. Accessed May 18, 2016.

Rovňanová, A. (2018). Konkurenčná diferenciácia v digitálnom prostredí. Dissertation. University of Zilina. Zilina.

Rostasova, M., Stofkova, J. (2003). Transregionálny marketing ako zatiaľ veľká neznáma mnohých slovenských podnikov a inštitúcií v euroregióne Beskydy (Transregional marketing as a great unknown of many Slovak companies and institutions in the Beskydy Euroregion). In: *Monitoring transhraničnej spolupráce a jej bariér v Euroregióne Beskydy (Monitoring trans-border cooperation and its bariers in the Beskydy Euroregion), Proceedings of the international scientific conference* (Ed.), ISBN 80-8070-151-2 (pp. 135–147). Zilina Zilinska univerzita v Ziline.

Samuelson, P., & Barnett, W. A. (2006). *Inside the economist's mind: Conversations with eminent economists* (1st ed.). Wiley-Blackwell. ISBN-10: 1405159170, ISBN-13: 978-1405159173.

Sedláčková, H., & Buchta, K. (2006) *Strategická analýza*. Praha: C. H. Beck, 121 s. ISBN 80-7179-367-1.

Special reports. Digital in 2016. http://wearesocial.com/uk/special-reports/digital-in-2016. Accessed April 14, 2019.

Trout, J., & Rivkin, S. (2008). *Differentiate or die: Survival in our era of killer competition* (2nd ed.). New Jersey: Wiley. 272 s. ISBN 978-0-470-22339-0.

Vaynerchurk, G. (2016). *One entrepreneur's take on leadership, social media, and self-awareness*. HarperCollins Publishers. ISBN 978-00-622-7312-3.

Web pages of social networks: www.facebook.com, www.googleplus.com, www.instagram.com, www.linkedin.com, www.twitter.com, www.youtube.com.

Chapter 48
The Effects of Crude Oil Price Volatility, Stock Price, Exchange Rate and Interest Rate on Malaysia's Economic Growth

Farah Rahim and Zarinah Hamid

Abstract This study examines the effects and relationships between Malaysia's economic growth and selected variables which are oil price volatility, stock price, real exchange rate and real interest rate. Using time-series data methodology, the study employs unit root test using Augmented Dickey–Fuller (ADF) and Phillips–Perron (PP), Auto-Regressive Distribution Lag (ARDL) model supplemented by Bounds F-Testing, Johansen-Julius Co-integration test and Granger causality test. The long-run equation derived from ARDL shows that there are positive relationships for stock price and real exchange rate whilst there are negative relationships between oil price volatility and real interest rate. Furthermore, Granger causality test shows that only stock price and real interest rates have an impact on Malaysia's gross domestic product (GDP) in the short run. Finally, sound policy recommendations are suggested, in particular, to address oil price volatility in a forward-looking manner as well as monetary-friendly measures to further support Malaysia's economic growth.

Keywords Economic growth · Malaysia · Oil price volatility

JEL Codes O44 · O47

48.1 Introduction

Oil and gas industry have been volatile since the 1970s. The sector experienced thick and thin for the past three (3) to four (4) decades which correspond to positive and negative impacts on the economic and financial activities. Starting with the "Energy Crisis" in 1973 where an oil embargo was imposed by the Organization of Arab Petroleum Exporting Countries (OAPEC) leading to short in supply and hence hike

F. Rahim (✉) · Z. Hamid (✉)
Kulliyyah of Economics and Management Sciences, International Islamic University of Malaysia, 53100 Gombak, Malaysia
e-mail: farah.rahim@live.iium.edu.my

Z. Hamid
e-mail: inahumkc@iium.edu.my

N. Tsounis and A. Vlachvei (eds.), *Advances in Cross-Section Data Methods in Applied Economic Research*, Springer Proceedings in Business and Economics,
https://doi.org/10.1007/978-3-030-38253-7_48

in oil prices, it was then followed by an oil glut in the 1980s whereby oil demand plummeted and hence forced the prices down. Another oil shock took place in the 1990s due to adverse economic conditions, perhaps after experiencing a 10-year cyclical oil shock persistently. During this era, the infamous "Asian Financial Crisis" hit the Asian region making the Asian countries suffering from slump and economic depression. There was a loss of demand and confidence in financial and economic development for the region.

As for Malaysia and as outlined by Kaplan (2001), Malaysia's effort to recovery was highly dependent on the imposition of capital control framework in September 1998 which was not eminent at that time. The trending was to borrow from the International Monetary Fund (IMF) but Malaysia had embarked on a different path by fixing the exchange rate, cutting the interest rate and adopting a policy to stimulate growth. It was found that this initiative had been proven worked for Malaysia as compared to taking funding from the IMF as faster recovery was formed. There were minimal declines in wages and employment coupled with more rapid retrieval in its stock market activity.

According to the World Bank (2017), Malaysia is a highly open, upper-middle-income country with over 31 million population. The country experiences escalation in economic growth throughout Q1 2017 at 5.6% as compared to the same quarter in 2016 at 4.5%. It was notable that the sources for this growth were on private investment on capital spending along with implementation of several large-scale projects. At the same time, inflation also peaked driven by high fuel prices as the oil and gas sector improves rapidly on cost efficiency and limiting its supply quantity. As a result, the reaction is to push up crude oil prices globally due to agreement between Organisation of Petroleum Exporting Countries (OPEC) and non-OPEC members to slightly curb on the supply side, Bank Negara Malaysia (2016). On the financial side, the indicators demonstrate that banking sectors are well-capitalised combined with strong liquidity performance in Q1 2017. The system remains resilient as the currency, i.e. the ringgit, reversing its downward trend towards appreciation against the US dollar, World Bank (2017).

As the ringgit volatility subsides, it promotes healthy rounds of exports and imports which simultaneously helping the nation's most highly dependable industry to grow and bounce back from the oil turmoil in recent years.

48.2 Literature Review

48.2.1 Oil Price Volatility and Economic Growth

Based on the economic theory, the behaviour of oil price volatility has the possibility to change over a short period of time, according to Narayan and Narayan (2007). Mohn and Misund (2009) investigated the relationship between investment and oil price volatility and they found that oil price volatility has the stimulating effect whereby oil shocks are temporary and transitory in nature. Over a longer period, Gadea et al. (2016), based on the study on the US' long term oil performance, found that the relationship between oil price and economic growth is not even significant. It could be due to important changes that occurred in the demand and supply that had actually led to a few structural breaks.

In another study on the relationship of energy sources namely electricity and oil, against economic growth, Sarwar et al. (2017) concluded that oil price shocks upsurge the economic risk. As a result, and in accordance with the fundamental of risk management whereby higher risk yields higher returns, they found that economic growth in low and middle-income countries somehow increase when oil price shocks happened. The scenario is however varied in other countries depending on their income and region.

Hamilton (2003) studied the non-linear relationship between oil prices and gross domestic product (GDP) growth. He used functional forms in his model as many economic analyses on oil shocks tend to begin with a production function and then relate it towards inputs such as capital, labour, and energy. This approach is appealing as it easily demonstrates linearity between log of GDP to the log of real oil prices. Therefore, the relationship between dependent variable and independent variable(s) could be clearly established and represented graphically by a straight line. He argued that the existing models interpret recession aftermath an oil shock as supply-driven rather than demand-driven, meaning that an oil prices increase would result in an increase in production cost.

48.2.2 Stock Price and Economic Growth

Stock market liquidity supports the hypothesis that it would positively predict growth. Indirectly, it indicates that banking and financial system play an important role to spur innovations by providing good prospective investment products, according to Levine (1998). Schumpeter and Backhaus (2003) further added that entrepreneurship would outgrowth economic development by vanishing savings and replacing it with funds. This marks a significant move towards generating funds by firms via financial market and stock market.

In a study by Silva et al. (2018) on stock market performance and economic growth of Sri Lanka using a linear model over a period of sixteen (16) years, they concluded that there is a positive relationship between the share prices that represented the stock market and economic growth. The same result is shared with Bangladesh on research performed by Mamun et al. (2018) using Granger causality test on the short-run dynamics and vector error correction model (VECM) on the long-run dynamics. Interestingly, the found a positive relationship between stock market development and economic growth for both short-run and long-run views though the long-run equilibrium is rather slow to be achieved.

Kuang (2008) conducted a holistic overview of Malaysian financial market situation to ascertain the underlying factors and risks that contribute to such an impact.

Blessed by stability economically and geopolitically, Malaysia managed to attract positive net inflow of foreign direct investment (FDI) at about 3.8% of GDP between 2004 and 2007 signifying ample capacity of Malaysian companies to expand and diversify their business operations. To support this development, the Central Bank of Malaysia, i.e. Bank Negara Malaysia, adopted several monitoring measures to enhance its surveillance and capital account transactions. Through sophisticated reporting and system, Malaysia portrays strong capital market performance alongside promotion of good governance and risk management. Therefore, Malaysia's monetary policy is then determined based on balanced risk assessment between inflation and growth. Sound intervention at both regulatory and supervisory levels would be initiated to address any fluctuation whether it is an appreciation or depreciation of Malaysian currency, to mitigate speculative exposure.

48.2.3 Real Exchange Rate and Economic Growth

There is a consensus agreement that high real exchange rate would encourage economic growth as outlined by Gala (2007), Rodrik (2008) and Rapetti et al. (2012). Taking example of China when the Yuan was undervalued in the 1970s, the country experienced rapid GDP growth owing to the fact that currency-undervaluation has driven its economic growth. Nonetheless, the key success to economic development in East and South Asia regions has been the competitive currency. They managed to smoothen their currency from over appreciating so that artificial high real wages could be prevented. This scenario is inferior such that consumption would increase but at the expense of high debt rather than generating resources to finance consumption. Bresser-Pereira (2002) termed this situation as 'saving displacement' which has the potential to worsen balance of payments simply attributable to overvaluation in exchange rate.

Rather supporting the above findings, Habib et al. (2017) confirmed a negative relationship between real exchange rate and economic growth only on developing countries and those countries with currency-pegged regime, while the result for advanced countries and currency-floating regime is not significant and weak. They also found that depreciation appears to have larger impact on economic growth than appreciation does. Similarly, Ribeiro et al. (2017) showed that the impact of exchange rate devaluation against economic growth is negatively signed and the effects of real exchange rate on economic growth are rather indirect, supported by income distribution and technological advancement.

On the contrary, devaluing a currency often invites recession according to Ito et al. (1999) with exception to rapidly developing countries. The contributing factor that relates to the success of the exchange rate and economic growth in international trade especially high exports which are then being translated into current account surplus. By referring to growth in Asia, they found that economic development within this region was due to upgrading from traditional industry such as mining and agriculture to manufacturing and hence these countries become modernised and advanced in technological inventiveness. They attract foreign direct investments and therefore could produce high quality yet cheap exports which then resulting in immense economic growth.

In Malaysia, a specific study on the impact of exchange rate misalignment on economic growth was conducted by Tsen Wong (2013). It was argued that an increase in the exchange rate misalignment would decrease economic growth, or in short, it reflects that uncontrolled appreciation would lead to slower growth, vice versa. In this study, it was also found that oil price and interest rate are important determinants to real exchange rate misalignment, in addition to currency reserve itself. As a nation with a managed floating exchange rate regime, it was evident that exchange rate policies undertaken by the Central Bank of Malaysia had been able to protect the exchange rate market from over-exposure to exchange rate risks.

48.2.4 Real Interest Rate and Economic Growth

By norm, investors in financial market are forward-looking, meaning that they consider expectations of future economic performance. Dotsey (1998) found that the use of the spread between long-term and short-term interest rates is still relevant to predict economic growth even though its accuracy has become more challenged recently due to several occurrences whereby spread has failed to anticipate the onset of likely recession. An example would be during 1990–91 where the economic downturn has seriously affected mostly the Western countries, yet spread has not functioned to forecast this occasion. Following this, Sims and Zha (2006) examined monetary policy shocks with attention towards interest rate-smoothing policy. Using the VAR model, they found that monetary policy shocks had little consequences on business cycle and growth as well as interest rate only accounts marginally as the contributing factor of the shock.

A study by Ramlan and Suhaimi (2017) on the relationship between the interest rate and economic growth in Malaysia during 2004–2013 was positive, meaning that an increase in interest rate would bring about an increase in economic growth. Conflicting with the act of Central Bank whereby they normally use high interest rate to moderate back the economy especially when inflation is expected to set-in, this study highlighted an interesting paradox, but this was understandable as Malaysia was undergoing a hard decade during this time both politically and economically. As a result, Malaysians did not reflect decrease in consumption despite interest rate was charged high therefore economic activities run as normal. Another interesting finding by Ang (2007) suggests that during macroeconomic shocks, real interest rate leads to a negative impact on Malaysia's financial deepening. This simultaneously shows that policy changes in real interest rates would not contribute to long-run growth of the country. Instead, they found that economic growth is the factor that leads to financial sector reformation in Malaysia in line with the demand-following hypothesis.

48.3 Materials and Methods

48.3.1 Model Specification

Since this study aims to resolve the question of what are the impacts of oil price volatility, stock price, real exchange rate and real interest rate on Malaysia's economic growth, it is imperative that a model specified for the empirical work shall be correct so that it supports the underlying intuition. The parameters chosen were derived from existing literature after thorough consideration of existing economic theory as well as the main factors that affect Malaysia's GDP itself. By implementing this thought, a strong connection between the model and the economic theory is established so that the selected variables are self-explanatory.

Therefore, there are five variables specified in the model and they are shown as below:

$$\mathrm{GDP} = f(\mathrm{OPV}, \mathrm{SP}, \mathrm{RER}, \mathrm{RIR}) \tag{48.1}$$

where GDP is Gross Domestic Product as a proxy to economic growth, OPV is Oil Price Volatility represented by the average in change in oil prices between two consecutive periods, SP is the Stock Price, RER is Real Exchange Rate and RIR is Real Interest Rate. Explicitly, the equation could be expressed as:

$$\mathrm{LGDP}_t = \alpha_0 + \alpha_1\mathrm{OPV}_t + \alpha_2\mathrm{SP}_t + \alpha_3\mathrm{RER}_t + \alpha_4\mathrm{RIR}_t + \varepsilon_t \tag{48.2}$$

where the model is in loglinear form. This model is chosen to address possibility of having a negative value for OPV based on the definition provided by Energy Information Administration (EIA) of the US in their May 2012 report. In addition, a loglinear model is a flexible and independent model which is normally used on raw data for data-smoothing purpose (Holland and Thayer 2000) and for considerate small sample analysis (Moreira et al. 2008). As such, α_i (i = 0, 1, 2, 3, 4) are the parameters to be estimated and ε_t is the disturbance term. In this model, the interpretation of α_i is such that it is in unit form, that is if the variables OPV, SP, RER and RIR change by 1 unit, LGDP is expected to change by α_i and to get it in percentage form, α_i would need to be times by hundred. In this model, the signs of the coefficients are sensitive to the level of GDP.

48.3.2 Testing Methodology

To pursue the empirical test, firstly, Ordinary Least Squared (OLS) of the model is estimated to understand the expected sign of each variable selected. Next, time-series property of each variable is verified using Augmented Dickey–Fuller (ADF) test to check their stationarity on the following form (Dickey and Fuller 1979).

In addition, Phillips–Perron (PP) Unit Root test (Phillips and Perron 1988) is also carried out to supplement ADF test. The advantage of using PP unit root test is such that it allows testing in a more general model and therefore both types of weak and strong variables are outfitted accordingly.

Second, Auto-Regressive Distributed Lag (ARDL) model (Pesaran and Shin 1998) and Bounds F-testing are conducted to extract both long-run and short-run relationships between independent and dependent variables for the former and to identify co-integration relationship for the latter. The expected outcome would yield consistent long-run coefficients despite stationarity of the regressors at I(0) or I(1), therefore valid interpretations may be developed from the result. Endogeneity is also minimised as there is no residual correlation (Nkoro and Uko 2016).

With a similar objective as ARDL test, co-integration test is carried out to avoid spurious regression. Once these tests have been fulfilled, the next step is to employ Granger causality test to analyse causality relationship between all variables. It is useful to determine causality property amongst the variables at least in one direction supported by Granger (1988). Upon existence of co-integration, there would be possible causal and effect relationship amongst the variables. Conditional to this outcome, Granger Causality test shall be proposed to ascertain the causality direction of the co-integrated variables.

48.3.3 Data Sources

Time series data from 1993 until 2017 were obtained quarterly from Q4:1993 until Q4:2017. The data for GDP was derived from International Monetary Fund (IMF) which represents the economic growth and it is in the form of real GDP. Real GDP indicates that the GDP data has been adjusted for inflation accordingly. Oil prices data was taken on the basis of Crude Brent Oil prices from Quandl database and it is measured in USD. From this data, oil price volatility (OPV) was calculated as follows based on EIA definition mentioned earlier.

$$\text{Average OP}_{t-2} = \frac{\text{Oil Price}_{t-2} - \text{Oil Price}_{t-3}}{\text{Oil Price}_{t-3}} \text{ Let this equation be A} \tag{48.3}$$

$$\text{Average OP}_{t-1} = \frac{\text{Oil Price}_{t-1} - \text{Oil Price}_{t-2}}{\text{Oil Price}_{t-2}} \text{ Let this equation be B} \tag{48.4}$$

$$\text{Average OP}_{t} = \frac{\text{Oil Price}_{t} - \text{Oil Price}_{t-1}}{\text{Oil Price}_{t-1}} \text{ Let this equation be C} \tag{48.5}$$

Then,

$$\text{OPV}_t = \frac{\text{A} + \text{B} + \text{C}}{3} \tag{48.6}$$

Stock price data was based on FTSE Bursa Malaysia from Kuala Lumpur Stock Exchange (KLSE) via Yahoo Finance. It is measured in Ringgit Malaysia (RM). For real exchange rate, the data was sourced from The Federal Reserve Bank of St. Louis and it is in index form with base 2010. Since the data is basing an index at a specified time, it is believed that this would eliminate the difficulty of carrying out regression on an indexed number (Bailey et al. 1963). Finally, real interest rate data was derived from IMF with slight modifications required since the data available for Malaysia are only on nominal interest rates. By also extracting the data on consumer price index (CPI) from IMF, real interest rate was derived as per the equation below.

$$\text{Real Interest Rate} = \text{Nominal Interest Rate} - \text{Inflation} \tag{48.7}$$

whereby inflation is calculated using CPI information as per the following equation.

$$\text{Inflation} = \frac{\text{CPI}_t - \text{CPI}_{t-1}}{\text{CPI}_{t-1}} \times 100 \tag{48.8}$$

48.4 Results and Discussion

48.4.1 Descriptive Statistics

Descriptive statistics is normally used to describe brief features of data employed for the study. The result is shown as per Table 48.1.

48.4.2 OLS Estimation of the Model

The OLS estimation of the model is as follows with t-stats are displayed in () parentheses and *p*-values are displayed in [] parentheses:

Table 48.1 Descriptive statistics

Variables	Mean	Maximum	Minimum	Standard deviation
LGDP	4.329	4.952	3.579	0.353
OPV	0.025	0.314	−0.236	0.095
SP	1157.6	1882.7	373.5	414.3
RER	100.2	130.7	84.57	10.37
RIR	6.635	12.82	0.42	2.458

$$\mathrm{LGDP}_t = 5.38 - 0.279\mathrm{OPV}_t + 0.0004\mathrm{SP}_t - 0.013\mathrm{RER}_t - 0.028\mathrm{RIR}_t \quad (48.9)$$

$$\begin{matrix} (-1.88) & (8.69) & (-7.40) & (-2.67) \\ [0.07] & [0.00] & [0.00] & [0.009] \end{matrix}$$

As shown in Eq. (48.9) above, all coefficients appear to be statistically significant.

48.4.3 Unit Root Test

Macroeconomic time series variables may exhibit trending behaviour and subsequently non-stationarity as the mean keeps on rising and not integrated. The problem with non-stationary data is that the OLS regression may lead to incorrect conclusions. Unit root test is carried out so that the time series data is differenced after d times to achieve stationarity and integrated at the order d (Asteriou and Hall 2015).

The findings of unit root test using ADF test and PP test are shown in Table 48.2 at level and first difference. Lag length of each series is automatically determined by the system tool using Akaike's Information Criterion (AIC). The null hypothesis is non-stationary. If the test statistic is greater than the critical values of the level of significance, the conclusion is that the variable has a unit root or a non-stationary series.

The null hypothesis of no unit root is rejected at first difference, hence the series are all stationary and integrated at the same order I(1).

Table 48.2 Unit root test

Variables	ADF	PP
At level		
LGDP	−0.309	1.322
OPV	−2.275**	−3.912*
SP	0.992	0.141
RER	−0.879	−1.221
RIR	−1.516	−1.453
At first difference		
ΔLGDP	−1.907***	−10.40*
ΔOPV	−4.729*	−20.76*
ΔSP	−5.342*	−10.18*
ΔRER	−8.373*	−8.342*
ΔRIR	−12.922*	−13.22*

Notes *denotes significant at 1% level using t-stats approach
**denotes significant at 5% level using t-stats approach
***denotes significant at 10% level using t-stats approach

48.4.4 Autoregressive Distributed Lag (ARDL) Model

In applying the ARDL approach, it is commendable to note that ARDL model has several advantages in comparison with other cointegration methods (Belloumi 2014). First, it does not need all variables to be integrated at the same order. As such, it could be applied to a mixture of stationary and non-stationary variables to get the estimated values of different parameters. Second, ARDL approach is more efficient to be used in a small and finite data sample and third, the long-run estimates are unbiased.

From the testing, the model outcome is given by ARDL (4,2,4,0,2) where the numbers in parentheses represent lags for each variable. It is a co-integration technique to ascertain the long-run relationship between all variables. The long-run coefficients of the variables are given as per below. Automated AIC is again used to select the optimum number of lags in this model.

Based on the ARDL result presented in Table 48.3, there is evidence of a unique long-run equilibrium relationship between Malaysia's economic growth and stock price as well as real interest rate. As for oil price volatility and real exchange rate, there is no any long-run relationship found. This situation would mean that causality examination would only be valid on stock prices and real interest rate, and there must exist Granger causality at least in one direction, whilst Granger causality would not bind for oil price volatility and real exchange rate (Ozturk and Acaravci 2011). More specifically in the long run, one unit increase in stock price would merely reduce Malaysia's real GDP by 0.02% and a one-unit increase in real interest rate would decrease Malaysia's real GDP by 2.02%. Despite that the nation relies heavily on its petroleum product, it shows that in the long term, Malaysia needs to overcome its dependency on these natural resources perhaps by diversifying the portfolio towards other types of energy as well as other income sources. This finding supports that Malaysia's growth in the long-run would not be vital upon crude oil price volatility and in fact, its economic growth strategy is therefore forward-looking and effective. It may also be argued that diversion from petroleum resources to other resources may improve overall productivity of Malaysia.

As for the more speculative variables which are stock price and real interest rate, it is not surprising that a long-run relationship exists since as a rapidly developing nation, other countries may find Malaysia as an attractive investment hub with huge

Table 48.3 ARDL test

Variables	Long run coefficient	t-stats [prob]
Dependent variable is LGDP		
ΔOPV_{t-2}	−0.174	−1.554 [0.1244]
ΔSP_{t-4}	0.0002	−2.825 [0.0060]*
RER_t	0.0019	1.335 [0.1860]
ΔRIR_{t-2}	−0.0202	−2.082 [0.0407]**

Notes *denotes significant at 1% level using prob. approach
**denotes significant at 5% level using prob. approach

profits potential to be explored, supported by positive looking stock market and interest rate management. In tandem with economic theory, lower real interest rate would indicate lower cost of borrowing. It, therefore, encourages investment spending that would boost Malaysia's economy further.

48.4.5 Bounds F-Testing

The Bounds F-testing using ARDL model is based on a technique outlined by Pesaran et al. (2001). The null hypothesis of no level relationship despite the variables are I(0) or I(1) would be evaluated using the critical value given. Rather than expected, the result suggests that there is compelling evidence of co-integration relationship between Malaysia's economic growth and the selected variables in this study which are oil price volatility, stock price, real exchange rate and real interest rate. The result is as follows in Table 48.4. Thus, it could be concluded that there is a relationship between Malaysia's economic growth and oil price volatility, stock price, real exchange rate and real interest rate.

48.4.6 Johansen-Julius Co-integration Test

Johansen-Julius co-integration method is carried out in this study for the purpose to confirm ARDL estimation earlier. Provided that all variables are stationary at I(1) as evidenced by ADF and PP unit root test method, this co-integration test is applied to learn if two or more time series variables have a long run or equilibrium relationship (Pillay 2013). By using 5% significant level, the test results indicate that the null hypothesis of no co-integrating variables is rejected at rank equals one which implies that there is indeed co-integration occurs in the model. The result is as per Table 48.5.

48.4.7 Granger Causality Test

To proceed with dynamic short-run causality relationships among all variables after having analysed the long-run relationship, the study employs Granger causality test.

Table 48.4 Bounds F-testing

Function of variables	F-stats ($k = 4$)	Decision
F(LGDP/OPV, SP, RER, RIR)	3.14*	Reject

Note *denotes significant at 10% level using t-stats approach at upper bound I(1)

Table 48.5 Johansen-Julius co-integration test

Hypothesised	Trace statistics	5% critical value
None*	79.85	69.82
At most 1	42.98	47.86
At most 2	18.71	29.80
At most 3	8.82	15.50
At most 4	3.21	3.84

Notes Trace test indicates 1 co-integrating equation at 5% level
*denotes rejection of the hypothesis at 5% level

Table 48.6 Granger causality test

Null hypothesis	F-stats	Prob.	Decision
OPV does not Granger Cause LGDP	1.204	0.315	Do not reject
LGDP does not Granger Cause OPV	1.10475	0.3356	Do not reject
SP does not Granger Cause LGDP	2.048	0.095*	Reject
LGDP does not Granger Cause SP	2.079	0.091*	Reject
RER does not Granger Cause LGDP	1.476	0.217	Do not reject
LGDP does not Granger Cause RER	2.186	0.078*	Reject
RIR does not Granger Cause LGDP	1.586	0.185	Do not reject
LGDP does not Granger Cause RIR	8.842	0.000005*	Reject

Note *denotes significant at 10% level or lower

The reason is that causal analysis is different from regression analysis in such a way that any regression model would lend itself for causality test. It suggests that regression result would portray consequences or effects whilst causality test results would give the idea of causes before a consequence happens (Kmenta 2010). In this spirit, Table 48.6 displays the Granger causality test result.

As uttered in ARDL analysis earlier, it is apparent that there is a causal relationship between two (2) variables found significant which are stock price and real interest rate. Even though real exchange rate tends to provide a similar view, it is considered invalid. Further explanation of the affected variables is in the subsequent sub-sections.

48.4.7.1 Bi-direction Causality Between Real GDP and Stock Price

The outcome suggests that causality relationship between Malaysia's economic growth and stock price is bi-directionally, indicating that there is a strong long run and Granger causality relationships between these two variables. For instance, stock price may play a vital role to cause any change towards the country's growth and it is therefore rather important to keep it stable.

48.4.7.2 Uni-direction Causality Between Real GDP and Real Interest Rate

In addition, causality relationship between Malaysia's economic growth and real interest rate is uni-directionally. It means that in the short run, a change in real GDP may alter real interest rate outlook depending on the degree of change and whether it is positive or negative.

48.5 Conclusion

The study has examined the impacts of oil price volatility, stock price, real exchange rate and real interest rate towards Malaysia's economic growth supplemented by a long-run relationship overview. Several tests had been carried out which are OLS estimation of the model, unit root test using ADF and PP, ARDL model and Bounds F-testing, Johansen-Julius co-integration test and Granger causality test.

All variables displayed the predicted signs and they are significant at 10% level or lower. Stock price and real interest rates are found to play a crucial role to contribute towards Malaysia's economic growth in the long term. Nonetheless, oil price volatility together with real exchange rate, would indicatively seem stable and also act as the substance for Malaysia's economic growth in the short run.

The negative relationship between oil price volatility and economic growth in Malaysia is a helpful sign that oil shocks are a mere short term and would not deprive the country's ambition towards a modern economy and society.

The positive relationship between stock price and Malaysia's economic growth is somewhat more than expected as generally, stock market would be an instance indicator of the economic condition of a country. This positive stance simply shows that firms are profitable and therefore making their shares more attractive as a result of growing dividends.

A negative relationship was detected for both relationships of Malaysia's economic growth with either real exchange rate or real interest rate. In other words, either an appreciation of Malaysian Ringgit or an increase in real interest rates would slow down economic growth. To some extent, this would not be of much impact as these two variables are common players in shaping every country's growth. Therefore, there are normally comprehensive policy measures in place to cushion the undesirable effect before it becomes inferior.

Nonetheless, the findings are limited to the sample period studied in this research as well as the choices of the variables as the determinants of Malaysia's economic growth.

References

Ang, J. B., & McKibbin, W. J. (2007). Financial liberalization, financial sector development and growth: Evidence from Malaysia. *Journal of Development Economics, 84*(1), 215–233.
Asteriou, D., & Hall, S. G. (2015). *Applied econometrics*. Palgrave Macmillan.
Bailey, M. J., Muth, R. F., & Nourse, H. O. (1963). A regression method for real estate price index construction. *Journal of the American Statistical Association, 58*(304), 933–942.
Belloumi, M. (2014). The relationship between trade, FDI and economic growth in Tunisia: An application of the autoregressive distributed lag model. *Economic Systems, 38*(2), 269–287.
Bresser-Pereira, L. C. (2002). Brazil's quasi-stagnation and the growth cum foreign savings strategy. *International Journal of Political Economy, 32*(4), 76–102.
Dickey, D. A., & Fuller, W. A. (1979). Distribution of the estimators for autoregressive time series with a unit root. *Journal of the American statistical association, 74*(366a), 427–431.
Dotsey, M. (1998). The predictive content of the interest rate term spread for future economic growth. Federal Reserve Bank of Richmond Economic Quarterly Volume 84/3.
EIA. (2012). Crude oil price volatility. Metric of the Month, May 2012.
Gadea, M. D., Gómez-Loscos, A., & Montañés, A. (2016). Oil price and economic growth: A long story? *Econometrics, 4*(4), 41.
Gala, P. (2007). Real exchange rate levels and economic development: theoretical analysis and econometric evidence. *Cambridge Journal of Economics, 32*(2), 273–288.
Granger, C. W. (1988). Some recent development in a concept of causality. *Journal of econometrics, 39*(1–2), 199–211.
Habib, M. M., Mileva, E., & Stracca, L. (2017). The real exchange rate and economic growth: Revisiting the case using external instruments. *Journal of International Money and Finance, 73*, 386–398.
Hamilton, J. D. (2003). What is an oil shock? *Journal of econometrics, 113*(2), 363–398.
Holland, P. W., & Thayer, D. T. (2000). Univariate and bivariate loglinear models for discrete test score distributions. *Journal of Educational and Behavioral Statistics, 25*(2), 133–183.
Ito, T., Isard, P., & Symansky, S. (1999). Economic growth and real exchange rate: An overview of the Balassa-Samuelson hypothesis in Asia. In: *Changes in exchange rates in rapidly developing countries: Theory, practice, and policy issues (NBER-EASE volume 7)* (pp. 109–132). University of Chicago Press.
Kaplan, E., & Rodrik, D. (2001). *Did the Malaysian capital controls work?* (p. w8142). No: National Bureau of Economic Research.
Kmenta, J. (2010). Mostly harmless econometrics: An empiricist's companion. *Business Economics, 45*(1), 75–76.
Kuang, O. S. (2008). Capital flows and financial assets in emerging markets: Determinants, consequences and challenges for central banks: The Malaysian experience. *BIS Papers, 44*(5), 321–339.
Levine, R., & Zervos, S. (1998). Stock markets, banks and economic growth. *American Economic Review*, 537–558.
Mamun, A., Basher, S., Hoque, N., & Ali, M. H. (2018). Does stock market development affect economic growth? Econometric evidence from Bangladesh. *Management & Accounting Review, 17*(1).
Mohn, K., & Misund, B. (2009). Investment and uncertainty in the international oil and gas industry. *Energy Economics, 31*(2), 240–248.
Moreira, E. E., Coelho, C. A., Paulo, A. A., Pereira, L. S., & Mexia, J. T. (2008). SPI-based drought category prediction using loglinear models. *Journal of Hydrology, 354*(1–4), 116–130.
Narayan, P. K., & Narayan, S. (2007). Modelling oil price volatility. *Energy Policy, 35*(12), 6549–6553.
Nkoro, E., & Uko, A. K. (2016). Autoregressive Distributed Lag (ARDL) cointegration technique: application and interpretation. *Journal of Statistical and Econometric Methods, 5*(4), 63–91.
OPEC. (2016). World oil outlook. October 2016. http://www.opec.org.

Ozturk, I., & Acaravci, A. (2011). Electricity consumption and real GDP causality nexus: Evidence from ARDL bounds testing approach for 11 MENA countries. *Applied Energy, 88*(8), 2885–2892.
Pesaran, M. H., & Shin, Y. (1998). An autoregressive distributed-lag modelling approach to cointegration analysis. *Econometric Society Monographs, 31,* 371–413.
Pesaran, M. H., Shin, Y., & Smith, R. J. (2001). Bounds testing approaches to the analysis of level relationships. *Journal of Applied Econometrics, 16*(3), 289–326.
Phillips, P. C., & Perron, P. (1988). Testing for a unit root in time series regression. *Biometrika, 75*(2), 335–346.
Pillay, S. (2013). The link between unemployment and inflation using Johansen's co-integration approach and vector error correction modelling. *Order, 1*, 1.
Ramlan, H., & Suhaimi, M. S. I. B. (2017). The relationship between interest rates and inflation toward the economic growth in Malaysia. *Journal of Humanities, Language, Culture and Business (HLCB), 1*(1), 55–63.
Rapetti, M., Skott, P., & Razmi, A. (2012). The real exchange rate and economic growth: are developing countries different? *International Review of Applied Economics, 26*(6), 735–753.
Ribeiro, R. S. M., McCombie, J. S., & Lima, G. T. (2017). Does real exchange rate undervaluation really promote economic growth? University of São Paulo (FEA-USP).
Rodrik, D. (2008). The real exchange rate and economic growth. *Brookings Papers on Economic Activity, 2008*(2), 365–412.
Sarwar, S., Chen, W., & Waheed, R. (2017). Electricity consumption, oil price and economic growth: Global perspective. *Renewable and Sustainable Energy Reviews, 76,* 9–18.
Schumpeter, J., & Backhaus, U. (2003). The theory of economic development. *Joseph Alois Schumpeter*, 61–116.
Silva, N. L., Perera, P. R., & Silva, N. C. (2018). Relationship between stock market performance & economic growth: Empirical evidence from Sri Lanka. *Journal for Accounting Researchers and Educators (JARE), 1*(1).
Sims, C. A., & Zha, T. (2006). Does monetary policy generate recessions? *Macroeconomic Dynamics, 10*(2), 231–272.
Tsen Wong, H. (2013). Real exchange rate misalignment and economic growth in Malaysia. *Journal of Economic Studies, 40*(3), 298–313.
World Bank. (2017). Data for development: Malaysia economic monitor, June 2017.

Author Index

N. Tsounis and A. Vlachvei (eds.), *Advances in Cross-Section Data Methods in Applied Economic Research*, Springer Proceedings in Business and Economics,
https://doi.org/10.1007/978-3-030-38253-7

Printed by Printforce, the Netherlands